T0190267

Lecture Notes in Computer Science   9339

Commenced Publication in 1973
Founding and Former Series Editors:
Gerhard Goos, Juris Hartmanis, and Jan van Leeuwen

More information about this series at http://www.springer.com/series/7409

Khalid Saeed · Władysław Homenda (Eds.)

Computer Information Systems and Industrial Management

14th IFIP TC 8 International Conference, CISIM 2015
Warsaw, Poland, September 24–26, 2015
Proceedings

 Springer

Editors
Khalid Saeed
Faculty of Computer Science
Bialystok University of Technology
BIALYSTOK
Poland

Władysław Homenda
Warsaw University of Technology
Poland

ISSN 0302-9743   ISSN 1611-3349   (electronic)
Lecture Notes in Computer Science
ISBN 978-3-319-24368-9   ISBN 978-3-319-24369-6   (eBook)
DOI 10.1007/978-3-319-24369-6

Library of Congress Control Number: 2015949265

LNCS Sublibrary: SL3 – Information Systems and Applications, incl. Internet/Web, and HCI

Springer Cham Heidelberg New York Dordrecht London

Printed on acid-free paper

Springer International Publishing AG Switzerland is part of Springer Science+Business Media
(www.springer.com)

Preface

CISIM 2015 was the 14th of a series of conferences dedicated to computer information systems and industrial management applications. The conference was supported by IFIP TC8 Information Systems. This year it was held during September 24–26, 2015, in Warsaw, Poland, at Warsaw University of Technology.

About 80 papers were submitted to CISIM by researchers and scientists from universities around the world. Each paper was assigned to three referees initially, and the decision was taken after receiving two positive or two negative reviews. In case of conflicting decisions, another expert's review was sought for a number of papers (over 35). In total, about 280 reviews were collected from the referees for the submitted papers. Because of the strict restrictions of Springer's Lecture Notes in Computer Science series, the number of accepted papers was limited. Furthermore, a number of electronic discussions were held between the Program Committee (PC) chairs and members to decide about papers with conflicting reviews and to reach a consensus. After the discussions, the PC chairs decided to accept for publication in the proceedings book about 65 % of the total submitted papers.

The main topics covered by the chapters in this book are biometrics, security systems, multimedia, classification and clustering with application, and industrial management. Besides these, the reader will find interesting papers on computer information systems as applied to wireless networks, computer graphics, and intelligent systems.

We are grateful to the four esteemed speakers for their keynote addresses. The authors of the keynote talks were Profs. Bożena Kostek (Gdańsk University of Technology, Poland), Jaroslav Pokorný (Charles University, Prague, Czech Republic), Agostino Cortesi (Università Ca' Foscari Venezia, Italy), and Radko Mesiar (Slovak University of Technology in Bratislava, Slovak Republic). Also Prof. Anna Bartkowiak from Wrocław University submitted a very interesting invited paper. All the keynote and invited papers are published in this proceedings volume.

We would like to thank all the members of the PC, and the external reviewers for their dedicated efforts in the paper selection process. We also thank the honorary chairs of the conference, Profs. Ryszard Tadeusiewicz and Witold Pedrycz. Special thanks are extended to the members of the Organizing Committee, both the International and the Local ones, and the Springer team for their great efforts to make the conference another success. We are also grateful to Andrei Voronkov, whose EasyChair system eased the submission and selection process and greatly supported the compilation of the proceedings. The proceedings editing was managed by Jiří Dvorský (VŠB-Technical University of Ostrava, Czech Republic), to whom we are indeed very grateful.

We hope that the reader's expectations will be met and that the participants enjoyed their stay in the beautiful city of Warsaw.

September 2015

Khalid Saeed
Władysław Homenda

Organization

Program Committee

Waleed Abdulla	University of Auckland, New Zealand
Raid Al-Tahir	The University of the West Indies, Trinidad and Tobago
Adrian Atanasiu	Bucharest University, Romania
Le Hoai Bac	Ho Chi Minh City University of Science, Vietnam
Anna Bartkowiak	Wrocław University, Poland
Aditya Bagchi	Indian Statistical Institute, India
Rahma Boucetta	National Engineering School of Gabes, Tunisia
Lam Thu Bui	Le Quy Don Technical University, Vietnam
Nabendu Chaki	Calcutta University, India
Rituparna Chaki	West Bengal University of Technology, India
Agostino Cortesi	Ca' Foscari University of Venice, Italy
Dipankar Dasgupta	University of Memphis, USA
Pierpaolo Degano	University of Pisa, Italy
Jan Devos	Ghent University, Belgium
Andrzej Dobrucki	Wrocław University of Technology, Poland
Jiří Dvorský	VŠB-Technical University of Ostrava, Czech Republic
David Dagan Feng	University of Sydney, Australia
Pietro Ferrara	IBM T.J. Watson Research Center, USA
Raju Halder	Ca' Foscari University of Venice, Italy
Christopher Harris	State University of New York, USA
Kauru Hirota	Tokyo Institute of Technology, Japan
Władysław Homenda	Warsaw University of Technology, Poland, Co-chair
Khalide Jbilou	Université du Littoral Côte d'Opale, France
Ryszard Kozera	The University of Western Australia, Australia
Flaminia Luccio	Ca' Foscari University of Venice, Italy
Romuald Mosdorf	Białystok University of Technology, Poland
Debajyoti Mukhopadhyay	Maharashtra Institute of Technology, India
Yuko Murayama	Iwate University, Japan
Hien Thanh Nguyen	Ton Duc Thang University, Vietnam
Nobuyuki Nishiuchi	Tokyo Metropolitan University, Japan
Andrzej Pacut	Warsaw University of Technology, Poland
Jerzy Pejaś	WPUT in Szczecin, Poland
Marco Pistoia	IBM T.J. Watson Research Center, USA
Igor Podolak	Jagiellonian University, Kraków, Poland
Jaroslav Pokorný	Charles University, Czech Republic
Piotr Porwik	University of Silesia, Poland

Jan Pries-Heje	The IT University of Copenhagen, Denmark
Tho Thanh Quan	Ho Chi Minh University of Technology, Vietnam
Isabel Ramos	University of Minho, Portugal
Khalid Saeed	Białystok University of Technology, Poland, Co-chair
Anirban Sarkar	National Institute of Technology, Durgapor, India
Ewa Skubalska-Rafajłowicz	Wrocław University of Technology, Poland
Václav Snášel	VŠB-Technical University of Ostrava, Czech Republic
Krzysztof Ślot	Lodz University of Technology, Poland
Marcin Szpyrka	AGH Kraków, Poland
Jacek Tabor	Jagiellonian University, Kraków, Poland
Andrea Torsello	Ca' Foscari University of Venice, Italy
Dao Trong Tran	Ton Duc Thang University, Vietnam
Nitin Upadhyay	BITS Pilani, India
Bay Dinh Vo	Ton Duc Thang University, Vietnam
Qiang Wei	Tsinghua University, Beijing, China
Sławomir Wierzchoń	Polish Academy of Sciences, Warsaw, Poland
Michał Woźniak	Wrocław University of Technology, Poland
Fusheng Yu	Beijing Normal University, China
Sławomir Zadrożny	Polish Academy of Sciences, Warsaw, Poland
Ivan Zelinka	VŠB-Technical University of Ostrava, Czech Republic

Additional Reviewers

Marcin Adamski	Białystok University of Technology, Poland
Tomáš Apeltauer	Brno University of Technology, Czech Republic
Alexander Barkalov	University of Zielona Góra, Poland
Stefano Bistarelli	University of Perugia, Italy
Chiara Bodei	University of Pisa, Italy
Mateusz Buczkowski	AGH Kraków, Poland
German Budnik	University of Białystok, Poland
Irena Bulatowa	Białystok University of Technology, Poland
Makoto Fukumoto	Fukuoka Institute of Technology, Japan
Hiroki Hasegawa	Mukogawa Women's University, Japan
Jun-Ichi Imai	Chiba Institute of Technology, Japan
Ondřej Jakl	VŠB-Technical University of Ostrava, Czech Republic
Jiří Jaroš	Brno University of Technology, Czech Republic
Bozena Kostek	Gdańsk University of Technology, Poland
Michal Krumnikl	VŠB-Technical University of Ostrava, Czech Republic
Miloš Kudelka	VŠB-Technical University of Ostrava, Czech Republic
Yasuo Kudo	Muroran Institute of Technology, Japan
Ewa Lukasik	Poznan University of Technology, Poland
Ladislav Maršík	Charles University, Czech Republic
Ilaria Matteucci	National Research Council, Italy
Hitomi Nakamura	Kinki University, Japan
Eliška Ochodková	VŠB-Technical University of Ostrava, Czech Republic
Akihiro Ogino	Kyoto Sangyo University, Japan

Contents

Biometrics and Biometrics Applications

Data Analysis and Information Retrieval

Pattern Recognition and Image Processing

Various Aspects of Computer Security

ICBAKE 2015 Workshop

Music Information Processing Workshop

Full Keynote and Invited Papers

Privacy Analysis of Android Apps: Implicit Flows and Quantitative Analysis

Gianluca Barbon[1], Agostino Cortesi[1(✉)], Pietro Ferrara[2], Marco Pistoia[2], and Omer Tripp[2]

[1] Università Cá Foscari Venezia, Venice, Italy
cortesi@unive.it
[2] IBM Thomas J.Watson Research Center, Yorktown Heights, USA

Abstract. A static analysis is presented, based on the theory of abstract interpretation, for verifying privacy policy compliance by mobile applications. This includes instances where, for example, the application releases the user's location or device ID without authorization. It properly extends previous work on datacentric semantics for verification of privacy policy compliance by mobile applications by (i) tracking implicit information flow, and (ii) performing a quantitative analysis of information leakage. This yields to a novel combination of qualitative and quantitative analyses of information flows in mobile applications.

1 Introduction

Security threats are increasing in the mobile space, in particular in the Android environment. Specifically, mobile devices contain different sorts of confidential information that software might access. Such information is usually protected by permissions. However, the solutions provided by current mobile operating systems are not satisfying, and expose the user to various threats [8]. In addition, various applications and (e.g., analytics and advertisement) libraries make use of and sometimes leak user confidential data. Mobile security is also a major concern in an enterprise environment, where firms allow the use of company applications in the employee's personal device, increasing the risk of leakage of confidential business data. Therefore, there is and increasing request and need to formally verify the behavior of mobile applications, and to assess (and possibly limit) the quantity of released data. On the opposite side, a complete absence of data leakage of data would compromise the functionalities of mobile software. For instance, a navigation app like Waze needs to access the user location and communicate it to its servers in order to show appropriate traffic information. However, the user might want to prevent to leakage of her location to the advertisement engine. Ideally, we would like to impose — via suitable privacy policies — constraints on levels of data release, and give the user better awareness of the direct and indirect actual information flow concerning her personal data.

In this context, current research follows two main approaches: a statistical one [14,17] and a language based one (e.g., information flow taint analysis) [1,11,21–24]. Both approaches suffer some weaknesses: the former does not

K. Saeed and W. Homenda (Eds.): CISIM 2015, LNCS 9339, pp. 3–23, 2015.
DOI: 10.1007/978-3-319-24369-6_1

fit well for qualitative analysis, while the latter as it is too strict, due to the fact that the non-interference notion [7] yields too many false positives limiting the effectiveness of the analysis.

In this paper, we extend our previous work [4]. This includes two primary contributions: (i) we investigate also implicit flows, where previously we considered only direct information release paths, and (ii) we relate explicit and implicit information flow to a quantitative notion of information leakage. We formalize our approach in the abstract interpretation framework. The advantage of such a method is that it enables a general abstraction of all possible executions of a given program. Therefore, following the abstract-interpretation framework [6], we design an enhanced concrete semantics that formalizes how the expressions generated by the program's execution maintain footprints of (possibly confidential) data stored in the local data-store of the mobile device. With this formalization of the concrete semantics, we show how to create a sound abstraction such that the analysis is computable.

This work leads to the definition of a framework that merges quantitative and qualitative approaches by taking advantage of their respective strengths. We exploited the evaluation of single operators for the former approach and the collection of quantities of released information for the latter. Last, but certainly not least, the definition of this method has revealed the important role of the implicit flow in the leakage of secret variables. We evaluated the effectiveness of this framework over some benchmark examples.

The paper is structured as follows. After a brief introduction that describes related research and fundamental notions in Section 2, Section 3 recalls the semantics introduced by Cortesi et al. [4] extending it to capture implicit flows as well. Section 4 introduces the new quantitative approach that is added to the semantics described in the previous Sections. Section 5 introduces an abstraction of the quantitative analysis. Finally, in Section 6 a few significant examples of real working applications are presented and analyzed. Section 7 concludes.

2   Background

This Section introduces some important notions that will be used throughout the rest of the paper, and briefly describes the current related research.

Implicit Flows. Implicit flows were described by Denning [7] in 1976. Implicit flows have origins from the so called control statements, like if and while statements, where they are generated by their conditional expression. For instance, consider the following example:

if b **then** x = 0 **else** x = 1;

Even if the final value of x does not allows to directly recover the value of b, the latter affects the value of x, and an indirect information flow occurs from b to x. Of course, implicit flows may yield to malicious effects[19].

Quantitative Approaches. A quantitative approach tracks some quantity, or measure, of leaked information. In [17] a new technique is proposed for determining the quantity of sensitive information that is revealed to public. The main idea presented by the authors consists in computing a maximum flow between the program inputs and the outputs, and by setting a limit on the maximum quantity of information revealed. The information flow is measured using a sort of network flow capacity, where the maximum rate of an imaginary fluid into this network represents the maximum extent of revealed confidential information. This method requires a dynamic approach in order to construct the graph, by performing multiple runs of the target program.

Quantitative Value Expressed as Bits. McCamant et al. [17] introduced a quantity concept in order to measure bits of information that can be released by the observation of a specific execution of a program. One of the first attempts to quantify information flow is the one of Lowe [14]. The author described quantity as number of bits, and defined the information flow as information passing between an high level user and a low level user through a *covert channel*. An interesting feature presented in this work consists in the assignment of *1 bit* of quantity also with absence of information flow. This means that the author considers the absence of information as having value 1 *bit*. Finally they also introduce a time notion in the flow analysis. Another interesting approach is the one by Clark et al.[2,3]. First, they analyse k *bit* variables, where 2^k are the values that can be represented from such variables. Second, they relate the maximum content of a variable to its data type, and they consider this as the possible quantity of leakage. Finally, they define the difference between the quantity of information of a confidential input and the amount of leaked information.

Security in Mobile Environments. Nowadays smartphones are used to store, modify and collect private and confidential data, e.g. location data or phone identifier. At the same time, a lot of malicious applications able to stole data or to track users exist. Mobile operating systems are not able to grant to users an appropriate control over confidential data and on how applications manage such data [8]. These limits make these platforms a potential target for attackers. An evolution of threats in mobile environments has been stressed also by the MacAfee Labs Threats Report [15]; in particular it underlines the existence of untrusted marketplaces and the increasing diffusion of open-source and commercial mobile malware source code, that facilitate the creation of such threats by unskilled attackers. Among mobile operating systems, Android is currently the most prevalent one [13], thus becoming the target of various threats. This mobile environment present different vulnerabilities. First, there is a lack of common definitions for securities and a high volume of available applications that guarantees the diffusion of malicious programs [9]. Second, many applications make use of private information, like the IMEI (International Mobile Station Equipment Identity), and of advertising and analytic libraries, that sends user data to remote servers for profiling. Third, the opportunity to install also applications coming from untrusted marketplaces makes the verification of these applications harder [18]. Last, but not least, even if Android requests to grant permission in order to install an application, this kind of control is not sufficient to avoid undesirable behaviour, because restrictions are not fine-grained [10,12].

Confidentiality Analysis in Mobile Environments. The importance of confidentiality analysis is growing in recent years, especially in the mobile space. In this field two main approaches can be found: dynamic and static analysis methods. Among the works that use the former method we can find those regarding the evaluation of permission-hungry mobile applications [1,18]. In particular, the work of Enck et al. [8] presents TaintDroid, a tool that monitors sensitive data by using real time tracking, avoiding the needing to get access to the applications source code. The main idea consists in tracking sensitive data that flows through systems interfaces, used by applications to get access to local data. This approach has some limitations. For instance, it does not allow the tracking of control flows, and generates false positives. Another approach is the one of Hornyack et al. with AppFence [12], which imposes privacy controls by retrofitting the Android environment, without the need to modify applications. Yet another approach, by Tripp and Rubin [25], is to reason about information release in terms of data values, rather than data flow, where the judgment is based on value similarity measures fed into a Bayesian learning algorithm. However, dynamic approaches present some weaknesses. First, they fail to discover some malicious behaviour, because applications have learned to recognize analysis during execution [10]. Second, the majority of dynamic approaches uses coarse-grained approximations that lead to false alarms and also missed leaks [1], while on the contrary static ones are able to discover potential leaks before the execution of the analysed application.

3   Collecting Semantics

In this section we introduce the collecting semantics, that consists in the first fundamental step of our framework design. We define the syntax, the domains, and the semantics with a specific focus on control statements.

3.1   Syntax

The formalization is focused onthree types of data: strings ($s \in \mathbb{S}$), integers ($n \in \mathbb{Z}$) and Booleans ($b \in \mathbb{B}$). $sexp$, $nexp$, and $bexp$ denotes string, integer, and Boolean expressions, respectively. ℓ is used to represent data-store entries, and $lexp$ denotes label expressions. For instance, string expressions are defined by: $sexp ::= s \mid sexp_1 \circ sexp_2 \mid encrypt(sexp, k) \mid sub(sexp, nexp_1, nexp_2) \mid hash(sexp) \mid read(lexp)$, where $\circ$ represents concatenation, $encrypt$ the encryption of a string with a key k, sub the substring of $sexp$ between n_1 and n_2, $hash$ the computation of the hash value, and $read$ the function that returns the value in the data-store that corresponds to the given label.

3.2 Domain

By *adexp* we denote an atomic data expression that tracks the data sources of a specific value. Formally, an atomic data expression *adexp* is a set of elements $\langle \ell_i, \{(op_j, l'_j) : j \in J\}\rangle$, representing that the datum corresponding to label ℓ_i has been combined with data corresponding to labels ℓ'_j through operators op_j to get the actual value of the expression.

The set of atomic data expressions is defined by: $\mathbb{D} = \{\langle \ell_i, L_i \rangle : i \in I \subseteq \mathbb{N}, \ell_i \in \mathsf{Lab}, L_i \subseteq \wp(\mathsf{Op} \times \mathsf{Lab})\}$, where Lab is the set of labels, and Op is the set of operators.

An environment relates variables to their values as well as to their atomic data expression. Formally, $\Sigma = D \times V$, where (i) $D : \mathbf{Var} \longrightarrow \wp(\mathbb{D})$ maps local variables in $\mathbf{Var}$ to a corresponding *adexp*, and (ii) $V : \mathbf{Var} \longrightarrow (\mathbb{Z} \cup \mathbb{S})$ is the usual environment that tracks value information. The special symbol $\star$ represents data coming from the user input and from the constants of the program. Instead, data coming from the *concrete data-store* C are represented by $= \{\langle \ell_i, \emptyset \rangle : i \in I\} \subseteq \mathbb{D}$ *such that* $\forall i,j \in I : i \neq j \Rightarrow \ell_i \neq \ell_j, and\ \ell_i \neq \star$.

3.3 Collecting Semantics

We extend the notion of atomic data expressions to collect also implicit flows generated by *if* and *while* statements. Such flows are treated in the same way as explicit flows by collecting the Boolean expression (*bexp*) of a conditional or loop statement, and considering it as an *adexp* with its operators and sources.

Definition 1 (Extended Atomic Data Expressions). *We redefine the set of atomic data expressions as:* $\mathbb{D} = \langle \{\langle \ell_i, L_i \rangle : i \in I\}, \{\langle \ell_j, L_j \rangle : j \in J\}\rangle$ *where* $L \subseteq \wp(\mathit{Op} \times \mathit{Lab})$.

An extended atomic data expression can be seen as a pair of two atomic data expressions, where the second one refers to the implicit flows (notice that also a Boolean or relational operator may appear). Formally, $d = \langle d^e, d^i \rangle$, where d^e and d^i correspond to the explicit and implicit flows, respectively. In this way we collect also the Boolean operators.

Consider the conditional statement: **if** *exp* **then** $x = case_1$ **else** $x = case_2$. We can interpret each expression as a combination of explicit and implicit flow:

$$d_{if\ cond} = \langle d^e,\ d^i \rangle$$
$$d_{case_1} = \langle d^e_{case_1},\ d^i_{case_1} \rangle$$
$$d_{case_2} = \langle d^e_{case_2},\ d^i_{case_2} \rangle$$

Notice that d^i in $case_1$ and $case_2$ expresses only the implicit flow generated inside the two branches of the **if** statement, and it does not include the implicit flow that comes from the evaluation of the Boolean expression **exp**. Then, if the $case_1$ is chosen, we obtain: $d_{result} = \langle d^e_{case_1},\ \{d^i_{case_1} \cup d^e_{if} \cup d^i_{if}\}\rangle$ where d^e_{if} and d^i_{if} represent the flows in the **if** condition, both collected in the implicit flow of all the subsequent expressions. The value associated to x after the **if-then-else** statement makes explicit that x has implicit dependence on the sources of the Boolean expression. For instance, if $exp = y \geq 0$, it will track that the value of x is dependent on the value of y.

We denote by $S_N : nexp \times V \to \mathbb{Z}$, $S_S : sexp \times V \to \$$, and $S_B : bexp \times V \to \{\mathsf{true}, \mathsf{false}\}$ the standard concrete evaluations of numerical, string, and Boolean expressions. In addition, $S_L : lexp \times \Sigma \to \mathsf{Lab}$ that returns a data label given a label expression. The semantics of expressions on atomic data $S_A : sexp \times \Sigma \to \wp(\mathbb{D})$ is described in Figure 1. The semantics has been improved w.r.t. [4] with a new operator, $checkpwd(sexp_1, sexp_2)$, that returns true if a secret password is equal to a given value. In addition, we track both explicit and implicit flows. In particular, we do not create any implicit flow, and we simply propagate the implicit flows generated by previous expressions: $\langle S[\![c]\!](a, v), \{\langle \ell_j, L_j \rangle : j \in J \} \rangle$.

Similarly, we rewrite the semantics of statements that create implicit flow, that is, the semantics of *if* and *while* statements (Fig. 2). The definition of this semantics is split into explicit (S_e) and implicit (S_i) flows. We add the *skip* statement to handle the exit from a loop statement like the *while*.

$$S_A[\![x]\!](a, v) = a(x)$$
$$S_A[\![read(lexp)]\!](a, v) = \{\langle S_L[\![lexp]\!](a, v), \emptyset \rangle\}$$
$$S_A[\![encrypt(sexp, k)]\!](a, v) = \{\langle \ell_1, L_1 \cup \{([encrypt, k], \ell_1)\}\rangle : \langle \ell_1, L_1 \rangle \in S_A[\![sexp]\!](a, s, n)\}$$
$$S_A[\![s]\!](a, v) = \{\langle \star, \emptyset \rangle\}$$
$$S_A[\![sexp_1 \circ sexp_2]\!](a, v) = \{\langle \ell_1, L_1 \cup \{(\circ, \ell_2)\}\rangle, \langle \ell_2, L_2 \cup \{(\circ, \ell_1)\}\rangle :$$
$$\langle \ell_1, L_1 \rangle \in S_A[\![sexp_1]\!](a, v), \langle \ell_2, L_2 \rangle \in S_A[\![sexp_2]\!](a, v)\}$$
$$S_A[\![sub(sexp, k_1, k_2)]\!](a, v) = \{\langle \ell_1, L_1 \cup \{([sub, k_1, k_2], \ell_1)\}\rangle : \langle \ell_1, L_1 \rangle \in S_A[\![sexp]\!](a, v)\}$$
$$S_A[\![hash(sexp)]\!](a, v) = \{\langle \ell_1, L_1 \cup (hash, \ell_1)\rangle : \langle \ell_1, L_1 \rangle \in S[\![sexp]\!](a, v)\}$$
$$S_A[\![checkpwd(sexp, s)]\!](a, v) = \{\langle \ell_1, L_1 \cup \{(checkpwd, \star)\}\rangle : \langle \ell_1, L_1 \rangle \in S_A[\![sexp_1]\!](a, v)\}$$

Fig. 1. Semantics of Expressions on Atomic Data

$$S[\![x := sexp]\!](a, v) = (a[x \mapsto S_A[\![sexp]\!](a, v)], v[x \mapsto S_S[\![sexp]\!](v)])$$
$$S[\![skip]\!](a, v) = (a, v)$$
$$S[\![send(sexp)]\!](a, v) = (a, v)$$
$$S[\![c_1; c_2]\!](a, v) = S[\![c_2]\!](S[\![c_1]\!](a, v))$$

$$S[\![\mathsf{if}\ c_1\ \mathsf{then}\ c_2\ \mathsf{else}\ c_3]\!](a, v) = \begin{cases} \langle S_e[\![c_2]\!](a, v),\ S_i[\![c_2]\!](a, v) \cup S_e[\![c_1]\!](a, v) \cup S_i[\![c_1]\!](a, v)\rangle \\ \qquad \text{if } S_B[\![c_1]\!](v) \\ \langle S_e[\![c_3]\!](a, v),\ S_i[\![c_3]\!](a, v) \cup S_e[\![\neg c_1]\!](a, v) \cup S_i[\![c_1]\!](a, v)\rangle \\ \qquad otherwise \end{cases}$$

$$S[\![\mathsf{while}\ c_1\ \mathsf{do}\ c_2]\!](a, v) = S[\![\ \mathsf{if}\ (c_1)\ \mathsf{then}\ (c_2; \mathsf{while}\ c_1\ \mathsf{do}\ c_2)\ \mathsf{else}\ skip\ ]\!](a, v)$$

Fig. 2. Concrete Semantics of Statements

Example. Suppose that y contains a value arising from a data store labeled ℓ_1, while x contains user input. We assume that $> y$.

```
1 y = read(ℓ₁);
2 x = userinput();
3 w = 9;
```

```
4 if (x <= y)
5     z = w;
6 else
7     z = y+3;
8 x = x + z;
```

The following are the expressions computed by the collecting semantics, where the subscript represents the code line of the expression:

$$
\begin{aligned}
y_1 &: \langle \{\langle \ell_1, \emptyset \rangle\}, \emptyset \rangle \\
(x<=y)_4 &: \langle \{\langle \ell_1, \{(>-, \star)\} \rangle\}, \emptyset \rangle \\
y+3_7 &: \langle \{\langle \ell_1, \{(+, \star)\} \rangle\}, \emptyset \rangle \\
z=y+3_7 &: \langle \underbrace{\{\langle \ell_1, \{(+, \star)\} \rangle\}}_{\text{explicit flow}}, \underbrace{\{\langle \ell_1, \{(<, \star)\} \rangle\}}_{\text{implicit flow}} \rangle \\
x=x+z_8 &: \langle \{\langle \ell_1, \{(+, \star)\} \rangle\}, \{\langle \ell_1, \{(<, \star)\} \rangle\} \rangle
\end{aligned}
$$

The first three expressions are not affected by implicit flows, so the implicit component in these expressions is $\emptyset$. The second expression refers to the if Boolean expression, and the fourth one refers to the assignment of the *else* branch, and it takes into account the implicit flow generated by the if statement.

4   Quantitative Semantics

In this Section, we extend the collecting semantics by introducing a quantitative notion of information flow.

4.1   Quantitative Concrete Domain

We begin by representing values having a binary form to express quantities of information flows. In this way, we adopt a standardized evaluation of quantities coming from different data types.

Definition 2 (Label Dimension). *Let ℓ_i be the label of a location in the datastore. ω returns the size of the memory location corresponding to the given label, and it is defined by $nbit_{\ell_i} := \omega(\ell_i)$, where nbit is the retrieved dimension in bits.*

The value returned ω depends on the particular type of the datum:

- *Numbers:* for the sake of simplicity we consider only integer numbers. The number of bits for a label containing such kind of data is: $nbits = \lfloor log_2(n) \rfloor + 1$,
- *String:* we adopt a simplified representation of characters. In particular, we consider an encoding representing only English alphabet (with uppercase and lowercase letters) and numerical digits. We then have 26+26+10 elements. Thus this encoding requires 6 bits for each character, and $nbits = 6 \times l_{str}$ where l_{str} represents the number of characters of string *str*, and
- *Boolean:* such values can be only 0 or 1, so they require only 1 bit.

We now extend the collecting semantics to take into account quantities of information by adding a new expression associated to the extended *adexp* to the concrete state.

Definition 3 (Quantitative Expression). *We define a quantitative expression* qadexp *as a sequence of pairs of labels associated with quantitative values* $\langle \ell, q \rangle$. *This collects the quantity of information generated by implicit flows for the given label* ℓ. *This sequence is combined with a* d_q *in* qadexp *in a unique expression as follows:*

$$d := (\ \langle d_e, d_i \rangle, \ d_q\ )$$

Therefore, we represent data expressions as follows:

$$\mathbb{D} = (\ \langle \{\langle \ell_i, L_i \rangle : i \in I\}, \{\langle \ell_j, L_j \rangle : j \in J\} \rangle, \ \{\langle \ell_k, q_k \rangle : k \in J\}\ )$$

where ℓ_k *are the labels used in statements that generate implicit flow, while* q_k *is the associated quantity of information.*

Every single pair $\langle \ell_k, q_k \rangle$ tracks the quantity of information that label ℓ_k potentially released through implicit flow. Notice that the expression $d :=$ $(\ \langle d_e, d_i \rangle, \ d_q\ )$ highlights how our analysis is the result of the combination of two approaches, and in particular (i) the first two components expression comes from a *qualitative* approach to explicit and implicit flows, and (ii) the last one is the result of a *quantitative* approach.

We define as Q the domain of quantities of information. We are now in position to introduce a function that describes how quantities are collected.

Definition 4 (Quantitative Function ϕ). *Let* ϕ *be a function that updates a quantitative value each time the associated label is involved in an implicit flow, such that:*

$$val_{post}^{\ell} := val_{pre}^{\ell} + \phi_{stm}(\ell)$$

where $\phi_{stm} : \ell \mapsto val$ *and pre and post refer to the statement (stm) execution.*

Quantities are represented as an interval $[val, val]$ were higher and lower bound coincide. This will allow an easier lift to the abstract value. Anyway, for the sake of readability, the singleton interval $[val, val]$ will be denoted by a single value val.

We have to track quantities of implicit flow generated by `if` and `while` statements. Conditional expressions can result only in *true* and *false*. Thus, the information obtained from the evaluation of a Boolean condition consists only of one *bit* [16].

For the sake of simplicity, we consider only the $>$ and $<$ (strict) operators. This avoids problems with equalities ($a == b$) allowing the collection of only one bit of information for each `if` statement [2,3]. Figure 3 defines the semantics of conditional expressions. Notice that we do not yet introduce quantities, while we only express how to collect equality in conditional statements using integers instead of Boolean values..

$$S[\![sexp]\!](a,v) = \{\langle \ell_1, L_1 \cup \{(>,\star)\}\rangle : \langle \ell_1, L_1\rangle \in S_A[\![sexp_1]\!](a,v)\}$$
$$S[\![\neg sexp]\!](a,v) = \{\langle \ell_1, L_1 \cup \{(<,\star)\}\rangle : \langle \ell_1, L_1\rangle \in S_A[\![sexp_1]\!](a,v)\}$$
$$S[\![sexp_1 > sexp_2]\!](a,v) = \{\langle \ell_1, L_1 \cup \{(>,\ell_2)\}\rangle, \langle \ell_2, L_2 \cup \{(<,\ell_1)\}\rangle :$$
$$\langle \ell_1, L_1\rangle \in S_A[\![sexp_1]\!](a,v), \langle \ell_2, L_2\rangle \in S_A[\![sexp_2]\!](a,v)\}$$
$$S[\![sexp_1 < sexp_2]\!](a,v) = \{\langle \ell_1, L_1 \cup \{(<,\ell_2)\}\rangle, \langle \ell_2, L_2 \cup \{(>,\ell_1)\}\rangle :$$
$$\langle \ell_1, L_1\rangle \in S_A[\![sexp_1]\!](a,v), \langle \ell_2, L_2\rangle \in S_A[\![sexp_2]\!](a,v)\}$$

Fig. 3. Concrete Semantics of Conditional Expressions

4.2 Quantitative Concrete Semantics

Let φ be function that maps variables to quantities ($\varphi : \mathtt{Var} \to qadexp$). We now introduce the quantity notion into our quantitative collecting semantics. The initial quantity value is $\phi_{stm}(\ell_i) = 0 \ \forall i$, and it is modified by ϕ_{stm} only for the statements that generate implicit flow. This means that in the other expressions the φ component will be carried as is. The new semantics is defined in Figures 4, 5 and 6.

$$S_A[\![x]\!](a,\varphi,v) = a(x)$$
$$S_A[\![read(lexp)]\!](a,\varphi,v) = \{\langle S_L[\![lexp]\!](a,\varphi,v),\emptyset\rangle\}$$
$$S_A[\![encrypt(sexp,k)]\!](a,\varphi,v) = \{\langle \ell_1, L_1 \cup \{([encrypt,k],\ell_1)\}\rangle :$$
$$\langle \ell_1, L_1\rangle \in S_A[\![sexp]\!](a,\varphi,s,n)\}$$
$$S_A[\![s]\!](a,\varphi,v) = \{\langle \star, \emptyset\rangle\}$$
$$S_A[\![sexp_1 \circ sexp_2]\!](a,\varphi,v) = \{\langle \ell_1, L_1 \cup \{(\circ,\ell_2)\}\rangle, \langle \ell_2, L_2 \cup \{(\circ,\ell_1)\}\rangle :$$
$$\langle \ell_1, L_1\rangle \in S_A[\![sexp_1]\!](a,\varphi,v),$$
$$\langle \ell_2, L_2\rangle \in S_A[\![sexp_2]\!](a,\varphi,v)\}$$
$$S_A[\![sub(sexp,k_1,k_2)]\!](a,\varphi,v) = \{\langle \ell_1, L_1 \cup \{([sub,k_1,k_2],\ell_1)\}\rangle :$$
$$\langle \ell_1, L_1\rangle \in S_A[\![scxp]\!](a,\varphi,v)\}$$
$$S_A[\![hash(sexp)]\!](a,\varphi,v) = \{\langle \ell_1, L_1 \cup (hash,\ell_1)\rangle :$$
$$\langle \ell_1, L_1\rangle \in S[\![sexp]\!](a,\varphi,v)\}$$
$$S_A[\![checkpwd(sexp,s)]\!](a,\varphi,v) = \{\langle \ell_1, L_1 \cup \{(checkpwd,\star)\}\rangle :$$
$$\langle \ell_1, L_1\rangle \in S_A[\![sexp_1]\!](a,\varphi,v)\}$$

Fig. 4. Quantitative Semantics of Expressions on Atomic Data

$$S[\![x := sexp]\!](a,\varphi,v) = (a[x \mapsto S_A[\![sexp]\!](a,\varphi,v)], v[x \mapsto S_S[\![sexp]\!](v)])$$
$$S[\![skip]\!](a,\varphi,v) = (a,\varphi,v)$$
$$S[\![send(sexp)]\!](a,\varphi,v) = (a,\varphi,v)$$
$$S[\![c_1;c_2]\!](a,\varphi,v) = S[\![c_2]\!](S[\![c_1]\!](a,\varphi,v)))$$

Fig. 5. Quantitative Concrete Semantics of Statements

$S[\![$if c_1 then c_2 else $c_3]\!](a, v) =$

- *if $S_B[\![c_1]\!](v)$ is* True *then:*

   let $(a', \varphi', v') = \langle S_e[\![c_2]\!](a, \varphi, v),$
   $$S_i[\![c_2]\!](a, \varphi, v) \cup S_e[\![c_1]\!](a, \varphi, v) \cup S_i[\![c_1]\!](a, \varphi, v)\rangle$$
   in $(a', \varphi'[(\ell_i, \ q_i)/(\ell_i, \ q_i + \phi_{stm}(c_1)) : \ell_i \in \mathtt{src}(c_1)], v')$

- *otherwise:*

   let $(a', \varphi', v') = \langle S_e[\![c_3]\!](a, \varphi, v),$
   $$S_i[\![c_3]\!](a, \varphi, v) \cup S_e[\![\neg c_1]\!](a, \varphi, v) \cup S_i[\![c_1]\!](a, \varphi, v)\rangle$$
   in $(a', \varphi'[(\ell_i, \ q_i)/(\ell_i, \ q_i + \phi_{stm}(c_1)) : \ell_i \in \mathtt{src}(c_1)], v')$

where ϕ_{stm} is the quantitative function in Def. 4

$S[\![$while c_1 do $c_2]\!](a, \varphi, v) =$

   $S[\![$ if (c_1) then $(c_2;$ while c_1 do $c_2)$ else *skip* $]\!](a, \varphi, v)$

Fig. 6. Quantitative Concrete Semantics of Control Statements

5   Abstract Semantics

We now extend the abstract semantics proposed by Cortesi et al. [4] to implicit flows and a quantitative analysis. Our abstract semantics is parameterized by a value domain V^a, and a label abstraction. First of all, we need to define a computable abstraction of quantities.

Definition 5 (Quantity Value Abstraction). *The quantity associate with label expressions is an interval. Each label ℓ^a is associated to an interval of quantities where the lower and the upper bounds are the minimum and the maximum quantities of information that can be released through the implicit flow for that specific label. Therefore, the abstract* qadexp *is defined as* $\langle \ell_k^a, q_{k_{min}}^a, q_{k_{max}}^a \rangle$.

If we have unbounded quantities, the analysis reveals a complete leakage of the associated label. In this case, the upper bound of the intervals is unbounded. Instead, for the lower bound the minimum quantity is zero.

5.1   Atomic Data Abstraction Extension

We now define the atomic data abstraction extended for handling implicit flows and quantities.

Definition 6 (Abstract Extended Atomic Data and Quantities). *Let us consider a set of atomic data and quantity values. We define abstract elements as*

$$(\langle \{\langle \ell_w^a, L_w^{a\sqcap}, L_w^{a\sqcup}\rangle : w \in W\}, \{\langle \ell_z^a, L_z^{a\sqcap}, L_z^{a\sqcup}\rangle : z \in Z\}\rangle, \ \{\langle \ell_g^a, q_g^{a\sqcap}, q_g^{a\sqcup}\rangle : g \in Z\})$$

where:

- ℓ_w^a *is an element that abstracts labels in* Lab *to track explicit flow,*
- ℓ_z^a *and* ℓ_g^a *are elements that abstract labels in* Lab *to track implicit flow,*
- $L_w^{a\sqcap} = \{(op_{iw}^a, \ell_{iw}^a) : i \in I\}$ *and* $L_z^{a\sqcap} = \{(op_{jz}^a, \ell_{jz}^a) : j \in J\}$ *represent the under-approximation of* ℓ_w^a *and* ℓ_z^a *with labels abstracted by* ℓ_{iw}^a *and* ℓ_{jz}^a, *and track explicit and implicit flows, respectively,*
- $L_w^{a\sqcup} = \{(op_{iw}^a, \ell_{iw}^a) : i \in I'\}$ *and* $L_z^{a\sqcup} = \{(op_{jz}^a, \ell_{jz}^a) : j \in J'\}$ *represent the over-approximation of* ℓ_w^a *and* ℓ_z^a *with labels abstracted by* ℓ_{iw}^a *and* ℓ_{jz}^a, *and track explicit and implicit flows, respectively,*
- $L_w^{a\sqcap} \subseteq L_w^{a\sqcup}$ *and* $L_z^{a\sqcap} \subseteq L_z^{a\sqcup}$,
- q_g^a *is an element that abstract quantites associated to a* ℓ_g^a *element,*
- $q_{kg}^{a\sqcap} : k \in J$ *is an under-approximation of the interval of possible quantities of information associated to* ℓ_g^a *with values represented by* q_{kg}^a,
- $q_{kg}^{a\sqcup} : k \in J'$ *is an over-approximation of the interval of possible quantities of information associated to* ℓ_g^a *with values represented by* q_{kg}^a, *and*
- $q_g^{a\sqcap} \leqslant q_g^{a\sqcup}$.

As a corollary, we define the source set of an atomic datum $\langle \{\ell_w^a : w \in W\}, \{\ell_z^a : z \in Z\}\rangle$ expressed as $\mathtt{src}(d)$.

Although we inherit the abstraction and concretization functions for the explicit flows [4], we have to extend them to handle quantities.

Definition 7 (Quantitative Abstraction Function). *We denote by* $\alpha_{\mathbb{Q}}$ *the abstraction function that given a set* $\{((\ell_k, q_k) : k \in J\}$ *returns* $\{(\alpha_{\mathtt{Lab}}(\ell_k), q_k^{a\sqcap}, q_k^{a\sqcup}) : k \in J\}$, *where* $q_k^{a\sqcap}, q_k^{a\sqcup}$ *represent the bounds of the interval that approximates all possible quantitative values in the abstract domain* Q^a.

Definition 8 (Quantitative Abstraction Function for Atomic Data). *Given a concrete atomic datum* $d = \big(\langle\{\langle\ell_i, L_i\rangle : i \in I\}, \{\langle\ell_j, L_j\rangle : j \in J\}\rangle, \{\langle\ell_k, q_k\rangle : k \in J\} \big)$, *we define an abstraction function* $\alpha : \wp(\mathbb{D}) \longrightarrow \mathbb{AD}$ *as:*

$$\alpha_s(d) = \big(\langle\{\langle\alpha_{\mathtt{Lab}}(\ell_i), \alpha_{\mathtt{Lab}}(L_i), \alpha_{\mathtt{Lab}}(L_i)\rangle : i \in I\},$$
$$\{\langle\alpha_{\mathtt{Lab}}(\ell_j), \alpha_{\mathtt{Lab}}(L_j), \alpha_{\mathtt{Lab}}(L_j)\rangle : j \in J\}\rangle,$$
$$\{\langle\alpha_{\mathtt{Lab}}(\ell_k), \alpha_{\mathbb{Q}}(q_k)\rangle : k \in J\}\big)$$

The abstraction function is then extended to sets by computing the upper bound of the point-wise application of α_s *to all the elements of the given set.*

5.2 Abstract Semantics of Statements

Expressions are abstracted via an abstract data label and an abstract value (AD^a and V^a, respectively). In Figure 7 the abstract semantics of statements taking into account implicit flows is defined Then, in Figure 8 this semantics is extended with the quantitative dimension. We omit here the abstract semantics of expressions, as it does not generate any implicit flow, and we refer the interested reader to Cortesi et. al [4] for more details.

$$S^a[\![x := sexp]\!](a^a, v^a) = (a^a, S_v^a[\![x := sexp]\!](v^a))$$
$$S^a[\![skip]\!](a^a, v^a) = (a^a, v^a)$$
$$S^a[\![send(sexp)]\!](a^a, v^a) = (a^a, v^a)$$
$$S^a[\![c_1; c_2]\!](a^a, v^a) = S^a[\![c_2]\!](S^a[\![c_1]\!](a^a, v^a))$$
$$S^a[\![\text{if } c_1 \text{ then } c_2 \text{ else } c_3]\!](a^a, v^a) =$$
$$\langle S_e^a[\![c_2]\!](a^a, S_e^a[\![c_1]\!](v^a)) \sqcup S_e^a[\![c_3]\!](a^a, S_e^a[\![\neg c_1]\!](v^a)),$$
$$S_i^a[\![c_2]\!](a^a, S_e^a[\![c_1]\!](v^a)) \sqcup S_i^a[\![c_1]\!](a^a, v^a) \sqcup$$
$$S_i^a[\![c_1]\!](a^a, v^a) \sqcup S_i^a[\![c_3]\!](a^a, S_e^a[\![\neg c_1]\!](v^a)) \sqcup$$
$$S_e^a[\![\neg c_1]\!](a^a, v^a) \sqcup S_i^a[\![c_1]\!](a^a, v^a)\rangle$$

$$S^a[\![\text{while } c_1 \text{ do } c_2]\!](a, v) =$$
$$fix(S^a[\![\text{ if } (c_1) \text{ then } (c_2; \text{while } c_1 \text{ do } c_2) \text{ else } skip \ ]\!](a^a, v^a))$$

Fig. 7. Abstract Semantics of Statements

$$S^a[\![x := sexp]\!](a^a, \varphi^a, v^a) = (a^a[x \mapsto S_A^a[\![sexp]\!](a^a, \varphi^a, v^a)], v^a[x \mapsto S_S^a[\![sexp]\!](v^a)])$$
$$S^a[\![skip]\!](a^a, \varphi^a, v^a) = (a^a, \varphi^a, v^a)$$
$$S^a[\![send(sexp)]\!](a^a, \varphi^a, v^a) = (a^a, \varphi^a, v^a)$$
$$S^a[\![c_1; c_2]\!](a^a, \varphi^a, v^a) = S^a[\![c_2]\!](S^a[\![c_1]\!](a^a, \varphi^a, v^a))$$

$$S^a[\![\text{if } c_1 \text{ then } c_2 \text{ else } c_3]\!](a^a, \varphi^a, v^a) =$$
$$let \ (a'^a, \varphi'^a, v'^a) = \langle S_e^a[\![c_2]\!](a^a, \varphi^a, S_e^a[\![c_1]\!](v^a)) \sqcup S_e^a[\![c_3]\!](a^a, \varphi^a, S_e^a[\![\neg c_1]\!](v^a)),$$
$$S_i^a[\![c_2]\!](a^a, \varphi^a, S_e^a[\![c_1]\!](v^a)) \sqcup S_e^a[\![c_1]\!](a^a, \varphi^a, v^a) \sqcup$$
$$S_i^a[\![c_1]\!](a^a, \varphi^a, v^a) \sqcup S_i^a[\![c_3]\!](a^a, \varphi^a, S_e^a[\![\neg c_1]\!](v^a)) \sqcup$$
$$S_e^a[\![\neg c_1]\!](a^a, \varphi^a, v^a) \sqcup S_i^a[\![c_1]\!](a^a, \varphi^a, v^a)\rangle$$
$$in \ (a'^a, \varphi'^a[(\ell_i^a, q_i^{a\sqcap}, q_i^{a\sqcup})/(\ell_i^a, q_i^{a\sqcap} + \phi_{stm}^{a\sqcap}(c_1), q_i^{a\sqcup} + \phi_{stm}^{a\sqcup}(c_1)) : \ell_i^a \in \text{src}(c_1)], v'^a)$$

where ϕ_{stm} is the quantitative function in Def. 4

$$S^a[\![\text{while } c_1 \text{ do } c_2]\!](a^a, \varphi^a, v^a) =$$
$$fix(S^a[\![\text{ if } (c_1) \text{ then } (c_2; \text{while } c_1 \text{ do } c_2) \text{ else } skip \ ]\!](a^a, \varphi^a, v^a))$$

Fig. 8. Quantitative Abstract Semantics of Statements

We need to abstract the number of iterations of a while loop to precisely approximate the quantity of information leaked by a loop. Our approach is composed by two steps: a *while* interval analysis approximating the number of iterations, followed by an *extended adexp* collection with quantitative values.

Step (a): while Interval Analysis. We add a counter initialized to 0 at the beginning, and we increment it by one at each loop iteration. In this way, we can apply a standard interval analysis to infer an upper bound on the number of iterations of a loop.

Example Consider the following program, where i represents the counter we added:

```
1 x=-2    (i = 0)
2 while (x<27)
3    x= x+2    (i = i + 1)
4 print (x)
```

At the end of the analysis, the interval domain can infer $i \mapsto [0..15]$ (e.g., by applying a narrowing operator after widening [5]). The upper bound of the interval of variable i returns the number of iterations of the loop, that is, 15. Then the upper bound on the number of iterations 15 becomes $[1,4]$, where 4 are the number of bits leaked in 15 iterations.

Step (b): *Extended Adexp* Collection with Quantitative Value. At the end of the while interval analysis, we apply a quantitative value analysis. *Example* Consider the following example:

```
1 secret = read(...)
2 found = false
3 while (!found) {
4    pwd = user_input()
5    found = checkpwd(pwd, secret)}
```

At the end of the first iteration of the analysis of the loop, we obtain:

$$secret_1 : \langle \{ \langle \ell_1, \emptyset, \emptyset \rangle \}, \emptyset \rangle$$
$$found_2 : \langle \emptyset, \emptyset \rangle$$
$$!found_3 : \langle \emptyset, \emptyset \rangle$$
$$pwd_4 : \langle \emptyset, \emptyset \rangle$$
$$found_5 : \langle \{ \langle \ell_1, \{(checkpwd, \star)\}, \{(checkpwd, \star)\} \rangle \}, \emptyset \rangle$$

Notice that no quantitative information has yet been released. In fact, the Boolean condition of the while loop is checked against a constant value (*false*) during the first iteration. However, *found* might be still false, and the loop would be iterated another time. Then, starting from the second iteration the implicit flow will contain the new definition of the variable *found*, thus each expression inside the scope of the while will be:

$$\langle \{ \dots explicit\ flow \dots \}, \{\langle \ell_1, \{(checkpwd, \star)\}, \{(checkpwd, \star), (<, \star), (>, \star)\} \rangle \} \rangle$$

Notice that the function $checkpw(p_1, p_2)$ returns a Boolean value, so *one bit*. This means that we are accumulating a bit of information at each iteration.

As soon as the implicit flow comes into the picture, we have to consider the quantity interval computed in *step (a)*:

$$\{ \ \langle\{ \dots explicit\ flow \dots \}, \ \{\langle \ell_1, \ \{(checkpwd, \star)\}, \ \{(checkpwd, \star), (<, \star), (> , \star)\}\rangle\}\rangle, \ \langle \ell_1, \ 1, \ 4\rangle \ \}$$

If inside a while loop there is an obfuscating operator (e.g., encryption or hashing) applied to confidential data, we need to know the quantity of information that is released by the operator. For instance, in the previous example the operator checkpwd(p_1,p_2) checks if the password given by the user is correct, and it returns a Boolean value. Thus the analysis accumulates a single bit at each iteration, and the quantitative value will depend on the number of iterations. However, other operators might release more information. In this case, we compute the product of the number of iterations and the released bits.

6 Applications

In this Section, we discuss the results of our analysis of some examples listed in the DroidBench application set [20], created by the Secure Software Engineering group of the Technische Universität Darmstadt. This set is open source, and it is a standard benchmark to test static and dynamic analyses. We chose the examples that specifically deal with implicit flows.

An interesting comparison can be made with the work by Tripp and Rubin [25], as they also used DroidBench as testing environment. Their approach performs very well on the whole test set (also with respect to other tools, like TaintDroid), but it suffers from false negatives in case of implicit flows. Our analysis instead allows to cope with these particular cases, for instance the ones due to custom transformations of private data in the ImplicitFlow1 test program. This is because we adopted a different approach, that instead of looking for privacy sinks, observes the whole flow of confidential data and operations applied to them.

For the sake of readability, we simplified some library functions, and we added some semantic rules to support some primitive functions contained in these examples, and that were not part of the minimal language we adopted in our formalization. For each example, we describe the results of the collecting semantics on a particular concrete state, and we then perform a two-stages static analysis. First we illustrate the results without the quantitative component *qadexp*, and we then discuss the results of the quantitative semantics.

6.1 ImplicitFlow1

The first example is an application that reads the device identifier (IMEI), obfuscates it, and then leaks it. The obfuscation can be performed with two functions with two different obfuscation powers (namely, low and high).

```
 1  public class ImplicitFlow1 extends Activity {      31   private String hardObfIMEI(String imei){
 2                                                      32     char [] imeiAsChar = imei.toCharArray();
 3    protected void onCreate (...) {                   33     String result = "";
 4      //...                                           34     int len = imeiAsChar.length();
 5                                                       35     int i = 0;
 6      String imei = getDeviceId(); //device id        36
 7      String obfuscatedIMEI                           37     while (i < len){
 8        = obfuscateIMEI(imei);                        38       result += (char)
 9      writeToLog(obfuscatedIMEI);                     39         (((int)imeiAsChar[i]) +1 + (i i)%62);
10                                                      40       i++;
11      obfuscatedIMEI                                  41     }
12        = hardObfIMEI(imei);                          42
13      writeToLog(obfuscatedIMEI);                     43     return result ;
14    }                                                 44   }
15                                                      45
16    private String obfuscateIMEI(String imei){        46   private void writeToLog(String message){
17      String result = "";                             47     Log.i("INFO", message); //sink
18      char [] imeiAsChar = imei.toCharArray();        48   }
19      int len = imeiAsChar.length();                  49 }
20      int i = 0;
21      int shift = 49;
22
23      while (i < len){
24        result += (char)
25          (((int)imeiAsChar[i]) + shift );
26        //returns 'a' for '0', 'b' for '1', ...
27        i++;
28      }
29      return result ;
30    }
```

First of all, we extend the semantics to the new functions contained in this example. For the most part, this extension is very intuitive and straightforward.

$$S_A[\![getDeviceId()]\!](u,v) = \{\langle S_L[\![lexp]\!](a,v), \emptyset \rangle\}$$
$$S_A[\![toCharArray(sexp)]\!](a,v) = \{\langle \ell_1, L_1 \cup \{(toCharArray, \ell_1)\}\rangle\} : \langle \ell_1, L_1 \rangle \in S_A[\![sexp_1]\!](a,v)\}$$
$$S_A[\![length(sexp)]\!](a,v) = \{\langle \ell_1, L_1 \cup \{(length, \ell_1)\}\rangle\} : \langle \ell_1, L_1 \rangle \in S_A[\![sexp_1]\!](a,v)\}$$
$$S_A[\![Log(sexp)]\!](a,v) = (a,v)$$
$$S_A[\![(typecast)sexp]\!](a,v) = \{\langle \ell_1, L_1 \cup \{(cast(type), \ell_1)\}\rangle\} : \langle \ell_1, L_1 \rangle \in S_A[\![sexp_1]\!](a,v)\}$$

$getDeviceId$ returns the IMEI from the datastore, $toCharArray$ convert the label to a char, $length$ returns the dimension (in integer) of an array and Log writes the argument to a log file. $cast(type)$ represents the type casting. We also add the modulo % operator to the semantics. We collect it as mod in our domain, and its behavior is similar to other arithmetic operators. As for arrays, when we refer to a single element of the array, we assume to perform a $S_A[\![sub(sexp, k_1, k_2)]\!](a,v)$ where k_1 and k_2 are the same element and are used as a sort of index in the array.

Concrete Analysis. The device identifier IMEI is contained in the datastore and can be retrieved through $getDeviceId$, that behaves like a $S_A[\![read(lexp)]\!](a,v)$. We also add a counter that allows to count the number of iterations in the loop. Trivially, at the end of each cycle this value will be equal to the dimension of the IMEI, that is, 14.

$$imei_6 \quad : \langle\{\langle\ell_1, \emptyset\rangle\}, \emptyset\rangle$$

$$imeiAsChar_{18} : \langle\{\langle\ell_1, \{(toCharArray, \ell_1)\}\rangle\}, \emptyset\rangle$$

$$len_{19} \quad : \langle\{\langle\ell_1, \{(length, \ell_1)\}\rangle\}, \emptyset\rangle$$

$$while\ cond_{23} : \langle\{\langle\ell_1, \{(length, \ell_1), (>, \star)\}\rangle\}, \emptyset\rangle \quad (count_1 = 0)$$

$$result_{24} \quad : \langle\{\langle\ell_1, \{([sub, \star, \star], \ell_1), (cast(int), \ell_1), (+, \star), (cast(char), \ell_1), (+, \star)\}\rangle\},$$
$$\{\langle\ell_1, \{(length, \ell_1), (>, \star)\}\rangle\}\rangle$$

$$i_{27} \quad : \langle\emptyset, \{\langle\ell_1, \{(length, \ell_1), (>, \star)\}\rangle\}\rangle$$

$$\dots \quad (after\ loop\ exit\ the\ condition\ in\ the\ flow\ is\ inverted), \quad (count_1 = 14)$$

$$log_{47} \quad : \langle\{\langle\ell_1, \{([sub, \star, \star], \ell_1), (cast(int), \ell_1), (+, \star), (cast(char), \ell_1), (+, \star), \dots\}\rangle\},$$
$$\{\langle\ell_1, \{(length, \ell_1), (>, \star)(<, \star)\}\rangle\}\rangle$$

$$imeiAsChar_{32} : \langle\{\langle\ell_1, \{(toCharArray, \ell_1)\}\rangle\}, \emptyset\rangle$$

$$len_{34} \quad : \langle\{\langle\ell_1 \{(length, \ell_1)\}\rangle\}, \emptyset\rangle$$

$$while\ cond_{37} : \langle\{\langle\ell_1, \{(length, \ell_1), (>, \star)\}\rangle\}, \emptyset\rangle \quad (count_2 = 0)$$

$$result_{38} \quad : \langle\{\langle\ell_1, \{([sub, \star, \star], \ell_1), (cast(int), \ell_1), (+, \star), (\times, \star), (mod, \star), (cast(char), \ell_1),$$
$$(+, \star)\}\rangle\}, \{\langle\ell_1, \{(length, \ell_1), (>, \star)\}\rangle\}\rangle$$

$$i_{40} \quad : \langle\emptyset, \{\langle\ell_1, \{(length, \ell_1), (>, \star)\}\rangle\}\rangle$$

$$\dots \quad (after\ loop\ exit\ the\ condition\ in\ the\ flow\ is\ inverted), \quad (count_2 = 14)$$

$$log_{47} \quad : \langle\{\langle\ell_1, \{([sub, \star, \star], \ell_1), (cast(int), \ell_1), (+, \star), (\times, \star), (mod, \star), (cast(char), \ell_1),$$
$$(+, \star), \dots\}\rangle\}, \{\langle\ell_1, \{(length, \ell_1), (>, \star)(<, \star)\}\rangle\}\rangle$$

As we can see from the concrete analysis, there is no noticeable difference between the two functions. Indeed, both example apply these function inside a loop, and in both the conditional expressions depend on the dimension of the secret label.

Abstract Analysis. The main differences between the concrete and abstract semantics consist in (i) considering when the loop condition holds and does not (unlike the concrete semantics that always knows a precise value), and (ii) the application of the interval analysis to over-approximate the number of iterations. Notice that since the dimension of the IMEI does not change, the corresponding label can be abstracted with full precision. The same applies to its dimension.

$$imei_6 \quad : \langle\{\langle\ell_1, \emptyset, \emptyset\rangle\}, \emptyset\rangle$$

$$imeiAsChar_{18} : \langle\{\langle\ell_1, \{(toCharArray, \ell_1)\}, \{(toCharArray, \ell_1)\}\rangle\}, \emptyset\rangle$$

$$len_{19} \quad : \langle\{\langle\ell_1, \{(length, \ell_1)\}, \{(length, \ell_1)\}\rangle\}, \emptyset\rangle$$

$$while\ cond_{23} : \langle\{\langle\ell_1, \{(length, \ell_1), (>, \star)\}, \{(length, \ell_1), (>, \star)\}\rangle\}, \emptyset\rangle$$

$$result_{24} \quad : \langle\{\langle\ell_1, \{([sub, \star, \star], \ell_1), (cast(int), \ell_1), (+, \star), (cast(char), \ell_1), (+, \star)\},$$
$$\{([sub, \star, \star], \ell_1), (cast(int), \ell_1), (+, \star), (cast(char), \ell_1), (+, \star)\}\rangle\},$$
$$\{\langle\ell_1, \{(length, \ell_1)\}, \{(length, \ell_1), (>, \star), (<, \star)\}\rangle\}\rangle$$

$$i_{27} \quad : \langle\emptyset, \{\langle\ell_1, \{(length, \ell_1)\}, \{(length, \ell_1), (>, \star), (<, \star)\}\rangle\}\rangle$$

$$log_{47} \quad : \langle\{\langle\ell_1, \{([sub, \star, \star], \ell_1), (cast(int), \ell_1), (+, \star), (cast(char), \ell_1), (+, \star)\},$$
$$\{([sub, \star, \star], \ell_1), (cast(int), \ell_1), (+, \star), (cast(char), \ell_1), (+, \star), \dots\}\rangle\},$$
$$\{\langle\ell_1, \{(length, \ell_1)\}, \{(length, \ell_1), (>, \star), (<, \star)\}\rangle\}\rangle$$

$$imeiAsChar_{32} : \langle\{\langle\ell_1, \{(toCharArray, \ell_1)\}, \{(toCharArray, \ell_1)\}\rangle\}, \emptyset\rangle$$

$$len_{34} \quad : \langle\{\langle\ell_1, \{(length, \ell_1)\}, \{(length, \ell_1)\}\rangle\}, \emptyset\rangle$$

$$while\ cond_{37} : \langle\{\langle\ell_1, \{(length, \ell_1), (>, \star)\}, \{(length, \ell_1), (>, \star)\}\rangle\}, \emptyset\rangle$$

$$result_{38} \quad : \langle\{\langle\ell_1, \{\langle\ell_1, \{([sub, \star, \star], \ell_1), (cast(int), \ell_1), (+, \star), (\times, \star), (mod, \star),$$
$$(cast(char), \ell_1), (+, \star)\}, \{([sub, \star, \star], \ell_1), (cast(int), \ell_1), (+, \star), (\times, \star),$$
$$(mod, \star), (cast(char), \ell_1), (+, \star)\}\rangle\},$$
$$\{\langle\ell_1, \{(length, \ell_1)\}, \{(length, \ell_1), (>, \star), (<, \star)\}\rangle\}\rangle$$

$$i_{40} \; : \; \langle \emptyset, \; \{ \langle \ell_1, \{(length, \ell_1)\}, \{(length, \ell_1), (>, \star), (<, \star)\} \rangle \} \rangle$$

$$log_{47} \; : \; \langle \{ \langle \ell_1, \{ \langle \ell_1, \{([sub, \star, \star], \ell_1), (cast(int), \ell_1), (+, \star), (\times, \star), (mod, \star),$$
$$(cast(char), \ell_1), (+, \star)\}, \{([sub, \star, \star], \ell_1), (cast(int), \ell_1), (+, \star), (\times, \star),$$
$$(mod, \star), (cast(char), \ell_1), (+, \star), \ldots \} \rangle \},$$
$$\{ \langle \ell_1, \{(length, \ell_1)\}, \{(length, \ell_1), (>, \star), (<, \star)\} \rangle \} \rangle$$

Quantitative Analysis. The interval analysis approximates the minimum and maximum number of iterations of the loop. Through these bounds, we compute an interval of quantities, that infers the minimum and the maximum amount of information revealed through implicit flows. However, in this particular example the number of iterations can be precisely inferred because it is performed on a fixed value (the dimension of the IMEI). Thus, we infer that the loop is iterated 14 times. Each iteration of the loop leaks one bit of information. We now infer the number of bits using the method described in the Section 5.2:

$$quantity = \lfloor log_2(n\_iterations) \rfloor + 1 \; = 4 \; bits$$

So, in both loops, the *qadexp* is $\langle \ell_1, 4, 4 \rangle$.

6.2   ImplicitFlow2

In this example, the user has to type a password. Then, this password is compared to the correct one, that comes from the data-store. After this evaluation, a message is saved to a log file. This operation leaks information through an implicit flow, since the logged message depends on the correctness of the password.

```
1  public class ImplicitFlow2 extends Activity {
2
3    protected void onCreate(...){
4      // ...
5    }
6
7    public void checkPassword(View view){
8      String userInputPassword = //user input
9      String superSecure = //secret password
10
11     if (checkpwd(superSecure,userInputPassword))
12       passwordCorrect = true;
13     else
14       passwordCorrect = false;
15
16     if (passwordCorrect)
17       Log.i("INFO", "Password_is_correct");
18     else
19       Log.i("INFO", "Password_is_not_correct");
20   }
21 }
```

Concrete Analysis. We reuse the semantics of *Log* defined for the previous example $(S_A \llbracket Log(sexp) \rrbracket (a, v) = (a, v))$. The abstract semantics is similar. We now shows the results of the concrete semantics, assuming that the password provided by the user is not correct. The concrete data-store contains only the label that corresponds to the variable *superSecure*, that is, $\langle \ell_1, \emptyset \rangle$.

$$\begin{aligned}
\text{superSecure}_9 &: \langle\{\langle\ell_1,\ \emptyset\rangle\},\ \emptyset\rangle \\
\textit{if condtion}_{11} &: \langle\{\langle\ell_1,\ \{(checkpwd,\star)\}\rangle\},\ \emptyset\rangle \\
\text{passwordCorrect}_{14} &: \langle\emptyset,\ \{\langle\ell_1,\ \{(checkpwd,\star),(<,\star)\}\rangle\} \\
2^{nd}\ \textit{if condition}_{16} &: \langle\emptyset,\ \{\langle\ell_1,\ \{(checkpwd,\star),(<,\star)\}\rangle\} \\
\log_{19} &: \langle\emptyset,\ \{\langle\ell_1,\ \{(checkpwd,\star),(<,\star)\}\rangle\}
\end{aligned}$$

Abstract Analysis. We now present the results of the abstract semantics. We adopt the same label of the concrete semantics.

$$\begin{aligned}
\text{superSecure}_9 &: \langle\{\langle\ell_1,\ \emptyset,\emptyset\rangle\},\ \emptyset\rangle \\
\textit{if condtion}_{11} &: \langle\{\langle\ell_1,\ \{(checkpwd,\star)\},\ \{(checkpwd,\star)\}\rangle\},\ \emptyset\rangle \\
\text{passwordCorrect}_{12,14} &: \langle\emptyset,\ \{\langle\ell_1,\ \{(checkpwd,\star)\},\{(checkpwd,\star),(>,\star),(<,\star)\}\rangle\}\rangle \\
2^{nd}\ \textit{if condition}_{16} &: \langle\emptyset,\{\langle\ell_1,\ \{(checkpwd,\star)\},\{(checkpwd,\star),(>,\star),(<,\star)\}\rangle\}\rangle \\
\log_{17,19} &: \langle\emptyset,\ \{\langle\ell_1,\ \{(checkpwd,\star)\}, \\
&\quad \{(checkpwd,\star),(>,\star),(<,\star),(>,\star),(<,\star)\}\rangle\}\rangle
\end{aligned}$$

Quantitative Analysis. We abstract quantities with an interval. In this case study, there is an implicit flow in the first `if` statement:

$$\textit{if condtion}_{11} : \big\{\langle\{\langle l_1,\ \{(checkpwd,\star)\},\ \{(checkpwd,\star)\}\rangle\},\ \emptyset\rangle, \langle\ell_1,1,1\rangle\big\}$$

This value is then propagated until the *Log* statement that leaks it.

6.3   ImplicitFlow3

Like in the previous example, this example checks if a password provided by a user matches the correct password. However, in this case the information is leaked through the creation of objects.

```
 1 public class ImplicitFlow3 extends Activity {      19    interface  Interface {
 2                                                     20       public void leakInfo ();
 3    protected void onCreate (...)  {                 21    }
 4      // ...                                         22
 5    }                                                23    public class ClassA implements Interface {
 6                                                     24       public void leakInfo (){
 7    public void leakData(View view){                 25          Log.i("INFO", "pwd_correct");
 8      String userIntPwd = //user input              26       }
 9      String superSecure = //secret password        27    }
10                                                     28
11      Interface  classTmp;                           29    public class ClassB implements Interface {
12      if (checkpwd(superSecure,userIntPwd))          30       public void leakInfo (){
13         classTmp = new ClassA();                    31          Log.i("INFO", "pwd_incorrect");
14      else                                           32       }
15         classTmp = new ClassB();                    33    }
16                                                     34 }
17      classTmp.leakInfo ();
18 }
```

Concrete Analysis. We reuse the `Log` semantic described in the previous example. We assume that the password typed by the user is correct. As in the previous example, the concrete data-store contains only one label $\{\langle\ell_1,\emptyset\rangle\}$ corresponding to *superSecure*.

$$\text{superSecure}_9 : \langle \{\langle \ell_1, \emptyset \rangle\}, \emptyset \rangle$$
$$\textit{if condtion}_{12} : \langle \{\langle \ell_1, \{(checkpwd, \star), (>, \star)\}\rangle\}, \emptyset \rangle$$
$$\text{classTmp}_{13} : \langle \emptyset, \{\langle \ell_1, \{(checkpwd, \star), (>, \star)\}\rangle\}\rangle$$
$$\textit{leakInfo}_{25} : \langle \emptyset, \{\langle \ell_1, \{(checkpwd, \star), (assert, l_1)\}\rangle\}\rangle$$

Abstract Analysis. We adopt the same label abstraction.

$$\text{superSecure}_9 : \langle \{\langle \ell_1, \emptyset, \emptyset \rangle\}, \emptyset \rangle$$
$$\textit{if condtion}_{12} : \langle \{\langle \ell_1, \{(checkpwd, \star), (>, \star)\}, \{(checkpwd, \star), (>, \star)\}\rangle\}, \emptyset \rangle$$
$$\text{classTmp}_{13,14} : \langle \emptyset, \{\langle \ell_1, \{(checkpwd, \star)\}, \{(checkpwd, \star), (>, \star), (<, \star)\}\rangle\}\rangle$$
$$\textit{leakInfo}_{25,31} : \langle \emptyset, \{\langle \ell_1, \{(checkpwd, \star)\}\rangle\}\}, \{\langle \ell_1, \{(checkpwd, \star), (>, \star), (<, \star)\}\rangle\}\rangle$$

Quantitative Analysis. In this example, there is only one *if* statement that generates implicit flow. This statement exposes *1 bit* of quantity of information:

$$\textit{if condtion}_{12} : \{\langle \{\langle \ell_1, \{(checkpwd, \star), (>, \star)\}, \{(checkpwd, \star), (>, \star)\}\rangle\}, \emptyset \rangle, \langle \ell_1, 1, 1 \rangle\}$$

This value will remain the same in all the following *qadexps*.

6.4 Discussion

As emphasized by the examples above, the adoption of a quantitative analysis allows the evaluation of quantities of confidential data that might be released. In ImplicitFlow1, the analysis tells that an implicit flows exists, that confidential labels are contained in it, and it also estimate the potential quantities of data released. This quantity is calculated by the operations implemented in the code, so by the operations that obfuscate the confidential label. The application of given policies [4] will allow to establish whether the released quantities are allowed or not. Any considerations about the safeness of the analyzed application are thus referred to the type of applied policy. In particular, as for ImplicitFlow1, we are able to calculate how much the while loop affects the produced quantity of data. Indeed, it allows to understand that, given a fixed (and possibly low) number of loop iterations, the quantity of confidential data that might be released will not be high. In conclusion, this analysis is not only capable of locating implicit flows, but also to evaluate their importance. In fact, if the released values will be low, with respect to a given policy, the implicit flow will be negligible.

7 Conclusions

In this paper, we extended the framework for tracking explicit flows introduced in [4] with respect to implicit flows and quantitative analysis, showing the effectiveness of this approach on significant examples. This framework can support complex hybrid policies, i.e. policies that can grant both qualitative and quantitative thresholds.

Acknowledgments. Work partially supported by the Italian MIUR project "Security Horizons".

References

1. Arzt, S., Rasthofer, S., Fritz, C., Bodden, E., Bartel, A., Klein, J., Le Traon, Y., Octeau, D., McDaniel, P.: Flowdroid: Precise context, flow, field, object-sensitive and lifecycle-aware taint analysis for android apps. SIGPLAN Not. **49**(6), 259–269 (2014)
2. Clark, D., Hunt, S., Malacaria, P.: Quantitative analysis of the leakage of confidential data. Electronic Notes in Theoretical Computer Science **59**(3), 1–14 (2002). Quantitative Aspects of Programming Languages (Satellite Event for PLI 2001)
3. Clark, D., Hunt, S., Malacaria, P.: Quantified interference for a while language. Electr. Notes Theor. Comput. Sci. **112**, 149–166 (2005)
4. Cortesi, A., Ferrara, P., Pistoia, M., Tripp, O.: Datacentric semantics for verification of privacy policy compliance by mobile applications. In: D'Souza, D., Lal, A., Larsen, K.G. (eds.) VMCAI 2015. LNCS, vol. 8931, pp. 61–79. Springer, Heidelberg (2015)
5. Cortesi, A., Zanioli, M.: Widening and narrowing operators for abstract interpretation. Computer Languages, Systems & Structures **37**(1), 24–42 (2011)
6. Cousot, P., Cousot, R.: Abstract interpretation: a unified lattice model for static analysis of programs by construction or approximation of fixpoints. In: Conference Record of the Fourth ACM SIGPLAN-SIGACT Symposium on Principles of Programming Languages, pp. 238–252. ACM Press (1977)
7. Denning, D.E.: A lattice model of secure information flow. Communications of the ACM **19**, 236–243 (1976)
8. Enck, W., Gilbert, P., Han, S., Tendulkar, V., Chun, B.-G., Cox, L.P., Jung, J., McDaniel, P., Sheth, A.N.: Taintdroid: An information-flow tracking system for realtime privacy monitoring on smartphones. ACM Trans. Comput. Syst. **32**(2), 5:1–5:29 (2014)
9. Enck, W., Octeau, D., Mcdaniel, P., Chaudhuri, S.: A study of android application security. In: Proc. USENIX Security Symposium (2011)
10. Fritz, C., Arzt, S., et al.: Highly precise taint analysis for android application. Technical report, EC SPRIDE Technical Report TUD-CS-2013-0113 (2013). http://www.bodden.de/pubs/TUD-CS-2013-0113.pdf
11. Hammer, C., Snelting, G.: Flow-sensitive, context-sensitive, and object-sensitive information flow control based on program dependence graphs. International Journal of Information Security **8**, 399–422 (2009)
12. Hornyack, P., Han, S., Jung, J., Schechter, S., Wetherall, D.: These aren't the droids you're looking for: retrofitting android to protect data from imperious applications. In: Proc. 18th ACM Conf. on Computer and Communications Security, pp. 639–652. ACM, New York (2011)
13. International Data Corporation. Worldwide Quarterly Mobile Phone Tracker 3q14. http://www.idc.com/tracker/showproductinfo.jsp?prod-id=37 (accessed January 2015)
14. Lowe, G.: Quantifying information flow In: Proc. IEEE Computer Security Foundations Workshop, pp. 18–31 (2002)
15. McAfee Labs. Threats Report. http://www.mcafee.com/ca/resources/reports/rp-quarterly-threat-q3-2014.pdf (accessed December 2014)
16. Mccamant, S., Ernst, M.D.: A simulation-based proof technique fordynamic information flow (2007)
17. McCamant, S., Ernst, M.D.: Quantitative information flow as network flow capacity. SIGPLAN Not. **43**(6), 193–205 (2008)

18. Rasthofer, S., Arzt, S., Lovat, E., Bodden, E.: Droidforce: enforcing complex, data-centric, system-wide policies in android. In: Proceedings of the 9th International Conference on Availability, Reliability and Security (ARES). IEEE, September 2014
19. Russo, A., Sabelfeld, A., Li, K.: Implicit flows in malicious and nonmalicious code. In: Logics and Languages for Reliability and Security. NATO Science for Peace and Security Series, vol. 25, pp. 301–322. IOS Press (2010)
20. Secure Software Engineering Group - Ec Spride. DroidBench. http://sseblog.ec-spride.de/tools/droidbench/ (accessed February 2015)
21. Smith, G.: Principles of secure information flow analysis. In: Christodorescu, M., et al. (eds.) Malware Detection. Advances in Information Security, vol. 27, pp. 291–307. Springer (2007)
22. Sridharan, M., Artzi, S., Pistoia, M., Guarnieri, S., Tripp, O., Berg, R.: F4f: taint analysis of framework-based web applications. In: OOPSLA. ACM (2011)
23. Tripp, O., Ferrara, P., Pistoia, M.: Hybrid security analysis of web javascript code via dynamic partial evaluation. In: Proc. of the 2014 Int. Symposium on Software Testing and Analysis, ISSTA 2014, pp. 49–59. ACM, New York (2014)
24. Tripp, O., Pistoia, M., Fink, S.J., Sridharan, M., Weisman, O.: Taj: effective taint analysis of web applications. In: ACM PLDI, pp. 87–97. ACM (2009)
25. Tripp, O., Rubin, J.: A bayesian approach to privacy enforcement in smartphones. In: USENIX Security (2014)

Probabilistic Principal Components and Mixtures, How This Works

Anna M. Bartkowiak[1,2]($\boxtimes$) and Radoslaw Zimroz[3]

[1] Institute of Computer Science, Wroclaw University, 50-383 Wroclaw, Poland
aba@ii.uni.wroc.pl
[2] Wroclaw School of Information Technology, 54-239 Wroclaw, Poland
[3] Diagnostics and Vibro-Acoustics Science Laboratory,
Wroclaw University of Technology, 50-421 Wroclaw, Poland

Abstract. Classical Principal Components Analysis (PCA) is widely recognized as a method for dimensionality reduction and data visualization. This is a purely algebraic method, it considers just some optimization problem which fits exactly to the gathered data vectors with their particularities. No statistical significance tests are possible. An alternative is to use probabilistic principal component analysis (PPCA), which is formulated on a probabilistic ground. Obviously, to do it one has to know the probability distribution of the analyzed data. Usually the Multi-Variate Gaussian (MVG) distribution is assumed. But what, if the analyzed data are decidedly not MVG? We have met such problem when elaborating multivariate gearbox data derived from a heavy duty machine. We show here how we have dealt with the problem.

In our analysis, we assumed that the considered data are a mixture of two groups being MVG, specifically: each of the sub-group follows a probabilistic principal component (PPC) distribution with a MVG error function. Then, by applying Bayesian inference, we were able to calculate for each data vector x its a posteriori probability of belonging to data generated by the assumed model. After estimation of the parameters of the assumed model we got means - based on a sound statistical basis - for constructing confidence boundaries of the data and finding outliers.

Keywords: Probabilistic principal components · Multi-variate normal distribution · Mixture models · Un-mixing multivariate data · Condition monitoring · Gearbox diagnostics · Healthy state · Probabilities a posteriori · Outliers

1 Introduction

Classical Principal Components Analysis (PCA) is widely recognized as a method for dimensionality reduction and data visualization. However, PCA is a purely algebraic method, it considers just some optimization problem which fits exactly to the gathered data vectors with their particularities.

Yet, without a proper probability model it is impossible to formulate statistically significant statements.

© IFIP International Federation for Information Processing 2015
K. Saeed and W. Homenda (Eds.): CISIM 2015, LNCS 9339, pp. 24–35, 2015.
DOI: 10.1007/978-3-319-24369-6_2

On the opposite, Probabilistic Principal Components Analysis (PPCA) permits to tackle the data in a smoothed holistic way. It is easy to introduce into its models (formulated in d-dimensional data space) some q dimensional sub-models with q lower than d. Additionally, probabilistic principal components may be combined into a mixture model, which permits to model the non-Gaussian data as a mixture of several sub-groups, each of them having its own Gaussian distribution. We will show below how such a model (embedding PPCA into mixtures) may be useful in analysis of real data.

We will consider data obtained from vibration signals of a heavy-duty machine being in good state. Say, the data are contained in a real data matrix B of size $n \times d$, that is with n rows (time segments) and d columns (variables characterizing the segments). It is common to imagine the data vectors of such a matrix as d-dimensional points located in the d-dimensional data space. During operation, the condition of the machine may deteriorate. The very important question is: **how to determine, whether the condition of the machine is good (healthy), or - whether it starts to be** (or is already) **faulty.**

Methods of multivariate data analysis permit to answer the above question, provided that it is formulated in strict mathematical language. For instance, one may be concerned with the following questions:

- Is the machine in good or bad condition? How to carry out the monitoring of the state the machine? To answer these questions, one needs also data sample from a 'bad' machine. The bad data sample should be provided as another data matrix with d columns containing values of the same variables as those measured for the 'good' matrix B. A survey of methods and papers dealing with this question may be found, for example, in [1,5,6,8,10,13,21].
- For the problem: How to detect the fault possibly early? see, e.g. [11].
- For very common and widely elaborated problems falling under the topics Feature selection and/or Dimensionality reduction see, e.g. [3,18,20], and references therein.
- Say, we have data only for a machine in good condition. For its monitoring, we might specifically ask for the boundary in the data space delimiting the 'normal', that is 'healthy' data. This problem is usually solved using methods like one class classification, novelty or anomaly detection, and outlier identification, see, for example, [2,8,12,14].

In the following we will be concerned only with the last item. We will consider only one machine being in good condition. Our novel contributions are related to a modelling of multidimensional diagnostic data using probabilistic approach. Our proposal is to combine *three* statistical models *into one common model*, which yields so called *probabilities a posteriori (posteriors)*. Under way, we are able to reduce dimensionality of the considered data. The posteriors obtained from the common model permit to perform - according to one's wish - condition monitoring, anomaly or novelty detection, identification of outliers (if any), and dimensionality reduction.

In this paper we show generally how the common model may be formulated and how its parameters may be estimated – this is illustrated using the mentioned data set B of the gearbox data. We show also - for the analyzed data set B - that the mentioned posteriors may be calculated directly and how they look like. The posteriors are the basis for further statistical inference - like anomaly detection, confidence boundaries construction, etc., however, for lack of space, this is not elaborated in the paper.

The paper is scheduled as follows. Actually, we are in Section 1, Introduction. Next Section 2 introduces the three basically used by us statistical methods, namely the Mixture model, Bayesian inference and the Probabilistic Principal Components – to construct a common model for the data. Some issues of dimensionality reduction are also considered. Section 3 contains a short description of essential features of the data serving as the basis for our analysis, also some details on constructing the learning and testing sample. In Section 4 we formulate the principles of our experiment and the goals to be achieved. We show, how the assumed common model works with our data. We show also, how the posteriors – calculated for our data look like – and what exactly they do mean. Section 5 contains some discussion and closing remarks.

2 Methodology of Un-Mixing Multivariate Data by Using Mixture Model with Probabilistic Principal Components

2.1 The Mixture Model

Suppose, we have M different groups of multivariate data, each of the groups containing data vectors x with d elements corresponding to d observed variables. Let $p(\mathbf{x} \mid j)$ denote the probability (probability density) that a given data vector x belongs to group j, $j = 1, \ldots, M$.

Next let us consider the overall probability distribution of all the data containing the M groups. The overall probability (probability density) function may be modelled as a mixture composed from these M groups [15]:

$$p(\mathbf{x}) = \sum_{j=1}^{M} P(j)p(\mathbf{x} \mid j), \tag{1}$$

where the symbols $P(j)$ are called *mixing coefficients*. They have the properties:

$$\sum_{j=1}^{M} P(j) = 1, \quad \text{and} \quad 0 \leq P(j) \leq 1, \quad j = 1, \ldots, M.$$

The *overall* probability distribution function $p(\mathbf{x})$ defined above in eq. (1) is a proper probability distribution function (pdf) describing the probabilities of all the data mixed together into one common group. The derived pdf given in (1) is called the *total* pdf. The mixing coefficients $P(j)$ are called *priors* or *probabilities á priori*.

Using Bayes' theorem, it is common to define *posterior probabilities* (*posteriors*) as:

$$P(j \mid \mathbf{x}) = \frac{p(\mathbf{x} \mid j)P(j)}{p(\mathbf{x})} \qquad (2)$$

In the following we will consider mixtures models composed only of two components, that is $M = 2$. The group-conditioned pdf's will be MVG with spherical covariance matrix $\boldsymbol{\Sigma}_j = \sigma_j^2 \boldsymbol{I}$:

$$p(\mathbf{x} \mid j) = \frac{1}{(2\pi\sigma_j^2)^{d/2}} \, exp\{-\frac{||\mathbf{x} - \boldsymbol{\mu}_j||^2}{2\sigma_j^2}\} \qquad (3)$$

2.2 Probabilistic Principal Components and Reduction of the Variables Space

The probabilistic principal components methodology is based on the assumption that the observed data vector $\mathbf{x}$ may be modelled as a linear combination of some latent variables defined in an - unobservable directly - latent variables space of dimension $q <= d$. The assumed model reads:

$$\mathbf{x} = \mathbf{W}\mathbf{z} + \boldsymbol{\mu} + \mathbf{e}. \qquad (4)$$

Meaning of symbols appearing in the assumed model:

$\mathbf{x}$ - the observed d-dimensional data vector, called also data instance,

$\mathbf{z}$ - q-dimensional latent factor variable, with $\mathbf{0}$ mean and unit isotropic variance; $\mathbf{z}$ is distributed as $N_q(\mathbf{0}, \mathbf{I})$,

$\mathbf{W}$ - so called matrix of loadings, consists of constant real numbers playing the role of parameters of the model; it may be estimated e.g. by the Maximum Likelihood (ML) method,

$\boldsymbol{\mu}$ - some constants playing the role of shift parameters; have to be estimated; the ML method yields here the data means as estimates,

$\mathbf{e}$ - independent noise process distributed as $N_d(\mathbf{0}, \sigma^2\mathbf{I})$.

Taking eq. (4) into account, the probability density model for the probabilistic principal component analysis (PPCA) reads:

$$p(\mathbf{x} \mid \mathbf{z}) = \frac{1}{(2\pi\sigma^2)^{d/2}} \, exp\{-\frac{||\mathbf{x} - \mathbf{W}\mathbf{z} - \boldsymbol{\mu}||^2}{2\sigma^2}\} \qquad (5)$$

Tipping and Bishop [17] have shown how to obtain estimates of the unknown parameters appearing in eq. (5). By integrating out the latent variables $\mathbf{z}$ they got that the distribution of the observed variables $\mathbf{x}$ is

$$\mathbf{x} \sim N(\boldsymbol{\mu}, \mathbf{C}), \quad \text{where} \quad \mathbf{C} = \mathbf{W}\mathbf{W}^\mathbf{T} + \sigma^2\mathbf{I}. \qquad (6)$$

Tipping and Bishop [17] have shown also that the ML methods yields the following estimates for the parameters $\mathbf{W}$ and σ^2 appearing in the probability model for PPCA shown in eq. (5):

$$\mathbf{W}_{ML} = \mathbf{U}_q(\Lambda_q - \sigma^2\mathbf{I})^{1/2}\mathbf{R}, \quad \text{where} \quad \sigma^2_{ML} = \frac{1}{d-q}\sum_{j=q+1}^{d}\lambda_j, \tag{7}$$

and $\Lambda_q, \mathbf{U}_q$ denote, up to a rotation matrix $\mathbf{R}$, the first q largest eigenvalues and the connected with them eigenvectors of the covariance matrix $\mathbf{C}$.

The dimension q is declared by the user. The variance σ^2_{ML} is interpreted as the variance lost in the projection from the data space (dimension d) to the latent space (dimension q).

After estimation of all the parameters appearing in the general mixture model (1) and its components, the posteriors defined in eq. (2) will be the most important. They will play an essential role in our analysis of real gearbox data, which are described in next section.

3 The Analyzed Data Sets: Learning Sample B500 and Test Sample Bres

In the following we will show an analysis conducted using true data from machines working in field conditions. The data were recorded by Bartelmus and Zimroz [1] from two gearboxes, one being faulty, i.e. in bad condition, the other being healthy, i.e. in good condition.

Taking as a new feature the sum of all the 15 variables, Bartelmus and Zimroz [1] were able to classify – on the base of the proposed feature – about 80 % of all data vectors. To classify the remainder, they needed an external variable, called ZWE, indicating for the actual load of the working machine.

The data were more thoroughly investigated in [2,19]. It appeared that the distribution of the variables is not Gaussian, the data contain a considerable number of outliers, moreover, the covariance structure in the two groups (faulty and healthy) is markedly different.

In the following we will consider only the healthy data containing $n = 951$ data vectors. The entire healthy gearbox data set $\mathbf{B}$ was subdivided into a learning sample called B500 and a testing sample called Bres. The learning sample B500 was obtained from randomly chosen 500 rows of the original data set $\mathbf{B}$. The remainder of the data called Bres containing 451 rows from $\mathbf{B}$, was designated for testing the built model.

Apart from this, we got also for each data instance (i.e. data vector $\mathbf{x}$) the value of another variable, called ZWE. The ZWE variable represents value of averaged speed for short (1s) observation period called segment (of signal), from which one 15D feature vector $\mathbf{x}$ was derived. Value of ZWE may belong to speed range: 940-1000 rpm (rotations per minute). Typically, values ZWE<= 990 denote a heavy load (HL); for ZWE> 990 the load is considered to be small or none (NL).

The number of heavy and small/none loads in the investigated $B500$-sample happened to be: 439 instances HL, 61 instances NL.

In Fig. 1 we show the distribution of the variable ZWE in the entire data set **B** (top graph), in the derived learning sample B500 (middle graph), and in the test sample Bres (bottom graphs). One may notice that all the three displays are very similar with respect of their ZWE distributions.

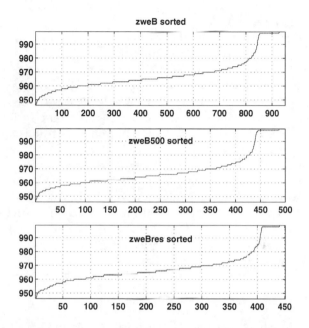

Fig. 1. Ordered values of ZWE in analyzed data **B** and its sub-samples B500 and Bres. *Top*: original set **B**. *Middle*: learning sample B500. *Bottom*: test sample Bres. Take notice that the distributions of ZWE visible in the three displays look similar.

For easiness of identifying the further results, the data instances (i.e. the data vectors) from both samples were sorted according the their ZWE values (each sample was sorted separately). After sorting, the heavy load data instances (HL) appear first, and the no-load instances (NL) last.

Our further analysis will consist of:

(i) building a two-group mixture model with embedded probabilistic principal components of dimension $q = 2$,

(ii) calculating the posteriors (see eq. 2) allowing for statistical inference on fitness of the assumed model and on the normality or abnormality of consecutive data vectors (abnormality means here outliers or atypical observations, which are not concordant with the assumed population model).

4   Application of Mixture Model with Embedded PPCs to Real Data; How This Works

4.1   Preliminary Settings

In this section we report our analysis when using the B500 and Bres samples of size 500×15 and size 451×15 appropriately. The rows $\mathbf{x} = [x_1, x_2, \ldots, x_{15}]$ of both samples are ordered according to increasing values of ZWE corresponding to their respective $\mathbf{x}$ vectors.

The B500 set is supposed to be the learning sample and the Bres set the test sample for the constructed probabilistic model.

Our first goal is to obtain for the data set B500 a decomposition into two Gaussian sub-samples numerated as $j = 1$ and $j = 2$. A second goal is to assert the connection of the derived sub-samples with the load variable ZWE. A third goal is to obtain an affirmation that the obtained decomposition (un-mixing of the data set B500 into two component sets from which it is composed) fits adequately to the gathered data.

We will show in next two subsections how these goals were realized for the B500 data set. Here we add only that we carried out the analysis using a special type neural network gmm from the Netlab library [15]. The network worked in an unsupervised way, that is it knew only that it has to divide the B500 sample into two sub-groups, however it did not know that the sub-groups are expected to be associated with the status of the variable ZWE, which was out of reach for the network during its work at this stage.

4.2   Modelling Data from the B500 Sample

The basic mixture model from eq. (1) with M=2 was applied. It says that we will consider the B500 sample as a mixture composed from two sub-groups, each of them having its own probability density function (pdf) denoted as $p(\mathbf{x}|j)$, $j = 1, 2$. Each of these pdf's is assumed be MVG with probabilistic principal components embedded into the expected values of the assumed MVG's – accordingly to eq. (3) and (4). There is a lot of parameters to estimate. The neural network gmm packs them into a structure called here mixB500. The structure contains in its subsequent fields values of the parameters needed for an analysis of the supplied data B500. The fields of mixB500 and their contents are shown in Table 1. After initialization of the structure, the fields are filled sequentially with advancing of the analysis.

The fields of the structure mixB500 are:
type - a kind of signature of the structure,
nin - number of the variables (columns) in the data matrix B500,
ncentres - how many sub-groups (components of the mixture) are desired,
covar_type - indicates how the covariance matrices have to be calculated; option 'ppca' means that the covariances should be calculated according to eq. (6),
ppca_dim - how many principal components (latent variables according eq. (4))

Table 1. The structure `mixB500` containing parameters used in the considered mixture model, before and after applying the EM algorithm

type: 'gmm'	type: 'gmm'
nin: 15	nin: 15
ncentres: 2	ncentres: 2
covar_type: 'ppca'	covar_type: 'ppca'
ppca_dim: 2	ppca_dim: 2
priors: [0.1285 0.8715]	priors: [0.1318 0.8682]
centres: [2x15 double]	centres: [2x15 double]
covars: [9.3489e-004 0.0090]	covars: [8.5744e-004 0.0093]
U: [15x2x2 double]	U: [15x2x2 double]
lambda: [2x2 double]	lambda: [2x2 double]
nwts: 98	nwts: 98

we wish to include into the model. We declared that we want to retain only 2 principal components,

priors - cardinalities of the two sub-groups of the mixture,

centres - means of the two initialized sub-groups after run of k-means (left structure), and re-adjusted after run of the EM algorithm (right structure),

covars - covariance matrices of the sub-model. In case of 'ppca' option the spherical covariance matrices are assumed by default. We have two sub-groups, each needs one real value as its variance,

U - eigenvectors from the matrix $\mathbf{C}$ given in eq. (6), for each sub-group separately.

lambda - the eigen-values associated with the eigen-vectors in $\mathbf{U}$,

nwts - the number of values memorized in the structure `mixB500`. In our case, the structure contains 98 constants, which are necessary when considering particular problems connected with the constructed mixture model. The parameters/weights are optimized by the Maximum likelihood method using the EM algorithm.

After finishing the estimation process, the structure `mixB500` is filled with some constants and with estimates of parameters necessary for further calculations. In particular, we may find there the parameters necessary for evaluation of the two sub-groups into which the entire data set B500 was split. The un-mix of the mixture appearing in set B500 is done.

Next steps of calculations are optional. We will be concerned with the content of subgroups established by the gmm network, also how this content is connected with the load variable ZWE. This is considered in next subsection.

4.3   The Content of Subgroups Obtained from the Mixture Model Memorized in mixB500

The gmm network fed with the B500 sample data has split the obtained data into two subgroups. Parameters useful for further calculations are stored in the structure `mixB500` (see Table 1).

We are mainly concerned, what is the content of these subgroups. To obtain answer to this question, we inspect for each $\mathbf{x} \in B500$ its group probability density (likelihood) $L(\mathbf{x}|j)$ and its posterior $P(j|\mathbf{x})$ for $j=1$ and $j=2$. The evaluated likelihoods and posteriors are shown in Fig 2.

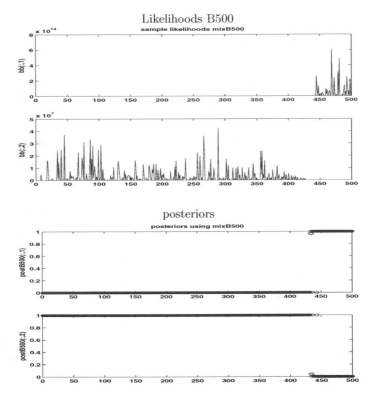

Fig. 2. Learning sample B500. Likelihoods and posterior probabilities of appearing data vectors $\mathbf{x}_i$, $i = 1, \ldots, 500$ in the mixture formed from two sub-groups. Counting from top to bottom: *First panel*: Likelihood of appearing in sub-group numbered $j = 1$. *Second panel*: Likelihood of appearing in sub-group numbered $j = 2$. *Third panel*: probability a posteriori of belonging to sub-group numbered $j = 1$. *Fourth panel*: probability a posterior of belonging to sub-group numbered $j = 2$.

The top graph in Fig. 2 shows likelihoods obtained as values of the probability density function $p(\mathbf{x} \mid j)$ (with parameters evaluated by the ML method). In our case we have in the mixture 2 groups of data. Each group has its Gaussian pdf with estimated parameters stored in the structure **mixB500**.Thus we are able to evaluate the value of the respective pdf (in other words, the likelihood) for every data vector $\mathbf{x}$.

Taking the pdf of the first derived sub-group numbered as $j=1$, we substitute into this pdf in turn all data vectors $\mathbf{x}$ contained in the set B500; this yields the set of likelihood values displayed in the first panel of Fig. 2. The displayed likelihoods are numbered $1, 2, \ldots, 500$, that is, similarly as the data vectors $\mathbf{x}$ serving to evaluation of the displayed likelihoods. Looking at the graph one may notice that the pronounced values of the likelihoods appear only for the (about)last 50 data instances of B500. Remembering that the sample B500 was sorted according its increasing ZWE values, one may deduce immediately: the subgroup $j=1$ contains data instances with highest ZWE values, which means NL category of the load.

Taking the pdf of the second derived sub-group numbered as $j=2$, and repeating the actions as above, we obtain the series of likelihoods evaluated for subsequent values $\mathbf{x}$ of the data B500, however now the likelihoods are evaluated from the pdf characterizing the subgroup numbered $j=2$. The likelihoods evaluated in such a way are shown in the second panel of Fig. 2. One may notice here, that pronounced values of the likelihoods appear for about first 450 data instances. It happens that just these 450 data instances are HL (i.e. heavy loaded). Thus the subgroup numbered $j=2$ contains data instances which are heavy loaded.

Analogous reasoning may be conducted when considering the probabilities a posteriori shown in the 3rd and 4th panel of Fig. 2. Here we see a clear group membership assignment. Moreover, the assignment is amazingly sharp. All data instances are allocated with a high probability. There are no doubtful assignments.

The final allocation of the 500 data instances is $66 + 434$ (to sub-group $j=1$ and $j=2$ appropriately).

4.4   Analysis of the Data Set Bres

The Bres data set, counting 451 data instances, is composed from the remnants of the entire data set B after removing from it the sample B500. It constitutes test data for the mixture model `mixB500` built previously in subsection 4.3 from the B500 data. Now the Bres data could be considered using two possibilities :

(i) Looking at the behavior of the testing vectors $x \in$Bres by evaluating their likelihoods and posteriors on the basis of the mixture model whose parameters are memorized in the structure `mixB500` obtained from an alien data set (B500).

(ii) Constructing a new, own data structure `mixBres`, and taking this new structure as basis for calculating the likelihoods and the posteriors for the Bres data.

We have performed the analysis according both (i) and (ii). The results, displayed in a similar way as those in Fig. 2, are amazingly similar; for lack of space they could not be shown here. Performing a similar analysis as for the B500 data set we got very similar results. For lack of space we show here only the final allocations of the data vectors $\mathbf{x}$ from Bres:

When making allocation using the alien `mixB500` structure: $51 + 400$.

When building own mixture model and own structure `mixBres`: $50 + 401$.

5   Discussion and Concluding Remarks

We have considered so far only the simplest probabilistic principal component mixture models assuming Gaussian rank-2 sub-models with a spherical covariance matrix. To our surprise, such a very simple model works amazingly well both for the learning sample B500 and the test sample Bres of the healthy gearbox data. Indeed, we got an un-mixing of the entire data set B into two sub-models, one of them corresponding to the heavy_load and the other to the light/none_load state of the instances belonging to set B. Moreover, this was achieved using only sub-models of dimension $q = 2$ (the original data are 15-dimensional).

The main results are: The data for the healthy gearbox can be modelled as a mixture of two separate sub-groups, each of them having its own multi-variate Gaussian distribution. The subgroups are associated with an external variable ZWE, namely one subgroup has ZWE of category HL (heavy load), the other subgroup has ZWE of category NL (no or light load). The outliers stated in [2] have disappeared.

However this simple model is not valid for data coming from a faulty gearbox. Faulty data are essentially different (see [19]) and have to be modelled separately using a more complex model.

All the calculations were done using raw data without any standardization. It is known that neural networks (its optimization procedures) are favoring standardized data. Also the results in [21] were obtained using standardized data. It would be interesting to repeat the analysis using standardized data. Also, we feel it worthy to look for a similar model for the data from a faulty gearbox, which seems to be for the gearbox data from [1] a much more difficult task.

References

1. Bartelmus, W., Zimroz, R.: A new feature for monitoring the condition of gearboxes in nonstationary operating systems. Mechanical Systems and Signal Processing **23**(5), 1528–1534 (2009)
2. Bartkowiak, A., Zimroz, R.: Outliers analysis and one class classification approach for planetary gearbox diagnosis. Journal of Physics: Conference Series **305** (1), art. no. 012031 (2011)
3. Bartkowiak, A., Zimroz, R.: Data dimension reduction and visualization with application to multidimensional gearbox diagnostics data: Comparison of several methods. Diffusion and Defect Data Pt.B: Solid State Phenomena **180**, 177–184 (2012)
4. Bishop, C.M.: Neural Networks for Pattern Recognition. Oxford University Press (1995)
5. Chen, J., Zhang, C., Zhang, X., et al.: Customized lifting multiwavelet packet information entropy for equipment condition identification. Smart Mater. Struct. **22**, 095022 (14pp). IOPPublishing (2013)
6. Chen, J., Zhang, C., Zhang, X., et al.: Planetary gearbox condition monitoring of ship-based satellite communication antennas using ensemble multiwavelet analysis methods. Mech. Syst. Signal Process. **54**, 277–292 (2014)

7. Cocconcelli, M., Zimroz, R., Rubini, R., Bartelmus, W.: Kurtosis over energy distribution approach for STFT enhancement in ball bearing diagnostics. In: Condition Monitoring of Machinery in Non-Stationary Operations 2012, Part I, pp. 51–59 (2012)
8. Heyns, T., Heyns, P.S., de Villiers, J.P.: Combining synchronous averaging with a Gaussian mixture model novelty detection scheme for vibration-based condition monitoring of a gearbox. Mech. Syst. Signal Process. **32**, 200–215 (2012)
9. Heyns, T., Heyns, P.S., Zimroz, R.: Combining discrepancy analysis with sensorless signal resampling for condition monitoring of rotating machines under fluctuating operations. Int. J. of Condition Monitoring **2**(2), 52–58 (2012)
10. Jardine, A.K.S., Lin, D., Banjevic, D.: A review on machinery diagnostics and prognostics implementing condition-based maintenance. Mech. Syst. Signal Process. **20**, 1483–1510 (2006)
11. Jedlinski, L., Jonak, J.: Early fault detection in gearboxes based on support vector machines and multilayer perceptron with a continuous wavelet transport. Applied Soft Computing Journal (2015) (in print)
12. Khan, S.S., Madden, M.G.: One-class classification: taxonomy of study. The knowledge Engineering Review. Cambridge Univ. Press (2014)
13. Lei, Y., Lin, J., Zuo, M.J., He, Z.: Condition monitoring and fault detection of planetary gearboxes: A review. Measurement **48**, 292–306 (2014)
14. Montechiesi, L., Cocconcelli, M., Rubini, R.: Artificial immune system via Euclidean Distance Minimization for anomaly detection in bearings. Mech. Syst. Signal Processing (2015) (in print). http://dx.doi.org/101016/j.ymssp.2015.04.017
15. Nabney, I.T.: NETLAB, Algorithms for Pattern Recognition. Springer, Heidelberg (2002)
16. Pimentel, M.A.F., Clifton, D.A., Clifton, L., Tarassenko, L.: A review of novelty detection. Signal Processing **99**, 215–249 (2014)
17. Tipping, M.E., Bishop, C.M.: Probabilistic principal component analysis. J. Roy. Statist. Soc. B **61**, 611–622 (1999)
18. Zheng, J., Zhang, H., Cattani, C., et al.: Dimensionality reduction by supervised neighbor embedding using Lapacian search. Computational and Mathematical Methods in Medicine (Hindawi) **2014**, 594379, 14pp (2014). http://dx.doi.org/10.1155/2014/594379
19. Zimroz, R., Bartkowiak, A.: Investigation on spectral structure of gearbox vibration signals by principal component analysis for condition monitoring purposes. Journal of Physics: Conference Series **305** (1), art. no. 012075 (2011)
20. Zimroz, R., Bartkowiak, A.: Multidimensional data analysis for condition monitoring: features selection and data classification. CM2012–MFPT2012. BINDT, June 11–14, London. Electronic Proceedings, art no. 402, pp. 1–12 (2012)
21. Zimroz, R., Bartkowiak, A.: Two simple multivariate procedures for monitoring planetary gearboxes in non-stationary operating conditions. Mech. Syst. Signal Process. **38**(1), 237–247 (2013)

Music Information Retrieval –
Soft Computing Versus Statistics

Bozena Kostek[✉]

Faculty of Electronics, Telecommunications and Informatics, Audio Acoustics Laboratory,
Gdańsk University of Technology, Narutowicza 11/12 80-233, Gdańsk, Poland
bokostek@audioakustyka.org

Abstract. Music Information Retrieval (MIR) is an interdisciplinary research area that covers automated extraction of information from audio signals, music databases and services enabling the indexed information searching. In the early stages the primary focus of MIR was on music information through Query-by-Humming (QBH) applications, i.e. on identifying a piece of music by singing (singing/whistling), while more advanced implementations supporting Query-by-Example (QBE) searching resulted in names of audio tracks, song identification, etc. Both QBH and QBE required several steps, among others an optimized signal parametrization and the soft computing approach. Nowadays, MIR is associated with research based on the content analysis that is related to the retrieval of a musical style, genre or music referring to mood or emotions. Even though, this type of music retrieval called Query-by-Category still needs feature extraction and parametrization optimizing, but in this case search of global online music systems and services applications with their millions of users is based on statistical measures. The paper presents details concerning MIR background and answers a question concerning usage of soft computing versus statistics, namely: why and when each of them should be employed.

Keywords: Music information retrieval (MIR) · Feature extraction · Soft computing · Collaborative filtering (CF) · Similarity measures

1 Introduction

Music Information Retrieval is a very well-exploited field. They are venues devoted to MIR only (e.g. ISMIR, MIREX) [18][20][24][34] in which state-of-the-art MIR methods and achievements are critically evaluated, also sessions, workshops, discussion panels dedicated to this domain occur within artificial intelligence, audio, multimedia and other symposia and conferences [14][16][17][23]. On the other hand, there exist many music recommendation services, commercial and non-commercial that are based on social networking rather than on MIR-related methods [31][38][39][40][41]. This is often the case when a query for specific song or music genre may be performed based on similarity measures retrieved from large music archives [23][31]. In this context the stress should be on 'large' because smaller databases could easily be managed by human resources. Most prior research done into the audio genre recognition within the field of Music Information Retrieval were based on rather small music databases with a few classes of music genres [1][8][9][17][25].

© IFIP International Federation for Information Processing 2015
K. Saeed and W. Homenda (Eds.): CISIM 2015, LNCS 9339, pp. 36–47, 2015.
DOI: 10.1007/978-3-319-24369-6_3

Even though collaborative (commercial) music services exist for many years, there are still some key problems that should be addressed in this field. This is especially important in cases when human-based evaluation doesn't always give correct answers or is far from giving correct answers, but nevertheless the user-based annotation is utilized in predicting the user's music preference. Moreover, there remains the key problem related to the scalability of the proposed solutions, regardless of the type of application (research- or commercial-based).

Applications that may be discerned within MIR area are: music genre classification, automatic track separation, music transcription, music recommendation, music generation, music emotion recognition (MER), music indexing, intellectual property rights management, and others. Many of the applications recalled above are based on a similar approach that consists in music pre-processing including parametrization, and the usage of soft computing methods [9][10][11][12][13][15][19][23][35]. These background notions are to be shortly reviewed with a focus on whether they need to be readdressed by MIR community.

The aim of this paper is paper is two-fold. First of it discusses MIR-related research and background measures utilized in music services. Secondly, it is to answer a question concerning usage of soft computing versus statistics, namely: why and when each of them should be employed. Section 2 reviews state-of-the-art in MIR in the context of search-based analysis, while in Section 3 issues related parametrization and soft-computing-based approach to genre classification are shown. Section 4 reviews background research that lies behind the song prediction in music services. Finally, summary remarks are formulated forming Conclusion Section.

2   Queries in MIR

Without any doubts one may say that MIR is a global research concentrated on the practical use of technical implementations and systems applications to music. Supported by soft computing, MIR evolved into a new domain, namely musical informatics. One of the crucial issues is the improvement of the efficiency of music recognition (e.g. in terms of performance), close to classification performed by human. However one of the problems is that human-based evaluation is not always able to give correct answers. Thus, we expect better soft-computing- than human-based performance. This concerns both music genre and emotion recognition.

During its early stages, MIR focus was on studies that allowed for searching for music information through QBH, *Query-by-Humming/Singing/Whistling*. Since singing or whistling is a natural ability of humans, humming to a microphone seemed to be the most convenient way to search for a given melody.

Full representation of a non-polyphonic piece is often called 'melody profile'. 'Sequence of frequencies' is a representation losing time-domain information, that is onsets and durations of sounds, but the information about pitches is preserved. In melodies represented as 'sequences of intervals', tonality information is lost, but the sizes of intervals between each pair of two consecutive sounds are known. The most simplified representation is the 'sequence of the directions of intervals' – only the directions of pitch of subsequent sounds in a melody are known. The last representation contains significantly reduced information, but at the same time preserves enough information for retrieval, i.e. it is resistant to rhythm changes (as no rhythm is retained), tonality and transposition errors. One of the most often cited work within QBH research studies is by Ghias *et al.* [5], who implemented a system able to detect coarse melodic contour based on Parsons code and retrieved by text string search. Even though the system had some constraints, i.e. usage of MIDI code, easily discerned notes, no rhythmic information, each pair of consecutive notes simply coded as "U" ("up") if the second note is higher than the first note, "R" ("repeat") if the pitches are equal, and "D" ("down") otherwise, it performed surprisingly well on a prepared database. This is especially interesting, when one takes into account fact that a human ability to recognize hummed melody is not very high. It was observed that the average human accuracy in recognizing hummed queries is approximately 66% [27][37]. This is why formulating queries in that way may not be fully sufficient, even though it is intuitive for humans or musicians, but still may be inconvenient for non-musicians.

A simple measure used for non-polyphonic pieces and single-channel melodies, which are common in the MIDI standard is based on the distance d between a query $q = q_1, q_2, ..., q_m$ and object $t = t_1, t_2, ..., t_n$ is calculated with Eq. 1. The length of the query equals to m, the length of the object is n. The average difference in pitch between the query and an object in the database is calculated, the minimum average difference is acknowledged to be the distance between the query and the object – the shifts of j positions in a melody and transpositions of Δ semitones are committed to minimize the value of the distance.

$$d(q,t) = \frac{1}{m} \min_{j=1}^{n-m} (\min_{\Delta} \sum_{i=1}^{i=m} | q_i - t_{i+j} + \Delta |) \tag{1}$$

In melody retrieval systems, a query is usually a fragment of a full melody, so the matching is done in many locations of a melody, the pattern given in the query is matched against all objects in the database. In addition, queries do not exactly match the melodies in the database, so time-consuming approximate string matching techniques should be used. All those factors enlarge the computational complexity of the music retrieval task. Although optimizations to the classical approach by Baesa-Yates to approximate string matching were proposed, algorithms for melody retrieval may still be time-consuming, especially if the database contains large amount of musical files or/and rhythm information by detecting periodicity in time domain [21] or by analyzing note duration is added to music database.

More advanced MIR applications support *Query-by-example* searching. They are strongly rooted in collaborative music social networking when a given song may be used as a query for similar music. However more broaden retrieval refers to *content-based* analysis. In particular, search for similar musical styles, genres or mood/emotions of a musical piece is called *Query-by-category: musical style, genre, mood/emotion* (content-based) [11]. These types of information retrieval are visible in both research-based and music services, however the most significant difference between these two approaches lies in the size of music databases. Research-based databases contain a few hundred or the most a few thousands music excerpts, typically 30 (or less) second-long because of their copyright situation which should allow processing and presenting them to the public, while music services offer million of songs. These facts translate straightforward into the answer when and why soft computing or similarity-based approach can be applied.

The need for user-centric music recommendation created music services. Search may use tags contained in the ID3v.2 format (a query may consist of the song title, artist, genre, composer, album title, song length, lyrics, etc.). Music databases contain songs assigned to music genres, described by low level feature vectors or higher level descriptors, such as an instrument name, lyrics, etc., often annotated manually. Music services collect also interaction traces between the user and the song or between the users. A simple "interaction" means to play a song by the user and save it to the list of the so-called "favorite songs" This is the way of creating the user's profile. This information can be sent from the user's computer in the form of an application (e.g. scrobbler - an application installed by the service last.fm [39], which involves automatic transmission of metadata for all of the music tracks for the user's computer for analysis and the so-called collaborative filtering (CF) [4][6][22][30].

With regard to the effectiveness of music search, when low level-feature-based approach is used for small databases, the achieved effectiveness varies depending on a feature vector of used parameters and decision algorithms and is in the range of 60-90% [20][16][17][37]. It should be noted that efficiency is comparable to results obtained in the process of musical genre classification by human. In the case of databases based on tags IDv3.2 format, the accuracy of searching depends on the efficiency of the search algorithm to search the database (e.g., SQL), which means that a typographical error contained in the query within the well-known music databases such as FreeDB or GRACENOTE may cause a lack of response.

Annotating music manually requires a large number of "experts" with musical background, and is time-consuming. However, when performed by statistically significant number of people participating in the process, this starts to be to some extent reliable and effective method. This method is also called social tagging and takes the form in which key words describing a musical piece are added by users. Of course, it must be remembered that manual annotation can also be problematic in the context of various musical tastes and preferences, which can lead to a situation where the same track is assigned to different genres by individuals with diverse musical experience. That is why, it is often observed that users are not able to fully objectively assign a given musical piece to appropriate musical styles.

3   Parametrization and Decision Systems

Paramerization, a part of the pre-processing, aims at differentiating objects between different classes, recognizing unclassified objects (from unknown class) and determining whether an object is a member of a certain class. The underlying need to parametrize musical signals is their redundancy, thus a parametrization process results in the creation of feature vectors. Therefore, the decision process can be based on a set of parameters that are characteristic for e.g. musical style. Feature vectors containing time-, frequency or time-frequency-domains descriptors are often completed by adding statistical parameters.

As mentioned already retrieval that performs based on a low-level description of music depends on the quality of parametrization and the associated decision system.

Low-level descriptors are usually based on the MPEG 7 standard, Mel-frequency cepstral coefficients (MFCC's) or, finally, dedicated parameters suggested by researchers [2][7][14][15][19][24][25]. Within this approach, feature descriptors are assigned to a given music excerpt in order to perform automatic annotation of a given piece. Thus, the adequate selection of parameters, the algorithm optimization in terms of signal processing and data exploration techniques serve as key technologies that provide effective music tagging automatically.

An example of a set of descriptors (191 in total) based on MPEG 7 standard, mel cepstral and dedicated parameters before optimization is given in Table 1 [7][10][28][29]. This was the feature vector created for the ISMIS'2011 (19th International Symposium on Methodologies for Intelligent Systems) music recognition contest. Prepared by the author and her collaborators was then incorporated into the ISMIS database [16]. The database contains over 1300 music excerpts, represented by 6 music genres (classical, Jazz, Blues, Rock, Heavy Metal, Pop). The winners of this competition got around 88% of correct classification [32]. As mentioned before the original FV contains 191 descriptors. Such a large number of parameters allows for an effective classification of musical genres, but at the same time it leads to a very high data redundancy, what results in a reduced classification effectiveness in terms of time consumption. That's why the author and her Ph.D. student applied PCA-based (Principal Component Analysis) optimization, and they obtained even higher accuracy in the classification process, but most important - classifying music genres was possible in real time based on buffered parts of the processed signals [7].

Table 1. Audio features an overview by the total number and description per type [7][29]

No. of param.	Audio Feature Description
1	Temporal Centroid
2	Spectral Centroid and its variance
34	Audio Spectrum Envelope (ASE) in 34 subbands
1	ASE mean
34	ASE variance in 34 subbands
1	Mean ASE variance
2	Audio Spectrum Centroid (ASC) and its variance
2	Audio Spectrum Spread (ASS) and its variance
24	Spectral Flatness Measure (SFM) in 24 subbands
1	SFM mean
24	SFM variance
1	SFM variance of all subbands
20	Mel Cepstral Coefficients (MFCC) –first 20
20	MFCC Variance –first 20
3	No. of samples higher than single/double/triple RMS value
3	Mean of THR_[1,2,3]RMS_TOT for 10 time frames
3	Variance of THR_[1,2,3]RMS_TOT for 10 time frames
1	A ratio of peak to RMS (Root Mean Square)
2	A mean/variance of PEAK_RMS_TOT for 10 time frames
1	Number of transition by the level Zero
2	Mean/Variance value of ZCD for 10 time frames
3	Number of transitions by single/double/triple level RMS
3	Mean value of [1,2,3]RMS_TCD for 10 time frames
3	Variance value of [1,2,3]RMS_TCD for 10 time frames

In general, the input signal is analyzed in the frequency sub-bands and then a set of parameters are calculated. That's why the optimization process of the feature vectors containing low-level features is further needed. Further, an important issue is that the available music excerpts represents typically 30 seconds (or less) of the whole track, which in most cases it is the beginning of the track (which not always is a perfect match for this music genre). Due to that fact even such a genre as Rap&HipHop which is quite easy to distinguish by the listener, can be hard to classify by the pre-trained system, since these 30 seconds can be represented either by the musical part or lyrics, differing much in style.

The same feature vector was applied to a larger database (but diminished to 173 parameters because not all frequency bands were present in the signal), called Synat, containing approximately 52,000 30 seconds-long music excerpts [7]. They are allocated to 22 music genres: Alternative Rock, Blues, Broadway&Vocalists, Children's Music, Christian&Gospel, Classic Rock, Classical, Country, Dance&DJ, Folk, Hard Rock&Metal, International, Jazz, Latin Music, Miscellaneous, New Age, Opera&Vocal, Pop, Rap&Hip-Hop, Rock, R&B, and Soundtracks. The database contains additional metadata, such as: artist name, album name, genre and song title. In addition to the items listed in the database, songs include also track number, year of recording and other parameters typically used for annotation of recordings. The user interface of this system is shown in Fig. 1.

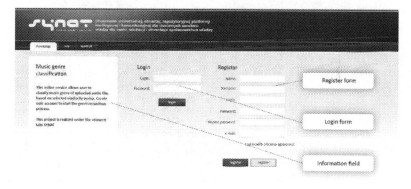

Fig. 1. Synat system user interface

From the whole Synat database 32,110 audio excerpts were chosen representing 11 genres (it is to note that this gives 5 555 030 parameters altogether, i.e. 32,110 x 173-element feature vector). That's why the PCA was applied to diminish this number for classification process. The system allows for an effective recommendation of music, experiments performed on 11 genres with an optimized feature vector returned classification accuracy of above 92% [11].

When reviewing MIR-related sources, one may see that among known classifiers the most often used are: SVMs (Support Vector Machines), minimum-distance methods, to which the k-Nearest Neighbor (k-NN) method belongs, Decision Trees, Random Forests, Rough Sets, etc. [15][17][26][34][35]. Each of these systems should ideally be considered in terms of high robustness and efficiency, not being computationally expensive, 'protecting' against overfitting, etc. Even though there is room to refine most of the given criteria, but when this list of criteria and conditions is reviewed one can say that the most problematic to achieve is the condition of not being computationally expensive when applied to large databases. That's why music recommendation services relies on statistics rather than on learning algorithms.

4   Music Recommendation

There are at least two layers of analysis when talking about music recommendation systems. It concerns both understanding and predicting user preferences. A recommender system must interact with the user, both to learn the user's preferences and provide recommendations based on the nearest neighbor for any query [4]. Systems should collect reliable data from which to compute their recommendations and preferences, reducing the noise in user preference data sets.

Before some background notions related to recommender systems are recalled, the problem of scalability should be pointed out, first. Scalability of search solutions imposes either small databases (utilized in research) and typically not showing results in real-time or utilizing techniques that reduce the number of users or items (or/and both) in search. One of the well-known solutions aimed to reduce the complexity and high dimensionality of database spaces is *Locality Sensitive Hashing* (LSH) belonging to randomized algorithms [33]. Its role is not to return exact answer but to guarantee a high probability that will bring in an answer close to the correct one. The algorithm builds a hash table, i.e., a data structure that allows for mapping between a symbol (i.e., a string) and a value. Then an arbitrary, pseudorandom function of the symbol that maps the symbol into an integer that indexes a table is calculated [33]. LSH is based on the idea that, if two points are close in a predefined space, then after the mapping operation these two points will remain close together [33].

The basis for a collaborative filtering is a collection of users' preferences for various (music) items (see Fig. 2 for explanation) [6][10][22][30][36]. Preference expressed by the user for an item is called a rating. The (user-item) matrix $\mathbf{X}$ with dimensions $K{\times}M$, is composed of K users, and M songs. A single matrix element is described by $x_{k,m} = r$, which means that the kth user assigns the r rate for the mth song. The matrix $\mathbf{X}$ may be decomposed into row vectors, representing each individual rating and may be treated as a separate prediction for the unknown rating [6][10][22][30][36]:

$$\mathbf{X} = [\mathbf{u}_1, \ldots , \mathbf{u}_K]^T, \mathbf{u}_k = [x_{k,1}, \ldots , x_{k,M}]^T, k = 1, \ldots , K \qquad (2)$$

Vector $\mathbf{u}_k^T$ describes the kth user's profile as it is a set of all ratings assigned (where: T denotes transpose of the matrix $\mathbf{X}$). Such decomposition of the matrix $\mathbf{X}$ constitutes a foundation for the users-based collaborative filtering.

It is also possible to present the matrix $\mathbf{X}$ as column vectors [6][10][22][30][36]:

$$\mathbf{X} = [\mathbf{i}_1, \ldots, \mathbf{i}_M], \mathbf{i}_m = [x_{1,m}, \ldots, x_{K,m}], m = 1, \ldots, M \qquad (3)$$

where $\mathbf{i}_m$ is a set of ratings of the mth song assigned by all K users. In this case this forms a basis for representing song(item)-based collaborative filtering (this process is illustrated in Fig. 3).

Both types of collaborative filtering need further processing, i.e. in the case of the *user-based collaborative filtering* each raw denoted above is sorted by its similarity towards the kth user's profile. The set of similar users can be identified by employing a threshold or selecting a group of top-N similar users. More detailed mathematical description of this method may be found in the work by Wang *et al.* [36].

For calculating a similarity between the users k and a in the collaborative filtering typically *Pearson correlation* (Eq. 4) or *cosine similarity* (Eq. 5) measures are used, which belong to memory-based algorithms:

$$s_{\mathbf{u}}(\mathbf{u}_k, \mathbf{u}_a) = \frac{\sum_{m \in M}(x_{k,m} - \overline{u}_k) \cdot (x_{a,m} - \overline{u}_a)}{\sqrt{\sum_{m \in M}(x_{k,m} - \overline{u}_k)^2} \cdot \sqrt{\sum_{m \in M}(x_{a,m} - \overline{u}_a)^2}} \qquad (4)$$

where:

- $x_{k,m}, x_{a,m}$ – is mth rate of a song assigned by the k and a users,
- $\overline{u}_k, \overline{u}_a$ – mean values of ratings assigned by the k and a users.

$$s_{\mathbf{u}}(\mathbf{u}_k, \mathbf{u}_a) = \cos(\mathbf{u}_k, \mathbf{u}_a) = \frac{\mathbf{u}_k \cdot \mathbf{u}_a}{\|\mathbf{u}_k\| * \|\mathbf{u}_a\|} \qquad (5)$$

where:

- $\mathbf{u}_k \cdot \mathbf{u}_a$ – scalar product of $\mathbf{u}_k$ and $\mathbf{u}_a$,
- $\|\mathbf{u}_k\|, \|\mathbf{u}_a\|$ – length of vectors $\mathbf{u}_k$ and $\mathbf{u}_a$.

Reassuming, the cosine similarity is represented by a scalar product and magnitude, in the information retrieval the resulting similarity ranges are within 0 (indicating decorrelation),1 (exactly the same). These are only examples of measures and metrics that are used, *adjusted cosine similarity* is another metric employed in the ranking area. To memory-based algorithms K-Nearest Neighbor also belongs.

Other techniques such as smoothing the estimate from the collection statistics, using the linear smoothing method are employed towards derivation of the ranking formulas [6][10][22][30][36]. Apart from memory-based and model-based algorithms among CF algorithms one may discern ranking-based and probabilistic model-based [6][10][22][30][36].

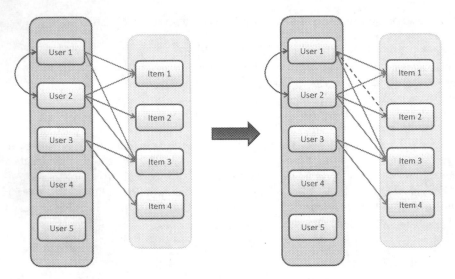

Fig. 2. Illustration of the user-based preference prediction for various (music) items (green lines indicate what the user listens to (and how many times), if two users (interconnected by a red arc) listen to the given song, and one of the pair listens to another one, then the implication is that the second one of the pair may want to listen to this one as well (violet dashed line)

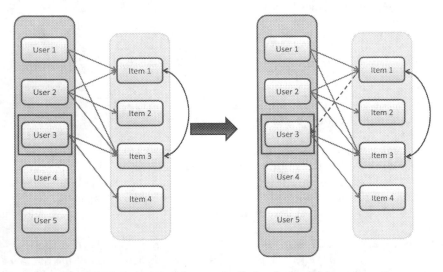

Fig. 3. Illustration of the item-based preference prediction (explanation as above, but concerning music items)

Due to the sparsity of the data, considering the co-occurrence statistics is unreliable. Thus in some recommender systems *Similar User Ratings*, *Similar Item Ratings* or *Similar User-Item Ratings* are used for diminishing the matrix **X**. For example in the *Similar User Ratings* approach for prediction only those songs are taken into account that were ranked highly in the ranked list, reducing the retrieval performance of the top-N returned items. In general, it is assumed that in systems with a sufficiently high user to item ratio, adding the user or changing ratings is unlikely to significantly change the similarity between two items, particularly when the items have many ratings. Therefore, pre-computing similarities between items in an item–item similarity matrix may be reasonable.

As brought by researchers working in the recommendation systems field, collaborative filtering is not risk-free. If there are millions of songs in a music service, then even very active users are not able to listen even to 1% of the music sources. This may result in unreliable recommendation. Thus, the fundamental question in modelling collaborative filtering is how to relate users and items through this usually very sparse user-item matrix.

When reviewing literature sources concerning collaborative filtering important issues related to sparsity, scalability, privacy of data, reliability, etc. are pointed out One of the very interesting ones lying at the roots of CF concerns how much confidence may be placed in the users' preferences, and whether it should be 'measured' with their consent or not. That's why the ultimate goal may be collaborative filtering without a community.

5   Conclusions

In this paper challenges in music retrieval and music recommendation systems were outlined. Also, reasons behind the answer to the question why and when statistics versus soft computing methods should be employed was given. Based on the review presented it may be concluded that issues of retrieval and recommendation are interconnected and these two approaches when joint together may make both processes more reliable. Also, new strategies such as for example separating music tracks at the pre-processing phase [3][8][28][29] and extending vector of parameters by descriptors related to a given musical instrument components that are characteristic for the specific musical genre to music genre classification should be more thoroughly pursued [3][28][29].

Acknowledgements. The study has been supported by the project no. PBS1/B3/16/2012 entitled "Multimodal system supporting acoustic communication with computers" financed by the Polish National Centre for R&D.

References

1. Aucouturier, J.-J., Pachet, F.: Representing musical genre: A state of art. J. New Music Research **32**(1), 83–93 (2003)
2. Bergstra, J., Casagrande, N., Erhan, D., Eck, D., Kegl, B.: Aggregate features and Ada-Boost for music classification. Machine Learning **65**(2–3), 473–484 (2006)
3. Eweret, S., Prado, B., Muller, M., Plumbley, M.: Score-Informed Source Separation for Musical Audio Recordings. Signal Processing Magazine, 116–124 (2014)
4. Ekstrand, M.D., Riedl, J.T., Konstan, J.A.: Collaborative Filtering Recommender Systems. Foundations and Trends in Human-Computer Interaction **4**(2), 81–173 (2011). doi:10.1561/1100000009

5. Ghias, A., Logan, J., Chamberlin, D., Smith, B.C.: Query by humming - musical information retrieval in an audio database. In: ACM Multimedia 1995, San Francisco (1995)
6. Guy, I., Zwerdling, N., Ronen, I., Carmel, D., Uziel, E.: Social media recommendation based on people and tags, pp. 194–201. ACM (2010)
7. Hoffmann, P., Kostek, B.: Music genre recognition in the rough set-based environment. In: Kryszkiewicz, M., Bandyopadhyay, S., Rybinski, H., Pal, S.K. (eds.) PReMI 2015. LNCS, vol. 9124, pp. 377–386. Springer, Heidelberg (2015)
8. Holzapfel, A., Stylianou, Y.: Musical genre classification using nonnegative matrix factorization-based features. IEEE Transactions on ASLP **16**(2), 424–434 (2008)
9. Hyoung-Gook, K., Moreau, N., Sikora, T.: MPEG-7 Audio and Beyond: Audio Content Indexing and Retrieval. Wiley & Sons (2005)
10. Konstan, J.L., Terveen, L.G., Riedl, J.T.: Evaluating Collaborative Filtering Recommender Systems Herlocker. ACM Transactions on Information Systems **22**(1), January 2004
11. Kostek, B.: Music information retrieval in music repositories. In: Skowron, A., Suraj, Z. (eds.) Rough Sets and Intelligent Systems - Professor Zdzisław Pawlak in Memoriam. ISRL, vol. 42, pp. 463–489. Springer, Heidelberg (2013)
12. Hoffmann, P., Kostek, B.: Music data processing and mining in large databases for active media. In: Ślęzak, D., Schaefer, G., Vuong, S.T., Kim, Y.-S. (eds.) AMT 2014. LNCS, vol. 8610, pp. 85–95. Springer, Heidelberg (2014)
13. Kostek, B.: Soft Computing in Acoustics, Applications of Neural Networks, Fuzzy Logic and Rough Sets to Musical Acoustics. Studies in Fuzziness and Soft Computing. Physica Verlag, Heildelberg (1999)
14. Kostek, B., Czyzewski, A.: Representing Musical Instrument Sounds for their Automatic Classification. J. Audio Eng. Soc. **49**, 768–785 (2001)
15. Kostek, B.: Perception-Based Data Processing in Acoustics. Applications to Music Information Retrieval and Psychophysiology of Hearing. Series on Cognitive Technologies. Springer Verlag, Heidelberg (2005)
16. Kostek, B., Kupryjanow, A., Zwan, P., Jiang, W., Raś, Z.W., Wojnarski, M., Swietlicka, J.: Report of the ISMIS 2011 contest: music information retrieval. In: Kryszkiewicz, M., Rybinski, H., Skowron, A., Raś, Z.W. (eds.) ISMIS 2011. LNCS, vol. 6804, pp. 715–724. Springer, Heidelberg (2011)
17. Li, T., Ogihara, M., Li, Q.: A comparative study on content-based music genre classification. In: Proceedings 26th Annual International ACM SIGIR Conference on Research and Development in Information Retrieval, Toronto, Canada, pp. 282–289 (2003)
18. Lidy T., Rauber A., Pertusa A., Inesta J.: Combining audio and symbolic descriptors for music classification from audio, Music Information Retrieval Information Exchange (MIREX) (2007)
19. Lindsay A., Herre J.: MPEG-7 and MPEG-7 Audio - An Overview **49**(7/8), pp. 589–594 (2001)
20. Mandel, M., Ellis, D.: LABROSA's audio music similarity and classification submissions, Music Information Retrieval Information Exchange (MIREX) (2007)
21. McNab, R.J., Smith, L.A., Witten, I.H., Henderson, C.L., Cunningham, S.J.: Toward the digital music library: tune retrieval from acoustic input. In: Proc. ACM Digital Libraries, pp. 11–18 (1996)
22. Mu, X., Chen, Y., Li, T.: User-based collaborative filtering based on improved similarity algorithm. In: Proceedings of the 3rd IEEE International Conference on Computer Science and Information Technology, Chengdu, China, vol. 8 pp. 76–80 (2010)

23. Ness, S., Theocharis, A., Tzanetakis, G., Martins, L.G.: Improving automatic music tag annotation using stacked generalization of probabilistic SVM outputs. In: 17 ACM Intern. Conf. on Multimedia, New York, NY (2009)
24. Pampalk, E., Flexer, A., Widmer, G.: Improvements of audio-based music similarity and genre classification. In: Proc. ISMIR, London, UK (2005)
25. Pachet, F., Cazaly, D.: A classification of musical genre. In: Proc. RIAO Content-Based Multimedia Information Access Conf., 2000 (2003)
26. Pawlak, Z.: Rough Sets. International J. Computer and Information Sciences **11**, 341–356 (1982)
27. Prechelt, L., Typke, R.: An interface for melody input. ACM Trans. on Computer Human Interaction **8** (2001)
28. Rosner, A., Schuller, B., Kostek, B.: Classification of Music Genres Based on Music Separation into Harmonic and Drum Components. Archives of Acoustics, 629–638 (2014)
29. Rosner, A., Weninger, F., Schuller, B., Michalak, M., Kostek, B.: Influence of low-level features extracted from rhythmic and harmonic sections on music genre classification. In: Gruca, A., Czachórski, T., Kozielski, S. (eds.) Man-Machine Interactions 3. AISC, vol. 242, pp. 467–473. Springer, Heidelberg (2014)
30. Sarwar, B., Karypis, G., Konstan, J., Riedl, J.: Item-based collaborative filtering recommendation algorithms. In: Proc. 10th International Conference on World Wide Web, New York, NY, USA, 285–295 (2001)
31. Schedl, M., Gomez, E., Urbano, J.: Music Information Retrieval: Recent Developments and Applications, vol. 8, no. 2–3, pp. 127–261. Now Publishers Inc., Boston (2014)
32. Schierz, A., Budka, M.: High–performance music information retrieval system for song genre classification. In: Kryszkiewicz, M., Rybinski, H., Skowron, A., Raś, Z.W. (eds.) ISMIS 2011. LNCS, vol. 6804, pp. 725–733. Springer, Heidelberg (2011)
33. Slaney, M., Casey, M.: Locality-Sensitive Hashing for Finding Nearest Neighbors. IEEE Signal Processing Magazine, March 2008. doi:10.1109/MSP.2007.914237
34. The International Society for Music Information Retrieval (ISMIR website). http://www.ismir.net/
35. Tzanetakis, G., Cook, P.: Musical genre classification of audio signal. IEEE Transactions on Speech and Audio Processing **10**(3), 293–302 (2002)
36. Wang, J., de Vries, A.P., Reinders, M.J.T.: Unifying user-based and item-based collaborative filtering approaches by similarity fusion. In: Proc. 29th Annual Intern. ACM SIGIR Conf. on Research and Development in Information Retrieval (2006)
37. Weinstein, E.: Query By Humming: A Survey. http://cs.nyu.edu/~eugenew/publications/humming-summary.pdf
38. http://www.amazon.com/
39. http://www.emusic.com/
40. http://www.last.fm/
41. http://musicovery.com/
42. http://www.pandora.com

Integrals Based on Monotone Measure: Optimization Tools and Special Functionals

Radko Mesiar[✉]

Slovak University of Technology, Bratislava, Slovakia
radko.mesiar@stuba.sk

Abstract. Integrals on finite spaces (e.g., sets of criteria in multicriteria decision support) based on capacities are discussed, axiomatized and examplified. We introduce first the universal integrals, covering the Choquet, Shilkret and Sugeno integrals. Based on optimization approach, we discuss decomposition and superdecomposition integrals. We introduce integrals which are universal and decomposition (superdecomposition) ones and integrals constructed by means of copulas. Several distinguished integrals are represented as particular functionals. Finally, we recall also OWA operators and some their generalizations.

Keywords: Capacity · Choquet integral · Copula · Copula–based integral · Decomposition integral · Sugeno integral · Universal integral

1 Introduction

Though integrals are, in general, introduced on general measurable spaces, in many computer–supported applications the finite spaces are considered, such as the sets of criteria, sets of rules, sets of players, etc. Therefore, in this paper we will consider universes $X_n = \{1, ..., n\}$, $n \in N$, and σ–algebras 2^{X_n}. More, we restrict our considerations into functions $f : X_n \to [0,1]$, i.e., we will consider n–dimensional vectors $\mathbf{x} = (x_1, ..., x_n) = (f(1), ..., f(n)) \in [0,1]^n$ as our integrands. Note that these integrands can be seen as membership functions of fuzzy subsets of X_n, too [24]. The information about the weights of subsets of X_n (e.g., groups of players, groups of criteria, etc.) is condensed into a capacity (fuzzy measure) $m : 2^{X_n} \to [0,1]$, which is supported to be monotone and $m(\emptyset) = 0$, $m(X_n) = 1$. Our overview of integrals on X_n, i.e., of discrete integrals is organized as follows. In Section 2, we bring the concept of universal integrals originally introduced in [8]. Section 3 is devoted to the decomposition integrals of Even and Lehrer [3] and the superdecomposition integrals of Mesiar et al [13]. Here we describe also all integrals which are simultaneously universal and decomposition (superdecomposition). In Section 4, we introduce several copula–based universal integrals. Section 5 brings the characterization of some distinguished integrals as particular functionals. Finally, some concluding remarks are added, recalling OWA operators and some of their generalizations.

© IFIP International Federation for Information Processing 2015
K. Saeed and W. Homenda (Eds.): CISIM 2015, LNCS 9339, pp. 48–57, 2015.
DOI: 10.1007/978-3-319-24369-6_4

2 Universal Integrals

Though universal integrals were introduced in [8] for any measurable space $(X, \mathcal{A})$, any monotone measure m and all $\mathcal{A}$-measurable functions $f\colon X \to [0, \infty]$, for our purposes we constrain them to act on finite spaces, and we will consider capacities and membership functions of fuzzy sets. For $n \in \mathbb{N}$, let $\mathcal{M}_n$ denote the set of all capacities on X_n.

Definition 1. *A mapping* $I\colon \bigcup\limits_{n-1}^{\infty} \mathcal{M}_n \times [0,1]^n \to [0,1]$ *is called a (discrete) universal integral whenever*

(i) *there is a semicopula* $\otimes\colon [0,1]^2 \to [0,1]$ *(i.e., an increasing binary function on $[0,1]$ with neutral element $e = 1$) such that for any $n \in \mathbb{N}$, $m \in \mathcal{M}_n$ and* $\mathbf{x} = c \cdot 1_A \in [0,1]^n$, $c \in [0,1]$, *it holds that*

$$I(m, \mathbf{x}) = c \otimes m(A),$$

(ii) *for any* $(m_i, \mathbf{x}_i) \in \mathcal{M}_{n_i} \times [0,1]^{n_i}$, $i = 1, 2$, *such that for any $t \in [0,1]$,*
$$m_1 \left(\{i \in X_{n_1} \mid x_i^{(1)} \geq t\} \right) \leq m_2 \left(\{j \in X_{n_2} \mid x_j^{(2)} \geq t\} \right) \ \text{it holds that}$$

$$I(m_1, \mathbf{x}_1) \leq I(m_2, \mathbf{x}_2).$$

Note that I is then increasing in both coordinates and $I(m_1, \mathbf{x}_1) = I(m_2, \mathbf{x}_2)$ whenever $m_1 \left(\{i \in X_{n_1} \mid x_i^{(1)} \geq t\} \right) = m_2 \left(\{j \in X_{n_2} \mid x_j^{(2)} \geq t\} \right)$ for each $t \in [0,1]$ (compare the equality of the expected values of random variables with the same distribution function). Moreover, $I(m, 1_A) = m(A)$ and $I(m, c \cdot 1_{X_n}) = c$ for all $m \in \mathcal{M}_n$, $A \subseteq X_n$ and $c \in [0,1]$.

We recall several distinguished examples:

- For an arbitrary semicopula $\otimes\colon [0,1]^2 \to [0,1]$, the smallest universal integral that is linked to $\otimes$, is given, for any $(m, \mathbf{x}) \in \mathcal{M}_n \times [0,1]^n$, by

$$\begin{aligned}
I_\otimes(m, \mathbf{x}) &= \sup \left\{ x_i \otimes m \left(\{j \in X_n \mid x_j \geq x_i\} \right) \mid i \in X_n \right\} \\
&= \sup \left\{ x_{\sigma(i)} \otimes m \left(\{\sigma(i), \ldots, \sigma(n)\} \right) \right\}, \quad (1)
\end{aligned}$$

where $\sigma\colon X_n \to X_n$ is an arbitrary permutation such that $x_{\sigma(1)} \leq \ldots \leq x_{\sigma(n)}$. In particular, if $\otimes = \wedge$ (minimum) then $I_\wedge = Su$ is the Sugeno integral [19], if $\otimes = \cdot$ (product) then $I. = Sh$ is the Shilkret integral [18], and if $\otimes = T$ is a strict norm, then I_T is the Weber integral [20], compare also N-integral of Zhao [23].
- The Choquet integral [1] that is given by

$$Ch(m, \mathbf{x}) = \sum_{i=1}^{n} \left(x_{\sigma(i)} - x_{\sigma(i-1)} \right) \cdot m \left(\{\sigma(i), \ldots, \sigma(n)\} \right) \quad (2)$$

$(x_{\sigma(0)} = 0$ by convention), is a universal integral linked to the product.

- The arithmetic mean of integrals Ch and Su, $I = \frac{1}{2}(Ch + Su)$, is also a universal integral, and it is linked to the semicopula $\otimes\colon [0,1]^2 \to [0,1]$, $a \otimes b = \frac{1}{2}(ab + \min\{a,b\})$.

Note that the class of all discrete universal integrals is a convex bounded partially ordered set. Its bottom I_{T_D} is linked to the drastic product t-norm T_D (the smallest semicopula), and, for all $(m,\mathbf{x}) \in \mathcal{M}_n \times [0,1]^n$, is given by

$$I_{T_D}(m,\mathbf{x}) = \max\left\{\max\left\{x_i \,|\, m\left(\{j \in X_n \,|\, x_j \geq x_i\}\right) = 1\right\}, m\left(\{i \in X_n \,|\, x_i = 1\}\right)\right\}.$$

Note that if $m(A) < 1$ whenever $A \neq X_n$, then

$$I_{T_D}(m,\mathbf{x}) = \max\left\{\min\left\{x_i \,|\, i \in X_n\right\}, m\left(\{i \in X_n \,|\, x_i = 1\}\right)\right\}.$$

On the other side, the top universal integral $I^\wedge$ is linked to the minimum $\wedge$ (which is the greatest semicopula) and given by

$$I^\wedge(m,\mathbf{x}) = \mathrm{essup}_m(\mathbf{x}) \wedge m(\mathrm{Supp}(\mathbf{x}))$$
$$= \min\left\{\max\left\{x_i \,|\, m\left(\{j \in X_n \,|\, x_j \geq x_i\}\right) > 0\right\}, m\left(\{i \in X_n \,|\, x_i > 0\}\right)\right\}.$$

Several other kinds of universal integrals will be discussed in Sections 3 and 4.

3   Decomposition and Superdecomposition Integrals

For $X_n = \{1,\ldots,n\}$, any non-empty subset $B \subseteq 2^{X_n}$ is called a collection, and any non-empty set $\mathcal{H} \subseteq 2^{2^{X_n}\setminus\{\emptyset\}}$ of collections is called a decomposition system. Denote by $\mathbb{X}_n$ the set of all decomposition systems.

We recall several examples of decomposition systems:

- $\mathcal{H}_i = \{(A_1,\ldots,A_i) \,|\, (A_1,\ldots,A_i) \text{ is a chain}\}$, $i = 1,\ldots,n$;
- $\mathcal{H}^i = \{(A_1,\ldots,A_i) \,|\, (A_1,\ldots,A_i) \text{ is a disjoint system of subsets}\}$, $i = 1,\ldots,n$;
- $\mathcal{H}^* = 2^{X_n} \setminus \{\emptyset\}$;
- $\mathcal{H}_A = \{B \subseteq X_n \,|\, A \subseteq B\}$.

Recently, Even and Lehrer [3] introduced decomposition integrals based on the idea of decomposition systems. These integrals can be viewed as a modification of the idea of the lower integral (inner measure). Similarly, the upper integral (outer measure) inspired the concept of superdecomposition integrals [13].

Definition 2. *For a given capacity* $m\colon 2^{X_n} \to [0,1]$ *and a fixed decomposition system* $\mathcal{H} \in \mathbb{X}_n$, *the corresponding decomposition integral* $I_{\mathcal{H},m}\colon [0,1]^n \to [0,\infty[$ *is given by*

$$I_{\mathcal{H},m}(\mathbf{x}) = \sup\left\{\sum_{j \in J} a_j m(A_j) \,|\, (A_j)_{j \in J} \in \mathcal{H}, \, a_j \geq 0, \, j \in J, \, \sum_{j \in J} a_j 1_{A_j} \leq \mathbf{x}\right\},$$

(3)

and the corresponding superdecomposition integral $I^{\mathcal{H},m}\colon [0,1]^n \to [0,\infty[$ is given by

$$I^{\mathcal{H},m}(\mathbf{x}) = \inf\left\{\sum_{j\in J} a_j m(A_j) \mid (A_j)_{j\in J} \in \mathcal{H},\ a_j \geq 0,\ j \in J,\ \sum_{j\in J} a_j 1_{A_j} \geq \mathbf{x}\right\}.$$
(4)

Note that:

- $I_{\mathcal{H}_1} = I_{\mathcal{H}^1} = Sh$ is the Shilkret integral [18];
- $I_{\mathcal{H}_n} = I^{\mathcal{H}_n} = Ch$ is the Choquet integral [1];
- $I_{\mathcal{H}^n} = PAN$ is the PAN integral of Yang [22];
- $I_{\mathcal{H}^*} = CVE$ is the concave integral of Lehrer [11];
- $I^{\mathcal{H}^*} = CEX$ is the convex integral introduced in [13];
- $I_{\mathcal{H}_{X_n}} = Min$;
- $I^{\mathcal{H}_{X_n}} = Max$.

The relationships between these integrals are visualized in Figure 1.

Example 1.

Let $n = 3$ and let m be a capacity on $X_3 = \{1,2,3\}$ given by $m(\{1\}) = 0.3$, $m(\{2\}) = 0.4$, $m(\{3\}) = 0.6$, $m(\{1,2\}) = m(\{2,3\}) = 0.7$, $m(\{1,3\}) = 0.6$ (and obviously, $m(X) = 1$). Consider the score vector $\mathbf{x} = (0.7, 0.5, 0.4)$. Then:

- $I_{\mathcal{H}_1,m}(\mathbf{x}) = I_{\mathcal{H}^1,m}(\mathbf{x}) = 0.4$ (Shilkret integral);
- $I_{\mathcal{H}_2,m}(\mathbf{x}) = 0.49$;
- $I_{\mathcal{H}_3,m}(\mathbf{x}) = I^{\mathcal{H}_3,m}(\mathbf{x}) = 0.53$ (Choquet integral);
- $I_{\mathcal{H}^2,m}(\mathbf{x}) = 0.59$;
- $I_{\mathcal{H}^3,m}(\mathbf{x}) = 0.65$ (PAN integral);
- $I_{\mathcal{H}^*,m}(\mathbf{x}) = 0.65$ (concave integral);
- $I^{\mathcal{H}^*,m}(\mathbf{x}) = 0.49$ (convex integral);
- $I_{\mathcal{H}_{X_3},m}(\mathbf{x}) = 0.4$;
- $I^{\mathcal{H}_{X_3},m}(\mathbf{x}) = 0.7$.

Decomposition and superdecomposition integrals are positively homogeneous. Hence, if a universal integral I is also a decomposition (superdecomposition) integral on each X_n, $n \in \mathbb{N}$, then it is necessarily linked to the product $\cdot$, $I(m, c \cdot 1_A) = c \cdot m(A)$. The integrals, which are both universal and decomposition integrals or universal and superdecomposition integrals, were characterized by Mesiar and Stupňanová in [14]. Note that we will use the same notation $\mathcal{H}_i$, $i \in \mathbb{N}$, for decomposition systems related to the chains of length at most i, independently of the underlying space X_n. Obviously, for a fixed $n \in \mathbb{N}$, then $\mathcal{H}_n = \mathcal{H}_{n+k}$ for each $k \in \mathbb{N}$.

Theorem 1. *Let I be a universal integral, $I \neq Ch$, which is also a decomposition (superdecomposition) integral on each X_n, $n \in \mathbb{N}$. Then $I = I_{\mathcal{H}_k}$ for some $k \in \mathbb{N}$ ($I = I^{\mathcal{H}_k}$ for some $k \in \mathbb{N}$).*

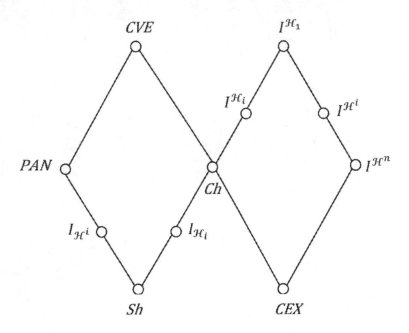

Fig. 1. Hasse diagram of some decomposition and superdecomposition integrals

Recall that $I_{\mathcal{H}_1} = Sh$ is the Shilkret integral. Moreover, for a fixed $n \in \mathbb{N}$, $I_{\mathcal{H}_n} = Ch$ is the Choquet integral on X_n, and then

$$I_{\mathcal{H}_n} = I_{\mathcal{H}_{n+1}} = I_{\mathcal{H}_k} \quad \text{for each } k \geq n.$$

Similarly,

$$I^{\mathcal{H}_n} = Ch = I^{\mathcal{H}_k} \quad \text{for each } k \geq n.$$

The family $(I_{\mathcal{H}_n})_{n \in \mathbb{N}} \bigcup (I^{\mathcal{H}_n})_{n \in \mathbb{N}}$ forms a chain of universal integrals

$$I_{\mathcal{H}_1} \leq I_{\mathcal{H}_2} \leq \ldots \leq I_{\mathcal{H}_k} \leq \ldots \leq Ch \leq \ldots \leq I^{\mathcal{H}_k} \leq \ldots \leq I^{\mathcal{H}_2} \leq I^{\mathcal{H}_1},$$

$$Ch = \sup_{k \in \mathbb{N}} I_{\mathcal{H}_k} = \inf_{k \in \mathbb{N}} I^{\mathcal{H}_k}.$$

Note also that the only integral on X_n, which is both decomposition and superdecomposition integral, is the Choquet integral.

4   Copula-Based Universal Integrals

Copulas (of dimension 2) are in fact joint distribution functions (restricted to $[0,1]^2$) of random vectors (X, Y) such that both X and Y are uniformly distributed over $[0,1]$. Two extremal copulas are the minimum M, $M(x,y) = \min\{x,y\}$ and the Fréchet-Hoeffding lower bound W given by $W(x,y) = \max\{0, x + y - 1\}$. The third distinguished copula is the independence copula Π, $\Pi(x,y) = x \cdot y$. For more details see [16]. Note that any copula $C\colon [0,1]^2 \to [0,1]$ is in a one-to-one correspondence with a probability measure $P_C\colon \mathcal{B}([0,1]^2) \to [0,1]$ with uniformly distributed margins. In particular, for a Borel subset $E \subseteq [0,1]^2$ we have:

- $P_M(E) = \mu_1\left(\{x \in [0,1] \mid (x,x) \in E\}\right)$,
- $P_W(E) = \mu_1\left(\{x \in [0,1] \mid (x,1-x) \in E\}\right)$,
- $P_\Pi(E) = \mu_2(E)$,

where μ_i is the standard Lebesgue measure on Borel subsets of $\mathbb{R}^i$, $i = 1, 2$. Inspired by Imaoka [7], Klement et al. [6] introduced copula-based integrals $I_C\colon \bigcup_{n\in\mathbb{N}} \mathcal{M}_n \times [0,1]^n \to [0,1]$ given by

$$I_C(m, \mathbf{x}) = P_C\left(\{(u,v) \in [0,1]^2 \mid v \le m(\{i \in X_n \mid x_i \ge u\})\}\right)$$

$$= \sum_{i=1}^{n}\left(C\left(x_{\sigma(i)}, m\left(\{\sigma(i),\ldots,\sigma(n)\}\right)\right) - C\left(x_{\sigma(i-1)}, m\left(\{\sigma(i),\ldots,\sigma(n)\}\right)\right)\right),$$

$$\tag{5}$$

σ being a permutation ensuring $x_{\sigma(1)} \le \ldots \le x_{\sigma(n)}$.

Note that $I_\Pi = Ch$ is the Choquet integral and $I_M = Su$ is the Sugeno integral, and that I_C is a universal integral linked to $\otimes = C$. Recently, we introduced [9] hierarchical families of copula-based universal integrals, which extend the results from Section 4.

Theorem 2. *Let* $C\colon [0,1]^2 \to [0,1]$ *be a copula and fix* $k \in \mathbb{N}$. *Then the mappings* $I_{C,k}$ *and* $I^{C,k}\colon \bigcup_{n\in\mathbb{N}} \mathcal{M}_n \times [0,1]^n \to [0,1]$, *given by*

$$I_{C,k}(m, \mathbf{x}) = \sup\left\{\sum_{j=1}^{k}\left(C\left(x_{\sigma(i_j)}, m\left(A_{i_j}\right)\right) - C\left(x_{\sigma(i_{j-1})}, m\left(A_{i_j}\right)\right)\right)\right\},$$

where $A_{i_j} = \{\sigma(i_j), \ldots, \sigma(n)\}$ *and* $0 = i_0 < i_1 < \ldots < i_k \le n$,
and

$$I^{C,k}(m, \mathbf{x}) = \inf\left\{\sum_{j=1}^{k}\left(C\left(x_{\sigma(i_j)}, m\left(\tilde{A}_{i_{j-1}}\right)\right) - C\left(x_{\sigma(i_{j-1})}, m\left(\tilde{A}_{i_{j-1}}\right)\right)\right)\right\},$$

where $\tilde{A}_{i_{j-1}} = \{\sigma(i_{j-1}) + 1, \ldots, \sigma(n)\}$ and $0 = i_0 < i_1 < \ldots < i_k \leq n$, with convention $\sigma(i_0) = 0$, are universal integrals linked to $\otimes = C$. Moreover,

$$I_{C,1} \leq I_{C,2} \leq \ldots \leq I_C \leq \ldots \leq I^{C,2} \leq I^{C,1},$$

and, for a fixed $n \in \mathbb{N}$,

$$I_{C,n} = I_C = I^{C,n}.$$

Obviously, if $C = \Pi$, then $I_{\Pi,k} = I_{\mathcal{H}_k}$ and $I^{\Pi,k} = I^{\mathcal{H}_k}$, $k \in \mathbb{N}$.

5   Integrals as Special Functionals

Recall that the discrete Lebesgue integral in our framework is just the weighted arithmetic mean, $L(\mathbf{x}) = \sum_{i=1}^n w_i x_i$, and it is related to the probability measure P on X_n, where $P(\{i\}) = w_i$. L can be seen as an additive aggregation function. Note that $A : [0,1]^n \to [0,1]$ is an aggregation function [5] if and only if A is nondecreasing in each coordinate and $A(0,\ldots,0) = 0$, $A(1,\ldots,1) = 1$. Hence an aggregation function is the Lebesgue integral once $A(\mathbf{x} + \mathbf{y}) = A(\mathbf{x}) + A(\mathbf{y})$ for all $\mathbf{x}, \mathbf{y}, \mathbf{x} + \mathbf{y} \in [0,1]^n$, and the corresponding capacity (probability) P is given by $P(E) = A(1_E)$. For several other distinguished integrals we have their characterization as special functionals:

- Choquet integral is a comonotone additive aggregation function [17];
- Sugeno integral is a comonotone maxitive and min–homogeneous aggregation function [12];
- Shilkret integral is a comonotone maxitive and positively homogeneous aggregation function [5];
- concave integral is the smallest concave functional on $[0,1]^n$ satisfying $I(1_E) \geq m(E)$ [3];
- convex integral is the greatest convex functional on $[0,1]^n$ such that $I(1_E) \leq m(E)$ [13].

Recall that two vectors $\mathbf{x}, \mathbf{y} \in [0,1]^n$ are comonotone if $x_i > x_j$ excludes $y_i < y_j$, i.e., $(x_i - x_j)(y_i - y_j) \geq 0$ for each $i, j \in X_n$.

6   Concluding Remarks

We have introduced and discussed several kinds of discrete integrals with respect to capacities. As a particular example, often exploited in numerous applications, we recall OWA operators [21] as the mappings $OWA_{\mathbf{w}} : [0,1]^n \to [0,1]$, which are defined by

$$OWA_{\mathbf{w}}(\mathbf{x}) = \sum_{i=1}^n w_i x_{\sigma(i)},$$

where $\mathbf{w} = (w_1, \ldots, w_n) \in [0,1]^n$ is a normed weighting vector, i.e., $\sum_{i=1}^n w_i = 1$.

Considering a capacity $m\colon 2^{X_n} \to [0,1]$ given by $m(A) = \sum_{i=1}^{\mathrm{card}(A)} w_{n-i+1}$, Grabisch [4] showed that $OWA_{\mathbf{w}} = Ch_m$ is the Choquet integral with respect to the capacity m. A capacity, which only depends on the cardinality of measured sets, is called a symmetric capacity. It can be viewed as a basis for generalizations of OWA operators. The first generalization yields OMA (Ordered Modular Average) operators, which were introduced by Mesiar and Zemánková in [15]:

Definition 3. *Let $m\colon 2^{X_n} \to [0,1]$ be a symmetric capacity generated by a normed weighting vector $\mathbf{w} = (w_1, \ldots, w_n)$, and let $C\colon [0,1]^2 \to [0,1]$ be a fixed copula. Then the integral $I_C(m, \cdot)\colon [0,1]^n \to [0,1]$ is called an OMA operator.*

Note that OMA operators were characterized axiomatically as comonotone modular symmetric idempotent aggregation functions, i.e., an $OMA\colon [0,1]^n \to [0,1]$ satisfies the following properties:

(i) $OMA(\mathbf{x} \vee \mathbf{y}) + OMA(\mathbf{x} \wedge \mathbf{y}) = OMA(\mathbf{x}) + OMA(\mathbf{y})$ for any comonotone couple $\mathbf{x}, \mathbf{y} \in [0,1]^n$ (i.e., for $\mathbf{x}$ and $\mathbf{y}$ with the property $(x_i - x_j)(y_i - y_j) \geq 0$ for any $i, j \in X_n$);
(ii) $OMA(\mathbf{x}) = OMA(x_{\sigma(1)}, \ldots, x_{\sigma(n)})$ for any permutation $\sigma\colon X_n \to X_n$;
(iii) $OMA(c, \ldots, c) = c$ for any $c \in [0,1]$.

By (5), $OMA_{C,m}$ is given by

$$OMA_{C,m}(\mathbf{x}) = \sum_{i=1}^{n} f_i(x_{\sigma(i)}),$$

where $f_i\colon [0,1] \to [0,1]$ is given by $f_i(t) = C(t, w_i + \ldots + w_n) - C(t, w_{i+1} + \ldots + w_n))$. Thus, f_i is an increasing 1-Lipschitz function that satisfies $f_i(0) = 0$, $f_i(1) = w_i$, and $\sum_{i=1}^{n} f_i(t) = t$ for any $t \in [0,1]$.

If $C = \Pi$ then $f_i(t) = w_i t$, and in that case OMA operators are simply OWA operators (and they are characterized by comonotone additivity, which is a genuine property of the Choquet integrals [17]).

For $C = M$, $f_i(t) = \max\{0, \min\{t - (w_{i+1} + \ldots + w_n), w_i\}\}$, and hence

$$OMA_{M,m}(\mathbf{x}) = \bigvee_{i=1}^{n} x_{\sigma(i)} \wedge (w_i + \ldots + w_n),$$

i.e., $OMA_{M,m}$ is the ordered weighted maximum [2].

Other kinds of OWA generalizations are based on Theorem 2, and again, they can be introduced for an arbitrary copula C. We restrict our considerations to the independence copula Π only. Then, for a fixed $n \in \mathbb{N}$ and a symmetric capacity m on X_n generated by a normed weighting vector $\mathbf{w} = (w_1, \ldots, w_n)$, all integrals $I_{\Pi,k}(m, \cdot)$ and $I^{\Pi,k}(m, \cdot)$, $k \in \{1, \ldots, n\}$, can be viewed as generalizations of OWA operators and

$$I_{\Pi,n}(m, \cdot) = I^{\Pi,n}(m, \cdot) = OWA_{\mathbf{w}}.$$

In general, for a fixed $k \in \{1, \ldots, n\}$, it holds

$$I_{\Pi,k}(m, \mathbf{x}) = \max \left\{ \sum_{j=1}^{k} \left(x_{\sigma(i_j)} - x_{\sigma(i_{j-1})} \right) \cdot \left(w_{i_j} + \ldots + w_n \right) \right\},$$

where $0 = i_0 < i_1 < \ldots < i_k \leq n$,
and

$$I^{\Pi,k}(m, \mathbf{x}) = \min \left\{ \sum_{j=1}^{k} \left(x_{\sigma(i_j)} - x_{\sigma(i_{j-1})} \right) \cdot \left(w_{i_{j-1}+1} + \ldots + w_n \right) \right\},$$

with $0 = i_0 < i_1 < \ldots < i_k \leq n$.

Acknowledgments. The support of grant APVV–14-0013 is kindly acknowledged.

References

1. Choquet, G.: Theory of capacities. Ann. Inst. Fourier **5**, 131–292 (1953–54)
2. Dubois, D., Prade, H.: A review of fuzzy aggregation connectives. Inform. Sci. **36**, 85–121 (1985)
3. Even, Y., Lehrer, E.: Decomposition-integral: unifying Choquet and concave integrals. Econ. Theory **56**(1), 33–58 (2014)
4. Grabisch, M.: Fuzzy integral in multicriteria decision making. Fuzzy Sets and Systems **69**, 279–298 (1995)
5. Grabisch, M., Marichal, J.-L., Mesiar, R., Pap, E.: Aggregation Functions. Cambridge University Press, Cambridge (2009)
6. Klement, E.P., Mesiar, R., Pap, E.: Measure-based aggregation operators. Fuzzy Sets and Systems **142**, 3–14 (2004)
7. Imaoka, H.: On a subjective evaluation model by a generalized fuzzy integral. Int. J. Uncertain. Fuzziness Knowledge-Based Systems **5**, 517–529 (1997)
8. Klement, E.P., Mesiar, R., Pap, E.: A universal integral as common frame for Choquet and Sugeno integral. IEEE Trans. Fuzzy Systems **18**, 178–187 (2010)
9. Klement, E.P., Mesiar, R., Spizzichino, F., Stupňanová, A.: Universal integrals based on copulas. Fuzzy Optimization and Decision Making **13**, 273–286 (2014)
10. Kolesárová, A., Stupňanová, A., Beganová, J.: Aggregation-based extensions of fuzzy measures. Fuzzy Sets and Systems **194**, 1–14 (2012)
11. Lehrer, E.: A new integral for capacities. Econ. Theory **39**, 157–176 (2009)
12. Marichal, J.-L.: An axiomatic approach of the discrete Sugeno integral as a tool to aggregate interacting criteria in a qualitative framework. IEEE Transactions on Fuzzy Systems **9**(1), 164–172 (2001)
13. Mesiar, R., Li, J., Pap, E.: Superdecomposition integrals. Fuzzy Sets and Systems **259**, 3–11 (2015)
14. Mesiar, R., Stupňanová, A.: Decomposition integrals. Int. J. Approximate Reasoning **54**(8), 1252–1259 (2013)
15. Mesiar, R., Mesiarová-Zemánková, A.: The Ordered Modular Averages. IEEE Transactions on Fuzzy Systems **19**(1), 42–50 (2011)

16. Nelsen, R.B.: An Introduction to Copulas, 2nd edn. Springer Verlag, New York (2006)
17. Schmeidler, D.: Integral representation without additivity. Proc. Amer. Math. Soc. **97**, 255–261 (1986)
18. Shilkret, N.: Maxitive measure and integration. Indag. Math. **33**, 109–116 (1971)
19. Sugeno, M.: Theory of Fuzzy Integrals and its Applications. PhD thesis, Tokyo Institute of Technology (1974)
20. Weber, S.: Two integrals and some modified versions - critical remarks. Fuzzy Sets and Systems **20**, 97–105 (1986)
21. Yager, R.R.: On ordered weighted averaging aggregation operators in multi-criteria decision making. IEEE Transactions on Systems, Man and Cybernetics **18**, 183–190 (1988)
22. Yang, Q.: The pan-integral on fuzzy measure space (in Chinese). Fuzzy Mathematics **3**, 107–114 (1985)
23. Zhao, R.: (N) fuzzy integral. J. Mathematical Research and Exposition **2**, 55–72 (1981)
24. Zadeh, L.A.: Fuzzy Sets. Information Control **8**, 338–353 (1965)

Graph Databases: Their Power and Limitations

Jaroslav Pokorný[✉]

Department of Software Engineering, Faculty of Mathematics and Physics, Charles University,
Prague, Czech Republic
pokorny@ksi.mff.cuni.cz

Abstract. Real world data offers a lot of possibilities to be represented as graphs. As a result we obtain undirected or directed graphs, multigraphs and hypergraphs, labelled or weighted graphs and their variants. A development of graph modelling brings also new approaches, e.g., considering constraints. Processing graphs in a database way can be done in many different ways. Some graphs can be represented as JSON or XML structures and processed by their native database tools. More generally, a graph database is specified as any storage system that provides index-free adjacency, i.e. an explicit graph structure. Graph database technology contains some technological features inherent to traditional databases, e.g. ACID properties and availability. Use cases of graph databases like Neo4j, OrientDB, InfiniteGraph, FlockDB, AllegroGraph, and others, document that graph databases are becoming a common means for any connected data. In Big Data era, important questions are connected with scalability for large graphs as well as scaling for read/write operations. For example, scaling graph data by distributing it in a network is much more difficult than scaling simpler data models and is still a work in progress. Still a challenge is pattern matching in graphs providing, in principle, an arbitrarily complex identity function. Mining complete frequent patterns from graph databases is also challenging since supporting operations are computationally costly. In this paper, we discuss recent advances and limitations in these areas as well as future directions.

Keywords: Graph database · Graph storage · Graph querying · Graph scalability · Big graphs

1   Introduction

A *graph database* is any storage system that uses graph structures with nodes and edges, to represent and store data. The most commonly used model of graphs in the context of graph databases is called a (*labelled*) *property graph model* [15]. The property graph contains connected *entities* (the *nodes*) which can hold any number of *properties* (*attributes*) expressed as key-value pairs. Nodes and edges can be tagged with *labels* representing their different roles in application domain. Some approaches refer to the label as the *type*. Labels may also serve to attach metadata—index or constraint information—to certain nodes.

© IFIP International Federation for Information Processing 2015
K. Saeed and W. Homenda (Eds.): CISIM 2015, LNCS 9339, pp. 58–69, 2015.
DOI: 10.1007/978-3-319-24369-6_5

Relationships provide directed, semantically relevant connections (*edges*) between two nodes. A relationship always has a *direction*, a *start node*, and an *end node*. Like nodes, relationships can have any properties. Often, relationships have quantitative properties, such as weight, cost, distance, ratings or time interval. Properties make the nodes and edges more descriptive and practical in use. Both nodes and edges are defined by a *unique identifier*.

As relationships are stored efficiently, two nodes can share any number or relationships of different types without sacrificing performance. Note that although they are directed, relationships can always be navigated regardless of direction. In fact, the property graph model concerns data structure called in graph theory *labelled and directed attributed multigraphs*.

Sometimes we can meet hypergraphs in graph database software. A *hypergraph* is a generalization of the concept of a graph, in which the edges are substituted by *hyperedges*. If a regular edge connects two nodes of a graph, then a hyperedge connects an arbitrary set of nodes.

Considering graphs as a special structured data, an immediate idea which arises is, how to store and process graph data in a database way. For example, we can represent a graph by tables in a relational DBMS (RDBMS) and use sophisticated constructs of SQL or Datalog to express some graph queries. Some graphs can be represented as JSON or XML structures and processed by their native database tools. A more general native solution is offered by graph databases.

One of the more interesting upcoming growth areas is the use of graph databases and graph-based analytics on large, unstructured datasets. A special attention is devoted to so-called *Big Graphs*, e.g. Facebook with 1 Billion nodes and 140 Billion edges, requiring special storage and processing algorithms [12].

Graph databases are focused on:

- processing highly connected data,
- be flexible in usage data models behind graphs used,
- exceptional performances for local reads, by traversing the graph.

Graph databases are often included among NoSQL databases[1].

We should also mention lower tools for dealing with graphs. They include frameworks, such as Google's Pregel [8] - a system for large-scale graph processing on distributed cluster of commodity machines, and its more advanced variant Giraph[2] suitable for analytical purposes. They do not use a graph database for storage. These systems are particularly suitable for OLAP and offline graph analytics, i.e. they are optimized for scanning and processing Big Graphs in batch mode. Also the notion of a *Big Analytics* occurs in this context.

In traditional database terminology, we should distinguish a *Graph Database Management Systems* (GDBMS) and a *graph database*. Unfortunately, the latter substitutes often the former in practice. We will also follow this imprecise terminology.

---

[1] http://nosql-database.org/
[2] http://giraph.apache.org/

There are a lot of papers about graph models, graph databases, e.g. [7], [12], [16], and theory and practise of graph queries, e.g. [4]. Now the most popular book is rather practically oriented work [15]. A performance comparison of some graph databases is presented, e.g., in [6], [9].

In this paper, a lot of examples from the graph database technology will be documented on the most popular graph database Neo4j[3], particularly in its version 2.2. In Section 2 we describe some basic technological features of graph databases. Section 3 presents an overview of graph databases categories as well as some their representatives, i.e., some commercial products. Section 4 presents some facts concerning the paper title and offers some research challenges. Finally, Section 5 concludes the paper.

2   Graph Database Technology

According to other DBMS, we can distinguish a number of basic components of graph database technology. They include graph storage, graph querying, scalability, and transaction processing. We will discuss them in the following subsections.

2.1   Graph Storage

An important feature of graph databases is that provide native processing capabilities, at least a property called *index-free adjacency*, meaning that every node is directly linked to its neighbour node. A database engine that utilizes index-free adjacency is one in which each node maintains direct references to its adjacent nodes; each node, therefore acts as an index of other nearby nodes, which is much cheaper than using global indexes. This is appropriate for local graph queries where we need one index lookup for starting node, and then we will traverse relationships by dereferencing physical pointers directly. In RDBMS we would probably need joining more tables trough foreign keys and, possibly, additional index lookups.

Obviously, more advanced indexes are used. For example, it is desirable to retrieve graphs quickly from a large database via *graph-based indices*, e.g. path-based methods. The approach used in [17] introduces so called *gIndex* using frequent substructures as the basic indexing features. Unfortunately, most of these techniques are usable only for small graphs.

Some graph stores offer a graph interface over non-native graph storage, such as a column store in the Virtuoso Universal Server[4] in application for RDF data. Often other DBMS is used as back-end storage. For example, the graph database FlockDB[5] stores graph data, but it is not optimized for graph-traversal operations. Instead, it is optimized for very large adjacency lists. FlockDB uses MySQL as the basic database storage system just for storing adjacency lists.

---

[3] http://www.neo4j.org/ (retrieved on 9.3.2015)
[4] http://virtuoso.openlinksw.com/ (retrieved on 9.3.2015)
[5] https://github.com/twitter/flockdb (retrieved on 9.3.2015)

2.2   Graph Querying

Query capabilities are fundamental for each DBMS. Those used in graph databases, of course, come from the associated graph model [2]. The simplest type of a query preferably uses the index-free adjacency. A node $v_k \in V$ is said to be at a *k-hop distance* from another node $v_0 \in V$, if there exists a shortest path from v_0 to v_k comprising of *k* edges. In practice, the basic queries are the most frequent. They include look for a node, look for the neighbours (1-hop), scan edges in several hops (layers), retrieve an attribute values, etc. Looking for a node based on its properties or through its identifier is called *point querying*.

Retrieving an edge by *id*, may not be a constant time operation. For example, Titan[6] will retrieve an adjacent node of the edge to be retrieved and then execute a node query to identify the edge. The former is constant time but the latter is potentially linear in the number of edges incident on the node with the same edge label.

As more complex queries we meet very often *subgraph* and *supergraph queries*. They belong to rather traditional queries based on exact matching. Other typical queries include *breadth-first/depth-first search, path* and *shortest path finding, finding cliques* or *dense subgraphs, finding strong connected components*, etc. Algorithms used for such complex queries need often iterative computation. This is not easy, e.g., with the MapReduce (MR) framework used usually in NoSQL databases for BigData processing. But the authors of [14] show for finding connected components that some efficient MR algorithms exist.   In Big Graphs often *approximate matching* is needed. Allowing structural relaxation, then we talk about *structural similarity queries*.

Inspired by the SQL language, graph databases are often equipped by a declarative query language. Today, the most known graph declarative query language is Cypher working with Neo4j database. Cypher commands are loosely based on SQL syntax and are targeted at ad hoc queries of the graph data. A rather procedural graph language is the traversal language Gremlin[7].

The most distinctive output for a graph query is another graph, which is ordinarily a transformation, a selection or a projection of the original graph stored in the database. This implies that graph visualization is strongly tied to the graph querying [13].

2.3   Scalability

Sharding (or *graph partitioning*) is crucial to making graphs scale. Scaling graph data by distributing it across multiple machines is much more difficult than scaling the simpler data in other NoSQL databases, but it is possible. The reason is the very nature way the graph data is connected. When distributing a graph, we want to avoid having relationships that span machines as much as possible; this is called the *minimum point-cut problem*. But what looks like a good distribution one moment may no longer be optimal a few seconds later. Typically, graph partition problems fall under the category of NP-hard problems. Scaling is usually connected with three things:

---

[6] http://thinkaurelius.github.io/titan/ (retrieved on 9.3.2015)
[7] http://gremlindocs.com/

- scaling for large datasets,
- scaling for read performance,
- and scaling for write performance.

In practice, the former is most often discussed. Today, it is not problem in graph databases area. For example, Neo4j currently has an arbitrary upper limit on the size of the graph on the order of 10^{10}. This is enough to support most of real-world graphs, including a Neo4j deployment that has now more than half of Facebook's social graph in one Neo4j cluster.

Scaling for reads usually presents no problem. For example, Neo4j has historically focused on read performance. In master-slave regime read operations can be done locally on each slave. To improve scalability in highly concurrent workloads, Neo4j uses two levels of caching.

Scaling for writes can be accomplished by scaling vertically, but at some point, for very heavy write loads, it requires the ability to distribute the data across multiple machines. This is the real challenge. For example, Titan is a highly scalable OLTP graph database system optimized for thousands of users concurrently accessing and updating one Big Graph.

2.4   Transaction Processing

As in any other DBMS, there are three generic use cases for graphs:

- CRUD (create, read, update, delete) applications,
- query processing - reporting, data warehousing, and real-time analytics,
- batch mode analytics or data discovery.

Graph databases are often optimized and focused on one or more of these uses. Particularly, the first two uses are focused on transactions processing, i.e. OLTP databases. When dealing with many concurrent transactions, the nature of the graph data structure helps spread the transactional overhead across the graph. As the graph grows transactional conflicts typically falls away, i.e. extending the graph tends to the more throughputs. But not all graph databases are fully ACID. However, the variant based on the BASE properties often considered in the context of NoSQL databases is not too appropriate for graphs.

In general, distributed graph processing requires the application of appropriate partitioning and replication strategies such as to maximise the locality of the processing, i.e., minimise the need to ship data between different network nodes.

For example, Neo4j uses master-slave replication, i.e. one machine is designated as the master and the others as slaves. In Neo4j, all writes directed towards any machine are passed through the master, which in turn ships updates to the slaves when polled. If the master fails, the cluster automatically elects a new master.

Neo4j requires a quorum in order to serve write load. It means that a strict majority of the servers in the cluster need to be online in order for the cluster to accept write operations. Otherwise, the cluster will degrade into read-only operation until a quorum can be established. Emphasize, that today's graph databases do not have the same level of write throughput as other types of NoSQL databases. This is a consequence of master-slave clustering and proper ACID transactions.

Some more complex architectures occur in the world of graph databases. Typically, a simple database is used to absorb load, and then feed the data into a graph database for refinement and analysis. The architecture Neo4j 2.2 contains even a bulk loader which operates at throughput of million records per second.

3   Categories of Graph Databases

There are a lot of graph databases. The well-maintained and structured Web site[8] included 20 products belonging among GDBMSs in 2011. The development of graph databases until 2011 is described in [1]. Wikipedia[9] describes 45 such tools. One half of them are ACID compliant.

We distinguish general purpose GDBMs, like Neo4j, InfiniteGraph[10], Sparksee[11], Titan, GraphBase[12], and Trinity[13], and special ones, e.g. the Web graph database InfoGrid[14] and FlockDB, or multimodel databases such as document-oriented databases enabling traversing between documents. For example, OrientDB[15] brings together the power of graphs and the flexibility of documents into one scalable database even with an SQL layer. HyperGraphDB[16] stores not only graphs but also hypergraph structures. All the graph information is stored in the form of key-value pairs.

An interesting question is which graph databases are most popular today. In June 2015, the web page DB-Engines Ranking of GDBMS[17] considering 17 graph products presented Neo4j, OrientDB, and Titan on the first three places. GDBMS Sparksee is on the 6th place.

In Section 3.1 we present two typical representatives of the general purpose category. From those special ones, more attention will be devoted to RDF triplestores in Section 3.2. The framework Pregel is explained in Section 3.3.

3.1   General Graph Purpose Databases - Examples

We describe shortly two successful graph GDBMSs - Neo4j and Sparksee - in some detail. In both GDBMSs a graph is a labelled directed attributed multigraph, where edges can be either directed or undirected.

---

[8] http://nosql-database.org/ (retrieved on 9.3.2015)

[9] http://en.wikipedia.org/wiki/Graph_database#cite_1 (retrieved on 12.6.2015)

[10] http://www.objectivity.com/infinitegraph#.U8O_yXnm9I0 (retrieved on 9.3.2015)

[11] http://sparsity-technologies.com/#sparksee (retrieved on 9.3.2015)

[12] http://graphbase.net/ (retrieved on 9.3.2015)

[13] http://research.microsoft.com/en-us/projects/trinity/ (retrieved on 9.3.2015)

[14] http://infogrid.org/trac/ (retrieved on 9.3.2015)

[15] http://www.orientechnologies.com/ (retrieved on 9.3.2015)

[16] http://www.hypergraphdb.org/index

[17] http://db-engines.com/en/ranking/graph+dbms (retrieved on 12.6.2015)

Example 1: Neo4j

Neo4j (now in version 2.2) is the world's leading GDBMS. It is an open-source, highly scalable, robust (fully ACID compliant) native graph database.

Neo4j stores data as nodes and relationships. Both nodes and relationships can hold properties in a key-value form. Values can be either a primitive or an array of one primitive type. Nodes are often used to represent entities, but depending on the domain the relationships may be used for that purpose as well. The nodes and edges have internal unique identifiers that can be used for the data search. Nodes cannot reference themselves directly [5]. The semantics can be expressed by adding directed relationships between nodes

Graph processing in Neo4j entails mostly random data access which can be unsuitable for Big Graphs. Graphs that cannot fit into main memory may require more disk accesses, which significantly influences graph processing. Big Graphs similarly to other Big Data collections must be partitioned over multiple machines to achieve scalable processing (see Section 2.3).

Example 2: Sparksee

In addition to the basic graph model, Sparksee also introduces the notion of a virtual edge that connects nodes having the same value for a given attribute. These edges are not materialized. A Sparksee graph is stored in a single file; values and identifiers are mapped by mapping functions into B+-trees. Bitmaps are used to store nodes and edges of a certain type.

The architecture of Sparksee includes the core, that manages and queries the graph structures, then an API layer to provide an application programming interface, and the higher layer applications, to extend the core capabilities and to visualize and browse the results. To speed up the different graph queries and other graph operations, Sparksee offers these index types:

- attributes,
- unique attributes,
- edges to index their neighbours, and
- indices on neighbours.

Sparksee implements a number of graph algorithms, e.g. shortest path, depth-first searching, finding strong connected components.

3.2   Triplestores

Some graph-oriented products are intended for special graph applications, mostly RDF data expressed in the form of *subject (S) - predicate (P) – object (O)*. RDF graphs can be viewed as a special kind of a property graph. At the logical level, an RDF graph is then represented as one table. For example, AllegroGraph[18] works with RDF graphs. BrightStarDB[19], Bigdata[20] and SparkleDB[21] (formerly known as

---

[18] http://franz.com/agraph/ (retrieved on 9.3.2015)
[19] http://brightstardb.com/ (retrieved on 9.3.2015)

Meronymy) serve for similar purposes. These *triple stores* employ intelligent data management solutions which combine full text search with graph analytics and logical reasoning to produce deeper results. Sometimes, *quad stores* are used holding a fourth attribute - the *graph name* (*N*) corresponding normally with the namespace of the ontology. AllegroGraph deals even with quints (*S, P, O, N, ID*), the ID can be used to attach metadata to a triple.

Now, GraphDB™[22] is the world's leading RDF triple store that can perform semantic inferring at scale allowing users to create new semantic facts from existing facts. GraphDB™ is built on OWL (Ontology Web Language). It uses ontologies that allow the repository to automatically reason about the data. AlegroGraph also supports reasoning and ontology modelling.

However, existing triple store technologies are not yet suitable for storing truly large data sets efficiently. According to the W3C Wiki, AllegroGraph leads the largest deployment with loading and querying 1 Trillion triples. The load operation alone took about 338 hours.

We remind also that triple stores create only a subcategory of graph databases. Rather a hybrid solution is represented by Virtuoso Universal Server[23]. Its functionality covers not only processing RDF data, but also relations, XML, text, and others.

A list of requirements often required by customers considering a triple store is introduced in [10]:

- inferring,
- integration with text mining pipelines,
- scalability,
- extensibility,
- enterprise resilience,
- data integration and identity resolution,
- semantics in the cloud,
- semantic expertise.

3.3   Pregel and Giraph

Pregel and Giraph are systems for large-scale graph processing. They provide a fault-tolerant framework for the execution of graph algorithms in parallel over many machines. Giraph utilizes Apache MR framework implementation to process graphs.

A significant approach to the design, analysis and implementation of parallel algorithms, hardware and software in Pregel is now the *Bulk Synchronous Processing* (BSP) model. BSP offers architecture independence and very high performance of parallel algorithms on top of multiple computers connected by a communication network.

---

[20] http://www.systap.com/ (retrieved on 9.3.2015)

[21] https://www.sparkledb.net/ (retrieved on 9.3.2015)

[22] http://www.ontotext.com/products/ontotext-graphdb/ (retrieved on 9.3.2015)

[23] http://virtuoso.openlinksw.com/ (retrieved on 9.3.2015)

BSP is a powerful generalization of MR. A subclass of BSP algorithms can be efficiently implemented in MR [11]. BSP is superfast on standard commodity hardware, orders of magnitude faster than the MR alone. It is an easy parallel programming model to learn, it has a cost model that makes it simple to design, analyse, and optimize massively parallel algorithms. It can be considered as a strong candidate to be the programming model for parallel computing and Big Data in the next years. For example, Google is already moving in its internal infrastructure from MR to BSP/Pregel.

4   Limitations of Graphs Databases

Despite of the long-term research and practice in this area, there are many important and hard problems that remain open in graph data management. They have influence on functionality restrictions of graph databases (Section 4.1). Others are specifically related to Big Analytics (Section 4.2). Challenges concerning some specific problems of graph database technology are summarized in Section 4.3.

4.1   Functionality Restrictions

Declarative querying: Most commercial graph databases cannot be queried using a declarative language. Only few vendors offer a declarative query interface. This implies also a lack of query optimization abilities.

Data partitioning: Most graph databases do not include the functionality to partition and distribute data in a computer network. This is essential for supporting horizontal scalability, too. It is difficult to partition a graph in a way that would not result in most queries having to access multiple partitions.

Vectored operations: They support a procedure which sequentially writes data from multiple buffers to a single data stream or reads data from a data stream to multiple buffers. Horizontally scaled NoSQL databases support this type of data access. It seems that it is not the case in graph databases today.

Model restrictions: Possibilities of data schema and constraints definitions are restricted in graph databases. Therefore, data inconsistencies can quickly reduce their usefulness. Often the graph model itself is restricted. Let us recall, e.g., Neo4j nodes cannot reference themselves directly. There might be real world cases where self-reference is required.

Querying restrictions: For example, FlockDB overcomes the difficulty of horizontal scaling the graph by limiting the complexity of graph traversal. In particular, FlockDB does not allow multi-hop graph walks, so it cannot do a full "transitive closure". However, FlockDB enables very fast and scalable processing of 1-hop queries.

4.2   Big Analytics Requirements

Graph extraction: A question is how to efficiently extract a graph, or a collection of graphs, from non-graph data stores. Most graph analytics systems assume that the graph is provided explicitly. However, in many cases, the graph may have to be constructed by joining and combining information from different resources which are not necessarily graphical. Even if the data is stored in a graph database, often we only need to load a set of subgraphs of that database graph for further analysis.

High cost of some queries: Most real-world graphs are highly dynamic and often generate large volumes of data at a very rapid rate. One challenge here is how to store the historical trace compactly while still enabling efficient execution of point queries and global or neighbourhood-centric analysis tasks. Key differences from temporal DBMSs developed in the past are the scale of data, focus on distributed and in-memory environments, and the need to support global analytics. The last task usually requires loading entire historical snapshots into memory.

Real time processing: As noted, graph data discovery takes place essentially in batch environments, e.g., in Giraph. Some products aimed at data discovery and complex analytics that will operate in real-time. An example is uRIKA[24] – a Big Data Appliance for Graph Analytics. It uses in-memory technology and multithreaded processor to support non-batch operations on RDF triples.

Graph algorithms: More complex graph algorithms are needed in practice. The ideal graph database should understand analytic queries that go beyond k-hop queries for small k. Authors of [9] did a performance comparison of 12 open source graph databases using four fundamental graph algorithms (e.g. simple source shortest path problem and Page Rank) on networks containing up to 256 million edges. Surprisingly, the most popular graph databases have reached the worst results in these tests. Current graph databases (like relational databases) tend to prioritize low latency query execution over high-throughput data analytics.

Parallelisation: In the context of Big Graphs there is a need for parallelisation of graph data processing algorithms when the data is too big to handle on one server. There is a need to understand the performance impact on graph data processing algorithms when the data does not all fit into the memory available and to design algorithms explicitly for these scenarios.

Heterogeneous and uncertain graph data: There is a need to find automated methods of handling the heterogeneity, incompleteness and inconsistency between different Big Graph data sets that need to be semantically integrated in order to be effectively queried or analysed.

---

[24] http://www.cray.com/products/analytics/urika-gd

4.3   Other Challenges

Other challenges in the development of graph databases include:

Design of graph databases: Similarly to traditional databases, some attempts to develop design models and tools occur in last time. In [3], the authors propose a model-driven, system-independent methodology for the design of graph databases starting from ER-model conceptual schema.

Need for a benchmark: Querying graph data can significantly depend on graph properties. The benchmarks built, e.g., for RDF data are mostly focused on scaling and not on querying. Also benchmarks covering a variety of graph analysis tasks would help towards evaluating and comparing the expressive power and the performance of different graph databases and frameworks.

Developing heuristics for some hard graph problems: For example, partitioning of large-scale dynamic graph data for efficient distributed processing belongs among these problems, given that the classical graph partitioning problem is NP-hard.

Graph pattern matching: New semantics and algorithms for graph pattern matching over distributed graphs are in development, given that the classical subgraph isomorphism problem is NP-complete.

Compressing graphs: Compressing graphs for matching without decompression is possible. Combining parallelism with compressing or partitioning is also very interesting.

Integration of graph data: In the context of Big Data, query formulation and evaluation techniques to assist users querying heterogeneous graph data are needed.

Visualization: Improvement of human-data interaction is fundamental, particularly a visualization of large-scale graph data, and of query and analysis results.

Graph streams processing: Developing algorithms for processing Big Graph data streams with goal to compute properties of a graph without storing the entire graph.

5   Conclusions

Graph databases are becoming mainstream. As data becomes connected in a more complicated way and as the technology of graph databases matures, their use will increase. New application areas occur, e.g. the Internet of Things, or rather Internet of Connected Things. Comparing to traditional RDBMS, there is a difficulty for potential users to identify the particular types of use case for which each product is most suitable. Performance varies greatly across different GDBMSs depending upon the size of the graph and how well-optimized a given tool is for a particular task. It seems that especially for Big Graphs and Big Analytics a lot of previous results and designs will have to be re-considered and re-thought in next research and development.

Acknowledgments. This paper was supported by the GAČR grant No. P103/13/08195S.

References

1. Angeles, R.: A comparison of current graph database models. In: Proc. of the 2012 IEEE 28th International Conference on Data Engineering Workshops, ICDEW 2012, pp. 171–177. IEEE Computer Society, Washington (2012)
2. Angeles, R., Gutierrez, C.: Survey of Graph Database Models. ACM Computing Surveys **40**(1), Article 1 (2008)
3. De Virgilio, R., Maccioni, A., Torlone, R.: Model-driven design of graph databases. In: Yu, E., Dobbie, G., Jarke, M., Purao, S. (eds.) ER 2014. LNCS, vol. 8824, pp. 172–185. Springer, Heidelberg (2014)
4. Holzschuher, F., Peinl, R.: Performance of graph query languages: comparison of cypher, gremlin and native access in Neo4j. In: Proc. of the Joint EDBT/ICDT 2013 Workshops, EDBT 2013, pp. 195–204. ACM, NY (2013)
5. Hurwitz, J., Nugent, A., Halper, F., Kaufman, M.: Big Data for Dummies. John Wiley & Sons, Inc. (2013)
6. Kolomičenko, V., Svoboda, M., Holubová – Mlýnková, I.: Experimental comparison of graph databases. In: Proc. of International Conference on Information Integration and Web-based Applications & Services, p. 115. ACM, NY (2013)
7. Larriba-Pey, J.L., Martínez-Bazán, N., Domínguez-Sal, D.: Introduction to graph databases. In: Koubarakis, M., Stamou, G., Stoilos, G., Horrocks, I., Kolaitis, P., Lausen, G., Weikum, G. (eds.) Reasoning Web. LNCS, vol. 8714, pp. 171–194. Springer, Heidelberg (2014)
8. Malewicz, G., Austern, M.H., Bik, A.J.C., Dehnert, J.C., Horn, I., Leiser, N., Czajkowski, G.: Pregel: a system for large-scale graph processing. In: Proc. of SIGMOD 2010 Int. Conf. on Management of data, pp. 135–146. ACM, NY (2010)
9. McColl, R., Ediger, D., Poovey, J., Campbell, D., Bader, D.A.: A performance evaluation of open source graph databases. In: Proc. of PPAA 2014, pp. 11–18. ACM, NY (2014)
10. Ontotext: The Truth about Triplestores. Ontotext (2014)
11. Pace, M.F.: BSP vs MapReduce. Procedia Computer Science **9**, 246–255 (2012)
12. Pallavi, M., Saxena, A.: Review: Graph Databases. Int. Journal of Advanced Research in Computer Science and Software Engineering **4**(5), 195–200 (2014)
13. Pokorny, J., Snášel, V.: Big graph storage, processing and visualization. In: Pitas, I. (ed.) Graph-Based Social Media Analysis, pp. 403–430. Chapman and Hall/CRC (in print, 2015)
14. Rastogi, V., Machanavajjhala, A., Chitnis, L., Sarma, A.D.: Finding Connected Components on Map-reduce in Logarithmic Rounds. CoRR, abs/1203.5387. ACM (2012)
15. Robinson, I., Webber, J., Eifrém, E.: Graph Databases. O'Reilly Media (2013)
16. Shimpi, D., Chaudhari, S.: An overview of Graph Databases. IJCA Proceedings on International Conference on Recent Trends in Information Technology and Computer Science 2012 ICRTITCS(3), 16–22 (2013)
17. Yan, X., Yu, P.S., Han, J.: Graph indexing: a frequent structure –based approach. In: Proc. of SIGMOD 2004 Int. Conf. on Management of Data, pp. 335–346. ACM, NY (2004)

Algorithms

Performance Analysis and Tuning for Parallelization of Ant Colony Optimization by Using OpenMP

Ahmed A. Abouelfarag, Walid Mohamed Aly$^{(\boxtimes)}$, and Ashraf Gamal Elbialy

^{1} College of Engineering and Technology, Arab Academy for Science and Technology, &
Maritime Transport, Alexandria, Egypt
abouelfarag@aast.edu
^{2} College of Computing and Information Technology, Arab Academy for Science,
Technology & Maritime Transport, Alexandria, Egypt
walid.ali@aast.edu, ashraf2k@gmail.com

Abstract. Ant colony optimization algorithm (ACO) is a soft computing metaheuristic that belongs to swarm intelligence methods. ACO has proven a well performance in solving certain NP-hard problems in polynomial time. This paper proposes the analysis, design and implementation of ACO as a parallel metaheuristics using the OpenMP framework. To improve the efficiency of ACO parallelization, different related aspects are examined, including scheduling of threads, race hazards and efficient tuning of the effective number of threads. A case study of solving the traveling salesman problem (TSP) using different configurations is presented to evaluate the performance of the proposed approach. Experimental results show a significant speedup in execution time for more than 3 times over the sequential implementation.

Keywords: Parallel metaheuristic · Ant colony optimization · Shared memory model · Openmp · Parallel threads

1 Introduction

Some of the real-life optimization problems cannot be tackled by exact methods which would be implemented laboriously and in a time-consuming manner. For such optimization problems, metaheuristics are used with less computational effort to find good solution from a set of large feasible solutions. Although other algorithms may give the exact solution to some problems, metaheuristics provide a kind of near-optimal solution for a wide range of NP-hard problems [1].

Since introduced in 1992 by Marco Dorigo [2], ACO algorithms have been applied to many combinatorial optimization problems, ranging from Scheduling Problems [3] to routing vehicles [4] and a lot of derived methods have been adapted to dynamic problems in real variables, multi-targets and parallel implementations.

ACO was proposed as a solution when suffering from limited computation capacity and incomplete information [3]. ACO metaheuristic proved a significant performance improvement compared with other metaheuristic techniques in solving many NP-hard problems such as solving the traveling salesman problem [5].

© IFIP International Federation for Information Processing 2015
K. Saeed and W. Homenda (Eds.): CISIM 2015, LNCS 9339, pp. 73–85, 2015.
DOI: 10.1007/978-3-319-24369-6_6

The multicore computation power encouraged the modification of the standard metaheuristic approaches to be applied in a parallel form.

In this paper, OpenMP is used on CPU with multi-cores to measure the performance speedup. To make the data accessible and shared for all parallel threads in global address space, a shared memory model is implemented in C++. OpenMP is implemented with its parallel regions, directives to control "*for*" loops. Scheduling clause for fine tuning. For eliminating race condition, omp critical sections have been also implemented.

The importance of TSP problem as a test case comes from its history of applications with many metaheuristics. TSP is also easy for mapping with real life problems.

The speedup gain in parallelization of a typical sequential TSP with ACO depends mainly on the proper analysis of where parallel regions should be placed in the algorithm. Theoretically, Amdahl's law [8] limits the expected speedup achieved to an algorithm by a relation between parts that could be parallel to the parts remain serial. One of the targets of the experiment is to assign the optimal number of parallel threads and tuning them dynamically with the available number of CPU cores to get effective speedup.

This paper is organized as the following: in Section 2, the related work to ACO and the research efforts towards its parallelization are presented. Section 3 presents the sequential ACO algorithm mapped to TSP. In section 4, the proposed ACO parallelization using OpenMP is presented where its sub-sections show the analysis of different elements of OpenMP and its effects on performance. In section 5, results and performance evaluation are investigated using the TSP problem as an implementation of parallel ACO algorithm. Finally, section 6 concludes the research and suggests the future work.

2   Related Work

Many strategies have been followed to implement ACO algorithm on different parallel platforms. In [9], Compute Unified Device Architecture (CUDA) is used to get the parallel throughput when executing more concurrent threads over GPUs. Results showed faster execution time with CUDA than OpenMP, but the main disadvantage of CUDA computing power is its dependence on GPU memory capacity related to problem size.

Marco Dorigo and Krzysztof Socha [10] addressed that the central component of ACO is the pheromone model. Based on the underlying model of the problem, parallelization of this component is the master point to the parallel ACO.

Bullnheimer et al. [11], introduced the parallel execution of the ants construction phase in a single colony. This research target was decreasing computations time by distributing ants to computing elements. They suggested two strategies for implementing ACO for parallelization: the synchronous parallel algorithm and the partially asynchronous parallel algorithm. Through their experiment, they used TSP and evaluated the speedup and efficiency. In the synchronous parallel algorithm, the speedup is poor for the small problem size and resulting to "slowdown" the efficiency close to zero. While in large problem size, the speedup is improved by increasing the number of workers (slaves). Communication and idle time have a great effect on limiting the overall performance. The authors conclude that the second approach, partially asynchronous parallel algorithm, implemented the concept of parallelism with better speedup and efficiency. The disadvantage of this model was the communication overhead for the master ant waiting for the workers to finish their task.

Stützle [12], introduced the execution of multiple ant colonies, where the ant colonies are distributed to processors in order to increase the speed of computations and to improve solution quality by introducing cooperation between colonies. This method would be implemented through distributed memory model which would require a huge communication that caused high overhead affecting the overall performance.

Xiong Jie et al. [13] used message passing interface MPI with C language to present a new parallel ACO interacting multi ant colonies. The main drawback of this approach is the coarse-granularity where the master node have to wait for all slave nodes to finish their work and then updates with the new low cost solution.

This paper proposes a solution with OpenMP to get the performance gain of parallel regions. These parallel regions provide parallelizing to the ACO algorithm by controlling the time-consuming loops, avoiding race hazards and maintain load balance.

3   The ACO Algorithm

In ACO as a metaheuristic, cooperation is a key design component of ACO algorithms [14]. The artificial cooperating ants build a solution for a combinatorial optimization problem by traversing a fully connected graph. Solution is built in a constructive method. The solution component is denoted by c_{ij}, c is representing a set of all possible solution components. When combining c components with graph vertices V or with set of edges E the result would be the graph $G_C(V,E)$.

3.1   ACO Solution Steps

ACO algorithm consists of three main procedures which are:
- **ConstructAntsSolutions(edge selection)** phase: the ants traversed through adjacent neighbor nodes of the graph is made by a stochastic local decision according to two main factors, pheromone trails and heuristic information. The solution construction phase starts with a partial solution $s^p=\phi$. From the adjacent neighbors a feasible solution component $N(s^p) \subseteq C$ is added to the partial solution. The partial built solution made by an ant is evaluated for the purpose of using it later in the UpdatePheromones procedure. Dorigo [14] formed an equation for the probability of selecting solution component:

$$p(c_{ij} \mid s^p) = \frac{\tau_{ij}^{\alpha} \cdot \eta_{ij}^{\beta}}{\sum_{c_{il} \in N(s^p)} \tau_{ij}^{\alpha} \cdot \eta_{ij}^{\beta}}, \forall c_{ij} \in N(s^p) \tag{1}$$

Where τ_{ij} is the deposited pheromone value in the transition from state i to state j, and η_{ij} is the heuristic value between i, j. Both τ_{ij} , η_{ij} associated with the component c_{ij}. Where α and β are two parameters which controls the parameters of τ_{ij} and ηij respectively, where $\alpha \geq 0, \beta \geq 1$

- **LocalSearch** phase: This step is started after solution construction phase and before pheromone update. The result of this step are locally optimized solutions. This is required - as a centralized action - to improve the solution construction phase.
- **UpdatePheromones** phase: is the most important phase where a procedure of pheromone level is increased or decreased. After all ants completed the solution, the following rule controls the pheromone update:

$$\tau_{ij} \leftarrow (1 - \rho)\tau_{ij} + \sum_k \Delta\tau_{ij}^k \qquad (2)$$

Where ρ is pheromone evaporation coefficient and $\Delta\tau_{ij}^k$ is the amount of pheromone released by k-th ants on the trip finished between i, j

$$\Delta\tau_{ij}^k = \{ \begin{matrix} \frac{Q}{L_k} if ant\ k\ traverse\ edge(i,j) \\ 0\ else \end{matrix} \qquad (3)$$

Where Q is a constant, L_k is tour length traversed by the ant k.
Continues increase in pheromone levels in each iteration would produce an attractive path to the following iterations. This leads to the trap of local optima ants discarding the exploration of other connections. To explore new areas, pheromone evaporation rate is activated to participate in lowering pheromone levels in each tour.

3.2   The ACO Algorithm for TSP

As the exemplary task, Traveling Salesman Problem TSP is considered to verify the efficiency of the proposed parallel approach as well as some related aspects like the scheduling of threads, the race hazards and tuning of the effective number of threads.
In the algorithm of TSP, the weighted graph G = (N, A) where N is the number of nodes representing cities. The connection between cities (i,j) $\square$ A and d_{ij} is the distance between (i,j). The τ_{ij} representing the desirability of visiting city j directly after visiting city i according to pheromone trails, η_{ij} depicts the heuristic information where $\eta_{ij} = 1/ d_{ij}$ and there will be a matrix of τ_{ij} which includes pheromone trails.
    The value of pheromone at initial state for TSP is:

$$\tau_{ij}(0) = m / C_{min} \qquad (4)$$

Where m is the number of ants, C_{min} is the minimum distance between any i, j. When ants planning to construct its path ant k determines the probability P of visiting the next city according to formula in (1).

The j is the city not visited yet by ant k, both α and β are two parameters which control the relative importance of pheromone (τ_{ij}) against heuristic information ($\eta_{ij} = 1/d_{ij}$), tabu$_k$ is the list of already visited cities by k-th ants. The update pheromone process starts after all ants have finished their tours construction. At first, pheromone values are lowered by a constant factor for all connections between cities. Then, pheromone levels are increased only for the visited connections by ants, pheromone evaporation determined by:

$$\tau_{ij} \leftarrow (1-\rho)\tau_{ij}$$

(5)

Consider ρ as pheromone evaporation rate, where $0 < \rho \leq 1$. After number of iterations, the ants release pheromone in all visited connections during their tour formula in (2) Where $\Delta\tau_{ij}^k(t)$ denotes the amount of pheromone deposited by ant k on the trip finished between nodes i and j defined as in formula (3).

4   Proposed ACO Parallelization by Using OpenMP

ACO is a potential candidate for parallelization for different reasons, including:
The individual independent behavior of ants.

- The large number of iterations required in updating pheromone trails.
- The computations needed for the single ant to construct a solution in the graph.
  Parallel ACO could be implemented with two different strategies [6]:
- Coarse-grained: single CPU is being used by many ants or even the whole colony with rarely information exchange between CPUs
- Fine-grained: few numbers of ants are to be assigned with each core of CPU with more communication and information exchange between them.

The main difference between previous two approaches is the amount of information exchange between the CPUs. Fine-grain model needs more communication which causes an overhead consuming most of the execution time. Coarse-grain parallelization model is most suitable for multiple colonies of ACO implementation [7]. Fine-grain parallelization strategy has been adopted in this paper to study the behavior of multithreading with relation to the multicores available in CPU with a single colony.

An improvement in ACO algorithm could be achieved mainly by using multithread programming with multi-core processors. This section introduces an implementation for parallel ACO using OpenMP platform. A shared memory model has been chosen to get the benefit of creating a common space sharing pheromone matrix without the overhead of communication, especially when applying both "ConstructAntSolutions" and "UpdatePheromones" processes. OpenMP is implemented   to reduce the execution time and not altering the ACO algorithm with major change.

The main effort here is to analyze and select the places which consume most execution time in the sequential ACO and to overcome the problem of communication overhead by using the OpenMP directives. Larger and in-place OpenMP parallel regions are used, because fragmented parallel regions would increase the overhead of creating and terminating threads.

4.1   Tuning Optimal Number of Threads

One of the major questions here when implementing parallel regions is: what is the optimal number of threads to execute through *for* loops? To answer this question, a hypothesis have been adopted. The optimal number of threads would depend on both parallel implementation of ACO and the number of multi-cores available in the CPU. This is according to two factors.

- Amdahl's law [8], which means that adding more threads would be neglected with no significant speedup because of sequential part.
- The number of threads can be chosen to be more than the number of cores. This is the case when a thread is in waiting/blocking condition. Hyperthreading availability in modern CPUs provides management for many threads per core.

4.2   Tuning Parallel Regions

The pseudocode of ACO is shown in Fig. 1, which simplifies the three main components of the algorithm. The "ConstructAntSolutions" is the function of asynchronous concurrent ants while visiting neighbor nodes of the graph. Ants progressively build their path towards the optimal solution with the help of "UpdatePheromones" function. In the function of "UpdatePheromones" the pheromone trails are updated with increased levels of pheromones by releasing more pheromone on connections between nodes, or the pheromone decreased by the effect of evaporation. Increasing pheromone levels means increasing the probability of successive future ants in their way to find the shortest path allowing only specific ants to release pheromone.

```
procedure ACOMetaheuristic
  Begin
  Set parameters, initialize pheromone trails
    while (termination condition not met) do
      ConstructAntSolutions
      ApplyLocalSearch   % optional
      UpdatePheromones
    end while
  end
```

Fig. 1. The pseudocode of ACO

The main experimental objective here is to apply a *pragma omp parallel* region to the main parts of ACO, first on *ConstructAntSolutions* only and then measure the performance. After that, the parallel region will be applied to *updatePheromone procedure*, where a parallel "for" applied with "n" number of threads. At the end of each parallel region there will be an implicit automatic barrier, its mission is to synchronize with the main thread before starting new parallel region.

4.3   Tuning OpenMP Scheduling Clause

Three types of OpenMP schedule clause could be experimented to control the granularity of thread execution: static (which is the default), dynamic, and guided schedule. The default scheduling used in *parallel for* is static, which distributes the work and iterations between threads. This is not the case of different jobs assigned to different ants. The proposed solution adds the schedule dynamic clause to the *"parallel for"* loops to give a full control for the distribution of iterations to the available threads. The iteration granularity is determined by the chunk size. The main benefit of dynamic scheduling is its flexibility in assigning more chunks to threads that can finish their chunks earlier. The rule is, the fastest thread shouldn't wait for the slowest.

4.4   Eliminating Race Condition Hazards

The race condition would occur when many threads update the same memory location at the same time. ACO algorithm may suffer from this problem, especially when two or more ants are trying to update the pheromone matrix at the same time. To avoid data race condition in the process of increasing/decreasing pheromone levels, critical sections are applied.

However, in our proposed parallelization, each thread will be responsible for updating pheromone level of each edge. Thus, the value of pheromone level update is the sole responsibility of a single thread. Accordingly, race hazards can be eliminated.

5   Results and Performance Analysis

In this paper, Travel Salesman Problem (TSP) NP-hard problem has been chosen as a well-known application of the generic ACO algorithm. In this paper, TSP parameters were initially set, and OpenMP was applied as a parallelization API. After that, results were gathered from the experiment. Finally, the performance of ACO algorithm with OpenMP was finally analyzed.

5.1   ACO Parallelization Environment

In the conducted experiment of this paper, OpenMP 4.0 and Visual Studio Ultimate 2013, ACO algorithm was implemented in C++. Computer configuration is Intel® Core™ i5-460M 2.53GHz, CPU– L3 cache 3MB, 4GB RAM.

The parallel regions of OpenMP with number of threads n=2, 4, 8, 16, 32, 64 are applied, utilizing 1000 ants. Different sizes for TSP problem with 40, 80, 130 cities are used to test the scalability of the parallelization. The test and the analysis would measure the speedup to gauge the parallelization impact on execution time and efficiency. The performance is measured by using speedup which shows the performance to determine the optimal solution in a specific computing time:

$$speedup = t_s / t_p \qquad (6)$$

In equation (6), t_s is the time required to solve the problem with the sequential version of code on a specific computer, t_p is the time to solve the same problem with the parallel version of code using p threads on the same computer. And the efficiency of the parallel implementation is calculated through the equation:

$$efficiency = speedup / P \qquad (7)$$

The strategy of implementation described before has been put under experiment by starting from an existing sequential implementation. Then, the appropriate OpenMP directives were added, the necessary changes were made as discussed before.

To achieve accurate results representing real execution time, code running was repeated ten times for every change in thread numbers. In this experiment, Sequential code was applied first to measure the difference between parallel and sequential versions of code. Tables 1, 2, 3 show the results of average execution time, speedup and efficiency when default schedule static was initially applied, then the application of dynamic schedule with n number of threads was compared showing the difference. By using k=1000 as number of ants, the experiment was sequentially executed with problem size of 40 cities of the ACO and the execution time was marked. Parallelization started with 2, 4, 8, 16, 32, and 64 threads respectively. Then, the same experiment was repeated with different problem sizes 80 and 130 cities. The speedup and efficiency are measured by equations (6) and (7).

Table 1. Ant colony size, 40 cities 1000 ants

Number of threads	Default Schedule Exec. time(sec)	Dynamic Schedule Execution time(sec)	Speedup (sequential to dynamic)	Efficiency
Sequential	1.5855	1.5855	-	-
2	1.2543	1.1264	1.41	0.70
4	1.0347	0.9427	1.68	0.42
8	1.0494	0.9338	1.70	0.21
16	1.0764	0.9430	1.68	0.11
32	1.0603	0.9454	1.68	0.05
64	1.0761	0.9650	1.64	0.02

Analyzing the results of execution times in table 2 has proved a better performance by using 4 and 8 threads, then no significant speedup was noticed on adding more threads. The colony size increased to 80 cities. A better performance took place with a leap in execution time especially after applying dynamic scheduling clause. The same could be addressed by increasing the TSP problem size to 130 cities as shown in Table 3. A fine tuning was done using schedule dynamic clause which caused a noticed performance speedup. This is due to the dynamically generated chunks at runtime which control the thread execution over iterations.

Table 2. Ant colony size, 80 cities, 1000 ants

Number of threads	Dynamic Exec. time(sec)	speedup	efficiency
Sequential	7.0755	-.	-
2	4.0492	1.75	0.87
4	2.7932	2.53	0.63
8	2.7204	2.60	0.33
16	2.7889	2.54	0.16
32	2.8113	2.52	0.08
64	2.8151	2.51	0.04

Table 3. Ant colony size, 130 cities 1000 ants

Number of threads	Default Schedule Execution time(sec)	Dynamic Schedule Execution time(sec)	speedup (sequential to dynamic)	efficiency
Sequential	25.9013	25.9013	-	-
2	17.764	10.6557	2.43	1.22
4	9.57293	7.3100	3.54	0.89
8	8.1691	7.2090	3.59	0.45
16	7.90743	7.2510	3.57	0.22
32	7.79117	7.3096	3.54	0.11
64	7.80114	7.3259	3.54	0.06

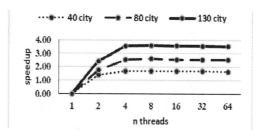

Fig. 2. The speedup with n number of threads applied on different ant colony sizes

After combining the results from the three tables 1, 2, and 3 in Fig. 2, a relative speedup for parallelization over sequential implementation was observed especially on increasing the TSP problem size 40, 80 and then 130 cities.

As shown in table 4, parallel regions of OpenMP wraps the most time consuming parts of ACO algorithm. When execution time was measured for each region, Updatepheromone was found to be the most time-consuming part. A speedup was achieved after applying OpenMP parallel. This is clearly illustrated in Fig. 3 which shows a significant time-consuming UpdatePheromone function and

AntSolutionConstruction is the second most time-consuming part. They both gain significant speedup after applying parallel regions of OpenMP.

Table 4. Execution time of Parallel regions against different n threads

number of threads	initialize PheromoneTrail	AntSolution Construction	update Pheromone	Overall execution time
1	0.000135	2.414022	9.531944	12.29551
2	0.000078	1.298681	4.116056	5.677514
4	0.000072	0.836327	3.056812	4.125318
8	0.000098	0.807538	3.000157	4.054615
16	0.000086	0.828095	3.060481	4.188573
32	0.000139	0.832196	3.0479	4.137231
64	0.000217	0.869248	3.024268	4.185221

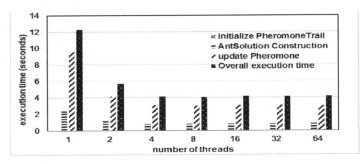

Fig. 3. Execution time of Parallel regions against different n threads with same problem size

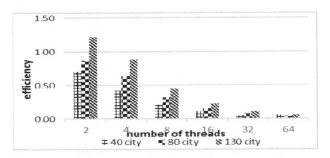

Fig. 4. Efficiency values when using 40, 80, and 130 city size

The experiment repeated with different numbers of threads 2, 4, 8, 16, 32, and 64 shown in Fig. 4 indicates an improvement in efficiency which occurred as a result of increasing problem size regarding the number of threads, since efficiency = speedup/ number of threads.

As the main goal is to provide better performance through parallelism, the experiments in this research would investigate the optimal number of threads needed. For this purpose, a tool of thread visualizing and monitoring the interaction and relation between threads and cores has been used. One selected tool is Microsoft concurrency visualizer which is a plug-in tool for Visual studio 2013. Different numbers of threads were implemented in each run and results have been collected and analyzed in the results section.

In the current experiment, 1, 4, and 8 threads have been selected to be analyzed by Concurrency Visualizer on a machine with 4 logical cores for the following reasons:

- Finding the optimal number of threads related to the available number of cores.
- Visualizing and analysis of concurrently executing 4 threads that's equal to the number of logical cores.
- Visualizing and analysis of concurrently executing 8 threads that's more than the number of cores.
- Visualizing and analysis of the behavior of multithreads and how they execute, block, and synchronize.

Executing the ACO with a bigger number of threads than the number of cores, an overhead of context switching, synchronization, and preemption of the threads is detected. In the meanwhile, OpenMP gives a better utilization of the multicore environment. Fig. 5, shows a detailed view of 4 and 8 threads on 2 cores CPU with hyper-threading which are logically equivalent to 4 cores. When the number of threads is equal to the number of cores, threads are distributed among the available cores. The advantage of this is less synchronization and preemption time. Most of this saved time is assigned to execution causing the parallel threads to achieve better speedup. Whereas, if the number of threads largely exceeds the number of available cores, an overhead and time wasting is detected. This is because of thread blocking, synchronization, and context switching. This experiment shows the fact that the optimal number of threads should not exceed the available number of cores. Consequently, if the possibility of thread blocking does not exist, the number of threads should be optimized according to the available number of cores, as each thread will utilize each CPU core.

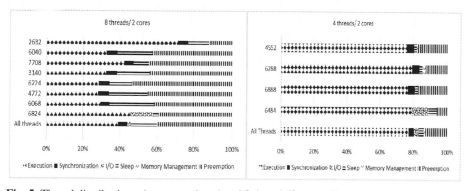

Fig. 5. Thread distribution when executing 4 and 8 threads/2 cores CPU with hyper-threading

6   Conclusion and Future Work

In this research, parallel implementation of ACO using OpenMP API directives effectively solves the common TSP problem. Results were evaluated, and comparison between sequential and parallel multithread were also analyzed. OpenMP parallel regions achieved a speedup more than 3X of sequential execution. The optimal number of threads was found to be equal to the number of processors available. With TSP sizes of 40, 80, and 130 cities, better speedup was detected with a larger number of cities. Moreover, tuning was added to the implementation of parallel ACO using OpenMP with different schedules clauses. Dynamic schedule was found to achieve better performance with average speedup 8-25% than default schedule clause especially on increasing the number of cities. This paper shows an upper border of speedup related to the available number of cores.

The future work would be oriented towards using this kind of parallel implementation using OpenMP for different newly metaheuristics such as Cuckoo search (CS) and to compare results to parallel ACO and measures which one positively affected more by the parallelization of OpenMP platform.

References

1. Alba, E.: Parallel Metaheuristics: A New Class of Algorithms. Wiley. ISBN 0-471-67806-6, July 2005
2. Dorigo, M.: Optimization, Learning and Natural Algorithms, PhD thesis, Politecnico di Milano, Italy (1992)
3. Chen, W.N., Zhang, J.: Ant Colony Optimization Approach to Grid Workflow Scheduling Problem with Various QoS Requirements. IEEE Transactions on Systems, Cybernetics-Part C: Applications and Reviews **31**(1), 29–43 (2009)
4. Donati, A.V., et al.: Time dependent vehicle routing problem with a multi ant colony system. European Journal of Operational Research **185**(3), 1174–1191 (2008)
5. Dumitrescu, I., Stützle, T.: Combinations of local search and exact algorithms. In: Raidl, G.R., Cagnoni, S., Cardalda, J.J., Corne, D.W., Gottlieb, J., Guillot, A., Hart, E., Johnson, C.G., Marchiori, E., Meyer, J.-A., Middendorf, M. (eds.) EvoIASP 2003, EvoWorkshops 2003, EvoSTIM 2003, EvoROB/EvoRobot 2003, EvoCOP 2003, EvoBIO 2003, and EvoMUSART 2003. LNCS, vol. 2611, pp. 211–223. Springer, Heidelberg (2003)
6. Xue-dong, X., et al.: The basic principle and application of ant colony optimization algorithm. In: Artificial Intelligence and Education (ICAIE) conference, Hangzhou, China (2010)
7. Dorigo, M., Gambardella, L.M.: Ant colony system: a cooperative learning approach to the traveling salesman problem. IEEE Transactions on Evolutionary Computation (2002)
8. Amdahl, G.: Validity of the single processor approach to achieving large Scale computing capabilities. In: AFIPS Conference Proceedings, vol. 30, pp. 483–485. Thompson Book, Washington, D.C., April 1967
9. Arnautovic, M., et al.: Parallelization of the ant colony optimization for the shortest path problem using OpenMP and CUDA (MIPRO), Opatija, Croatia (2013)

10. Dorigo, M., Socha, K.: An Introduction to Ant Colony Optimization. Universit de Libre de Bruxelles, CP 194/6, Brussels (2007). http://iridia.ulb.ac.be
11. Bullnheimer, B., Kotsis, G., Strauss, C.: Parallelization strategies for the ant system. In: De Leone, R., Murli, A., Pardalos, P., Toraldo, G. (eds.) High Performance Algorithms and Software in Nonlinear Optimization. Applied Optimization, vol. 24, Dordrecht (1997)
12. Stützle, T.: Parallelization strategies for ant colony optimization. In: Eiben, A.E., Bäck, T., Schoenauer, M., Schwefel, H.-P. (eds.) PPSN 1998. LNCS, vol. 1498, pp. 722–731. Springer, Heidelberg (1998)
13. Xiong, J., Liu, C., Chen, Z.: A new parallel ant colony optimization algorithm based on message passing interface. In: Computational Intelligence and Industrial Application, PACIIA 2008. Pacific-Asia Workshop, Wuhan (2008)
14. Dorigo, M., Stutzle, T.: "Ant colony optimization" A Bradford Book. The MIT Press, Cambridge (2004)

Acceleration of Blender Cycles Path-Tracing Engine Using Intel Many Integrated Core Architecture

Milan Jaroš[1,2]([✉]), Lubomír Říha[1], Petr Strakoš[1], Tomáš Karásek[1],
Alena Vašatová[1,2], Marta Jarošová[1,2], and Tomáš Kozubek[1,2]

[1] IT4Innovations, VŠB-Technical University of Ostrava, Ostrava, Czech Republic
milan.jaros@vsb.cz
[2] Department of Applied Mathematics, VŠB-Technical University of Ostrava,
Ostrava, Czech Republic

Abstract. This paper describes the acceleration of the most computationally intensive kernels of the Blender rendering engine, Blender Cycles, using Intel Many Integrated Core architecture (MIC). The proposed parallelization, which uses OpenMP technology, also improves the performance of the rendering engine when running on multi-core CPUs and multi-socket servers. Although the GPU acceleration is already implemented in Cycles, its functionality is limited. Our proposed implementation for MIC architecture contains all features of the engine with improved performance. The paper presents performance evaluation for three architectures: multi-socket server, server with MIC (Intel Xeon Phi 5100p) accelerator and server with GPU accelerator (NVIDIA Tesla K20m).

Keywords: Intel xeon phi · Blender Cycles · Quasi-Monte Carlo · Path Tracing · Rendering

1 Introduction

The progress in the High-Performance Computing (HPC) plays an important role in the science and engineering. Computationally intensive simulations have become an essential part of research and development of new technologies. Many research groups in the area of computer graphics deal with problems related to an extremely time-consuming process of image synthesis of virtual scenes, also called rendering (Shrek Forever 3D – 50 mil. CPU rendering hours, [CGW]).

Beside the use of HPC clusters for speeding up the computationally intensive tasks hardware accelerators are being extensively used as well. They can further increase computing power and efficiency of HPC clusters. In general, two types of hardware accelerators could be used, GPU accelerators and MIC coprocessors.

The new Intel MIC coprocessor is composed of up to 61 low power cores in terms of both energy and performance when compared to multi-core CPUs. It can be used

© IFIP International Federation for Information Processing 2015
K. Saeed and W. Homenda (Eds.): CISIM 2015, LNCS 9339, pp. 86–97, 2015.
DOI: 10.1007/978-3-319-24369-6_7

as a standalone Linux box or as an accelerator to the main CPU. The peak performance of the top-of-the line Xeon Phi is over 1.1 TFLOP (10^{12} floating point operations per second) in double precision and over 2.2 TFLOPS in single precision.
MIC architecture can be programmed using both shared memory models such as
OpenMP or OpenCL (provides compatibility with codes developed for GPU) and
distributed memory models such as MPI.

The implementation presented in this paper has been developed and tested
on Anselm Bullx cluster at the IT4Innovations National Supercomputing Centre
in Ostrava, Czech Republic. Anselm cluster is equipped with both Intel Xeon
Phi 5110P and Tesla K20m accelerators [AHW]. For production runs, once the
algorithm is fully optimized, new IT4Innovations Salomon system will be used.
Salomon will be equipped with 432 nodes, each with two coprocessors Intel Xeon
Phi 7120P [SHW].

1.1 Rendering Equation and Monte Carlo Path-Tracing Method

In 1986 Kajiya first introduced the rendering equation in computer graphics
[KAJ]. One of the last versions of this equation is represented as

$$L_o(x, \omega_o) = L_e(x, \omega_o) + \int_\Omega L_i(x, \omega_i) f_r(x, \omega_i, \omega_o)(\omega_i \cdot n) d\omega_i, \qquad (1)$$

where ω_o is direction of outgoing ray, ω_i is direction of incoming ray, L_o
is spectral radiance emitted by the source from point x in direction ω_o, L_e is
emitted spectral radiance from point x in direction ω_o, Ω is the unit hemisphere
in direction of normal vector n with center in x, over which we integrate, L_i is
spectral radiance coming inside to x in direction ω_i, $f_r(x, \omega_i, \omega_o)$ is distribution
function of the image (BRDF) in point x from direction ω_i to direction ω_o, $\omega_i \cdot n$
is angle between ω_i and surface normal.

Rendering equation is fundamental algorithm for all algorithms of image synthesis based on ray tracing principle such as Path-Tracing. Solving the rendering
equation is computationally extensive in general. The most common solution
methods are based on numerical estimation of the integral (1). One of the most
commonly used methods for numerical solution of equation (1) is Monte Carlo
(MC) method. More information about this method can be found in the dissertation thesis of Lafortune [LAF]. MC is also employed in different areas beside
the computer graphics, e.q. in statistics [GRE].

1.2 Quasi-Monte Carlo and Sobol's Sequence

One of the MC drawbacks is slow convergency, which is $O\left(\frac{1}{\sqrt{N}}\right)$, where N is
number of simulations. Due to this reason techniques that speed up the convergency and effectivity of the whole computation have been developed.

Deterministic form of Monte Carlo method is called quasi-Monte Carlo
(QCM) and its convergency speed is $O\left(\frac{(\log N)^s}{N}\right)$, where s is dimension of the

integral. In order for $O\left(\frac{(\log N)^s}{N}\right)$ to be smaller than $O\left(\frac{1}{\sqrt{N}}\right)$, s needs to be small and N needs to be large [LEM]. In QMC method pseudo-random numbers are replaced by quasi-random numbers that are generated by deterministic algorithms. Typical property of such numbers is that they fill in the unit square more uniformly. This property is called low-discrepancy (LD). More details about it can be found in [MOR], [NIE].

Let elements $x_1, \ldots, x_N$ are sequence of s-dimensional space $[0,1]^s$, then approximation is expressed as

$$\int_{[0,1]^s} f(u)\, du \approx \frac{1}{N} \sum_{i=1}^{N} f(x_i). \tag{2}$$

Well known types of LD sequences are Halton's, Faure's, Sobol's, Wozniak's, Hammersly's or Niederreiter's sequence. Blender uses Sobol's sequences [JO3], [JO8], since they fit their needs - runs well on the CPU and accelerators, supports high path depth and can perform adaptive sampling.

Due to its property Sobol's sequences can be used for progressive sampling. Unlike the Halton's sequence which can be used for progressive sampling as well, Sobol's sequences are not correlated in higher dimensions, and so do not need to be scrambled. The algorithm for generating Sobol's sequences is explained in [BRA].

Any number from any dimension can be queried without per path precomputation. Each dimension has its own sequence and when rendering the i-th pass, Blender gets element i from the sequence. A sequence is defined by a 32×32 binary matrix, and getting the i-th element in the sequence corresponds to multiplying the matrix by i. With binary operations this ends up being quite quick.

These matrices are not as simple to compute, but the data to generate them up to dimension 21201 is available online. Blender currently uses 4 dimensions initially to sample the subpixel location and lens and 8 numbers per bounce, so that limits us to a maximum path depth of 2649 [BLS].

2   Implementation and Parallelization for MIC Accelerator

The implementation presented in this paper is based on source code of the Blender version 2.73 that has been obtained from [BLE]. The code of Blender is compiled using GNU compiler version gcc/4.9.0 and the library running on MIC coprocessor was compiled using intel/14.0.1 compiler. In order to enable newly developed OpenMP and MIC accelerated rendering engines new OMP computing device has been added to GUI setting of Blender.

2.1   Parallelization for Multi-core CPU's with Shared Memory

The core of the Cycles engine computation method implements quasi-Monte Carlo method with Sobol's sequence. Rendered scene is represented as a C++ global variable. If GPU or MIC acceleration is used this global variable has to be transferred to the accelerator before rendering (solving the rendering equation (1)) is started. The synthesized image of size $x_r \times y_r$ is decomposed into tiles of size $x_t \times y_t$ (see Fig. 1). The way rendering algorithm itself is executed inside a tile differs for each computing device. We compare the performance of the following computing devices: CPU (POSIX threads for CPU only, this is the original computing device used by Blender Cycles), OpenMP (for CPU and MIC – newly developed computing device by our group), OpenCL (for CPU, MIC and GPU) and CUDA (for GPU only).

Original Implementation. The original computing device from Blender Cycles uses POSIX threads for parallelization. Parallelization is done in the following way: the synthesized image of resolution $x_r \times y_r$ is decomposed into tiles of size $x_t \times y_t$. Each tile is then computed by one POSIX thread/one CPU core. The situation is shown in the Fig. 1.

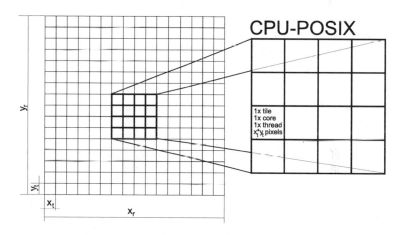

Fig. 1. The decomposition of synthesized image with resolution $x_r \times y_r$ to tiles with size $x_t \times y_t$ by original implementation. The one tile is computed by one POSIX thread on one CPU core for $x_t \times y_t$ pixels. This is an example of CPU16 - see Section 3.

2.2 OpenMP Parallelization of Intra Tile Rendering for CPU and MIC Architecture

The newly proposed OpenMP parallelization is implemented in the OMP computing device. A hierarchical approach is used where each POSIX thread forked by the Cycles renderer is further parallelized using OpenMP threads. In order to provide enough work for each core of MIC coprocessor we need to decompose the larger tile $x_t \times y_t$ to smaller sub-tile $x_o \times y_o$ to fully utilize the CPU hardware (this is an example of OMP15MIC or OMP8CPU2MIC - see Section 3). The OpenMP parallelizes the loop of calculation across sub-tiles of the tile in a way that single OpenMP thread is processing single sub-tile of a tile. An example in

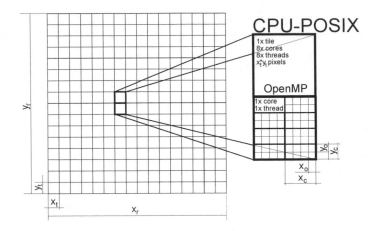

Fig. 2. The decomposition of synthesized image with resolution $x_r \times y_r$ to tiles with size $x_t \times y_t$ and to sub-tiles with size $x_o \times y_o$ by OpenMP implementation. One tile $x_t \times y_t$ is computed by eight threads using eight cores for $x_t \times y_t$ pixels. Each sub-tile $x_o \times y_o$ is computed by one OpenMP thread. This is an example of OMP8CPU2 - see Section 3.

Fig. 2 shows the case with two tiles or POSIX threads and predefined number of OpenMP threads per tile.

The computation time of each sub-tile is different. To achieve an effective load balancing we have to adjust the workload distribution by setting up the OpenMP runtime scheduler to `schedule(dynamic, 1)` and the values of x_o and y_o have to be set to small number (ex. $x_o = 32$ and $y_o = 32$). This setup produces the most efficient work distribution among processor cores and therefore minimizes processing time.

As of now the POSIX threads are used to control the tiles, but in our future work, we would like to use MPI processing for computer clusters, so that single image can be processed by multiple computers or computing nodes of the HPC cluster. For this scenario the POSIX threads will be substituted by the MPI threads.

The acceleration of the rendering process using Intel Xeon Phi accelerators is built on the similar basis as the approach to multi-core CPUs. In this case one POSIX thread is used to control single MIC accelerator. This means that one accelerator works on a single tile and multiple accelerators can be used in parallel to render multiple tiles.

The architecture of the Intel Xeon Phi is significantly different from the regular Xeon processors. It is equipped with 61 processing cores where each core can run up to 4 threads, which gives 244 threads in total. This means that in order to fully utilize the hardware and to provide enough work for each core to enable load balancing, each tile has to be significantly larger than in case of CPU processing (see Fig. 3). In addition, the computation of each pixel takes

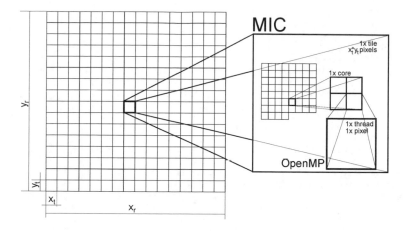

Fig. 3. The decomposition of synthesized image with resolution $x_r \times y_r$ to tiles with size $x_t \times y_t$ by MIC implementation. The entire tile is computed by the coprocessor. Every pixel of the synthesized image is computed on one thread of the coprocessor.

different time. To enable load balancing using OpenMP runtime engine we have to set the scheduler to `schedule(dynamic, 1)`.

Using the coprocessor with separate memory also requires the data transfer between CPU memory and the memory of the coprocessor. Blender uses complex C++ structure that represents entire scene (`KernelGlobals`) and therefore in order to transfer data it has to be retyped to binary array (`mic_alloc_kg()`). When computation ends, allocated memory of the coprocessor is cleaned (`mic_free_kg()`).

```
//Structure that represents entire scene
struct KernelGlobals
{
  texture_image_uchar4 texture_byte_images[MAX_BYTE_IMAGES];
  texture_image_float4 texture_float_images[MAX_FLOAT_IMAGES];

  #define KERNEL_TEX(type, ttype, name) ttype name;
  #define KERNEL_IMAGE_TEX(type, ttype, name)
  #include "kernel_textures.h"

  KernelData __data;
}

//Declaration of variable for data transfer to MIC
__declspec(target(mic : 0)) char *kg_bin = NULL;

//Transfer of data to MIC
void mic_alloc_kg(KernelGlobals *kgPtr, size_t kgSize)
{
  kg_bin = (char *) kgPtr;

  #pragma offload target(mic:0) \
    in(kg_bin:length(kgSize) alloc_if(1) free_if(0))
  {
    KernelGlobals* kg_mic = (KernelGlobals *)kg_bin;
    //...
```

```
  }
}

//Main rendering process
void mic_path_trace(int tile_h, int tile_w, int start_sample, int end_sample)
{
  int size = tile_h*tile_w;

  #pragma offload target(mic:0) \
  nocopy(kg_bin:length(0) alloc_if(0) free_if(0))
  {
    for (int sample = start_sample; sample < end_sample; sample++)
    {
      #pragma omp parallel for schedule(dynamic, 1)
      for (int i = 0; i < size; i++)
      {
        int y = i / tile_w;
        int x = i - y * tile_w;
        kernel_path_trace(x,y);
      }
    }
  }
}

//Allocated memory of the coprocessor is cleaned
void mic_free_kg(...)
{
  #pragma offload target(mic:0) \
    nocopy(kg_bin:length(0) alloc_if(0) free_if(1))
}
```

2.3   Parallelization by OpenCL and CUDA

The OpenCL computing device can be used for multi-core CPU's as well as for MIC or GPU accelerators. Scene decomposition is similar to OpenMP processing for MIC. Only one POSIX thread with a large tile for optimal performance is used due to previously discussed reasons. The parallelization is based on task parallelism where for computing of one pixel a separate task is created (see Fig. 4). The original code had to be modified in order to run on Intel Xeon Phi devices. Unfortunately rendering with textures did not work on MIC coprocessor. Due to this shading and advance shading had to be disabled. There is no intention to fix this malfunction, because the OpenCL is not a targeted platform for us (the OpenCL is limited like CUDA and it is hard to use for development and optimization).

As OpenCL and CUDA programing model are very similar, so is the decomposition. There is again one POSIX thread for main computation per accelerator. On GPU a rendering kernel uses single CUDA thread to render single pixel of a tile. The GPU needs thousands threads for better performance. This is reason, why we need the large tile (see Section 3).

The GPU acceleration is a part of the original render engine. When compared to the our proposed approach it has limited functionality: the maximum amount of individual textures is limited, Open shading language (OSL) is not supported, Smoke/Fire rendering is not supported, GPU has smaller memory then MIC, GPU does not support cooperative rendering with CPU. We need

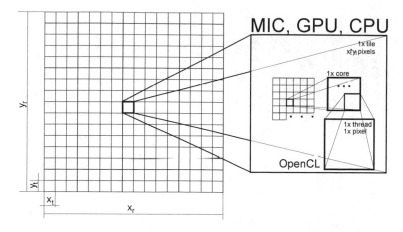

Fig. 4. The decomposition of synthesized image with resolution $x_r \times y_r$ to tiles with size $x_t \times y_t$ by OpenCL implementation. The entire tile is computed by the device. For computing of one pixel is created one task.

the all feature from CPU - that's reason, why the combining of the CPU and GPU is useless for us.

3   Benchmark

In this paper two scenes are used for all benchmarks; one scene with and one without textures. The first scene with Tatra T87 has 1.2 millions triangles and uses HDRI lighting (see Fig. 5). The other scene with bones was generated from CT images and has 7.7 millions triangles (see Fig. 5). It does not use textures. This scene is used to evaluate the performance of the OpenCL implementation for Xeon Phi as it does not support textures.

The benchmark was run on single computing node of the Anselm supercomputer equipped with two Intel Sandy Bridge E5-2470 CPU's (used by CPUn, OMPn engines - n is number of cores used) and one Intel Xeon Phi 5110P (MIC) or one NVIDIA Tesla K20m coprocessor (GPU).

In the next test we exploited the CPU-MIC hybrid system (OMP15MIC). The two tiles with large size are computed at the same time (2×POSIX threads were created, one for CPU and one for MIC). First tile is computed by CPU using 15× OpenMP threads and the other tile is computed by MIC coprocessor (1× core is used to manage MIC), see the results in the Table 1 and 4.

Another test we performed was a combination of OMP8 and CPU2. That means the computation of two tiles was parallelized (2×POSIX threads were created) and each tile was computed by 8×OpenMP threads, see the results in the Table 1 and 4.

We also combined the CPU2 (2×tiles, each has one POSIX thread), OMP8 (the each POSIX thread has 8×OpenMP threads) and MIC, see the results in

Fig. 5. *(left)* Benchmark 1: Model of Tatra T87. *(right)* Benchmark 2: Model of bones generated from CT images.

the Table 1 and 4. This combination is designed for the systems with multiple MIC accelerators (this will be the architecture of the Salomon – see Section 5).

For all tests, when OMP is used (OMP16, OMP8CPU2, OMP15MIC, OMP8CPU2MIC), the size of sub-tile 32×32px (see Section 2.2).

The division of the image into tiles has to be made carefully. You can see the big time when CPU16 is used and the size of tile is 1024×1024. In this example the 12×cores are idle (see the Table 1 and 4).

3.1   Benchmark 1: Tatra T87

For this scene resolution 2048×2048px was used. First we compared the calculation for different size of tiles for the same resolution (see Table 1). In next two tests the resolution and count of samples were changed (see Table 2 and 3).

Table 1. Benchmark 1: In the table we can see the time in minutes for different size of tiles. The test was executed for: Samples: 256, and Resolution: 2048×2048px.

	32×32	64×64	128×128	256×256	512×512	1024×1024
CPU16	03:08	03:10	03:12	03:19	06:54 (8cores)	13:10 (4cores)
OMP16	44:42	12:41	04:08	03:31	03:12	03:09
OMP8CPU2	22:01	06:39	03:34	03:17	03:12	03:25
GPU	34:58	12:11	05:42	03:43	03:09	03:06
MIC	25:40	11:30	07:38	06:38	06:22	06:17
OMP15MIC	14:08	05:52	03:21	02:30	**02:18**	02:30
OMP8CPU2MIC	10:41	04:07	02:40	02:22	02:21	03:01

3.2   Benchmark 2: Bones

The original implementation of OpenCL does not work on Intel Xeon Phi. The problem is with shading and advance shading which has to be disabled. For this reason, we created a new scene, just for OpenCL testing. The Table 4 compares runtimes (in minutes) for different numbers of tiles. The Table 5 shows the result using OpenCL.

Table 2. Benchmark 1: In the table we can see the time in minutes for different resolutions. The test was executed for: Samples: 256, Tiles:512 × 512px.

	256	512	1024	2048
CPU16	00:47	03:03	03:16	06:48 (8cores)
OMP16	**00:05**	**00:14**	00:50	03:11
GPU	00:07	00:15	00:53	03:09
MIC	00:09	00:27	01:39	06:23
OMP15MIC	00:09	00:27	**00:40**	**02:20**

Table 3. Benchmark 1: In the table we can see the time in minutes for count of samples. The test was executed for: Tiles: 512 × 512px, Resolution: 2048 × 2048px.

	32	64	128	256	512	1024
CPU16	00:55	01:46	03:30	06:50	13:35 (8cores)	27:18 (4cores)
OMP16	00:28	00:51	01:38	03:12	06:19	12:40
GPU	00:39	01:14	02:22	04:40	09:16	18:31
MIC	00:59	01:44	03:17	06:22	12:34	24:59
OMP15MIC	**00:23**	**00:40**	**01:12**	**02:18**	**04:31**	**09:05**

Table 4. Benchmark 2: In the table we can see the time in minutes for different numbers of tiles. The test was executed for: Samples: 256, Resolution: 2048 × 2048px.

	32×32	64×64	128×128	256×256	512×512	1024×1024
CPU16	03:28	03:30	03:36	03:53	05:50 (8cores)	17:20 (4cores)
OMP16	49:08	13:37	04:20	03:49	03:39	03:36
OMP8CPU2	24:35	07:07	03:52	03:42	03:37	03:36
GPU	30:42	09:17	04:45	03:28	03:15	03:17
MIC	57:56	20:43	10:37	07:50	07:06	06:54
OMP15MIC	25:54	08:17	04:02	02:54	02:39	**02:32**
OMP8CPU2MIC	17:10	05:27	03:12	02:43	02:39	02:36

Table 5. Benchmark 2: In the table we can see the time in minutes for different numbers of tiles using OpenCL. The test was executed for: Samples: 256, Resolution: 2048 × 2048px.

	32×32	64×64	128×128	256×256	512×512	1024×1024	2048×2048
CPUCL	06:44	05:46	05:18	05:06	05:01	05:02	05:07
GPUCL	35:58	11:08	04:46	04:03	**03:47**	03:49	03:50
MICCL	01:04:34	21:23	14:37	10:34	09:41	09:10	08:47

4   Conclusion

Both benchmarks show that the best performance could be obtained in case when combination of CPU and MIC coprocessor (OMP15MIC) is used. We can see from the results that the MIC coprocessor behaves like a 6-cores CPU unit. On the other hand, the MIC accelerator adds only 1.37 speedup over CPU implementation, which is less than expected. We would expect at least the same performance boost as in case of GPU accelerators. The reason why Intel MIC does not provide the expected performance boost is due to insufficient vectorization in the code for calculation the rendering equation (512 bit registers (able to hold 16 floats) are wasted now).

We also show that the combination of full CPU utilization and MIC (OMP15MIC) has the advantage over GPU parallelization. Advantages are as follows:

- GPU parallelization does not use all CPU cores
- GPU does not offer all features of our MIC implementation, which has identical feature set as the original CPU implementation
- The combination of 2 POSIX threads, each thread running on one socket, and 2× MIC is designed for the systems with multiple MIC accelerators (this will be the architecture of the Salomon – see Section 5)

5   Future Work

In the future work we will focus on vectorization of the code to improve its performance on Intel Xeon Phi devices. We will also modify the existing implementation of the Path-Tracing method using MPI technology. Our new benchmarks will target the new supercomputer Salomon which will be equipped with two Intel Xeon Phi for better performance.

Acknowledgments. This paper has been elaborated in the framework of the project New creative teams in priorities of scientific research, reg. no. CZ.1.07/2.3.00/30.0055, supported by Operational Programme Education for Competitiveness and cofinanced by the European Social Fund and the state budget of the Czech Republic. The work was also supported by the European Regional Development Fund in the IT4Innovations Centre of Excellence project (CZ.1.05/1.1.00/02.0070), the Project of major infrastructures for research, development and innovation of Ministry of Education, Youth and Sports with reg. num. LM2011033 and by the VSB-TU Ostrava under the grant SGS SP2015/189.

References

[CGW] Intel: Animation Evolution: A Biopic Through the Eyes of Shrek, Computer Graphic World, December 2010
[KAJ] Kajiya, J.: The rendering equation. In: Computer Graphics, vol. 20, pp. 143–150, August 1986

[LAF] Lafortune, E.: MathematicalModels and Monte Carlo Algorithms for Physically Based Rendering, Cornell University, PhD. Dissertation, February 1996

[GRE] Gregor, L.: Ověření ocenění opcí metodou quasi-Monte-Carlo, 5. mezinárodní konference Finanční řízení podniku a finančních institucí, VŠB-TU Ostrava (2005)

[NIE] Niederreiter, H.: Random number Generation and quasi-Monte Carlo Methods. SIAM, Philadelphia (1992). ISBN 0-89871-295-5

[MOR] Morokoff, W.J.: Generating quasi-Random Paths for Stochastic Processes, Working Paper, Mathematics Dept. of UCLA (1997)

[JO3] Joe, S., Kuo, F.Y.: Remark on Algorithm 659: Implementing Sobol's quasi-random sequence generator. ACM Trans. Math. Softw. **29**, 49–57 (2003)

[JO8] Joe, S., Kuo, F.Y.: Constructing Sobol sequences with better two-dimensional projections. SIAM J. Sci. Comput. **30**, 2635–2654 (2008)

[BRA] Bratley, P., Fox, B.L.: Algorithm 659: Implementing Sobol's quasi-random sequence generator. ACM Trans. Math. Software **14**, 88–100 (1988)

[LEM] Lemieux, Ch.: Monte Carlo and Quasi-Monte Carlo Sampling. Springer (2009). ISBN 978-1441926760

[AHW] https://docs.it4i.cz/anselm-cluster-documentation/hardware-overview

[SHW] https://docs.it4i.cz/salomon/hardware-overview

[BLE] http://www.blender.org/

[BLS] http://wiki.blender.org/index.php/Dev:2.6/Source/Render/Cycles/Sobol

A Modified Complete Spline Interpolation and Exponential Parameterization

Ryszard Kozera[1,3], Lyle Noakes[2], and Magdalena Wilkołazka[3]($\boxtimes$)

[1] Faculty of Applied Informatics and Mathematics, Warsaw University of Life
Sciences - SGGW, Nowoursynowska str. 159, 02-776 Warsaw, Poland
ryszard.kozera@gmail.com, ryszard_kozera@sggw.pl
[2] School of Mathematics and Statistics, The University of Western Australia,
35 Stirling Highway, Crawley, Perth, WA 6009, Australia
lyle.noakes@maths.uwa.edu.au
[3] Faculty of Mathematics, IT and Landscape Architecture, John Paul II Catholic
University of Lublin, Konstantynów str. 1H, 20-708 Lublin, Poland
magda.wilkolazka@gmail.com

Abstract. In this paper a modified complete spline interpolation based
on reduced data is examined in the context of trajectory approximation.
Reduced data constitute an ordered collection of interpolation points in
arbitrary Euclidean space, stripped from the corresponding interpolation knots. The exponential parameterization (controlled by $\lambda \in [0, 1]$)
compensates the above loss of information and provides specific scheme
to approximate the distribution of the missing knots. This approach is
commonly used in computer graphics or computer vision in curve modeling and image segmentation or in biometrics for feature extraction.
The numerical verification of asymptotic orders $\alpha(\lambda)$ in trajectory estimation by modified complete spline interpolation is performed here for
regular curves sampled more-or-less uniformly with the missing knots
parameterized according to exponential parameterization. Our approach
is equally applicable to either sparse or dense data. The numerical experiments confirm a slow linear convergence orders $\alpha(\lambda) = 1$ holding for all
$\lambda \in [0, 1)$ and a quartic one $\alpha(1) = 4$ once modified complete spline is
used. The paper closes with an example of medical image segmentation.

Keywords: Spline interpolation · Curve approximation and modeling ·
Reduced data · Biometrics and feature extraction · Computer graphics
and vision · Medical image processing

1 Problem Formulation

Let $\gamma : [0, T] \to E^n$ be a smooth regular parametric curve, i.e. the curve with
$\dot{\gamma}(t) \neq \mathbf{0}$ over $t \in [0, T]$ (here $T < \infty$). Reduced data represent a sequence of $m+1$
interpolation points $Q_m = \{q_i\}_{i=0}^m$ in arbitrary Euclidean space E^n satisfying
$q_i = \gamma(t_i)$ and $q_{i+1} \neq q_i$. The corresponding interpolation knots $\{t_i\}_{i=0}^m$ fulfilling
$t_0 < \ldots < t_i < \ldots < t_m$ are assumed here to be unknown. Any data fitting

© IFIP International Federation for Information Processing 2015
K. Saeed and W. Homenda (Eds.): CISIM 2015, LNCS 9339, pp. 98–110, 2015.
DOI: 10.1007/978-3-319-24369-6_8

scheme $\hat{\gamma}$ based on reduced data Q_m is called *non-parametric interpolation*. In order to construct $\hat{\gamma}$ explicitly, first the knot estimates $\{\hat{t}_i\}_{i=0}^m \approx \{t_i\}_{i=0}^m$ need to be somehow guessed (here one naturally sets $\hat{\gamma}(\hat{t}_i) = q_i$). Upon selecting a specific interpolation scheme $\hat{\gamma} : [0, \hat{T}] \to E^n$ and the substitutes $\{\hat{t}_i\}_{i=0}^m$ of the missing knots $\{t_i\}_{i=0}^m$, the analysis yielding the order α in γ approximation by $\hat{\gamma}$ needs to be carried out (for $m \to \infty$). The appropriate choice of $\{\hat{t}_i\}_{i=0}^m$ should ensure convergence of the interpolant $\hat{\gamma}$ to the unknown curve γ with possibly fast order α.

We recall now a necessary background information (see e.g. [1]). In fact, reduced data $Q_m = \{\gamma(t_i)\}_{i=0}^m$ are formed from the set of admissible samplings:

Definition 1. *The interpolation knots $\{t_i\}_{i=0}^m$ are called admissible if they satisfy:*

$$\lim_{m\to\infty} \delta_m \to 0^+, \quad \text{where} \quad \delta_m = \max_{1\le i \le m} \{t_i - t_{i-1} : i = 1, 2, \ldots, m\}. \tag{1}$$

In this paper a special subfamily of admissible samplings i.e. the so-called *more-or-less uniform samplings* is considered (see also [2]):

Definition 2. *The sampling $\{t_i\}_{i=0}^m$ is more-or-less uniform if for some constants $0 < K_l \le K_u$ and sufficiently large m the following holds:*

$$\frac{K_l}{m} \le t_i - t_{i-1} \le \frac{K_u}{m}, \tag{2}$$

for all $i = 1, 2, \ldots, m$. Alternatively, condition (2) can be replaced by the equivalent inequality $\beta\delta_m \le t_{i+1} - t_i \le \delta_m$ satisfied for some $0 < \beta \le 1$ and sufficiently large m.

Recall now the next definition (see e.g. [1] or [3]):

Definition 3. *Consider a family $\{f_{\delta_m}, \delta_m > 0\}$ of functions $f_{\delta_m} : [0, T] \to E$. We say that f_{δ_m} is of order $O(\delta_m^\alpha)$ (denoted as $f_{\delta_m} = O(\delta_m^\alpha)$), if there is a constant $K > 0$ such that, for some $\bar{\delta} > 0$ the inequality $|f_{\delta_m}(t)| < K\delta_m^\alpha$ holds for all $\delta_m \in (0, \bar{\delta})$, uniformly over $[0, T]$. In case of vector-valued functions $F_{\delta_m} : [0, T] \to E^n$ by $F_{\delta_m} = O(\delta_m^\alpha)$ it is understood that $\|F_{\delta_m}\| = O(\delta_m^\alpha)$ (here $\|\cdot\|$ denotes a standard euclidean norm).*

To examine the asymptotics in trajectory estimation (i.e. the coefficient α from Def. 3) in case of classical *parametric interpolation* $\tilde{\gamma} : [0, T] \to E^n$, where both $q_i = \tilde{\gamma}(t_i)$ and $\{t_i\}_{i=0}^m$ are given, one sets $F_{\delta_m} = \gamma - \tilde{\gamma}$. On the other hand, for *non-parametric interpolation* a slight adjustment in the last expression for F_{δ_m} is required (see [1]). Indeed, the latter stems from the fact that both domains $[0, T]$ of γ and $[0, \hat{T}]$ of $\hat{\gamma}$ do not generically coincide (here $T = t_m$ and $\hat{T} = \hat{t}_m$). Consequently, for the *non-parametric* interpolant $\hat{\gamma}$ (given $\{\hat{t}_i\}_{i=0}^m$ are somehow guessed) a reparameterization $\psi : [0, T] \to [0, \hat{T}]$ is needed so that the asymptotics

$$(\hat{\gamma} \circ \psi)(t) - \gamma(t) = O(\delta_m^\alpha) \tag{3}$$

can be examined over a common domain $[0,T]$. Noticeably, the reparametriza-
tion issue (given fixed $\hat{\gamma}$ and $\{\hat{t}_i\}_{i=0}^m$) is essential to both theoretical and numerical examination determining an intrinsic asymptotics built in (3). In addition,
preferably ψ should be a genuine reparameterization (i.e. $\dot{\psi} > 0$) e.g. if length of
γ is to be estimated by the length of $\hat{\gamma}$. Evidently, on its own the construction
of the interpolant $\hat{\gamma}$ does rely on explicit formula standing for ψ. Independently
from ψ, the derivation of any non-parametric interpolant $\hat{\gamma}$ requires an the appropriate choice of the estimates $\{\hat{t}_i\}_{i=0}^m$ mimicking the missing knots $\{t_i\}_{i=0}^m$. In
doing so, recall now a definition of *exponential parameterization* (e.g. in [4]):

$$\hat{t}_0^\lambda = 0 \quad \text{and} \quad \hat{t}_j^\lambda = \hat{t}_{j-1}^\lambda + \|q_j - q_{j-1}\|^\lambda, \tag{4}$$

where $j = 1, 2, \ldots, m$ and $\lambda \in [0,1]$. If $\lambda = 0$ a blind guess yielding uniform
knots $\hat{t}_i^0 = i$ follows. On the other hand, the case of $\lambda = 1$ results in *a cumulative
chord parameterization* $\hat{t}_j^1 = \hat{t}_{j-1}^1 + \|q_j - q_{j-1}\|$ (see [4] or [5]). From now on we
suppress the superscript notation with λ in (4), unless needed otherwise. The
term *exponential parameterization* stands for the determination of a discrete
set of knots $\{\hat{t}_i\}_{i=0}^m \approx \{t_i\}_{i=0}^m$, whereas a similar term i.e. *a reparameterization*
represents a piecewise-smooth mapping $\psi : [0,T] \to [0,\hat{T}]$.

Previous result [6] proved that for $\lambda = 1$ and for an arbitrary admissible
sampling (1) a Lagrange piecewise-quadratic(-cubic) $\hat{\gamma}_r$ ($r = 2,3$ - see e.g. [3])
interpolation combined with (4) yields $\alpha_r(1) = r + 1$. Hence for cumulative
chords the interpolant $\hat{\gamma}_r$ ($r = 2,3$) renders either cubic or quartic convergence
orders in trajectory estimation (see (3)). Interestingly, opposite to the parametric
interpolation $\tilde{\gamma}_r$, the convergence orders in question do not necessarily increase
for $r > 3$ and $\lambda = 1$ - see [1] or [7]. In addition, a recent result by [8] (see also [9])
proves that $\hat{\gamma}_2$ combined with (4) and more-or-less uniformly sampled (2) reduced
data Q_m yields $\alpha(1) = 3$ and $\alpha(\lambda) = 1$ for $\lambda \in [0,1)$. The latter demonstrates an
unexpected left-hand side discontinuity of $\alpha(\lambda)$ at $\lambda = 1$. Interestingly, such trend
continues once (4) is combined with piecewise-cubics $\hat{\gamma}_3$. Indeed the following
holds (see [10]):

Theorem 1. *Suppose γ is a regular $C^4([0,T])$ curve in E^n sampled more-or-
less uniformly (2). Assume that $\{\hat{t}_i^\lambda\}_{i=0}^m$ are computed from Q_m according to (4).
Then there exists a piecewise-cubic C^∞ mapping $\psi : [0,T] \to [0,\hat{T}]$, such that
over $[0,T]$, we have for either $\lambda \in [0,1)$:*

$$\hat{\gamma}_3 \circ \psi - \gamma = O(\delta_m) \tag{5}$$

or for $\lambda = 1$ (and (1)):

$$\hat{\gamma}_3 \circ \psi - \gamma = O(\delta_m^4). \tag{6}$$

Undesirably, the interpolants $\hat{\gamma}_r$ ($r = 2,3$), are generically non-smooth at
junction points, where both neighboring local quadratics (cubics) are glued
together over two consecutive segments $[t_i, t_{i+r}]$ and $[t_{i+r}, t_{i+2r}]$ (with $r = 2,3$).
In order to alleviate such deficiency, a modified C^1 Hermite interpolation $\hat{\gamma}_3^H$

based on Q_m, cumulative chords and general admissible samplings (1) is introduced and examined in [11] or [12]. Here the unknown derivatives at all interpolation points $\{q_i\}_{i=0}^m$ are approximated with high accuracy via special procedure (see [11]). This permits to obtain quartic order $\alpha(1) = 4$ in trajectory estimation once $\hat{\gamma}_3^H$ and (1) are coupled together. Analogously to Th. 1, the latter extends to all remaining $\lambda \in [0, 1)$ (for samplings (2)) resulting in $\alpha(\lambda) = 1$ (see [13]). Recurrent left-hand side discontinuity in convergence order $\alpha(\lambda)$ at $\lambda = 1$ is here manifested again.

For certain applications (e.g. approximation of curvature of γ, image segmentation or other feature extraction in biometrics) the interpolant $\hat{\gamma}$ should be at least *continuously twice differentiable*. Such constraint is not generically fulfilled by so-far discussed interpolants at any junction point. The remedy guaranteeing C^2 smoothness is met upon applying various hybrids of C^2 cubic spline interpolants $\hat{\gamma}_3^S$ (see [3]) based on Q_m and (4). One of them (called a *complete cubic spline* $\hat{\gamma}_3^C$) relies on the provision of initial and terminal velocities $\gamma'(t_0 = 0) = v_0$ and $\gamma'(t_m = T) = v_m$ usually not accompanying reduced data Q_m. This special case is discussed in [14] (also limited exclusively to $\lambda = 1$), where quartic order $\alpha(1) = 4$ for trajectory estimation by $\hat{\gamma}_3^C$ is established.

In this paper we extend the latter (at least with the aid of numerical tests) to a twofold more general situation. Similarly to $\hat{\gamma}_3^H$, we estimate first both missing velocities $\gamma'(t_0) \approx v_0^a$ and $\gamma'(t_m) \approx v_m^a$. Next a modified complete spline interpolant $\hat{\gamma}_3^C$ based on Q_m, v_0^a, v_m^a and (4) is introduced for all $\lambda \in [0, 1]$ - see Section 2. The conjectured asymptotics reads as:

Theorem 2. *Let γ be a regular $C^4([0, T])$ curve in E^n sampled more-or-less-uniformly (4). Approximate $(\gamma'(t_0), \gamma'(T))$ with $v_0^a = \hat{\gamma}_3'(0)$ and $v_m^a = \hat{\gamma}_3'(\hat{T})$, where $\hat{\gamma}_3$ defines a piecewise cubic based on Q_m and (4) with $\lambda \in [0, 1]$. Assume also that $\hat{\gamma}_3^C : [0, \hat{T}] \to E^n$ define a modified complete spline constructed on Q_m, estimated velocities (v_0^a, v_m^a) and exponential parameterization (4). Then there is a piecewise-C^∞ mapping $\psi : [0, T] \to [0, \hat{T}]$ such that over $[0, T]$ we either have for all $\lambda \in [0, 1)$:*

$$\hat{\gamma}_3^C \circ \psi - \gamma = O(\delta_m) \tag{7}$$

or for $\lambda = 1$:

$$\hat{\gamma}_3^C \circ \psi - \gamma = O(\delta_m^4). \tag{8}$$

In Section 3 the asymptotics from Th. 2 is *numerically verified as sharp* and specific application of modified C^2 complete spline $\hat{\gamma}_3^C$ is given. In addition, we compare our interpolant $\hat{\gamma}_3^C$ against $\hat{\gamma}_3^H$. Finally, our paper concludes with hints for possible extension of this work. Extra literature references concerning related work and spin-off applications are also provided.

2   Modified Complete Spline on Reduced Data

A modified complete spline interpolant $\hat{\gamma}_3^C$ based on reduced data Q_m (see also [3]) and exponential parameterization (4) is introduced below. This scheme applicable to both dense and sparse Q_m falls into the following steps:

1. Calculate the estimates $\{\hat{t}_i\}_{i=0}^{m}$ of the missing knots $\{t_i\}_{i=0}^{m}$ according to the exponential parameterization (4) (with $\lambda \in [0,1]$).
2. The so-called general C^2 piecewise-cubic spline $\hat{\gamma}_3^S$ interpolant (a sum-track of cubics $\{\hat{\gamma}_{3,i}^S\}_{i=0}^{m-1}$ - see [3]) fulfills the following constraints over each segment $[\hat{t}_i, \hat{t}_{i+1}]$:

$$\hat{\gamma}_{3,i}^S(\hat{t}_i) = q_i, \qquad \hat{\gamma}_{3,i}^S(\hat{t}_{i+1}) = q_{i+1},$$

$$\hat{\gamma}_{3,i}^{S'}(\hat{t}_i) = \boldsymbol{v}_i, \qquad \hat{\gamma}_{3,i}^{S'}(\hat{t}_{i+1}) = \boldsymbol{v}_{i+1}, \qquad (9)$$

where $\boldsymbol{v}_0, \dots, \boldsymbol{v}_m$ represent the unknown slopes $\boldsymbol{v}_i \in \mathbb{R}^n$. The internal velocities $\{\boldsymbol{v}_1, \boldsymbol{v}_2, \dots, \boldsymbol{v}_{m-1}\}$ can be uniquely computed from C^2 constraints imposed on $\hat{\gamma}_3^S$ at junction points $\{q_1, \dots, q_{m-1}\}$ i.e. by enforcing:

$$\hat{\gamma}_{3,i-1}^{S''}(\hat{t}_i) = \hat{\gamma}_{3,i}^{S''}(\hat{t}_i), \qquad (10)$$

provided both $\boldsymbol{v}_0$ and $\boldsymbol{v}_m$ are somehow computed (or a priori given). The computational method to determine all slopes $\{\boldsymbol{v}_i\}_{i=0}^{m}$ (including initial and terminal ones) is discussed next.
3. Assuming temporarily the provision of all velocities $\{\boldsymbol{v}_i\}_{i=0}^{m}$, each cubic $\hat{\gamma}_{3,i}^S$ over $\hat{t} \in [\hat{t}_i, \hat{t}_{i+1}]$ reads as:

$$\hat{\gamma}_{3,i}^S(\hat{t}) = c_{1,i} + c_{2,i}(\hat{t} - \hat{t}_i) + c_{3,i}(\hat{t} - \hat{t}_i)^2 + c_{4,i}(\hat{t} - \hat{t}_i)^3, \qquad (11)$$

where its respective coefficients (with $\Delta\hat{t}_i = \hat{t}_{i+1} - \hat{t}_i$) are equal to:

$$c_{1,i} = q_i, \quad c_{4,i} = \boldsymbol{v}_i,$$

$$c_{3,i} = \frac{\frac{q_{i+1}-q_i}{\Delta\hat{t}_i} - \boldsymbol{v}_i}{\Delta\hat{t}_i} - c_{4,i}\Delta\hat{t}_i, \quad c_{4,i} = \frac{\boldsymbol{v}_i + \boldsymbol{v}_{i+1} - 2\frac{q_{i+1}-q_i}{\Delta\hat{t}_i}}{(\Delta\hat{t}_i)^2}. \qquad (12)$$

If additionally $\boldsymbol{v}_i = \gamma'(t_i)$ are given then formulas (11) and (12) yield a well-known C^1 Hermite spline. However, the required velocities $\{\boldsymbol{v}_0, \boldsymbol{v}_1, \dots, \boldsymbol{v}_m\}$ are not usually supplemented to Q_m. A scheme for computing the corresponding missing internal velocities $\{\boldsymbol{v}_1, \boldsymbol{v}_1, \dots, \boldsymbol{v}_{m-1}\}$ is recalled next (see [3]). Following the latter a method of estimating $\{\boldsymbol{v}_0, \boldsymbol{v}_m\}$ is given. It is inspired by the approach adopted in [11].
4. Formulas (11) and (12) render $\hat{\gamma}_{3,i}^{S''}(\hat{t}_i) = 2c_{3,i}$ and $\hat{\gamma}_{3,i-1}^{S''}(\hat{t}_i) = 2c_{3,i-1} + 6c_{4,i-1}(\hat{t}_i - \hat{t}_{i-1})$ which combined with (10) leads to the linear system:

$$\boldsymbol{v}_{i-1}\Delta\hat{t}_i + 2\boldsymbol{v}_i(\Delta\hat{t}_{i-1} + \Delta\hat{t}_i) + \boldsymbol{v}_{i+1}\Delta\hat{t}_{i-1} = b_i, \qquad (13)$$

where

$$b_i = 3\left(\Delta\hat{t}_i\frac{q_i - q_{i-1}}{\Delta\hat{t}_{i-1}} + \Delta\hat{t}_{i-1}\frac{q_{i+1} - q_i}{\Delta\hat{t}_i}\right).$$

Assuming that the end-slopes $\boldsymbol{v}_0$ and $\boldsymbol{v}_m$ are somehow given the system (13) solves uniquely in $\{\boldsymbol{v}_i\}_{i=1}^{m-1}$. The latter yields a C^2 spline $\hat{\gamma}_3^S$ (which fits reduced data Q_m) defined as a track-sum of $\{\hat{\gamma}^S_{3,i}\}^{m-1}_{i=0}$ introduced in (11). If extra conditions hold, i.e. $\gamma'(t_0) = v_0$ and $\gamma'(T) = v_m$ then $\hat{\gamma}^S_3$ is called a *complete cubic spline* (denoted here as $\hat{\gamma}^C_3$).

5. Since Q_m are usually deprived from both initial and terminal velocities $\{\gamma'(t_0) = v_0, \gamma'(T) = v_m\}$ a good estimate $\{v^a_0, v^a_m\}$ is therefore required. Of course, any choice of $\{v^a_0, v^a_m\}$ renders a unique explicit formula for $\hat{\gamma}^C_3$. This however is insufficient for our consideration. Indeed, still a proper estimate of these two velocities is needed so that (7) and (8) follow. In doing so, we invoke Lagrange cubic $\hat{\gamma}^L_{3,0} : [0, \hat{t}^\lambda_3] \to E^n$ (and $\hat{\gamma}^L_{3,m\ 3} : [\hat{t}^\lambda_{m-3}, \hat{T}] \to E^n$), satisfying $\hat{\gamma}^L_{3,0}(\hat{t}^\lambda_i) = q_i$ (and $\hat{\gamma}^L_{3,m-3}(\hat{t}^\lambda_{m-3+i}) = q_{m-3+i}$), with $i = 0, 1, 2, 3$ - here the same $\lambda \in [0, 1]$ is applied in the derivation of $\hat{\gamma}^L_{3,0}$, $\hat{\gamma}^L_{3,m-3}$ and $\hat{\gamma}^C_3$. Set now for $v^a_0 = \hat{\gamma}^{L'}_{3,0}(0)$ and for $v^a_m = \hat{\gamma}^{L'}_{3,m-3}(\hat{T})$, respectively.

This completes *a description of a modified C^2 complete spline $\hat{\gamma}^C_3$* based on reduced data Q_m and exponential parameterization (4).

However, to verify the asymptotics from (7) and (8) (either numerically or theoretically) a candidate for *a reparameterization $\psi : [0, T] \to [0, \hat{T}]$* is still required, as justified in Section 1. In doing so, consider a C^2 complete spline $\psi = \psi^C_3 : [0, T] \to [0, \hat{T}]$ satisfying the knots' interpolation constraints $\psi^C_3(t_i) = \hat{t}_i$, where $\{\hat{t}_i\}^m_{i=0}$ are defined according to (4). In addition, the initial and terminal velocities of $s_0 = \psi^{C'}_3(0)$ and $s_m = \psi^{C'}_3(T)$ are set similarly to the construction from above. More specifically, define two Lagrange cubics $\psi_{3,0} : [0, t_{i+3}] \to [0, \hat{t}^\lambda_{i+3}]$ and $\psi_{3,m-3} : [t_{m\ 3+i}, T] \to [\hat{t}^\lambda_{m-3+i}, \hat{T}]$ satisfying interpolation conditions $\psi_{3,0}(t_i) = \hat{t}^\lambda_i$ and $\psi_{3,m-3}(t_{m-3+i}) = \hat{t}^\lambda_{m-3+i}$ (with $i = 0, 1, 2, 3$ and the same $\lambda \in [0, 1]$ as for the construction of $\hat{\gamma}^C_3$), respectively. One sets here for $s_0 = \psi^{C'}_3(0) = \psi'_{3,0}(0)$ and for $s_m = \psi^{C'}_3(T) = \psi'_{3,m-3}(T)$.

We pass now to the experimental section of this paper which tests the asymptotics from Th. 2. As already indicated, a sole derivation of a modified C^2 complete spline $\hat{\gamma}^C_3$ relies exclusively on reduced data Q_m (either dense or sparse) and (4). On the other hand, any numerical verification or theoretical proof of the asymptotics $\alpha(\lambda)$ involved (e.g. from Th. 2), requires an extra introduction of reparameterization ψ (proposed here as ψ^C_3) as well as an admittance of sufficiently densely more-or-less uniformly sampled points Q_m. The latter enables to assess a desired asymptotics controlling the decrease in difference $\hat{\gamma}^C_3 \circ \psi^C_3 - \gamma$, uniformly over $[0, T]$ (once $m \to \infty$).

3   Experiments

In this section, a numerical verification of the asymptotics $\alpha(\lambda)$ (and its *sharpness*) claimed in Th. 2 is conducted. Recall that, given fixed $\lambda \in [0, 1]$, by *sharpness* we understand the existence of at least one curve $\gamma \in C^4([0, T])$ and one special family of more-or-less uniform sampling (2) such that the asymptotics in differences $\hat{\gamma}^C_3 \circ \psi^C_3 - \gamma$ (over $[0, T]$) is not faster than predicted $\alpha(\lambda)$. A positive verification of (7) and (8) would point out again to a bizarre phenomenon. Namely, the existence of the left-hand side discontinuity in $\alpha(\lambda)$ at $\lambda = 1$.

All tests for this paper are carried out in Mathematica 8.0[1] (see also [15]) and resort to two types of skew-symmetric more-or-less uniform samplings (2). The first one selected (for $t_i \in [0,1]$) reads as:

$$t_i = \begin{cases} \frac{i}{m} + \frac{1}{2m}, & \text{for } i = 4k+1; \\ \frac{i}{m} - \frac{1}{2m}, & \text{for } i = 4k+3; \\ \frac{i}{m}, & \text{for } i \text{ even;} \end{cases} \quad (14)$$

with $K_l = (1/2)$ and $K_u = (3/2)$ as introduced in (2). The second one is defined according to:

$$t_i = \frac{i}{m} + \frac{(-1)^{i+1}}{3m}, \quad (15)$$

with constants $K_l = (1/2)$ and $K_u = (5/3)$ from (2). For a given m, the error E_m, between γ and reparameterized modified complete spline $\hat{\gamma}_3^C \circ \psi_3^C$ reads as:

$$E_m = \max_{t \in [0,1]} \|(\hat{\gamma}_3^C \circ \psi_3^C)(t) - \gamma(t)\|. \quad (16)$$

The latter is computed over each sub-interval $[t_i, t_{i+1}]$ (for $i = 0, \ldots, m-1$) by using Mathematica function - *FindMaximum* and then upon taking the maximal values from all segments' optima. In order to approximate $\alpha(\lambda)$ we calculate first E_m for $m_{min} \le m \le m_{max}$, where m_{min} and m_{max} are sufficiently large fixed constants. Then a linear regression yielding a function $y(x) = \bar{\alpha}(\lambda)x + b$ is applied to $\{(\log(m), -\log(E_m))\}_{m_{min}}^{m_{max}}$. Mathematica built-in function *LinearModelFit* extracts a coefficient $\bar{\alpha}(\lambda) \approx \alpha(\lambda)$. A full justification of this procedure to approximate $\alpha(\lambda)$ by $\bar{\alpha}(\lambda)$ is given in [1]. Note also that since both (7) and (8) have asymptotic character the constants $m_{min} < m_{max}$ should be taken as sufficiently large. On other hand, a potential negative impact of machine rounding-off errors stipulates these two constants not to exceed big values. In practice, the appropriate choices for $m_{min} < m_{max}$ are adjusted each time during the experimental phase. The tests conducted here employ three types of C^∞ regular curves: *a spiral* γ_{sp} and *a cubic* γ_c both in E^2 as well as *a helix* γ_h in E^3. They are sampled more-or-less uniformly according to either (14) or (15). For comparison reasons we also test here the asymptotic orders $\alpha_H(\lambda)$ in trajectory estimation for modified C^1 Hermite interpolant $\hat{\gamma}_3^H$ examined in [11] and [12] (here $\alpha_H(1) = 4$ and $\alpha_H(\lambda) = 1$ for $\lambda \in [0,1)$). However, since the interpolant $\hat{\gamma}_3^H \in C^1$ (over Q_m) it does not permit to approximate the curvature of γ at interpolation points. However, the latter can be accomplished with the aid of $\hat{\gamma}_3^C$ due it is higher order of smoothness (i.e. $\hat{\gamma}_3^C \in C^2$ over $\hat{t} \in [0, \hat{T}]$).

Example 1. Consider a regular planar spiral $\gamma_{sp} : [0,1] \to E^2$,

$$\gamma_{sp}(t) = ((0.2 + t)\cos(\pi(1-t)), (0.2 + t)\sin(\pi(1-t))). \quad (17)$$

Figure 1 (or Figure 2) contains the plots of γ_{sp} (or of $\hat{\gamma}_3^C$) with $\lambda = 0$ sampled (here $m = 15$) according to either (14) or (15).

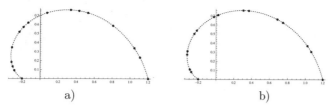

Fig. 1. A spiral γ_{sp} from (17) sampled along (dotted): a) (14) or b) (15), for $m = 15$.

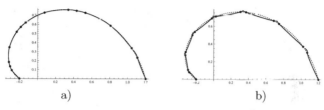

Fig. 2. A spiral γ_{sp} from (17) for: a) (14) b) (15) fitted by $\hat{\gamma}_3^C$ (here $m = 15$ and $\lambda = 0$).

The respective linear regression based estimates $\bar{\alpha}(\lambda) \approx \alpha(\lambda)$ (for various $\lambda \in [0, 1]$) are computed here for $m_{min} = 60 \leq m \leq m_{max} = 120$. The numerical results contained in Table 1 confirm the sharpness of (7) and (8) for $\lambda \in \{0.0, 0.1, 0.3, 0.5, 0.7\}$ and yield marginally faster (though still consistent with asymptotics from Th. (2)) $\alpha(\lambda)$ for $\lambda \approx 1$. For comparison reasons, Table 1 contains also the corresponding numerical results established for estimating γ with modified C^1 Hermite interpolant $\hat{\gamma}_3^H$ based on the same reduced data Q_m and exponential parameterization.

Table 1. Computed $\bar{\alpha}(\lambda) \approx \alpha(\lambda)$ in (7) & (8) for γ_{sp} from (17) and various $\lambda \in [0, 1]$.

λ	0.0	0.1	0.3	0.5	0.7	0.9	1.0
$\bar{\alpha}(\lambda)$ for (14)	1.0067	1.0085	1.0134	1.0218	1.0409	1.1463	4.2537
$\bar{\alpha}(\lambda)$ for (15)	1.0121	1.0128	1.0160	1.0248	1.0506	1.2099	3.9912
$\alpha(\lambda)$ in Th. 2	1.0	1.0	1.0	1.0	1.0	1.0	4.0
$\bar{\alpha}_H(\lambda)$ for (14)	1.0070	1.0084	1.0129	1.0205	1.0371	1.1282	3.9192
$\bar{\alpha}_H(\lambda)$ for (15)	1.0009	1.0023	1.0113	1.0484	1.0499	4.8304	4.0584

We pass now to the example with a helix having a trajectory in E^3.

Example 2. Let $\gamma_h : [0, 1] \to E^3$ be defined as

$$\gamma_h(t) = (1.5\cos(2\pi t), \sin(2\pi t), 2\pi t/4). \qquad (18)$$

Figure 3 (or Figure 4) illustrates the trajectories of γ_h (or of $\hat{\gamma}_3^C$) for $\lambda = 0.3$ sampled according to either (14) or (15), with $m = 15$. As previously, a linear

---

[1]   *This research was supported in part by computing resources of ACC Cyfronet AGH.*

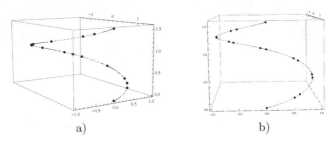

Fig. 3. A helix from (18) sampled along (dotted): a) (14) b) (15), for $m = 15$.

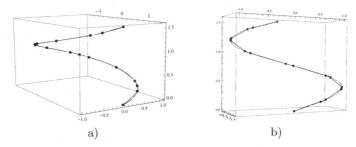

Fig. 4. A helix γ_h from (18) for: a) (14) b) (15) fitted by $\hat{\gamma}_3^C$ (here $m = 15$ and $\lambda = 0.3$).

regression estimating $\bar{\alpha}(\lambda) \approx \alpha(\lambda)$ from Th. 2 is used here, for m ranging over $60 \leq m \leq 120$ with various $\lambda \in [0,1]$. The coefficients $\bar{\alpha}(\lambda)$ (see Table 2) computed numerically all sharply coincide with those specified in (7) and (8). Again, for comparison reasons, Table 2 presents the corresponding numerical results derived for estimating γ with modified C^1 Hermite interpolant $\hat{\gamma}_3^H$ based on the same reduced data Q_m and exponential parameterization.

Table 2. Computed $\bar{\alpha}(\lambda) \approx \alpha(\lambda)$ in (7) & (8) for γ_h from (18) and various $\lambda \in [0,1]$.

λ	0.0	0.1	0.3	0.5	0.7	0.9	1.0
$\bar{\alpha}(\lambda)$ for (14)	1.0000	1.0000	1.0002	1.0006	1.0009	1.0065	3.9949
$\bar{\alpha}(\lambda)$ for (15)	1.0000	1.0000	1.0001	1.0005	1.0015	1.0127	3.9992
$\alpha(\lambda)$ in Th. 2	1.0	1.0	1.0	1.0	1.0	1.0	4.0
$\bar{\alpha}_H(\lambda)$ for (14)	1,0000	1,0000	1.0002	1.0003	1.0008	1.0049	3.9833
$\bar{\alpha}_H(\lambda)$ for (15)	1.0002	1.0001	1.0001	1.0026	1.0043	1.0317	3.9888

Finally, a planar cubic γ_c is tested.

Example 3. Let $\gamma_c : [0,1] \to E^2$ be defined as follows:

$$\gamma_c(t) = (\pi t, (\pi t + 1)^3 (\pi + 1)^{-3}). \tag{19}$$

Figure 5 (or Figure 6) contains the plots of γ_c (or of $\hat{\gamma}_3^C$) sampled along either (14) or (15), with $\lambda = 1$ and $m = 15$. In order to compute $\bar{\alpha}(\lambda) \approx \alpha(\lambda)$ estimat-

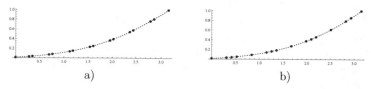

Fig. 5. A cubic planar curve (19) sampled along (dotted): a) (14) b) (15), for $m = 15$.

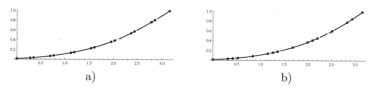

Fig. 6. A cubic from γ_c (19) for: a) (14) b) (15) fitted by $\hat{\gamma}_3^C$ (here $m = 15$ and $\lambda = 1$).

ing the asymptotics from Th. 2 again a linear regression is used (as explained at the beginning of this section) for $60 \leq m \leq 120$ and varying $\lambda \in [0, 1]$. Table 3 enlists numerically computed estimates $\bar{\alpha}(\lambda) \approx \alpha(\lambda)$ for various $\lambda \in [0, 1]$ and samplings (14) and (15). Evidently these numerical results re-emphasize the sharpness of the asymptotics determined by (7) and (8), with marginally faster case of $\alpha(1)$. Similarly to the previous examples, Table 3 contains also the corresponding numerical results obtained for estimating γ with modified C^1 Hermite interpolant $\hat{\gamma}_3^H$ based on the same reduced data Q_m and exponential parameterization.

Table 3. Computed $\alpha(\lambda) \approx \alpha(\lambda)$ in (7) & (8) for γ_c from (19) and various $\lambda \in [0, 1]$.

λ	0.0	0.1	0.3	0.5	0.7	0.9	1.0
$\bar{\alpha}(\lambda)$ for (14)	1.0001	1.0001	1.0001	1.0002	1.0003	1.0011	4.1612
$\bar{\alpha}(\lambda)$ for (15)	1.0001	1.0001	1.0002	1.0002	1.0003	1.0017	4.1196
$\alpha(\lambda)$ in Th. 2	1.0	1.0	1.0	1.0	1.0	1.0	4.0
$\bar{\alpha}_H(\lambda)$ for (14)	1.0001	1.0001	1.0001	1.0002	1.0003	1.0010	4.2868
$\bar{\alpha}_H(\lambda)$ for (15)	0.9999	1.0000	1.0001	1.0002	0.9998	0.9991	4.3044

The examples presented herein demonstrate *the sharpness* of (7) and (8) resulting in *a left-hand side discontinuity* of $\alpha(\lambda)$ at $\lambda = 1$ which is consistent with Th. 2. We close this section with an application of $\hat{\gamma}_3^C$ to medical image processing.

Example 4. A medical image of a kidney is shown in Figure 7. A segmentation of an image of any human organ from its image background (e.g. from a digital image) permits to focus on vital geometrical or other properties (like γ perimeter, section internal area, average curvature) of the examined organ. This ultimately can be exploited in medical diagnosis and further treatment. Indeed, a physician can mark $m+1$ selected consecutive points on the kidney's boundary (represent-ing the trajectory of the unknown curve γ). Such input points, positioned along trajectory of γ, form the set of available interpolation points Q_m. Naturally, the corresponding knots $\{t_i\}_{i=0}^{m}$ parameterizing Q_m are here defaulted. A modified complete spline $\hat{\gamma}_3^C$ based on (4) and Q_m can be applied now. The relevant points' coordinates are determined here by using *Get Coordinate Tool in Mathematica*. Figure 7 contains of a plot a modified complete spline $\hat{\gamma}_3^C$ based on 67 marked points (here as $q_0 = q_{67}$ we have 67 different points) with either $\lambda = 0$ or $\lambda = 1$ set in (4) - see Figure 7 a) or b), respectively. Note that the boundary of the kidney forms a loop which re-translates e.g. into $q_0 = \gamma(0) = \gamma(T) = q_m$. Con-sequently the interpolant $\hat{\gamma}_3^C$ is generically not smooth at a single point $q_0 = q_m$ unless $v_0 = v_m$, for which C^1 class follows. This weakness can be removed e.g. by taking the average of v_0 and v_m at both overlapping "ends" of the curve γ. Finally, for comparison reasons, Fig. 8 a) or b) presents the trajectory of the cor-responding modified Hermite interpolant $\hat{\gamma}_3^H$ constructed on the same reduced data Q_m and exponential parameterization.

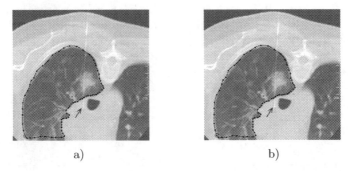

a)   b)

Fig. 7. The shape of a kidney determined by $\hat{\gamma}_3^C$ with a) $\lambda = 0$ b) $\lambda = 1$, for $m = 67$.

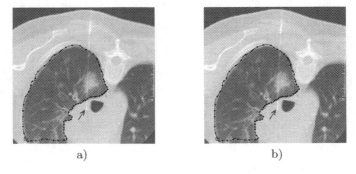

a)   b)

Fig. 8. The shape of a kidney determined by $\hat{\gamma}_3^H$ with a) $\lambda = 0$ b) $\lambda = 1$, for $m = 67$.

4   Conclusion

The tests in Section 3 confirm *the sharpness* of the asymptotics from Th. 2 to approximate γ via modified complete spline $\hat{\gamma}_3^C$ based on reduced data Q_m, more-or-less uniform samplings (2) and exponential parameterization (4). A possible extension of this work includes e.g. an analytical proof of Th. 2 (including investigation of asymptotic constants) or determination of sufficient conditions imposed on samplings $\{t_i\}_{i=0}^m$ to render ψ_3^C as a genuine piecewise-C^∞ reparameterization of $[0, T]$ into $[0, \hat{T}]$. The investigation of the asymptotics in curvature estimation by $\hat{\gamma}_3^C$ is also an open problem. The case with $\lambda = 1$ offers the fastest quartic asymptotics in trajectory estimation for $\hat{\gamma}_3^C$ and (4). However, one can also focus on enforcing specific geometrical properties or constraints by selecting the best $\hat{\gamma}_3^C$ (depending on $\lambda \in [0, 1]$ from (4)) to optimize newly adopted criteria (criterion). This paper shows that if the speed of γ approximation is not the main issue then a decisive factor in choosing optimal $\hat{\gamma}_3^C$ should stem from such extra requirement(s) as almost all $\hat{\gamma}_3^C$ have an identical $\alpha(\lambda)$ for γ approximation. Related work on ε-uniform samplings combined with (4) can be found in [16]. More specific applications on interpolating (or approximating) reduced data are provided e.g. in [4], [17], [18], [19] or [20]. Splines can also be used in trajectory planning [21], finding algebraic and implicit curves [22] and [23] or in bifurcating surfaces [24]. To supplement (4), there are also other parameterizations applied predominantly on sparse data (applicable also on dense Q_m) - see e.g. the so-called *blending parameterization* [25], *monotonicity or convexity preserving ones* [4] or [26].

References

1. Kozera, R.: Curve modeling via interpolation based on multidimensional reduced data. Studia Informatica **25**(4B–61), 1–140 (2004)
2. Noakes, L., Kozera, R.: More-or-less uniform samplings and length of curves. Quarterly of Applied Mathematics **61**(3), 475–484 (2003)
3. de Boor, C.: A Practical Guide to Spline. Springer-Verlag, Heidelberg (1985)
4. Kvasov, B.I.: Methods of Shape-Preserving Spline Approximation. World Scientific, Singapore (2000)
5. Lee, E.T.Y.: Choosing nodes in parametric curve interpolation. Computer-Aided Design **21**(6), 363–370 (1989)
6. Noakes, L., Kozera, R.: Cumulative chords piecewise-quadratics and piecewise-cubics. In: Klette, R., Kozera, R., Noakes, L., Weickert, J. (eds.) Geometric Properties of Incomplete Data. Computational Imaging and Vision, vol. 31, pp. 59–75. Kluver Academic Publishers, The Netherlands (2006)
7. Kozera, R.: Asymptotics for length and trajectory from cumulative chord piecewise-quartics. Fundamenta Informaticae **61**(3–4), 267–283 (2004)
8. Kozera, R., Noakes, L.: Piecewise-quadratics and exponential parameterization for reduced data. Applied Mathematics and Computation **221**, 620–638 (2013)
9. Kozera, R., Noakes, L., Szmielew, P.: Trajectory estimation for exponential parameterization and different samplings. In: Saeed, K., Chaki, R., Cortesi, A., Wierzchoń, S. (eds.) CISIM 2013. LNCS, vol. 8104, pp. 430–441. Springer, Heidelberg (2013)

10. Kozera, R., Noakes, L., Wilkołazka, M.: Piecewise-cubics and exponential parameterization for reduced data (submitted)
11. Kozera, R., Noakes, L.: C^1 interpolation with cumulative chord cubics. Fundamenta Informaticae **61**(3–4), 285–301 (2004)
12. Kozera, R., Noakes, L., Szmielew, P.: Quartic orders and sharpness in trajectory estimation for smooth cumulative chord cubics. In: Chmielewski, L.J., Kozera, R., Shin, B.-S., Wojciechowski, K. (eds.) ICCVG 2014. LNCS, vol. 8671, pp. 9–16. Springer, Heidelberg (2014)
13. Kozera, R., Noakes, L., Wilkołazka, M.: C^1 interpolation with cumulative chord cubics and exponential parameterization (submitted)
14. Floater, M.S.: Chordal cubic spline interpolation is fourth order accurate. IMA Journal of Numerical Analysis **26**, 25–33 (2006)
15. Wolfram Mathematica 9, Documentation Center. reference.wolfram.com/mathematica/guide/Mathematica.html
16. Noakes, L., Kozera, R., Klette, R.: Length estimation for curves with different samplings. In: Bertrand, G., Imiya, A., Klette, R. (eds.) Digital and Image Geometry. LNCS, vol. 2243, pp. 339–351. Springer, Heidelberg (2001)
17. Janik, M., Kozera, R., Kozioł, P.: Reduced data for curve modeling - applications in graphics, computer vision and physics. Advances in Science and Technology **7**(18), 28–35 (2013)
18. Piegl, L., Tiller, W.: The NURBS Book. Springer, Heidelberg (1997)
19. Yan-Bin, J.: Polynomial Interpolation. Computer Science Notes 477/577, Fall, Iowa State University (2014)
20. Jupp, D.L.P.: Approximation to data by splines with free knots. Journal on Numerical Analysis **15**(2), 328–343 (1978)
21. Budzko, D.A., Prokopenya, A.N.: Symbolic-numerical methods for searching equilibrium states in a restricted four-body problem. Programming and Computer Software **39**(2), 74–80 (2013)
22. Kozera, R.: Uniqueness in shape from shading revisited. Journal of Mathematical Imaging and Vision **7**(2), 123–138 (1997)
23. Taubin, G.: Estimation of planar and non-planar space curves defined by implicit equations with applications to edge and range segmentation. IEEE Transactions in Pattern Analysis and Machine Intelligence **13**(11), 1115–1138 (1991)
24. Circularly symmetrical eikonal equations and non-uniqueness in computer vision. Journal of Mathematical Analysis and Applications **165**, 192–215 (1992)
25. Kocić, L.M., Simoncelli, A.C., Della Vecchia, B.: Blending parameterization of polynomial and spline interpolants. Facta Universitatis (NIŠ), Series Mathematics and Informatics **5**, 95–107 (1990)
26. Mørken, K., Scherer, K.: A general framework for high-accuracy parametric interpolation. Mathematics of Computation **66**(217), 237–260 (1997)

Chaotic Properties of Gait Kinematic Data

Michal Piorek[✉]

Department of Computer Engineering, Wroclaw University of Technology,
Janiszewskiego 11/17, 50-372 Wroclaw, Poland
michal.piorek@pwr.edu.pl

Abstract. Time delay reconstruction for real systems is a widely explored area of nonlinear time series analysis. However, the majority of related work relates only to univariate time series, while multivariate time series data are common too. One such example is human gait kinematic data. The main goal of this article is to present a method of nonlinear analysis for kinematic time series. This nonlinear analysis is designed for detection of chaotic behavior. The presented approach also allows for the largest Lyapunov's exponent estimation for kinematic time series. This factor helps in judging the stability of the examined system and its chaotic properties.

Keywords: Deterministic chaos · Nonlinear time series analysis · Quaternions · Human motion analysis · Human gait data

1 Introduction

Multivariate time series data are common in real systems. Many of those systems are results of the evolution of nonlinear systems dynamics. To assess the chaotic origin of time series, time delay reconstruction of a phase space is required. This step provides a view of the dynamics of the underlying system and allows the estimation of other properties of the investigated system (e.g. Lyapunov's largest exponent or one of the fractal dimensions of the reconstructed attractor). Based on the estimations of several parameters characterizing nonlinear processes, a decision about chaotic origin of time series may be taken.

According to the embedding theorem ([27]), for recovering dynamics only a univariate time series is needed, but often measurements of more than one quantityes related to the same dynamical system are available. One such case is the gait kinematic data for patients suffering from various diseases affecting walking ability.

In related work, there is a large number of applications of embedding theorem including univariate time series embedding ([24], [25], [28]), multivariate time series embedding ([3], [10], [18]), modelling ([1], [9], [11]), chaos control ([2], [5], [22]), noise reduction ([4], [12], [19]) and signal classification ([26]).

The method presented in this paper is designed for a nonlinear analysis procedure for gait kinematics time series (Euler Angles or Quaternion) aimed at computing the Largest Lyapunov Exponent for reconstructed dynamics for the purpose of identifying of deterministic chaos in gait kinematic data.

© IFIP International Federation for Information Processing 2015
K. Saeed and W. Homenda (Eds.): CISIM 2015, LNCS 9339, pp. 111–119, 2015.
DOI: 10.1007/978-3-319-24369-6_9

The presented method does not assume that investigated system is a deterministic chaotic system in the first place. This empirical approach is aimed to investigate the origin of the examined time series.

In this approach the Largest Lyapunov Exponent is also treated as a measure of human locomotion stability. In this case stability is defined as the sensitivity of a dynamic system to perturbations. This is a very popular factor in biomedical applications ([7], [6]).

The second section describes gait kinematic data time series - a subject of further investigations. It also includes information about conversion to quaternion's angle time series which allows for further efficient computations. The third section includes information about methods used in a nonlinear analysis procedure. The fourth section presents the numerical results. The conclusions are presented in section five.

2   Gait Kinematics Data Time Series

There are three kinds of parameterisation of orientation space. Euler angles are good for human understanding of angular position. Matrices are able to do the calculations. However, quaternions are computationally efficient whilst also avoiding the singularities of Euler angles ([20]).

Quaternion parameterisation describes human motion which requires significant amounts of information about rotational displacement of selected segments. The method presented in this paper is designed for data captured from physical systems. We assumed that, to make a proper estimate of finite-time Lyapunov exponents experimentally, it is necessary to collect time series data captured from a large number of consecutive strides of gait ([14]).

The data are recorded as time series formed by Euler Angles. It is the most common parameterisation especially for biomedical applications.

$$s(n) = [\beta_1(t_0 + n\Delta t), \beta_2(t_0 + n\Delta t), \beta_3(t_0 + n\Delta t)] \tag{1}$$

where $s(n)$ is a n-th sample of Euler angles measured in interval time Δt from initial time t_0 and β_1, β_2, β_3 are Euler angles in a X-Y-Z sequence. Axes X, Y and Z are defined as unit vectors:

$$\boldsymbol{X} = (1,0,0), \boldsymbol{Y} = (0,1,0), \boldsymbol{Z} = (0,0,1) \tag{2}$$

Due to the fact that an Euler Angles time series is a multivariate time series, the following procedure was used to obtain better efficiency of computations.

Based on the assumption that axes X, Y and Z are unit vectors, rotation coding in Euler's Angles and in quaternions are identical. We can define quaternions for each base rotation in a Euler sequence:

$$
\begin{aligned}
q_x(\beta_1) &= \cos(\tfrac{\beta_1}{2}) + \overrightarrow{(sin(\tfrac{\beta_1}{2}),0,0)} \\
q_y(\beta_2) &= \cos(\tfrac{\beta_2}{2}) + \overrightarrow{(0,sin(\tfrac{\beta_2}{2}),0)} \\
q_z(\beta_3) &= \cos(\tfrac{\beta_3}{2}) + \overrightarrow{(0,0,sin(\tfrac{\beta_3}{2}))}
\end{aligned}
\tag{3}
$$

Finally a quaternion equivalent to Euler angles representation can be calculated from three consecutive rotations described by the following quaternions:

$$q_{xyz}(\beta_1, \beta_2, \beta_3) = q_x(\beta_1)q_y(\beta_2)q_z(\beta_3) =$$

$$(cos(\tfrac{\beta_1}{2})cos(\tfrac{\beta_2}{2})cos(\tfrac{\beta_3}{2}) - sin(\tfrac{\beta_1}{2})sin(\tfrac{\beta_2}{2})sin(\tfrac{\beta_3}{2}))+$$

$$i(sin(\tfrac{\beta_1}{2})cos(\tfrac{\beta_2}{2})cos(\tfrac{\beta_3}{2}) - cos(\tfrac{\beta_1}{2})sin(\tfrac{\beta_2}{2})sin(\tfrac{\beta_3}{2}))+ \qquad (4)$$

$$j(cos(\tfrac{\beta_1}{2})sin(\tfrac{\beta_2}{2})cos(\tfrac{\beta_3}{2}) - sin(\tfrac{\beta_1}{2})cos(\tfrac{\beta_2}{2})sin(\tfrac{\beta_3}{2}))+$$

$$k(cos(\tfrac{\beta_1}{2})cos(\tfrac{\beta_2}{2})sin(\tfrac{\beta_3}{2}) - sin(\tfrac{\beta_1}{2})sin(\tfrac{\beta_2}{2})cos(\tfrac{\beta_3}{2}))$$

Quaternion's time series is formed by conversion of each value of a Euler's angles time series to unit quaternion

$$q(n) = q_{xyz}(s(n)) = q_{xyz}(\beta_1(t_0 + n\Delta t), \beta_2(t_0 + n\Delta t), \beta_3(t_0 + n\Delta t)) \quad (5)$$

Based on the assumption that there is greater variability in the quaternion's angle than its axis, nonlinear analysis directed at identifying the presence of deterministic chaos and local stability investigation is performed on the time series formed by angles of quaternion $q(n)$

$$\alpha(n) = 2arccos(real(q(t_0 + n\Delta t))) \qquad (6)$$

3 Nonlinear Analysis Procedure for Quaternion Angle Time Series

The nonlinear analysis procedure consists of two steps: time delay reconstruction and the largest Lyapunov exponent estimation.

3.1 Time Delay Reconstruction

According to the Takens embedding theorem ([27]), its possible to reconstruct the state trajectory from a single time series using the algorithm below:

$$y(n) = [s(n), s(n + T), \ldots, s(n + (d - 1))T], \qquad (7)$$

where T is a time delay and d is an embedding dimension, which estimates a real dimension of the observed system. The main point of the state space reconstruction method is T and d estimation. To estimate time delay T, the average mutual information I has been used, while for the embedding dimension the false nearest neighbor method ([1]).

The mutual information approach is based on information theory and transformation of linear autocorrelation to non-linear systems. More precisely, this method consists of 2-dimensional adaptive histogram ([9]).

Let's assume that there are two nonlinear systems: A and B. The outputs of these systems are denoted as a and b, while the values of these outputs are represented by a_i and b_k. The mutual information factor describes how many bits of b_k could be predicted where a_i is known.

$$I_{AB}(a_i, b_k) = log_2\left(\frac{P_{AB}(a_i, b_k)}{P_A(a_i)P_B(b_k)}\right),\tag{8}$$

where $P_A(a_i)$ is the probability that $a = a_i$ and $P_B(b_k)$ is the probability that $b = b_k$ and $P_{AB}(a_i, b_k)$ is the joint probability that $a = a_i$ and $b = b_k$.

The average mutual information factor can be described by:

$$I_{AB}(T) = \sum_{a_i, b_k} P_{AB}(a_i, b_k)I_{AB}(a_i, b_k).\tag{9}$$

In order to use this method to assess the correlation between different samples in the same time series, the Average mutual information factor is finally described by the equation:

$$I(T) = \sum_{n=1}^{N} P(S(n), S(n+T))$$
$$log_2\left(\frac{P(S(n), S(n+T))}{P(S(n))P(S(n+T))}\right).\tag{10}$$

Fraser and Swinney ([9]) propose that T_m where the first minimum of $I(T)$ occurs as a useful selection of time lag T_d. This selection guarantees that the measurements are somewhat independent, but not statistically independent. In case of absence of the average mutual information clear minimum, this criterion needs to be replaced by choosing T_d as the time for which the average mutual information reaches four-fifths of its initial value:

$$\frac{I(T_d)}{I(0)} \approx \frac{4}{5}.\tag{11}$$

The false nearest neighbours method is based on determining an acceptable minimum embedding dimension by looking at the behaviour of near neighbours under changes in the embedding dimension from d to $d+1$. The most important assumption is that all points in the attractor that are close in $\Re^m$ should be also close in $\Re^{m+1}$. The false nearest neighbour is a point that appears to be a nearest neighbor because the embedding space is too small. When the number of false nearest neighbors arising through projection is zero in dimension d_E, the attractor has been unfolded in this dimension ([17]).

Assume that the dimension of space is d. The r-th nearest neighbor of $y(n)$ is denoted by $y^r(n)$. The distance between point $y(n)$ and it's r-th nearest neighbor is a square of the Euclidean distance.

$$R_d^2(n, r) = \sum_{k=0}^{d-1} [x(n + kT) - x^r(n + kT)]^2\tag{12}$$

In going from dimension d to $d+1$ by time delay embedding new coordinate $x(n+Td)$ is added onto each delayed vectors $y(n)$. The distance between points before and after adding new coordinates is now compared. A point is designated as a false neighbour when increase of distance is too large and the criteria below are fulfilled.

$$\left[\frac{R_{d+1}^2(n,r) - R_d^2(n,r)}{R_d^2(n,r)}\right]^{\frac{1}{2}} = \left|\frac{x(n+Td) - x^r(n+Td)}{R_d(n,r)}\right| > R_{Tol} \qquad (13)$$

where R_{Tol} is some threshold.

Authors of the method ([17]), in numerical investigations, proved that for $R_{Tol} \geq 10$ the false nearest neighbors are clearly identified.

An acceptable minimum embedding dimension is chosen by looking at the percentage of false nearest neighbors during the addition of $d+1$ components to the delayed vectors. When the percentage of false nearest neighbors drops to zero, a proper embedding dimension may be obtained.

3.2 The Largest Lyapunov's Exponent

Lyapunov's exponents examine the action of the dynamics defining the evolution of trajectories. The largest Lyapunov exponent describes the mean divergence between neighboring trajectories in the phase space by the following formula

$$d(t) = De^{\lambda_1 t} \qquad (14)$$

where D is the initial separation between neighboring points and λ_1 is the largest Lyapunov exponent. There are a few algorithms designed for the Largest Lyapunov's exponent estimation ([29], [23] and [16]). In this investigation Rosenstein's algorithm was used.

The first stage of the Rosenstein algorithm is time delay reconstruction. After reconstruction, for each point on the trajectory, the nearest neighbor $x_{\hat{j}}$ is found. This point minimizes the distance to the particular reference point, x_j as described below

$$d_j(0) \approx \min_{x_{\hat{j}}} \left\| x_j - x_{\hat{j}} \right\| \qquad (15)$$

where $d_j(0)$ is the initial distance from the j-th point to its nearest neighbor, and $\|...\|$ is the Euclidean norm.

From the definition of λ_1 in eq. (14) authors ([23]) assumed the j-th pair of nearest neighbors diverge approximately at a rate given by the largest Lyapunov exponent.

$$d_j(i) \approx D_j e^{\lambda_1(i\Delta t)} \qquad (16)$$

where D_j is the initial separation. We can take the logarithm of both sides eq. (17)

$$ln(d_j(i)) \approx ln(D_j) + \lambda_1(i\Delta t) \qquad (17)$$

Eq. (17) represents a set of approximately parallel lines (for j = 1,2,...,M), each with a slope roughly proportional to λ_1. The largest Lyapunov exponent is calculated then by linear regression

$$y(i) = \frac{1}{\Delta t} \langle ln(d_j(i)) \rangle \qquad (18)$$

where $\langle ... \rangle$ denotes the average over all values of j.

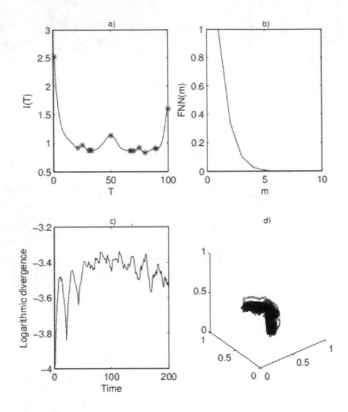

Fig. 1. Stages of the nonlinear analysis procedure: mutual information, percentage of false nearest neighbors, logarithmic divergence reconstructed attractor

4   Numerical Results

The experiment involves the analysis of gait sequences which were recorded in the Human Motion Laboratory (HML) of the Polish-Japanese Institute of Information Technology by means of the Vicon Motion Kinematics Acquisition and Analysis System ([21], [15] , [13], [8]).

Gait sequences were recorded in Euler angles. Six kinds of time series were recorded - movements of femurs, tibias and feet (left and right). The Experiment's aim was the investigation of local (associated with body parts) chaotic behaviour occurring in a human's gait. There were six investigations associated with movement of all the mentioned parts of the body's skeleton.

Fig. 1 illustrates results of successive stages of the nonlinear analysis procedure for the left femur: a) mutual information, b) percentage of false nearest neighbors, c) divergence, d) reconstructed attractor. Based on the above figure one can see that from the mutual information chart time delay embedding $T = 21$ could be obtained when the first minimum of $I(T)$ occurs. From the false nearest neighbours chart embedding dimension $d = 4$ is obtained when the percentage of nearest neighbours drops to zero. From the linear regression of the logarithmic divergence the largest Lyapunov exponent is estimated $\lambda_1 = 0.3157$.

Table 1 includes results of the nonlinear analysis procedure for all mentioned body parts. For each of them the time delay T, embedding dimension d and the largest Lyapunov exponent have been estimated. For right foot and left tibia negative LLEs values have been observed. It could be caused by too large value of the estimated embedding dimension. However, negative value of the largest Lyapunov exponent does not undermine the possible chaotic nature of the investigated data. The positive value of the Largest Lyapunov exponent is only one indicator of the presence of deterministic chaos. The others are fractal structure of the reconstructed attractor or limited prediction of the investigated system.

Table 1. Results from nonlinear analysis procedure for each body part

Body part	Time delay	Embedding dimension	LLE
Left femur	21	4	0.3157
Right femur	20	4	0.0084
Left foot	15	4	0.0476
Right foot	16	5	−0.0206
Left tibia	33	7	−0.0450
Right tibia	23	5	0.1600

5   Conclusion

In this article, six time series captured from a large number of consecutive strides of gait were examined. Measurements came from three parts of the body: femur, foot and tibia. For each time series time delay reconstruction and largest Lyapunov's exponent estimation has been carried out. Values of all of the computed parameters for all examined time series are gathered in table 1.

Time delay embedding for time series has already been widely explored by various contributors. However, most of the work in the published literature concerns only scalar time series. In this paper the method for multivariate kinematic's time series is presented. The results are promising for practical applications in human gait analysis.

Analyzing time delays estimated for these time series, it can be stated that proper time delay is different for each time series. On the other hand all of the values are in the range $[15; 33]$. Embedding dimension values are from the range $[4; 7]$. However the most frequent values are 4 and 5. It is probable that the embedding dimension value for left tibia is a numerical error. One factor to consider is the averaging time delay and embedding dimension values in further investigations.

Most of the largest Lyapunov's exponents calculated values are positive. Due to this fact human gait kinematics data exhibit the properties of chaotic behavior. It could be also stated that during human locomotion, all mentioned body parts are highly sensitive to initial conditions.

Acknowledgments. The author is grateful for the reviews, which certainly helped raise the quality of the work. The author would like to acknowledge the Polish-Japanese Institute of Information Technology for the gait sequences recorded in the Human Motion Laboratory (HML).

References

1. Abarbanel, H.: Analysis of observed chaotic data. Springer-Verlag New York (1996)
2. Andrievskii, B.R., Fradkov, A.L.: Control of chaos: Methods and applications. Automation and Remote Control **64**(5), 673–713 (2003)
3. Cao, L., Mees, A., Judd, K.: Dynamics from multivariate time series. Physica D **121**, 75–88 (1998)
4. Casdagli, M., Eubank, S., Farmer, J.D., Gibson, J.: State space reconstruction in the presence of noise. Physica D: Nonlinear Phenomena **51**(1), 52–98 (1991)
5. Cordoba, A., Lemos, M.C., Jiménez-Morales, F.: Periodical forcing for the control of chaos in a chemical reaction. Journal of Chemical Physics **124**(1), 1–6 (2006)
6. Dingwell, J.B., Cusumano, J.P., Cavanagh, P.R., Sternad, D.: Local dynamic stability versus kinematic variability of continuous overground and treadmill walking. Journal of Biomechanical Engineering **123**(1), 27–32 (2001)
7. Dingwell, J.B., Marin, L.C.: Kinematic variability and local dynamic stability of upper body motions when walking at different speeds. Journal of Biomechanics **39**(3), 444–452 (2006)
8. Filipowicz, W., Habela, P., Kaczmarski, K., Kulbacki, M.: A generic approach to design and querying of multi-purpose human motion database. In: Bolc, L., Tadeusiewicz, R., Chmielewski, L.J., Wojciechowski, K. (eds.) ICCVG 2010, Part I. LNCS, vol. 6374, pp. 105–113. Springer, Heidelberg (2010)
9. Fraser, A.M., Swinney, H.L.: Independent coordinates for strange attractors from mutual information. Physical Review A (1986)
10. Garcia, S.P., Almeida, J.S.: Multivariate phase space reconstruction by nearest neighbor embedding with different time delays. Phys. Rev. E **72**, August 2005
11. Grassberger, P., Procaccia, I.: Measuring the strangeness of strange attractors. Physica D9 **9** (1983)
12. Grassberger, P., Hegger, R., Kantz, H., Schaffrath, C., Schreiber, T.: On noise reduction methods for chaotic data. Chaos: An Interdisciplinary Journal of Nonlinear Science **3**(2), 127–141 (1993)
13. Jabłoński, B.: Application of quaternion scale space approach for motion processing. In: Choraś, R.S. (ed.) Image Processing & Communications Challenges 3. AISC, vol. 102, pp. 141–148. Springer, Heidelberg (2011)
14. Jablonski, B.: Quaternion dynamic time warping. IEEE Transactions on Signal Processing **60**(3), 1174–1183 (2012)

15. Josiński, H., Michalczuk, A., Świtoński, A., Mucha, R., Wojciechowski, K.: Quantifying chaotic behavior in treadmill walking. In: Nguyen, N.T., Trawiński, B., Kosala, R. (eds.) ACIIDS 2015. LNCS, vol. 9012, pp. 317–326. Springer, Heidelberg (2015)

16. Kantz, H.: A robust method to estimate the maximal lyapunov exponent of a time series. Physics Letters A **185**, 77–87 (1994)

17. Kennel, M.B., Brown, R., Abarbanel, H.D.: Determining embedding dimension for phase-space reconstruction using a geometrical construction. Physical Review A **45**(6), 3403 (1992)

18. Kocak, K., Saylan, L., Eitzinger, J.: Nonlinear prediction of near surface temperature via univariate and multivariate time series embedding. Ecological Modelling **173**, 1–7 (2004)

19. Kostelich, E.J., Schreiber, T.: Noise reduction in chaotic time-series data: a survey of common methods. Physical Review E **48**(3), 1752 (1993)

20. Kuipers, J.B.: Quaternions and rotation sequences, vol. 66. Princeton University Press, Princeton (1999)

21. Kwolek, B., Krzeszowski, T., Wojciechowski, K.: Real-time multi-view human motion tracking using 3d model and latency tolerant parallel particle swarm optimization. In: Gagalowicz, A., Philips, W. (eds.) MIRAGE 2011. LNCS, vol. 6930, pp. 169–180. Springer, Heidelberg (2011)

22. Parmananda, P.: Controlling turbulence in coupled map lattice systems using feedback techniques. Physical Review E **56**(1), 239–244 (1997)

23. Colins, J.J., Rossenstein, M.T., de Luca, C.J.: A practical method for calculating largest lyapunov exponents from small data sets. Physica D **65**, 117–134 (1993)

24. Sauer, T., Yorke, J.A., Casdagli, M.: Embedology. Journal of Statistical Physics (1991)

25. Stark, J.: Delay Embeddings for Forced Systems. I. Deterministic Forcing. Journal of Nonlinear Science, New York (1999)

26. Sugihara, G.: Nonlinear forecasting for the classification of natural time series. Philosophical Transactions of the Royal Society of London. Series A: Physical and Engineering Sciences **348**(1688), 477–495 (1994)

27. Takens, F.: Detecting strange attractors in turbulence. Springer, Berlin (1981)

28. Whitney, H.: Differentiable manifolds. Ann. Math. (1936)

29. Wolf, A., Swift, J.B., Swinney, H.L., Vastano, J.A.: Determining lyapunov exponents from a time series. Physica 16D **16**, 285–317 (1985)

Comparison of ASIM Traffic Profile Detectors and Floating Car Data During Traffic Incidents

Lukáš Rapant[1]([✉]), Kateřina Slaninová[1], Jan Martinovič[1],
Marek Ščerba[2], and Martin Hájek[1]

[1] IT4Innovations, VŠB - Technical University of Ostrava, 17. listopadu 15/2172,
Ostrava, Czech Republic
{lukas.rapant,katerina.slaninova,jan.martinovic,martin.hajek}@vsb.cz
[2] Transport Research Centre, Líšeňská 33a, Brno, Czech Republic
marek.scerba@cdv.cz

Abstract. Intelligent Transportation Systems are highly dependent on the quality and quantity of road traffic data. The complexity of input data is often crucial for effectiveness and sufficient reliability of such systems. Recent days, the fusion of various data sources is the topic which attracts attention of several researchers. The algorithms for data fusion take benefit of the advantages and disadvantages of each technology, resulting in an optimal solution for traffic management problems. The paper is focused on finding relations between two main data sources, floating car data and ASIM traffic profile detectors. Time series of speed and other information obtained from these data sources were analysed by Granger causality with intention to use both data sources efficiently for traffic monitoring and control during traffic incidents.

Keywords: Traffic analysis · Granger causality test · Traffic incident detection · Floating car data · ASIM sensors

1 Introduction

Intelligent Transportation Systems (ITS) are highly dependant on the quality and quantity of road traffic data. The complexity of input data is often crucial for effectiveness and sufficient reliability of such systems. Recent days, the fusion of various data sources is under the development and new algorithms for data fusion are discussed. Common data input is traffic information such as vehicle speed or traffic flow collected through fixed detectors placed along the road network at strategic points. Other valuable data source based on collecting traffic data through mobile devices and on-board units has become important as a source that can provide accurate real-time information over a large road network and overcomes some problems related to fixed detectors.

The floating car data (FCD) technique is based on the exchange of information between floating cars travelling on a road network and a central data system. The floating cars periodically send the recent accumulated data on their

© IFIP International Federation for Information Processing 2015
K. Saeed and W. Homenda (Eds.): CISIM 2015, LNCS 9339, pp. 120–131, 2015.
DOI: 10.1007/978-3-319-24369-6_10

positions, whereas the central data system tracks the received data along the travelled routes. The frequency of sending/reporting is usually determined by the resolution of data required and the method of communication.

The most common and useful information that FCD techniques and ITS provide is average travel times and speeds along road links or paths [6,7,11, 16,17]. They deploy FCD in order to predict short-term travel conditions, to automatically detect incident or critical situations [3,13,15], or determine Origin-Destination traffic flow patterns [10,12].

The reliability of all types of estimates based on FCD highly depends on the percentage of floating cars participating in the traffic flow. Several FCD systems were presented, integrating short-term traffic forecasting based on current and historical FCD. However, these systems exploit data mostly from car flotillas to deliver real-time traffic speed information throughout large cities, signalized urban arterials or particular parts of traffic network, for example Italian motorway [1], Berlin [8], Beijing [9], Vienna [5], and many others.

The RODOS Transport Systems Development Centre[1] operates the system viaRODOS [2] which covers the whole traffic network of the Czech Republic [2]. Therefore, we are able to monitor traffic situation from the global perspective. On the other hand, this globalisation brings us several restrictions. To cover the whole traffic network, the system viaRODOS uses segmentation system which divides the highways and speed ways onto smaller parts - segments. The location code table from Traffic Message Channel (TMC) - a technology for delivering traffic and travel information to drivers - is used for identification of real world objects localization. Each row in location code table is strongly connected to a specific geographical entity (crossroads, roads, important objects, etc.). Locations used by TMC system are set by the rules for location identification defined by the international standard EN ISO 14819-3:1999. The location code tables for Czech Republic is created by Central European Data Agency (CEDA), which also addresses their certification on the international level.

The viaRODOS system operates the complex database of people and goods mobility database integrating various types of data sources like traffic data consisted of data from toll gates electronic system and ASIM traffic detectors, floating car data, meteodata, and data from Uniform system of traffic information for the Czech Republic. The appropriate combination of all the data sources and their usage after suitable preprocessing allow us to obtain more accurate results for traffic monitoring and control and for short-time predictions.

FCD data are usually used for quality control of static sensor infrastructure like identifying faulty traffic detectors [5], for assessment of traffic message system quality [14], or for traffic state analysis to evaluate the effectiveness of traffic control measures (signalling optimization). The published contributions are focused on the exact position of the traffic detectors, mainly within urban networks. We do not have opportunity to influence the distribution of the traf-

---

[1] RODOS Transport Systems Development Centre: http://www.it4i-rodos.cz/defaultEN.aspx

[2] viaRODOS is available on http://www.viarodos.eu

fic detectors, mainly due to its expensiveness, and have a set network of TMC segments to measure FCD data. However, using appropriate methods and algorithms, it is possible to obtain sufficient outputs for traffic management and short-time prediction.

The paper is focused on finding relations between time series obtained from ASIM traffic profile detectors and floating car data with intention to use both data sources for traffic monitoring and control during traffic incidents. The compared data sources are described in more detail in Section 2. The comparison was done by identifying Granger causality, see Section 3. The experimental results are then described in Section 4, and Section 5 concludes the paper.

2   Data Sources

Generally, data sources describing actual traffic situation on Czech motorways can be divided into two groups - stationary data sources and floating car data sources. Stationary data sources contain data provided by toll gates and the data provided by ASIM sensors. However, the value of the data from the toll gates is severely reduced by the fact, that they only contain information about large vehicles (trucks, buses, etc.). Data from toll gates thus only describes this specific part of the traffic, and is not usable for the description of general traffic situation. The following text briefly describes both ASIM sensor data and floating car data and summarizes their advantages and disadvantages.

2.1   ASIM Sensors

In the Czech Republic, the traffic situation is mostly monitored and evaluated using the stationary data. One of the most important source of stationary data is ASIM sensor network. ASIM sensors are placed on certain toll gates (all these toll gates are placed on the highways). They comprise of various sensors like passive infrared detectors and radars. They are able to distinguish individual vehicle types, and measure their speed and intensity. Their measurements are aggregated every five minutes and mean speed and intensity are calculated.

They have number of advantages. One of the biggest advantages is the fact that there is no need for equipping vehicles with additional electronic devices. Consequently, speeds of all vehicles going through a sensor are measured. Another important advantage is detail of the data. ASIM sensors provide separate information about every lane of the monitored road. Moreover, since the ASIM sensor is able to distinguish type of the passing vehicle, it is only data source which is able to provide speeds and intensities for each type of the vehicle.

There are, however some serious disadvantages of these sensors. In the Czech Republic, this network of measuring points is very sparse. There are only about 120 toll gates equipped with ASIM sensors; all of these are placed on the motorways. This low density is caused by related necessary expenses – installation of such measuring points is quite expensive. There are also other limitations. Electronic toll gates divide roads into fragments of various length, some of them may extend to many kilometres. Thus, data obtained from ASIM sensors exactly describe only traffic situation around the tollgate.

2.2   Floating Car Data

The opposite to stationary data is Floating Car Data (FCD). This approach is based on the measurements of location, speed, travel direction and time information from certain vehicles in the traffic. These information are obtained from the GPS receiver inside the car and broadcast by radio unit or cell phone. Nowadays, an on-board unit including a GPS receiver becomes a standard equipment of corporate fleet cars. Moreover, increasing expansion of smart phones brought GNSS technology to our personal lives, where with combination of cheap connectivity, each vehicle can become a source of this type of data. FCD have specific discretization. For example, D1 highway is divided into the sections (TMC segments) with length from several hundred meters to few kilometres. The traffic speed is calculated each minute as a mean of speed of all floating cars that passed through the section in the last minute.

This approach again has several advantages and drawbacks. The number of cars equipped with a GPS unit has doubled over the past five years. It can be expected that the trend will continue. It implies that the number of potential data sources will increase. Moreover, data from GPS receivers is not limited to the predefined places so the coverage is much larger than in the case of the stationary data.

Disadvantages come mainly from the GNSS technology itself. GPS device as a part of GNSS technology, fails to provide precise outputs or the outputs can be intentionally distorted. The quality of outputs can also be influenced by many factors such as the device quality, location, weather or other unpredictable and uncontrollable phenomena. All of this can have an impact on positioning, ranging from meters to tens of meters. Because GNSS is based on satellite technology, GPS receiver has to be able to receive signals from several satellites. This can prove to be difficult in some cases. Typical example is an urban area with tall buildings which form obstacles between receiver and satellites. Then, GPS receiver is not able to report its position.

3   Granger Causality

A variable x is said to Granger cause another variable y if past values of x help predict the current value of y. This definition is based on the concept of causal ordering [4]. Two variables can be correlated by chance but it is improbable that the past values of x will be useful in predicting y, given all the past values of y, unless x does in some way actually cause y. Granger causality is not identical to causation in the philosophical sense, but it does demonstrate the likelihood of such causation or the lack of such causation more forcefully than does simple correlation. For example, where the third variable drives both x and y, x might still appear to drive y though there is no actual philosophical causal mechanism directly linking the variables. However, there can be still Granger causality as one variable may be useful for predicting the other. The simplest test of Granger causality requires estimating the following two regression equations:

$$y_t = \gamma_{1,0} + \sum_{i=1}^{l} \gamma_{1,i} y_{t-i} + \sum_{j=1}^{l} \gamma_{1,l+j} x_{t-j} + \varepsilon_t \tag{1}$$

$$x_t = \gamma_{2,0} + \sum_{i=1}^{l} \gamma_{2,i} x_{t-i} + \sum_{j=1}^{l} \gamma_{2,l+j} y_{t-j} + \varepsilon_t \tag{2}$$

where l is the number of lags that adequately models the dynamic structure so that the coefficients of further lags of variables are not statistically significant and the error terms ϵ are white noise. Number of lags l is usually chosen using an information criterion, in our case Bayesian information criterion. If the l parameters $\gamma_{1,l+j}$ are jointly significant according to the F-test then the null hypothesis that x does not Granger cause y can be rejected. Similarly, if the l parameters $\gamma_{2,i}$ are jointly significant according to the F-test, then the null hypothesis that y does not Granger cause x can be rejected. This test is Granger causality test.

4 Experimental Results

Two toll gates with ASIM sensors and their appropriate FCD segments were chosen for the experiments. The first toll gate (labeled 34.1) is placed on 195.7th km of D1 motorway in direction to Ostrava and the other (labeled 15.2) is placed on 117.7th km of D1 in direction to Prague. Lengths of their corresponding FCD segments are roughly 2 km in both cases and the gates are placed in the middle of the segments. These gates and segments were chosen because of higher frequency of traffic incidents in these locations. These locations are also interesting because the first one is located near the city and the other one is not. Data comes from period of March to April 2014.

As it was mentioned in the introduction, our main interest is in determination of relationship between FCD and ASIM data also during the traffic incidents, respectively, whether this relation is causal or not. In case of longer time series without any incidents it can be quite unsurprisingly shown that there exists a causal relationship. This causality in case of gate 34.1 and its corresponding segment can be seen in Figure 1.

From the perspective of Granger causality test, both relations are causal (i.e. ASIM contains significant information about FCD and vica versa). In case of ASIM time series causing FCD time series, test statistic has value of 51.82 with critical value of 2.7 and in case of FCD causing ASIM, value test statistic was 12.36 with critical value 2.3. Therefore, in both cases we can reject null hypothesis that there is no causality between the time series. Similar results were received in case of other sensors-segments and time periods.

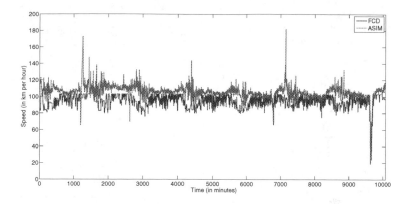

Fig. 1. Time series of speed from ASIM sensor 34.1 and corresponding FCD segment form the third week of march 2014

Based on this we can declare that ASIM time series can be used for completion and prediction of FCD series and vice versa. It would not be difficult as, most of the time, traffic is periodic and easily predictable. This is, however, of little use as the most interesting part of the traffic are the traffic incidents. It is quite possible that margin of error allowed by the Granger causality can come from these rare events. Therefore, it is important to know whether these causal relations work even in case of traffic incidents on shorter time series. There were 16 incidents detected by our method during observed period (six in case of sensor 34.1 and ten in case of sensor 15.2). Results from Granger causality tests performed on these incidents can be seen in Tables 1 and 2 (T is test statistic and k is critical value; tests which have not confirmed causality are marked by red colour).

Table 1. ASIM sensor 34.1 causality

Time of incident	ASIM causes FCD $[T/k]$	FCD causes ASIM $[T/k]$
8. 3. 2014 14:36-17:20	0.84/3.85	3.69/3.87
21. 3. 2014 16:19-17:55	6.49/3.89	9.7/3.04
16. 4. 2014 16:11-17:21	1.04/3.87	17.34/3.87
18. 4. 2014 16:49-18:48	0.51/3.87	19.07/3.1
23. 4. 2014 9:46-10:27	44.28/3.89	7.17/3.04
29. 4. 2014 17:00-18:33	18.51/3.87	5.92/3.88

Three different kinds of outcome can be seen in Table 1 and Table 2. The first one is that both causality tests were passed. This is the most usual outcome and it implies that both ASIM data and FCD data react on the incident at roughly the same time. It probably means that incident happened somewhere near the

Table 2. ASIM sensor 15.2 causality

Time of incident	ASIM causes FCD [T/k]	FCD causes ASIM [T/k]
24. 3. 2014 9:17-21:05	14.02/3.85	21.75/3.85
25. 3. 2014 7:13-12:15	5.14/3.02	15.89/3.86
25. 3. 2014 17:05-21:07	16.73/3.01	0.63/3.86
26. 3. 2014 9:01-10:16	1.55/3.87	0.7/3.87
26. 3. 2014 14:13-15:05	0.16/3.92	3.42/3.93
26. 3. 2014 15:36-20:17	7.35/3.88	3.03/3.02
28. 3. 2014 15:55-19:16	0.88/3.86	5.24/3.86
1. 4. 2014 16:05-16:46	8.41/3.89	9.71/2.05
10. 4. 2014 16:40-17:33	14.07/3.87	16.20/3.02
22. 4. 2014 7:30-9:56	12.89/2.40	9.52/3.88

toll gate with ASIM sensor. Such incident can be seen in Figure 2. The fact that this outcome represents more then a half of the detected incidents means, that most of the time, both of the sensors react well and at the similar time on the development of the traffic.

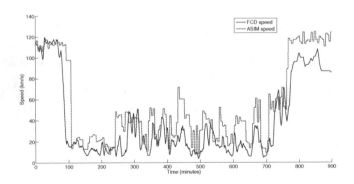

Fig. 2. Time series of speed from ASIM sensor 15.2 and corresponding FCD segment form 24. 3. 2014

The second possible outcome is that there is only one way causality between the time series. Such example is in Figure 3. It happens either when the incident is further from the toll gate with ASIM and is sooner registred by FCD or is located in the close vicinity of the ASIM sensor. Due to the sparsity of the ASIM sensor network (sensors on D1 are placed about 12 km apart), it is much more usual that FCD data detects the incident sooner than ASIM sensors and are therefore usable for the predictions of speeds in ASIM sensor time series. Opposite scenario is much rarer. If we take into account the fact that most of the time both series are roughly equivalent, we can assume that it is quite safe

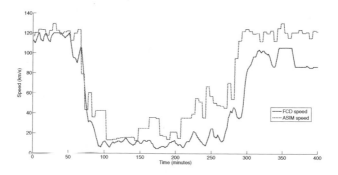

Fig. 3. Time series of speed from ASIM sensor 15.2 and corresponding FCD segment form 25. 3. 2014

to predict ASIM speed time series from FCD time series. If we try it other way, there is greater possibility of failure due to the sensor sparsity.

The third possible outcome is that there is no causality either way. These outcomes prove to be problematic because they cannot be easily explained and can imply some problems regarding predictability. Because of this fact, they will be thoroughly analyzed.

The first of the three analysed incidents is the incident from 8.3.2014 from 195.7th km of D1 in the direction to Ostrava. Time series from FCD and ASIM are shown in Figure 4. The figure shows an apparent disparity in the data between FCD and ASIM data. This is a very busy part of the D1 motorway. This FCD segment is placed between major motorway ramps. One ramp leads to the motorway to Vienna and the other one to motorway to Bratislava. The segment is approximately 2300 m long and ASIM sensor is installed 1400 m from the beginning of the segment.

There was short-term closure of the left lane realized on this segment on 8.3.2014. This meant a reduction in the number of lanes. Beginning of this short-term closure was on 195.2 km and end of this closure was on 195.6 km, approximately 700 meters before the ASIM sensor. The short-term closure was implemented between 3:00 p.m. and 6:00 p.m. A traffic column was created in the front of the closure, which is visible in the FCD data in Figure 4. However, data from ASIM sensor show no traffic problem. This is because the column was created in front of traffic restrictions, but ASIM sensor is placed behind the restriction where the traffic flow is not restricted. Despite relative closeness of the incident to the ASIM sensor, it has failed to detect it. This situation confirms fact that to predict FCD time series from ASIM can be inaccurate. On the other hand, the FCD data source can be used to monitor the situation.

On 24. 3. 2014 at 9:00 at 112th km started the modernization of the D1 motorway. The repaired section started at 112th km and ended at 104th km in the direction to Prague. In the period between the 24.3. and 30.3. 2014, the traffic was restricted to one lane. Such traffic engineering measures at places with

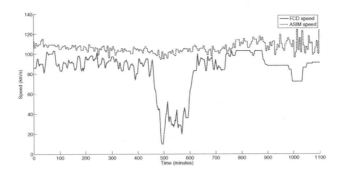

Fig. 4. Time series of speed from ASIM sensor 34.1 and corresponding FCD segment form 8. 3. 2014

so intense traffic always cause problems and so it was in this case. Both traffic incidents with no causality happened during this period. Bottleneck, the place where two lanes were merging into one was placed at 112.5th km. Beginning (or more exactly the end) of TMC segment was distanced approximately 3500 m against the road direction (116th km) from the bottleneck and ASIM sensor was placed additional approximately 1500 meters from the beginning of the segment. This TMC segment was about 3500 meters long.

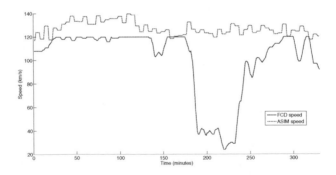

Fig. 5. Time series of speed from ASIM sensor 15.2 and corresponding FCD segment form 9:00 26. 3. 2014

The exported data from FCD and ASIM sensor show that in the first and the second day of reconstruction (24. 3. and 25. 3.) there were long traffic columns with length of more than 5 km almost all the day in the front of the merge. In those days, the speeds from FCD data and ASIM sensor were almost identical. This phenomenon was caused by the very rapid formation of traffic columns, which reached the ASIM sensor within minutes. The next day (26. 3.), it is already evident that after a series of media reports a certain percentage of drivers chose to postpone their trip, or chose another type of transport. This fact caused formation of shorter columns and their slower formation, which is evident in the difference between the speed of FCD and ASIM sensor (see Figure 5). Because the column has started reaching FCD segment, but has not reached the ASIM sensor, the speed of the FCD reduced, but the monitored detection sensor was still recording the speed of freely moving traffic flow. This is evident from the incident that happened on 26. 3. 2014 between 9:00 and 10:00 when the column intervened into the FCD segment, but has not reached the measured profile. In case of the next incident (14:00 on the same day), the column reached ASIM sensor yet.

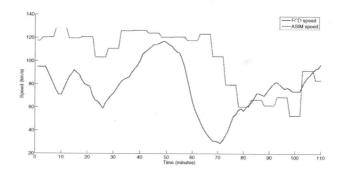

Fig. 6. Time series of speed from ASIM sensor 15.2 and corresponding FCD segment form 14:00 26. 3. 2014

From Figure 6 there is apparent delay in detection on the column by ASIM sensor. This is caused by slow formation of the column. The same is true in case of the dissolution of the column. The speed at first rises in ASIM sensor measurements and then gradually increases in FCD data. Only at the moment when the column does not interfere with the measured segment, traffic speeds again start to match. This again proves that prediction of FCD time series from ASIM is problematic due to the many specific configurations where profile sensor fails to detect traffic incident.

5   Conclusion

In this article, we have analysed Granger causality of speed time series from FCD and ASIM sensors with special focus on the traffic incidents. It was determined from the obtained results that in more than a half of incidents, there is Granger causality between FCD and ASIM data in both ways. In the other cases, there was only one way causality. It was mostly due to the fact, that when the incident happens some distance from the ASIM sensor, FCD is usually much swifter to record this incident than ASIM. Sometimes there is no causality at all between these time series but by thorough analysis of these incidents, we have proven that again this is caused by static nature of ASIM detectors which fails to detect some phenomena that can happen even in its close vicinity. Therefore, we can summarize that it is quite reliable to predict values of ASIM time series from FCD during the traffic incidents. Predicting FCD from ASIM can work most of the time too but is nowhere as reliable due to the nature of the sensor.

Results of this analysis underline importance of FCD data in Czech motorway traffic. ASIM sensors provide valuable information, but due to their sparsity are not able to describe accurately traffic in its entirety. They are failing especially when the traffic column is not long enough to reach the ASIM sensor or in the areas with many ramps. Due to this fact, it is very important to incorporate FCD data to any traffic model for Czech motorways. FCD-based analyses are very flexible, especially in an environment where it would be difficult (for economic or organizational reasons) to install dedicated static sensor infrastructure such as ASIM.

The intelligent combination of FCD with on-road sensors represents the perfect inputs to dynamic traffic models. New algorithms for data fusion will take benefit of the advantages and disadvantages of each technology, resulting in an optimal solution for traffic management problems.

In the near future, we are planning to find and implement methods for prediction in the analysed time series. These methods will be based on advanced approaches like Bayesian networks and Neural networks and will utilize results from this article.

Acknowledgments. This work was supported by the European Regional Development Fund in the IT4Innovations Centre of Excellence project (CZ.1.05/ 1.1.00/02.0070) and the national budget of the Czech Republic via the Research and Development for Innovations Operational Programme, by the project New creative teams in priorities of scientific research (reg. no. CZ.1.07/2.3.00/30.0055), supported by Operational Programme Education for Competitiveness, and co-financed by the European Social Fund and supported by 'Transport Systems Development Centre' co-financed by Technology Agency of the Czech Republic (reg. no. TE01020155) and by the internal grant agency of VŠB Technical University of Ostrava, Czech Republic, under the project no. SP2015/114 'HPC Usage for Analysis of Uncertain Time Series'.

References

1. de Fabritiis, C., Ragona, R., Valenti, G.: Traffic estimation and prediction based on real time floating car data. In: Proceedings of 11th International IEEE Conference on Intelligent Transportation Systems, ITSC 2008, pp. 197–203 (2008)
2. Fedorčák, D., Kocyan, T., Hájek, M., Szturcová, D., Martinovič, J.: viaRODOS: monitoring and visualisation of current traffic situation on highways. In: Saeed, K., Snášel, V. (eds.) CISIM 2014. LNCS, vol. 8838, pp. 290–300. Springer, Heidelberg (2014)
3. Ghosh, B., Basu, B., O'Mahony, M.: Multivariate short-term traffic flow forecasting using time-series analysis. IEEE Transactions on Intelligent Transportation Systems **10**(2), 246–254 (2009)

4. Granger, C.: Some recent development in a concept of causality. Journal of Econometrics **39**(1–2), 199–211 (1988)
5. Graser, A., Dragaschnig, M., Ponweiser, W., Koller, H., Marcinek, M.-S., Widhalm, P.: Fcd in the real world – system capabilities and applications. In: Proceedings of 19th ITS World Congress, Vienna, Austria, p. 7 (2012)
6. Jones, M., Geng, Y., Nikovski, D., Hirata, T.: Predicting link travel times from floating car data. In: Proceedings of International IEEE Conference on Intelligent Transport Systems (ITSC) (2013)
7. Khan, R.-A.-I., Landfeldt, B., Dhamdher, A.: Predicting travel times in dense and highly varying road traffic networks using starima models. Technical report, School of Information Technologies, The University of Sydney and National ICT Australia (2012)
8. Kuhns, G., Ebendt, R., Wagner, P., Sohr, A., Brockfeld, E.: Self evaluation of floating car data based on travel times from actual vehicle trajectories. In: IEEE Forum on Integrated and Sustainable Transportation Systems (2011)
9. Li, M., Zhang, Y., Wang, W.: Analysis of congestion points based on probe car data. In: Proceedings of International IEEE Conference on Intelligent Transportation Systems, ITSC 2009, pp. 1–5 (2009)
10. Ma, Y., van Zuylen, H.J., van Dalen, J.: Freight origin-destination matrix estimation based on multiple data sources: methodological study. In: TRB 2012 Annual Meeting (2012)
11. McLeod, D.S., Elefteriadou, L., Jin, L.: Travel time reliability as a performance measure: applying florida's predictive model on the state's freeway system. In: TRB 2012 Annual Meeting (2012)
12. Schäfer, R.-P., Thiessenhusen, K.-U., Wagner, P.: A traffic information system by means of real-time floating-car data. In: Proceedings of ITS World Congress 2002, Chicago, USA (2002)
13. Vlahogianni, E.I.: Enhancing predictions in signalized arterials with information on short-term traffic flow dynamics. Journal of Intelligent Transportation Systems **13**(2), 73–84 (2009)
14. Widhalm, P., Koller, H., Ponweiser, W.: Identifying faulty traffic detectors with floating car data. In: IEEE Forum on Integrated and Sustainable Transportation System (2011)
15. Wu, Y.-J., Chen, F., Lu, C.-T., Smith, B.: Traffic flow prediction for urban network using spatio-temporal random effects model. In: 91st Annual Meeting of the Transportation Research Board (2011)
16. Zeng, W., He, Z., Lu, R., Zhuang, L., Xia, X.: Freeway segment speed estimation model based on distribution features of floating-car data. In: TRB 2012 Annual Meeting (2012)
17. Zheng, J.: Road travel time estimation with gps floating car data. In: Stander Symposium Posters. Book 191 (2012)

Verification of ArchiMate Behavioral Elements by Model Checking

Piotr Szwed$^{(\boxtimes)}$

AGH University of Science and Technology, Kraków, Poland
pszwed@agh.edu.pl

Abstract. In this paper we investigate the problem of verification of business processes specified with ArchiMate language. The proposed solution employs model checking techniques. As a verification platform the state of the art symbolic model checker NuSMV is used. We describe a method of fully automated translation of behavioral elements embedded in ArchiMate models into a representation in NuSMV language, which is then submitted to verification with respect to requirements expressed in CTL. The requirements specification can be entered by user, but we also propose to derive some of them automatically, based on analysis of control flows within business processes. The solution was implemented as a plugin to Archi, a popular ArchiMate modeling tool. Application of the method is presented on an example of a small business process.

Keywords: Formal verification · Model checking · Business process · ArchiMate · NuSMV

1   Introduction

In this paper we investigate an application of model checking techniques to automated verification of behavioral description embedded within ArchiMate models. ArchiMate is a lightweight language providing a uniform representation of enterprise architecture [22]. The language comprises elements of various types, however, constructs allowing to model behavior can be found only in the *Business* layer. They include events, processes (also understood as activities), interactions, collaborations and several types of junctions. Therefore, the verification of ArchiMate behavioral elements falls into a wide domain of business process verification [17].

Business models can comprise a large number of processes. For clarity reasons they are often depicted in form of several *views*, that cover only selected parts of the model. In consequence, behaviors embedded in the model are distributed among the views, what often makes them difficult to track. Although modeling tools offer support for local syntax checking, e.g. correct use of links between elements of the graphical language, some structural errors remain undetected, especially those resulting from incorrect use of synchronization mechanisms [17]. Partial analysis of model behavior can be performed by simulation techniques,

© IFIP International Federation for Information Processing 2015
K. Saeed and W. Homenda (Eds.): CISIM 2015, LNCS 9339, pp. 132–144, 2015.
DOI: 10.1007/978-3-319-24369-6_11

however, only application of formal methods can give unequivocal answer that the verified model exhibits desired properties.

Formal system verification can by done either by deductive reasoning or model checking [9]. Deductive reasoning consists in formulating theorems specifying desired system properties and proving or falsifying them using manual or automated techniques. The advantage of deductive reasoning methods is their ability to verify systems with infinite domains (number of states). However, they give very little information on causes, if the verified property does not hold.

Model checking allows to verify a concurrent system modeled as a finite state transition graph against a set of specifications expressed in a propositional temporal logic. It employs efficient internal representations and quick search procedures to determine automatically, whether the specifications are satisfied along the computational paths. Moreover, if a specification is not met, the procedure delivers a counterexample that can be used to analyze the source of the error. The main problem faced by model checking is the state explosion [8]. At the very beginning only small examples could have been processed. A significant progress in this technique was achieved with application of ordered binary decision diagrams (OBBD) [4] allowing to model systems consisting of millions of states and transitions.

Although formal tools reached state of the art, they are not commonly used in engineering practice. According to Huuck [13] three factors decide on successful application of formal tools: they should be simple to use, the time spent on model preparation and verification should be comparable with other user activities, and, finally, a tool should provide a real value, i.e. deliver information that was previously not available.

The goal of our work was to develop a software tool that fully automatically translates behavioral elements of a business model expressed in ArchiMate language to a corresponding finite-state graph required by a model checker. We were also attracted by an idea of deriving automatically requirements specifications based on control flows within business processes.

As a verification platform the state of the art symbolic model checker NuSMV [5] is used. NuSMV allows to enter a model being a set of communicating finite state machines (FSM) and automatically check its properties specified as Computational Tree Logic (CTL) or Linear Temporal Logic (LTL) formulas. For a given temporal logic formula $\mathcal{F}$, NuSMV provides the answer that $\mathcal{F}$ is satisfied by the model or it delivers a counterexample falsifying it.

The concept of verification system is presented in Fig. 1. The business model is defined within Archi [2], a well known ArchiMate modeling tool. We have developed an Archi plugin that extracts a subgraph of ArchiMate behavioral elements and transforms it into NuSMV model descriptions.

As a specification language CTL is used. Basically, a specification of system properties is entered by a user. This is a manual task, that requires a certain insight into the business process, as well a knowledge of mapping of its elements onto NuSMV model. However, a part of the specification is generated automatically by an analysis of the process structure.

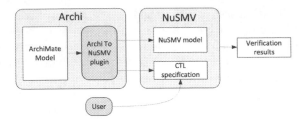

Fig. 1. The concept of the verification system

The paper is organized as follows: next Section 2 discusses various approaches to data verification of business models. It is followed by Section 3, which presents ArchiMate language. In Section 4 the translation procedure is described. Application of the presented approach to a business process verification is presented in Section 5. Section 6 provides concluding remarks.

2   Related Works

Application of formal methods to verification of business processes was surveyed by Morimoto [17]. Author distinguished three prevalent approaches: based on automata, Petri nets and process algebras. The first approach consists in translating the process description into a set of communicating automata (state machines) and performing model checking with such tools, as SPIN or UPPAAL In analysis of Petri net models basically simulation techniques are used, especially in case of more expressive colored Petri nets.

Model checking has an established position in verification of business processes. I was applied in [23] to BPMN models extended with temporal and resource constraints. In [1] verification of of e-business processes was achieved by translation to CSP language and checking refinement between two specifications. In [16] authors implemented a system that translates BPEL specification into NuSMV language and then allows to check properties defined as CTL formulas. Three types of correctness properties were analyzed: invariants, properties of final states and temporal relations between activities. The first two can be classified as *safeness*, the last as the *liveness* property. Similarly, in work by Fu et al. [11] CTL was applied to the verification of e-services and workflows with both bounded and unbounded number of process instances. Work [10] discusses verification of data-centric business processes. The correctness problem was expressed in the LTL-FO, an extension to the Linear Temporal Logic, in which propositions were replaced by First Order statements about data objects.

In our previous works [14,15] we proposed a method for verification of ArchiMate behavioral specifications based on deductive reasoning. The described approach consisted in transforming ArchiMate model into a set of LTL formulas, then extending it with formulas defining desired system properties and formally proving them using semantic tableaux method.

NuSMV [5] is a state of the art model checker that has been succesfully used for various verification tasks including formal protocol analysis [7], verification of requirements specification [12] or planning tasks [3]. The package uses a special language (named also NuSMV) to define the verified model as a set of linked finite state machines, as well as its specification in form of temporal logic formulas. The model submitted to the verification tool must be manually coded in NuSMV language or generated from another language amenable to state transition system, e.g a state charts [6] or reachability graphs of Petri nets [20].

3   Archimate

ArchiMate [22] is a contemporary, open and independent language intended for description of enterprise architectures. It comprises five main modeling layers shortly characterized below. The *Business* layer includes business processes and objects, functions, events, roles and services. The *Application* layer contains components, interfaces, application services and data objects. The *Technology* layer gathers such elements as artifacts, nodes, software, devices, communication channels and networks. Elements of the *Motivation* layer allow to express business drivers, goals, requirements and principles. Finally, *Implementation&Migration* layer contains such elements, as work package, deliverable and gap.

ArchiMate allows to present an architecture in the form of views which, depending on the needs, can include only items in one layer or can show vertical relations between layers, e.g.: a relationship between a business process and a function of the component software.

ArchiMate was built in opposition to UML [19], which can be seen as a collection of unrelated diagrams, and Business Process Modeling Notation BPMN [18] which covers mainly behavioral aspect of enterprise architecture. The definition of a language has been accompanied by an assumption, that in order to build an expressive business model, it is necessary to use the relationships between completely different areas, starting from business motivation to business processes, services and infrastructure.

Archimate provides a small set of constructs that can be used to model behavior. It includes *Business Processes, Functions, Interactions, Events* and various connectors (*Junctions*), which can be attributed with a logical operator specifying, how inputs should be combined or output produced. According to language specification casual or temporal relationships between behavioral elements are expressed with use of *triggering* relation. On the other hand, Archimate models frequently use *composition* and *aggregation* relations, e.g. to show that a process is built from smaller behavioral elements (subprocesses or functions).

Although the set of behavioral elements seems to be very limited when compared with BPMN [18], after adopting a certain modeling convention its expressiveness can be similar [21]. An advantage of the language is that in allows to comprise in a single model a broad context of business processes including roles, services, processed business objects and elements of lower layers responsible for implementation and deployment.

4   Model Generation

This section discusses language patterns that can be used to model ArchiMate elements in NuSMV, as well as details of the translation procedure.

4.1   ArchiMate Model

The internal structure of an Archimate model constitutes a graph of nodes linked by directed edges. Both nodes and edges are attributed with information indicating a type of element or relation. Generating NuSMV code describing behavioral aspects of Archimate model we focus on components of the *Business layer*: processes (interactions, functions), events and various junctions.

It should be noted that Archimate behavioral constructs have no precisely defined semantics. In fact, translation from Archimate specification to NuSMV assigns a semantics, which, although arbitrarily selected, follows a certain intuition, e.g. how to interpret an activity or an event.

Definition 1 (Archimate Model). *ArchiMate model AM is a tuple $\langle V, E, C, R, v, e \rangle$, where V is a set of vertices, $E \subset V \times V$ is a set of edges, C is a set of ArchiMate element types, R is a set of relations, $vt \colon V \to C$ is a function that assigns element types to graph vertices $et \colon E \to R$ assigns relation types to edges.*

As we focus on business layer elements that are used to specify behavior, it is assumed that $C = \{$*Process, Function, Interaction, Event, Junction, AndJunction, OrJunction, Other*$\}$ and $R = \{$*triggering, association, composition, other*$\}$.

4.2   NuSMV Model

The basic structural unit in NuSMV language is *module* understood as a set of variables and statements that assign to them initial values and define a transition relation. Depending on the module definition, we may distinguish input variables corresponding to stimuli, internal state variables and output variables (actions).

Definition of a module introduces a new type that can be instantiated. Hence, it is possible to declare a variable of a module type and bind it during declaration resembling a constructor call to a number of input variables. Subsequent variables definitions may reference outputs of other modules instances as their inputs. This allows to define a system of communicating state machines of desired complexity, which propagates input stimuli to its components causing subsequent state changes and generation of output signals. Typically, the model integration is achieved within the special *main* module, however, it can be distributed among lower level modules, which are referenced from *main*.

After an analysis of components used to describe ArchiMate processes the following basic modules were identified and implemented:

- *atomicProcess$_n$*: n-ary atomic process has exactly one input, one primary output and n additional outputs, which can be activated if one of n exceptions occurs. The exception should be modeled in ArchiMate as an event linked with the process by an association relation.
- *event*: has only one input and one output (a boolean flag). Multiple recipients may use this flag as trigger.
- *andFork*: used to model AndJunction in Archmate. The module construction is analogous to event.
- *andJoin$_n$*: n-ary andJoin produces output signal, if all n inputs are set to TRUE.
- *xorFork$_n$*: n-ary xor-fork have one input and n outputs. Upon module activation, only one from outputs will be triggered.
- *xorJoin$_n$*: n-ary xor-join has n inputs and sets the output flag if any of them is set. Moreover it tracks the number of inputs, e.g. if two from n inputs are activated, the output flag will be set twice.

Fig. 2 shows the state diagram of the module `atomicProcess1`. The number 1 indicates the number of additional outputs activated as a result of exception occurrence. The process is activated by the input signal *trigger*. Upon signal arrival it makes the state transition from *idle* to *started*. Then a choice can be made between the states *finished* and *interrrupted1*. Synchronously, the corresponding output variable is set: either *outflag* or *exccptflag1* to *TRUE*. The output variable, whichever is set, will be cleared during the transition to *idle* state.

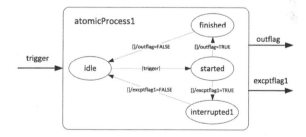

Fig. 2. State machine modeling an atomic process

The NuSMV code for the module is given in Fig. 3. It should be mentioned, that n exceptional outputs, we generate module `atomicProcess_n` with states *interrupted1,..., interrruptedn* and n output flags *exceptflag1,..., exceptflagn*.

4.3   Generation Procedure

The generation procedure consists of the following stages:

1. *Refactoring.* With relation to the numbers of inputs and outputs, it is expected that elements fall into one of two classes: $1 : m$ (one input and

138   P. Szwed

```
MODULE atomicProcess1(trigger)
VAR
    state : {idle,started,finished,interrupted1};
    outflag : boolean;
    excptflag1 : boolean;
ASSIGN
    init(state) := idle;
    next(state) :=
        case
            state = idle & trigger: {started};
            state = started : {finished,interrupted1};
            state = finished & !outflag : idle;
            state = interrupted1 & !excptflag1 : idle;
            TRUE : state;
        esac;
    init(outflag) := FALSE;
    next(outflag) :=
        case
            state = finished : TRUE;
            state = idle : FALSE;
            TRUE : outflag;
        esac;
    init(excptflag1) := FALSE;
    next(excptflag1) :=
        case
            state = interrupted1 : TRUE;
            state = idle : FALSE;
            TRUE : excptflag1;
        esac;
SPEC
    AG (trigger = TRUE -> AF (outflag = TRUE | excptflag1 = TRUE))
```

Fig. 3. NuSMV code of the module `atomicProcess1` (the number 1 indicates number of exceptional outputs)

m outputs) or $n : 1$ (m inputs and one output). Hence elements with the arity $n : m$ are replaced by two two elements: the first is an appropriate xorJoin or andJoin of arity $n : 1$. The second is an atomic process, event or fork of arity $1 : n$.

2. *Assigning representation.* For each element, based on its type and numbers of inputs/outputs, an appropriate NuSMV module type is selected and configured. Only required modules are generated. E.g. if the specification uses only processes with one and three exceptional outputs, only modules defining `atomicProcess1()` and `atomicProcess3()` will be generated.

3. *Main module generation.* This step comprises declaration of variables and linking them. For roots (modules without inputs) appropriate initial variables and transitions are added as well.

4. *Specification generation.* The implemented procedure analyses the graph of elements and generates CTL specifications. See Section 4.5.

4.4 Small Example

We will discuss the effects of the generation procedure on a small process example presented in Fig. 4. The whole process is activated upon occurrence of the event *Start*. Then the subprocess *P1* is launched. If *P1* terminates correctly, the event *Stop* is produced. However, *P1* execution can be interrupted by the event *Excpt*, which triggers the subprocess *P2*. After finishing *P2* a decision is made, whether the whole process should terminate (*abort*) or *P1* should be launched once again (*retry*).

The generated NuSMV code for the *main* module is presented in Fig. 4 below the ArchiMate diagram. It can be noticed, that variables definition

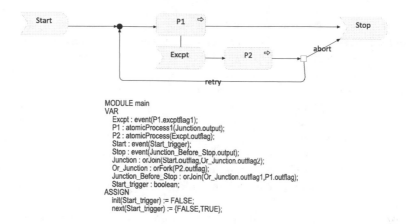

Fig. 4. Sample ArchiMate specification and corresponding NuSMV main module code

are unordered and the code contains forward references, e.g. the output variable `P1.excptflag1` is referenced before `P1` definition. The event *Stop* has two inputs. As the result of model refactoring an OrJunction (variable `Junction_Before_Stop`) was introduced into the model. For the event *Start* constituting a root element, the boolean variable `Start_trigger` with corresponding transition was added.

4.5 Generation of Specification

As a specification language we use CTL, which allows to formulate properties applying to a tree of computations (paths) starting from a given state. As the tree defines a set imaginable futures, CTL is called the branching time logic. CTL formulas are combinations of two types of operators *path quantifiers* and *linear-time operators*. The path quantifiers are: A (for every path in a tree) and E (there exists a path in a tree). Temporal operators include: G ($G\,p$ means that p holds true globally in the future) and F ($F\,p$ means that p holds true sometime in the future).

Typically a specification formally describing requirements is entered by a user. However, we tried to derive some *liveness* requirements based on control flows within ArchiMate model (see Definition 1). The implemented procedure generating a set of specifications comprises the following steps:

1. Build a set of paths $\Pi = \{\pi_i\}$ within the Archimate model,
2. Restrict elements in π_i to events only (elements from the set Evt)
3. Build a partial mapping $R\colon Evt \to 2^{Evt}$
4. Generate the specification for each pair $(e_i, R(e_i))$ in R

In the first step (1) a depth-first search starting from *roots* (ArchiMate elements having no predecessors) is performed. It returns a set of paths $\Pi = \{\pi_i\}$ comprising ArchiMate elements linked by control flow relation. For a path

$\pi_i = (e_{ib}, \ldots, e_{ie})$, its last element e_{ie} is either a final element in the model (without successors) or a branching element (already present in π_i). The set of obtained paths reflects only topological relations within the process model. The procedure does not attempt to interpret the model according to any behavioral semantics. This is left to the verification tool.

In the step (2) the paths from Π are restricted to ArchiMate elements being events. We decided to focus in requirements specification on elements of *Event* type, because in business process definitions they are typically used to mark important process states (e.g. initial, final and intermediate events).

In the next step (3) a partial mapping $R: Evt \to 2^{Evt}$ is built. The mapping R assigns all (potentially) reachable events to first events appearing in paths from Π

Finally, in the step (4) for each event $e \in \operatorname{dom} R$, a pair $(e, R(e))$ is converted into a set of specifications taking the form of (1), where $\mathcal{G} = \{AG, EG\}$, $\mathcal{F} = \{AF, EF\}$ and $\mathcal{O} = \{\bigvee, \bigwedge\}$.

$$\mathcal{G}((f \to \mathcal{F}(\underset{l_i \in R(f)}{\mathcal{O}} l_i))) \tag{1}$$

For the process presented in Fig. 4 an example of generated CTL specification is: `AG (Start.outflag -> EF (Stop.outflag | Excpt.outflag))`. It is equivalent to the statement: *for every path, starting with Start event, it is possible to reach a state, where Stop or Excpt events occur*. This requirement is obviously true. Another generated specification: `AG( Start.outflag -> AF( Stop.outflag & Excpt.outflag ))` is false, as justified by a counterexample path comprising 14 elements produced by NuSMV.

5   Business Process Example

In this section we present a more realistic example of ArchiMate specification describing a process of selling a product (a service) to a client. The process is divided into two stages: preparation presented in Fig. 5 and finalization (Fig. 6) separated by the event *Contract Prepared*. The finalization phase is far more complex. During execution of the *Acceptance* subprocess two events: *Timeout* and *Rejection* may occur and in consequence loop back the whole process to a previous stage. Contract signing by both parties, as well as *Implementation* and *Signed contract scanning* are placed between ArchiMate AndJunctions (forks and synchronization joins.)

Based on this specification the NuSMV model was generated. During refactoring phase second AndJoin in Fig. 6 was split into two (serving as join and fork). Another join was added before the interaction *Terms negotiation*. The *main* module of NuSMV comprised 22 finite state machines, whereas the flattened model consisted of 47 state variables. Considering their ranges, the whole state space comprised $3^9 \cdot 2^{37} \cdot 5 = 1.35 \cdot 10^{16}$ states, whereas the number of reachable states calculated by NuSMV based on the internal OBDD representation was equal to $7.039 \cdot 10^7$. The transition relation was total, i.e. no deadlocks were present.

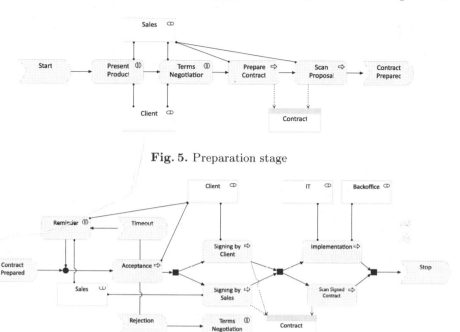

Fig. 5. Preparation stage

Fig. 6. Finalization stage

Examples of automatically generated specifications based on control flow are:

1. AG(Start.outflag ->
   AF(Stop.outflag | Timeout.outflag | Rejection.outflag))
2. AG(Start.outflag ->
   AF(Stop.outflag & Timeout.outflag & Rejection.outflag))

The first was checked to be true, whereas the second, as expected, occurred false. The path constituting a counterexample for the second specification comprised 42 states.

An example of a user-defined CTL specification equivalent to the statement that *all contracts signed by a client are finally scanned* is:
AG (Signing_by_Client.outflag ->(AF Scan_Signed_Contract.outflag)).
NuSMV reported is as true.

For the presented example verification of one CTL specification took about 43 seconds. However, after applying dynamic variable ordering this time decreased to 6.64 sec. We may conclude that although the state explosion is alleviated in NuSMV by employing internal OBDD representation, it seems that it still remains a problem. Hence, dedicated model generation techniques focusing on keeping models compact, e.g. generating partial models, should be employed.

6   Conclusions

This paper investigates the problem of automatic verification of behavioral specification embedded within ArchiMate models. We were motivated by an idea of developing a solution tightly integrated with Archi modeling tool that would allow to extract behavioral elements from an ArchiMate specification, then fully automatically translate it into a model in NuSMV language and finally verify it with the NuSMV model checker. Requirements specification in form of CTL formulas can be entered by user, but the implemented tool is capable of generating specifications based on analysis of control flows. We discuss methods of model transformation applied in the implemented software: language patterns used to model atomic processes and other elements, as well as rules for translating them into NuSMV modules. Finally, application of the method is presented on an example of a business process.

An issue that requires closer investigation is the time efficiency of the verification process. Surprisingly, papers discussed in Section 2, which claim to use the NuSMV model checker, do not provide evaluation data on complexity of verified processes and verification times. On the other hand, sample specifications distributed with NuSMV are built manually and optimized. The main factor influencing memory usage is the ordering of OBDD variables used in internal representation. Many NuSMV models are distributed with files defining ordering, which was determined by performing a separate optimization task.

ArchiMate is primarily a modeling language. It does not define semantics of behavioral elements. Application of certain modeling patterns and methods of translating them to a NuSMV language is an arbitrary decision related to assumed semantics. Probably, several options and alternatives controlled by program parameters should be considered.

References

1. Anderson, B., Hansen, J.V., Lowry, P., Summers, S.: Model checking for e-business control and assurance. IEEE Transactions on Systems, Man, and Cybernetics, Part C: Applications and Reviews **35**(3), 445–450 (2005)
2. Beauvoir, P.: Archi, archimate modelling tool (2015). http://www.archimatetool. com/ (accessed March 2015)
3. Bertoli, P., Cimatti, A., Pistore, M., Roveri, M., Traverso, P.: Mbp: a model based planner. In: Proc. of the IJCAI 2001 Workshop on Planning Under Uncertainty and Incomplete Information (2001)
4. Bryant, R.E.: Symbolic boolean manipulation with ordered binary-decision diagrams. ACM Computing Surveys (CSUR) **24**(3), 293–318 (1992)
5. Cimatti, A., Clarke, E., Giunchiglia, E., Giunchiglia, F., Pistore, M., Roveri, M., Sebastiani, R., Tacchella, A.: NuSMV 2: an opensource tool for symbolic model checking. In: Brinksma, E., Larsen, K.G. (eds.) CAV 2002. LNCS, vol. 2404, pp. 359–364. Springer, Heidelberg (2002)

6. Clarke, E., Heinle, W.: Modular translation of statecharts to smv. Tech. rep., Cite-seer (2000)
7. Clarke, E.M., Grumberg, O., Hiraishi, H., Jha, S., Long, D.E., McMillan, K.L., Ness, L.A.: Verification of the futurebus+ cache coherence protocol. Formal Methods in System Design 6(2), 217–232 (1995)
8. Clarke, E.M., Klieber, W., Nováček, M., Zuliani, P.: Model checking and the state explosion problem. In: Meyer, B., Nordio, M. (eds.) LASER 2011. LNCS, vol. 7682, pp. 1–30. Springer, Heidelberg (2012)
9. Clarke, E.M., Wing, J.M.: Formal methods: State of the art and future directions. ACM Computing Surveys (CSUR) 28(4), 626–643 (1996)
10. Deutsch, A., Hull, R., Patrizi, F., Vianu, V.: Automatic verification of data-centric business processes. In: Proceedings of the 12th International Conference on Database Theory, pp. 252–267. ACM (2009)
11. Fu, X., Bultan, T., Su, J.: Formal verification of e-services and workflows. In: Bussler, C.J., McIlraith, S.A., Orlowska, M.E., Pernici, B., Yang, J. (eds.) CAiSE 2002 and WES 2002. LNCS, vol. 2512, pp. 188–202. Springer, Heidelberg (2002)
12. Fuxman, A., Pistore, M., Mylopoulos, J., Traverso, P.: Model checking early requirements specifications in tropos. In: Proceedings of the Fifth IEEE International Symposium on Requirements Engineering, pp. 174–181. IEEE (2001)
13. Huuck, R.: Formal verification, engineering and business value. In: Olveczky, P.C., Artho, C. (eds.) Proceedings First International Workshop on Formal Techniques for Safety-Critical Systems, Kyoto, Japan, November 12, 2012. Electronic Proceedings in Theoretical Computer Science, vol. 105, pp. 1–4. Open Publishing Association (2012)
14. Klimek, R., Szwed, P.: Verification of ArchiMate process specifications based on deductive temporal reasoning. In: Ganzha, M., Maciaszek, L.A., Paprzycki, M. (eds.) Proceedings of the 2013 Federated Conference on Computer Science and Information Systems, Kraków, Poland, September 8–11, 2013, pp. 1103–1110 (2013). http://fedcsis.org/2013/
15. Klimek, R., Szwed, P., Jedrusik, S.: Application of deductive reasoning to the verification of ArchiMate behavioral elements. Informatyka Ekonomiczna 29, 76–97 (2013)
16. Mongiello, M., Castelluccia, D.: Modelling and verification of BPEL business processes. In: Fourth and Third International Workshop on Model-Based Development of Computer-Based Systems and Model-Based Methodologies for Pervasive and Embedded Software, MBD/MOMPES 2006, p. 5-pp. IEEE (2006)
17. Morimoto, S.: A survey of formal verification for business process modeling. In: Bubak, M., van Albada, G.D., Dongarra, J., Sloot, P.M.A. (eds.) ICCS 2008, Part II. LNCS, vol. 5102, pp. 514–522. Springer, Heidelberg (2008)
18. OMG: Business Process Model and Notation (BPMN) version 2.0. Tech. rep., OMG, January 2011. http://www.omg.org/spec/BPMN/2.0
19. Rumbaugh, J., Jacobson, I., Booch, G.: Unified Modeling Language Reference Manual, 2nd edn. Pearson Higher Education (2004)
20. Szpyrka, M., Biernacka, A., Biernacki, J.: Methods of translation of Petri nets to NuSMV language. In: Popova-Zeugmann, L. (ed.) Proceedings of the 23th International Workshop on Concurrency, Specification and Programming, Chemnitz, Germany, September 29 - October 1, 2014. CEUR Workshop Proceedings, vol. 1269, pp. 245–256. CEUR-WS.org (2014). http://ceur-ws.org/Vol-1269/paper245.pdf

21. Szwed, P., Chmiel, W., Jedrusik, S., Kadluczka, P.: Business processes in a distributed surveillance system integrated through workflow. Automatyka/Automatics **17**(1), 127–139 (2013)
22. The Open Group: Open Group Standard. Archimate 2.1 Specificattion. Van Haren Publishing, Zaltbommel (2013)
23. Watahiki, K., Ishikawa, F., Hiraishi, K.: Formal verification of business processes with temporal and resource constraints. In: 2011 IEEE International Conference on Systems, Man, and Cybernetics (SMC), pp. 1173–1180. IEEE (2011)

Time-Dependent Route Planning
for the Highways in the Czech Republic

Radek Tomis[(⊠)], Jan Martinovič, Kateřina Slaninová, Lukáš Rapant,
and Ivo Vondrák

IT4Innovations, VŠB - Technical University of Ostrava, 17. listopadu 15/2172,
708 33 Ostrava, Czech Republic
{radek.tomis,jan.martinovic,katerina.slaninova,lukas.rapant,
ivo.vondrak}@vsb.cz

Abstract. This paper presents an algorithm for dynamic travel time
computation along Czech Republic highways. The dynamism is represented by speed profiles used for computation of travel times at specified time. These speed profiles have not only the information about an
optimal speed, but also a probability of this optimal speed and the probability of the speed which represents the possibility of traffic incident
occurrence. Thus, the paper is focused on the analysis of paths with the
uncertainty created by traffic incidents. The result of the algorithm is
the probability distribution of travel times on a selected path. Based on
these results, it is possible to plan a departure time with the best mean
travel time for routes along the Czech Republic highways for a specified
maximal acceptable travel time. This method will be a part of a larger
algorithm for dynamic traffic routing.

Keywords: Time-dependent route planning · Speed profiles ·
Uncertainty · Traffic events · Floating car data

1   Introduction

Finding the fastest paths by travel time is a common feature of navigation services, because the efficient route planning on a road network saves time and
money of drivers. Traffic data about road networks can be used to obtain more
accurate results. However, most navigation services use only simple statistical
aggregates of historic travel times on roads for computation of the paths, even
though this is not sufficient if there are traffic incidents on the roads, so likely
on real road networks.

Finding the best route within the real road network is affected by a departure
time of the vehicle. Some roads can be congested at the time of rush hours, which
leads to larger delays. In such environment, route planning can be modelled as
time-dependent shortest path problem [14] with variable travel times as edge
weights. The resulting path is then determined by the departure time.

Dijkstra's algorithm [6] solves this problem if the non overtaking property
is guaranteed [4], stating that later departure can not lead to earlier arrival.

© IFIP International Federation for Information Processing 2015
K. Saeed and W. Homenda (Eds.): CISIM 2015, LNCS 9339, pp. 145–153, 2015.
DOI: 10.1007/978-3-319-24369-6_12

There are many adaptations and extensions of time-dependent Dijkstra's algorithm, for example Contraction Hierarchies [1] and SHARC [5]. These algorithms use some precomputed information to speed up the shortest path queries.

The main disadvantage of time-dependent route planning is that it does not take uncertain events into account. Travel times on the edges are computed as aggregates of available traffic data [15], even though this is not sufficient in many cases [7,9]. For example, if there are irregular but recurrent traffic congestions at some road, we should consider it in computation of the path and try to find another route [12]. Even though the probability of the congestion can be very low, the delay in the case the congestion happens can be very long. For this reason, we have to consider uncertain traffic events and their probabilities in the computation of the path [13,17].

Traffic incidents and congestions cause uncertainty of travel times. The main idea of this paper is to analyze paths with the uncertainty created by traffic incidents. Some paths are driven through more frequently than others and therefore it is desirable for drivers to know how travel times on these paths are affected by the traffic incidents. To achieve this, we need to extract information about the traffic incidents from the traffic data. The process of incident extraction as well as our algorithm and its continuity on traffic routing is described at section 3. Section 4 presents experiments of our algorithm.

We use the road network created from Traffic Message Channel (TMC) segments in the Czech republic, because it represents the backbone of the real road network and it covers the whole Czech republic evenly. TMC is also a standard used in GPS navigations.

2   Time-Dependent Route Planning with Probability

Some algorithms [2,3,10,16] try to find a solution for time-dependent shortest path problem in uncertain networks from the global point of view. The algorithms work on the whole network and try to minimize travel time with a set probability or to maximize the arrival probability with a set travel time. However, even in case of small traffic networks, the global approach is very time demanding. In the case of very large networks, it is impossible to compute all the possibilities across all the possible paths. There are broadly two approaches how to deal with this problem.

The first one is to use some form of precomputed results [11,17]. We do not consider this approach attractive. Thanks to the access to all sensors on Czech Republic highways, we can recompute speed profiles quite often, depending on the situation on the road. For example, it is sensible to recompute these profiles when the highway is undergoing reconstruction. Such frequent speed profile recomputation compromises all the performance advantages of routing based on pre-computation.

Therefore, we propose to use the second possible approach. This approach is based on some form of the problem simplification. It does the same as other algorithms, but from the different point of view. In the first step of our algorithm, several time-dependent shortest paths between two vertices are found (without their travel time uncertainty). In the second step, a probability function of travel time is computed on these paths. As the next step, we can analyze these results, compare them with each other, and suggest detours by identification of edges with the biggest travel time slow down or the arrival probability decrease. The choice of the best path can be based on various characteristics, like mean travel time or its variance. The progress of the algorithm can be summarized into the following steps:

1. Input origin, destination and desired departure time.
2. Perform deterministic dynamic routing to receive n best paths.
3. **Perform probabilistic travel time computation on these paths.**
4. Analyse received paths and their travel times to propose improvements (short detours or better departure time).
5. Recommend the best route and departure time based on preferred criterion.

The main aim of this paper is to propose a solution to the third step of the algorithm (highlighted by the bold font). The rest of the algorithm is currently under the development and will be published in the near future.

3   Probabilistic Travel Time Computation

The focus of this paper is on the computation of travel times and their probabilities on the selected path. Let $G = \{V, E\}$ be a directed graph created from a road network, where vertices represent intersections and edges represent roads. Our selected path starts at a vertex u and ends at a vertex v. We choose departure time t_d and compute time-dependent shortest path with optimal speed profiles as edge weights to obtain optimal path $P_o = \{u = v_0, e_0, v_1, e_1, \ldots, v_{n-1}, e_{n-1}, v_n = v\}$ by travel time for t_d, let's denote travel time of this path as t_o. Then we compute travel times and their probabilities for other combinations of speed profiles, which means travel times and their probabilities grow as binary tree with root node represented by u, leaf nodes represented by v and each path between u and v represents one specific combination of speed profiles. Binary tree is a tree data structure in which each node has at most two children. There can be any number of nodes in between u and v and exact number depends on a number of speed profiles.

The tree can be very large, so we have to introduce some constraints. We choose s as a percentage constraint of a maximum allowed slow down of computed paths compared to t_o. The computation of travel times and their probabilities is based on depth-first search on the sequence of edges $e_0, e_1, \ldots, e_{n-1}$ and at each vertex $v_i : i = 1, 2, \ldots, n$, we compute the actual travel time t_a to this vertex. Then we compute the remaining optimal time t_r as optimal time from v_i to v. The computation of the path for some given combination of speed profiles can be stopped if $t_a + t_r > (1 + s)t_o$, which means the tree does not have to be expanded at these vertices and is effectively truncated. The example of travel time tree is presented on Fig. 1. Some nodes are not expanded because

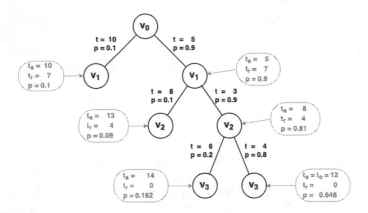

Fig. 1. Example of the specific travel time tree

they do not satisfy certain slow down condition s. See Algorithm 1 for pseudo code of our algorithm.

Algorithm 1 Compute travel time probabilities for given array of edges, departure time and slow down

```
 1: procedure TRAVELTIMEPROBABILITIES(edges, t_d, s)
 2:     t_m = maximum allowed time for given edges, t_d and s
 3:     push to stack {edge = edges[0], time = t_d, probability = 1}
 4:     while stack is not empty do
 5:         actual = pop from stack
 6:         edgeResults = GetTravelTimeProbabilities(actual)
 7:         for r in edgeResults do          ▷ r is a pair of t_a and probability
 8:             t_r = optimal remaining time from actual to end
 9:             t = r → t_a + t_r
10:             if t < t_m then
11:                 if actual → edge is last edge then
12:                     add r to result
13:                 else
14:                     push to stack {actual → nextEdge, r → t_a, r → probability}
15:                 end if
16:             end if
17:         end for
18:     end while
19: end procedure
```

The sum of all the leaf node probabilities is always 1. The probability of the situation in which the slow down is exceeded can be calculated as the sum of probabilities of the nodes not expanded to the end of the path.

4   Experiment

The experimental results of presented algorithm and their evaluation are presented in this section. The path from Praha to Brno along the highway D1 was chosen, because it is known that there are many traffic incidents on the highway D1, especially during its reconstruction. The path is composed of 84 road segments which means there are 84 edges on the path. Visualization of the path is presented on Fig. 2.

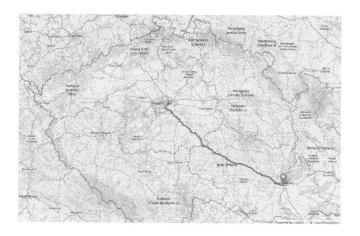

Fig. 2. Selected path from Praha to Brno

The speed profiles used in our experiments were computed from data, which was obtained due to online traffic monitoring by viaRODOS system [8]. The experimental set of data was extracted from two months (October and November 2014) with traffic work on the highway D1. Speed profiles contain sets of pairs of data in 15 minutes interval for each day of the week and each measured place. The first pair contains average speed from values equal or higher than 50 percent of LoS (Level-of-Service - the measured speed divided by the normal free flow speed) and probability of the occurrence of this state. The second pair is computed by the similar way, but from the values under 50 percent of LoS. The values with reliability equal to 0 were excluded from the speed profiles computation. You can see probability intensity computed from values under 50 percent LoS (traffic problems) in the Fig. 3.

Table 1 shows the comparison of our algorithm for three different departure times on Wednesday with maximum slowdown $s = 0.9$. The percentage of acceptable travel times indicates travel times lower than $(1 + s)t_o$. The expected value E and the standard deviation σ are computed only for acceptable travel times. As expected, E is higher at peak hours and higher values of σ points out to a bigger number of traffic incidents at that time.

Figures 4, 5 and 6 show probability distributions of acceptable travel times for previously mentioned departure times. We can observe that the distribution of

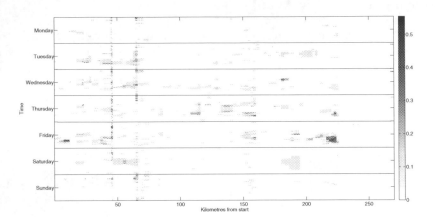

Fig. 3. Probability Intensity for values < 50% LoS

Table 1. Comparison of Different Departure Times

Travel Time	Departure Time		
	8:00	14:00	20:00
Acceptable [%]	89.3	67.7	100.0
Unacceptable [%]	10.7	32.3	00.0
E [min]	105.1	107.5	101.4
σ [min]	3.5	3.4	0.6

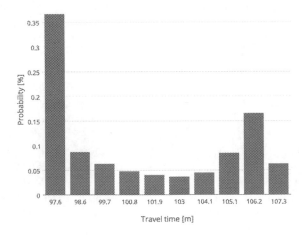

Fig. 4. Travel time probability distribution for departure time 8:00

probability is dependent on the departure time. As we can see in Fig. 5, bigger portion of probability is located around lower travel times. It is obvious that

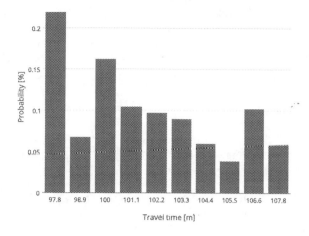

Fig. 5. Travel Time Probability Distribution for Departure Time 14:00

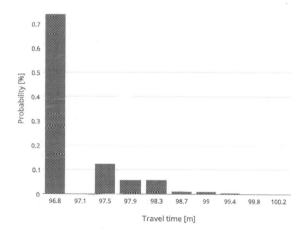

Fig. 6. Travel Time Probability Distribution for Departure Time 20:00

during afternoon is much higher traffic flow which often cause traffic incidents than in the morning or in the evening. Fig. 6 shows that evenings are much suitable for travelling.

5   Conclusion

In this paper, the method for time-dependent route planning with probability was presented. This method is based on the computation of the truncated binary tree. While it would be nigh impossible to compute the full binary tree for any sensible number of road segments, this truncation allows us to compute it efficiently even for long highways with many road segments. Our experiments on the D1 highway from Praha to Brno proved, that our algorithm is able to swiftly compute the percentage of arrivals faster than the threshold and presents their probability distribution. This algorithm has two main applications. It can either serve as a stand alone module for dynamic route planning or it can be a part of a larger dynamic routing algorithm, which is our goal for a near future. We are also planning to compare the results of our algorithm with Monte Carlo simulation, which seems to be a feasible solution to this problem.

Acknowledgments. This work was supported by the European Regional Development Fund in the IT4Innovations Centre of Excellence project (CZ.1.05/1.1.00/02.0070) and the national budget of the Czech Republic via the Research and Development for Innovations Operational Programme, by the project New creative teams in priorities of scientific research (reg. no. CZ.1.07/2.3.00/30.0055), supported by Operational Programme Education for Competitiveness, and co-financed by the European Social Fund and supported by "Transport Systems Development Centre" co-financed by Technology Agency of the Czech Republic (reg. no. TE01020155) and by the internal grant agency of VŠB Technical University of Ostrava, Czech Republic, under the project no. SP2015/157 'HPC Usage for Transport Optimisation based on Dynamic Routing.

References

1. Batz, G.V., Geisberger, R., Neubauer, S., Sanders, P.: Time-dependent contraction hierarchies and approximation. In: Festa, P. (ed.) SEA 2010. LNCS, vol. 6049, pp. 166–177. Springer, Heidelberg (2010)
2. Chen, B., Lam, W., Sumalee, A., Li, Q., Shao, H., Fang, Z.: Finding reliable shortest paths in road networks under uncertainty. Networks and Spatial Economics **13**(2), 123–148 (2013)
3. Chen, B.Y., Lam, W.H.K., Sumalee, A., Li, Q., Tam, M.L.: Reliable shortest path problems in stochastic time-dependent networks. Journal of Intelligent Transportation Systems **18**(2), 177–189 (2014)
4. Cooke, K.L., Halsey, E.: The shortest route through a network with time-dependent internodal transit times. Journal of Mathematical Analysis and Applications **14**(3), 493–498 (1966)
5. Delling, D.: Time-dependent SHARC-routing. In: Halperin, D., Mehlhorn, K. (eds.) ESA 2008. LNCS, vol. 5193, pp. 332–343. Springer, Heidelberg (2008)
6. Dijkstra, E.: A note on two problems in connexion with graphs. Numerische Mathematik **1**(1), 269–271 (1959)
7. Fan, Y., Kalaba, R., Moore, J.E.: Arriving on time. Journal of Optimization Theory and Applications **127**(3), 497–513 (2005)
8. Fedorčák, D., Kocyan, T., Hájek, M., Szturcová, D., Martinovič, J.: viaRODOS: monitoring and visualisation of current traffic situation on highways. In: Saeed, K., Snášel, V. (eds.) CISIM 2014. LNCS, vol. 8838, pp. 290–300. Springer, Heidelberg (2014)
9. Hofleitner, A., Herring, R., Abbeel, P., Bayen, A.: Learning the dynamics of arterial traffic from probe data using a dynamic bayesian network. IEEE Transactions on Intelligent Transportation Systems **13**(4), 1679–1693 (2012)

10. Hua, M., Pei, J.: Probabilistic path queries in road networks: traffic uncertainty aware path selection. In: Proceedings of the 13th International Conference on Extending Database Technology, pp. 347–358. ACM (2010)
11. Lim, S., Sommer, C., Nikolova, E., Rus, D.: Practical route planning under delay uncertainty: stochastic shortest path queries. In: Robotics: Science and Systems, vol. 8, pp. 249–256 (2013)
12. Miller-Hooks, E.: Adaptive least-expected time paths in stochastic, time-varying transportation and data networks. Networks, 35–52 (2000)
13. Nikolova, E., Brand, M., Karger, D.R.: Optimal route planning under uncertainty. In: ICAPS, vol. 6, pp. 131–141 (2006)
14. Orda, A., Rom, R.: Shortest-path and minimum-delay algorithms in networks with time-dependent edge-length. J. ACM 37(3), 607–625 (1990)
15. Rice, J., Van Zwet, E.: A simple and effective method for predicting travel times on freeways. IEEE Transactions on Intelligent Transportation Systems 5(3), 200–207 (2004)
16. Sun, S., Duan, Z., Sun, S., Yang, D.: How to find the optimal paths in stochastic time-dependent transportation networks? In: 2014 IEEE 17th International Conference on Intelligent Transportation Systems (ITSC), pp. 2348–2353. IEEE (2014)
17. Yang, B., Guo, C., Jensen, C.S., Kaul, M., Shang, S.: Multi-cost optimal route planning under time-varying uncertainty. In: Proceedings of the 30th International Conference on Data Engineering (ICDE), Chicago, IL, USA (2014)

Self Organizing Maps with Delay Actualization

Lukáš Vojáček[1,2]([✉]), Pavla Drázdilová[2], and Jiří Dvorský[2]

[1] IT4Innovations, VŠB - Technical University of Ostrava, 17. listopadu 15/2172,
708 33 Ostrava, Czech Republic
lukas.vojacek@vsb.cz
[2] Department of Computer Science, VŠB – Technical University of Ostrava,
17. listopadu 15/2172, 708 33 Ostrava, Czech Republic
{pavla.drazdilova,jiri.dvorsky}@vsb.cz

Abstract. The paper deals with the Self Organizing Maps (SOM).
The SOM is a standard tool for clustering and visualization of high-
dimensional data. The learning phase of SOM is time-consuming especially for large datasets. There are two main bottleneck in the learning
phase of SOM: finding of a winner of competitive learning process and
updating of neurons' weights. The paper is focused on the second problem. There are two extremal update strategies. Using the first strategy,
all necessary updates are done immediately after processing one input
vector. The other extremal choice is used in Batch SOM – updates are
processed at the end of whole epoch. In this paper we study update
strategies between these two extremal strategies. Learning of the SOM
with delay updates are proposed in the paper. Proposed strategies are
also experimentally evaluated.

Keywords: Self organizing maps · High-dimensional dataset · High
performance computing

1 Introduction

Recently, the issue of high-dimensional data clustering has arisen together with
the development of information and communication technologies which support
growing opportunities to process large data collections. High-dimensional data
collections are commonly available in areas like medicine, biology, information
retrieval, web analysis, social network analysis, image processing, financial transaction analysis and many others.

Two main challenges should be solved to process high-dimensional data collections. One of the problems is the fast growth of computational complexity
with respect to growing data dimensionality. The second one is specific similarity measurement in a high-dimensional space. Beyer et al. presented in [1]
that for the expected distance any point in a high-dimensional space, computed
by the Euclidean distance to the closest and to the farthest point, shrinks with
growing dimensionality. These two reasons reduce the effectiveness of clustering
algorithms on the above-mentioned high-dimensional data collections in many
actual applications.

© IFIP International Federation for Information Processing 2015
K. Saeed and W. Homenda (Eds.): CISIM 2015, LNCS 9339, pp. 154–165, 2015.
DOI: 10.1007/978-3-319-24369-6_13

The paper is organized as follows. In Sect. 2 we will describe one Self Organizing Maps. Section 3 describes parallel design of SOM learning algorithm. Modification of weights' update process is given in Sect. 4. Some experimental results are presented in Sect. 5. The paper is summarized and conslusions are made in Sect. 6.

2   Self Organizing Maps

Self Organizing Maps (SOMs), also known as Kohonen maps, were proposed by Teuvo Kohonen in 1982 [3]. SOM consists of two layers of neurons: an *input layer* that receives and transmits the input information, and an *output layer*, that represents the output characteristics. The output layer is commonly organized as a two-dimensional rectangular grid of nodes, where each node corresponds to one neuron. Both layers are feed-forward connected. Each neuron in the input layer is connected to each neuron in the output layer. A real number, *weight*, is assigned to each of these connections. i.e. weights of all connections for given neuron form *weight vector*. SOM is a kind of artificial neural network that is trained by unsupervised learning. Learning of the SOM is competitive process, in which neurons compete for the right to respond to a training sample. The winner of the competition is called *Best Matching Unit* (BMU).

Using SOM, the input space of training samples can be represented in a lower-dimensional (often two-dimensional) space [4], called a *map*. Such a model is efficient in structure visualization due to its feature of topological preservation using a neighbourhood function.

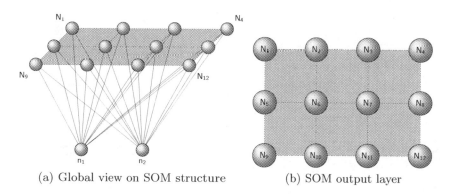

(a) Global view on SOM structure   (b) SOM output layer

Fig. 1. Basic Schema of SOM

3   Parallel SOM Learning Algorithm

A *network partitioning* is the most suitable implementation of the parallelization of an SOM learning algorithm. Network partitioning is an implementation of the learning algorithm, where the neural network is partitioned among the processes. Network partitioning has been implemented by several authors [2,9]. The parallel implementation proposed in this work is derived from the standard sequential SOM learning algorithm.

After analysing the serial SOM learning algorithm we have identified the two most processor time-consuming areas. These parts were selected as candidates for the possible parallelization. The selected areas were:

Finding BMU – this part of SOM learning can be significantly accelerated by dividing the SOM output layer into smaller pieces. Each piece is then assigned to an individual computation process. The calculation of Euclidean distance among the individual input vector and all the weight vectors to find BMU in a given part of the SOM output layer is the crucial point of this part of SOM learning. Each process finds its own, partial, BMU in its part of the SOM output layer. Each partial BMU is then compared with other BMUs obtained by other processes. Information about the BMU of the whole network is then transmitted to all the processes to perform the updates of the BMU neighbourhood.

Weight Actualization – Weight vectors of neurons in the BMU neighbourhood are updated in this phase. The updating process can also be performed using parallel processing. Each process can effectively detect whether or not some of its neurons belong to BMU neighbourhood. If so, the selected neurons are updated.

A detailed description of our approach to the parallelization process is described in Fig. 2.

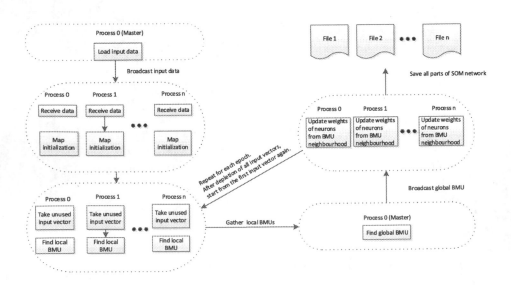

Fig. 2. Improved Parallel SOM Algorithm

Before any implementation of an experimental application began, we had to decide how the parallelization would be done. Initially, we supposed that the most effective approach is to divide the SOM into several parts or blocks, where each block is assigned to the individual computational process. For example, let's suppose that an SOM with neurons $N = 20$ in the output layer is given. The output layer is formed as a rectangular grid with number of rows $N_r = 4$ and number of columns $N_c = 5$. Then the output layer of the SOM is divided into 3 continuous blocks which are associated with three processes[1].

To remove the unbalanced load, the approach to the parallelization process has been modified. The division of the SOM output layer was changed from a block load to a cyclic one. The individual neurons were assigned to the processes in a cyclic manner. A nearly uniform distribution of the output layer's neurons among processes is the main advantage of this kind of parallelization. The uniform distribution of the neurons plays an important role in weight actualization because there is a strong assumption that neurons in the BMU neighbourhood will belong to different processes. An example of a cyclic division of the SOM output layer with a dimension of 4×5 neurons can be seen in Fig. 3, where each neuron is labeled with a color of assigned process. A more detailed description of parallelization can be found in our previous papers (including a full notation)[6,8].

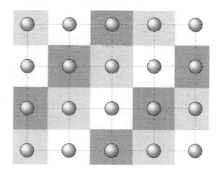

Fig. 3. Cyclic Division

4   Delay Actualization

In this modification of the SOM algorithm we focused on the area called *finding BMU*. Only in the parallel version is it necessary to find the global BMU from the local BMUs in each iteration and here are two areas, by which we will discuss:

1. To find the global BMU we must transfer a lot of data between processes.

---

[1] If there is no possibility of dividing the output layer into a block with the same number of neurons, some blocks have one extra neuron.

2. This waiting mode (blocking communication), where other processes and threads awaiting the outcome, will decrease the efficiency of parallel computation.

The method described below is based on information that with the same amount of data it is effective to send data all at once instead of sending in portions. Both problems mentioned above are solved this way. The proof about transfer data is in Table 1, where 1 to 64 processes are used and transferred 50 thousand and 500 thousand numbers of all processes on a single process, but in one case we send all of these numbers together and in the second case separately - at one time two numbers together. For clarity, the number of data that are transfer from individual processes is always the same. Only the total number of data that are finally placed on the target process is changing. For example, if we have 6 processes and 50k numbers, so we have on the target process saved $6 \times 50k$ numbers. From these results it is possible to see that the final times for both amounts (50k and 500k) and for sending data together are the very similar.

For data transmission, the MPI functions *Gather*[2] are used and the processes are running on separate computing nodes, which are connected by the Infiniband network.

Table 1. Comparison of data transmission

Processes	Time [sec]			
	50k		500k	
	Separate data	Together data	Separate data	Together data
1	0.0199089	0.0000188	0.197716	0.000154018
2	0.146948	0.030802	2.06079	0.031806
4	0.316004	0.062149	3.14302	0.0727129
8	0.487644	0.142774	5.09625	0.153242
16	0.67049	0.304665	6.58546	0.30529
32	0.785121	0.627432	8.63451	0.633787
64	0.959224	1.26573	9.81402	1.25528

The second point, which we mentioned above, concerns the utilization of individual processes or threads (both parallelization operate on the same principle, see previous article [6]). As we mentioned earlier we divide the SOM algorithm into two parts: The first part concerns the search for the BMU (the fast part) and the second part concerns updating weight (time-consuming part). The delay occurs in the situation where some processes (threads) must update more neurons than the other processes (threads), an example can be seen in Fig. 4. Where the process number two must update three neurons, but other processes must update only two neurons. If the update does not occur after each iteration, but only after a certain time, it is possible to reduce the impact of blocking communication. Individual processes will not have to wait for other processes and utilization processes should be uniform. It is because of two reasons:

1. A BMU is usually different with each iteration and therefore neurons which must be updated are different.
2. The number of neurons to be updated decreases, but at the beginning of the algorithm 1/4 of all neurons are updated. An important factor that affects the distribution is training data and unfortunately this cannot be anticipated.

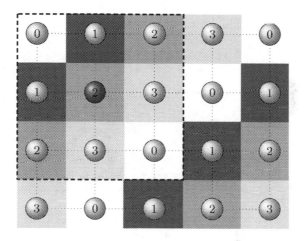

Fig. 4. Example of actualization area

According to the above examples our goal is aggregate data which are transmitted and we propose the following approach to update the weights:

The base is the parallel solution which we described in Sect. 3, where at the beginning limit of delay – L is set for how many local BMU can be kept in the local memory in each process. Each processes find the local BMU and save the result in the local memory. If the limit is not reached, it is necessary to read the new input vector and find a new local BMU. If the limit is reached all local BMUs are moved to a process with rank 0, which finds a global BMU for each iteration and then sends results to all processes. After this step each process gradually updates the weights.

We worked with three variants of the above described algorithm:

1. *Constant delay (Cons)* – Size of L is the same throughout the calculation.

2. *Decreasing delay (Dec)* – Size of L is decreasing by ζ at the start of each epoch to 1.

3. *Increasing delay (Inc)* – The value of how many local BMUs can be kept in the local memory is set at 1 and increases by ζ at the end of the each epoch until it reaches L.

For a complete description of the algorithm is to be noted that ζ is applied at the end of each epoch (only for variants *Dec* and *Inc*). Setting the value of ζ, for variants *Dec* and *Inc* largely depends on the number of input vectors M. Therefore we are working with a percentage of M. It is used for settings L and ζ. In the chapter experiments we attempted to show how much influence the value of ζ is. For example: $L = 10\%$ of M, $\zeta = 0.1\%$ of M.

Here it is necessary to briefly recall the behaviour of the neural network SOM. Over time, the number of updated neurons is changing – decreases. At the beginning, most of the neurons are updated but at the end only the few neurons or only one neuron are. If variant *Dec* is used, delay gradually decreases by ζ and also the number of neurons that must be updated. In variant *Inc* it is the opposite, by the number of updated neurons still decreases but the delay increases.

5   Experiments

We will describe different datasets and we will provide experiments with bigger and smaller limit of delay – L. The mean quantization error (MQE) is used to compare the quality of the neural network method which it is described in paper [5].

5.1   Experimental Datasets and Hardware

Weblogs Dataset. A Weblogs dataset was used to test learning algorithm effectiveness on high dimensional datasets. The Weblogs dataset contained web logs from an Apache server. The dataset contained records of two months worth of requested activities (HTTP requests) from the NASA Kennedy Space Center WWW server in Florida[2]. Standard data preprocessing methods were applied to the obtained dataset. The records from search engines and spiders were removed, and only the web site browsing option was left (without download of pictures and icons, stylesheets, scripts etc.). The final dataset (input vector space) had a dimension of 90,060 and consisted of 54,961 input vectors. For a detailed description, see our previous work [7], where web site community behaviour has been analyzed.

On the base of this dataset 15,560 user profiles were extracted and the number of profile attributes is 28,894 (this number corresponds to the dimension of input space) for the final dataset.

Experimental Hardware. The experiments were performed on a Linux HPC cluster, named Anselm, with 209 computing nodes, where each node had 16 processors with 64 GB of memory.The processors in the nodes were Intel Sandy

---

[2] This collection can be downloaded from http://ita.ee.lbl.gov/html/contrib/NASA-HTTP.html.

Bridge E5-2665. Compute network is InfiniBand QDR, fully non-blocking, fat-tree. Detailed information about hardware can be found on the website of Anselm HPC cluster[3].

In this section we describe experiments which are based on delay actualizations. For the experiment, we examine the quality of the resulting neural networks and the time that is required for calculation. The type of parallelization of SOM is a combination of MPI and OpenMP.

5.2   First Part of the Experiment

The first part of the experiments was oriented towards an examinination of the quality of neural networks which depends on the size of the delay. The dataset used is Weblogs. All the experiments in this section were carried out for 1000 epochs; the random initial values of neuron weights in the first epoch were always set to the same values. The tests were performed for SOM with rectangular shape – 400×400 neurons. All three variants shown in section 4, are tested. If variants *Inc* or *Dec* are used, then the steps ζ are as follows 0.1%, 0.01%, 0.005%. MQE errors are presented for limit of delays L equal 5%, 10% and 20% in Table 2. Step size does not affect the variant *Cons*. Therefore, this method has only one value instead of three in the above table.

Table 2. MQE depends to limit of delay actualization

Steps	MQE								
[%]	Delay L = 5%			Delay L = 10%			Delay L = 20%		
	Inc	Dec	Cons	Inc	Dec	Cons	Inc	Dec	Cons
0.100	1.71474	0.54016	1.71477	1.7792	0.55492	1.77917	1.79262	0.56304	1.87535
0.010	1.66801	0.55741	1.71477	1.68754	1.10173	1.77917	1.69227	1.68584	1.87535
0.005	1.66795	1.08419	1.71477	1.67759	1.67199	1.77917	1.68192	1.69745	1.87535

5.3   Second Part of the Experiment

The second part of the experiments were oriented towards scalability. As in the previous test, experiments are carried out on three types of delays (increasing, decreasing and constant). The parallel version of the learning algorithm was run using 16, 32, 64, 128, 256, 512, and 1024 cores respectively. The achieved computing time is presented in the Table 3 for step $\zeta = 0.1\%$, in Table 4 for step $\zeta = 0.01\%$, in Table 5 for step $\zeta = 0.005\%$. In the above tables the variant *Cons* is presented (it is not affected by the step – all three tables contains same values), the reason is comparison resulting times. For comparison, the standard SOM algorithm (without any delay) takes 32:10:30 computing time and MQE is 0.4825.

---

[3] https://support.it4i.cz/docs/anselm-cluster-documentation/hardware-overview

Table 3. Scalability of delay actualization – step $\zeta = 0.1\%$

Cores	Computing Time [hh:mm:ss]								
	Delay L = 5%			Delay L = 10%			Delay L = 20%		
	Inc	Dec	Cons	Inc	Dec	Cons	Inc	Dec	Cons
16	12:24:19	27:04:58	12:13:49	12:17:21	23:47:34	11:53:06	12:11:46	18:35:00	11:47:09
32	5:11:19	13:11:54	5:05:59	5:10:21	11:30:02	5:00:52	5:32:45	8:41:41	5:04:13
64	1:45:20	6:13:49	1:42:12	1:43:16	5:14:24	1:38:14	1:51:56	3:43:40	1:39:23
128	0:45:11	3:15:36	0:43:53	0:43:37	2:44:05	0:41:10	0:47:00	1:53:40	0:40:44
256	0:24:08	1:57:26	0:23:18	0:22:57	1:38:43	0:21:13	0:23:43	1:10:33	0:20:50
512	0:15:53	1:24:03	0:15:21	0:14:34	1:11:20	0:13:18	0:15:53	0:53:07	0:12:59
1024	0:17:34	1:25:12	0:16:54	0:15:36	1:17:37	0:14:23	0:17:25	1:03:08	0:14:05

Table 4. Scalability of delay actualization – step $\zeta = 0.01\%$

Cores	Computing Time [hh:mm:ss]								
	Delay L = 5%			Delay L = 10%			Delay L = 20%		
	Inc	Dec	Cons	Inc	Dec	Cons	Inc	Dec	Cons
16	13:54:21	14:19:45	12:13:49	13:18:46	13:04:25	11:53:06	13:20:08	12:21:52	11:47:09
32	5:28:27	6:17:04	5:05:59	5:36:31	5:29:52	5:00:52	6:03:48	5:36:57	5:04:13
64	1:54:03	2:20:04	1:42:12	1:57:10	1:57:31	1:38:14	2:12:01	1:57:21	1:39:23
128	0:49:31	1:10:31	0:43:53	0:50:53	0:53:14	0:41:10	0:59:19	0:50:42	0:40:44
256	0:24:29	0:43:56	0:23:18	0:24:48	0:29:53	0:21:13	0:29:52	0:24:51	0:20:50
512	0:15:42	0:35:07	0:15:21	0:15:57	0:21:29	0:13:18	0:19:33	0:16:00	0:12:59
1024	0:17:21	0:46:27	0:16:54	0:16:36	0:25:57	0:14:23	0:21:34	0:16:50	0:14:05

Table 5. Scalability of delay actualization – step $\zeta = 0.005\%$

Cores	Computing Time [hh:mm:ss]								
	Delay L = 5%			Delay L = 10%			Delay L = 20%		
	Inc	Dec	Cons	Inc	Dec	Cons	Inc	Dec	Cons
16	13:09:47	13:01:33	12:13:49	14:09:51	12:24:42	11:53:06	14:09:44	12:11:29	11:47:09
32	6:03:58	5:31:41	5:05:59	6:03:42	5:14:13	5:00:52	6:00:06	5:10:09	5:04:13
64	2:12:38	1:53:28	1:42:12	2:12:17	1:47:21	1:38:14	2:10:08	1:42:41	1:39:23
128	0:59:15	0:53:32	0:43:53	0:59:27	0:44:41	0:41:10	0:57:51	0:42:06	0:40:44
256	0:31:50	0:28:44	0:23:18	0:30:36	0:23:02	0:21:13	0:28:24	0:21:46	0:20:50
512	0:21:17	0:19:46	0:15:21	0:20:01	0:14:46	0:13:18	0:17:56	0:13:46	0:12:59
1024	0:22:38	0:22:14	0:16:54	0:21:46	0:16:07	0:14:23	00:19:04	0:14:06	0:14:05

Conclusion of Delay Experiments. In this section an evaluation of the above described experiments can be found. The reason this evaluation is discussed in a separate part is that the overall evaluation of effectiveness can not only be based on individual results. It is necessary to focus on a combination of outcomes for finding the optimal solution.

From the first experiment, which was focused on the quality of the final neural network, we can deduce the following conclusions:

1. As we expected, with the increasing size of the local memory, the overall quality of the neural networks is deteriorating. This behavior is evident in all three types of delays.

2. The variant *Cons* was in all three cases the worst.

3. According to these results, the variants *Inc* and *Dec* fundamentally differ from each other. When we use the variant *Dec*, the subsequent decrease of the value of the delay deteriorates the quality of the neural networks, but when we use the variant *Inc*, the quality of the neural network improves; it is not a significant change in the same way as in the *Dec*.

The second experiment was focused on the scalability and the time consumption of the above variants. We describe the results of the experiments as follows:

1. Even though the variant *Cons* is independent of the value steps ζ it still achieves the fastest computing time.

2. When the variant *Cons* and the variant *Inc* are used, the time difference between the delay (5%, 10% and 20%) is only a small percent - almost negligible. However, the variant *Dec* reaches time differences of up to 60%.

3. When 16 cores are used and step $\zeta = 0.1\%$ so the variant *Inc* is much faster (more than twice) than the variant *Dec*. Again, using 16 cores and at step $\zeta = 0.01\%$ times are in both the above variants almost comparable. However, when step $\zeta = 0.005\%$ is used, the variant *Dec* is slightly faster than the variant *Inc*.

If we look only at the individual results according to the first experiment, the overall best results are obtained with the variant *Dec* (delay $L = 5\%$ and step $\zeta = 0.1\%$) and the worst results are obtained with the variant *Cons*. The second experiment shows that the variant *Cons* is the fastest and the variation *Inc* is minimally affected by the delay amount. After comparing all the achieved results and the required time to calculate them, we have identified as the best variant *Dec* (delay $L = 5\%$ and step $\zeta = 0.01\%$) with computing time 0:35:07 and MQE 0.55741.

An example of limit values achieved for delay $L = 5\%$ is possible to see in Fig. 5 where we can see the methods *Inc* and *Dec* with step $\zeta = 0.1\%, 0.01\%$

and 0.005%. The step ζ value has a major impact on the overall result, because it determines the time when the above method reaches the maximum permitted delay or vice versa, when they reach the minimum delay.

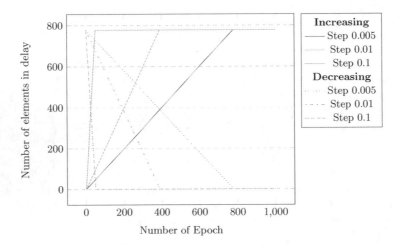

Fig. 5. Example of achievement delay 5%

6   Conclusion

The experiments have shown the possibility of speeding up the computation of actualizing the weights while maintaining the sufficient quality of the final neural network. Speeding up the calculation of the SOM algorithm is based on updating the weights after several (delay L) input vectors. It is similar to Batch SOM, which updates the weights after one epoch. The actualization process for variant *Dec* calculates the values of the weight roughly at the beginning and the next calculation in this variant leads to a more accurate calculation of the weights using the decreasing value of the delay. Overall, the best results are achieved for the variant *Dec* with the smallest test delay ($L = 5\%$) and a mean step ($\zeta = 0.01\%$). This variant is quickly approaching the standard SOM with weight actualization after each input vector. With the initial actualization for the smallest test number of delays, this variant *Dec* is faster than the standard SOM (*Dec* for cores = 16, $L = 5\%$, $\zeta = 0.01\%$ takes 14:19:45 and the standard SOM for 16 cores takes 32:10:30). Further acceleration is due to the massive parallelization, when the best time is achieved for 512 cores (0:35:07). Even faster is the variant with $\zeta = 0.005\%$, but the MQE of this variant is twice as big and therefore less accurate.

Acknowledgments. This work was supported by the IT4Innovations Centre of Excellence project (CZ.1.05/1.1.00/02.0070), funded by the European Regional Development

Fund and the national budget of the Czech Republic via the Research and Development for Innovations Operational Programme, as well as Czech Ministry of Education, Youth and Sports via the project Large Research, Development and Innovations Infrastructures (LM2011033), supported by the internal grant agency of VŠB Technical University of Ostrava, Czech Republic, under the project no. SP2015/114 "HPC Usage for Analysis of Uncertain Time Series" and also this work was supported by SGS, VSB - Technical University of Ostrava, Czech Republic, under the grant No. SP2015/146 "Parallel processing of Big Data 2".

References

1. Beyer, K., Goldstein, J., Ramakrishnan, R., Shaft, U.: When is "nearest neighbor" meaningful? In: Beeri, C., Bruneman, P. (eds.) ICDT 1999. LNCS, vol. 1540, pp. 217–235. Springer, Heidelberg (1998)
2. Gropp, W., Lusk, E., Skjellum, A.: Using MPI: portable parallel programming with the message-passing inferace. MIT Press (1999)
3. Kohonen, T.: Self-Organization and Associative Memory. Springer Series in Information Sciences, vol. 8, 3rd edn. Springer, Heidelberg (1989)
4. Kohonen, T.: Self Organizing Maps, 3rd edn. Springer-Verlag (2001)
5. Lawrence, R., Almasi, G., Rushmeier, H.: A scalable parallel algorithm for self-organizing maps with applications to sparse data mining problems. Data Mining and Knowledge Discovery **3**(2), 171–195 (1999)
6. Martinovič, J., Slaninová, K., Vojáček, L., Draždilová, P., Dvorský, J., Vondrák, I.: Effective Clustering Algorithm for High-Dimensional Sparse Data based on SOM. Neural Network World **23**(2), 131–147 (2013)
7. Slaninová, K., Martinovič, J., Novosád, T., Dráždilová, P., Vojáček, L., Snášel, V.: Web site community analysis based on suffix tree and clustering algorithm. In: Proceedings - 2011 IEEE/WIC/ACM International Conference on Web Intelligence and Intelligent Agent Technology - Workshops, WI-IAT Workshops 2011, pp. 110–113 (2011)
8. Vojáček, L., Dvorský, J., Slaninová, K., Martinovič, J.: Scalable parallel som learning for web user profiles. In: International Conference on Intelligent Systems Design and Applications, ISDA, pp. 283–288 (2014)
9. Wu, C.H., Hodges, R.E., Wang, C.J.: Parallelizing the self-organizing feature map on multiprocessor systems. Parallel Computing **17**(6-7), 821–832 (1991)

Biometrics and Biometrics Applications

Person Identification Technique Using RGB Based Dental Images

Soma Datta[✉] and Nabendu Chaki

Department of Computer Science and Engineering, University of Calcutta, 92 APC Road,
Kolkata 700009, India
soma21dec@yahoo.co.in, nabendu@ieee.org

Abstract. Dental signature captures information about teeth, including tooth contours, relative positions of neighboring teeth, and shapes of the dental work. However, this is complicated as dental features change with time. In this paper, we proposed a new, safe and low cost dental biometric technique based on RGB images. It uses three phases: image acquisition with noise removal, segmentation and feature extraction. The key issue that makes our approach distinct is that the features are extracted mainly from incisor teeth only. Thus the proposed solution is low cost besides being safe for human.

Keywords: HSI color format · Wiener filtering · Opening · Watershed · Snake

1 Introduction

Person identification based on human teeth is very popular in the world. Generally, dental records have been used to identify the victims of disasters like 9/11 terrorist attack, Asian tsunami [1] etc. According to these facts there are many advantages of using dental biometrics. It is very possible to identify an unidentified (mutilated) body by comparing the post-mortem (PM) records against ante-mortem records. This will produce the closest match of multiple identities [2]. Dental biometric system based on radiograph images are also able to identify the correct person from a large set of database where manual method fails. Dental biometrics is worked upon the radiograph images. Frequently taken x-ray is very injurious to our health. The radiation of used X-Ray changes our DNA structure that leads to cancer [3]. One question naturally comes to our mind that can we use dental biometric on living people? The answer is 'yes' off-course we can by taking the RGB based dental image. The other reasons for choosing dental biometrics are as follows

1. It is very precise and correct.
2. We don't need an expert to treat and compare the result.
3. It is not easy to replicate the dental signature.

The primary contribution of this research work is to propose a three phase novel technique for RGB dental image based authentication and verification using biometrics. Our proposed method takes the RGB images of human teeth, extract the features

© IFIP International Federation for Information Processing 2015
K. Saeed and W. Homenda (Eds.): CISIM 2015, LNCS 9339, pp. 169–180, 2015.
DOI: 10.1007/978-3-319-24369-6_14

[1] like shape; contour; length etc. Depending on the features system will take the decision whether record is matched or not. This will be the extended version of this re-search work. There are so many good biometrics methods other than dental are exist. Among them retina scan is invasive in nature and it is injurious to our eyes. For finger print, iris detection [4, 5, 6, 7] special type of device set-up is needed where as dental image can be taken by any kind of camera. Hence to identify a person at any place is possible by only carrying the camera and this application. However this system does not require any extra high cost device like retina scan requires Topcon retinal camera and its cost is $15,995. Hence it is very less cost device comparative to other biometrics devices. This method is safe to our health. For this reason dental signature based biometrics method is helpful. Here we extracted the features of five incisor teeth. Hence we can say that RGB based dental biometrics is advantageous with respect to speed, storage requirement and human health.

2   Related Review Work on Dental Biometrics

Before starting of this work, we have gone through many good dental biometrics methods. Most of these methods work upon the dental radiographs. Here some of them are explained shortly. Anil K. Jain and Hong Chen dedicated a concept of semi-automatic contour extraction method for shape extraction and pattern matching [8]. The main problems in their approach are if the image is too blurred, their algorithm will not work and slight angle deviation in the database image and incoming images may not be handled with this approach. Said et al. [9] offered a mathematical morphology approach, which used a series of morphology filtering operations to improve the segmentation. Morphological filters like top hat and bottom filters are used for tooth segmentation. Nomir and Adbel-Mottaleb introduced a fully automated segmentation technique [10]. It starts by applying iterative thresholding followed by adaptive thresholding to segment the teeth from both the background and the bone areas. After adaptive thresholding, horizontal integral projection followed by vertical integral projection is applied to separate each individual tooth. And this method can achieve the position of each tooth precisely. All of the above method works on the radiograph dental images where as our proposed method works on dental RGB image.

3   Proposed Method

This research work describes up to the dental biometrics features extraction procedure. Fig 1 shows the entire system. Image acquisition and filtering is the first step. For de-noising Winer filter is used. In the first phase of this method conventional methods are used that are described in the next sub sections in short. In the segmentation phase only the tooth region are segmented based on morphological operations. Segmentation of individual tooth is done by using the 'watershed' and 'snake' algorithm. In the last step the features like volume, size, area etc are extracted from the incisors teeth.

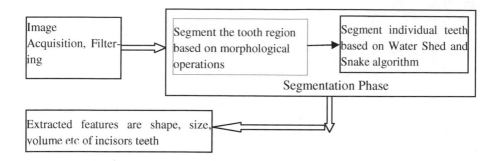

Fig. 1. Block diagram of the system.

3.1   Image Acquisition and Filtering

We worked upon freely available database named 'Labial Teeth and Gingiva Image Database' [11]. Here dental images are different for resolution, file format and image scene type. Due to easiness of our research work we transform each image into jpeg format. All the rest of the works are based on these jpeg images. The qualities of the images that are obtained from the sensor camera are not so good, some noises exist. To remove these noises we used 'Winer' filter.

3.2   Segmentation

Segmentation phase contains two sub phases. The phases are 'Segment the tooth region based on morphological operations' and 'Segment individual teeth based on Water Shed and Snake algorithm'. The next subsections describe how the teeth are extracted finally.

Information Extraction

It is not so easy to extract only tooth region from the entire input image. The input image contains white space surrounded by the green color, lips, some part of face etc. These regions should be eliminated from the ROI. It is very challenging to separate the teeth and non-teeth region based on Red, Green and Blue component. Sometimes it fails to find the exact ROI due to the variation of white color that present in the teeth. Hence we have used HSI color model [12]. The meaning of HSI color model is Hue (H), Saturation (S) and Intensity (I). The HSI color model described more exact color than the RGB color. Though HIS color model is non-uniform in perception, still it is one of the most popular color models for color image processing. The another advantage of using HSI color model is that it has human-intuitional advantages such as color image enhancement, fusion, skin area detection, segmentation, color based object detection etc. The RGB to HSI color model conversation is done by using the following equations:-

$$H = \begin{cases} \theta & if \ B <= G \\ 360^{0} - \theta & otherwise \end{cases} \tag{1}$$

Where

$$\theta = \cos^{-1}\left\{ \frac{\frac{1}{2}[(R-G)+(R-B)]}{\sqrt{(R-G)(R-B)+(R-B)(G-B)}} \right\}$$

$$S = 1 - \frac{3}{(R+G+B)} * [\min (R,G,B)] \qquad (2)$$

$$I = (R+G+B)/3 \qquad (3)$$

Where, H stands for Hue i.e. pure color, S for saturation, i.e. the degree by which the pure color is diluted using white light and I for intensity i.e. Gray level. Fig 2.a shows the corresponding saturation image of the input image in fig 3. Saturation component contains a lot of information for both tooth and background region. So it is very difficult to extract only teeth region from background from saturation component. As a consequence hue and intensity components are used to segment ROI and after that saturation component is used for feature extraction.

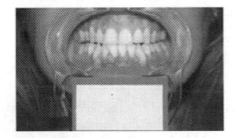 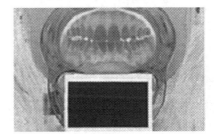

Fig. 2. Input Image   **Fig. 2a.** Corresponding saturation Image

Region of Interest (ROI) Extraction

After information extraction, the initial segmentation is done based on the hue and intensity component of the image. In this phase the hue and intensity component are multiplied pixel-wise. Now this is converted into binary image using self updating threshold method [13]. It stores the intensities of the pixels in an array. The threshold is calculated by using total mean and variance. Based on this threshold value each pixel is set to either 0 or 1. i.e. background or foreground. Thus here the change of image takes place only once. Suppose f(i,j) is the gray-scale value at pixel (i, j), and Ti is the segmentation threshold value at step i. To obtain a new threshold value, we have to threshold the original image using Ti to separate the image into teeth areas and non-teeth areas, where μ_i^0 and μ_i^1 are the mean gray values for the two areas.

$$\mu_i^0 = \left(\sum ((i,j) \in f(i,j))/no\_pixel \right) \qquad (4)$$

$$\mu_i^1 = \left(\sum ((i,j) \in background - f(i,j)) / no\_pixel \right) \qquad (5)$$

The threshold value for step i+1 can be obtained as

$$T_{i+1} = (\mu_0 + \mu_1)/2 \qquad (6)$$

Procedure: Binarization
Assumption: Null
Input: Teeth image
Output: Binary image of the given teeth image

> *Step 1. Select an initial estimate of the threshold T.*
> *Step 2. Calculate the mean grey values $\mu0$ and $\mu1$ of the partition, R1, R2.*
> *Step 3. Partition the image into two groups, R1, R2, using the threshold T.*
> *Step 4. Select a new threshold as T= ($\mu0 + \mu1$)/2 *
> *Step 5. Repeat step 2-3 until the mean value $\mu0, \mu1$ values in successive iteration are equal.*
> *Step 6. End*

Fig. 3a. Output after using Binarization.   **Fig. 3b.** After applying *Fainting_Nameplate*

In Fig3.a the name plate portion of the image is mostly visible. This is not required at all, hence to remove this unwanted region we used the following procedure remove_nameplate.

Procedure: Fainting_Nameplate
Assumption Presence of the Nameplate as specified in [11]
Input: hue and intensity image of the given teeth image, threshold_value obtain in Binarization algorithm
Output: Teeth image where Nameplate area is filled with threshold_value

> *Step 1 temp= image(hue)*image(intensity) // Pixel wise multiplication of hue and saturation and store it into temp variable.*
>
> *Step 2 Take the size of temp and store them in two different variable, [r, c] =   size(temp).*
> *Step 3 Start loop i=1 to r*
> *Start loop j=1 to c*
> *if(g(i,j)>=1)*
> *temp2(i,j)= threshold_value / Ti+1;*
> *End Loop*
> *End Loop*
> *Step4 End*

Again we used procedure Binarization upon Fig 3.b to get the image where teeth region and name plate both are present. Next task is to remove the name plate region. It is done by subtracting fig 3.a from fig 4.a, shown in fig 4.b.

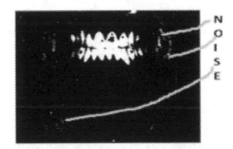

Fig. 4a. After applying 2 times Binarization   **Fig. 4b**. Only teeth region with noise

In fig 5.b some noise are present. Noises have been removed using erosion followed by dilation [12] technique. Erosion erodes contours so small contours are removed but it also shrinks the desired contours. Dilation recovers the looses areas. Now the contours contains only tooth region. Algorithm3 is used to find the final ROI which is a subset of input image. Algorithm 3 accepts the saturation components (Sat_Mat) and binary mask (B_Mask) of tooth region which is cleaned by erosion and dilation techniques. The dilation of A by B, denoted, is defined as the set operation.

$$A \oplus B = \left\{ z \mid \hat{B}_z \cap A \neq \phi \right\} \tag{7}$$

Where Ø is the empty set and B is the structuring element. In words, the dilation of A by B is the set consisting of all the structuring element origin locations where the reflected and translated B overlaps at least one element of A. The erosion of A by B, denoted, is defined as

$$A \ominus B = \left\{ z \mid (B)_z \cap A^c = \phi \right\} \tag{8}$$

Here, erosion of A by B is the set of all structuring element origin locations where no part of B overlaps the background of A.

Procedure: Find_ROI
Assumption: Nameplate should be removed from the binary image.
Input: saturation matrix, binary matrix after applying Remove_Nameplate
Output: exact teeth image

Step1: *// Averaging is required to suppress the detail information*
$(Avg\_Sat\_Mat)_{40*40} = average\_filter(Sat\_Mat)_{40*40}$
Step2:   for all point in b_mask where b_mask(row,col)==1
        V_Point (index,1)= row
        V_Point(index,2)=col   *// Storing row and col-*
umn
Step3: $\forall(I,j)$ do
       {
    Avg_Sat_Mat(V_Point.row,V_Point.col)=
    Sat_Mat(V_Point.row,V_Point.col)
    }
    //End Loop
Step4: *// Avg_Sat_Mat contains detail information about the tooth region and   suppress information for background.*
    $Max\_row = max(V\_Point_{1st}\,column)$
     $Min\_row=min(V\_Point_{1st}\,column)$
    $Max\_Col=max(V\_Point_{2nd}\,column)$
    $Min\_Col=min(V\_Point_{2nd}\,column)$
Step6:   *ROI_sub_image =*
    Avg_Sat_Mat[(Min_row,Min_row+1,.....,Max_row),
    (Min_Col, Min_col+1,....,Max_col)]
Step7: End

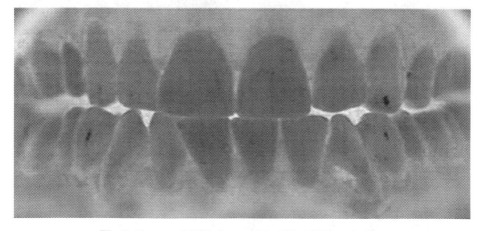

Fig. 5. The actual ROI after applying *Find_ROI* on fig 5.b

Segment Individual Tooth

In this step the individual teeth are segmented using mainly watershed [14] and snake active contour model [15] followed by some morphological preprocessing. Fig 5 is converted into its equivalent binary image using algorithm1 shown in Fig 6. Now we have segmented each contour using opening operation [12] shown in Fig 7.

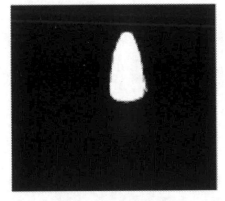

Fig. 6a. Binary image of Fig 5   **Fig. 6b.** After applying Opening on Fig 5

In dental biometry it is not required to find the features of all the teeth. We have taken five incisors tooth for which features have been extracted. These teeth are shown in Fig 8. After opening operation we have pointed out the incisors tooth.

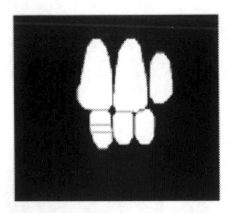

Fig. 7. After applying Watershed incisor are segmented

Fig. 8. Segmented contour after label matrix are Technique.

Now each contour has been identified by applying the label matrix technique [12] shown in Fig 8. The boundary of the contour is detected by using boundary detection algorithm as follows.

Procedure: Find_boundary
Assumption: Input image contains only single teeth.
Input: Teeth image after applying Watershed algorithm
Output: Boundary points of the teeth region.

Step 1 Set A to be empty ; From bottom to top and left to right scan the cells of T until a black pixel, s, of x is found.
Step 2 Insert s in A ; Set the current boundary point x to s or x=s
Step 3 Move to the pixel from which s was entered. Set c to be the next   pixel in M(x).
Step 4 While c not equal to s do
$$If\ c = 0$$
insert c in A
set x=c
Move the current pixel c to the pixel from which x was entered

else
add the current pixel c to the next clock-wise pixel in M(x)

end if
End While
Step 5 End

The label matrix technique has used for getting the approximate boundary points of the tooth. After that snake active contour algorithm has been used to detect the exact individual tooth region as shown in Fig 9, Fig 10.

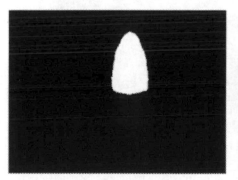
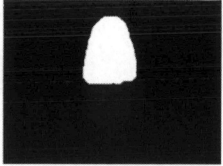

Fig. 9. incisors_central_1 Contour   **Fig. 10.** incisors_central_2 Contour

In the last phase the features are extracted teeth wise. We have extracted features of the incisor teeth from right maxilla, left maxilla, right mandible and left mandible. The binary contour of each tooth (teeth_contour) is given as the input of the system. The algorithm returns the features of the teeth.

Procedure: Feature_Extraction
Assumption: Input image must contains only one teeth.
Input: Individual tooth image

Output: Features like height, width, CG_Row (CG_Row and CG_Col points are the row and column value of the centre points of a tooth) etc

---

Step1 Determine the position of each segmented teeth; i.e. upper jaw or lower jaw. In teeth_contour find the number of pixel whose value is 1 for each row. Store the result in jaw_vector_array. If (jaw_vector(i) <= jaw_vector(i+1)) is true for almost all element of jaw_vector then that tooth belongs in the upper jaw.

Step2 // finding the width and height of each teeth.

$\qquad\qquad$ *Width = maximum _value(jaw_vector)*

$\qquad\qquad$ *Height = number of non zero elements in jaw-vector*

$\qquad\qquad$ *The ratio of these two is independent to zoom.*

Step3 //find volume of each teeth

$$Volume = \sum_{i=1}^{i=sizeof(jaw\_vector)} jaw\_vector(i)$$

Step4 // find the CG co-ordinate for each teeth contour

$$CG\_row = (\sum row\_no\_nonzero\_pixel)/total\_pixel\_positions$$

$$CG\_col = (\sum col\_no\_nonzero\_pixel)/total\_pixel\_positions$$

Relative positions of CG points vary with the width of the teeth. CG points are helpful to determine the relative position.

$\quad$*Step5 Stop*

---

4   Result

After applying procedure Feature_Extraction we got the following data for five teeth that mentioned in the table given below. This method can be applied on all of the remaining tooth. If we apply this algorithm to all 32 teeth then processing time will be much more higher than the proposed method and storage space requirement will be again coonsiderably high. However that case accuracy will be much higher. Similarly we can find the features of the tooth. Here for simplicity we have mentioned the features of incisors_central_1, incisors_central_2, incisors_central_3, incisors_central_1 and incisors_lateral (discussed in introduction).

Table 1. The calculated featured of individual teeth

Teeth Name	Width	Height	Volume	CG-Row	CG-Col
incisors_central_1	208	256	38100	240	427
incisors_central_2	196	256	36965	243	615
incisors_central_3	156	245	32145	495	625
incisors_central_4	150	244	31120	495	480
incisors_lateral	157	242	31560	493	405

5   Discussion and Conclusion

In this research work we proposed a system by which the features of the incisors tooth have been extracted. We have worked upon Labial Teeth and Gingiva Image Database [20]. We have applied the algorithm upon 270 data from set 1 to set 6 in Labial Teeth and Gingiva Image Database. Our proposed method can correctly find out the features from these sample dental images. In the next phase of this research work these features will be matched with the database. To extract the tooth contour from the entire tooth region we have used watershed and snake algorithm. Sometimes it happens that these methods are unable to detect exact tooth contour due to the less 'gap-valley' area. Even if the proposed dental biometrics approach is a low cost solution, dental signatures do change with time. A dental signature change due to accidents, dental work and as human grows up. Hence biometrics method based on dental signature is not 100% accurate. Our future plan is to develop low cost, multimodal biometrics method based on dental signature and ear pattern which will be more accurate towards identifying a person.

Acknowledgement. Authors are thankful to Dr. Satyabrata Biswas for providing relevant knowledge and the "TEQIP Funded CoE Project", at Computer Science & Engineering Department, Calcutta University, for providing infrastructural facilities during the progress of the work.

References

1. Choorat, P., Chiracharit, W., Chamnongthai, K..: A single tooth segmentation using structural orientations and statistical textures. In: Biomedical Engineering International Conference (BMEiCON), 2011, pp. 294–297. IEEE (2012)
2. Chen, H., Jain, A..: Dental biometrics: alignment and matching of dental radiographs. In: Application of Computer Vision WACV/MOTIONS 2005, vol. 1, pp. 316–321. IEEE (2005)
3. Siltanen, S., et al.: Statistical inversion for medical x-ray tomography with few radiographs: I. General theory. Physics in medicine and biology **48**(10), 1437–1464 (2003)
4. http://www.topconmedical.com/categories/imaging-retinalcameras.htm
5. Ito, K., et al.: A fingerprint recognition algorithm using phase-based image matching for low-quality fingerprints. In: IEEE International Conference on Image Processing, ICIP 2005, vol. 2, pp. 2–33 (2005)
6. Jea, T.Y., Govindaraju, V.: A minutia-based partial fingerprint recognition system. Pattern Recognition **38**(10), 1672–1684 (2005). Elsevier
7. Javad, H., Fatemizadeh, E.: Biometric identification through hand geometry. In: The International Conference on Computer as A Tool, EUROCON, 2005, vol. 2, pp. 1011–1014. IEEE (2005)
8. Jain, A.: Matching of dental X-ray images for human identification. Pattern recognition **37**(7), 1519–1532 (2004)

9. Shah, S., et al.: Automatic tooth segmentation using active contour without edges. In: Biometrics Symposium: Special Session on Research at the Biometric Consortium Conference, 2006. IEEE (2006)
10. Nomir, O., Mottaleb, A..: Human identification from dental X-ray images based on the-shape and appearance of the teeth. IEEE Transactions on Information Forensics and Security 2(2) (2007)
11. Labial Teeth and Gingiva Image Database, Color Imaging Laboratory, Department of Optics University of Granada, Spain, Set 1: undried oral cavity, Part 1/1
12. Gonzalez, R.C., Richard, R.E.: Woods, digital image processing, 2nd edn. Prentice Hall Press (2002). ISBN 0-201-18075-8
13. Liu, Y., Sargur, N.: Document image binarization based on texture features. IEEE Transactions Pattern Analysis and Machine Intelligence 19(5), 540–544 (1997)
14. Kass, M.: Snakes:Active Contour Models. International Journal of Computer Vision, 321–331 (1988)
15. Roerdink, J., Meijster, A.: The Watershed Transform – Definition Algorithm and parallelization Strategies. Foundamental Informatica, vol. 41, pp. 187–228. IOS Press (2001)

A Novel Double Fault Diagnosis and Detection Technique in Digital Microfluidic Biochips

Sagarika Chowdhury[1(✉)], Rajat Kumar Pal[2], and Goutam Saha[3]

[1] Department of Computer Science and Engineering,
Narula Institute of Technology, Kolkata, India
sagsaha2004@gmail.com
[2] Department of Computer Science and Engineering,
University of Calcutta, Kolkata, India
pal.rajtk@gmail.com
[3] Department of Information Technology,
North Eastern Hill University, Shillong, India
dr_goutamsaha@yahoo.com

Abstract. This paper presents a rigorous offline double fault diagnosis as well as a detection technique for Digital Microfluidic Biochips (DMFBs). Due to the underlying mixed technology biochips exhibit unique failure mechanisms and defects. Thus, offline and online test mechanisms are required to certify the dependability of the system. In this paper, the proposed algorithm detects double faults anywhere in the chip satisfying the dynamic fluidic constraints and improves the fault diagnosis time to an extent.

Keywords: Biochip · Droplet · LOC · Micro-fluidic technology · Fluidic constraints

1 Introduction

An integrated microfluidic device incorporates many of the necessary components and functionality of a typical room-sized laboratory onto a small chip [1]. These composite micro-systems, also known as lab-on-a-chip (LOC) (or bio-MEMS), offer a number of advantages over the conventional laboratory procedures and enable the handling of small amounts, e.g., micro- and nanolitres of fluids [2].

Droplet routing on the surface of the microfluidic biochip has been attracting much attention in recent years as it is one of the key issues to make use of the digital microfluidic device efficiently [3].

Microfluidic biochips have been characterized for the detection of faults [4], [5], [6], [7]. The test planning problem was formulated in terms of Euler circuit in [6], [7]. In [8], a functional testing has been proposed, referring to [4], [10], [11] that targets the functional operations of the microfluidic modules. Su *et al.* have proposed a defect tolerance based on graceful degradation and dynamic reconfiguration [9]. A network flow based routing algorithm has been proposed in [12] for the droplet routing problem on biochips [13]. An efficient diagnosis technique has been enhanced in [14] by

© IFIP International Federation for Information Processing 2015
K. Saeed and W. Homenda (Eds.): CISIM 2015, LNCS 9339, pp. 181–192, 2015.
DOI: 10.1007/978-3-319-24369-6_15

Xu *et al.* such that multiple defect sites can be efficiently located using parallel scan-like testing. A more advanced multiple fault detection technique has been proposed in [16] by Chowdhury *et al.* in much less time compared to some previous techniques. However, it is not supported by the concept of Fluidic constraints, which has been explained in [15].

This paper addresses the issue of double fault diagnosis and detection technique in digital microfluidic based biochips through a graph-theoretic formulation.

The rest of the paper is organized as follows: Section 2 presents the preliminaries of microfluidic arrays, their defect characterization, and the graph-theoretic formulation. Section 3 explains the proposed technique. Experimental results are reported in Section 4. Conclusions are drawn in Section 5.

2   Preliminaries

2.1   Structure of a Microfluidic Array

In digital microfluidic biochips, each droplet can be independently controlled by the electrodynamic forces generated by an electric field [13]. Compared to the first generation biochips (analog), droplets can move anywhere in a 2D array to perform the desired chemical reactions, and electrodes can be re-planned for the different bioassays.

There are three key components in a biochip: 2D microfluidic array, dispensing ports/reservoirs, and optical detectors [13]. The 2D microfluidic array contains a set of basic cells, which handle droplet movement. The dispensing ports/reservoirs handle droplet generation, and the optical detectors are used for reaction detection.

2.2   Defect Characterization

As has been described in [4], faults in digital microfluidic systems can be classified as being either catastrophic or parametric. Catastrophic faults cause a complete breakdown of the system while parametric faults degrade the system performance. To detect a fault, we need to pass a droplet across the cells so that it can traverse the whole path and reach towards the sink. If there is any defect within the microarray, the droplet gets stuck there. Otherwise, it reaches the sink at a predefined time.

With the use of electrowetting phenomenon, droplets can be moved to any location in the given 2D array. However, it should be taken care that each of the droplets is satisfying the observable fact of fluidic constraints described in [15]. Only then the incidence of droplet collision is reduced.

3   Proposed Technique

Detection of a single fault in the biochip has reached at its end. However, diagnosis and detection of multiple faults are complex. Thus, let us start with more than one fault. Assume that, there are at most two faults in the biochip. The proposed technique takes a greedy approach to solving double fault detection technique. It tries to visit all the boundary nodes of $G_{m \times n}$ during the first and second pass (that are P1 and P2) starting from source to sink. Remaining edges and nodes are traversed in subsequent passes P3, P4, and so on through certain movement patterns, which are explained below.

3.1 Movement Patterns

Column traversal from the source to the sink is based on one kind of movement expressed in Fig. 1 as Down-Left-Down-Right (DLDR). Let $v_{i,j}$ be the current node during a traversal.

See Fig. 1(a) to understand the movement Down-Left-Down-Right (DLDR) as follows, where the value of i (j) increases from top to bottom (left to right):

$$v_{i,j} \xrightarrow{D} v_{i+1,j} \xrightarrow{L} v_{i+1,j-1} \xrightarrow{D} v_{i+2,j-1} \xrightarrow{R} v_{i+2,j}$$

The sink can be reached from the source by the following appropriate sequence of movements mentioned above. Example 1 presents such a journey from source to sink.

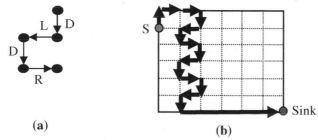

(a) (b)

Fig. 1. (a) Movement patterns. (b) A path from source to sink following the proposed movement pattern of DLDR.

Example 1: Fig. 1(b) shows a graph dual $G_{7 \times 7}$ digital microfluidic array. The source is at position (2, 1), and the sink is at (7, 7). The graph has 36 nodes and 60 edges. The journey from source to sink with the proposed pathway is indicated with solid arrows.

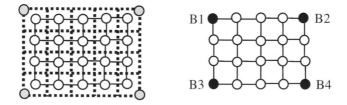

Fig. 2. Four base nodes at a graph dual of $G_{4 \times 4}$.

3.2 Strategy

We locate four fixed nodes as the 'base' nodes from where the journey with the prescribed movement patterns begins. For the graph dual $G_{m \times n}$ these base nodes are $B_1 = v_{1,1}$, $B_2 = v_{1,n}$, $B_3 = v_{m,1}$, and $B_4 = v_{m,n}$. These four base nodes are shown in Fig. 2 for $G_{m \times n}$.

It is proposed that, irrespective of the source position, the traversal of the cells starts from any one of the nearest base point following the complete procedure.

3.3   The Complete Procedure

The complete process is as follows for a test array of size *M×N*.

Procedure

Begin /* Assume source is at Base 1 and sink at (M, N) */

Step I: **Boundary Test 1:** A test droplet is dispensed from the source, and it traverses the boundary region clockwise and moves to the sink, as shown in Fig. 3(a).

Step II: **Boundary Test 2:** The second test droplet is dispensed with a delay of two units' time slice from the source and it traverses the boundary region anti-clockwise and moves to the sink, as shown in **Error! Reference source not found.**(b).

If BT1 and BT2 fail, it ensures at most two faults are at the boundary region. Hence, go for *Detect_Fault_UB* algorithm and *Detect_Fault_SB* algorithm. Skip steps three and four. Otherwise, proceed to step three.

Step III: **Row Test:** Two iterations of parallel scan-like test with one row shift are carried out, having the time delay of two units during dispense of each droplet. The test movement pattern of row test is shown in Fig. 4. Thus, in iteration 1, all the even rows are traversed and in iteration 2 all the odd rows are covered. After the first iteration, there should be a delay of two units' time.

After row test, the defected rows can be identified easily, following the arrival report of the droplets at the sink.

Now to further *reduce* the testing area of the chip, let us identify the region of the affected rows following algorithm *Reduce_Area* (Fig. 5).

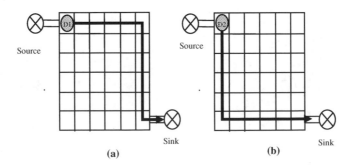

Fig. 3. (a) Boundary Test I, where droplet #1 and time slice T_1. **(b)** Boundary Test II where droplet #2 and time slice T_4.

Algorithm *Reduce_Area*

1. If the affected rows are in the upper region, i.e. between row #1 to floor ($M/2$) of the chip, then divide it into two halves in such a way, so that, the divider passes just next to the one row, which is affected last (Fig. 5(a)).
2. Else if the affected rows are in the lower region, i.e. after floor ($M/2$) row number of the chip, then divide the chip into two halves in such a way, so that the divider passes just before the row, which is affected first (Fig. 5(b)).
3. Else divide the chip into two halves keeping faulty rows in both the halves (Fig. 5(c)), so that column test can be carried out in those two halves in parallel.

If the row test is satisfactory but BT1 and/or BT2 are not adequate, then consider Case 1.

Else if, row test is not agreeable, but BT1 and BT2 are satisfactory, then consider Case 2 and go to Step IV.

Else if row test is not acceptable and so for BT1 and/or BT2, then consider Case 3 and go to Step IV.

Else it ensures that the row test, BT1 and BT2 all are good enough. Thus, the chip is free from any fault.

Step IV: **Column Test:** Delay for two units. Repeat parallel scan-like test (for two iterations) for the columns, following DLDR movement patterns. Three units of time delay against dispersion of every droplet and four units of time delay during second iteration are required. These movements are explicitly shown in Fig. 6.
End Procedure

3.4 Analysis and Detection of Faults

The total time required for the entire process is the sum of the required time for Step I, Step II, Step III, and Step IV if they are carried out sequentially. Step III and Step IV are to be performed if only they are required.

As there can be double faults anywhere in the chip, including *boundary*, let us discuss their possible positions on the chip sequentially.

Case 1: Assuming two faults are anywhere at the boundary, i.e. the rest of the chip is fault free. Thus, the faults may be in the following locations:

- Two faults at the upper/lower boundary, or
- Two faults at the right/left side boundary, or
- One fault at the upper/lower boundary, other at the side boundary, or
- One fault at the upper boundary, other at the lower boundary.

If BT1 fails, but BT2 succeeds, then there may be one / two faults at the boundary. Consequently, go for Row Test. If Row Test succeeds, follow *Reduce_Area* algorithm described earlier. Then go for the following:

1. Consider sink at the end of the first row and perform boundary checking, starting from source to sink.
2. If the droplet does not reach, then the upper boundary region is faulty.

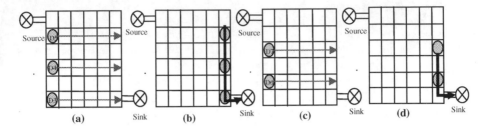

Fig. 4. Row_Test. (**a**) Iteration 1: droplet #3 at time slice T_7, droplet #4 at time slice T_{10}, and droplet #5 at time slice T_{13}. (**b**) Three droplets follow the last column to the sink. (**c**) Iteration 2: droplet #6 at time slice T_{18} and droplet #7 at time slice T_{21}. (**d**) Two droplets follow the last column to the sink.

3. Follow algorithm *Detect_Fault_UB*.
4. Next, delay for two units of time and send another droplet, from second row towards the end of that row and then downwards to sink, following side boundary. If it reaches properly, no fault in the right side region. Otherwise, there is a fault. Then follow algorithm *Detect_Fault_SB* .

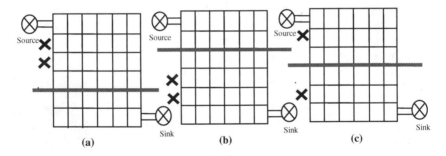

Fig. 5. Chip divider algorithm. (**a**) Affected rows are in the upper region. (**b**) Affected rows are in the lower region. (**c**) Affected rows are in any of the regions.

Algorithm *Detect_Fault_UB: /* Detect Fault(s) in Upper Boundary region*/*
Assume the source at $(1, 1)$ location and the sink at (M, N) location.

1. Disperse a droplet from source to the second column.
2. Go downwards by one row.
3. Go to the last column of that row and then to the sink.
4. After dispensing a droplet, a next droplet is dispersed after two units' delay.
5. Repeat Steps 1 through 4 incrementing the column number by one until a droplet fails to reach the sink in proper time.
6. When a droplet does not reach to the sink, then the interleaving column of the first row is detected as the *defective* cell.
   Once an affected cell is found, do the following:
7. Send the next droplet just before to the affected cell.
8. Go downwards by one row.

9. Follow the right way and go upwards, so that the very next cell to the affected one at the boundary get touched.
10. Go to the last column of that row and then to sink.
11. After dispensing a droplet, a next droplet is dispersed after two units' delay.
12. Repeat Steps 7 through 11 as shown in Fig. 7, until a droplet succeeds to reach the sink in proper time.

Following the last droplet that may fail to reach the sink in time, we can straightwardly identify the *defective* cell.

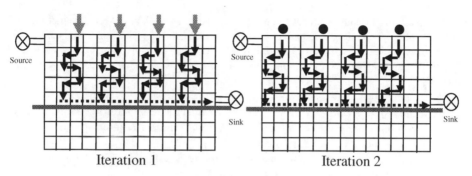

Iteration 1   Iteration 2

Fig. 6. Column_Test following *DLDR* movement patterns.

Algorithm *Detect_Fault_SB: /* Detect Fault in Side Boundary region */*

1. If the upper boundary is satisfactory, but the side boundary is not all right, then make source at $(1, n-1)$ location and follow algorithm *Detect_Fault_UB* to identify fault at the side boundary.
2. Else if the upper boundary is faulty as well as the side boundary, then go for Row Test and detect the faulty row.

It is justified that the intersecting points of row and side boundary are treated as the faulty cell, as we have assumed that there can be at most two faults in the chip.

E.g., if the fault is at $(M-3, N)$ location, then more than one droplet set for row test must fail to reach the sink. In that case, for the last droplet, which fails to reach the sink, the intersecting point of row path and side boundary can be detected as faulty (Fig. 8).

Case 2: Boundary is passable. Thus, two faults are anywhere in the chip, other than the boundary.

Go for the Complete Procedure as discussed in Section 3.3. After performing column test, we can have several scenarios to be discussed further.

1. If two adjacent column tests fail to pass droplets against one affected row, then there must be one common intersecting point, which is affected definitely (Fig. 9(a)).
2. Else, if two adjacent column tests fail to pass droplets, against two of the affected rows, then we are getting six considerable points among which two may be faulty (Fig. 9(b)). Thus, detection can be done afterward. Fig. 10 shows it clearly.

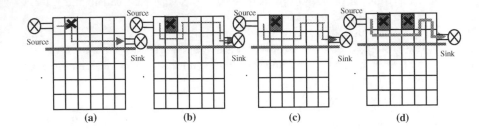

Fig. 7. Detection of double faults at the upper boundary of the chip. (**a**) First droplet fails to reach the sink, so the fault is at cell #2. (**b**) Second droplet fails to reach the sink, but cannot say whether the fault is on cell #3. (**c**) Third droplet fails to reach the sink, but cannot say whether the fault is on cell #4. (**d**) Fourth droplet succeeds to reach the sink. Thus, cell #4 is certainly faulty.

3. Else if one column test fails to pass droplet against one affected row, then two considerable points are there, of which one has not gone for column test. Thus, that non-traversed point is the faulty one (Fig. 9(c)).
4. Else if one column test fails, against two of the affected rows, then there are exactly two infected cells to be identified for sure (Fig. 9(d)).

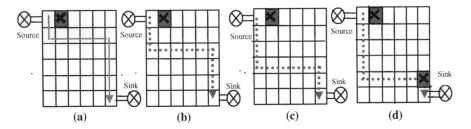

Fig. 8. Traversing through (a) to (d) while detecting the fault at the side boundary.

Case 3: One fault is at the boundary and the other is anywhere in the chip.

Consider an example 2, where the graph dual of $G_{7\times7}$ depicts that it has an error at cell #2, i.e. on the upper boundary and at cell #25. Now, according the proposed method, BT1 will fail while BT2 will succeed to reach towards the sink in specified time. Therefore, we go for Row test and definitely, we will get row #4 as faulty. Hence, after performing algorithm *Reduce_Area*, it looks like the picture as shown in Fig. 11(a).

Now, perform algorithm *Detect_Fault_UB* and it will detect a fault at cell #2.

At this instant, droplet #D_1 of Column Test at Iteration 2 fails to reach the sink. Thus, the intersecting point of row #4 and the path traversed by D_1 during column test at iteration 2 is cell #25, as discussed in *Case 2(b)*. Fig. 11(b) shows this clearly.

The detection time is compared with some existing technique. It shows that the proposed one is much superior compared to the other. Moreover, the proposed technique satisfies the dynamic fluidic constraints as well.

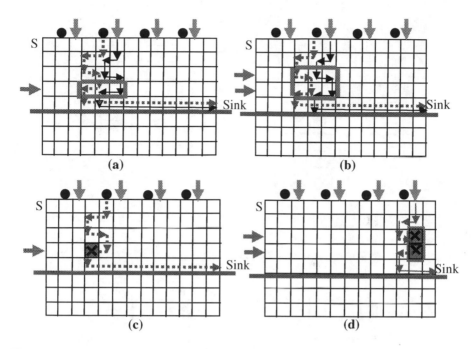

Fig. 9. Fault analysis for Case 2, where ➡ indicates affected row, ➡ indicates column traversed in the first iteration, and ● indicates column traversed in the second iteration.

4   Experimental Results

Extensive offline testing has been done with a large number of arrays varying from 4×4 to 60×60 electrodes. Table I reports the details of the microarray. Table II reports the performance of the proposed technique, viz. the existing technique [14]. The performance of the proposed technique is divided into two columns: Proposed (min) and Proposed (max).

The proposed method not only diagnoses double faults in the chip, but it also detects the location. To test $N \times N$ target array, Boundary Test 1 and Boundary Test 2 are carried out first, and the methods take $2N+2$ units' time. Next, row test is performed; in each iteration, this takes N units of time. Thus, up to this step, the proposed technique takes $4N$ units' time slice. After that, the $N \times N$ target array be partitioned into two halves, and the column test is performed in parallel. Here, if one has to go for column test, then it takes $2N/2$, i.e. N units time slice in each iteration. Hence, as a whole it takes $6N$ units time slice. Therefore, the total fault diagnosis procedure includes $6N$ steps, i.e. $O(N)$, and compared to parallel scan-like test and multiple defect diagnosis [14], which has $8N$ steps, the time needed for this diagnosis is reduced.

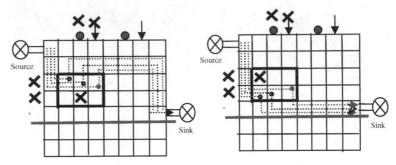

Fig. 10. Detection of double fault for Case 2(b).

Columns 6 and 7 of Table II show the percentage (%) improvement in each case. This is defined as:

% improvement = ((Existing Time − Proposed Time) × 100) / Existing Time

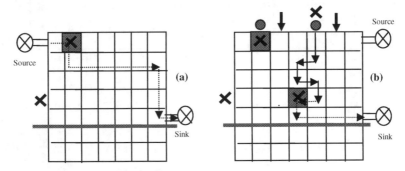

Fig. 11. Double Fault Detection through Example 2 for Case 3.

It can be seen that the proposed method has an improvement over time at about 12.5% minimum and 37.5% maximum. Table II shows the case-wise result, as discussed earlier. It shows that the proposed technique achieves improvement to a great extent.

Table 1. Test case details

Sl. No.	Size	Source	Sink	Total Edge
1	4×4	1, 1	4, 4	24
2	5×5	1, 1	5, 5	40
3	6×6	1, 1	6, 6	60
4	10×10	1, 1	10, 10	180
5	20×20	1, 1	20, 20	760
6	20×25	1, 1	20, 25	980
7	30×30	1, 1	30, 30	1740
8	40×40	1, 1	40, 40	3120
9	50×50	1, 1	50, 50	4900
10	60×60	1, 1	60, 60	7080

Table 2. Performance of the proposed technique

Sl. No.	Existing [14]	Time Slice Required						% improvement in Diagnosis	
		Proposed							
		Case 1		Case 2		Case 3		(Min)	(Max)
		Diag-nosis	Detec-tion	Diag-nosis	Detection (max)	Diag-nosis	Detec-tion		
1	32	20	24	24	32	28	28	12.5	37.5
2	40	25	30	30	40	35	35	12.5	37.5
3	48	30	36	36	48	42	42	12.5	37.5
4	80	50	60	60	80	70	70	12.5	37.5
5	160	100	120	120	160	140	140	12.5	37.5
6	200	125	150	150	200	175	175	12.5	37.5
7	240	150	180	180	240	210	210	12.5	37.5
8	320	200	240	240	320	280	280	12.5	37.5
9	400	250	300	300	400	350	350	12.5	37.5
10	480	300	360	360	480	420	420	12.5	37.5

5   Conclusion

Efficient fault detection in a microfluidic biochip is an indispensable activity, as it is often used to operate in critical circumstances. In this paper, an advanced double fault detection technique has been proposed, which yields better results compared to some existing methods. Also, it satisfies the phenomenon of dynamic fluidic constraints. Thus, the chances of collision between two droplets are reduced. The proposed algorithm can detect any fault in the boundary region too. Therefore, further case studies can be done so that, not only double fault at the boundary, but more than two faults can be identified.

References

1. Erickson, D., Li, D.: Integrated Microfluidic Devices. Proc. Elsevier, Analytica Acta **507**, 11–26 (2004)
2. Chakrabarty, K., Su, F.: Design Automation Challenges for Microfluidics based Biochips. DTIP of MEMS & MOEMS, Montreux, Switzerland, June 1–3, (2005)
3. Zhang, X., Proosdij, F., Kerkhoff, G.: A Droplet Routing for Fault-Tolerant Digital Microfluidic Devices. In: The research has been partly funded by DfMM, FP6 NoE PATENT, in the framework of the BioDrop Flagship. IEEE (2008)
4. Su, F., Ozev, S., Chakrabarty, K.: Testing of droplet based microfluidic systems. In: Proc. IEEE Int. Test Conf., pp. 1192–1200 (2003)
5. Su, F., Ozev, S., Chakrabarty, K.: Test planning and test resource optimization for droplet based microfluidic systems. In: Proc. IEEE Eur. Test Sym., pp. 72–77 (2004)
6. Su, F., Hwang, H., Mukherjee, A., Chakrabarty, K.: Testing and diagnosis of realistic defects in digital microfluidic biochip. In: Proc. Springer Science + Business Media (2007)
7. Srinivasan, V., Pamula, V., Pollack, M., Fair, R.: A digital microfluidic biosensor for multianalyte detection. In: Proc. IEEE MEMS Conference, pp. 327–330 (2003)
8. Su, F., Chakrabarty, K.: Defect Tolerance based on Graceful Degradation and Dynamic Reconfiguration for Digital Microfluidics based Biochips. IEEE TCAD **25**(12) (2006)

9. Xu, T., Chakrabarty, K.: Functional Testing of Digital Microfluidic Biochip. ITC (2007)
10. Su, F., Ozev, S., Chakrabarty, K.: Ensuring the Operational Health of Droplet based Microelectrofluidic Biosensor Systems. IEEE Sensors **5**, 763–773 (2005)
11. Su, F., Ozev, S., Chakrabarty, K.: Concurrent testing of droplet based microfluidic systems for multiplexed biomedical assays. In: Proc. Int. Test Conf., pp. 883–892 (2004)
12. Kerkhoff, H.G.: Testing of microelectronic-biofluidic systems. IEEE D&T for Computers **24**, 72–82 (2007)
13. Yuh, P.-H., Yang, C.-L., Chang, Y.-W.: BioRoute: A Network-Flow-Based Routing Algorithm for the Synthesis of Digital Microfluidic Biochips. IEEE TCAD **27**(11), 1928–1941 (2008)
14. Xu, T., Chakrabarty, K.: Parallel Scan-Like Test and Multiple-Defect Diagnosis for Digital Microfluidic Biochips. IEEE Transactions on Biomedical Circuits and Systems **1**(2) (2007)
15. Roy, P., Rahaman, H., Giri, C., Dasgupta, P.: Modelling, detection and diagnosis of multiple faults in cross referencing DMFBs. In: Proc. IEEE ICIEV, pp. 1107–1112 (2012)
16. Chowdhury, S., Majumder, S., Mondal, K.: Multiple fault detection technique for digital microfluidic based biochip. In: Proc. IET and Int. Conf. ArtCom, pp. 117–125 (2013)

Biometric Swiping on Touchscreens

Orcan Alpar and Ondrej Krejcar[✉]

Faculty of Informatics and Management, Center for Basic and Applied Research,
University of Hradec Kralove, Rokitanskeho 62 500 03, Hradec Kralove, Czech Republic
orcanalpar@hotmail.com, ondrej@krejcar.org

Abstract. Touchscreen devices have become very popular in the last decade and eased our modern life. It is now possible to automatically log in to any web page connected to our touchscreen phones, such as social networks, e-commerce sites and even mobile banking. Given these facts, the emerging touchscreen technology brings out a potential security issue: weakness of authentication protocols. Therefore, we put forward a biometric enhancement on "swiping" authentication, which is one of the options to log in a touchscreen phone however with the lowest security. We created a ghost password by extracting the features of coordinates and swipe durations to use them as the inputs of the Levenberg-Marquardt based neural network and adaptive neuro-fuzzy classifiers which both discriminate real attempts from fraud attacks after training.

Keywords: Touchscreen · Biometric · Authentication · Swiping · Security

1 Introduction

Biometrics is the general term for human traits which are so unique that makes them really hard to mimic. The biometric authentication systems are developed for extracting physical, biological or behavioral characteristics to identify or discriminate the users when necessary. Among the several types of biometric systems, keystroke recognition has an unusual enhancement since the features could be designed intentionally and changed on request. Considering other well-known biometric systems, such as iris, gait, fingerprint, finger veins, hand geometry, the traits are biological or physical that cannot be changed, but in keystroke systems, the password design can be natural or a ghost password can be designed.

Keystroke recognition is basically based on the uniqueness of entering an alphanumeric password. The infrastructure of keystroke authentication systems is more or less similar; collecting inter-key durations as the main feature. Moreover, keystroke techniques are extended subsequent to emerging technologies of touchscreens and now it is comprising a basis for touchscreen authentication and related. However the kernel stays same, no matter the input device is a keyboard or a touchscreen. In addition to alphanumeric passwords, the touchscreens have various authentication methods such as pattern passwords and swiping.

Despite the security issues, swiping is the easiest method to authenticate to a touchscreen. In this process, the users only need to do a fingertip gesture on the screen

© IFIP International Federation for Information Processing 2015
K. Saeed and W. Homenda (Eds.): CISIM 2015, LNCS 9339, pp. 193–203, 2015.
DOI: 10.1007/978-3-319-24369-6_16

and simply drawing a line while touching is enough to authenticate. In spite of the given ease of use, this procedure however has a security drawback since most new generation mobile phones and tablets remember passwords of very crucial websites, like e-banking, e-commerce or all kind of social networks. Therefore, what we briefly propose in this research is to strength the swiping authentication systems using bio-metrical features.

There are three major subsystems introduced in this paper, namely; Feature Extraction, Training and Classifying which could be seen in Figure 1 below,

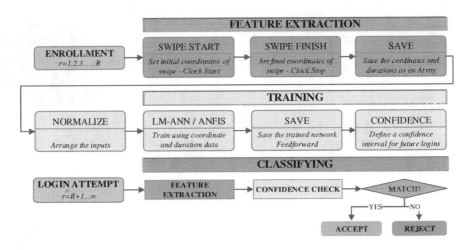

Fig. 1. Workflow of Enhanced Swiping Authentication System

Initially, an interface is written to emulate the screen dimensions of Samsung I8262 Galaxy Core Duos smartphone, which is 800x480 pixel-square. As the swiping starts in enrollment step, the feature extraction subsystem marks the initial coordinates. The subsystem also records the touch duration until the swipe is over and points the final coordinates. Using these five inputs, Swipe Start x, Swipe Start y, Swipe Finish x, Swipe Finish y and the time data, the neural networks based classifiers, Levenberg-Marquardt based artificial neural (LM-ANN) and adaptive neuro-fuzzy (ANFIS), are trained.

Although numerous articles have been published in the last decade regarding keystroke recognition like [1] [2] [5] [7] [8] [9] [11] [12] [13] [14] [15] [16] [17] [20] [21], there are several papers in the literature that are relevant of our research.

Very briefly; Sae-bae et.al. [4] introduced a gesture-based authentication method using five-finger touch gestures. They collected the biometric data from the movement characteristics of the palm and created a classifier to recognize unique biometric gesture features and to check the future logins. They achieved an equal error rate (EER) of 5% – 10%. Chang et al. [3] utilized the pressure feature for a graphical authentication system for touchscreens with an EER of 6.9% – 14.6%.

Furthermore, Angulo and Wästlund [6] dealt with lock pattern dynamics and developed an application for the Android mobile platform to collect data. As a result of the experiments they made, an EER of 10.39% was revealed. Maiorana et al. [10] proposed a method of keystroke recognition to enhance keypad authentication for mobile devices and reached 13.59% – 24.15% EER. Tasia et. al [22] also proposed a twelve key virtual keypad as an interface for users to enter their biometric pins. The result is encouraging that they achieved a constant 8.4% EER. Kang and Cho [23] presented three different interfaces for touchscreens to collect biometric data and their experiment resulted in 5.64% – 16.62% EER.

Moreover; Kambourakis et al. [24] implemented a biometric keystroke system for touchscreens using for traits: speed, distance, hold-time and inter-time and achieved an EER of 13.6% – 26%. Sae-bae et. al. [18] dealt with multi touch gestures, especially hand and finger muscle behavior. They pointed the initial points of the five fingers, traced the movement as the fingers move, calculated the distances to propose a gesture based user authentication system and reached 5.14% – 27.73% EER. Finally, Zhao et al [19] determined gesture types for single and multiple touches and introduced the "Graphical Touch Gesture Feature" with an EER of 4.1% – 10.5%.

Comparing with these enhancements, what we put forward is two types of intelligent classifiers to strengthen the swiping process on touchscreens.

2   Feature Extraction

Since the major concern of this research is enhancing the existing and built-in authentication algorithm in touchscreens, the swiping process is considered not as a gesture as in previous works, but as a simple and basic motion. Therefore and initially, an invisible interface is created to collect coordinate and duration data. The ghost password beneath the swipes is 5-bit array which can be represented by

$$P = \left[x_i, y_i, x_f, y_f, t\right] \tag{1}$$

where x represents the horizontal axis, y represents the vertical axis, i is initial, f is final point and t is the duration and $x_i\ y_i\ x_f\ y_f \in \mathbb{Z}^+, \forall x_i, x_f \in [0\ 480]\ \forall y_i, y_f \in [0\ 800]$.

3   Training Algorithms

As the classifier system, we firstly selected artificial neural network (ANN) which is a learning system that simulates the neurological processing ability of the human brain and can be used in correlating the nonlinearity between inputs and outputs. The ANNs are usually trained by the backpropagation algorithms however we used the Levenberg-Marquardt [25] [26] algorithm, which is actually a nonlinear optimization protocol since it has lower dissolution time.

Like the quasi-newton models, the LM algorithm is designed to find x_{k+1} from x_k using the Hessian and gradient matrices however in LM, the Hessian matrix is approximated by Jacobian matrix. On the other hand, we're dealing with the optimization of the weights therefore the equation is written for the weights, namely,

$$w_{n+1} = w_n - [J_n^T J_n + \mu_n I]^{-1} J_n e_n \tag{2}$$

where e is the vector form of errors for n^{th} iteration, μ is initial leaning rate, $J_n e_n$ is the gradient, $J_n^T J_n$ is the approximation of Hessian and J_n is the Jacobian matrix:

$$J = \begin{bmatrix} \dfrac{\partial e_{1,1}}{\partial w_1} & \dfrac{\partial e_{1,1}}{\partial w_2} & \cdots & \dfrac{\partial e_{1,1}}{\partial w_N} \\ \dfrac{\partial e_{1,2}}{\partial w_1} & \dfrac{\partial e_{1,2}}{\partial w_2} & \cdots & \dfrac{\partial e_{1,2}}{\partial w_N} \\ \cdots & \cdots & \cdots & \cdots \\ \dfrac{\partial e_{P,M}}{\partial w_1} & \dfrac{\partial e_{P,M}}{\partial w_2} & \cdots & \dfrac{\partial e_{P,M}}{\partial w_N} \end{bmatrix} \tag{3}$$

When the initial leaning rate μ is zero, this gives the Newton method with approximated Hessian. The main difference in LM is the general procedure of forcing the Hessian to be positive definite by $J_n^T J_n + \mu_n I$ such that; in each iteration, μ_n is adjusted to make the Hessian positive if it is not.

The errors are computed by sum of squares namely;

$$E(w) = \frac{1}{2} \sum_{p=1}^{P} \sum_{m=1}^{M} e^2{}_{p,m} \tag{4}$$

where p is the index of inputs for P inputs, m is the index of outputs for M outputs and $e_{p,m} = \dot{o}_{p,m} - o_{p,m}$ where $\dot{o}_{p,m}$ is expected and $o_{p,m}$ is the actual output.

As the initiation of the experiment, 10 real attempts are saved to train the network. Although the right thumb movement is simulated which should reveal a trace like a nonlinear curve, since only the initial and final coordinates of the swipes are extracted, the swipes therefore look like straight lines as in Figure 2.

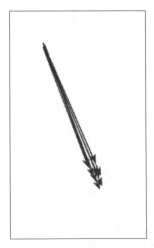

Fig. 2. Training set consisting of 10 swipes.

The data includes the coordinates in pixel numbers such as $\forall x_i \, y_i \, x_f \, y_f \in \mathbb{Z}^+$ where $\forall x_i, x_f \in [0 \; 480] \; \forall y_i, y_f \in [0 \; 800]$ however these values are normalized to; $\forall \dot{x}_i \, \dot{y}_i \, \dot{x}_f \, \dot{y}_f \in \mathbb{R}^+$ where $\forall \dot{x}_i, \dot{x}_f, \dot{y}_i, \dot{y}_f \in [0 \; 1]$ namely;

$$\dot{P} = \left[\dot{x}_i = x_i/480, \; \dot{y}_i = y_i/800, \; \dot{x}_f = x_f/480, \; \dot{y}_f = y_f/800, \; t \right] \qquad (5)$$

We trained the network with 10 input arrays and for initial learning rate $\mu_0 = 0.5$ by iterating the network, involving standard sigmoid perceptron and 5 nodes in one hidden layer, for 200 epochs and optimized the weights using LM. The input matrix is also used as the checking data to determine the confidence interval by feedforwarding the network and the following values are achieved in Figure 3.

Given the maximum and minimum levels of the Figure 3, the confidence interval is determined as $o_{max} = 1.0008$ and $o_{min} = 0.9995$ however we extended the interval by doubling the range as $\dot{o}_{max} = 1.0016$ and $\dot{o}_{min} = 0.9990$ and therefore if the results of feedforward process of succeeding attempts result in outside of this region, they will be rejected.

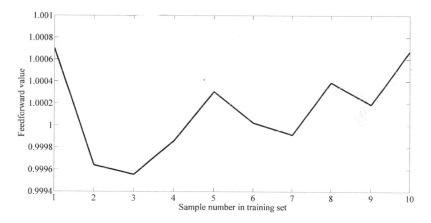

Fig. 3. Feedforward values of the input matrix as the confidence region

These values also represent the correspondence between the individual value and the whole training set.

In addition, we developed an ANFIS structure to utilize as the second classifier with generating a Sugeno style fuzzy inference system (FIS) with gird partitioning for 30 epochs. The membership function styles are selected as Gaussian, with three members each. However, ANFIS itself is not capable of differentiating the attempts, since, as a curve fitting algorithm, it is not designed for biometric classification. Therefore an imaginary fraud training set is computed and concatenated to (1) namely;

$$P = \left[x_i, y_i, x_f, y_f, t \right] \to 1 \qquad (5)$$

$$P' = [480 - x_i, 800 - y_i, 480 - x_f, 800 - y_f, 2 - t] \rightarrow 0 \qquad (6)$$

so we achieve;

$$P_{new} = [P; P'] \qquad (7)$$

Using P_{new} as the main training set consisting of 20 trials, the ANFIS is trained and the training set is tested to validate the success of training by plotting the FIS output vs training data in Figure 4. The generated Sugeno-FIS has 5 inputs and Gaussian membership functions which are shown in Figure 5.

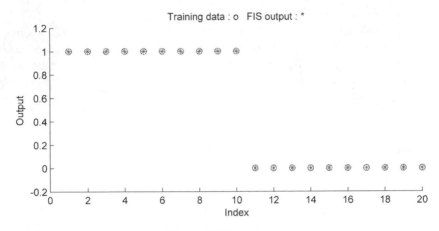

Fig. 4. ANFIS testing.

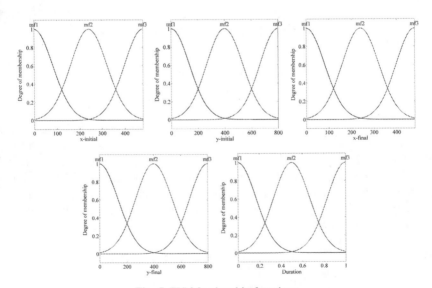

Fig. 5. FIS Membership functions

Although the expected result to validate the attempt is 1, we again defined a confidence interval between $o_{max} = 1.02$ and $o_{min} = 0.98$. Given the results of training session, both systems are perfectly adjusted to discriminate real attempts from fraud attacks.

4   Experimental Results

In the testing phase, 100 fraud and 100 real attempts are collected to check the performance of the systems. 100 fraud attacks are completely unbiased and totally random, however real attempts are made by the owner himself, therefore the paths and durations are more or less similar with the training set, which could be seen in Figure 6.

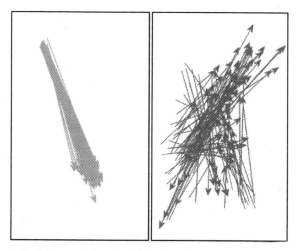

Fig. 6. Real Attempts (on the left) vs Fraud Attacks (on the right)

Initially, the LM-ANN results are analyzed to find false reject rate (FRR), false accept rate (FAR) and EER. According to the classification of LM-ANN, the FRR=8% which is higher than expected, in contrast FAR=1% which means that only 1% percent of the fraud attacks are granted. Equal error rate, which corresponds the intersection points of FRR and FAR, is linearly interpolated as EER=2.2%.

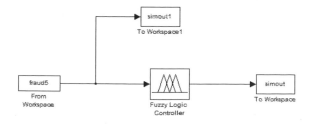

Fig. 7. Simulink Design for ANFIS

By the help of Simulink, the fraud and real attempts were easily calculated by the FIS that the ANFIS generated.

The results of ANFIS are a little reverse that FRR=0%, FAR=10% and EER is estimated as 5.4%. The consolidated EER points of output curves for both classifiers are shown in Figure 8.

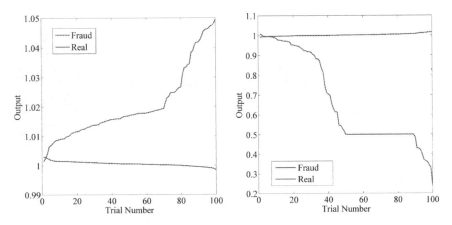

Fig. 8. Output Curves and EER points (LM-ANN on the left, ANFIS on the right)

Beside of these methods, two curves are mandatory to evaluate the performance of biometric authentication systems. Receiver Operating Characteristic (ROC) curve is a general tool to summarize the results using 1-FRR and FAR percentages while, Detection Error Trade-off (DET) curve is a useful tool to plot the error rates on both axes by FAR% and FRR% with a special scale-free diagram as in Figure 9.

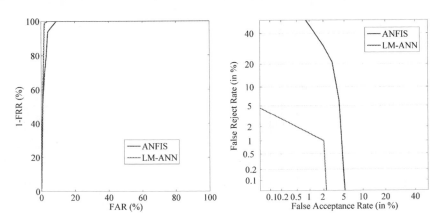

Fig. 9. ROC Curves on the left, DET curves on the right

The ROC curves also provide an insight for sensitivity since they are calculated by altering the $\dot{o}_{max}$ and $\dot{o}_{min}$ values to check the system performance within various intervals. However for each new interval the calculated FAR and FRR rates could be the same and we selected the points that will start from (0,0),end in (100,100) and reveal a continuous line. The infrastructure beneath the ROC concept is briefly the unconditional existence very narrow and very large intervals to make the FAR and FRR both 0 and 100.

According to the ROC curves, the performance of the LM-ANN is slightly better than ANFIS since it is increasing more sharply and ANFIS is closer to the x=y axis. Moreover, the DET curves prove the same argument: in ANFIS to reduce FAR by 3% we need to sacrifice 30% FRR, however in LM-ANN only 5% FRR will be sacrificed for %2 reduction of FAR.

5   Conclusions and Discussions

As a brief summary, we introduced two types of artificial intelligence based classifier to strengthen the swiping authentication. According to the results, both seems useful on enhancing swiping process by biometric features since the equal error rates are promising though LM-ANN had slightly better EER. ROC and DET curves are encouraging for both classifiers yet LM-ANN is again superior.

Regarding LM-ANN, the network is trained by 200 epochs however the number of iterations could be extended or reduced based on the desired narrowness level. If extended, the resulting interval would be so narrow that the FAR will be higher however if reduced FRR will increase. In contrast we trained ANFIS by 30 epochs which seems enough to fit the training data and FIS outputs. However the main disadvantage of ANFIS is necessity of an imaginary set to generate the FIS.

As future research, whole trace could be extracted instead of initial and final coordinates. If LM-ANN is desired to be the major training algorithm then it is possible to create a skip-layer network to give importance to the duration data. Although our network is fully connected, it is plausible to erase some connections to achieve more precise results however it is not recommended for this project since the coordinate data we're using is in order. Additionally the kernel seems suitable for nearest neighbor algorithms if the features will be the coordinates. On the other hand, the points could be turned into angles to reduce the number of inputs however the starting point of swiping will be lost this time.

Acknowledgment. This work and the contribution were supported by project "SP/2014/05 - Smart Solutions for Ubiquitous Computing Environments" from University of Hradec Kralove.

References

1. Zheng, N., Bai, K., Huang, H., Wang, H.: You are how you touch: User verification on smartphones via tapping behaviors. Technical Report, College of William and Mary (2012)
2. Kwapisz, J., Weiss, G., Moore, S.: Cell phone-based biometric identification. In: Proceedings IEEE Int. Conf. on Biometrics: Theory Applications and Systems (2010)
3. Chang, T.Y., Tsai, C.J., Lin, J.H.: A graphical-based password keystroke dynamic authentication system for touch screen handheld mobile devices. Journal of Systems and Software **85**(5), 1157–1165 (2012)
4. Sae-Bae, N., Ahmed, K., Isbister, K., Memon, N.: Biometric-rich gestures: a novel approach to authentication on multi-touch devices. In: CHI 2012 Proceedings of the 2012 ACM Annual Conference on Human Factors in Computing Systems, New York (2012)
5. De Luca, A., Hang, A., Brudy, F., Lindner, C., Hussmann, H.: Touch me once and i know it's you!: implicit authentication based on touch screen patterns. In: CHI 2012 Proceedings of the 2012 ACM Annual Conference on Human Factors in Computing Systems, New York (2012)
6. Angulo, J., Wästlund, E.: Exploring touch-screen biometrics for user identification on smart phones. In: Camenisch, J., Crispo, B., Fischer-Hübner, S., Leenes, R., Russello, G. (eds.) Privacy and Identity Management for Life. IFIP AICT, vol. 375, pp. 130–143. Springer, Heidelberg (2012)
7. Shahzad, M., Liu, A.X., Samuel, A.: Secure unlocking of mobile touch screen devices by simple gestures: you can see it but you can not do it. In: Proceedings of the 19th Annual International Conference on Mobile Computing & Networking. ACM (2013)
8. Schaub, F., Deyhle, R., Weber, M.: Password entry usability and shoulder surfing susceptibility on different smartphone platforms. In: Proceedings of Mobile & Ubiquitous Multimedia (2012)
9. Shahzad, M., Zahid, S., Farooq, M.: A hybrid GA-PSO fuzzy system for user identification on smart phones. In: ACM, Proceedings of the 11th Annual Conference on Genetic and Evolutionary Computation, pp. 1617–1624 (2009)
10. Maiorana, E., Campisi, P., González-Carballo, N., Neri, A.: Keystroke dynamics authentication for mobile phones. In: Proceedings of the 2011 ACM Symposium on Applied Computing, pp. 21–26. ACM (2011)
11. Rao, M.K., Aparna, P., Akash, G.A., Mounica, K.: A Graphical Password Authentication System for Touch Screen Based Devices. International Journal of Applied Engineering Research **9**(18), 4917–4924 (2014)
12. Jeanjaitrong, N., Bhattarakosol, P.: Feasibility study on authentication based keystroke dynamic over touch-screen devices. In: 2013 13th International Symposium on Communications and Information Technologies (ISCIT), pp. 238–242. IEEE (2013)
13. Do, S., Hoang, T., Luong, C., Choi, S., Lee, D., Bang, K., Choi, D.: Using Keystroke Dynamics for Implicit Authentication on Smartphone. 멀티미디어학회논문지 **17**(8), 968–976 (2014)
14. Trojahn, M., Arndt, F., Ortmeier, F.: Authentication with time features for keystroke dynamics on touchscreens. In: De Decker, B., Dittmann, J., Kraetzer, C., Vielhauer, C. (eds.) CMS 2013. LNCS, vol. 8099, pp. 197–199. Springer, Heidelberg (2013)
15. Rogowski, M., Saeed, K., Rybnik, M., Tabedzki, M., Adamski, M.: User authentication for mobile devices. In: Saeed, K., Chaki, R., Cortesi, A., Wierzchoń, S. (eds.) CISIM 2013. LNCS, vol. 8104, pp. 47–58. Springer, Heidelberg (2013)

16. Bours, P., Masoudian, E.: Applying keystroke dynamics on one-time pin codes. In: 2014 International Workshop on Biometrics and Forensics (IWBF), pp. 1–6. IEEE (2014)
17. Frank, M., Biedert, R., Ma, E., Martinovic, I., Song, D.: Touchalytics: On the applicability of touchscreen input as a behavioral biometric for continuous authentication. IEEE Transactions on Information Forensics and Security 8(1), 136–148 (2013)
18. Sae-Bae, N., Memon, N., Isbister, K., Ahmed, K.: Multitouch Gesture-Based Authentication. IEEE Transactions on Information Forensics and Security 9(4), 568–582 (2014)
19. Zhao, X., Feng, T., Shi, W., Kakadiaris, I.: Mobile User Authentication Using Statistical Touch Dynamics Images. IEEE Transactions on Information Forensics and Security 9(11), 1780–1789 (2014)
20. Alpar, O.: Keystroke recognition in user authentication using ANN based RGB histogram technique. Engineering Applications of Artificial Intelligence 32, 213–217 (2014)
21. Campisi, P., Maiorana, E., Bosco, M.L., Neri, A.: User Authentication Using Keystroke Dynamics for Cellular Phones. IET Signal Processing - Special Issue on Biometric Recognition 3(4), 333–341 (2009)
22. Tasia, C.J., Chang, T.Y., Cheng, P.C., Lin, J.H.: Two novel biometric features in keystroke dynamics authentication systems for touch screen devices. Security and Communication Networks 7(4), 750–758 (2014)
23. Kang, P., Cho, S.: Keystroke dynamics-based user authentication using long and free text strings from various input devices. Information Sciences (2014). http://dx.doi.org/10.1016/j.ins.2014.08.070
24. Kambourakis, G., Damopoulos, D., Papamartzivanos, D., Pavlidakis, E.: Introducing touchstroke: keystroke-based authentication system for smartphones. Security and Communication Networks (2014). doi:10.1002/sec.1061
25. Levenberg, K.: A method for the solution of certain problems in least squares. Quarterly of Applied Mathematics 2, 164–168 (1944)
26. Marquardt, D.W.: An algorithm for least-squares estimation of nonlinear parameters. Journal of the Society for Industrial & Applied Mathematics 11(2), 431–441 (1963)

Simple Displaying Method for Genealogy with Assisted Reproductive Technologies

Seiji Sugiyama[1]([⊠]), Daisuke Yokozawa[1], Atsushi Ikuta[1], Satoshi Hiratsuka[2], Miyuki Shibata[1], and Tohru Matsuura[3]

[1] Otani University, Kyoto, Japan
{seijisan,a.ikuta}@sch.otani.ac.jp, dyokozawa@gmail.com,
neko@res.otani.ac.jp
[2] Ritsumeikan University, Kusatsu, Shiga, Japan
hiratsuka@spice.ci.ritsumei.ac.jp
[3] Hokkaido University Hospital, Sapporo, Hokkaido, Japan
macchan@med.hokudai.ac.jp

Abstract. In this research, a new layout style, 'Nodes of Effects and/or Way through for TYing Particular Elements (NeWTYPe)', for displaying genealogy with assisted reproductive technologies (ART) that include a sperm/ovum donor and/or a surrogate mother using our WHIteBasE method is proposed. The NeWTYPe is a node with symbols; 'Arrow', 'Pipe', and 'Arrow and Pipe'. Using the NeWTYPe, complex relations of the ART can be understood easily. Note that previous WHIteBasE method has perfectly been able to integrate each relation that includes a married couple and their children, and has been able to display complex relations with segment intersections and various layout styles easily, and also, our JaBBRoW method for abbreviating some jointed relations on the WHIteBasE has been proposed. As a result, displaying both regular complex genealogy and the ART can be realized simultaneously. Our improved software that can display the NeWTYPe automatically and seamlessly by only mouse operations is presented.

Keywords: Family trees · Pedigrees · Sperm or ovum donor · Surrogate mother · GEDCOM · WHIteBasE

1 Introduction

There is a lot of genealogy display software these days[1]-[18]. However, almost all of them cannot display complex relations perfectly. In the case of writing complex genealogy on paper media, one individual is written only once in most cases using segment intersections and various layout styles. In contrast, in the case of using the software, one individual is often displayed in multiple places because the software considers no complex layouts even if GEDCOM[19], a de facto standard for recording genealogy data exchange format, can store them perfectly. These displaying results are very difficult to understand complex relations correctly.

To cope with the difficulty, new genealogy display software has already been proposed on our previous research by using the WHIteBasE (Widespread Hands

© IFIP International Federation for Information Processing 2015
K. Saeed and W. Homenda (Eds.): CISIM 2015, LNCS 9339, pp. 204–215, 2015.
DOI: 10.1007/978-3-319-24369-6_17

Fig. 1. A regular family layout in genealogy **Fig. 2.** Connection model of WHIteBasE

to InTErconnect BASic Elements) method[20]. The WHIteBasE is a hidden node for intcgrating relations that include not only a married couple and their children but also information of those positions. As a result, one individual have been displayed only once using segment intersections easily. In addition, not only various layouts such as paper media have been displayed but also intuitive inputs and inspections such as map display systems have been realized[21],[22]. Moreover, JaBBRoW (Joint ABBReviation for Organizing WHIteBasE) method has also been proposed for abbreviating a part of genealogy[23]. As a result, arbitrary relations with horizontal and vertical connections in genealogy can be abbreviatcd easily.

On the other hand, there is different complex relations these days such as Assisted Reproductive Technologies (ART) that include a sperm or ovum donor, and a surrogate mother[24]. This work said that ART symbols and pedigree lines can be displayed on many existing genealogy display software. However, these software cannot display regular complcx relations with segment intersections perfectly mentioned abovc. In addition, these layout styles has slant lines between a parent gcncration and a child generation. Using slant lines makes displaying genealogy complicated in the case of using segment intersections. Displaying all situations both of regular genealogy and medical pedigree such as the ART cannot be realized using the existing medical line definitions.

In this paper, a new layout style, 'Nodes of Effects and/or Way through for TYing Particular Elements (NeWTYPe)', is added to the WHIteBasE method. The NeWTYPe is a node with symbols; 'Arrow', 'Pipe', and 'Arrow and Pipe'. Using the NeWTYPe, complex relations of the ART can be understood easily. As a result, displaying both regular complex genealogy and the ART can be realized simultaneously. Our improved software that can display the NeWTYPe automatically and seamlessly by only mouse operations is presented.

2   WHIteBasE and JaBBRoW

In this section, the WHIteBasE method and the JaBBRoW method that are our previous proposal [20]-[23] are briefly introduced. A regular family relation between a married couple and their child is managed as an event by a Hidden Node, WHIteBasE as shown in Fig. 1. The connection model of WHIteBasE is shown in Fig. 2. WHIteBasE has three keyholes, S_L, S_R (Substance) and D (Descendant). Individuals have two keys, A (Ascendant) and M (Marriage). A can connect with D, and M can connect with S_L or S_R, where denote one family.

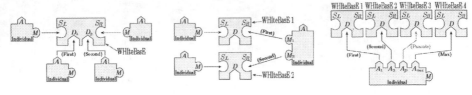

Fig. 3. Brothers and sisters   **Fig. 4.** Multiple Remarriages   **Fig. 5.** Adoptions

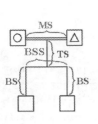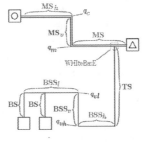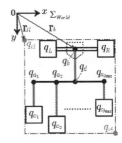

Fig. 6. Regular layout   **Fig. 7.** Various Layouts   **Fig. 8.** Coordinate System

For brothers and sisters, D is extended to multiple keyholes D_j as shown in Fig. 3. For multiple remarriages, M is extended to multiple keys M_k and plural WHIteBasEs are used as shown in Fig. 4. For adoptions, A is extended to multiple keys A_l as shown in Fig. 5 where A_p, one of A_l, denotes ID for handling the biological parents, and the others denote IDs for handling social parents.

Fig. 6 shows the regular Japanese layout style. It includes a double horizontal segment MS (Marriage Segment), a vertical segment TS (Trunk Segment), a horizontal segment BSS (Brothers and Sisters Segment), and a vertical segment BS (Branch Segment). The '$\triangle$' denotes a male, and the '$\bigcirc$' denotes a female that are a couple connected by using MS. For various layouts, MS is extended to MS, MS_v, and MS_h named DB (Double Bend), and BSS is extended to BSS_h, BSS_v, and BSS_l named HS (Hooked Segment), as shown in Fig. 7.

A set of W_i that defines WHIteBasEs and a set of I_j that defines Individual Nodes are represented by

$$
\begin{aligned}
W_i &= \{S_L, S_R, D_j, \mathbf{Q}\} \\
I_j &= \{M_k, A_l\}
\end{aligned}
\qquad
\begin{cases}
i = 0, 1, \cdots, i_{max} \\
j = 0, 1, \cdots, j_{max} \\
k = 0, 1, \cdots, k_{max} \\
l = 0, 1, \cdots, p, \cdots, l_{max}
\end{cases}
\tag{1}
$$

where i, j, k, l and $i_{max}, j_{max}, k_{max}, l_{max}$ denote the IDs and their maximum values on the data table respectively, p denotes the ID for handling a biological parents, S_L and S_R denote the IDs for handling a couple, D_j denote the IDs for handling descendants, M_k denote the IDs for handling marriages, and A_l denote the IDs for handling ascendants. Individuals are managed by using data table including names and annotation data. WHIteBasEs are managed by using data table separated from Individuals.

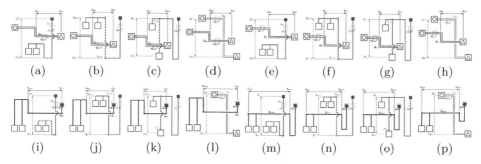

Fig. 9. Search pattern of segment intersections for various layouts

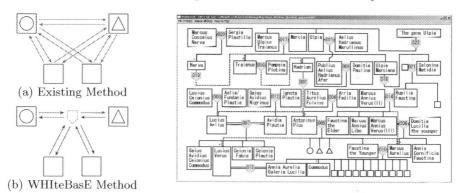

(a) Existing Method

(b) WHIteBasE Method

Fig. 10. Number of references

Fig. 11. Displaying Result by using WHIteBasE [25]

A set of **Q** that defines coordinate values for each position managed by a WHIteBasE measured from the origin in the displaying area is represented by

$$\mathbf{Q} = \{q_b, q_L, q_R, q_d, q_{c_j}, q_{a_j}, q_{vl}, q_{vh}, q_m, q_e, q_{tl}, q_{rb}\} \tag{2}$$

where q_b denotes the WHIteBasE's position, q_L, q_R denote the parents' positions, q_d denotes a junction's position between MS and TS, q_{c_j} denotes children's positions, q_{a_j} denotes junctions' positions between BSS and BS, q_{vl}, q_{vh} denote the corners on DB, q_m, q_e denote the corners on HS, q_{tl}, q_{rb} denote positions of top-left and bottom-right of all area managed by a WHIteBasE, as shown in Fig. 7 and Fig. 8.

There are only four kinds of horizontal segments and four kinds of vertical segments in the WHIteBasE method. The positions of segment intersections can be calculated by using only 16 patterns of line crossing as shown in Figs. 9(a)-(p). The half arcs are displayed on the positions of segment intersections. The detailed information has already been written in our previous research [22].

This algorithm is very fast because it skips when two WHIteBasEs' areas do not overlap. In addition, when adoptions are set, the segment style changes to the dashed segments named AS (Adopted Segment) and the arcs are not used.

One of advantages using WHIteBasE is the decreased reference volume. If the existing software is used, all of individuals connect with other individuals as

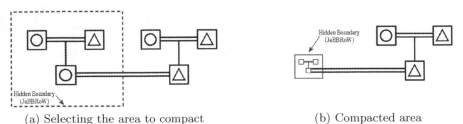

(a) Selecting the area to compact   (b) Compacted area

Fig. 12. Compacted and Recovered Operation by using the Hidden Node, JaBBRoW

shown in Fig. 10(a). In contrast, if the WHIteBasE is used, two reference links per a child decrease as shown in Fig. 10(b). Moreover, the users can understand the complex relations intuitively and can input and inspect them easily.

Fig. 11 shows the sample demonstrations by using our previous genealogy display software that can display complex relations with segment intersections automatically and seamlessly by only mouse operation [25].

In addition, the JaBBRoW method can be used for abbreviating a part of genealogy. A selected area of genealogy with abbreviation is managed as an event by a Hidden Boundary as shown in Fig. 12(a). When the area is compacted, the dotted rectangle becomes the solid rectangle as shown in Fig. 12(b). All of relations in genealogy can be maintained while compacting, and all of relations in the Hidden Boundary can be scaled down to the very small area.

JaBBRoW is defined using a set of hyper-graph G represented by

$$G = (\ V,\ \epsilon\ ) \tag{3}$$

where ϵ denotes a hyper-edge given by

$$\epsilon = \{\ J_0,\ J_1,\ J_2,\ \cdots\ \in V \mid J_i \cap J_j = 0,\ i \neq j\ \} \tag{4}$$

where J_k ($k = 0, 1, 2, \cdots$) denote a Hidden Boundary JaBBRoW, each JaBBRoW is a disjoint set, and one node is not managed by plural JaBBRoW. On the other hand, V denotes a set of each node inside the JaBBRoW represented by

$$V = \{\ V_0,\ V_1\ \} \tag{5}$$

where V_0 and V_1 denote a set of Individuals and a set of WHIteBasE respectively represented by

$$V_0 = \{\ I_0,\ I_1,\ I_2,\ \cdots,\ \mid I_j \notin J_k \text{ then } I_j \notin V_0,\ k = 0, 1, 2, \cdots\ \} \tag{6}$$

$$V_1 = \{\ W_0,\ W_1,\ W_2,\ \cdots,\ \mid W_i \notin J_k \text{ then } W_i \notin V_1,\ k = 0, 1, 2, \cdots\ \} \tag{7}$$

where I_j are coordinate values on the $\sum_{world}$, and W_i are coordinate values of only corner points in the WHIteBasE represented by

$$W_i = \{q_b, q_d, q_{vl}, q_{vh}, q_m, q_e \mid q_b \notin J_k \text{ then } q_d, q_{vl}, q_{vh}, q_m, q_e \notin W_i, k = 0, 1, 2, \cdots\}. \tag{8}$$

As a result, a set of each node inside the JaBBRoW is scaled in each J_k. Note that q_{vl}, q_{vh}, q_m, q_e are not calculated when various layouts are not used.

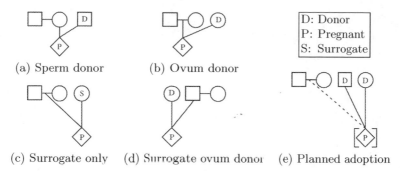

(a) Sperm donor   (b) Ovum donor

D: Donor
P: Pregnant
S: Surrogate

(c) Surrogate only   (d) Surrogate ovum donor   (e) Planned adoption

Fig. 13. Assisted Reproductive Technology Symbols and Definitions[26]

3 Layout style for Assisted Reproductive Technologies

3.1 Existing Definitions

The common pedigree symbols have been defined in the medical pedigree[26].
It is very important to discuss these symbols, however, it is not necessary to
calculate segment positions for displaying these symbols because they are only
symbols instead of displaying individuals' names. Therefore, only segment layout
styles are considered for calculating segment intersections in this research.

There are five segment styles in the ART as shown in Figs. 13(a)–(e)[26]
where 'D' denotes Donor, 'P' denotes Pregnant and 'S' denotes Surrogate, '○'
denotes woman, '□' denotes man, and '◇' denotes sex unknown. The five layout
styles (a)–(c) mean as the following:

(a) Couple in which woman is carrying pregnancy using donor sperm.
(b) Couple in which woman is carrying pregnancy using a donor egg and part-
    ner's sperm.
(c) Couple whose gametes are used to impregnate a woman (surrogate) who
    carries the pregnancy.
(d) Couple in which male partner's sperm is used to inseminate.
(e) Couple contracts with a woman to carry a pregnancy using ovum of the
    woman carrying the pregnancy and donor sperm.

3.2 Problem of these Definitions

It is necessary to draw slant lines between parents and a child in these definitions.
It is thought that the reason why slant lines are necessary is to display parents
and a donor on the same horizontal position and to display genetic relations with
reproductive technologies. However, if the display distance between a couple and
a donor is long and there is a lot of relations near the couple, the angle of slant
lines becomes small and the segment layout becomes complicated because a lot
of horizontal and vertical segments are crossing on the slant lines. In addition, it
takes more times to calculate positions of segment intersections with slant lines
than using only horizontal and vertical segments. Moreover, these definitions are
special transcription specialized in medical pedigree and are not general.

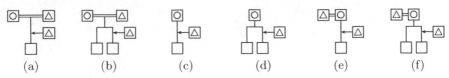

Fig. 14. Sperm donor layouts using Regular Layouts and Direct Segments

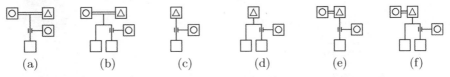

Fig. 15. Ovum donor layouts using Regular Layouts and Direct Segments

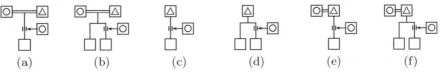

Fig. 16. Surrogate only layouts using Regular Layouts and Direct Segments

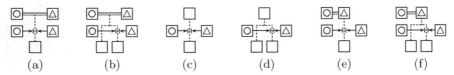

Fig. 17. Surrogate ovum donor layouts using Regular Layouts and Direct Segments

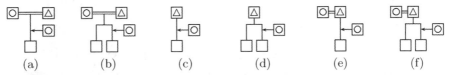

Fig. 18. Planned adoption layouts using Regular Layouts and Direct Segments

4   NeWTYPe

It is important to realize the requirement both of regular genealogy layouts such as the WHIteBasE method and pedigree layouts for the ART. To realize this requirement, a new layout style, 'Nodes of Effects and/or Way through for TYing Particular Elements (NeWTYPe)', is proposed in this research. It can be said that persons other than a couple and a child are only added in the ART treatment. This scenario only includes connections of donors and/or surrogates from third persons to the stream between a couple and a child. Existing ART layouts can be changed to the following new layout styles.

Sperm Donor: Figs. 14(a)–(f) show sperm donor layouts where (a) and (b) denote Regular Layout for a child and children respectively, (c) and (d) denote Direct Segment from a single parent for a child and children respectively, and (e) and (f) denote Direct Segment from parents for a child and children respectively. The horizontal arrow from a third person denotes a sperm donor. These

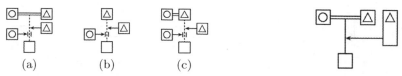

(a)   (b)   (c)

Fig. 19. Different Vertical Positions   **Fig. 20.** Generation alignment

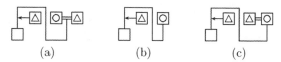

(a)   (b)   (c)

Fig. 21. The sample using Hooked Segments

layouts correspond to Fig. 13(a), however, only horizontal and vertical segments are used. Note that these six layouts without arrows (donors) have already displayed on the WHIteBasE method. The node of the vertical segment BS (see Fig. 6) and the arrow segment is one of NeWTYPe. These layouts are very simple to understand the meaning.

Ovum Donor: Figs. 15(a)–(f) show ovum donor layouts where (a)–(f) mean the same mentioned above. The difference between sperm donor layouts and ovum donor layouts is only the sex display of donors that includes a man '△' and a woman '○'. These layouts correspond to Fig. 13(b).

Surrogate Only: Figs. 16(a)–(f) show surrogate only layouts where (a)–(f) also mean the same. In this case, genetically parents are the couple and the surrogate person only takes her place. Considering this meaning, a pipe symbol is used instead of the arrow. These layouts correspond to Fig. 13(c).

Surrogate Ovum Donor: Figs. 17(a)–(f) show surrogate ovum donor layouts where (a)–(f) also mean the same. In this case, the event has not only surrogate but also donor. Considering this meaning, both an arrow and a pipe symbol are used together. These layouts correspond to Fig. 13(d).

Planned Adoption: Figs. 18(a)–(f) show planned adoption layouts where (a)–(f) also mean the same. In this case, two arrows from two persons other than a couple and a child to the node are used. Note that all donor/surrogate persons of (a)–(f) are placed at the same vertical position. In contrast, Figs. 19(a)–(c) show the sample of different vertical positions. Both cases use two arrows and one pipe symbol. These layouts correspond to Fig. 13(e).

Generation Alignment: Fig. 20 shows the sample of generation alignment. Using the long size of individual's text-box vertically, the top position of a couple and a donor/surrogate person can be aligned even though the NeWTYPe is used.

Using Hooked Segments: Figs. 21(a)–(c) show the sample of sperm donor using Hooked Segments. Using these styles, various layouts with the NeWTYPe can be displayed. The other samples using Hooked Segments including ovum

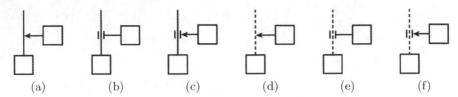

Fig. 22. Symbols for the NeWTYPe

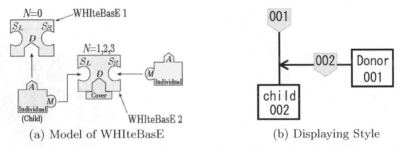

(a) Model of WHIteBasE   (b) Displaying Style

Fig. 23. Improved WHIteBasE model for the NeWTYPe

donor, surrogate only, surrogate ovum donor, and planned adoption, are similar to these samples, because the node is located on the BS using both regular layout, Direct segments, and Hooked segments. Therefore, the figures of the other samples are omitted in this paper.

As a result, the necessary symbols for the NeWTYPe can be only six types; 'Arrow', 'Pipe', and 'Arrow and Pipe' using solid segment BS or dotted segment BS as shown in Figs. 22(a)–(f).

5   Improved WHIteBasE Model

Symbols 'Arrow', 'Pipe', and 'Arrow and Pipe' are necessary to display the NeWTYPe. NeWTYPe flag N is added to the WHIteBasE represented by

$$W_i = \{S_L, S_R, D_j, \mathbf{Q}, N\}. \tag{9}$$

If $N = 0$, the WHIteBasE is the normal mode that equals previous model. If $N = 1, 2, 3$, the WHIteBasE changes the NeWTYPe mode and the keyhole D is covered, that means connecting descendants is not allowed as shown in Fig. 23(a). The numbers of N mean 'Arrow' ($N = 1$), 'Pipe' ($N = 2$), and 'Arrow and Pipe' ($N = 3$). The left individual that has connected with ascendant WHIteBasE denotes a child of reproductive treatment. The meaning of key M in the left individual changes to the NeWTYPe connection.

One of this displaying style is shown in Fig. 23(b). In this case, the right individual in (a) equals to the individual 001 in (b), the left individual in (a) equals to the individual 002 in (b), and $N = 1$. If the top position of text box in the individual is lower than the vertical position of the WHIteBasE that is NeWTYPe mode, the NeWTYPe (arrow node) is displayed automatically.

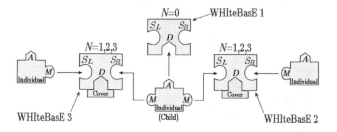

Fig. 24. Connection model of the WHIteBasE for planned adoptions

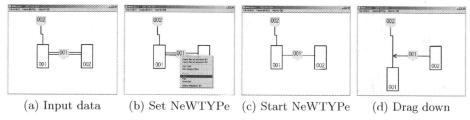

(a) Input data   (b) Set NeWTYPe   (c) Start NeWTYPe   (d) Drag down

Fig. 25. Instruction for setting NeWTYPe

The horizontal segment (arrow) is single segment, however, the layout is similar to MS. Therefore, the same search method for segment intersections as shown in Figs. 9(a)–(p) can be used for the NeWTYPe in a little change between single segment and double segment. As a result, the advantages of the WHIteBasE and the JaBBRoW can be maintained as in the past.

For planned adoptions, plural WHIteBasEs that are set to the NeWTYPe mode and multiple keys M_k in the child are only used as shown in Fig. 24. In this case, the definition of WHIteBasE does not change at all.

6   Demonstration of Our New Software

Figs. 25(a)–(d) show the instruction for setting the NeWTYPe. The detailed sequence is as the following:

(a) Input data; two Individuals and two WHIteBasEs and connect them.
(b) Select NeWTYPe menu that includes 'Arrow' or 'Pipe' or 'Arrow Pipe' on the WHIteBasE 001.
(c) The WHIteBasE 001 changes to the NeWTYPe mode and the MS becomes a single segment automatically.
(d) Drag down the individual 001, the NeWTYPe appears automatically. In this case, 'Arrow' is selected in (b).

Fig. 26(a) shows the sample of five NeWTYPe test on WHIteBasE where Individuals 001/002 are a couple, Individual 004 is a sperm donor, Individual 006 is a ovum donor, Individual 008 is a surrogate mother, Individual 010 is a surrogate ovum donor, and Individuals 012/013 are the case of planned adoption. In this sample, a lot of arcs for segment intersections are automatically displayed.

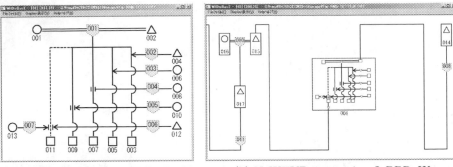

(a) NeWTYPe test on WHIteBasE   (b) NeWTYPe test using JaBBRoW

Fig. 26. Our new Genealogy Display Software for ART Layouts

Fig. 26(b) shows the sample of five NeWTYPe test using JaBBRoW. The JaBBRoW 001 manages the five NeWTYPe area to abbreviate. The ascendant of JaBBRoW 001 is WHIteBasE 008 and the descendant of JaBBRoW 001 is Individual 015. The stream line from WHIteBasE 008 to Individual 015 can be seen directly. Note that the JaBBRoW method does not change at all, however, the function of JaBBRoW can be used even though the NeWTYPe is used, because the difference between previous method and new method is only to add the NeWTYPe flag to the WHIteBasE. The definition of the JaBBRoW is the same as our previous research.

7   Conclusion

In this research, a new layout style, 'Nodes of Effects and/or Way through for TYing Particular Elements (NeWTYPe)', that includes 'Arrow', 'Pipe', and 'Arrow and Pipe', could be added to our previous WHIteBasE method.

As a result, not only regular complex genealogy with segment intersections but also the ART can be displayed simultaneously. Using the NeWTYPe layout, relations of the ART can be understood easily because slant segments are not used. In addition, the calculation time of the NeWTYPe is less than the case using slant segments. Moreover, the layout style of the NeWTYPe is not special transcription specialized in medical pedigree and this method has wide variety of use.

Future plan will be conducted to construct grid layouts on semi-automatic, displaying mythology genealogy, multi OS application, and new genealogy data format for automatic layouts.

References

1. The Generations Network: Genealogy, Family Trees and Family History Records on line. http://ancestry.com
2. MyHeritage. http://myheritage.jp

3. Jurek Software. http://www.pedigree-draw.com/
4. He, M., Li, W.: PediDraw: a web-based tool for drawing a pedigree in genetic counseling. In: BMC Medical Genetics, pp. 1–4 (2007)
5. Brun-Samarcq, L., et al.: CoPE: a collaborative pedigree drawing environment. Bioinformatics 'Applications Note' **15**(4), 345–346 (1999)
6. Dudbridge, F., et al.: Pelican: pedigree editor for linkage computer analysis. Bioinformatics 'Applications Note' **20**(14), 2327–2328 (2004)
7. Trager, E.H., et al.: Madeline 2.0 PDE: a new program for local and web-based pedigree drawing. Bioinformatics 'Applications Note' **23**(14), 1854–1856 (2007)
8. Makinen, V.P., et al.: High-throughput pedigree drawing. European Journal of Human Genetics **13**, 987–989 (2005)
9. Mancosu, G., Ledda, G., Melis, P.M.: PedNavigator: a pedigree drawing servlet for large and inbred populations. Bioinformatics 'Applications Note' **19**(5), 669–670 (2003)
10. Torcs, F., Barillot, E.: The art of pedigree drawing: algorithmic aspects. Bioinformatics **17**(2), 174–179 (2001)
11. Loh, A.M., et al.: Celestial3D: a novel method for 3D visualization of familial data. Bioinformatics 'Applications Note' **24**(9), 1210–1211 (2008)
12. Bennett, R.L., et al.: Recommendations for Standardized Human Pedigree Nomenclature. Journal of Genetic Counseling **4**(4), 267–279 (1995)
13. PED Pedigree Software. http://www.medgen.de/ped/
14. PAF. http://www.familysearch.org/
15. ScionPC. http://homepages.paradise.net.nz/scionpc/
16. XY Family Tree. http://www.xy-family-tree.com/
17. WeRelate. http://www.werelate.org/wiki/Main_Page/
18. GenoPro. http://www.genopro.com/
19. GEDCOM LETTER. http://en.wikipedia.org/wiki/GEDCOM
20. Sugiyama, S., Ikuta, A., Shibata, M., Matsuura, T.: A Study of An Event Oriented Data Management Method for Displaying Genealogy: Widespread Hands to InTERconnect BASic Elements (WHIteBasE). International Journal of Computer Information Systems and Industrial Management Applications (IJCISIM), 280–289 (2011). ISSN: 2150–7988/2
21. Sugiyama, S., Ikuta, A., Yokozawa, D., Shibata, M., Matsuura, T.: Displaying Genealogy with Various Layouts by using the "WHIteBasE" Method. International Journal of Computer Information Systems and Industrial Management Applications (IJCISIM), 102–115 (2014). ISSN: 2150–7988/6
22. Sugiyama, S., Ikuta, A., Yokozawa, D., Shibata, M., Matsuura, T.: Displaying genealogy with adoptions and multiple remarriages using the WHIteBasE. In: Saeed, K., Chaki, R., Cortesi, A., Wierzchoń, S. (eds.) CISIM 2013. LNCS, vol. 8104, pp. 325–336. Springer, Heidelberg (2013)
23. Sugiyama, S., Yokozawa, D., Ikuta, A., Hiratsuka, S., Saito, S., Shibata, M., Matsuura, T.: Abbreviation method for some jointed relations in displaying genealogy. In: Saeed, K., Snášel, V. (eds.) CISIM 2014. LNCS, vol. 8838, pp. 339–350. Springer, Heidelberg (2014)
24. Voon, F.W., Meow, K.T., Siew, H.O.: An Overview of Computer-Aided Medical Pedigree Drawing Systems. Proc. of CMU. J. Nat. Sci. **7**(1), 95–108 (2008)
25. Nerva-Antonine dynasty. http://en.wikipedia.org/wiki/Nerva
26. Robin, L.B., Kathryn, S.F., Robert, G.R., Debra, L.D.: Standardized Human Pedigree Nomenclature: Update and Assessment of the Recommendations of the National Society of Genetic Counselors. Journal of Genetic Counseling **18**(5), 424–433 (2008)

Data Analysis and Information Retrieval

U-Stroke Pattern Modeling for End User Identity Verification Through Ubiquitous Input Device

Tapalina Bhattasali[1(✉)], Nabendu Chaki[1], Khalid Saeed[2], and Rituparna Chaki[3]

[1] Department of Computer Science & Engineering, University of Calcutta, Kolkata, India
tapolinab@gmail.com, nabendu@ieee.org
[2] Faculty of Computer Science, Bialystok University of Technology, Bialystok, Poland
k.saeed@pb.edu.pl
[3] A.K.Choudhury School of Information Technology, University of Calcutta, Kolkata, India
rchaki@ieee.org

Abstract. Identity verification on ubiquitous input devices is a major concern to validate end-users, because of mobility of the devices. User device interaction (UDI) is capable to capture end-users' behavioral nature from their device usage pattern. The primary goal of this paper is to collect heterogeneous parameters of usage patterns from any device and build personal profile with good-recognition capability. This work mainly focuses on finding multiple features captured from the usage of smart devices; so that parameters could be used to compose hybrid profile to verify end- users accurately. In this paper, U-Stroke modeling is proposed to capture behavioral data mainly from smart input devices in ubiquitous environment. In addition to this, concept of CCDA (capture, checking, decision, and action) model is proposed to process U-Stroke data efficiently to verify end-user's identity. This proposal can draw attention of many researchers working on this domain to extend their research towards this direction.

Keywords: U-Stroke · Smart device · Touch screen · Ubiquitous input device · Identity verification

1 Introduction

Nowadays, mobile devices become smarter by offering multiple types of computing services at any place and at any time. Ubiquitous input devices [1] (smart phone, tablet, phablet, PDA, laptop, netbook etc.) become rich source of personal data, due to its support towards "any" paradigm. Sensitive personal data (such as password, financial information, health records [2]), stored in mobile devices are growing day by day. As a result, they are becoming attractive target to be attacked. Accurate identity verification of end-user is becoming a major requirement to preserve confidentiality and integrity in uncontrolled environment.

Traditional authentication mechanism (PIN/Password based) can be easily compromised. Anyone can access all services and can misuse personal information stored in the device, if device is misplaced. Implicit authentication mechanism needs to be considered without affecting normal usage pattern to overcome existing weak authentication

© IFIP International Federation for Information Processing 2015
K. Saeed and W. Homenda (Eds.): CISIM 2015, LNCS 9339, pp. 219–230, 2015.
DOI: 10.1007/978-3-319-24369-6_18

methods. Typing on computer keyboard is completely different from typing on smart devices having small keypads [3] and sensors enabled touch screen. Today, user-friendly touch screens are widely used on many devices such as mobile phones, tablets, and computers. As smart devices can perform multiple tasks at the same time, data acquisition only during typing is not efficient to build user profile. Beside this, typing on touch-screen based smart devices becomes more error-prone compared to computer keyboard based typing. Only temporal data based keystroke analysis is not sufficient to build unique user profile for any ubiquitous device. Therefore, keystroke analysis needs to be merged with touch screen based gesture analysis to enhance success rate of identity verification. Keystroke dynamics is mainly considered for desktop computers [2]. Since touch devices comprise sensors to capture environmental changes, they offer more capabilities to authenticate users accurately. Ubiquitous devices consider a different type of Human to Machine (H2M) communication by changing traditional way of human-computer interaction (HCI).

The major contribution of this paper is to propose a novel H2UID (human to ubiquitous input device) interaction mechanism U-Stroke (ubiquitous stroke) that can be applied to any computing device. This type of H2M communication is considered here to verify identity of end-user either by using distinct model or authentication model. Here human to human verification (H2HV) is defined by proposed CCDA (capture, checking, decision, and action) processing model. Different types of U-Strokes and their multiple features are discussed here along with collected data through Android device, which may attract researchers to work on this domain in future.

The rest of the paper is organized as follows. Section 2 presents a brief survey of existing works on this domain. Section 3 describes proposed U-Stroke analysis to verify end-user identity through ubiquitous devices. Section 4 presents brief analysis part followed by conclusion in section 5.

2   Literature Survey

Researchers are very much interested to work on human computer interaction to be considered as a means of verification of end-user identity [3, 4, 5, 6, 7, 8, 9]. Nowadays, HCI interaction with ubiquitous computing device becomes popular. Instead of considering end user authentication by means of only PINs or passwords, researchers are working on this area in recent years. Related works can be considered from different aspects such as user's identity verification by keystroke dynamics, by finger movements and tapped information on sensor based touch screens. "Touch Sensor" is the predecessor [10] of modern touch screens. In a few recent studies, touch-based biometrics is proposed for mobile devices instead of keystroke dynamics. There exists several finger gestures based authentication on touch screen of mobile devices. According to literature survey, very few works are based on continuous authentication on smart devices. Software like Touch logger can detect usage pattern of device owner and block unauthorized access to the device. Biometric touch information can be considered to enhance the security by using screen unlock. Interaction data are captured by sensors without affecting normal activities. If it is detected that the current end-user is different from the device owner, explicit access policy needs to be triggered.

PIN authentication method is strengthened with sensor data and timings. Different parameters can be collected like acceleration values, touching pressure, touched area on the screen, different temporal values like key-hold time or inter-key time. Flexible authentication can be implemented without considering predefined text. After a learning phase, end - users are authenticated while entering normal text. Touch dynamics may extract features like priority of usage of left and right hand, one-hand or both hand, use of thumb or index finger, stroke size, stroke timing, stroke speed, and timing regularity. Another way of implicit authentication is through learning behavior of a user- based on sent and received text messages, phone calls, browser history, and location of the smart phone. Instead of entering text into a soft keyboard, gestures like sliding towards a special direction or taps are most efficiently used. Generally, target acquisition tasks are carried out with a stylus that is much smaller than the targets. Among various information processing model, Fitt's model is dependent on finger size and type of stroke [11]. Complexity of Welford's model [12] is high compared to Whiting's model, but Welford model is more efficient to define information processing task. A major challenge is to apply Fitts' law to finger input, which may not be efficient for small-sized targets. This is mainly due to "Fat Finger" problem. Fitts' law fails if targets are small. As finger touch on smart phones and tablets becomes popular, examining Fitts' law [11] for finger touch attracts attention of many HCI researchers. Other information processing models [12] are not utilized effectively to model touch gesture till date.

After studying various existing works on this domain, it can be said there is no suitable model exists till date, which can be applied to any device for end-user verification. Most of the touch screen based authentication techniques consider few parameters or includes the features that are only available to costly devices. Considering few strokes with few parameters may not give accurate result. However, processing too many parameters may slow down the procedure. In order to improve the efficiency and accuracy of end-user identity verification, proposed work mainly focuses on finding physical or virtual UDI parameters of individual users and build hybrid personal profiles for accurate identification of end-users through ubiquitous input devices.

3   Proposed Work

Any type of user to input device interaction is proposed as U-Stroke, which is analyzed to identify end-users to any device in ubiquitous environment. U-Stroke analysis considers typing on numerical keypad or QWERTY keypad of mobile phone, external keyboard of tablet, and physical keyboard of desktop or laptop as physical keystroke; typing on on-screen QWERTY keypad of smart devices or any interaction with touch screen as touch stroke. The concept of U-Stroke pattern is proposed to model any human interaction with ubiquitous input device (H2UID).

Definition (U-Stroke). It is designed for any type of end-user to input device interaction (UDI) on user-friendly interface of smart devices {smart phone, tablet, phablet (phone + tablet)} in ubiquitous environment to validate H2M communication. U-Stroke is implicitly used to create hybrid profile of end-user (HPEU) for identification as well as verification.

Classification of proposed U-Stroke pattern is presented in figure 1.

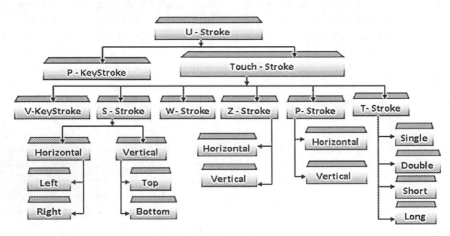

Fig. 1. U-Stroke Pattern

H2UID identity verification triggers multiple times during usage. Detailed classification of proposed U-Stroke pattern is described below.

P- KeyStroke (Physical KeyStroke)–It behaves as keystroke dynamics on physical (hard) keyboards of desktops or laptops or keypads of mobile phones. This type of keystroke mainly considers temporal (key press event, latency, typing speed etc.) data. As keypad of mobile devices may differ with physical keyboards, P-Keystroke patterns may differ.

Touch Stroke– It is based on the usage pattern on touch screen. To recognize valid user, multiple sensor data are integrated to model user variation.

V- KeyStroke (Virtual KeyStroke)–It considers typing on soft keyboard (virtual) on touch screen. Distance between neighbor keys of soft keyboard is much lesser than distance between neighbor keys of hard keyboard. V-Keystroke mainly includes touch_down, and touch_up events.

S-Stroke (Slide Stroke)– If finger movement on touch screen is either in horizontal direction (left or right) or in vertical direction (top or bottom), it is a type of S-Stroke. It is unidirectional and probability of touch_move event is high.

W-Stroke (Write Stroke) –If finger (mainly index) acts just like stylus, used normally for writing or drawing on the screen, it is a type of W-Stroke. This stroke is similar to handwriting. W-Stroke includes touch_down, touch_move and touch_up events.

Z-Stroke (Zoom Stroke)– If two fingers (mainly thumb and index of right hand) start from the same point and move towards opposite directions, it is a type of Z-Stroke. It is considered as open stroke as it moves outwards. Z-Stroke is bi-directional and probability of occurrence for touch_move event is high.

P-Stroke (Pinch Stroke) – If two fingers (mainly thumb and index of right hand) start from two opposite directions and move towards same point, it is a type of P-Stroke. It is considered as close stroke as it moves inwards on touch-screen. P-Stroke is bi-directional and probability of occurrence for touch_move event is high.

T-Stroke (Tap stroke) –If touch_down, and touch_up events occur due to the stroke similar to single click, double lick, long tap or short tap on touch screen and screen unlock, it is a type of T-Stroke. Probability of occurrence for touch_down event is high.

3.1   U-Stroke Pattern Modeling through Ubiquitous Input Device (UID)

This section presents detailed idea about how U-Stroke pattern processing model can be defined in terms of information processing model like Welford's model [12]. Here proposed U-Stroke Pattern Processing Model is defined by CCDA (capture, checking, decision, and action) concept with self-loop to identify end-user. This CCDA concept is mapped to the identity verification of end-user. Capture process is mainly used to collect U-Stroke data. Checking process is mainly used to classify U-Stroke pattern. Decision process is used mainly to take decision. Action process is used to take necessary steps according to final decision. Short term memory is considered as local memory store and long term memory is considered as remote memory store. Self-loop (feedback) is used to update template profile. Figure 2 represents CCDA processing model for UID.

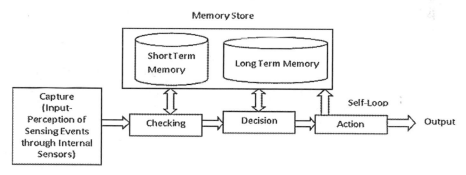

Fig. 2. CCDA Processing Model for UID

CCDA processing model of UID enables effective modeling of end-user's usage pattern from U-Stroke and creation of hybrid profile of end-user after extracting multiple features. Considering more than one feature can enhance accuracy level of classification. End-User's usage pattern is monitored multiple times to avoid malicious use. Less complex computation such as checking only device owner's validity can be performed through short term memory store (local). Short term memory can store device owner's log file. However, other complex computations are performed through long term memory store (remote server) to reduce computational overhead from limited resource device. CCDA process model may slow down if multiple features are processed compositely. For this reason, composite features are separated before processing and then fused as a whole to speed up the process. Significant variation of user's profile is managed by frequent update of template through feedback path of CCDA processing model.

3.2   End-User Identity Verification by U-Stroke Pattern Processing Model

In this section, identity verification procedure of end-users through ubiquitous input devices is briefly presented. Definition of end-user identity verification is given below.

Definition (n class H2HV). A type of H2UID interaction based on U-Stroke pattern processing model CCDA, is classified into two sub-classes- distinction class (1: m verification, where n = m) and authentication class (1:2 verification, where n = 2).

In 1: m distinction logic (where m = number of enrolled end-users), identity of valid end-user is accurately determined among all other end-users. In 1:2 authentication logic (1st class →valid user, 2nd class→ invalid user), identity of claimed owner of the device is determined. U-Stroke can produce raw events at every few milliseconds. One single operation generates a series of raw events to create secure hybrid profile of end-user (HPEU).

1:2 authentication logic can be processed on ubiquitous input device, depending on its capacity. Only owner's usage patterns are stored in short term memory of CCDA for verification. 1: n distinction logic is processed on web server, where usage patterns of n number of enrolled users are stored in long term memory of CCDA for verification. H2HV works in two phases- initial phase and verification phase.

Initial phase includes U-Stroke data acquisition task, multiple features extraction and processing, learning of data-set from environment and template generation. Verification phase includes U-Stroke data collection for claimed identity, multiple features extraction and processing, classification, fusion, match logic, decision logic. Capture process of CCDA model includes data acquisition task, multiple features extraction and processing, learning of data-set from environment and template generation of H2HV. Checking process of CCDA model includes classification, fusion, match logic. Decision process of CCDA includes decision logic and finally action needs to be taken according to security rule. Here main focus is given to data collection from touch screen enabled smart phones or tablets. However, U-Stroke pattern can be collected from any type of devices from traditional desktop computer to smart phone.

Multiple Features Collected for Capture Process of CCDA Model

At first, H2UID interaction captures U-Stroke data according to device usage. Event e in U-Stroke consists of multiple parameters. Capture process of CCDA processing model includes raw data collection. U-Stroke raw data includes {activity, timestamp, X-coordinate, Y-coordinate, pressure, area covered}. Figure 3 represents U-Stroke analysis framework to verify identity of end-user in ubiquitous environment.

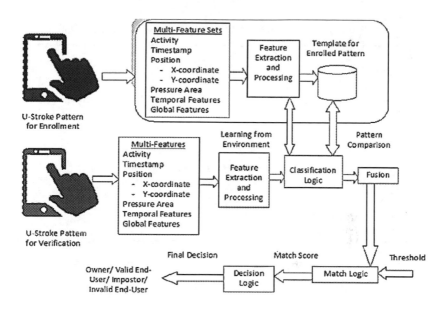

Fig. 3. U-Stroke Analysis for End-User Identity Verification (H2HV)

Features of U-Stroke pattern are presented below.

Activity- P- KeyStroke, Touch-Stroke, V-KeyStroke, S-Stroke, W-Stroke, Z-Stroke, P-Stroke, T stroke - all are under activity category. Three types of activity are touch_down (0), touch_move (0.5) and touch_up (1).

Timestamp - Absolute time of recorded action is measured in milliseconds. Timestamp depends on clock resolution of used devices [13].It is measured by Android API Date.getTime()[14]. Device clock is characterized by sampling rate of 1ms.

Position (X-coordinate, Y-coordinate) - On screen X-axis and Y-axis values of location of each touch point are recorded. When end-user touches the screen, one finger_touch point (part of fingertip) is created. It is measured by Android API ImageView.getLocationOnScreen()[14].

Pressure- Finger pressure ranges from 0 to 1. 0 implies no pressure and 1 implies normal pressure on the screen. However, few touch points hold the same value of finger pressure. Finger pressure force can be obtained by multiplying pressure and size of each touch point. It is measured by Android API MotionEvent.getPressure() [14]. To enhance usability of finger pressure data, values of pressure are expanded 1000 times.

Covered Area- Part of fingertip touched on the screen is considered as size of finger_touch point. It is measured by Android API MotionEvent.getSize().The area covered by fingertip varies with the size of the finger or type of the finger.
Mapping of H2HV procedure with CCDA model is presented in table 1.

Table 1. Mapping of H2HV Procedure with CCDA Model

begin
check H2HV phase
if H2HV phase:= initial then,
enable CCDA(capture)
else if H2HV phase:= verification then,
enable CCDA (capture, checking, decision, action)
if n=m in H2HV then, // n ← number of end-users needs to be
checked for H2HV and m ← number of enrolled user
activate 1:m distinction model
else if n=2 in H2HV then,
activate 1:2 authentication model
end

Table 2 represents procedural logic of CCDA model to identify end-users in ubiquitous environment through any device.

Table 2. Procedural Logic of CCDA for H2HV

begin
process capture()
begin
collect_UStroke(P-KeyStroke, T-KeyStroke)   // data collection
aggregate X (activity, time, position$_x$, position$_y$, pressure, area) // data of
raw event
fragment X into {X$_1$, X$_2$, ...,X$_n$} based on time // feature extraction and
processing
construct feature vector F
fragment F into {f$_1$, f$_2$, ...,f$_n$}
map X {X$_1$, X$_2$, ...,X$_n$} to F {f$_1$, f$_2$, ...,f$_n$}
learn_context (CCDA self loop)
find frequency (used pattern)
store_template(F)
update(CCDA feedback)
if template_size<= local_storge then,
encode and store (short_term_memory)
else
encode, transmitted through secure protocol and store (long_term_memory)
end
process checking()
begin
calculate_closeness (U, F) // U → enrolled user's feature vector during veryfi-
cation, F → feature vector stored at template
evaluate similarity_score() and assign to to s
fusion()

```
 begin
 assign w to each factor of U-Stroke  //w →weight
 calculate confidence_level(w,s)and assign to c
 end
 evaluate match score(s, c, th) and assign to rank  // th →tolerance level
 end
 process decision()
  begin
   if rank=1 then,
    set validity = true  // valid end-user
    assign valid identity of end-user
   else
    set validity = false // invalid end-user
  end
 process action()
  begin
    generate_warning() or block_user() // based on security context
  end
```

4   Analysis

Overall data collection task is performed here by Spice Dual Core Phablet (screen size 5 inches or 12.7 cm), having easy to use touch based user interface with Android version 4.2 Jelly Bean. Here Android data acquisition device id is 37d4d7ddd0b99bdf. As U-Stroke contains heterogeneous strokes, multiple features are not processed as a whole; because it may consume more energy in low-cost devices. As for example, S-Stroke or W-Stroke with one finger move or a T- Stroke with one finger hit is quite different from P-Stroke or Z-Stroke with two fingers. It is seen from the collected raw data that there exists relation between two sets. Set 1 includes {activity, position (X-coordinate, Y-coordinate), timestamp} and set 2 includes {pressure, area}. Set 1 is considered as fine-grained set, whereas set 2 is considered as coarse-grained set. Coarse grained set member "area" is proportional to finger-tip size of end-user. Fingertip size of thumb is greater than index. Frequency of use of thumb and index fingers are higher compared to other fingers. As multiple features are considered, FTA (failure to acquire) and FTE (failure to enroll) rate for H2UID interaction are almost equal to zero compared to other behavioral usage pattern analysis. However, probability of error for device usage (like V-Keystroke, W-Stroke, T-Stroke) is directly proportional to the size of fingertip. Fat finger also affects FTE and FTA parameters. Table 3 represents sample of U-Stroke raw data. Table 4 represents few strokes of U-Stroke pattern for user U1. To build strong profile of user U1 all raw data are collected such as T-Stroke, S-Stroke, and then are grouped according to type of stroke and are processed separately. Finally outputs of all features are fused to generate final decision.

Table 3. U-Stroke Raw Data Collected from Two End-Users

User-ID	Fine Grained Features				Coarse Grained Features	
	Activity	Timestamp (ms)	X-coordinate	Y-coordinate	Pressure	Area
U1	0	4893336544	272	269	0.21	0.04444445
U1	0.5	4893336790	262	271	0.32	0.04444445
U1	0.5	4893336795	123	327	0.28	0.04444445
U1	0.5	4893336952	98	336	0.17	0.13333336
U1	0	4893337798	108	339	0.48	0.04444445
U2	0	4626934695	138	242	0.71	0.15555558
U2	0.5	4626934713	140	241	0.71	0.1777778
U2	0.5	4626934727	180	225	0.71	0.20000002
U2	0.5	4626934744	230	220	0.71	0.1777778
U2	1	4626934790	293	216	0.55	0.13333336

Table 4. Few Strokes of U-Stroke Pattern for User U1

Stroke	Timestamp(ms)	X	Y	Pressure	Area
T-Stroke	78864458	73	541	0.1	0.070588
S-Stroke (right)	79073654	125	656	0.133333	0.109804
S-Stroke (left)	79137343	433	595	0.133333	0.129412
S-Stroke(up)	79107024	392	600	0.141176	0.133333
S-Stroke (down)	79168990	405	351	0.2	0.160784
W-Stroke	79203117	244	271	0.233333	0.156863
Z-stroke	59021345	240	481	0.266667	0.133333
P-Stroke	37581872	394	55	0.137255	0.2

Compared to existing works [15, 16], proposed model works well by collecting heterogeneous data, reduces resource consumption by using CCDA model, and works well for low-cost devices for considering only basic sensor features. Here only 1:2 authentication model is considered, where user U1 is treated as valid end-user (owner) of the device, whereas user U2 is treated as invalid one. Figure 4 represents end-user identification through coarse-grained features. It is seen that inter-user variability between user U1 and U2 is much higher than intra-user variability that can identify owner U1 of Spice Dual Core Phablet efficiently.

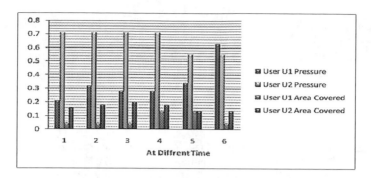

Fig. 4. Coarse-grained Features for End-User Identification H2HV

Remote healthcare application is considered as a use case [2] of our proposed work. In this case, data owner (patients or local caregivers) can use smart device to upload health related data towards remote web server or cloud server. Similarly healthcare professionals from remote locations can access health related data of patients through smart devices at any time. Here authentication through ubiquitous input device is most important step to validate remote health service. Our proposed model works on this direction.

5   Conclusion

Existing works focus on either traditional keystroke logic or touch-stroke logic. We are designing a system model, which is capable to identify user at any place. This paper determines various patterns to build strong hybrid profile of end-users that is capable to reduce false detection, which is very harmful in uncontrolled environment. For touch stroke based authentication, multiple features are collected through user-friendly interface of Android device. This is useful to enhance the flexibility of end-user verification. Multiple features are processed separately and then fused to build user profile. Requirement of computational power is minimized by proposing CCDA model running on the background of limited resource mobile device. Proposed logic can process multiple features in a way that end-user can be identified accurately with less time and computational overhead. User profiles are frequently updated by self-loop. Procedural logic of proposed CCDA model is given in paper and result shows that owner of Spice Dual Core Phablet can be successfully identified through coarse grained features (along with fine grained features consideration) with high accuracy and less resource consumption. Detailed analysis is not given here due to shortage of space. Target of our proposed work is to apply end-user verification (H2HV) on cheap smart devices that can be used by any people within budget.

Work is on to evaluate the performance of proposed model compared to other well-known works on this domain. Various security features, scalability, processor and memory overhead, battery consumption, and timeliness are also need to be considered to implement U-Stroke analysis in ubiquitous environment. Hopefully, direction of this research will be valuable for the further research on this domain.

Acknowledgement. This research work was partially supported by CoE, Centre of System Biology and Biomedical Engineering, and grant no. UGC/452/DST Purse of University of Calcutta, India and Faculty of Mathematis and Information Science, Warsaw University of Technology, Poland.

References

1. Ballagas, R., Borchers, J., Rohs, M., Sheridan, J.G.: The smart phone: a ubiquitous input device. IEEE Journal of Pervasive Computing **5**(1), 70–77 (2006)
2. Bhattasali, T., Saeed, K., Chaki, N., Chaki, R.: Bio-authentication for layered remote health monitor framework. Journal of Medical Informatics & Technologies **23**, 131–140 (2014)
3. Maxion, R., Killourhy, K.: Keystroke biometrics with number-pad input. In: Proceedings of IEEE International Conference on Dependable Systems & Networks, pp. 201–210 (2010)
4. Xu, H., Zhou, Y., Lyu, M.R.: Towards continuous and passive authentication via touch biometrics: an experimental study on smartphones. In: Proceedings of Symposium on Usable Privacy and Security, pp. 187–198 (2014)
5. Shahzad, M., Liu, A.X., Samuel, A.: Secure unlocking of mobile touch screen devices by simple gestures – you can see it but you cannot do it. In: Proceedings of International Conference on Mobile Computing and Networking, pp. 39–50 (2013)
6. Feng, T., Liu, Z., Kwon, K.-A., Shi, W., Carbunar, B., Jiang, Y., Nguyen, N.: Continuous mobile authentication using touchscreen gestures. In: Proceedings of IEEE International Conference on Biometrics: Theory, Applications and Systems, pp. 451–456 (2013)
7. Xu, Z., Bai, K., Zhu, S.: TapLogger: inferring user inputs on smartphonetouchscreens using on-board motion sensors. In: Proceedings of International conference on Security and Privacy in Wireless and Mobile Networks, pp. 113–124. ACM (2012)
8. Frank, M., Biedert, R., Ma, E., Martinovic, I., Song, D.: Touchalytics: On the Applicability of Touchscreen Input as a Behavioral Biometric for Continuous Authentication. IEEE Transactions on Information Forensics and Security **8**(1), 136–148 (2013)
9. Luca, A.D., Hang, A., Brudy, F., Lindner, C., Hussmann, H.: Touch me once and i know it's you! Implicit authentication based on touch screen patterns. In: Proceedings of the SIGCHI Conference on Human Factors in Computing Systems, pp. 987–996. ACM (2012)
10. Touch Screen. http://inventors.about.com/library/inventors/bltouch.htm
11. Bi, X., Li, Y., Zhai, S.: FFitts law: modeling finger touch with fitts' law. In: Proceedings of SIGCHI Conference on Human Factors in Computing Systems, pp. 1363–1372. ACM (2013)
12. Welford, A.T., Norris, A.H., Shock, N.W.: Speed and Accuracy of Movement And Their Changes with Age. Elsevier Journal Acta Psychologica. **30**, 3–15 (1969)
13. Killourhy, K.S., Maxion, R.A.: The effect of clock resolution on keystroke dynamics. In: Lippmann, R., Kirda, E., Trachtenberg, A. (eds.) RAID 2008. LNCS, vol. 5230, pp. 331–350. Springer, Heidelberg (2008)
14. Rogers, R.: Android Application Development. O'Reilly (2009)
15. Zheng, N., Baiy, K., Huangy, H., Wang, H.: You are how you touch: user verification on smartphones via tapping behaviors. In: Proceedings of IEEE International Conference on Network Protocols (ICNP), pp. 221–232 (2014)
16. Bo, C., Zhang, L., Li, X.Y., Huang, Q., Wang, Y.: SilentSense: silent user identification via touch and movement behavioral biometrics. In: Proceedings of Annual International Conference on Mobile Computing & Networking (MobiCom), pp. 187–190 (2013)

A Geometrical Approach to Rejecting Option in Pattern Recognition Problem

Jakub Ciecierski[1], Bartomiej Dybisz[1], Agnieszka Jastrzebska[1(✉)],
and Witold Pedrycz[2,3]

[1] Faculty of Mathematics and Information Science,
Warsaw University of Technology, ul. Koszykowa 75, 00-662 Warsaw, Poland
a.jastrzebska@mini.pw.edu.pl
[2] Systems Research Institute, Polish Academy of Sciences, ul. Newelska 6,
01-447 Warsaw, Poland
[3] Department of Electrical & Computer Engineering, University of Alberta,
Edmonton, AB T6R 2G7, Canada

Abstract. Frequently it happens that during symbols recognition, not all of them are the proper ones. This may cause deterioration of a classifying process. In this paper we present a way to "separate the wheat from the chaff", by constructing a rejector, based on geometrical figures enclosing "wheat" and excluding "chaff". We assume that entities of wheat, called native elements, are structured in some way and that there is no a priori knowledge about chaff, named foreign symbols. For the purpose of this study we present simple geometrical figures to generalize the distribution of symbols and to govern the rejection process.

Keywords: Pattern recognition · Rejecting option · Native and foreign elements

1 Introduction

In a standard attempt to pattern recognition an object is classified into one of given classes. However, in practice, this assumption is often too optimistic. Unfortunately, in important practical applications we do not only have elements belonging to one of proper classes, but also elements that do not belong to any of these classes, cf. [2,5]. Such elements, which we shall not classify into any of proper classes, could appear for example due to an error in input signal segmentation.

Surprisingly, the issue of rejecting foreign symbols is rarely considered in otherwise very impressive research volume on pattern recognition, despite its obvious importance. We may refer to [2] and [3], where the issue of contaminated datasets is recalled. Among few recent papers, dealing with the issue of contaminated datasets we can list [1] and [4]. The literature study reveals that dominating technique for classification with rejection proposes to issue "flexible" decisions regarding class belongingness. This does not necessarily entail application of fuzzy sets, though in [11] authors point out that this is a viable method. Among studies oriented on rejection in pattern recognition problems we may refer to [8,9].

© IFIP International Federation for Information Processing 2015
K. Saeed and W. Homenda (Eds.): CISIM 2015, LNCS 9339, pp. 231–243, 2015.
DOI: 10.1007/978-3-319-24369-6_19

Since elements not belonging to any of proper classes are usually not known a priori, i.e. at the stage of recognizer construction. Moreover, we cannot assume that they form their own class(es) and we cannot use them at this stage. To distinguish between these two types of elements the following terms are used:

- *native* elements for elements of recognized classes and
- *foreign* elements for ones not belonging to any given class.

Objectives of this study are aimed on inventing and exploring geometrical methods that could be employed for rejecting foreign elements, to test proposed methods on synthetic data and validate them on real data. In addition, the study focuses on comparison of different geometrical figures used for symbol rejection. In particular, two figures are considered: n-dimensional ellipsoid and hyperrectangle. As a working hypothesis we assume that the latter one will perform worse.

Let us emphasise that it is not our goal to elaborate and work on native symbols classification, i.e. determining their class belongingness. Such techniques are already well wrought. Nonetheless, when the need occurs we allow ourselves to use some well-known methods of this area.

The paper is structured as follows. In Section 2 mathematical rudiments of presented work are presented. Section 3 contains information about conducted experiments for both synthetic (3.1) as well real data and with their transformations (3.1). Eventually, Section 4 concludes the work.

2   Preliminaries

2.1   Basic Concepts

Conventionally, a pattern recognition problem is an action of dividing a set of objects $\mathbf{S} = \{s_1, s_2 \ldots, s_{|\mathbf{S}|}\}$ into subsets, which include similar objects. Let us assume that $\mathbf{S} = \{S_1, S_2, \ldots, S_{|\mathbf{C}|}\}$ such that $(\forall i \neq j)(S_i \cap S_j = \emptyset)$. Mapping $\sigma : \mathbf{S} \to \mathbf{C}$, where $\mathbf{C} = \{1, 2, \ldots, |\mathbf{C}|\}$, constitutes a basic model for a task of splitting.

In order to compare and assign class labels to each object we identify them with a vector of some measurable characteristics, which are called features, and then perform a classification. Such approach can be split into two mappings: $\phi : \mathbf{S} \to \mathbf{X}$ and $\omega : \mathbf{X} \to \mathbf{C}$, where the first one goes from the space of object to the space of features and the second one from the space of features to the space of classes. It can be easily seen that $\sigma = \omega \circ \phi$ and from now on σ can be referred to as a classifier. In addition, throughout this paper we assume that $\mathbf{X} = X_1 \times X_2 \times \ldots \times X_n = \mathbb{R} \times \mathbb{R} \times \ldots \times \mathbb{R}$ i.e. space of features is the real coordinate space of n-dimensions - $\mathbb{R}^n$ and we use lower-case and upper-case letters to distinguish vectors and sets, respectively.

Since set $\mathbf{S}$ is commonly not available as a whole, we will construct the rejector only on some part of considered space. Let $\mathbf{S} \supset \mathbf{L} = L_1 \cup L_2 \cup \ldots \cup L_{|\mathbf{C}|}$ such that $(\forall i \in \langle 1, |\mathbf{C}|\rangle)(L_i \subset S_i)$. We call $\mathbf{L}$ a learning set. Furthermore we split the learning set into training set($\mathbf{Tr}$) and testing set($\mathbf{Ts}$) in the following fashion: $\mathbf{L} = (Tr_1 \cup Ts_1) \cup (Tr_2 \cup Ts_2) \cup \ldots \cup (Tr_{|C|} \cup Ts_{|C|})$ such that every class of the learning set is split into a training set and a testing set, namely: $(\forall i,j \in \langle 1, |C| \rangle)(Tr_i \cup Ts_i = L_i \wedge Tr_i \cap Ts_j = \emptyset)$ and $\mathbf{Tr} = Tr_1 \cup Tr_2 \cup \ldots \cup Tr_{|C|}$ along with $\mathbf{Ts} = Ts_1 \cup Ts_2 \cup \ldots \cup Ts_{|C|}$.

It is also worthy to note that the word *element* is used all over this paper to indicate examined object, as well as its features vector. Usually difference can be distinguished from the context, but wherever it may cause any doubts we explicitly state which is which.

2.2   Rejector Construction

Since we are interested only in evaluating whether given element belongs or not to any of the proper classes (rather than specifying to which one exactly), each element will be classified either as a native or a foreign one. In this case we assume that the rejector is represented by following mapping: $\rho : \mathbf{S} \to \mathbf{X} \to \bar{\mathbf{C}} = \{native, foreign\}$.

Let $\mathbf{Z} = Z_1 \cup Z_2 \cup \ldots \cup Z_{|C|}$ represent a geometrical region in $\mathbb{R}^n$ being a union of some figures Z_i. This region is assumed to enclose all points in training sets, such that Z_i is created based on training set T_i, for all $i \in \langle 1, |C| \rangle$. For convenience we assume that figures Z_i are convex and compact. Such a region will be used to determine if a feature vector from $\mathbf{X}$ represents native or foreign element. We will write $x \in \mathbf{Z}$ to indicate the fact that some x from $\mathbb{R}^n$ belongs to one or more figures from $\mathbf{Z}$. Since precise information about geometrical objects are defined in Section (2.3) - we are not covering any further details about $\mathbf{Z}$.

Clearly, we are interested in a mapping:

$$\lambda : \mathbf{X} \to \mathbf{C} \quad \text{such that} \quad (\forall x \in \mathbf{X}) \ \lambda(x) = \begin{cases} native & \text{if } x \in \mathbf{Z} \\ foreign & \text{otherwise} \end{cases}$$

In other words if a vector of features belongs to the region $\mathbf{Z}$, we classify it as native. Otherwise it will be treated as a foreign element. To sum up, we complete ρ with a new mapping λ: $\rho : \mathbf{S} \xrightarrow{\phi} \mathbf{X} \xrightarrow{\lambda} \bar{\mathbf{C}}$, where λ is the object of our study.

2.3   Geometry

As mentioned in the previous Section, there is still a need to precise, which geometrical figures we will use to construct the rejector, i.e. the region $\mathbf{Z}$. We have chosen n-dimensional ellipsoids and hyperrectangles and in what follows we define how to establish a membership to each of them. Choice of figures has been motivated by their simplicity (hyperrectangles are really straight-forward to compute) and intuitiveness (using ellipsoidal figures rely on the expectation that features vectors will be normally distributed among each class).

Ellipsoids. An n-dimensional ellipsoid E can be defined as follows:

$$E = \{x \in \mathbb{R}^n \ : \ (x - x_0)^T A(x - x_0) \leq 1\}, \tag{1}$$

where $x_0 \in \mathbb{R}^n$ is the center of the ellipsoid E and A is a positive definite matrix, cf. [10, 13]. Having this in mind, it is obvious that any ellipsoid is uniquely represented by its center x_0 and matrix A.

Given volume of the unit n-dimensional hypersphere V_0, we can compute volume of the ellipsoid E in the following way:

$$Vol(E) = \frac{V_0}{\sqrt{det(A)}}, \tag{2}$$

Referring to Section 2.2, we define a region $\mathbf{Z}$ as union of ellipsoids:

$$\mathbf{Z} = E_1 \cup E_2 \cup \ldots \cup E_{|\mathbf{C}|}$$

such that the ellipsoid E_i encloses all elements of the training set Tr_i and has minimal volume, for all classes in $\mathbf{C}$. Let us notice that according to Formula (2) volume minimization is equivalent to maximization of the determinant. The task of finding minimal volume ellipsoids enclosing given sets of elements was solved by implementation of methods given in [13].

Finally, let us state that for any $x \in \mathbf{X}$, $x \in \mathbf{Z}$ if and only if it is enclosed by at least one ellipsoid from $\mathbf{Z}$.

Hyperrectangles. Alike in the case of ellipsoids, we now construct a rejection region $\mathbf{Z}$ as union of n-dimensional hyperrectangles enclosing training sets of native elements:

$$\mathbf{Z} = H_1 \cup H_2 \cup \ldots \cup H_{|\mathbf{C}|}$$

such that the hyperrectangle H_i encloses all elements of the training set Tr_i, its edges are parallel to axes and it has minimal volume, for all classes in $\mathbf{C}$.

More precisely, the hyperrectangle H_i enclosing the training set Tr_i is a Cartesian product of the following finite intervals:

$$H_i = I_i^1 \times I_i^2 \times \cdots \times I_i^n$$

where, for all classes $i \in \mathbf{C}$, the interval I_i^k is the minimal interval containing values of k-th parameter for all points of the training set Tr_i. Assuming that $f_k(x)$ is the value of k-th feature of an elements x, we get:

$$I_i^k = \big\langle \min \big\{ f_k(x) \big) : x \in Tr_i \big\}, \max \big\{ f_k(x) : x \in Tr_i \big\} \big\rangle$$

Again, let us state that for any $x \in \mathbf{X}$, $x \in \mathbf{Z}$ if and only if it is enclosed by at least one hyperrectangle from $\mathbf{Z}$.

2.4   Evaluation

For a better understanding of how quality of classification with rejection should be measured we adopt parameters and quality measures used in signal detection theory. Since these parameters are widely utilized, we do not refer to their original sources here. The following parameters were used in defining several measures outlining classification's quality. These parameters create so called confusion matrix, which is given in Table 1. The parameters given in the matrix are numbers of elements of a testing set, which have the following meaning:

- TP - the number of elements of the considered class correctly classified to this class,
- FN - the number of elements of the considered class incorrectly classified to other classes,
- FP - the number of elements of other classes incorrectly classified to the considered class,
- TN - the number of elements of other classes correctly classified to other classes (no matter, if correctly, or not).

Table 1. Confusion matrix for rejecting in pattern recognition problem

	Classification to the class	Classification to other classes
The class	True Positives (TP)	False Negatives (FN)
Other classes	False Positives (FP)	True Negatives (TN)

In this study, original pattern recognition problem is a multiclass problem. However, from the point of view of rejection task, it is important whether a native element is classified to any native class, even to an incorrect native class. Therefore, the question if a native element is classified to the correct or any other native class is not considered here. Hence, a multiclass pattern recognition with rejection is turned to a two-class problem. Finally, the following measures were used assess the quality of the classifier:

$$\text{Accuracy} = \frac{TP+TN}{TP+FN+FP+TN}$$
$$\text{Sensitivity} = \frac{TP}{TP+FN}$$
$$\text{Precision} = \frac{TP}{TP+FP}$$
$$\text{F-measure} = 2 \cdot \frac{\text{Precision} \cdot \text{Sensitivity}}{\text{Precision} + \text{Sensitivity}} \tag{3}$$

The following comments help to understand these characteristics:

- Accuracy is a measure of a rejecting performance. This measure describes the ability to distinguish between native and foreign elements. Of course, the higher the value of this measure, the better the identification.
- Precision is the ratio of the number of not rejected native elements to the number of all elements (native and foreign) not rejected. Precision evaluates the rejection ability to separate foreign elements from native ones. The higher the value of this measure, the better ability to distinguish foreign elements from native ones.

- Sensitivity is the ratio of the number of not rejected native elements to the number of all native ones. This measure evaluates the rejection ability to identify native elements. The higher the value of Sensitivity, the more effective identification of native elements. Unlike the Precision, this measure does not evaluate the effectiveness of separation between native and foreign elements. The higher the value of this measure, the better ability to identify native elements.

- Precision and Sensitivity are complementary: increasing sensitivity can cause a drop in precision since, along with increasing the number of not rejected native elements, there might be more not rejected foreign ones. It is there to express the balance between precision and sensitivity since, in practice, these two affect each other. There exists yet another characteristic that combines them: the F–measure. The higher the value of this measure, the better balance between identification of native elements along with separation native elements from foreign ones.

3   Experiment

Experiments are performed for two kinds of data: synthetic and real, both described in Section 3.1. Elements of both kinds are characterized by 24 features. In both, ellipsoids and hyperrectangles were built on chosen set of elements, cf. Sections 2.2 and 2.3, and effectiveness of rejectors has been checked. Both kinds of datasets have been split into learning and testing set.

In addition, we observe how rejection behaves when we start to remove some of points from training classes and reconstruct geometric figures according to shrunken training sets. We shrink number of elements 4 times; at each stage we subtract 5% of points from the current cardinality of training set.

Figure 1 depicts the process of ellipsoids and hyperrectangles shrinking. In this Figure, elements of two classes are presented in the 2-dimensional space of features in order to keep explanation as lucid as possible.

3.1   Datasets

Synthetic Data. For this kind of data randomizing symbols demands several stages. First of all we are generating 24 intervals (using uniform distribution), where each interval can take values from 0 to 20 inclusively. These intervals serve as a scope of possible values for each of features. Next, we are creating 10 different classes of symbols by assigning to them random vectors of features, as well drawn from a uniform distribution. At this stage we have 10 points in our features space. Next, we distort them by creating clouds of points around each symbol. Process of spreading points is done as follows: take features vector of some symbol and for every value of this vector add a number drawn from $N(0,1)$. This is done 1500 times per each previously generated symbol. It gives us 10 clouds of points, each having 1500 elements. We treat clouds as learning sets, where 1000 points belong to training set and remaining 500 to testing set.

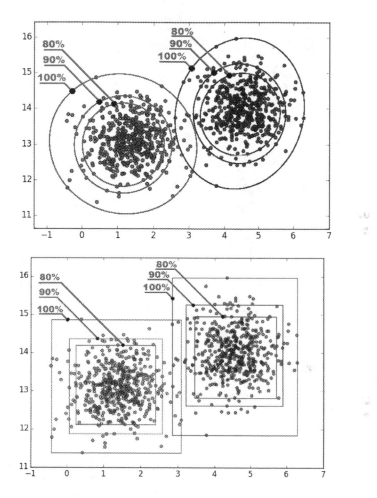

Fig. 1. Consecutive shrinking process applied for: ellipsoids (upper part) and hyper-rectangles (bottom part).

As for foreign symbols, two approaches were applied:

- homogeneous distribution in the space of features, which spreads elements uniformly around the Cartesian product of features intervals. Elements accidentally overlapping with natives were redrawn.
- non-homogeneous distribution - created by applying following process: for each segment between a pair of native clouds centers find its middle point. Treat the points as a centre of new cloud of 1000 foreign points, created using the normal distribution.

In this way, in both manners, we get 10000 foreign points.

Real and Semi-synthetic Data. The datasets were constructed based on the MNIST database of handwritten digits [12]. The following figure (2), represents a sample of natives elements used in the experiments:

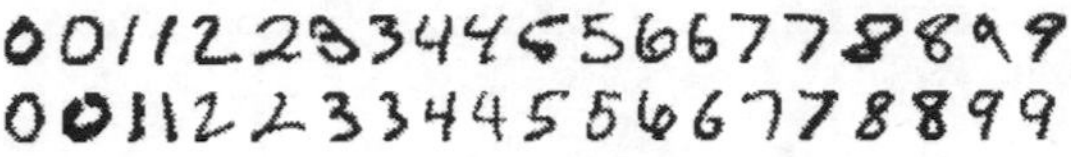

Fig. 2. Samples of elements of native classes.

Then, based on this database, two sets of foreign elements were constructed. Sample of such set is represented by Figure 3.

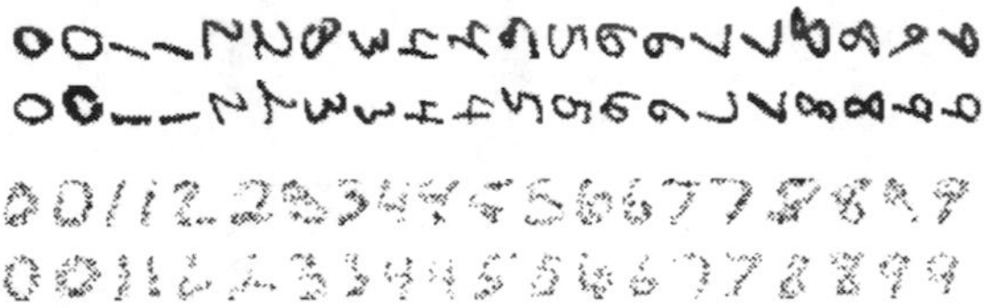

Fig. 3. Transformed native elements: rotated by 90 degrees (upper part) and randomly distorted (bottom part).

On the other hand, we refer to collection of foreign symbols as 'semi-synthetic', because they are neither pure real, nor pure synthetic objects. They have been created by modifying in some specific fashion (therefore synthetic) the native set of symbols (therefore real). In this paper we incorporate two such sets: A and B. First one comprises of native symbols rotated by 90 degrees, while the second one of uniformly distorted native elements, cf. Figure 3.

3.2   Results

This Section is built mostly upon tables, which present results of the experiments. Although we separate synthetic data measurements from real/semi-synthetic ones, at the end there is an array concluding both of them.

Synthetic Data. First of all we present Tables 2 and 3. Each of them is divided into considered geometric figure (upon which rejector has been based on), type of foreign symbols distribution and consecutive steps of shrinking figures numbered as 1000, 950, 903, 858, 816 (number of points in each figure at each stage). The only difference between them is that both training and testing sets are used in the first case, while test set in the second case. One can observe natural behaviour of hyperrectangles, which in the end of the volume minimizing, enclose more native points than ellipsoids. What is more, ellipsoids have better foreign recognition properties, as mostly they are smaller (in terms of volumes) than hypperrectangles. In addition, both figures work better with homogeneous distributed foreign, which is caused by an assumption that feature's vectors of foreign symbols are equally likely to appear within the considered space.

Table 2. Confusion matrices for consecutive shrinking of hyperrectangle (h-r) and ellipsoid (ell) at training set (in %).

training set	Rejector built for synthetic data sets						
data set	homogeneous				non-homogeneous		
figure	h-r		ell		h-r		ell	
confusion	TP	FN	TP	FN	TP	FN	TP	FN
matrix	FP	TN	FP	TN	FP	TN	FP	TN
-0%	100.00	0.00	100.00	0.00	100.00	0.00	100.00	0.00
	0.67	99.33	0.14	99.86	25.39	74.61	14.96	85.04
-5%	98.46	1.54	94.84	5.16	98.46	1.54	94.84	5.16
	0.48	99.52	0.07	99.93	21.67	78.33	10.54	89.46
-10%	96.98	3.02	90.10	9.90	96.98	3.02	90.10	9.90
	0.38	99.62	0.03	99.97	17.62	82.38	7.91	92.09
-15%	95.53	4.47	85.64	14.36	95.53	4.47	85.64	14.36
	0.31	99.96	0.02	99.98	17.13	82.87	5.38	94.62
-20%	94.23	5.77	81.56	18.44	94.23	5.77	81.56	18.44
	0.29	99.71	0.01	99.99	16.99	83.01	4.83	95.17

Table 3. Confusion matrices for consecutive shrinking of hyperrectangle (h-r) and ellipsoid (ell) at testing set (in %).

testing set	Rejector built for synthetic data sets						
data set	homogeneous				non-homogeneous		
figure	h-r		ell		h-r		ell	
confusion	TP	FN	TP	FN	TP	FN	TP	FN
matrix	FP	TN	FP	TN	FP	TN	FP	TN
-0%	95.10	4.90	87.96	12.04	95.10	4.90	87.97	12.03
	0.71	99.29	0.03	99.97	31.03	68.97	8.33	91.67
-5%	93.36	6.64	80.66	19.34	93.36	6.64	80.66	19.34
	0.47	99.53	0.02	99.98	27.64	72.36	6.31	93.69
-10%	92.12	7.88	76.16	23.84	92.12	7.88	76.16	23.84
	0.39	99.61	0.00	100.0	24.32	75.68	5.63	94.37
-15%	91.02	8.98	71.68	28.32	91.02	8.98	71.68	28.32
	0.33	99.67	0.00	100.0	22.55	77.45	4.55	95.45
-20%	89.52	10.48	66.74	33.26	89.52	10.48	66.74	33.26
	0.26	99.74	0.00	100.0	21.43	78.57	3.84	96.16

Real and Semi-synthetic Data. As for this type, we provided only one Table (4), which concerns both sets: A and B. 'h-r' is an abbreviation for hyperrectangle, while 'ell' means ellipsoid. In this case each stage of shrinking is marked as '-0%', '-5%', '-10%', '-15%' or '-20%', because our samples contain approximately 1000 features' vectors per symbol class, which causes slight

Table 4. Confusion matrices for consecutive shrinking in ellipsoid (ell) and hyperrect-angle (h-r) approach. Considered are sets A and B of foreign elements.

testing set	Rejector built for real data set							
data set	A				B			
geometry	h-r		ell		h-r		ell	
confusion	TP	FN	TP	FN	TP	FN	TP	FN
matrix	FP	TN	FP	TN	FP	TN	FP	TN
-0%	98.42	1.58	85.06	14.93	98.45	1.55	85.98	14.02
	62.41	37.59	12.10	87.90	3.18	96.82	0.11	99.89
-5%	96.45	3.55	80.82	19.18	96.74	3.26	81.83	18.17
	54.16	45.84	7.53	92.47	2.57	97.43	0.10	99.90
-10%	95.60	4.40	77.25	22.75	95.45	4.55	76.93	23.07
	49.96	50.04	5.51	94.49	1.95	98.05	0.05	99.95
-15%	93.92	6.08	73.61	26.39	93.88	6.12	73.37	26.63
	46.41	53.59	4.27	95.73	1.87	98.13	0.02	99.98
-20%	92.77	7.23	69.53	30.47	66.74	33.26	93.15	6.85
	43.20	56.80	3.18	96.82	0.00	100.0	1.80	98.20

differences in number of points enclosed by each of geometrical figure, hence it can not be generalized. Of course '-0%' symbolizes situation, in which geometric figures are based on all points in training sets. As in the previous Section, data are presented in confusion matrices built with testing set.

First remark is that in both foreign sets hyperrectangle approach is not always worse than the ellipsoid one - we have got 100% rejected foreign symbols in case of hyperrectangles in B, while ellipsoids rejected 98.20%. Second observation is that for two sets ellipsoid-based rejectors works well, while hyperrectangles acquire rather average results in A. Hyperrectangle approach in sets A and B manifests difference in points classified as true positive. In the first one, at stage '-20%', it is 92.77% while in the second 66.74%. This reveals difference in native elements distribution i.e. in set B they are more 'compressed' than in A, hence shrinking process has created hyperectangles of a bigger volume in the case of set A than in B. In addition in set A, ellipsoid technique, we achieved high foreign symbols rejection rate, but at the same time the rate of native elements' classification decreased.

Summary. As stated in Section 1, one of the main aims of this study is to measure differences between approach based on ellipsoids and hyperretangles. In this Section we present Table 5, which is the resume of performed tests, based on measuring sensitivity, accuracy, precision and F-measure features, as described in 2.4. This array helps us observing behaviour of both considered geometrical figures.

Table 5. Measuring rejecting results for synthetic and real data for shrunken figures ('-0%', '-5%', '-10%', '-15%' or '-20%'). h-r -hyperrectangle, ell - ellipsoid.

testing sets	synthetic				real/semi-synthetic			
data	homogeneous		non-homogen.		90ccl		AND	
figure	h-r	ell	h-r	ell	h-r	ell	h-r	ell
Sensitivity	95.10	87.96	95.10	87.96	98.41	85.06	98.45	85.98
Accuracy	97.89	95.97	77.68	90.43	57.99	86.95	97.37	95.23
Precision	98.52	99.93	60.51	84.07	44.32	78.01	93.97	99.75
F-measure	96.78	93.56	73.96	85.97	61.11	81.38	96.16	92.35
Sensitivity	93.36	80.66	93.36	80.66	96.45	80.82	96.74	81.83
Accuracy	97.47	93.54	79.36	89.35	62.82	88.56	97.20	93.85
Precision	99.00	99.95	62.81	86.47	47.33	84.42	94.99	99.76
F-measure	96.10	89.27	75.10	83.46	63.50	82.58	95.86	89.90
Sensitivity	92.12	76.16	92.12	76.16	95.60	77.25	95.45	76.93
Accuracy	97.11	92.05	81.16	88.30	65.32	88.70	97.18	92.24
Precision	99.16	100.0	65.44	87.12	49.13	87.62	96.10	99.87
F-measure	95.51	86.47	76.52	81.27	64.90	82.11	95.78	86.91
Sensitivity	91.02	71.68	91.02	71.68	99.91	73.61	93.88	73.37
Accuracy	96.79	90.56	81.97	87.53	67.12	88.31	96.71	91.07
Precision	99.28	100.0	66.87	88.73	50.53	89.69	96.19	99.94
F-measure	94.97	83.50	77.10	79.30	65.70	80.86	95.02	84.62
Sensitivity	89.52	66.74	89.52	66.74	92.77	69.52	93.15	69.53
Accuracy	96.33	88.91	82.22	86.35	68.86	87.66	96.50	89.79
Precision	99.42	100.0	67.62	89.68	52.01	91.69	96.30	99.97
F-measure	94.21	80.05	77.05	76.53	66.65	79.08	94.70	82.02

We have divided the array into datasets types, foreign types (homogeneous, non-homogeneous; set A, set B), rejector kind which has been used ('h-r' means hyperrectangle; 'ell' describes ellipsoid) and results for consecutive shrinking of geometrical figures.

First, we observe that in ellipsoid approach sensitivity decreases quicker than in hyperrectangle one. Also, interesting is fact that for non-homogeneous foreign symbols, F-measure of hyperrectangle technique actually elevates, while in all others is getting smaller (especially in the ellipsoid type of rejectors). In all cases during shrinking process precision rises, but some of the accuracy is lost.

4   Conclusion and Future Research Directions

We have proposed an approach to native elements recognition/foreign elements rejection. Native elements belong to proper classes, which we plan to process, while foreign elements may appear in a data set due to an unexpected error. Because classification itself has not been in the scope of this study, presented methods may play crucial role for example in data preprocessing, where one can firstly dispose of foreign elements and then focus on proper classification. Foreign elements removed early from a dataset would not be subjected to a classification process and therefore the proposed technique could improve the overall pattern recognition process.

Two methods have been analysed: based on hyperrectangles and on ellipsoids. Despite the fact that ellipsoid-based rejector exhibits high precision in detecting foreign elements, it forfeits significant amount of native elements (especially in shrinking process). On the other hand, hyperrectangular rejector detects native elements on acceptable level but its ability to discern foreign ones is closely related to the learning set layout. As for real life application, it is beneficial to use ellipsoid-based rejector, without shrinking technique, but one must keep in mind that with this method approximately 14% of native points may be wrongly rejected.

As to future directions, we plan to employ models of bipolar uncertainty to features and their aggregation [6,7]. Since final decision is crisp (a pattern is either native, or foreign) preferred are univariate bipolar models based on the uncertainty interval [-1,1] rather than bivariate models based on two unit intervals representing negative/positive uncertainties.

Acknowledgement. The research is supported by the National Science Center, grant No 2012/07/B/ST6/01501, decision no UMO?1?72012/07/B/ST6/01501.

References

1. Bertolami, R., Zimmermann, M., Bunke, H.: Rejection strategies for offline handwritten text line recognition. Pattern Recognition Letters **27**(16), 2005–2012 (2006)
2. Bromley, J., Denker, J.S.: Improving rejection performance on handwritten digits by training with rubbish. Neural Computing **5**, 367–370 (1993)
3. Chow, C.: On optimum recognition error and reject tradeoff. IEEE Transactions on Information Theory **16**(1), 41–46 (1970)
4. Elad, M., Hel-Or, Y., Keshet, R.: Pattern detection using a maximal rejection classifier. In: Arcelli, C., Cordella, L.P., Sanniti di Baja, G. (eds.) IWVF 2001. LNCS, vol. 2059, pp. 514–524. Springer, Heidelberg (2001)
5. Homenda, W.: Optical music recognition: the case study of pattern recognition. In: Kurzynski, M., Puchala, E., Wozniak, M., et al. (eds.) Computer Recognition Systems. Advances in Soft Computing, pp. 835–842 (2005)
6. Homenda, W.: Balanced Fuzzy Sets. Information Sciences **176**, 2467–2506 (2006)
7. Homenda, W., Pedrycz, W.: Processing of uncertain information in linear space of fuzzy sets. Fuzzy Sets & Systems **44**, 187–198 (1991)
8. Homenda, W., Lesinski, W.: Optical music recognition: a case of pattern recognition with undesirable and garbage symbols. In: Choras, R., et al. (eds.) Image Processing and Communications Challenges, pp. 120–127 (2009)
9. Koerich, A.: Rejection strategies for handwritten word recognition. In: Proc. of the 9th International Workshop on Frontiers in Handwriting Recognition (2004)
10. Kumar, P., Yildirim, E.A.: Minimum-Volume Enclosing Ellipsoids and Core Sets. Journal of Optimization Theory and Applications **126**(1), 1–21 (2005)

11. Meel, A., Venkat, A.N., Gudi, R.D.: Disturbance classification and rejection using pattern recognition methods. Ind. Eng. Chem. Res. **42**(14), 3321–3333 (2003)
12. LeCun, Y., Cortes, C., Burges, C.: The MNIST database of handwritten digits (1996). http://yann.lecun.com/exdb/mnist/
13. Todda, M.J., Yildirim, E.A.: On Khachiyan's algorithm for the computation of minimum-volume enclosing ellipsoids. Discrete Applied Mathematics **155**(13), 1731–1744 (2007)

Identification Effectiveness of the Shape Recognition Method Based on Sonar

Teodora Dimitrova-Grekow[✉] and Marcin Jarczewski

Faculty of Computer Science, Bialystok University of Technology, Wiejska 45A,
15-351 Bialystok, Poland
t.grekow@pb.edu.pl, m.jarczewski@o2.pl

Abstract. Sonars are among the most popular navigation elements used in autonomous vehicles. Beside their well known properties, they have unexplored specifics offering interesting information. In this paper, we present the results of an experiment with the drawbacks of sonars. Our approach combined the regular information obtained from a sonar system with information deriving from measurement aberration. The experiments with an ultrasonic range measurement system of a mobile robot showed that the usually neglected sonar drawbacks could be unusually helpful. This paper emphasizes the effectiveness of identification, which was calculated based on the ratio of the quantities of parallelepipeds to cylinders. The experimental results are presented. Further work aims to implement this idea on a robot on an HCR base. Another possibility is also suitable implementation of map building with a relative degree of confidence.

Keywords: Shape recognition · Sonar signal · Features extraction · Signal analysis · Mobile robotics

1 Introduction

Sonar sensors are famous for their robustness and unambiguous acting for quite narrow and strictly defined work conditions. To obtain satisfying accuracy in distance measurement, one has to pay attention mainly to the applied sensor, the send signal, and the method of processing the received echo-information. All attempts to identify objects using sonar have to deal with the following problems:

- physical properties of objects: size, shape, material of which the object is made, the surface of the object;
- relationship between the sensor and the object, such as distance, angle;
- complexity and number of objects to recognize;
- repositioning, the physical properties of objects at a time;
- external factors, such as temperature and humidity.

The most common way to use ultrasonic sensors today are sonar arrays, containing from 3 to 16 and more sensors. In contrast to a quite irrelevant, single

© IFIP International Federation for Information Processing 2015
K. Saeed and W. Homenda (Eds.): CISIM 2015, LNCS 9339, pp. 244–254, 2015.
DOI: 10.1007/978-3-319-24369-6_20

sonar sensor measurement, a data sequence from a sonar array allows compensation of the drawbacks of the acoustic signals to some level. In this paper, we present a complimentary attempt: in addition to the classical signal recovery and ridding of bad echoes, we sorted them and brought them into use. In our experiment, we tested shape distinguishing using simple objects, such as cylinders and parallelepipeds. A set of shape recognition rules was set and implemented in a real-time system: NXT robot. The tests have proved the off-line assumptions and calculations.

An important aspect of the study was to estimate the possibility of not only identifying the objects, but also their exact orientation and collocations. Hence, building maps to a relative degree of confidence [1] is a future aim.

2   Related Work

The most popular uses of ultrasonic signals are distance establishment and obstacle detection [2], localization [3] and avoidance [4]. It should not be forgotten, though, that sonar sequences contain much information about the environment [5] from such sources as inferential echo signals from all possible reflection surfaces in the environment the robot is acting in [6].

Although the sonar possesses a set of well known advantages, such as its wide accessibility, relative good accuracy and low costs, its main disadvantage are connected with the conical emission area of the signal. That is the orgin of faked measurements occurring in the signal sequences. The more complex the structure of the environment, the more additional complicating and disturbing echoes arise. That complicates too much for direct use of sonar data for object recognition or topological localization. An well-known way to solve these problems is using neural networks [7], [8], [9], genetic algorithms [10], Fuzzy Artmap [11], Hough transform [12] or an extended Kalman filter [13]. Researches involved the analysis of a two objects based on Continuously Transmitted Frequency Modulated ultrasonic sensor [14].

All these methods require quite many calculations and the real-time work of sonar-based systems at times significantly slows down. But on the other hand all these approaches consider only ultrasonic echoes, neglecting measurements in which a non echo comes back etc.

In our work, we took into account not only the 'regular' information, delivered from sonar sensors, but also 'hidden' information. We acted on signal features, which were the result of the specific interaction between the sonar sensor and certain objects. In comparison to the mentioned methods, we used minimal computation, simultaneously keeping a very high identification effectiveness of shape recognition.

The first information about use of sonar shortcomings are described in [15]. In this article, we present enriched experience and extended explanation of the identification effectiveness using our shape recognition method.

3   System Structure

We present a complimentary attempt: beside the classical signal recovery and ridding of the bad echos, we sorted them and brought them in use. In our experiment, we tested shape distinguishing using simple objects, such as cylinders and parallelepipeds. A set of shape recognition rules was set and implemented in a real-time system: NXT robot. Each of the mobile robots was used as an independent data collecting vehicle. So far, the tests have proved the offline assumptions and calculations.

Considering the specificity of sonar signals, the first stage of research involved data processing (Fig. 1). The information gathered from the sonar system was treated in different ways while searching for the most relevant interpretation. The robot route is straight passing beside the obstacles. The robot maintains a path parallel to the wall.

Observing the collected data gathered from the sonar sensors, we noticed a number of interesting dependencies between the received reflections and the history of scanning. Finally, a set of object features enabling effective object recognition emerged. This can be considered the separate second stage of the study. The most essential features are described in the next section.

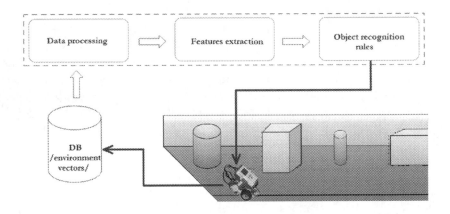

Fig. 1. Stages of the system

We used a simple set of objects: two types of solids - parallelepipeds and cylinders. The tests shown in the third section were done on several different sizes of each type. The final, third stage of our system was developing recognition rules, which had been applied to the real-time test vehicle and proved the primary idea - to get more than the usual noise using only very simple tools.

In our experiments, we achieved over 80% accuracy in shape recognition. The experimental results are shown in the last section. The further work aims an implementation in mobile robot localization. A hybrid location method is being developed to test the pattern recognition approach in real-time conditions.

Its main point is building a relative confidence degree map to defining the vehicle location. The method is described generally at the end of the article.

4   Simple Shape Recognition Method

The most common approach to shape recognition is to consider shape context. The features used in this methodology are based on complex data related directly to the analyzed objects. We present a shape recognition method that also uses indirect data, such as reflections, which we called "glitters" in this paper. To implement our approach, we consider the following steps: (1) primary data collection, (2) initial features extraction, (3) final features extraction (4) shape recognition rules building.

For all these phases, the robot passed a distance D scanning the environment along its path and gathering data (Fig. 1).

4.1   Primary Data Collection

Walking a certain distance, the experimental vehicle collects a set of distance measurements. The raw data are processed twice:

a First, the raw sonar data it was smoothed so that the registered shapes became sharper and more reliable. The results of this smoothing was very appreciable and observable if one visualizes the data stream.

b Simultaneously, all data exceptions and irregularity were counted exactly, related, and compared.

All data irregularities were removed (Fig. 2). Among the registered values, there were many 'glitters' - reading exceptions observed by comparison with neighboring ones. Their quick smoothing facilitated further processing of the received signal. Simultaneously, these irregularities were statistically assessed.

4.2   Initial Features Extraction

The first features extraction was based on regularly shaped data, obtained from double smoothed sonar sequences. The secondary correction was focused on larger 'exceptions' and smoothing of the discovered shapes (Fig. 2). The so-called 'exceptions' were a result of overlapping echoes from various objects and measurements made in sequence. This will be especially useful in the future development of the system in the navigation area.

The very first phase of the research used a single object scene: the robot scanned and saved data from a single object. It was indispensable to extract all the necessary information for effective object recognition. After many observations, based on the acoustic rules and simplification derived from the chosen work conditions, several important dependencies were found.

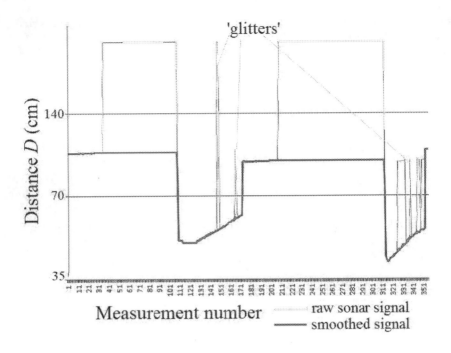

Fig. 2. Raw sonar measurements and real objects

The adjustment scheme was empirically determined during the experiments and was part of a continued refinement-cast. The primary consideration allowed to appoint one of the most important features, used in further features determination.

Minimal measured distance: D_{MIN} The meaning of this parameter is useful for detecting if it is an edge, side or cylinder. The minimal value itself is very important, but it becomes meaningful only after colligation with 10 to 30 contiguous distances.

4.3   Final Features Extraction

The main idea of our approach is based on investigating the irregularities in sonar measurements, taking into account the sequences in which they appear and the rules of this irregularity. The extracted features were used for building the shape recognition rules. Every file with data saved from the sonar was interpreted as a vector. The most important selected characteristics were:

Wall-greater Distances: D_{OV} - percentage of measurements greater than the distance to the wall N_W

The source of such values can be different: NXT sonars use value '255' as an error measurement; normally it should mean 255 cm, but in fact it means non-response was registered; even if the obstacle is so near that the reflections of the send signal cannot reach the receiver. The total value of D_{OV} is calculated as follows:

$$D_{OV} = \frac{(N_{255} + N_{GW})}{N} \tag{1}$$

Where:

N_{255} - number of '255' values,

N_{GW} - number of values greater than the distance to the wall,

N - total number of measurements.

Alien Echos: D_{NR} - percentage of measured distances less than N_W although no object is displaced at the spot

Obviously, this is the result of delayed or side reflections:

$$D_{NR} = \frac{N_{LLW}}{N} \tag{2}$$

Where:

N_{LLW} - number of values less than the distance to the wall, cached in the object's free space.

4.4 Shape Recognition Rules

A set of $D_{NR} = f(D_{OV})$ characteristics for ca. several hundred vectors were built. Some of them will be shown in the next section. A linear dependence (Fig. 3), which was implemented and loaded on the robot for online tests, resulted from the characteristic families. This is the most important, next to the extraction of features, step in the process of object recognition. When the optimal set of features has been selected, it is time to create a classifier. There are three different methods:

1. The concept of similarity - the simplest and most common approach, known as 'template matching'.
2. Probabilistic approach: includes methods based on the Bayesian decision rule, maximum likelihood or density estimation.
3. Building of decision limitations based on optimizing some error criteria: Fisher's linear discriminant, multilayer perceptions, decision tree.

Our approach was based on the first method. We studied the features extracted out in the previous subsection, as well as their behavior and relations to each other. This allowed us to discriminate parallelepipeds and cylinders with minimum calculations. An optimization of these observations is proof of the simple reliance between D_{OV} and D_{NR}.

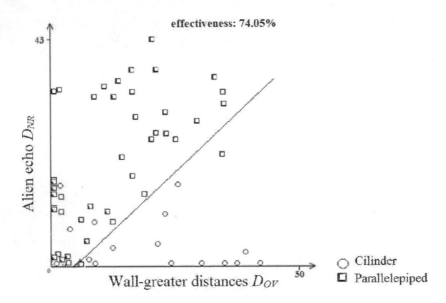

Fig. 3. Distinguishing parallelepipeds and cylinders

Example of the dependency $D_{NR} = f(D_{OV})$ is visualized in Fig. 3. The optimal clustering generated a linear function which was different for every group of objects. In fact, a rule generalizing these differences can be found. Objects clustering was determined by linear function $F_{CL}(x) = ax + b$. Points located on the same side of the line belong to the same cluster.

Finding the best function consists of several steps:

1. Defining points in a certain distance from each other on the x and y axes: the parameters D_{OV} and D_{NR} got integer values from 0 to 100. Thus, we assumed that if the distance between two points is greater than 1, it is a sufficient condition to set an optimal line.
2. Then, a collection of lines for each of these points is appointed. Or for each point a dozen simple lines are determined. They all differ by a factor. The difference between the lines is 2. In a single group, at least a few thousand had been checked.
3. By evaluating the test collection, the best of the lines was selected.

5   Identification Effectiveness

Because of observations of various orientations of the parallelepipeds, the difference in the number of scanned cylinders and parallelepipeds was significant. Therefore, in order to ensure objective evaluation, a secondary factor S was introduced, depending on the total number of cylinders C, and the total number of parallelepipeds P. In this way, we could save the $S = P/C$. Thanks to the difference in the number of measurements, it will not affect final effectiveness.

The effectiveness of R identification was calculated based on the ratio of the quantity of parallelepipeds to cylinders on the same side of the line. Indexes O stand for objects over the line and U for those under. So, for both cases R_U and R_O we obtain:

$$R_U = S_U(S_U + C_U P) \qquad (3)$$

$$R_O = C_O \frac{P}{S_O + C_O P} \qquad (4)$$

Hence, we get R_1:

$$R_1 = (R_U \frac{C_U P + S_U}{S + C} + R_O \frac{C_O P + S_O}{S + C})100 \qquad (5)$$

Later, you could make the opposite assumptions that under the line there are cylinders and over parallelepipeds:

$$R_2 = 1 - R_1 \qquad (6)$$

And finally:

$$R = max(R_1, R_2) \qquad (7)$$

6   Tests and Experimental Results

Through the experiments we conducted, we found that the most appropriate way to obtain satisfactory and relevant shape recognition requires splitting the measurements into several groups, considering the minimum read distance. This range clustering was determined during the hundreds of tests. We generalized several variants considering the specific effectiveness for separate distance fractions and the complex effectiveness for the total experiment.

Here we present an optimal division of the distance ranges, where the complex effectiveness manifest stability. Groups, to which we assigned individual points were:

a) 8 - 25 cm,
b) 26 - 40 cm,
c) 41 - 60 cm,
d) 61 - 80 cm,
e) 81 - 120 cm.

In the realization of this study, we conducted over 500 tests divided into two sets:

– Teaching set - used exclusively for deriving proprer clustering for the objects,
– Testing set - serving only for the evaluation of clustering effectiveness.

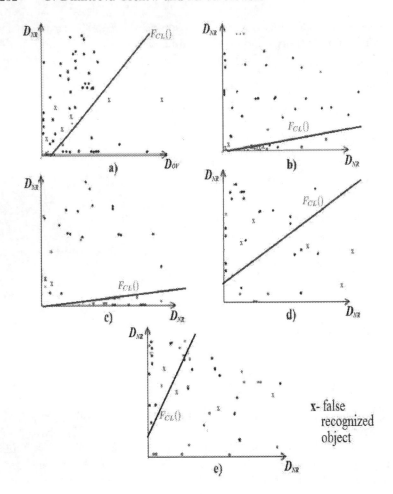

Fig. 4. Clustering functions for different data groups: a) 8-25 cm; b) 26-40 cm; c) 41-60 cm; d) 61-80 cm; e) 81 - 125 cm

The results of the clustering function derive are shown as a set of graphs. The tests, repeated several hundred times, proved the calculated accuracy. When interpreting them, you should take into account that for the largest distances ($> 100cm$) most of the test objects were hardly 'visible' thus parameters D_{OV} and D_{NR} were almost the same. Figure 4 shows the end selected separating lines or clustering function $F_{CL}()$ for all five distance groups. The dependency between the function parameters are not the center of attention for this issue. To make things more clear, X-points are all unrecognized or incorrectly recognized figures.

The lowest effectiveness of the clustering function $F_{CL}()$ was 74.05% - refers to the nearest group of objects (Fig. 5). Its main weaknesses were parallelepipeds parallel to the robot path. The best effectiveness 96.15% was reached in the third

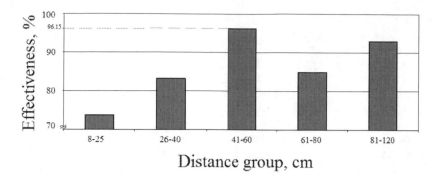

Fig. 5. Effectiveness for the distance groups

group 41-60 cm. The linearity is changing is non linear, but possesses a logical rule: The hardware unfortunately disallows work with longer distances.

7   Conclusions

The focus of this paper was identification effectiveness, which was calculated using the ratio of the number of parallelepipeds to cylinders. We considered not only the 'regular' information, delivered from sonar sensors, but also 'hidden' information and acted on signal features, which were the result of the specific interaction between the sonar sensor and certain objects.

The results of our experience with sonar drawbacks substantiate the developed method of simple shape recognition. Our approach combines the regular information obtained from the sonar system with measurements of aberration derivative. This original approach minimizes calculations for real-time implementation.

We presented a shape recognition rule: linear function $F_{CL}()$ expressing the dependencies between the sonar signal features in the described conditions. The average accuracy we achieved was 86.28%. The tests on the robot Lego Mindstoms NXT proved the effectiveness of function $F_{CL}()$.

Our further plans are to find general rules for shape distinguishing and also position recognition, which we partly touched on in our studies.

We intend to explore new features based on acoustic signal dependencies and additionally to increase the number of ultrasonic receivers. Further work also aims to use a new mobile robot on the HCR base, which will allow to implement this shape recognition method in building building a relative degree of confidence maps.

Acknowledgments. This paper is supported by the S/WI/1/2013.

References

1. Dimitrova-Grekow, T.: A hybrid algorithm for self location. In: PAK, vol. 11, pp. 1163–1166 (2013)
2. Del Castilloa, G., Skaara, S., Cardenasb, A., Fehr, L.: A sonar approach to obstacle detection for a vision-based autonomous wheelchair. Robotics and Automation IEEE Journal **54**, 967–981 (2006)
3. Choi, J., Choi, M., Nam, S.Y., Chung, W.K.: Autonomous topological modeling of a home environment and topological localization using a sonar grid map. Autonomous Robots Journal **30**, 351–368 (2011)
4. Lenser, S., Veloso, M.: Visual sonar: Fast obstacle avoidance using monocular vision. Intelligent Robots and Systems **1**, 886–891 (2003)
5. Ohtani, K., Baba, M.: Shape recognition for transparent objects using ultrasonic sensor array. In: Annual Conference SICE 2007, pp. 1813–1818 (2007)
6. Kiyoshi, O., Masamichi, M., Hiroyuki, T., Keihachiro, T.: Obstacle arrangement detection using multichannel ultrasonic sonar for indoor mobile robots. Journal Artificial Life and Robotics **15**, 229–233 (2010)
7. Vossiek, M., et al.: An ultrasonic multi-element sensor system for position invariant object identification. In: IEEE Ultrasonics Symposium Proceedings, pp. 1293–1297 (1994)
8. Dror, I.E., et al.: Three-dimensional target recognition via sonar: a neural network model. Neural Networks **8**, 149–160 (1995)
9. Kuc, R.: Biomimetic sonar locates and recognizes objects. IEEE Journal of Oceanic Engineering **22**, 616–624 (1997)
10. Baba, M., et al.: 3D shape recognition system by ultrasonic sensor array and genetic algorithms. In: Proceedings of the 21st IEEE Instrumentation and Measurement Technology Conference, pp. 1948–1952 (204)
11. Streilein, W.W., et al.: A neural network for object recognition through sonar on a mobile robot. In: Intelligent Control, Held Jointly with IEEE International Symposium on Computational Intelligence in Robotics and Automation, Intelligent Systems and Semiotics, pp. 271–276 (1998)
12. Yap, T.N., Shelton, CR.: SLAM in large indoor environments with low-cost, noisy, and sparse so-nars. In: Proceedings of IEEE International Conference on Robotics and Automation, pp. 1395–401 (2009)
13. Joong-Tae, P., Jae-Bok, S., Se-Jin, L., Munsang, K.: Sonar Sensor-Based Effcient Exploration Method Using Sonar Salient Features and Several Gains. Journal of Intelligent and Robotic Systems **63**, 465–480 (2011)
14. Worth, P., McKerrow, P.: An approach to object recognition using CTFM sensing. Sensors and Actuators **179**, 319–327 (2012)
15. Dimitrova-Grekow, T., Jarczewski, M.: Sonar method of distinguishing objects based on reflected signal specifics. In: Andreasen, T., Christiansen, H., Cubero, J.-C., Raś, Z.W. (eds.) ISMIS 2014. LNCS, vol. 8502, pp. 506–511. Springer, Heidelberg (2014)

MRI Texture Analysis for Differentiation Between Healthy and Golden Retriever Muscular Dystrophy Dogs at Different Phases of Disease Evolution

Dorota Duda[1]([✉]), Marek Kretowski[1], Noura Azzabou[2,3],
and Jacques D. de Certaines[2,3]

[1] Faculty of Computer Science, Bialystok University of Technology,
Wiejska 45a, 15-351 Bialystok, Poland
{d.duda,m.kretowski}@pb.edu.pl
[2] Institute of Myology, Nuclear Magnetic Resonance Laboratory, Paris, France
[3] CEA, I2BM, MIRCen, NMR Laboratory, Paris, France

Abstract. In this study, a texture analysis is applied to T2-weighted Magnetic Resonance Images (MRI) of canine pelvic limbs in order to differentiate between Golden Retriever Muscular Dystrophy (GRMD) dogs and healthy ones. The differentiation is performed at three phases of canine growth and/or disease development: 2-4 months (the first phase), 5-6 months (the second phase), and 7 months and more (the third phase). Eight feature extraction methods (statistical, model-based, and filter-based) and five classifiers are tested. Four types of muscles are analyzed: the *Extensor Digitorum Longus* (EDL), the *Gastrocnemius Lateralis* (GasLat), the *Gastrocnemius Medialis* (GasMed) and the *Tibial Cranialis* (TC). The experiments were performed on five healthy and five GRMD dogs. Each of the muscles was considered separately. The best classification results were 95.81% (the EDL muscle), 97.19% (GasLat), and 91.37% (EDL) correctly recognized cases, for the first, second and third phase, respectively. These results were obtained with an SVM classifier.

Keywords: Golden Retriever Muscular Dystrophy (GRMD) · Duchenne Muscular Dystrophy (DMD) · Texture analysis · Tissue characterization · Muscles · Classification · Dog · MRI T2 · Computer-Aided Diagnosis (CAD)

1 Introduction

The Golden Retriever Muscular Dystrophy (GRMD) canine model is acknowledged to be the closest to human Duchenne Muscular Dystrophy (DMD, the most common and most severe form of muscular dystrophy) [1]. For this reason it is commonly used for various pre-clinical and therapeutic trials. In research on GRMD development or its response to treatment, great hope is placed in Magnetic Resonance (MR) image analysis, performed with various

© IFIP International Federation for Information Processing 2015
K. Saeed and W. Homenda (Eds.): CISIM 2015, LNCS 9339, pp. 255–266, 2015.
DOI: 10.1007/978-3-319-24369-6_21

(semi)automatic, computer-aided techniques. Other diagnostic methods (such as needle biopsy followed by histopathological analysis), while providing more reliable diagnoses, are to be avoided here. They can alter muscle integrity and weaken muscles which are already degenerated and poorly functioning due to disease progression.

It has been shown that image texture can be a very important source of information contained in the image [2]. Texture analysis has already been successfully applied to many diagnostic problems, concerning a variety of tissue types and/or imaging modalities. A broad review of texture analysis methods and applications in the field of medical image classification can be found in several articles [3–5].

The aim of this study is to assess the potential of various MRI texture analysis techniques (statistical, model-based, and filter-based) for characterization of different types of muscles in canine pelvic limbs: the *Extensor Digitorum Longus* (EDL), the *Gastrocnemius Lateralis* (GasLat), the *Gastrocnemius Medialis* (GasMed) and the *Tibial Cranialis* (TC). In total, eight methods of texture analysis are used. A texture-based differentiation between healthy and GRMD dogs is performed at three different phases of canine growth and/or disease development: 2-4 months (the first phase), 5-6 months (the second phase), and 7 months and more (the third phase). The division into three phases is made in reference to histological changes in muscle structure resulting from disease progression. As early as the first 3-4 months of age, GRMD skeletal muscles display hypercontracted, degenerating or regenerative isolated fibers [6]. After this period (up to the age of about 6 months), the number of degenerating necrotic fibers dramatically increases [7]. At this stage, varying degrees of fibrosis and adipose infiltration can occur. Finally, from 6 months of age, GRMD is in its third phase, which is characterized by rather slow muscular changes, with a lower level of degeneration and regeneration, and progressive intensity of fibrosis and fat tissue infiltration [8]. As such changes may alter the structure of each muscle type in different ways, each type of muscle is considered separately in this study.

The experiments are repeated using five well-known classifiers: Support Vector Machines, Back-Propagation Neural Networks, Logistic Regression, Random Forest, and Adaptive Boosting. To the best of our knowledge, this is the first comparative study of texture-based classification of the Canine Hindlimb Muscles involving such a large number of texture analysis techniques and classifiers, and comparing the usefulness of the textural information extracted from different types of muscles and at each phase of canine growth / disease development.

2   Related Work

Texture analysis of different human muscle types has already been studied in some works (for a review, please refer to [9,10]). However, there are few studies dealing with its application to GRMD tissue characterization or characterization of disease development over time.

One of the earliest studies on MRI texture analysis applied to characterization of dystrophic muscles was presented in [11]. The work assessed the potential of several texture analysis techniques (based on the gray-level histogram, co-occurrence matrices, gradients, and run length matrices) in comparison to the potential of visual analyses of the same ROIs carried out by several radiologists (each radiologist analyzed a single ROI). Textural features were extracted from T1-weighted images and analyzed by Correspondence Factorial Analysis (CFA). Automated classification of dystrophic and healthy patients resulted in 70% and 86% sensitivity and specificity, respectively. The results achieved by the radiologists assessments were less accurate (sensitivity of 56% and specificity of 71%).

The aim of another work [12] was to evaluate the usefulness of MRI texture analysis methods in the characterization of diseased and healthy calf muscles. In addition, these methods were compared to standard radiological evaluation. The authors tested a total of 282 textural features (statistical and model-based) derived from T1-weighted images. Four different classes of calf muscle were considered, depending on the severity of the pathology affecting the muscles. The classification results obtained with the best (selected) 7 textural features were in 80% agreement with the categorization made by the radiologists.

Fan et al. [13] analyzed different MRI biomarkers (non-textural MR imaging-based and texture analysis-based) for seven muscles of the proximal pelvic limbs in GRMD and healthy control dogs. All the dogs were imaged at 3, 6, and 9-12 months of age. The aim of the study was to quantify longitudinal disease progression and to differentiate between two groups of dogs in different stages of canine growth and/or disease development. Texture features, based on the gray-level histogram and run length matrices, were calculated from T2-weighted images. The statistical test (Mann-Whitney-Wilcoxon) found all the texture features to be significantly higher in the GRMD dogs than in the healthy controls, in each dog age group. Moreover, classification based on Linear Discriminant Analysis (LDA) showed that RLM-based texture features had on average better discriminatory power than other MRI biomarkers (such as fat content and T2 relaxation time). Nevertheless, for certain muscles, texture features did not show significant correlations with the histopathology indices.

In the work [14] texture analysis of T2-weighted MR images was used to describe the structure of thigh soft tissues in five groups of athletes (representing differently loading sport types: repetitive non-impact, repetitive low impact, odd impact, high impact, and high magnitude) and non-athletes. Five thigh muscles at two anatomical levels of the dominant leg were characterized with co-occurrence matrix-based texture features. Statistical analyses showed differences in thigh muscle textures, especially between the athletes performing high impact and odd impact loading sports.

Another study [15], performed on a similar database (five athlete groups and non-athletic controls), analyzed the differences in MRI texture properties of hip muscles (on T1-weighted images). Four different muscle types were considered in the study. Six methods for extraction of texture features were used to characterize muscular tissues (based on the gray level histogram, gradient matrices, co-occurrence matrices, run length matrices, wavelets, and an autoregressive model). Significant differences in texture properties between athletes and non-athletes were observed for the four considered sport types for at least one muscle type. Only between the non-magnitude loading athletes and the non-athlete controls no significant differences were found in muscle texture.

3   Texture-Based Classification of the Canine Hindlimb Muscles

Two stages can be distinguished in a typical system for texture-based classification of medical images [16]. The first stage is preparation of the learning set used to construct the classifiers. In this stage a database of images, as large as possible, is gathered and preprocessed (if necessary). Then the *Regions of Interest* (ROIs, the image regions subjected to the analysis) are delineated, either manually, or by (semi)automated segmentation methods. Each ROI is assigned a label that refers to a tissue class (e.g., healthy or pathologically changed) and is based on a verified diagnosis. Afterwards various methods are applied in order to characterize each ROI. In our case, these methods are based on texture analysis and result in the creation of vectors of textural features. Each feature is a numerical measure of a specific texture property, such as coarseness, granularity, regularity, entropy, or frequency of stripes, waves, edges, etc. Labeled feature vectors form a *training set*, based on which several classifiers can be constructed.

Once the classifiers are created, the system can be used for recognition of new cases that have not yet been diagnosed. In this second stage of operation of the system, a suspicious image region is delineated by a physician or segmented (semi)automatically by the methods incorporated in the system. Then it is characterized by texture features, the same as were used in the first stage. Finally, the system classifiers are used to indicate the most probable tissue class. These two stages of work with the system are depicted schematically in Figure 1. This work-flow was used in our experiments, aimed at recognition of healthy and GRMD dogs based on muscle MRI texture analysis.

3.1   Database Description

The experiments were performed on the database provided by [17]. Five GRMD dogs and five healthy controls were considered in the study. The dogs were bred in a dedicated gene therapy facility at the National Veterinary School of Alfort, France. All procedures were carried out in accordance with the *Guide for the Care and the Use of Laboratory Animals* and approved by the Institutional Animal Use and Care Committee, in accordance with European legislation regarding the use of laboratory animals. The image database was created at the Nuclear Magnetic Resonance Laboratory of the Institute of Myology, Pitie-Salpetriere University Hospital in Paris, France (its full description, as well as a description of all the acquisition protocols, can be found in [17]). Each acquisition was performed on a 3T Siemens Magnetom Trio TIM imager/spectrometer (Siemens Healthcare, Erlangen, Germany) with a standard circularly polarized extremity coil. The in-plane resolution was 0.56 mm × 0.56 mm, the slice thickness

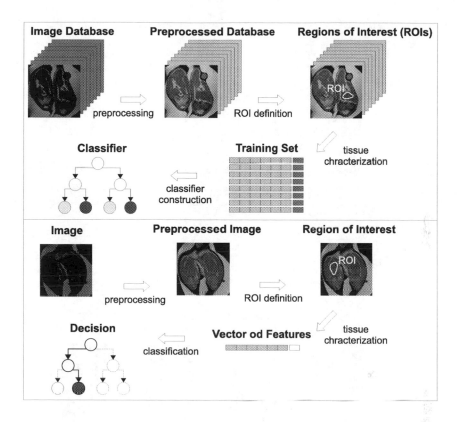

Fig. 1. Typical system for texture-based classification. Two stages of operation of the system: training (the upper part of the figure) and learning (the lower part)

was 3 mm, and the inter-slice gap was 7.5 mm. The slice orientation was axial with respect to the long axis of the muscle. Anesthesia was induced in the dogs with propofol (Rapinovet®, Schering-Plough), injected intravenously at a dose of 0.65 ml/kg. The T2-weighted Spin Echo sequences (used in our analyses) were acquired with the following parameters: repetition time TR = 3,000 ms, echo time TE1 = 6.3 ms, and TE2 = 50 ms. Each image series comprised from 12 to 14 images. For each dog, from 3 to 5 examinations were performed over a maximum of 14 months. In total, 38 examinations were used in the study. Each examination was assigned to one of the three considered phases of canine growth and/or disease development. In total, 14, 9, and 15 examinations were available for the first, second and third phase, respectively.

Only 4 types of muscle were considered in our analyses (EDL, GasLat, GasMed, and TC). Other muscle types were ignored because they occupied very small areas on the images (less than 50 pixels within a ROI), or due to unsuitable geometry (areas that were too narrow). For each muscle a minimum of 3 images were segmented. Only ROIs larger than 40 pixels and having each dimension

Table 1. Average sizes of ROIs used in our experiments

muscle \class	Phase 1 GRMD	Phase 1 healthy	Phase 2 GRMD	Phase 2 healthy	Phase3 GRMD	Phase3 healthy
EDL	102	127	156	213	142	271
GasLat	144	123	204	170	158	212
GasMed	244	267	266	395	311	420
TC	116	162	241	248	227	314

Table 2. Numbers of ROIs used in our experiments

muscle \class	Phase 1 GRMD	Phase 1 healthy	Phase 2 GRMD	Phase 2 healthy	Phase3 GRMD	Phase3 healthy
EDL	96	104	77	47	95	149
GasLat	67	46	38	28	45	90
GasMed	82	68	45	37	64	115
TC	104	107	92	67	105	178

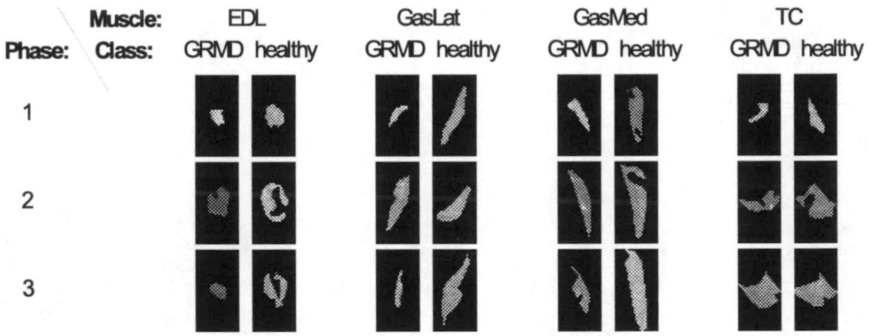

Fig. 2. Examples of ROIs for each tissue type, tissue class, and phase of canine growth and/or disease development. The size of each black square is 30 × 47 pixels

greater than four pixels were kept for further analysis. The numbers of analyzed ROIs and their average dimensions are given in Tables 1 and 2, respectively. In Figure 2 exemplary ROIs for each muscle type and for each muscle class (GRMD, healthy) are presented.

Due to the differences in average image intensities between different examinations, and even between different images within the same series, the images had to be preprocessed. The preprocessing consisted in a linear image transformation, performed separately for each image, so that the reference object was of the same average pixel intensity on all images. Owing to this procedure the gray level interval covering all the pixels belonging to the ROIs did not exceed 256 values.

3.2   Texture Analysis

Eight texture analysis methods (statistical, model-based and filter-based) were considered for our investigation. They were implemented in our homemade software *MIP* (*Medical Image Processing*). In total, 39 features were calculated:

- *average, variance, skewness,* and *kurtosis* – first order statistics (FOS), obtained from a gray-level histogram,
- *normalized autocorrelation coefficient* (AC) [18],
- *average, variance, skewness, kurtosis,* from the gradient matrix (GM) [19],
- *energy, inverse difference moment, entropy, correlation, sum average, difference average, sum variance, difference variance, sum entropy, difference entropy,* and *contrast,* from the co-occurrence matrices (COM) [20],
- *short run emphasis, long run emphasis, gray level non-uniformity, run length non-uniformity, fraction of image in runs, low gray level runs emphasis, high gray level runs emphasis,* and *run length entropy,* from the run length matrices (RLM) [21–23],
- *average, entropy, angular second moment, inverse difference moment,* and *contrast,* form the gray level difference matrices (GLDM) [24],
- *fractal dimension* based on the fractional Brownian motion model (FB) [25],
- *entropy* of an image region filtered with the following pairs of the Laws' masks: (*E3L3* and *L3E3*), (*S3L3* and *L3S3*), (*S3E3* and *E3S3*), (*E3E3* and *E3E3*), and (*S3S3* and *S3S3*) [26].

Each of the aforementioned sets of features was considered separately. In addition, a set of all the possible features (calculated with the eight enumerated texture analysis methods) was tested. The use of a relatively large number of texture characteristics was dictated by two facts. Firstly, various stages of the disease were considered, and each stage results in other changes in the muscle structure. These latter alter in different way the muscle texture of an MRI image. Secondly, the observed changes are not the same for each type of muscle. In turn, each texture feature is a numerical measure of other texture property, related to the type of muscle and and/or disease development. A detailed comparative study on various MRI texture analysis techniques in muscular dystrophy of GRMD dogs, explaining the histological meaning of MRI textures, and justifying the use of various texture features can be found in [9]).

The choice of parameter settings for each method (such as maximum pixel distance) was strictly dependent on the properties of the ROIs. Most of the ROIs were rather thin and narrow, so the use of some methods would have required further elimination of dozens of ROIs. For example, in the first phase of canine growth, the percentages of ROIs unsuitable for Laws' method with a mask of size 5×5 were 31.50%, 42.48%, 18.67%, and 28.91% for EDL, GasLat, GasMed, and TC, respectively. A similar problem pertained to the co-occurrence matrix-based, gray level matrix-based, autocorrelation-based, and fractal-based approach. For all of them the maximum considered pixel distance was set at 2.

The co-occurrence matrices and the gray level difference matrices were constructed separately for 4 standard directions (0°, 45°, 90°, and 135°) and for

2 considered distances between pixel pairs (1 and 2). The same four directions and/or two pixel distances were also considered in the run length matrix-based method and during calculation of the normalized autocorrelation coefficients. For all four aforementioned methods, features corresponding to different directions of pixel arrangement and/or different pixel distances were averaged. All possibilities of averaging (or not) of the features corresponding to different directions and/or to different pixel distances were tested.

3.3   Classification

Classification experiments were performed with *Weka* software [27]. Five classifiers were used to compare the potential of different feature sets and the usefulness of the information extracted from each of the 4 considered muscles:

- Support Vector Machines (SVM) [28] using a Sequential Minimal Optimization (SMO) algorithm [29] and a second degree polynomial kernel,
- Neural Network (NN) [30] with a backpropagation and sigmoidal activating function, having a hidden layer wherein the number of neurons was equal to the average value of the number of features and the number of classes,
- Logistic Regression (LR) [31],
- Random Forest (RF) [32] comprising a set of 50 trees,
- Adaptive Boosting (AB) [33] using the C4.5 tree [34].

Classification accuracies were estimated by 10-fold cross-validation, repeated 10 times. The 100 partial results were averaged.

4   Results and Discussion

The best results obtained by each classifier for each type of muscle and at each phase of canine growth / disease progression are presented in Table 3.

It can be seen from Table 3 that the usefulness of textural information is different for each muscle. It also changes over time, with canine growth (and/or disease development). In the earliest phase of canine life (2-4 months), the most important information could be extracted from the EDL muscle texture. For all the classifiers, the best classification result at this first phase was obtained for this muscle – from 93.44% for the AB classifier to 95.81% for the SVM. For comparison, at the same phase, only 81.70% (AB) to 83.91% (SVM) of cases were correctly recognized with the textural features extracted from the GasLat muscle. In contrast, the texture of the GasLat muscle proved the most useful (or nearly the most useful) for classification at the second phase of canine life. The highest percentage of correctly diagnosed cases (97.19%) was observed for the GasLat-based textural features combined with the SVM classifier. Still, at the second phase, it was the GasMed muscle that outperformed the other muscles in terms of classification when the RF and the AB classifier were used. In the latter case, the GasLat muscle gave slightly inferior results (by about 1% – 2%) than the GasLat muscle. Finally, at the third phase, no clear advantage of any

Table 3. Differentiation between healthy and GRMD dogs at different phases of canine growth / disease evolution. The best classification accuracies [%] (and standard deviations) achieved with five different classifiers ("Cl") and for each considered muscle of canine pelvic limbs. Each result is followed by the corresponding texture analysis method

Cl	Phase	Muscle			
		EDL	GasLat	GasMed	TC
SVM	1	95.81 (4.63) RLM	83.91 (11.44) GLDM	86.72 (8.89) All	85.40 (8.42) All
	2	90.72 (8.10) COM	97.19 (6.38) COM	94.92 (7.91) COM	91.65 (7.95) COM
	3	91.37 (4.79) RLM	89.45 (9.00) COM	89.55 (6.82) RLM	90.81 (5.78) All
NN	1	94.83 (5.22) RLM	82.87 (12.01) GLDM	83.84 (9.61) All	85.69 (7.75) All
	2	91.62 (7.52) COM	96.93 (6.20) COM	93.33 (8.86) All	89.10 (7.32) All
	3	90.81 (5.87) COM	87.82 (8.38) All	89.81 (7.12) RLM	89.83 (5.86) COM
LR	1	94.72 (5.78) RLM	83.36 (11.34) GLDM	83.79 (9.64) All	83.19 (6.67) COM
	2	89.83 (9.66) All	95.50 (8.11) COM	91.38 (9.40) FOS	87.30 (9.93) FOS
	3	86.82 (6.38) RLM	89.76 (7.34) RLM	86.83 (7.45) COM	89.58 (5.13) COM
RF	1	93.59 (6.22) All	83.15 (10.26) COM	81.84 (9.02) RLM	83.51 (7.86) COM
	2	90.83 (8.58) All	91.36 (11.15) RLM	93.14 (8.63) RLM	89.05 (8.80) RLM
	3	88.94 (6.16) COM	88.03 (7.62) RLM	89.24 (5.66) RLM	89.82 (5.17) All
AB	1	93.44 (6.52) All	81.70 (11.46) COM	84.27 (9.38) All	84.65 (7.28) COM
	2	92.08 (7.34) All	91.90 (10.65) COM	92.83 (9.84) COM	86.75 (8.36) All
	3	88.60 (6.51) COM	87.82 (8.15) All	86.25 (8.12) RLM	90.91 (5.03) COM

one muscle could be observed, and the differences in the results obtained with different muscles were the smallest. For the SVM and the NN classifiers, the best results were achieved with the GasLat muscle (91.37% and 90.81%, respectively). For the RF and AB classifiers, the best third-phase results were obtained for the TC muscle (89.82% and 90.91%, respectively).

Given the above results, it can be concluded that the classification results are not strongly correlated with the size of the characterized ROIs. The crucial textural information, in terms of tissue differentiation, could be extracted from even very small ROIs. For example, the EDL muscle occupied the smallest image regions in almost all cases, and it was with this muscle that the classification experiments often gave the best results.

The best overall classification results at the first, second, and third phase were 95.81%, 97.19%, and 91.37% correctly recognized cases, respectively. The significant difference between the two latter phases is not surprising, if we consider that the set of ROIs corresponding to the third phase was two times greater than the one used for the second phase (see Table 1). Direct comparisons between phases could be more reliable if equally numerous datasets were used for each phase-problem. In our case, the original number of ROIs was small, so we preferred not to truncate the datasets.

Finally, it could be seen that the best texture analysis methods were those based on the co-occurrence matrices and on the run length matrices. It is difficult to say which of these is better, as their application very often resulted in similar classification accuracies. The use of the COM method led to better results for the GasLat muscle type, whereas the RLM method was the most frequently selected for the TC muscle. In the case of the first- and second-phase classification problem, the sets composed of all the possible textural features (derived from the 8 classification methods) were also frequently selected as the best ones.

5   Conclusion

The study investigated the possibility of using MRI texture analysis in the process of distinguishing between healthy and GRMD dogs at various stages of canine growth and/or disease development. Four types of muscle located in canine pelvic limbs were considered: EDL, GasLat, GasMed, and TC. Eight texture analysis methods were used for their characterization, including statistical, model-based, and filter-based methods. The experiments, while conducted on a small sample, showed that several texture analysis methods have great potential. The best ones proved to be those based on co-occurrence matrices and run-length matrices. Satisfactory results were also obtained with the sets comprising features provided by all of the eight considered texture analysis methods. In this case, the calculations required more memory to store data and more time for classifier construction.

The classification results for each muscle were compared in order to evaluate which type of muscle may provide the most useful information in terms of disease detection in different phases of canine growth. At the earliest phase (2-4 months of canine life), the best differentiation between healthy and GRMD dogs was observed for the EDL muscle (for all classifiers used). In the second phase (5-6 months), the GasLat and the GasMed muscles were found to provide slightly better texture characteristics than the other two muscles. Finally, in the third phase (7 months and more), the best results corresponded either to the EDL muscle texture analysis (with the SVM and NN classifiers), the TC muscle (RF, AB), or the GasLat muscle (LR).

6   Future Work

Some problems occurring during our investigations are still unresolved an will be the subject of our future research. For example, the choice of minimum acceptable ROI size remains problematic. Moreover, it is not only the ROI size, but also its shape that determines its suitability for texture analysis. The choice of distances between pixel pairs should also be assessed. Certain texture properties will not be captured when only small distances (such as 1 or 2) are considered for the COM, GLDM, FB, or AC method. If distances were too large (5 or more pixels), many more ROIs would have to be discarded due to their size – too small to guarantee a large enough number of pixel pairs for feature calculation. Having only 10 dogs for the analyses, we had to limit ourselves to consideration of only small distances, in order not to reject too many ROIs. Similar experiments should be conducted on a larger data base. It will also be interesting to explore other types of MR images (e.g. T1-weighted, fat-suppressed, acquired using the Dixon technique, diffusion tensor sequences, etc.) and perform a multiparametric texture classification. Other texture analysis methods (such as those based on wavelets, the Fourier transform, or the Gabor transform) could also be tested. Finally, it will be interesting to study the evolution of textural features during canine growth / disease development.

Acknowledgments. This work was performed under the auspices of the European COST Action BM1304, MYO-MRI. It was also supported by grant S/WI/2/2013 from the Bialystok University of Technology, Bialystok, Poland.

References

1. Kornegay, J.N., Bogan, J.R., Bogan, D.J., Childers, M.K., Li, J., et al.: Canine models of Duchenne muscular dystrophy and their use in therapeutic strategies. Mamm. Genome **23**(1–2), 85–108 (2012)
2. Haralick, R.M.: Statistical and structural approaches to texture. Proc. of the IEEE **67**(5), 786–804 (1979)
3. Castellano, G., Bonilha, L., Li, L.M., Cendes, F.: Texture analysis of medical images. Clin. Radiol. **59**(12), 1061–1069 (2004)
4. Hajek, M., Dezortova, M., Materka, A., Lerski, R.A. (eds.): Texture Analysis for Magnetic Resonance Imaging. Med4Publishing, Prague (2006)
5. Nailon, W.H.: Texture analysis methods for medical image characterisation. In: Mao, Y. (ed.) Biomedical Imaging, pp. 75–100. InTech Open (2010)
6. Nguyen, F., Cherel, Y., Guigand, L., Goubault-Leroux, I., Wyers, M.: Muscle lesions associated with dystrophin deficiency in neonatal golden retriever puppies. J. Comp. Pathol. **126**(2–3), 100–108 (2002)
7. Valentine, B.A., Cooper, B.J., Cummings, J.F., de Lahunta, A.: Canine X-linked muscular dystrophy: morphologic lesions. J. Neurol. Sci. **7**(1), 1–23 (1990)
8. Nguyen, F., Guigand, L., Goubault-Leroux, I., Wyers, M., Cherel, Y.: Microvessel density in muscles of dogs with golden retriever muscular dystrophy. Neuromuscul. Disord. **15**(2), 154–163 (2005)
9. De Certaines, J.D., Larcher, T., Duda, D., Azzabou, N., Eliat, P.A., et al.: Application of texture analysis to muscle MRI: 1-What kind of information should be expected from texture analysis? EPJ Nonlinear Biomed. Phys. **3**(3), 1–14 (2015)
10. Lerski, R.A., de Certaines, J.D., Duda, D., Klonowski, W., Yang, G., et al.: Application of texture analysis to muscle MRI: 2 technical recommendations. EPJ Nonlinear Biomed. Phys. **3**(2), 1–20 (2015)
11. Herlidou, S., Rolland, Y., Bansard, J.Y., Le Rumeur, E., de Certaines, J.D.: Comparison of automated and visual texture analysis in MRI: characterization of normal and diseased skeletal muscle. Magn. Reson. Imaging **17**(9), 1393–1397 (1999)
12. Skoch, A., Jirak, D., Vyhnanovska, P., Dezortova, M., Fendrych, P., et al.: Classification of calf muscle MR images by texture analysis. Magn. Reson. Mater. Phy. **16**(6), 259–267 (2004)
13. Fan, Z., Wang, J., Ahn, M., Shiloh-Malawsky, Y., Chahin, N., et al.: Characteristics of magnetic resonance imaging biomarkers in a natural history study of golden retriever muscular dystrophy. Neuromuscul. Disord. **24**(2), 178–191 (2014)

14. Sikio, M., Harrison, L.C., Nikander, R., Ryymin, P., Dastidar, P., et al.: Influence of exercise loading on magnetic resonance image texture of thigh soft tissues. Clin. Physiol. Funct. Imaging **34**(5), 370–376 (2014)

15. Nketiah, G., Savio, S., Dastidar, P., Nikander, R., Eskola, H., Sievanen, H.: Detection of exercise load-associated differences in hip muscles by texture analysis. Scand. J. Med. Sci. Sports **25**(3), 428–434 (2015)

16. Duda, D.: Medical image classification based on texture analysis. Ph.D. Thesis, University of Rennes 1, Rennes, France (2009)

17. Thibaud, J.L., Azzabou, N., Barthelemy, I., Fleury, S., Cabrol, L., et al.: Comprehensive longitudinal characterization of canine muscular dystrophy by serial NMR imaging of GRMD dogs. Neuromuscul. Disord. **22**(Suppl. 2), S85–S99 (2012)

18. Gonzalez, R.C., Woods, R.E.: Digital Image Processing, 2nd edn. Addison-Wesley, Reading (2002)

19. Lerski, R., Straughan, K., Shad, L., Boyce, D., Bluml, S., Zuna, I.: MR image texture analysis - an approach to tissue characterization. Magn. Reson. Imaging **11**(6), 873–887 (1993)

20. Haralick, R.M., Shanmugam, K., Dinstein, I.: Textural features for image classification. IEEE Trans. Syst., Man, Cybern., Syst. SMC **3**(6), 610–621 (1973)

21. Galloway, M.M.: Texture analysis using gray level run lengths. Comp. Graph. and Im. Proc. **4**(2), 172–179 (1975)

22. Chu, A., Sehgal, C.M., Greenleaf, J.F.: Use of gray value distribution of run lengths for texture analysis. Pattern Recogn. Lett. **11**(6), 415–419 (1990)

23. Albregtsen, F., Nielsen, B., Danielsen, H.E.: Adaptive gray level run length features from class distance matrices. In: Sanfeliu, A., Villanueva, J.J., Vanrell, M., Alqukzar, R., Crowley, J., Shirai, Y. (eds.) 15th International Conf. on Pattern Recogn., vol. 3, pp. 738–741. IEEE Press, Los Alamitos (2000)

24. Weszka, J.S., Dyer, C.R., Rosenfeld, A.: A comparative study of texture measures for terrain classification. IEEE Trans. Syst., Man Cybern. **6**(4), 269–285 (1976)

25. Chen, E.L., Chung, P.C., Chen, C.L., Tsai, H.M., Chang, C.I.: An automatic diagnostic system for CT liver image classification. IEEE Trans. Biomed. Eng. **45**(6), 783–794 (1998)

26. Laws, K.I.: Textured image segmentation. Ph.D. Thesis, University of Southern California, Los Angeles, CA, USA (1980)

27. Hall, M., Frank, E., Holmes, G., Pfahringer, B., Reutemann, P., Witten, I.H.: The WEKA data mining software: an update. SIGKDD Explorations **11**(1), 10–18 (2009)

28. Vapnik, V.N.: The Nature of Statistical Learning Theory, 2nd edn. Springer, New York (2000)

29. Platt, J.C.: Fast training of support vector machines using sequential minimal optimization. In: Scholkopf, B., Burges, C.J.C., Smola, A.J. (eds.) Advances in Kernel Methods - Support Vector Learning, pp. 185–208. MIT Press, Cambridge (1998)

30. Rojas, R.: Neural Networks: A Systematic Introduction. Springer, Berlin (1996)

31. Hosmer, D.W., Lemeshow, S., Sturdivant, R.X.: Applied Logistic Regression, 3rd edn. John Wiley & Sons Inc., Hoboken (2013)

32. Breiman, L.: Random Forests. Mach. Lear. **45**(1), 5–32 (2001)

33. Freund, Y., Shapire, R.: A decision-theoretic generalization of online learning and an application to boosting. J. Comput. System Sci. **55**(1), 119–139 (1997)

34. Quinlan, J.: C4.5: Programs for Machine Learning. Morgan Kaufmann, San Francisco (1993)

Policy-Based Slicing of Hibernate Query Language

Angshuman Jana[1]([⊠]), Raju Halder[1], Nabendu Chaki[2],
and Agostino Cortesi[3]

[1] Indian Institute of Technology Patna, Patna, India
{ajana.pcs13,halder}@iitp.ac.in
[2] University of Calcutta, Kolkata, India
nabendu@ieee.org
[3] Università Ca' Foscari Venezia, Venezia, Italy
cortesi@unive.it

Abstract. This paper introduces a policy-based slicing of Hibernate Query Language (HQL) based on a refined notion of dependence graph. The policies are defined on persistent objects, rather than transient objects, which are stored in an underlying database. We extend the Class Dependence Graph (ClDG) of object-oriented languages to the case of HQL, and we refine it by applying semantics-based Abstract Interpretation framework. This leads to a slicing refinement of HQL programs, producing more precise slices $w.r.t.$ policies and we refine by using semantics equivalence, according to the Abstract Interpretation framework.

Keywords: Program slicing · Hibernate Query Language · Dependence graphs · Abstract interpretation

1 Introduction

Program slicing is a widely used static analysis technique which extracts from programs a subset of statements which is relevant to a given behavior [24]. Some of its worth mentioning applications are debugging, testing, code-understanding, code-optimization, etc. [21,23]. Many program slicing algorithms are proposed during last four decades, referring to various language paradigms, such as imperative, object-oriented, functional, logical, etc. [9,22–24]. Recently, [10,25] extended the slicing approaches to the case of applications interacting with external database states. Various forms of program slicing, like static, dynamic, quasi-static, conditioned, etc. are proposed by tuning it towards specific program analysis aim [23].

Hibernate query language (HQL) is an Object-Relational Mapping (ORM) language which remedies the paradigm mismatch between object-oriented languages and relational database models [2]. Various `Session` methods are used to convert transient objects into persistent ones by propagating their states from memory to the database (or vice versa) and to synchronize both states when

© IFIP International Federation for Information Processing 2015
K. Saeed and W. Homenda (Eds.): CISIM 2015, LNCS 9339, pp. 267–281, 2015.
DOI: 10.1007/978-3-319-24369-6_22

a change is made to persistent objects. HQL has gained popularity to software developers in recent years as it provides a unified platform to develop database applications without knowing much details about the database.

Reduction of software failure rate which may happen due to the frequent change of enterprise policies or customers requirements, always remains a serious challenge in software industry [8]. Let us consider an enterprise scenario where new policies are often defined or existing policies are often modified in order to ensure that the real business-data meet business challenges and goals. This forces software developers to maintain and incorporate appropriate changes to the associated program code even after their deployment in real world. Since new or modified policies may also lead to an inconsistent database state, the identification of inconsistent database parts *w.r.t.* the policies is also an important issue. This motivates us to propose a slicing framework for HQL programs, aiming at extracting a subset of program statements affecting enterprise-policies defined on underlying databases. Unfortunately none of the existing approaches are directly applicable to the case of HQL where high-level variables interact with database attributes through hibernate (Session) interface – particularly when we slice HQL programs *w.r.t.* the behavior of persistent objects rather than just transient objects.

The main contributions in this paper are:

1. We construct syntax-based dependence graph of HQL, considering (a) intra-class intra-method dependences, (b) intra-class inter-method dependences, (c) inter-class inter-method dependences, and (d) session-database dependences.
2. We apply semantics-based analysis to refine syntax-based dependence graphs of HQL. To this aim, we define an abstract semantics of Hibernate Session methods in a relational abstract domain (the domain of polyhedra).
3. Finally, we propose a policy-based slicing technique on semantically refined dependence graph.

The structure of the rest of paper is as follows: Section 2 describes a running example. In section 3, we describe the syntax-based dependence graphs of HQL. A semantics-based refinement approach of syntax-based dependence graphs is presented in section 4. Section 5 illustrates the running example. Finally, section 6 concludes the work.

2   A Running Example

Consider an enterprise information system where the HQL program Prog (Figure 1a) performs three different operations (select, update, delete) on employees information stored in the database dB (Figures 1b and 1c) based on the user choice. Observe that the fields *eid, jid, sal, age* of POJO class emp in Prog correspond to the attributes *teid, tjid, tsal, tage* of dB table temp respectively. Similarly the fields *jobid, jname, jcat, maxsl* of POJO class Job in Prog correspond to the attributes *tjobid, tjname, tjcat, tmaxsl* of dB table tjob

```
1. class service {
2. public static void main(String arg[]){
3.         Configuration cfg =new Configuration();
4.         cfg.Configure("hibernate.cfg.xml");
5.         Session ses =(cfg.buildSessionFactory()).openSession();
6.         Transaction tr = ses.beginTransaction();
7.         int i = (new Scanner(System.in)).nextInt();
8.         if(i==1){
9.             int id_v = getparam(...);
10.            List ls = ( ses.createQuery("SELECT a.jname from emp e INNER JOIN e.Job
     a WHERE e.eid
                   = :xid").setParameter("xid", id_v)).list();
11.            Object obj = (Object)ls;
12.            System.out.println((String)obj),}
13.        if(i==2){
14.            int id_v = getparam(...);
15.            int sal_v = getparam(...);
16.            int r_1 = (ses.createQuery("UPDATE emp e SET e.sal= e.sal+:xsal WHERE
     e.eid ⩾:xid")
                   .setParameter("xsal",sal_v).setParameter("xid",id_v)).executeUpdate();}
17.        if(i==3){
18.            int id_v = getparam(...);
19.            int r_2 = (ses.createQuery("DELETE from emp e WHERE e.eid=:xid")
                   .setParameter("xid",id_v)).executeUpdate();}
20.        tr.commit();
21.        ses.close(); } }
```

(a) HQL program Prog

teid	tjid	tsal	tage
1	3	1200	35
2	2	600	28
3	4	1000	30
4	1	2500	45
5	1	1600	20

tjobid	tjname	tjcat	tmaxsl	tminsl
1	Asst.Prof	A	3000	1000
2	HR	C	1000	500
3	Asso.Prof	A	3000	1000
4	Registrar	B	2000	800
5	Prof.	A	3000	1000

(b) Database dB: Table temp   (c) Database dB: Table tjob

Fig. 1. Running example

respectively. This mapping is defined in a configuration file of hibernate framework in XML format. Let us suppose that the company decides to introduce a new policy ψ_1 which respects the consistency of employees salary structure, defined below:

The salary of employees of age less or equal to 40 cannot have a salary greater than 75% of the maximum salary of the same category.

The policy is defined on the persistent objects which have permanent representation in the dB. We observe that Prog may violate ψ_1 because statement 16 updates employee's salary without checking his/her age.

Our slicing algorithm will allow us to identify the subset of HQL statements responsible for such policy violation.

3   Syntax-Based Dependence Graph of HQL

In this section, we extend the notion of dependence graph representation to the case of HQL. Let us describe its construction using our running example whose

dependence graph is depicted in Figure 2. We consider the following three types
of dependences in HQL programs:

Intra-class Intra-method Dependences: These represent the dependences
within the same method of a class, and it follows the Program Dependence
Graph-based approach [20]. We denote these dependences by dotted edges. Edges
7 - 13, 7 - 17, 7 - 8, 18 - 19, etc. in Figure 2 are of this type.

Intra-class Inter-method Dependences: These represent the dependences
between statements of two different methods within same class and are constructed by following System Dependence Graph-based approach [13]. We denote
these dependences by long-dash-dotted edges. There is no edge of this type in
Figure 2.

Inter-class Inter-method Dependences:

Through Transient Objects. Inter-class Inter-method dependences occur in OOP
when a method in one class calls another method in other class. This is done by
calling the method through an object of the called-class. Therefore, additional
in-parameters corresponding to the object-fields through which the method is
called, must be considered [16]. Note that, in this scenario, a constructor-call
during object creation is also a part of the graph which follows the same representation as of other inter-class inter-method calls. We denote these dependences
by long-dash-dotted edges (as in the case of Intra-class Inter-method Dependences). Edges 3 - 4, 5 - 21, 6 - 20, 5 - 6, 4 - 5, etc. in Figure 2 are of this type.
Observe that node 4 calls "`configure()`" method on the object "cfg" which
is received from node 3. It configures the "cfg" object using "XML" file and
acts as a source for newly-configured "cfg" object. For the sake of simplicity,
we do not include here the details of the calling scenario at node 4. Similarly,
we hide the details of the calling-scenarios at nodes 5 (which creates the session
object by calling `openSession()`), 6 (which creates the transaction object by
calling `beginTransaction()`), 20 (when calling `commit()`) and 21 (when calling
`close()`) respectively.

Through Session Objects. Various `Session` methods are used to convert objects
from transient state to persistent state and to perform various operations, like
select, update, delete on the persistent objects in the database. In other words,
Hibernate `Session` serves as an intermediate way for the interaction between
high-level HQL variables and the database attributes. As creation of a `Session`
object implicitly establishes connection with the database, we consider the nodes
which create `Session` objects as the sources of the database (hence database-
attributes). For instance, in Figure 2 the node 5 acts as a source of dB. When
`Session` methods (`save()`, `creatQuery()`) are called through `Session` objects,
either a transient object (in case of `save()`) or an object-oriented variant of
SQL statement (in case of `createQuery()`) are passed as a parameter. For
instance, see nodes 10, 16, 19. The presence of HQL variables in the parameter
which have mapping with database attributes leads to a number of dependences

shown by dash-lines between 5 - 10, 5 - 16 and 5 - 19. We call such dependences as session-database dependences. These edges are labeled with used- and defined- HQL variables present in the parameter. For instance, in case of "obj" passed to save(), all database attributes corresponding to object fields act as defined variables. Similarly, in case of update and delete as parameters in the createQuery(), the variables in the WHERE clause act as used variables and the variables in the action part act as defined variables. In case of select, all variables in the parameter act as used variables.

Observe that for the sake of simplified representation, we hide the detail calling scenario of "createQuery()" by nodes 10, 16, 19. The edges connecting node 5 and dB indicates the propagation and synchronization of memory and database states. Although we connect node 4 with XML file "hibernate.cfg.xml" by an edge, it has no role in slicing and we may omit it also.

4 Semantics-Based Refinement of HQL Dependence Graphs

The syntax-based dependence graphs represent dependences based on the syntactic presence of a variable in the definition of another variables. However, this is not the case always if we focus on the actual values instead of variables. For instance, although the expression "$e = x^2 + 4w \bmod 2 + z$" syntactically depends on w, semantically there is no dependency as the evaluation of "$4w \bmod 2$" is always zero. This motivate researchers towards semantics-based dependence computation [12, 17].

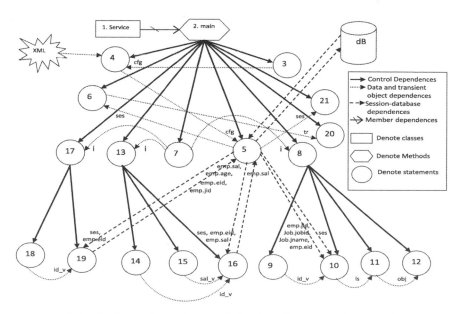

Fig. 2. Dependence Graph of the class "service" (Figure 1)

In [12], authors applied three notions: Semantic relevancy, Semantic data-dependences and conditional dependences. This leads to a refinement of syntax-based dependence graphs into more refined semantic-based dependence graphs, producing more precise slices.

The extension of these notions to the case of HQL is not straight-forward because of the existence of transient objects, persistent objects and `Session` methods. Therefore, we have to treat transient objects and persistent objects differently when we apply these semantics-based computations to HQL.

In the rest of this section, we use the following: Let `Var` and `Val` be the set of variables and the domain of values. The set of states is defined as $\Sigma = $ `Var` $\longmapsto$ `Val`$_\perp$, where by `Val`$_\perp$ we denote `Val`$\cup\{\perp\}$ and $\perp$ is undefined value.

4.1   Semantic Relevancy of HQL Statements *w.r.t* Policies

Consider the following HQL statement on the POJO class `Cls` which corresponds to the database table `Tab` in Figure 3a.

$$Q = \texttt{ses.CreateQuery(UPDATE Cls SET } age = age\texttt{+1 WHERE } age \leqslant \texttt{60).executeUpdate()}$$

Consider a company policy ψ_2 (defined on `Tab`) which says that employees ages must belong to the range 18 and 62 (*i.e.* $18 \leqslant tage \leqslant 62$). We denote by σ_D the state of the database D which includes the state of `Tab`. The semantics[1] of `Q` in σ_D, *i.e.* $S[\![Q]\!]\sigma_D$ yields the result shown in Figure 3b. We observe that the policy ψ_2 is satisfied before and after the execution of `Q`, *i.e.* $\psi_2(\sigma_D) = \psi_2(S[\![Q]\!]\sigma_D)$. Therefore, Q is *irrelevant w.r.t.* ψ_2, assuming σ_D is the only state that occurs at the program point of Q.

teid	tsal	tage
1	1200	55
2	1600	62
3	2000	45
4	800	18

(a) Table **Tab**

teid	tsal	tage
1	1200	56
2	1600	62
3	2000	46
4	800	19

(b) Result after execution of Q on **Tab**

$teid^\sharp$	$tsal^\sharp$	$tage^\sharp$
[1, 4]	[800, 2000]	[18, 62]

(c) Abstract table **Tab**$^\sharp$ corresponding to **Tab**

$teid^\sharp$	$tsal^\sharp$	$tage^\sharp$
[1, 4]	[800, 2000]	[19, 62]

(d) Result after execution of $Q^\sharp$ on **Tab**$^\sharp$

Fig. 3. Concrete and Abstract Query Semantics.

---

[1] Interested readers may refer [11] for more details on concrete and abstract semantics of query languages.

Although this example is trivial to compute the irrelevancy of Q in concrete domain, in case of very large database (or even when database state depends on run-time inputs) the irrelevancy can be computed in an abstract domain of interest following the Abstract Interpretation framework [6]. The Abstract Interpretation framework is a semantics-based overapproximation technique to infer program's behavior during static time. The aim is to lift concrete semantics to an abstract setting by replacing concrete values by suitable properties of interest, and simulating the concrete operations by sound abstract operations. The mapping between concrete semantics domain (D^c) and abstract semantics domain (D^a) is formalized by Galois Connection $\langle D^c, \alpha, \gamma, D^a \rangle$, where $\alpha : D^c \to D^a$ and $\gamma : D^a \to D^c$ represent concretization and abstraction functions respectively.

To illustrate, let us consider the abstract domain of intervals. The abstract table $\mathsf{Tab}^\sharp$ corresponding to Tab in the domain of intervals is shown in Figure 3c. The corresponding abstract state which includes $\mathsf{Tab}^\sharp$ is denoted by $\sigma_D^\sharp$. The abstract semantics $S^\sharp[\![Q^\sharp]\!]\sigma_D^\sharp$ where $Q^\sharp$ is

```
ses.CreateQuery (UPDATE Cls♯ SET age♯=age♯+[1,1] WHERE age♯ ⩽♯[60,60]).executeUpdate()
```

yields the abstract result depicted in Figure 3d. We observe that $\psi_2(\sigma_D^\sharp) = \psi_2(S^\sharp[\![Q^\sharp]\!]\sigma_D^\sharp)$. By following [11], we can prove the soundness, *i.e.*

$$(\psi_2(\sigma_D^\sharp) = \psi_2(S^\sharp[\![Q^\sharp]\!]\sigma_D^\sharp)) \implies \forall Q \in \gamma(Q^\sharp), \forall \sigma_D \in \gamma(\sigma_D^\sharp) : \psi_2(\sigma_D) = \psi_2(S[\![Q]\!]\sigma_D)$$

where γ is the concretization function [6].

There exist various relational and non-relational abstract domain in the abstract interpretation framework. The efficiency and preciseness of static analysis vary depending on the abstract domain chosen [6]. As our objective is to consider enterprise policies on database, we choose a relational abstract domain – the domain of polyhedra [7] – to compute semantic relevancy of HQL code.

Domain of Polyhedra. Convex polyhedra are regions of some n-dimensional space $\mathbb{R}^n$ that are bounded by a finite set of hyperplanes. Let $\vec{x} = \langle x_1, x_2, \ldots, x_n \rangle$ and $\vec{v} = \langle v_1, v_2, \ldots, v_n \rangle \in \mathbb{R}^n$ be the program variables of real numbers and an n-tuple (vector) of real numbers. By $\beta = \vec{v}.\vec{x} \otimes c$ where $\vec{v} \neq \vec{0}$, $c \in \mathbb{R}$, $\otimes \in \{=, \geqslant\}$, we denote a set of linear restraints over $\mathbb{R}^n$. Given a set of linear restraints β on $\mathbb{R}^n$, a set of solutions or points $\{\sigma | \sigma \models \beta\}$ defines the polyhedron $P = (\beta, n)$. We denote this set of points by $\gamma(p)$ [4,7].

Let $\mathfrak{p}$ be a set of all polyhedra on $\mathbb{R}^n$. We define a complete lattice $L_A = \langle \mathfrak{p}, \sqsubseteq, \emptyset, \mathbb{R}^n, \sqcup, \sqcap \rangle$ where $\emptyset$ and $\mathbb{R}^n$ are bottom and top elements respectively. Given $P_1, P_2 \in \mathfrak{p}$: $P_1 \sqsubseteq P_2 \Rightarrow \gamma(P_1) \subseteq \gamma(P_2)$, $P_1 \sqcap P_2 \Rightarrow \gamma(P_1) \cap \gamma(P_2)$ and $P_1 \sqcup P_2$ returns convex polyhedron hull which is the least polyhedron covering both P_1 and P_2 [4]. Various operations of convex polyhedra are emptiness checking, projection, *etc* [4].

Given a complete lattice $L_C = \langle \wp(\mathsf{Val}), \subseteq, \bot, \mathsf{Val}, \cup, \cap \rangle$ of the concrete domain of values Val, the correspondence between concrete and abstract domains is formalized by Galois Connection $\langle L_C, \alpha, \gamma, L_A \rangle$ where α and γ are abstraction and concretization functions respectively [6].

Abstract Semantics. The transition relation is defined as $\mathscr{T}: \text{Com} \times \mathfrak{p} \to \wp(\mathfrak{p})$ where Com is the set of commands and $\mathfrak{p}$ is the set of all polyhedra. It defines the abstract semantics of a command in the domain of polyhedra by specifying how application of a command on a polyhedron results into a set of new polyhedra.

Example 1. **(Assignment)** Given $P=(\beta, n)=(\{x \geqslant 3, y \geqslant 2\}, 2)$. The transition semantics of assignment statement $x := x+y$ is defined as: $\mathscr{T}[\![x := x+y]\!]P = \{P'\}$ where $P' = (\{x - y \geqslant 3, y \geqslant 2\}, 2)$.

Example 2. **(Test)** Given $P= (\beta, n)= (\{x \geqslant 4, y \geqslant 3\}, 2)$. The transition semantics of boolean expression $x \geqslant 10$ is defined as: $\mathscr{T}[\![x \geqslant 10]\!]P = \{P_T, P_F\}$ where
$$P_T = (\{ x \geqslant 10, \ y \geqslant 3 \}, 2) \quad \text{and} \quad P_F = (\{ x \geqslant 4, \ -x \geqslant -9, \ y \geqslant 3 \}, 2).$$

We are now in position to define abstract transition semantics of Hibernate Session methods. We denote the abstract syntax of Session methods by triplet $\langle C, \phi, \text{OP} \rangle$ where OP is the operation to be performed on a set of tuples satisfying ϕ in database tables corresponding to a set of classes C. The condition ϕ is a first order logic formula. Four basic OP that cover a wide range of operations are SAVE, UPD, DEL, and SEL [5].

- $\langle C, \phi, \text{SAVE(obj)} \rangle = \langle \{c\}, false, \text{SAVE(obj)} \rangle$: Stores the state of the object obj in the database table t, where t corresponds to the POJO class c and obj is the instance of c. The pre-condition ϕ is $false$ as the method does not identify any existing tuples in the database.
- $\langle C, \phi, \text{UPD}(\vec{x}, \vec{exp}) \rangle = \langle \{c\}, \phi, \text{UPD}(\vec{v}, \vec{exp}) \rangle$: Updates the attributes corresponding to the class fields $\vec{x}$ by $\vec{exp}$ in the database table t for the tuples satisfying ϕ, where t corresponds to the POJO class c.
- $\langle C, \phi, \text{DEL}() \rangle = \langle \{c\}, \phi, \text{DEL}() \rangle$: Deletes the tuples satisfying ϕ in t, where t is the database table corresponding to the POJO class c.
- $\langle C, \phi, \text{SEL}(f(\vec{exp'}), \ r(\vec{h}(\vec{x})), \ \phi', \ g(\vec{exp})) \rangle$: Selects information from the database tables corresponding to the set of POJO classes C, and returns the equivalent representations in the form of objects. This is done only for the tuples satisfying ϕ. As of [11], we denote by g, h, r, f, ϕ' the GROUP BY, Aggregate Functions, DISTINCT/ALL, ORDER BY, and HAVING clause respectively.

Observe that as SAVE(), UPD() and DEL() always target single class, the set C is a singleton $\{c\}$. However, C may not be singleton in case of SEL().

As there is a correspondence between HQL variables and database attributes, we define the transition semantics $\mathscr{T}_{hql}$ of Hibernate Session methods in terms of the transition semantics $\mathscr{T}_{sql}$ in the corresponding database domain as follows:

$$\mathscr{T}_{hql}[\![\langle C, \phi, \text{OP} \rangle]\!] = \begin{cases} \mathscr{T}_{sql}[\![\langle T, \phi_d, \text{OP}_d \rangle]\!] & \\ \text{if } C = \{c_1, \ldots, c_n\} \wedge (\forall i \in 1 \ldots n. \ t_i = \text{Map}(c_i)) \wedge T = \{t_1, t_2, \ldots, t_n\}. & \\ \\ \bot \quad otherwise. & \end{cases}$$

Map() is a function which maps any HQL component into an equivalent database component involving only database tables and attributes. Thus, $\phi_d = $ Map(ϕ), OP$_d = $ Map(OP) are the condition-part (WHERE clause) and the database operations (UPDATE, DELETE, INSERT, SELECT) defined on the underlying database.

Example 3. Consider Figure 3 and the following Session method:

$m_{upd} ::= $ ses.CreateQuery (UPDATE Cls SET $sal = sal$+100 WHERE $age \geqslant$30).executeUpdate()

The equivalent abstract syntax is $\langle \{\text{Cls}\}, age \geqslant 30, \text{UPD}(\langle sal \rangle, \langle sal + 100 \rangle) \rangle$. The function Map$(m_{upd})$ converts m_{upd} into an equivalent database operation whose abstract syntax is $\langle \{\text{Tab}\}, tage \geqslant 30, \text{UPDATE}(\langle tsal \rangle, \langle tsal + 100 \rangle) \rangle$ where

$$\text{Map}(\{\text{Cls}\}) = \{\text{Tab}\}, \qquad\qquad \text{Map}(age \geqslant 30) = tage \geqslant 30,$$
$$\text{Map}(\text{UPD}(\langle sal \rangle, \langle sal + 100 \rangle)) = \text{UPDATE}(\langle tsal \rangle, \langle tsal + 100 \rangle)$$

Let us define abstract transition semantics of four different database operations corresponding to the four aforementioned Session methods in the domain of polyhedra.

1. Update:

$$\mathscr{T}_{hql}[\![\langle \{c\}, \phi, \text{UPDATE}(\vec{x}, e\vec{x}p) \rangle]\!]\text{P} = \mathscr{T}_{sql}[\![\langle \{t\}, \phi_d, \text{UPDATE}(\vec{x}_d, e\vec{x}p_d) \rangle]\!]\text{P} = \{\text{P}'_T , \ \text{P}_F\}$$

where
$\quad \text{P}_T = (\text{P} \sqcap \phi_d).$
$\quad \text{P}'_T = \mathscr{T}_{sql}[\![\text{UPDATE}(\vec{x}_d, e\vec{x}p_d)]\!]\text{P}_T = \mathscr{T}_{sql}[\![\vec{x}_d := e\vec{x}p_d]\!]\text{P}_T.$
$\quad \text{P}_F = (\text{P} \sqcap \neg\phi_d).$
By the notation $\vec{x}_d := e\vec{x}p_d$ we denote $\langle x_1 := exp_1, \ x_2 := exp_2, \ \ldots, \ x_n := exp_n \rangle$ where $\vec{x}_d = \langle \ x_1, \ x_2, \ \ldots, \ x_n \rangle$ and $e\vec{x}p_d = \langle \ exp_1, \ exp_2, \ \ldots, \ exp_n \rangle$, which follow transition semantic definition for assignment statement.

Example 4. Consider table Tab in Figure 3a. The abstract representation of Tab in the form of polyhedron is:

$$\text{P} = \langle \{teid \geqslant 1, -teid \geqslant -4, tsal \geqslant 800, -tsal \geqslant -2000, tage \geqslant 18, -tage \geqslant -62\}, 3 \rangle$$

Consider the following Session method defined on class Cls:

$m_{upd} ::= $ ses.CreateQuery (UPDATE Cls SET $sal = sal$+100 WHERE age $\geqslant$30).executeUpdate().

The equivalent abstract syntax is $\langle \{\text{Cls}\}, age \geqslant 30, \text{UPD}(\langle sal \rangle, \langle sal + 100 \rangle) \rangle$. The abstract transition semantics of m_{upd} on P is:

$$\mathscr{T}_{hql}[\![m_{upd}]\!]\text{P} = \mathscr{T}_{hql}[\![\langle \{\text{Cls}\}, age \geqslant 30, \text{UPD}(\langle sal \rangle, \langle sal + 100 \rangle) \rangle]\!]\text{P}$$
$$= \mathscr{T}_{sql}[\![\langle \{\text{Tab}\}, tage \geqslant 30, \text{UPDATE}(\langle tsal \rangle, \langle tsal + 100 \rangle) \rangle]\!]\text{P} = \{\text{P}'_T, \text{P}_F\} \ where$$

$\text{P}'_T = \langle \{teid \geqslant 1, -teid \geqslant -4, tsal \geqslant 900, -tsal \geqslant -2100, tage \geqslant 30, -tage \geqslant -62\}, 3 \rangle.$
$\text{P}_F = \langle \{teid \geqslant 1, -teid \geqslant -4, tsal \geqslant 800, -tsal \geqslant -2000, tage \geqslant 18, -tage \geqslant -29\}, 3 \rangle.$

2. Delete: $\mathscr{T}_{sql}[\![\langle\{t\}, \phi_d, \text{DELETE}()\rangle]\!]P = \{(P \sqcap \neg\phi_d)\}$

Example 5. Consider the following `Session` method:

$m_{del} ::= \text{ses.CreateQuery (DELETE from Cls WHERE } age \geqslant 30\text{).executeUpdate()}.$

The transition semantics of m_{del} on P is:

$$\begin{aligned}
\mathscr{T}_{hql}[\![m_{del}]\!]P &= \mathscr{T}_{hql}[\![\langle\{\text{Cls}\}, age \geqslant 30, \text{DEL}()\rangle]\!]P \\
&= \mathscr{T}_{sql}[\![\langle\{\text{Tab}\}, tage \geqslant 30, \text{DELETE}()\rangle]\!]P \\
&= \{P \sqcap \neg(tage \geqslant 30)\} = \{P'\} \quad where
\end{aligned}$$

$P' = \langle\{teid \geqslant 1, -teid \geqslant -4, tsal \geqslant 800, -tsal \geqslant -2000, tage \geqslant 18, -tage \geqslant -29\}, 3\rangle$

3. Insert: Let $\vec{x}$ be the fields of a class c. Given an object `obj` of c, suppose $\vec{v}$ be the values in $\vec{x}$ of the object. The transition relation is defined as

$$\mathscr{T}_{hql}[\![\langle\{c\}, false, \text{SAVE}(obj)\rangle]\!]P = \mathscr{T}_{sql}[\![\langle\{t\}, false, \text{INSERT}(attribute(t), \vec{v})\rangle]\!]P = \{P'\}$$

where $P' = P \sqcup \{attribute(t) = \vec{v} \mid \vec{v} \in \mathbb{R}^n\}$.

Example 6. Let `obj` be an object of POJO class `Cls` in Figure 3 whose fields $\vec{x} = \langle eid, sal, age\rangle$ are set to values $\vec{v} = \langle5, 600, 35\rangle$. Consider the following `Session` method $m_{ins} ::= \text{ses.save(obj)}$. The transition semantics is:

$$\begin{aligned}
\mathscr{T}_{hql}[\![m_{ins}]\!]P &= \mathscr{T}_{hql}[\![\langle\{\text{Cls}\}, false, \text{SAVE}(obj)\rangle]\!]P \\
&= \mathscr{T}_{sql}[\![\langle\{\text{Tab}\}, false, \text{INSERT}(\langle teid, tsal, tage\rangle, \langle5, 600, 35\rangle)\rangle]\!]P = \{P'\}
\end{aligned}$$

where $P' = P \sqcup \{teid = 5, tsal = 600, tage = 35\} = \langle\{teid \geqslant 1, -teid \geqslant -5, tsal \geqslant 600, -tsal \geqslant -2000, tage \geqslant 18, -tage \geqslant -62\}, 3\rangle$

4. Select: The select operation does not modify any information in a polyhedron. Therefore, the transition relation is defined as:

$$\mathscr{T}_{sql}[\![\text{T}, \phi_d, \text{SELECT}(f(\vec{exp}'_d), \, r(\vec{h}(\vec{x}_d)), \, \phi'_d, \, g(\vec{exp}_d)]\!]P = \{P\}$$

5   Illustration on the Running Example

Let us illustrate our proposed approach on the running example (Figure 1) in section 2.

Syntax-Based Slicing. The backward slice of `Prog` w.r.t. ψ_1 is depicted in Figure 4. This is done by traversing the syntax-based dependence graph (Figure 2) in backward direction w.r.t. the slicing criteria $\langle21, \{sal, age, maxsl\}\rangle$. Observe that the sliced-database on which the slice performs its computation, is a part of the original database. This has crucial role in data-provenance applications.

```
1.   class service {
2.   public static void main(String arg[]){
3.            Configuration cfg =new Configuration();
4.            cfg.Configuration("hibernate.cfg.xml");
5.            Session ses =(cfg.buildSessionFactory()).openSession();
7.            int i = (new Scanner(System.in)).nextInt();
13.           if(i==2){
14.                int id_v = getparam(...);
15.                int sal_v = getparam(...);
16.                int r1 = (ses.createQuery("UPDATE emp e SET e.sal=
                   e.sal+:xsal WHERE e.eid=:xid").setParameter("xsal",sal_v)
                   .setParameter("xid",id_v)).executeUpdate();}
17.           if(i==3){
18.                int id_v = getparam(...);
19.                int r2 = (ses.createQuery("DELETE from emp e WHERE
                   e.eid=:xid").setParameter("xid",id_v)).executeUpdate();}
21.           ses.close(); } }
```

(a) Slice of **Prog** w.r.t ψ_1

teid	tsal
1	1200
2	600
3	1000
4	2500
5	1600

(b) Slice of **temp** w.r.t ψ_1

Fig. 4. Syntax-based Slice w.r.t. ψ_1.

Semantic-Based Slicing. The initial polyhedron[2] corresponding to the database dB (Figure 1b) is $P_{dB} = \langle \{teid \geqslant 1, -teid \geqslant -5, tsal \geqslant 600, -tsal \geqslant -2500, tage \geqslant 20, -tage \geqslant -45\}, 3 \rangle$. The pictorial representation is shown in Figure 5(a).

The abstract syntax of **Session** methods m_{sel}, m_{upd} and m_{del} at program points 10, 16, 19 respectively in **Prog** are:

$m_{sel} ::= \langle C, \phi, OP \rangle$ where $C = \{$emp, Job$\}$, $\phi = \{eid = jobid,\ eid = id\_v\}$,

$\qquad OP = \text{SEL}(f(\vec{exp'}),\ r(\vec{h}(\vec{x})),\ \phi',\ g(\vec{exp})) = \text{SEL}(id, \text{ALL}(id(jname)), true, id))$,

$\qquad$ and id denotes identity function.

$m_{upd} ::= \langle \{$emp$\}, \{eid = id\_v\}, \text{UPD}(\langle sal \rangle, \langle sal + sal\_v \rangle) \rangle$

$m_{del} ::= \langle \{$emp$\}, \{eid = id\_v\}, \text{DEL}() \rangle$

The transition semantics on P_{dB} are:

$\mathscr{T}_{hql} [\![m_{sel}]\!] P_{dB}$

$\quad = \mathscr{T}_{hql} [\![\langle \{emp, Job\}, \{eid = jobid, eid = id\_v\}, \text{SEL}(id, \text{ALL}(id(jname)), true, id) \rangle]\!] P_{dB}$

$\quad = \mathscr{T}_{sql} [\![\langle \{$temp, tjob$\}, \{teid = tjobid, teid = tid\_v\}, \text{SELECT}(id, \text{ALL}(id(tjname)), true, id) \rangle]\!] P_{dB}$

$\quad = \{ P_{dB} \}$

---

[2] For the sake of simplicity, we consider the polyhedron in the space involving only three attributes *teid*, *tsal* and *tage*.

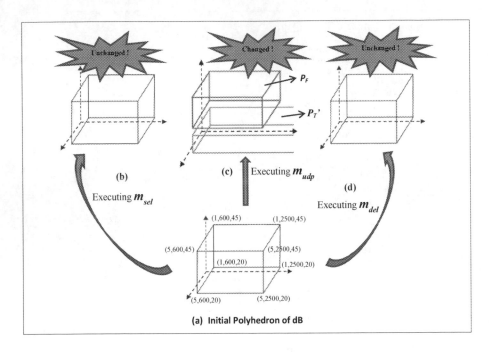

Fig. 5. Polyhedra representation of `temp` on various operation $(m_{sel}, m_{udp}, m_{del})$.

Note that, select operation does not change the database, hence the polyhedron remains unchanged (see Figure 5(b)).

$$\mathcal{T}_{hql}[\![m_{upd}]\!] = \mathcal{T}_{hql}[\![\langle\{\texttt{emp}\}, \{eid \geqslant id\_v\}, \texttt{UPD}(\langle sal\rangle, \langle sal + sal\_v\rangle)\rangle]\!]\text{P}_{dB}$$
$$= \mathcal{T}_{sql}[\![\langle\{\texttt{temp}\}, \{teid \geqslant id\_v\}, \texttt{UPDATE}(\langle tsal\rangle, \langle tsal + sal\_v\rangle)\rangle]\!]\text{P}_{dB}$$
$$= \{\text{P}'_T, \text{P}_F\} \quad where$$

$$\text{P}_T = \text{P}_{dB} \sqcap \{teid \geqslant id\_v\}$$
$$\text{P}'_T = \mathcal{T}_{sql}[\![tsal := tsal + sal\_v]\!](\text{P}_T)$$
$$\quad = \langle\{teid \geqslant 1,\ -teid \geqslant -5,\ tage \geqslant 20,\ -tage \geqslant -45,\ tsal \geqslant 600\},\ 3\rangle.$$
$$\text{P}_F = \{\text{P}_{dB} \sqcap \neg(teid \geqslant id\_v)\} = \{\text{P}_{dB}\}$$

Note that, since the updation of $tsal$ depends on run-time input, we project-out the upper bound of the attribute from the set of restraints in P'_T in order to guarantee the soundness. The polyhedron representation of P'_T is shown in Figure 5(c). Also note that, P_F is sound-approximated by disregarding the effect of "$teid = id\_v$" as it depends on run-time input.

$$\mathcal{T}_{hql}[\![m_{del}]\!] = \mathcal{T}_{hql}[\![\langle\{\texttt{emp}\}, \{eid = id\_v\}, \texttt{DEL}()\rangle]\!]\text{P}_{dB}$$
$$= \mathcal{T}_{sql}[\![\langle\{\texttt{temp}\}, \{teid = id\_v\}, \texttt{DELETE}()\rangle]\!]\text{P}_{dB} = \{\text{P}_{dB}\}$$

Note that, the semantics of m_{del} is sound-approximated by disregarding the effect of "$teid = id\_v$" as it depends on run-time input (see Figure 5(d)).

```
 1. class service {
 2. public static void main(String arg[]){
 3.        Configuration cfg =new Configuration();
 4.        cfg.Configuration("hibernate.cfg.xml");
 5.        Session ses =(cfg.buildSessionFactory()).openSession();
 7.        int i = (new Scanner(System.in)).nextInt();
13.        if(i==2){
14.            int id_v = getparam(...);
15.            int sal_v = getparam(...);
16.            int r₁ = (ses.createQuery("UPDATE emp e SET e.sal=e.sal+:xsal WHERE
       e.eid=:xid")
                   .setParameter("xsal",sal_v).setParameter("xid",id_v)).executeUpdate();}
21.        ses.close(); } }
```

Fig. 6. Semantics-based slice of Prog $w.r.t$ ψ_1

Observe that the initial polyhedron of dB is covered by the polyhedron representing ψ_1. This can verified by performing the operations, e.g. interaction, emptiness checking, etc. on the polyhedra domain. Therefore, initially ψ_1 is satisfied by dB. The abstract semantics-based analysis proves that m_{del} does not change the initial polyhedron P_{dB} (see Figure 5). Therefore it is semantically irrelevant $w.r.t.$ ψ_1. The semantics-based slice is shown in Figure 6 which disregards the semantically irrelevant statements $w.r.t.$ ψ_1, yielding to a slice more accurate than the syntax-based one (Figure 4).

6   Conclusion

In this paper, we introduce a policy-based slicing of Hibernate Query Language where the policies are defined on persistent objects, rather than transient objects. We extend the Class Dependence Graph (ClDG) [16] of object-oriented languages to the case of HQL, and propose a refinement of dependence graph for removing false dependences by analyzing programs in relational or non-relational abstract domains by following the Abstract Interpretation framework.

Our approach is comparable with conditioned slicing and specification-based slicing (several variants exist, e.g. precondition−, postcondition−, contract−, assertion−based, etc.) [3]. The method defined for finding a conditioned slice is to use symbolic execution and reject infeasible paths based on the constraints defined by the first order logic equations. Specification-based slicing approach is proposed based on the axiomatic semantics (weakest precondition or strongest postcondition computations) in program verification. All these approaches use SMT solver which has exponential complexity [15]. Our proposal is based on the semantic analysis in an abstract domain following the Abstract Interpretation framework. The framework allows to perform analysis in a relational or nonrelational abstract domain based on the properties of interest. Analysis in the domain of polyhedra uses Linear Problem Solver [1]. Although in some cases the worst-case computational complexity in polyhedron domain is exponential [14, 18], but there is an opportunity to chose another less costlier weakly relational domains such as the domain of octagons [19].

References

1. Bagnara, R., Hill, P.M., Zaffanella, E.: The ppl: Toward a complete set of numerical abstractions for the analysis and verification of hardware and software systems. Tech. rep., Dipartimento di Matematica, Universit'a di Parma, Italy (2006)
2. Bauer, C., King, G.: Hibernate in Action. Manning Publications Co. (2004)
3. Canfora, G., Cimitile, A., Lucia, A.D.: Conditioned program slicing. Information and Software Technology 40(11–12), 595–607 (1998)
4. Chen, L., Miné, A., Cousot, P.: A sound floating-point polyhedra abstract domain. In: Ramalingam, G. (ed.) APLAS 2008. LNCS, vol. 5356, pp. 3–18. Springer, Heidelberg (2008)
5. Cortesi, A., Halder, R.: Information-flow analysis of hibernate query language. In: Dang, T.K., Wagner, R., Neuhold, E., Takizawa, M., Küng, J., Thoai, N. (eds.) FDSE 2014. LNCS, vol. 8860, pp. 262–274. Springer, Heidelberg (2014)
6. Cousot, P., Cousot, R.: Abstract interpretation: a unified lattice model for static analysis of programs by construction or approximation of fixpoints. In: Proc. of the POPL 1977, pp. 238–252 (1977)
7. Cousot, P., Halbwachs, N.: Automatic discovery of linear restraints among variables of a program. In: Proceedings of the POPL 1978, pp. 84–96 (1978)
8. Glass, R.L.: It failure rates-70% or 10–15%? IEEE Software 22(3), 112–111 (2005)
9. Gyimóthy, T., Paakki, J.: Static slicing of logic programs. In: Automated and Algorithmic Debugging, pp. 87–103 (1995)
10. Halder, R., Cortesi, A.: Abstract program slicing of database query languages. In: Proc. of the 28th Annual ACM SAC, pp. 838–845 (2013)
11. Halder, R., Cortesi, A.: Abstract interpretation of database query languages. Computer Languages, Systems & Structures 38, 123–157 (2012)
12. Halder, R., Cortesi, A.: Abstract program slicing on dependence condition graphs. Sci. Comput. Program. 78(9), 1240–1263 (2013)
13. Horwitz, S., Reps, T., Binkley, D.: Interprocedural slicing using dependence graphs. ACM Transactions on PLS 12(1), 26–60 (1990)
14. Kelner, J.A., Spielman, D.A.: A randomized polynomial-time simplex algorithm for linear programming. In: Proc. of the Theory of Computing, pp. 51–60 (2006)
15. King, T., Barrett, C., Tinelli, C.: Leveraging linear and mixed integer programming for smt. In: Proc. of the 14th ICFMCAD lausanne, Switzerland (to appear) (2014)
16. Larsen, L., Harrold, M.J.: Slicing object-oriented software. In: Proc. of the 18th ICSE, pp. 495–505 (1996)
17. Mastroeni, I., Zanardini, D.: Data dependencies and program slicing: from syntax to abstract semantics. In: Proc. of the ACM symposium on PEPM, pp. 125–134 (2008)
18. Megiddo, N.: Linear programming in linear time when the dimension is fixed. Journal of the ACM 31(1), 114–127 (1984)
19. Minè, A.: The octagon abstract domain. Higher Order Symbol. Comput. 19(1), 31–100 (2006). http://www.astree.ens.fr/
20. Ottenstein, K.J., Ottenstein, L.M.: The program dependence graph in a software development environment. ACM SIGPLAN Notices 19(5), 177–184 (1984)
21. Podgurski, A., Clarke, L.A.: A formal model of program dependences and its implications for software testing, debugging, and maintenance. IEEE Transactions on Software Engineering 16(9), 965–979 (1990)

22. Rodrigues, N.F., Barbosa, L.S.: Slicing functional programs by calculation. In: Beyond Program Slicing, November 06–11, 2005 (2005)
23. Tip, F.: A survey of program slicing techniques. Tech. rep. (1994)
24. Weiser, M.: Program slicing. IEEE Trans on SE **SE–10**(4), 352–357 (1984)
25. Willmor, D., Embury, S.M., Shao, J.: Program slicing in the presence of a database state. In: Proc. of the 20th Int. Conf. on Software Maintenance, pp. 448–452 (2004)

Uncovering Document Fraud in Maritime Freight Transport Based on Probabilistic Classification

Ron Triepels[1]([⊠]), Ad Feelders[2], and Hennie Daniels[1]

[1] CenTER, Tilburg University, Warandelaan 2, Tilburg, The Netherlands
{r.j.m.a.triepels,h.a.m.daniels}@uvt.nl
[2] Department of Information and Computing Sciences, Utrecht University,
Princetonplein 5, Utrecht, The Netherlands
a.j.feelders@uu.nl

Abstract. Deficient visibility in global supply chains causes significant risks for the customs brokerage practices of freight forwarders. One of the risks that freight forwarders face is that shipping documentation might contain document fraud and is used to declare a shipment. Traditional risk controls are ineffective in this regard since the creation of shipping documentation is uncontrollable by freight forwarders. In this paper, we propose a data mining approach that freight forwarders can use to detect document fraud from supply chain data. More specifically, we learn models that predict the presence of goods on an import declaration based on other declared goods and the trajectory of the shipment. Decision rules are used to produce miscoding alerts and smuggling alerts. Experimental tests show that our approach outperforms the traditional audit strategy in which random declarations are selected for further investigation.

Keywords: Data mining · Fraud detection · Freight forwarding · Global supply chains

1 Introduction

International trade is going through an impressive growth. Eurostat estimated the total value of goods imported by the member states of the European Union over 2014 at 1.6 trillion euros, which constitutes an increase of almost 64 percent compared to 2004 [8]. Increased trade is an indication of improved economic integration and world prosperity, but at the same time suggests that fraud is more likely to happen with more serious consequences. Particularly, freight forwarders face problems when trade increases. The focal position of freight forwarders in global supply chains restricts their visibility and control on shipment documentation while budget and manpower for customs brokerage are also limited. Freight forwarders must blindly trust externally generated shipping documents and declare goods they usually do not even see [12]. Without clear overview

© IFIP International Federation for Information Processing 2015
K. Saeed and W. Homenda (Eds.): CISIM 2015, LNCS 9339, pp. 282–293, 2015.
DOI: 10.1007/978-3-319-24369-6_23

or effective risk controls in place, fraudulent declarations easily vanish in the extensive volume that needs to be processed.

The rise of information technology (IT) proposes a shift towards automation, risk management and intelligence in the customs brokerage practices of freight forwarders [11]. IT allows more detailed supply chain data to be recorded. Take radio frequency identification (RFID) as an example. The small size of the RFID tags and their low production costs makes them useful for tracking and tracing international cargo flows [2] and reducing delays at customs clearance locations [14]. At the same time, IT also provides tools to share data among supply chain participants in a fast and reliable way. Several technologies have been proposed to connect shippers and freight forwarders in global supply chains, like electronic data interchange (EDI) [17]. The rich supply chain data that freight forwarders are able to collect can be analyzed to manage customs brokerage risks.

In this paper, we present a data mining approach to detect miscoding and smuggling from supply chain data. Our approach can be applied by freight forwarders for signaling and internal auditing purposes. Customs agents can consult our data mining models during customs brokerage to determine if the documentation of a shipment has high potential to involve fraud. Potentially fraudulent declarations can thereby be prevented from being sent to customs. In addition, our data mining models can improve existing auditing and risk management procedures. Usually, freight forwarders take random samples of declarations and audit these declarations to ensure procedural compliance. Instead of taking random samples, our data mining models can be consulted to specifically audit only those declarations that likely involve miscoding or smuggling.

In summary, the contributions of this paper are as follows:

1. We define decision rules for miscoding alarms and smugling alarms.
2. We present a data mining approach to automatically produce alarms for miscoding and smuggling from supply chain data.
3. We conduct a comparative study on the performance of different classification models.
4. We demonstrate that our data mining approach performs significantly better at detecting miscoding and smuggling than the random audit strategy.

2   Background

2.1   Document Fraud in International Shipping

One of the oldest and most common fraud schemes in international shipping is document fraud. Document fraud is the act of manipulating facts in contracts or agreements with the intent to benefit by commercial gain [13]. International logistics is an attractive target for document fraud because it heavily relies on the exchange of formal shipping agreements. Although shipment agreements are issued and checked by different actors in a supply chain, the exchange of agreements takes the form of a serial connection. Thus, fraudulent agreements at the beginning of a supply chain are simply adopted by others and are hard to detect at the end [12]. According to the World Customs Organization, the incentive to commit document fraud in international shipping is to evade customs duties and tax payments, or to circumvent shipping restrictions and sanctions [21].

2.2   Types of Document Fraud

Two types of document fraud are commonly committed in international shipping documentation:

Miscoding is the act of providing incorrect or incomplete information about the nature of goods that are being shipped. To keep track of the variety of goods, the World Customs Organization introduced the harmonized system (HS). The HS is an international system of codes to classify goods. Fraudsters commonly specify HS-codes of other goods with similar properties but which are not prohibited or require to pay lower customs duties.

Smuggling is the act of secretly shipping goods under conditions that are against the law by any of the countries that are crossed by a shipment. Usually, goods are secretly put inside a container somewhere along the supply chain and removed after goods have been cleared at the destination country. Drugs, weapons, cigarettes and alcohol are goods that are frequently smuggled because they are prohibited or require to pay higher customs duties.

2.3   Related Research

Research dedicated to the task of detecting document fraud from supply chain data uses supervised and unsupervised learning techniques. Supervised learning techniques assume that data about fraudulent cases is available a priori which can be used to predict fraud in future observations. Bayesian classifiers have been applied to detect miscoding of HS-codes [9]. The researchers built an hierarchical Bayesian model based on values of the consignee, country of origin and destination country that are listed on import declarations. Fraudulent behavior is learned by training the model on a sample of correctly and incorrectly classified goods. A comparable study constructed a classifier based on association rules [22]. The classifier aims to predict the overall risk level of shipments based on inconsistencies in product features like prices and weights.

Unsupervised learning techniques assume that there is no a priori knowledge about document fraud available. These techniques focus on observations that significantly deviate from a statistical norm. Outlier detection is applied to detect deviating product properties of goods marked for clearance [6]. The researchers developed an application that highlights the statistical distributions of product properties in a set of diagrams. Customs agents can use these diagrams to inspect how much goods on an import declaration deviate from others. In addition, ranking may help freight forwarders to prioritize outliers. A related study proposes a method to calculate a numerical ranking for price outliers in trade data [16]. Freight forwarders can use such a ranking to identify risky declarations that require further investigation.

2.4   Hidden Information in Shipment Trajectories

Existing research demonstrates the ability of data mining to detect document fraud from supply chain data. However, proposed applications mainly ignore the trajectory by which shipments find their way through the supply chain network. Including trajectory details in the analysis may improve the detection rate due to two recent changes in international trade. First of all, international trade is moving towards vertical specialization in which each country produces particular goods for the stages of a production sequence [15]. Second, logistic services are subject to optimization by which the trajectory of a shipment is chosen based on a trade-off between economic considerations, like price, flexibility and service level [4] [20]. These changes are expected to create distinct patterns in shipment behavior which can be used to highlight cases of document fraud. Our approach differs from existing research in that we specifically use these patterns in shipment trajectories to predict the goods that should be listed on the corresponding import declarations.

3   Fraud Detection in Supply Chain Data

3.1   Detecting Miscoding and Smuggling

We propose to detect miscoding and smuggling using an unsupervised learning approach. Fraudulent declarations are identified by learning shipping behavior from supply chain data, in terms of probabilities that HS-codes are declared on a trajectory, and determining the extent to which an import declaration deviates from this norm. We introduce some notation to formalize this problem.

Let L be the state space of all possible locations between which goods can be transported. A trajectory is defined as a sequence consisting of a set of random variables $X = \{x_1, \ldots, x_n\}$, where each variable $x_i \in L$ represents a location in a supply chain and n is fixed for all trajectories. Moreover, let G be a set of indicators of HS-codes, that is, $G_i = 1$ if the good with HS-code i is listed on the import declaration, and $G_i = 0$ otherwise.

We learn a model from data that estimates the probability of goods on an import declaration given all other declared goods and the trajectory of the shipment. Predictions of goods are compared with the goods listed on the import declaration to determine if the declaration involves miscoding or smuggling. An alarm is produced for miscoding when a good is declared but the probability of this good estimated by model M is very low:

$$G_i = 1 \wedge P_M(G_i = 1 | G_{j \neq i}, X) \leq \alpha \tag{1}$$

Here, $G_{j \neq i}$ represents all goods other than the good that is currently evaluated on the import declaration and α represents a threshold. We define the alarm for smuggling in a similar fashion. An alarm for smuggling is produced when a good has not been declared but the probability of this good estimated by model M is very high:

$$G_i = 0 \wedge P_M(G_i = 1 | G_{j \neq i}, X) \geq (1 - \alpha) \tag{2}$$

3.2   Construction of the Classification Models

We built probabilistic classification models to estimate the conditional probabilities in equation 1 and 2. Our modelling approach is similar to the one proposed in [23] for the construction of Bayesian chain classifiers, except that, unlike our model, Bayesian chain classifiers are intended for multi-label classification. For that reason the authors of [23] need to impose an order on the labels, where predicted values of labels that are prior in the order are used to predict subsequent labels. They use a Bayesian network to define the order, and use the parents of a node as predictors for the child node. Unlike in the multi-label classification scenario, we observe all labels (declared HS-codes) during prediction, and can use the Markov blanket instead of just the parent set. The construction of our models can be broken down into two main steps.

In the first step we define associations between goods in a shipment. We do this by learning an undirected graphical model (Markov random field) from a data table where each row lists the goods that are contained in a shipment, that is, $G_i = 1$ if good i is contained in the shipment, and $G_i = 0$ otherwise. To avoid overfitting, we score candidate models using Akaike information criterion (AIC) which penalizes model complexity. Unfortunately, finding the model with the best AIC score from data is NP-hard [3]. To find a good (locally optimal) model, we perform a hill-climbing search with forward selection. Still, it can take a considerable amount of time to find such a model when the algorithm needs to start from the mutual independence model (empty graph). Therefore, we first generate a minimal AIC forest [7] and then use this simplified model as initial model to speed up the hill climbing.

In the second step we evaluate two types of probabilistic classifiers: Naive Bayes (NB) and Tree-Augmented Naive Bayes (TAN). NB is a simple classifier that uses Bayes rule of conditional probability to compute the probability of a label given a set of features. This computation is simplified under the assumption that all features are independent of each other given the label. A NB classifier is constructed for each good by determining its Markov blanket in the undirected graphical model (Fig. 1A), and estimating the probability of the good given the goods in its Markov blanket and locations in the shipping trajectory. The resulting classifier is depicted as a Bayesian network in (Fig. 1B). We incorporate only dependent goods as additional features in the classification models to avoid features that have poor prediction power with respect to the target good. Therefore, term $G_{j \neq i}$ in equation 1 and 2 is substituted by $MB(G_i)$. Here, $MB(G_i)$ refers to the Markov blanket of good G_i in the undirected graphical model.

The main drawback of a NB classifier is that it fails to capture the dependencies between features due to its strong independence assumption. A TAN relaxes this assumption by specifying a tree structure on the feature set in which each feature only has as parent the label and at most one other feature. We use Chow and Liu's algorithm [5] to automatically generate TAN classifiers from data. The structure of a TAN is generated by creating a weighted spanning tree with mutual information weights. This spanning tree is transformed to a directed tree by picking a root node and pointing all edges away from this root. Finally, the

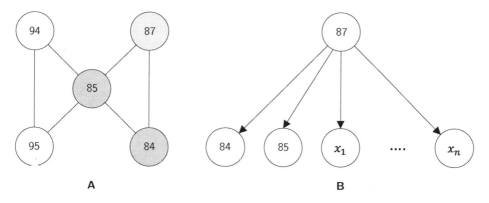

Fig. 1. An example graphical model with dependencies between HS-codes (A) and the corresponding Naive Bayes classifier for HS-code 87 (B).

structure of the TAN is obtained by making all nodes in the directed tree dependent on the label. The advantage of modeling features in a tree structure is that it allows to make an optimal trade off between the ability to incorporate feature dependencies and the corresponding computational complexity [10].

4   Performance Evaluation

4.1   Sample Data

We extracted a large sample from the supply chain repository of an international freight forwarder. The sample contains data of 11,044 maritime shipments that were shipped to the Netherlands in the period of April 2012 and June 2013. Each shipment has data about the bill of lading that was issued by the sea carrier and the import declaration that was send to the Dutch customs authorities. Bills of lading related to the inland transportation were not available. For our application we focus on six features in the sample (Table 1).

From the bill of lading we extracted the bill of lading number (BLN) and four trajectory locations, the: origin (ORG), port of loading (POL), port of discharge (POD) and destination (DES). The origin represents the location where goods are produced. The port of loading is the first port in the shipment trajectory and the place where goods are loaded and secured on a cargo ship. The port of discharge is the last port in the shipment trajectory and the place where goods are unloaded for transloading. This is also the place where the goods in our sample are cleared by the Dutch customs authorities. Finally, the destination represents the location of the consignee. From the import declaration we extracted the HS-codes (HSC) that are declared for the shipments.

Table 1. Three example shipments in the sample data that transported goods to the port of Rotterdam and Antwerp. The goods are transshipped from these ports to consignees located in Amsterdam and Tilburg. The bill of lading numbers are anonymized for confidentiality reasons.

BLN	HSC	ORG	POL	POD	DES
01234567890123	69	Shenzhen	Yantian	Rotterdam	Amsterdam
01234567890123	94	Shenzhen	Yantian	Rotterdam	Amsterdam
01234567890123	39	Chicago	Montreal	Antwerp	Amsterdam
01234567890123	83	Delhi	Mundra	Rotterdam	Tilburg
01234567890123	94	Delhi	Mundra	Rotterdam	Tilburg
01234567890123	76	Delhi	Mundra	Rotterdam	Tilburg

4.2   Data Pre-processing

After collecting supply chain data, we performed pre-processing to transform the sample to the right format for analysis. We aggregated the shipments based on their bill of lading number and transformed the HS-codes to individual binary features. Then, we performed filter operations to ensure that we would be able to take stratified samples to partition the sample into training sets and test sets with equally distributed shipping trajectories. We used the following filters on the sample: each shipping trajectory must have been taken by at least 3 shipments, and each HS-code must have been declared for at least 15 shipments. Finally, we extracted the first two digits of the HS-codes. This was necessary given the small size of the sample. There are not enough observations to learn four digit or six digit HS-codes without over-fitting the classification models. The sample after pre-processing includes data of 10,154 shipments that transported 50 types of goods over 625 shipment trajectories. The bnlearn package [19] in R is used to construct the NB and TAN classifiers on this sample.

4.3   Evaluation Procedure

We evaluated the performance of the classification models by generating artificial declaration errors and counting how many times the models produced a correct alarm. The sample was first divided in a training set and test set based on a 75-25 percent split ratio. Then, artificial declaration errors were generated for ten percent of the declarations in the test set. Miscoding errors were generated by determining the joint Markov blanket of all goods listed on a declaration and adding a random good from this blanket to the declaration. If all goods from this blanket were already listed on the declaration, then a random good outside the blanket was added. Smuggling errors were generated by randomly removing a good from the declaration.

The accuracy of the miscoding alerts and smuggling alerts are reported by calculating corresponding confusion matrices. From these confusion matrices, we derived three additional performance measures: precision, recall and F_1. Precision and recall are defined as [18]:

$$Precision = \frac{TP}{TP+TN} \qquad Recall = \frac{TP}{TP+FP} \qquad (3)$$

Here, TP denotes true positives, TN denotes true negatives and FP denotes false positives. Precision measures the fraction of alarms in which declarations indeed contain miscoding or smuggling. Recall measures the fraction of fraudulent declarations for which an alarm is produced. These two measures are combined to form the F_1 score [18]:

$$F_1 = 2 \cdot \frac{precision \cdot recall}{precision + recall} \qquad (4)$$

The F_1 score constitutes the harmonic mean of precision and recall. It provides a single measure to score competing classification models. We compare the F_1 scores of our modes and the audit strategies and determine the model or strategy that scores the highest F_1 score.

The evaluation procedure of our models can be summarized as follows:

1. *Generate training set and test set* - take a stratified sample and generate a training set and test set based on a 75-25 percent split ratio.
2. *Construct the classification model* - construct a classification model on the training set. Estimate the parameters of the classifiers using Laplace smoothing [10].
3. *Generate miscoding and smuggling errors* - generate two separate test sets, one having a smuggling error in 10 percent of the declarations, and the other having a miscoding error in 10 percent of the declarations.
4. *Predict miscoding and smuggling* - use the classification model to predict whether the declarations in the test sets involve miscoding or smuggling.
5. *Calculate confusion matrices* - use the predictions to calculate corresponding confusion matrices for the miscoding and smuggling alarms.

5   Results

The results of the performance evaluations of the NB and TAN models are shown in the confusion matrices in Table 2. Alarms are produced at an alpha value of $\alpha = 0.05$. This means that the models must be: at most 5 percent certain that a good should be declared to produce a miscoding alert, and at least 95 percent certain that a good should be declared to produce a smuggling alert. Given these criteria, we performed 25 iterations of the evaluation procedure and calculated the mean prediction rates for the confusion matrices.

We compare the performance of our models with the post audit strategy that suggests to audit the same number of declarations as our models but choose declarations at random. We denote these strategies RNB and RTAN. The confusion matrices for the strategies are shown in Table 3. In this table, prediction rates of RNB for miscoding are calculated as follows. Let A be the probability of choosing a declaration for investigation according the prediction rate of the NB model, and E the probability that a declaration contains a miscoding error. Given Table 2, the values for A and E are:

$$A = 0.0886 + 0.1297 = 0.2183 \quad \neg A = 1 - (0.0886 + 0.1297) = 0.7817 \quad (5)$$
$$E = 0.0886 + 0.0112 = 0.0998 \quad \neg E = 1 - (0.0886 + 0.0112) = 0.9002 \quad (6)$$

Because A and E are independent of each other, the confusion matrix can be calculated by multiplying the following combinations:

$$TP = A \cdot E \qquad TN = A \cdot \neg E \qquad FP = \neg A \cdot E \qquad FN = \neg A \cdot \neg E \qquad (7)$$

Here, TP denotes true positives, TN denotes true negatives, FP denotes false positives and FN denotes false negatives. After calculating the confusion matrices for the models and audit strategies, we derived their precision, recall and F_1 score and compared their scores, see Table 4.

Table 2. Confusion matrices for the alarms produced by the NB and TAN models with an alpha value of $\alpha = 0.05$. Rows indicate whether an alarm goes off, columns indicate whether something is actually wrong with the declaration.

	Miscoding				Smuggling			
	NB		TAN		NB		TAN	
	True	False	True	False	True	False	True	False
True	0.0886	0.1297	0.0944	0.0938	0.0441	0.1376	0.0500	0.0410
False	0.0112	0.7705	0.0054	0.8063	0.0558	0.7626	0.0498	0.8592

Table 3. Confusion matrices for the alarms produced by the RNB and RTAN audit strategies. Rows indicate whether an alarm goes off, columns indicate whether something is actually wrong with the declaration.

	Miscoding				Smuggling			
	RNB		RTAN		RNB		RTAN	
	True	False	True	False	True	False	True	False
True	0.0218	0.1965	0.0188	0.1695	0.0181	0.1635	0.0091	0.0819
False	0.0780	0.7036	0.0810	0.7307	0.0817	0.7367	0.0907	0.8183

Table 4. Precision, recall and F_1 scores for the NB and TAN models and their corresponding random audit strategies denoted as RNB and RTAN.

	Miscoding				Smuggling			
	NB	RNB	TAN	RTAN	NB	RNB	TAN	RTAN
Precision	0.4059	0.0998	0.5015	0.0998	0.2426	0.0998	0.5494	0.0998
Recall	0.8877	0.2183	0.9457	0.1882	0.4415	0.1816	0.5007	0.0910
F_1	0.5570	0.1370	0.6554	0.1305	0.3131	0.1288	0.5239	0.0952

6   Discussion

The F_1 scores show that the TAN model outperforms the other models and the random audit strategies on both miscoding and smuggling. The model produced close to 19 percent miscoding alarms and 9 percent smuggling alarms for the declarations in the test set. Miscoding alerts are produced with an average precision of 50 percent and a recall of 95 percent. This means that half of the time the model produced an incorrect miscoding alarm although almost each declaration with miscoding is detected. Smuggling seems more difficult to detect. Alerts for smuggling are produced with an average precision of 55 percent and a recall of 50 percent. Or in other words, the model produced less than half of the time an incorrect smuggling alarm and detected only half of the total declarations in the test set that contained smuggling.

Alarms produced by the NB model are of lower quality. The model produced more alarms for miscoding and smuggling, respectively 22 percent and 18 percent, while the precision and recall of these alarms are lower. Miscoding alerts are produced with an average precision of 41 percent and a recall of 89 percent, while smuggling alerts are produced with an average precision of 24 percent and recall of 44 percent. The NB model suggests to audit more declarations while it captures less fraudulent declarations than the TAN model. This inaccuracy can be attributed to the strong independence assumption of the NB model, which assumes that the goods on an import declaration and the locations in the shipping trajectories are independent of each other given the good that is being predicted, while there clearly seems to exist interaction between these features.

Although the TAN model also does not have an exceptionally high precision and recall, it performs substantially better than the corresponding random audit strategy. Using the random audit strategy leads in our experiment to anti-fraud investigations that are only worthwhile for 10 percent of the suspected declarations. Furthermore, the strategy is only able to detect 19 percent of the total miscoding errors and 9 percent of the total smuggling errors. Therefore, we argue that the use of our TAN model is a substantial improvement over the random audit strategy.

7   Conclusion

In this paper, we have proposed a data mining approach that freight forwarders can apply to detect miscoding and smuggling. We performed an experiment to determine the extent to which these types of document fraud can be automatically detected from supply chain data. The experiment shows that our approach outperforms the audit strategy in which the same number of declarations would be audited but declarations are chosen at random. Therefore, we conclude that our approach is a substantial improvement over this audit strategy.

We learned models from supply chain data that predict the presence of a HS-code on an import declaration based on other declared HS-codes and the trajectory of the corresponding shipment. Decision rules are defined to produce alarms for miscoding and smuggling when declared goods deviate too much from the expected norm. We proposed two different classification models for this task and evaluated their performance. Performance is measured by generating artificial declaration errors and counting how often the models produced a correct alarm. The classification model based on TAN achieved the highest F_1 score.

8   Future Research

Our approach to detect miscoding and smuggling from supply chain data could be further improved. Trajectories in our models have a fixed length and therefore ignore stops at intermediate ports or warehouses. Intermediate stops in a trajectory may reflect critical patterns of document fraud that, when including them in our classification models, may improve the quality of the miscoding and smuggling alarms. The decision rules that raise these alarms should thereby also consider prohibited goods and incorporate the magnitude of the potential fraud in terms of costs. Prohibited goods usually do not show up in the import declarations and therefore remain undetectable by our models. In addition, including costs is important because businesses need to find a balance between the costs to undertake anti-fraud investigation and the savings that can potentially be achieved [1]. We leave these issues open for future research.

References

1. Bolton, R.J., Hand, D.J.: Statistical fraud detection: A review. Statistical Science, 235–249 (2002)
2. Chang, Y.S., Son, M.G., Oh, C.H.: Design and implementation of rfid based aircargo monitoring system. Advanced Engineering Informatics **25**(1), 41–52 (2011)
3. Chickering, D.M.: Learning bayesian networks is np-complete. In: Learning from-data, pp. 121–130. Springer (1996)
4. Choi, T.Y., Hartley, J.L.: An exploration of supplier selection practices across the supply chain. Journal of Operations Management **14**(4), 333–343 (1996)
5. Chow, C., Liu, C.: Approximating discrete probability distributions with dependence trees. IEEE Transactions on Information Theory **14**(3), 462–467 (1968)

6. Digiampietri, L.A., Roman, N.T., Meira, L.A., Ferreira, C.D., Kondo, A.A., Constantino, E.R., Rezende, R.C., Brandao, B.C., Ribeiro, H.S., Carolino, P.K., et al.: Uses of artificial intelligence in the brazilian customs fraud detection system. In: Proceedings of the 2008 International Conference on Digital Government Research, pp. 181–187. Digital Government Society of North America (2008)
7. Edwards, D., De Abreu, G.C., Labouriau, R.: Selecting high-dimensional mixed graphical models using minimal aic or bic forests. BMC Bioinformatics **11**(1), 18 (2010)
8. Eurostat: EU trade since 1995 by HS6 (2015)
9. Filho, J., Wainer, J.: Using a hierarchical bayesian model to handle high cardinality attributes with relevant interactions in a classification problem. In: IJCAI, pp. 2504–2509 (2007)
10. Friedman, N., Geiger, D., Goldszmidt, M.: Bayesian network classifiers. Machine Learning **29**(2–3), 131–163 (1997)
11. Gordhan, P.: Customs in the 21st century. World Customs Journal **1**(1), 49–54 (2007)
12. Hesketh, D.: Weaknesses in the supply chain: who packed the box. World Customs Journal **4**(2), 3–20 (2010)
13. Hill, H.: Nolo's Plain-English Law Dictionary. Nolo (2009)
14. Hsu, C.I., Shih, H.H., Wang, W.C.: Applying rfid to reduce delay in import cargo customs clearance process. Computers & Industrial Engineering **57**(2), 506–519 (2009)
15. Hummels, D., Ishii, J., Yi, K.M.: The nature and growth of vertical specialization in world trade. Journal of International Economics **54**(1), 75–96 (2001)
16. Kopustinskas, V., Arsenis, S.: Risk analysis approaches to rank outliers in trade data. In: Advanced Statistical Methods for the Analysis of Large Data-Sets, pp. 137–144. Springer (2012)
17. Murphy, P.R., Daley, J.M.: Edi benefits and barriers: comparing international freight forwarders and their customers. International Journal of Physical Distribution & Logistics Management **29**(3), 207–217 (1999)
18. Olson, D.L., Delen, D.: Advanced data mining techniques. Springer Science & Business Media (2008)
19. Scutari, M.: Learning bayesian networks with the bnlearn r package. arXiv preprint arXiv:0908.3817 (2009)
20. Tongzon, J.L.: Port choice and freight forwarders. Transportation Research Part E: Logistics and Transportation Review **45**(1), 186–195 (2009)
21. World Customs Organization: Illicit trade report (2012). http://www.wcoomd.org/en/topics/enforcement-and-compliance/~/media/WCO/Public/Global/PDF/Topics/Enforcement%20and%20Compliance/Activities%20and%20Programmes/Illicit%20Trade%20Report%202012/WCO%20REPORT%202013%20-%20BR.ashx
22. Yaqin, W., Yuming, S.: Classification model based on association rules in customs risk management application. In: 2010 International Conference on Intelligent System Design and Engineering Application (ISDEA), vol. 1, pp. 436–439. IEEE (2010)
23. Zaragoza, J.H., Sucar, L.E., Morales, E.F., Bielza, C., Larranaga, P.: Bayesian chain classifiers for multidimensional classification. IJCAI **11**, 2192–2197 (2011)

Modelling and Optimization

Telerobotic Surgery: Fuzzy Path Planning Control for a Telerobotic Assistant Surgery

Rahma Boucetta[⊠]

Laboratory on Control and Energy Management (CEM Lab),
National Engineering School of Sfax, University of Sfax, BP W, 3038 Sfax, Tunisia
boucetta.rahma@gmail.com

Abstract. A strategy of path planning with fuzzy logic for a telerobotic assistant surgery is presented in this paper. Telerobotic surgery occurred a long track in its short history. While teleconsultation proceeds to be used today, the advent of high speed communications and increased computational competence is making long distance remote control of operating instruments, called telepresence surgery, a reality. Based on laparoscopic technology, telerobotic surgery was tested first on animals and, more recently, on humans with success. The technology offers several advantages, including improved accuracy and the capability to bring difficult procedures to rural and remote locations where trained surgeons are not available. A dynamic model is computed first for the telerobots using Lagrange formulation. A fuzzy control strategy is used in order to validate the path planning method and the theoretical developments in motion constraints analysis. The paper is ended with a conclusion.

Keywords: Telerobotic surgery · Dynamic model · Path planning · Fuzzy logic · Laparoscopic surgery

1 Introduction

Surgery has evolved from the early rough days of trepanation and battlefield amputations to modern procedures such as complex neurosurgeries and minimally invasive laparoscopic interventions. However, the surgeon is virtually useless without his tools, and it is perhaps the development of these tools, which has directly lead the evolution of surgery. While several tools such as scalpels, stitches, loops, anaesthesia and antiseptics have each amplified the set of possibilities for procedures, some of the newest tools to enter the surgical instrumentation are robots and computers.

While the advantages of computer and robotic assistance in surgery, in terms of improved accuracy and control may seem evident, one of the most interesting and useful applications of this technology is to perform surgeries remotely. Patients in rural and remote locations often do not have access to advanced surgical care due to an absence of qualified personnel [1]. This is the case in both wartime battlefields and third world countries, and many remote areas

K. Saeed and W. Homenda (Eds.): CISIM 2015, LNCS 9339, pp. 297–304, 2015.
DOI: 10.1007/978-3-319-24369-6_24

as Canada country. Surgical care in these emplacements is either impossible or requires transportation to an urban center upon long distances.

The prime essays at remote care were really what would be appealed teleconsultation. The 1960s saw the beginning of electronic transmission of radiological films, while the 1970s brought the ability for medicaster to consult with experts remotely over video-conference systems [3]. In a surgical implementation of teleconsultation, a remote video-conferencing system was set up in the operating room and was linked to an expert physician at an urban center [2]. This apart surgeon did not actively participate in the process, but instead suggested advice or guidance to the attending surgeon at critical points. At best, electronic remote control of the video camera was available, but little else. While accurate benefits in terms of transmitting expertise and training inexperienced surgeons could be realized with this setup, true remote surgical control was impossible.

This changed with the advent of a robotic system tested at assisting in laparoscopic procedures. Laparoscopic surgery uses a miniature camera (i.e., laparoscope) and small surgical tools which are introduced into the body via tiny incisions and controlled through external manipulators. Minimally invasive surgery performed using laparoscopy provided various advantages to the patient : less pain, a shorter hospital stay, better cosmetic outcome and faster recovery [4]. Unfortunately, this surgical technique, in its original conception, had several shortcomings. The laparoscope produced only a 2-dimensional view of the surgical area, and hand-eye coordination was difficult due to the need to look at a monitor instead of ones hands. Even, the laparoscope was held by an assistant, and therefore direct was taken out of the hands of the surgeon. Perhaps most importantly yet, laparoscopy, by its very nature, introduced amplification of vibration, loss of degrees of freedom (dof) in manipulation, and the brought the requirement for making non-intuitive motions when performing a process [4].

To cross the inherent limitations of laparoscopic surgery, research supported by the US Defense Departments Star Wars program was undertaken in the early 1990's to develop a *master-slave tele-manipulator*, consisted on a computer and robotic instrumentation intervened between the surgeon and the patient [4]. The original goal of this technology was to allow actual manipulation of surgical instruments by telepresence surgery [5]. This technology is hoped to be useful in performing remote trauma surgeries on the battlefield or outer space, where surgeons could not venture [5]. Unfortunately, while a system was developed, it missed the required dof necessary for efficient surgery, and its large size stopped expanded use.

In 1994, a private company developed the da Vinci robot system. This robot builds on traditional laparoscopic technology, rectifying some of its faults while introducing the capacity for remote manipulation. The first refinement is that the camera platform is stable, and can be controlled by the surgeons feet or voice commands, eliminating the need for an assistant. Second, visualization is greatly enhanced with a 3-dimensional magnified system to simulate natural vision, or alternately 2-dimensional displays positioned near the hand controls [6]. Moreover, since physical manipulation of the controls is processed by a computer, shaking can be digitally filtered out preventing excessive error. Finally, the use of motion scaling, which reduces large movements to fine ones, allows surgeons to perform actions which were previously impossible due to their delicacy [6].

Early telepresence surgery research was extremely limited, and being hampered by technical limitations, was carried out only on animal models. Advanced manipulation techniques were not possible due to lack of adequate computational power and communication bandwidth. An early procedure was performed in 1993 by issuing keyboard and mouse commands to manipulate an echographic sonde, biopsy needle and scalpel over a transatlantic fiber optic telephone link to remove a cyst from a pigs liver. Unfortunately, transfer of real-time video over the wired network was technologically impossible at the time due to bandwidth constraints; consequently, relatively expensive satellite links were required [2].

One of the leading difficulties in developing clinically viable telerobotic surgery has been the requirement of minimal time lag between the issuing of commands, actual surgical action, and reception of visual confirmation on the screen. This lag is influenced by multiple factors including time required for converting video and movements into the appropriate signals and the inherent delay in the communication network itself. Experiments have determined that the acceptable limit for safe surgery is $330ms$ [7]. Even with the satellite video link in early experiments, overall delays of approximately $2s$ [2] were inherent in the technology, obviously far from acceptable for a real-time surgical procedure. Accordingly, it was estimated that feasible distances for remote surgery could not exceed several hundred kilometers [8]. This was, however, disproved in subsequent years.

This paper is composed of the following sections : after an introduction, the dynamic model is computed in the second paragraph using the Lagrange equations. The development of a fuzzy path planning control is given by the next section to analyse the telerobotic surgery behavior. the paper is ended with a conclusion.

2 Dynamic Modelling of the Surgical Robot

2.1 Concepts

Safety, control convenience, and flexibility for use in an ample variety of surgical applications were important factors in determining the manipulator design. In laparoscopic applications, rigid instruments are inserted into the patient's body through small cannulas slotted into the abdominal wall. This settlement creates a swivel effect, so that the instrument has only four significant motion dof (three rotations and depth of penetration) centered at the gate. Only very constrained lateral motions are acceptable.

If a robot is keeping an instrument, its motions obey these constraints, necessary. A conventional industrial robot can, of course, be programmed move an instrument about such a fulcrum. Unfortunately, such motions usually require a lot of manipulator joints to make large, tightly coordinated excursions. Thus, even relatively slow end-effector motions can require rapid joint motions. Any control or coordination failure can thereby represent a potential safety hazard both for the patient and for the surgeon. Simply slowing down the actuators can cause the entire functioning of the robot to be painfully boring. Consequently, manipulator designs that require only low velocity actuation are preferred, they do not have motion singularities in the normal working volume, and permit simple stable controls. Similarly, the motions required to perform a task should be reasonably intuitive for the surgeon. Even if the control computer is handling all the details, it is desirable not to surprise the surgeon with unanticipated complex motions. Finally, a great agreement of modularity allow us to reconfigure the system for different procedures.

The 4 dof Robotic Arm chosen in our study delivers fast, accurate, and repeatable movement. The robot features are the Z-base rotation, the single X-plane shoulder, the X-elbow, the X-wrist motion, and a functional gripper.

Fig. 1. 4-dof Surgical Robot architecture.

The dynamic model of the surgical robot was developed using the Lagrange formulation. The robot is described by Figure 1, using a right-handed inertial frame $(B_0 - frame)$ represented by (X_0, Y_0, Z_0), and three right-handed body frames $(B_i - frame)$ represented by (X_i, Y_i, Z_i), where i is the number of dof $i = 1..4$. The positive direction of the first angle θ_1 is decided by a right handed rotation about positive Z axis, the others angles θ_2, θ_3 and θ_4 are about X axis respectively.

Each vector V_0 in the $B_0 - frame$ can be transformed into a vector V_i in the $B_i - frame$ by the following relation

$$q_0 = R_{0,i}.q_i \tag{1}$$

where $R_{0,i}$ is the rotation matrix of the $B_i-frame$ relative to the $B_0-frame$ determined as

$$R_{0,1} = \begin{pmatrix} C_1 & -S_1 & 0 \\ S_1 & C_1 & 0 \\ 0 & 0 & 1 \end{pmatrix}, R_{i,i+1} = \begin{pmatrix} 1 & 0 & 0 \\ 0 & C_{i+1} & -S_{i+1} \\ 0 & S_{i+1} & C_{i+1} \end{pmatrix} \tag{2}$$

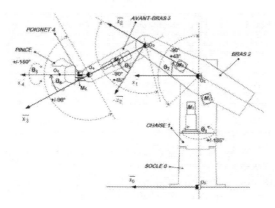

Fig. 2. Cinematics of the Surgical Robot.

2.2 Dynamics

The dynamic behavior can be generated using the Lagrange formulation given
by the expression as

$$\frac{d}{dt}\left(\frac{\partial L}{\partial \dot{q}_i}\right) - \frac{\partial L}{\partial q_i} = \Gamma \tag{3}$$

where L, the lagrangian, that is the difference between kinetic and potential
energies given by $L = T - V$. T is the kinetic energy of the overall system and V
is the potential energy due to the internal deformation of the robot that is equal
to zero. So, the Lagrangian becomes equal to the sum of the kinetic energies
of the moving bodies. The kinetic energy of each body with mass M_i has the
general expression as follows

$$T_i = \frac{1}{2}\left(M_i V_{G_i}^2 + \Omega_i^T I^{(i)} \Omega_i\right) \tag{4}$$

where V_{G_i} is the translation velocity vector of the center of inertia of the moving
link i and has the following form

$$V_{O_{i+1}}^{(0)} = V_{O_i}^{(0)}(R_i) + \Omega_i^{(0)}(R_i) \wedge \overrightarrow{O_i O_{i+1}}(R_i) \tag{5}$$

and $\Omega_i^{(0)}(R_i)$ is the rotation velocity vector given by

$$\Omega_i^{(0)}(R_i) = \breve{\Omega}_i^{(i-1)}(R_{i-1}) + [R_{i-1,i}]^T \Omega_{i-1}^{(0)}(R_{i-1}) \tag{6}$$

The dynamic model can be deduced from the computation of the kinetic
energies and the derivation of Lagrange equations. It has the following expression

$$M\ddot{\theta} + K\dot{\theta}^2 + C\dot{\theta}\dot{\theta} = \Gamma \tag{7}$$

where M, K and C are the inertial, centrifugal and coupling forces matrices,
respectively. To simulate the surgical robot model, the real dimensions values
are given as $L_2 = 0.175m$, $L_3 = 0.28m$, $M_2 = 0.64kg$, and $M_3 = 0.6kg$.

3   Fuzzy Path Planning Control

A fuzzy controller (FC) consists of a set of linguistic conditional statements that are derived from human operators, and which represent knowledge about the system being controlled. These statements define a set of control actions using if-then rules. The FC can be considered as a fuzzy reasoning process to manifest itself in the form of qualitative information about the process, and this information is articulated in the if-then rules, [9].The first step to be performed by the FC is to fuzzify each input, which is done by associating each input with a set of fuzzy variables. In order to give semantics of a fuzzy variable a numerical sense, a membership function is assigned to each variable. The form of a membership function can be either discrete or continuous, and its range is varied from zero to one. Two types of continuous membership functions commonly adopted in fuzzy logic control are triangle and exponential forms. Fuzzified inputs are then associated with knowledge base of the fuzzy controller, containing a set of control rules. By matching the fuzzified inputs with each control rule activates a set of control actions. Since the control actions are in the fuzzy sense, defuzzification is required to transform fuzzy control actions into an exact output value of the controller, [9].

Figure 3 illustrates the block diagram of a direct fuzzy controller applied to the flexible manipulator. Control rules process the error between hub angle and its desired value (e) and the change in error (ce) to synthesize a change in control for improving system performance and vibration suppression. Membership functions are chosen triangular and symmetric. The universes of discourse are divided to 7 fuzzy sets for the inputs and 7 fuzzy sets for the output and chosen between [-1, +1]. So, scaling gains are introduced to normalize the control system. Knowledge rule-base is composed of $7 \times 7 = 49$ rules.

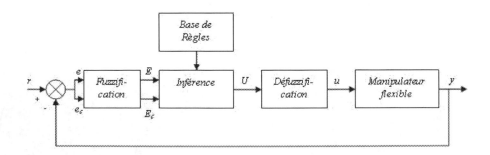

Fig. 3. Diagram of Fuzzy Controller.

4   Simulation Results

The models of master-slave surgical robots are inserted in a *simulink* file. The fuzzy controllers are then established and placed in the closed loop of the robots.

The consign signals are chosen to put the end-point in a desired position. The slave receive the same information after a second. Simulation results are given by the next figures 4, 5 and 6.

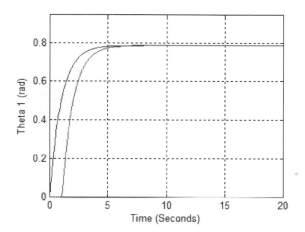

Fig. 4. Responses and first angle θ_1.

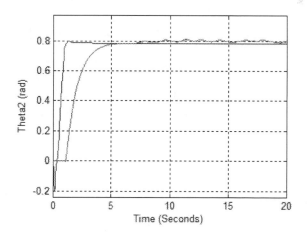

Fig. 5. Responses and second angle θ_2.

The first Z-angle θ_1 for the master and the slave robots are stables and reach consign slowly without overshoots. The second X-angle θ_2 is more fast for the master robot and slow with some fluctuations for the slave robot. The third X-angle θ_3 is very fast with some overshoots for the master robot, and slow and stable for the slave robot. The slave robot can easily pursuit the master robot in its path planning in spite of the delay between the robots operations.

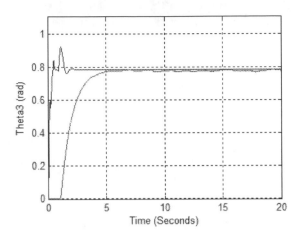

Fig. 6. Responses and third angle θ_3.

5   Conclusion

This paper deals with telerobotic surgery. The main task is to determine a dynamic model of a serial surgical robot using the Lagrange formulation. A fuzzy path planning control is then developed to command a master-slave robot for a surgery application. Simulations results are given to compare different outputs variations. This work can be improved with other types of controllers and real environment in the near future.

References

1. Anvari, M.: Reaching the rural world through robotic surgical programs. Eur. Surg. **37**(5), 284–292 (2005)
2. Rovetta, A.: Remote Control in Telerobotic Surgery. IEEE Transactions on Systems, Man and Cybernetics **26**(4), 438–444 (1996)
3. Benger, J.: A review of telemedicine in accident and emergency: The story so far. Emerg. Med. J. **17**, 157–164 (2000)
4. Broeders, I., Ruurda, J.: Robotics revolutionizing surgery: the Intuitive Surgical "Da Vinci" system. Industrial Robot **28**(5), 387–391 (2001)
5. Bowersox, J., Cordts, P., LaPorta, J.: Use of an intuitive telemanipulator system for remote trauma surgery: An experimental study. J. Am. Coll. Surg. **186**(6), 615–621 (1998)
6. Costello, A., Haxhimolla, H., Crowe, H., Peters, J.: Installation of telerobotic surgery and initial experience with telerobotic radical prostatectomy. BJU Int. **96**, 34–38 (2005)
7. Marescaux, J., Leroy, J., Gagner, M., Rubino, F., Mutter, D., Vix, M., Butner, S., Smith, M.: Transatlantic robot-assisted telesurgery. Nature **413**, 279–380 (2001)
8. Marescaux, J., Rubino, F.: Robotic surgery: potentials, barriers and limitations. Eur. Surg. **37**(5), 279–283 (2005)
9. Passino, K.M., Yurkovich, S.: Fuzzy Control. Addison-Wesley, Longman (1998)

A Model for an Aggression Discovery Through Person Online Behavior

Germanas Budnikas[1,2](✉)

[1] Faculty of Economics and Informatics in Vilnius, University of Bialystok, Vilnius, Lithuania
german.budnik@uwb.edu.pl
[2] Faculty of Informatics, Kaunas University of Technology, Kaunas, Lithuania

Abstract. Reports on aggression acts are quite often in modern community. Its bigger part actively uses Internet resources. The paper considers a hypothesis on a presence of the relationship between real world aggressive behavior and behavior in Internet. The presented model assumes a conduction of aggression tests and monitoring web user online behavior. Gathered data serves as a training data set required for machine learning, which will let to classify an aggression through a person online behavior.

Keywords: Online behavior · Tracking · Aggression · Machine learning

1 Introduction

One of the problems of nowadays community is aggressive behavior of its members. "Aggression is a forceful behavior, action, or attitude that is expressed physically, verbally, or symbolically. It may arise from innate drives or occur as a defense mechanism. It is manifested by either constructive or destructive acts directed toward oneself or against others" [1].

Aggressive behavior leads to negative outcomes and has a direct impact on a welfare of the society. These facts are continuously evidenced by mass media reports. Investigation of aggression at persons of all ages is important. This paper deals with aggression discovery model at adolescent persons of 17-18 years old through their online behavior.

The following is an outline of online activities that have a relationship to aggressive behavior found in psychological literature:

- Usage of violent media that includes viewing action films, playing violent computer games, and visiting violence-oriented Internet sites [2,3], – Playing violent game [4,5].
- Listening to aggressive music [6,7]. Some research have discovered that aggressive lyrics are more significant in forecasting hostile behavior than just an aggressive tone [7, 8].
- Cyber bullying [9, 10].

© IFIP International Federation for Information Processing 2015
K. Saeed and W. Homenda (Eds.): CISIM 2015, LNCS 9339, pp. 305–315, 2015.
DOI: 10.1007/978-3-319-24369-6_25

In other words, activities and interactions with the following Internet based resources can be associated with an aggressive behavior if it possess a violent content:

- Internet sites,
- Online games,
- Forums, posts in social media,
- Online music and video.

In order to be able to perceive a kind of activities performed onsite – violent and aggressive or friendly, it is vital to be able to track web user online actions with its content. Next, these data can be used for classification of a behavior.

Some recent works in online behavior tracking, classification of common patterns and prediction are outlined further (see Table 1) with respect to (w.r.t.) four parts: outcomes to be achieved, monitored online activities, experiment and used methods and techniques.

Table 1. Some recent works in the field (Source: self-made)

	Work by Gutschmidt [11]
Goals/outcomes:	To find significant behavioral differences between web task categories.
Monitored activity:	Mouse pointing, clicking, scrolling.
Experiment (data source, time):	Users documented a kind of task they implemented during browsing – fact-finding, information gathering, just browsing (45 users, 1 month).
Methods:	Descriptive analysis, mean value comparison and correlation analysis, testing hypotheses with mean value comparisons, machine learning methods, descriptive statistics of behavioral attributes, discriminant analysis.

	Work by Xian *et al* [12]
Goals/outcomes:	To predict undesirable network behaviors; to find a relationship between network services and types of services provided; to find trends and types of services provided in the same period.
Monitored activity:	Specific patterns and rules in network user behavior; time of using campus network; times and trends of using types of services provided; network use in different periods.
Experiment (data source, time):	Web site classification based on Open Directory Project (ODP) (ODP catalogue, information from calendar, class, institute, user's IP address, log data of router, DNS catalogue, E-card log data; 1 month).
Methods:	Data mining, statistical analysis.

	Work by Canali *et al* [13]
Goals/outcomes:	Risk prediction based on user web browsing behavior only (probability of visiting malicious web pages).
Monitored activity:	74 features grouped in: how much a user surfs the web; how diversified is the set of websites visited by a user; which website categories the user is mostly interested in; computer type; how popular are the websites visited by the user; how stable is the set of visited pages.
Experiment (data source, time):	Antivirus software on each of user computers that monitors user activity (160.000 users, 3 months).
Methods:	A correlation analysis (to see if any of the browsing factors is correlated with the probability of visiting malicious web pages); machine learning techniques to provide a prediction model that can be used to estimate the risk class of a given user.

Table 1. (*Continued*)

	Work by Ho *et al* [14]
Goals/outcomes:	Model for interpreting online dialogues; classification of anomalous online behavior w.r.t. predefined model.
Monitored activity:	Online user social interaction through emails, blogs, online conversation.
Experiment (data source, time):	Analysis of dialogs in computer-mediated communication environments.
Methods:	Attribute assignment to certain words or actions; dyadic attribute model; computational analysis.

	Work by Vachirapanang *et al* [15]
Goals/outcomes:	To classify online game addiction level among adolescents; to find relationship between the playing data recorded and game addiction risk conditions and risk behaviors.
Monitored activity:	Game-playing periods and frequency, game-playing times, text-based chatting, mouse clicks and keyboard typing during the game.
Experiment (data source, time):	Real-time interaction-based behavior data from a program agent installed in PC (20 users, 2 months).
Methods:	Semi-structured interviews; constructing the user model using Waikato Environment for Knowledge Analysis (WEKA); validation method by decision tree; backpropagation neural networks.

Main objective of the paper is to propose a model that could enable to verify an existence of a relation between an aggression and person online activities in virtual environments using techniques of computer processing and recognition.

A research hypothesis – collected data about person behavior in virtual environments will permit to state about patterns of an aggressive behavior.

Need and *actuality* of the suggested investigation topic are defined by:

- Actual issues influenced by aggressive behavior of persons,
- Announced in the end of 2014 and actual call of Defense Advanced Research Projects Agency in the field of *Detection and computational analysis of psychological signals* [16],
- Recent works in the field of classification and interpretation of a behavior in virtual environments [11,12,13,14,15],
- Existence of theoretical [17] and practical [18] techniques for implementation of behavioral change. This fact permits to consider a possibility to influence aggressive persons online that can be discovered using the model proposed in the given paper.

The paper is structured in the following manner. Section 2 describes general schema of the model proposed in the paper and gives details on implementing the model too. Differences and similarities of the proposed model to the works in the alike topic are presented in the succeeding section. Conclusion summaries the proposed approach.

2   Model Construction

2.1   General Schema

In order to recognize a kind of aggressive behavior in virtual environments like those that were mentioned in the Introduction section – web portals, online games and social media, a supervised machine learning can be applied. A training data set for such a system is composed in two steps.

At the first one, respondents are assigned with unique identifiers and are interviewed using psychological aggression questionnaires[1]. An outcome of the interviews is a division of respondent groups into subgroups with respect to their aggression types or non-aggression property. Additionally, each respondent possesses some psychological portrait drawn by conclusions of filled-out questionnaires in terms of discovered additional aggression types.

At the second step, respondents are asked to log to a dedicated web portal that contains elements of the following types (see first layer at Figure 1):

- Online game,
- Online chat, forum, text,
- Image gallery,
- Hyperlinks,
- Media clips (sound and video).

Web portal collects data about web user interactions with or within a specific portal element. For example, it is possible to monitor user actions undertaken during online game, either to collect user votes on images of different categories. All these data joined with the data from the first step produce a training set (see second layer at Figure 1), which is used by a supervised machine learning. The later technique permits to develop a model for an aggression type discovery (see third layer at Figure 1). Additionally, as each respondent might been classified by additional aggression types, like proactive and reactive aggression [20], another classification and analysis experiments with the training data set are possible in order to define a behavioral pattern w.r.t. aggression types discovered during the first step. While building a model for machine learning, initial experiments are to be performed using representative training set that are generated using the special technique [23] based on k-nn and genetic algorithms.

---

[1] As stated in [19], efficiency of the revised version of the inventory of psychological aggression syndrome IPSA-II [20] increases in case of application of additional inventories. Two more questionnaires might be applied – the aggression questionnaire by Buss & Perry [21] and multi-scale inventory of aggression by Choynowski [22]. Mentioned questionnaires cover aggression types analyzed in the paper, i.e. physical, verbal, without physical or verbal contact and inward aggression [19], and may discover additional aggression types like proactive and reactive aggression.

Data view	Technique view
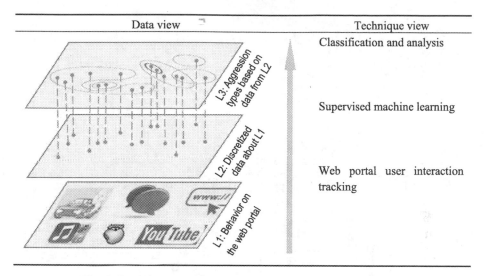	Classification and analysis
	Supervised machine learning
	Web portal user interaction tracking

Fig. 1. General schema of the proposed model (Source: self-made)

Next sub-section explains model implementation issues in more detail.

2.2   Details on Model Implementation

A key functional point in the proposed approach is a monitoring of web user onsite behavior. Such data gathering is quite popular and useful for achievement of stated goals [11], [24].

User behavior with web portal elements is context specific and needs to be represented in such a general form to compose a joint training data set. Such representation is offered in a form of a semantic network, presented in Figure 2. Here, in the Figure 2, an action category is defined with respect to the characteristic property of the applied aggression type as shown in Table 2.

Table 2. Characteristic properties of aggression types considered in the work (Source: self-made using [1], [19])

Aggression type			
Physical	Verbal	Without physical or verbal contact	Inward
° beating, ° pushing, ° spitting ° destruction of property, ° forcing to perform some activities.	° insults, ° threats, ° blackmailing.	° grimaces, ° hostile gestures, ° isolation – limitation of actions (e.g. blocking in the rooms).	° destructive behavior directed against oneself.

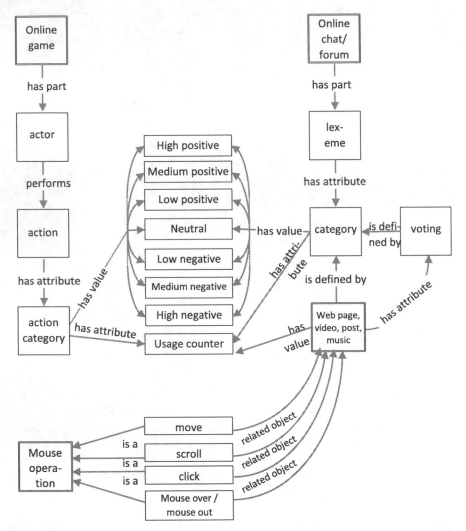

Fig. 2. Discretization of different activities on the web portal for composition of a training data (Source: self-made)

The semantical network shows how user behavior in web portal elements is discretized into pieces of data, which are used for an analysis. The model foresees a creation of an online role-playing game (RPG), which players interact between themselves and with game bots by actions enlisted in Table 2. As seen from the Figure 2, action category may have negative or positive values[2]. A number of application of actions belonging to certain categories is recorded in corresponding usage counters. An online chat consists of exchange of predefined lexemes that are of a certain category and its

---

[2] In order to evaluate a certain aggression type, its two marginal behaviors must present – an aggressive and a friendly.

usage counters are employed in the analysis too. A number of visited web pages and/or read web posts of a certain category is evaluated during the analysis as well. Web pages and/or web posts may be assessed by certain category votes. In addition, as it was mentioned in the review (see Table 1), mouse operations have to be taken into account.

Another important issue in this approach is assignment of categories for those web portal elements, which content is continuously updated or has a bigger volume – text and video clips. Following table briefly outlines techniques to be applied for categorization of big volumes of text and video content (see Table 3).

Table 3. Suggested categorization techniques for text and video information sources (Source: self-made)

Web portal content type(s)	Suggested categorization technique
° text (song lyrics, chat post, news feeds), ° hyperlinks to web sites.	Text categorization using aggressive feature selection [25] permits a solution of text categorization problem that are characterized by many redundant features using classification technique C4.5.
° video clips.	Multimodal and ontology-based fusion approaches of audio and visual processing for violence detection in movies [26] uses multimodal approach that provides binary decisions on the existence of violence or not, and employs machine learning techniques and an ontological and reasoning techniques, that combine the audio-visual cues with violence and multimedia ontologies.

The approach presented above outlines a model construction based on training data. However, in order to successfully use the model in practice, the following must be taken into consideration. Recent research [27,28] has shown a correlation between demographic variables like sex and location, thus, these parameters must be derived from behavioral data too. Location data may be obtained by querying IP address location function, while mining gender information from visited web pages and read texts is possible using Support Vector Machine Regression technique [29,30] as described in [31].

Data about user online behavior can be gathered from a website by means of Event Tracking method (a part of Google Analytics Tracking Code) that enables recording user interaction with website elements, such as embedded AJAX page element, page gadgets, Flash-driven element and so on which are the parts of online game.

Planned period of data collection is influenced by a desired model accuracy and is equal to minimum two months duration in case of daily use of the web portal. Collected data from the web portal will be analyzed by methods that were outlined in Table 1.

3   Related Works

A review of the related works is given in Table 4 with respect to the three criteria – research model, differences and similarities with the topics presented in this paper.

Table 4. Review of the related works (Source: self-made)

Goals	Model	Similarities	Differences
Work by Law *et al* [32]			
to investigate reactive and proactive online aggression.	completion of self-reported questionnaires.	use of aggression test inventories.	three is no tracking of online behavior; there is no machine learning (ML).
Work by France *et al* [33]			
to identify prevention efforts to impact reasons for cyberbullying.	completion of self-reported questionnaires.	online survey on web portal elements similar to ones listed in Sec. 2.1.	the same as previous.
Work by Canali *et al* [13]			
to test an aggression in an online game.	completion of self-reported questionnaires before and after playing the game	use of aggression test inventories, use of game.	the same as previous.
Work by Ho *et al* [14]			
to interpret online dialogues; to classify anomalous online behavior w.r.t. predefined model.	online RPG game, provocation of online user communication and behavior	interpretation of texts, behavior tracking.	used techniques for text classification.
Work by Bidel *et al* [34]			
to investigate various statistical ML models for the categorization and tracking of user navigation behaviors in rich hypermedia systems.	questionnaire based generation of data related to user behavior on the web; application of various ML methods.	tracking of user behavior on the web; behavior models and behavior categorization are similar to discovering different behaviors w.r.t. aggression types.	application area; scope and depth of analyzed web media.

4   Conclusions and Discussion

Pros and cons of the suggested model are discussed in this section. Although the paper does not contain experimental part – only the model has been proposed, some assumptions can be made on the applicability of the proposed model. It may serve as a basis for:

- development of machine learning techniques for an analysis of a relationship between behavior in virtual environments and properties of aggressive behavior,
- succeeding investigations of dependencies between other psychological patterns and actual person behavior in virtual environments,

- enabling a selection and classification of persons, who should be covered by actions of prophylactic either therapeutic nature with respect to discovered aggression types,
- development of behavior impact methods using virtual environments similar to [17,18].

Weaknesses of the suggested approach are twofold – issues of implementation and scalability. Creation of the web portal to be so interesting and continuously updating in order adolescents would use it in a natural way during all period of investigations is a challenging task. An agreement with the existing popular web resource might be a solution. Another issue is that the suggested model assumes application of several methods, which computational complexity has not been evaluated yet. This sets prerequisites for the future work.

Acknowledgement. I express a gratitude to Professor Władysław Homenda from Warsaw University of Technology for his opinion and remarks on the topic presented in this paper.

References

1. Mosby's Medical Dictionary. http://medical-dictionary.thefreedictionary.com/
2. Slater, M.D.: Alienation, aggression, and sensation seeking as predictors of adolescent use of violent film, computer, and website content. Journal of Communication 53(1), 105–121 (2003)
3. Slater, M.D., Henry, K.L., Swaim, R.C., Anderson, L.L.: Violent media content and aggressiveness in adolescents a downward spiral model. Communication Research 30(6), 713–736 (2003)
4. Anderson, C.A., Sakamoto, A., Gentile, D.A., Ihori, N., Shibuya, A., Yukawa, S., Kobayashi, K.: Longitudinal effects of violent video games on aggression in Japan and the United States. Pediatrics 122(5), e1067–e1072 (2008)
5. Willoughby, T., Adachi, P.J., Good, M.: A longitudinal study of the association between violent video game play and aggression among adolescents. Developmental Psychology 48(4), 1044 (2012)
6. Coyne, S.M., Padilla-Walker, L.M.: Sex, violence, & rock n' roll: Longitudinal effects of music on aggression, sex, and prosocial behavior during adolescence. Journal of Adolescence 41, 96–104 (2015)
7. Mast, J.F., McAndrew, F.T.: Violent lyrics in heavy metal music can increase aggression in males. North American Journal of Psychology 13, 63–64 (2011)
8. Lennings, H.I.B., Warburton, W.A.: The effect of auditory versus visual violent media exposure on aggressive behaviour: the role of song lyrics, video clips and musical tone. Journal of Experimental Social Psychology 47(4), 794–799 (2011)
9. Moore, M.J., Nakano, T., Enomoto, A., Suda, T.: Anonymity and roles associated with aggressive posts in an online forum. Computers in Human Behavior 28(3), 861–867 (2012)
10. Buelga, S., Cava, M.J., Musitu, G.: Cyberbullying: adolescent victimization through mobile phone and internet. Psicothema 22(4), 784–789 (2010)
11. Gutschmidt, A.: Classification of User Tasks by the User Behavior: Empirical Studies on the Usage of On-Line Newspapers. Logos Verlag, Berlin GmbH (2013)

12. Xian, X., Chen, F., Wang, J.: An insight into campus network user behavior analysis decision system. In: Computer, Consumer and Control (IS3C), pp. 537–540. IEEE (2014)
13. Canali, D., Bilge, L., Balzarotti, D.: On the effectiveness of risk prediction based on users browsing behavior. In: Proceedings of the 9th ACM Symposium on Information, Computer and Communications Security, pp. 171–182. ACM, New York (2014)
14. Ho, S.M., Timmarajus, S.S., Burmester, M., Liu, X.: Dyadic attribution: a theoretical model for interpreting online words and actions. In: Kennedy, W.G., Agarwal, N., Yang, S.J. (eds.) SBP 2014. LNCS, vol. 8393, pp. 277–284. Springer, Heidelberg (2014)
15. Vachirapanang, K., Sinthupinyo, S., Tuisima, S., Sirivunnabood, P.: The Classification of the Real-Time Interaction-Based Behavior of Online Game Addiction in Children and Early Adolescents in Thailand. International Journal of Advanced Research in Artificial Intelligence 1(7), 7–13 (2012)
16. Defence Advanced Research Projects Agency: Detection and computational analysis of psychological signals (DCAPS). NY. Information Innovation Office (2014)
17. Bosse, T., Provoost, S.: Towards aggression de-escalation training with virtual agents: a computational model. In: Zaphiris, P., Ioannou, A. (eds.) LCT. LNCS, vol. 8524, pp. 375–387. Springer, Heidelberg (2014)
18. Klein, M., Mogles, N., van Wissen, A.: Intelligent mobile support for therapy adherence and behavior change. Journal of Biomedical Informatics 51, 137–151 (2014)
19. Sajewicz-Radtke, U., Radtke, B.M., Kalka, D.: Kwestionariusz agresywności młodzieży-reaktywność emocjonalna: normy dla młodzieży ponadgimnazjalnej. Pracownia Testów Psychologicznych i Pedagogicznych SEBG (2014)
20. Gaś, Z.B.: Zrewidowana wersja Inwentarza psychologicznego syndromu agresji–IPSA-II. Przegląd Psychologiczny 30(4), 1003–1016 (1987)
21. Buss, A.H., Perry, M.P.: The aggression questionnaire. Journal of Personality and Social Psychology 63, 452–459 (1992)
22. Choynowski, M.: Agresywność: pomiar i analiza psychometryczna. Polskie Towarzystwo Psychologiczne, Warszawa (1998)
23. Gabryel, M., Woźniak, M., K. Nowicki, R.: Creating learning sets for control systems using an evolutionary method. In: Rutkowski, L., Korytkowski, M., Scherer, R., Tadeusiewicz, R., Zadeh, L.A., Zurada, J.M. (eds.) EC 2012 and SIDE 2012. LNCS, vol. 7269, pp. 206–213. Springer, Heidelberg (2012)
24. Budnikas, G.: Research on user online behavior. Statistics in Transition (2015) (in press)
25. Gabrilovich, E., Markovitch, S.: Text categorization with many redundant features: using aggressive feature selection to make SVMs competitive with C4.5. In: Proceedings of the Twenty-First International Conference on Machine Learning, pp. 41–50. ACM (2004)
26. Perperis, T., Giannakopoulos, T., Makris, A., Kosmopoulos, D.I., Tsekeridou, S., Perantonis, S.J., Theodoridis, S.: Multimodal and ontology-based fusion approaches of audio and visual processing for violence detection in movies. Expert Systems with Applications 38(11), 14102–14116 (2011)
27. Sakellaropoulos, A., Pires, J., Estes, D., Jasinski, D.: Workplace aggression: assessment of prevalence in the field of nurse anesthesia. AANA Journal 79(4 Suppl), S51–S57 (2011)
28. Lemmens, J.S., Valkenburg, P.M., Peter, J.: The effects of pathological gaming on aggressive behavior. Journal of Youth and Adolescence 40(1), 38–47 (2011)
29. Homenda, W., Luckner, M., Pedrycz, W.: Classification with rejection based on various SVM techniques. In: Proceedings of the 2014 International Joint Conference on Neural Networks (IJCNN), pp. 3480–3487. IEEE (2014)

30. Homenda, W., Jastrzebska, A., Pedrycz, W., Piliszek, R.: Classification with a limited space of features: improving quality by rejecting misclassifications. In: Proceedings of the 2014 Fourth World Congress on Information and Communication Technologies (WICT), pp. 164–169. IEEE (2014)
31. Hu, J., Zeng, H.J., Li, H., Niu, C., Chen, Z.: Demographic prediction based on user's browsing behavior. In: Proceedings of the 16th International Conference on World Wide Web, pp. 151–160. ACM (2007)
32. Law, D.M., Shapka, J.D., Domene, J.F., Gagné, M.H.: Are cyberbullies really bullies? An investigation of reactive and proactive online aggression. Computers in Human Behavior **28**(2), 664–672 (2012)
33. France, K., Danesh, A., Jirard, S.: Informing aggression–prevention efforts by comparing perpetrators of brief vs. extended cyber aggression. Computers in Human Behavior **29**(6), 2143–2149 (2013)
34. Bidel, S., Lemoine, L., Piat, F., Artieres, T., Gallinari, P.: Statistical machine learning for tracking hypermedia user behavior. In: Proceeding of the 2nd Workshop on Machine Learning, Information Retrieval and User Modeling (2003)

Modeling On-demand Transit Transportation System Using an Agent-Based Approach

Olfa Chebbi[1]([✉]) and Jouhaina Chaouachi[2]

[1] Institut Supérieur de Gestion de Tunis, Université de Tunis,
41, Rue de la Liberté - Bouchoucha, 2000 Bardo, Tunisie
olfaa.chebbi@gmail.com

[2] Institut des Hautes Etudes Commerciales de Carthage, Université de Carthage,
IHEC Carthage Présidence, 2016 Tunis, Tunisie

Abstract. We consider the real-time routing of driverless vehicles in an on-demand transit transportation system with time window. Because fast dispatching decisions are required, decentralized decisions system are generally used in these contexts. For that purpose, we introduce a new multi agent-based simulation model where intelligent vehicle agents determine their specific routes and which transportation requests to serve. They interact with passengers, who strive for minimum waiting time. Our approach offers several advantages: it is fast, make it easy for vehicles to determine their specific routes and needs little information for vehicles. We propose also a specific algorithm for the independent vehicles'agent in order to determine their specific routes. Preliminaries computational tests of our multi-agent model and our developed algorithm prove that our approach is very promising.

Keywords: On-demand transit transportation system · Pubic transportation · Simulation · Multi-agent systems

1 Introduction

1.1 Simulation Context

Transportation tools are in general very complex systems that are intertwined with technology. They consists mainly of several decisions that involves different entities such as vehicles, passengers, etc. These systems are generally also the subjects of several decisions and different policies that affect their operational behavior and level of service. Decisions makers related to these complex systems are often faced with the dilemma of exploring the different effect of their long lasting strategic decisions without to actually implement them. That is why, policies makers, scientists and analysts would use distinctive approaches to understand the system under study. These approaches include benchmarking, historical analysis [12], computational modeling and **simulation**[4]. Indeed, these approaches are very useful in order to find effective policies for managing complex transportation systems.

© IFIP International Federation for Information Processing 2015
K. Saeed and W. Homenda (Eds.): CISIM 2015, LNCS 9339, pp. 316–326, 2015.
DOI: 10.1007/978-3-319-24369-6_26

Simulation program is mainly developed to imitate and shows the operation of a specific system over and how it evolves . In the literature, there exists different simulation approaches. We could note for instance discrete event simulation, dynamic system, etc . However, there exists one specific simulation approach that has the ability to study complex systems at the level of individual behavior. This approach is named the agent-based modeling and simulation (ABMS).

1.2   Background of the Paper

On the other hand, due to the huge advance in computers, robotic, communication, control, location, information, sensors, and artificial intelligence, we have observed a growth in the development of intelligent transportation systems (ITS). ITS is generally a term used to define complex systems to improve transportation and drivers experience. Examples and applications of ITS include the in-vehicle eCall [5], collision avoidance systems, dynamic traffic light sequence, Personal Rapid Transit (PRT), etc.

A specific focus could be given to the PRT system. PRT have emerged as a very effective and intelligent transportation system. PRT is a concept a personalized urban mass transit system. PRT can be seen as the combination of individualized passengers transportation tool and mass public transit transportation mean. In fact, PRT use small electric driverless vehicles that could take from one to six passengers. PRT have been introduced to many urban contexts such as the Heathrow airport London UK, Morgan town West Virginia USA, Masdar City Abu Dhabi UAE, etc. PRT is seen as an efficient and sustainable transportation tool which has the ability to bring a new insight to the way that people are moved in cities. However, PRT literature is at its infancy.

1.3   Related Literature

For managerial aspects, there exists a few studies that tackled the PRT system. One could note network design [13], station locations [14], fleet size [8], the waiting time for passengers [6], [3] and energy consumption [10], [9]. As for simulation, many simulation approaches have been developed to simulate PRT system [1]. **However, these models does not tackle battery issues for the PRT electric vehicles.** Batteries for PRT represents an important feature as they provide energy supplies for the system and need to be periodically charged in specific locations. Simulation model that developed battery issues for PRT was developed by Mueller and Sgouridis [11]. **However, they used discrete event simulation approach to model the PRT system.** According to us, ABMS requires a specific attention in the PRT literature due to its huge ability to simulate the PRT'vehicles behavior. In fact as the PRT vehicles are driverless, agent based simulation represents the perfect tool to model efficiently how the PRT vehicles are operated in this system.

1.4   Contributions of the Paper

Starting from the statements that the PRT system deserves a more decentralized management approach and the related simulation literature to PRT have been focused on discrete event simulation, we:

1. Define a Multi Agent simulation model for simulating PRT systems.
2. Suggest a decentralized management strategy to solve the problem of managing driverless vehicles in PRT systems.
3. Validate our model on data sets generated following a field study in the case study of Corby in the United Kingdom.

1.5   Outlines of the Paper

The structure of this paper is as follows. In Section 2, we present briefly the PRT system. In Section 3, we present our problem definition. Section 4 explains the model-driven development process for simulating PRT system. In Section 5, we present results and analysis of our simulation model. Finally, Section 6 concludes and gives directions for future research.

2   The Personal Rapid Transit System

Personal rapid transit (PRT) is an automated transit system in which small vehicles move to transport small number of passengers on demand to their desired destinations. Transportation service in PRT is done by means of non-transfer, nonstop and on its own right-of-way. PRT vehicles (also called pods) run on exclusive small tracks also called guideways.

The guideways are designed as elevated facilities above the ground, for purpose of eliminating at-grade crossings or interferences with other transportation modes.

A PRT system offers a taxi-like transportation service. In fact in PRT, users are served only on demand. There isn't any predetermined schedule for PRT as by other conventional mass transportation system such as bus or train. More specifically, the transportation service is done as follow: at PRT station, a passenger or a group of passengers first select the desired PRT destination station. Then, the control system dispatch a specific PRT vehicle to the station to take the passenger of the group of passengers to their desired destination. Transportation service in PRT is done without any intermediate stops. In fact, PRT stations are placed offline. This feature allows PRT vehicles to embark/disembark passengers on auxiliary guideways without interfering with the vehicles movements on the main line. Consequently, PRT vehicles could move without any unnecessary stops at intermediate stations.

Due to the latest advances in technology and robotics, PRT vehicles are electric and are under computer control. Therefore, PRT vehicles don't need a human driver. The size of a PRT vehicle can accommodate one to six passengers in general. PRT systems was developed in several real world applications recently, including in Korea, Sweden, London and United Arab Emirates.

2.1   Related PRT Literature

In recent decades, different microsimulators have been developed to model the behavior of individuals and automated vehicles. One could note the PRT International (USA)[1], RUF International (Denmark)[2] TrakEdit: PRT Simulator from Taxi 2000 (USA)[3], Mueller and Sgouridis PRT simulator in 2011 [11], etc. More details about PRT simulators are given in [1].

However, what is missing in the literature is a powerful agent based simulator that could take into account different characteristics of the PRT systems in term of battery management, dispatching decisions and route choice. Mainly, the main difference that battery vehicles bring is the additional movement for the vehicles to charge their battery in the specific charging locations. One should note also that routing and dispatching decisions for PRT vehicles follows strictly central control system decisions. These decisions concern specifically the empty vehicle management (EVM). EVM is a specific control function that has big influence on the routing and dispatching of empty PRT movement. In fact, the empty vehicles flows in station need to be balanced between inbound and outbound flows. Using agent based simulation approach has the possibility to offer a more decentralized control option for PRT system and therefore, bring new insight into PRT management options.

3   Problem Definition of Distance Minimization and Waiting Time of PRT with Multi-agent System

In this section, we present the formal problem definition to be treated in this work.

Within the PRT transportation system network N, passengers arrive at stations and ask the PRT system in order to request to carry them from their specific departure PRT station origin to a specific PRT destination station. N is composed by a set of M stations and one depot station. Passengers arrive in each station following a poisson process of rate λ. Transportation requests should be done immediately and served as soon as possible. No rejection is allowed. PRT system satisfy the transportation requests using a set of electric PRT vehicles. The vehicles are supposed to have a limited battery capacity denoted by B. We consider also to have a specific cost matrix that defines the cost of moving between each couple of stations. All vehicles are supposed to be initially located at the depot. Vehicles charging operations are supposed to be done only in the depot. In this paper, the vehicles are supposed to be autonomous. A dispatching decisions refer to assigning a vehicle to a specific transportation request. The dispatch decisions in a PRT system must be decided quickly and as soon as the passenger requests are received. This ensures a reduced waiting time for passengers and therefore a high quality of service. However, the decision of dispatching a

---

[1] www.prtnz.com
[2] http://www.ruf.dk/
[3] http://www.taxi2000.com/

vehicle to a specific transportation request requires all the current PRT'network data. That is why the dispatching decisions should be made while evaluating all the possible dispatching alternatives in order to optimize the vehicle behavior and the overall system performance.

The information of the coming of the passengers is known gradually as the PRT system serves its passengers. This is the most crucial point in assigning vehicles to transportation requests because the limited battery capacity don't allow the vehicles to serve all the transportation requests. Therefore, a limit is imposed on the PRT vehicles while traveling a route to serve passengers.

3.1   Objectives

The following two objectives have to be achieved in regard to the problem context formulated above.

1. On the one hand, a minimization of travel and transportation costs has to be faced. This objective can be subdivided into the sub-objectives of minimizing travel distances and minimizing the number of vehicles in use. Concerning travel distance, this objective could be reached by minimizing the total empty movement for PRT vehicles as the distance of satisfying transportation request is considered as a fixed cost. Whereas the evaluation of the needed number of PRT pods could be more complicated as it is pre-defined and related to the strategic level of decisions of PRT system. However, one should note that saving in the exact number of used vehicles in a pre-optimization step could offer a high flexibility to the system. In fact, as we could save in the exact number of used vehicles, the system could enhance its customer service as more free vehicles would be available.
2. On the other hand, a maximization of customer satisfaction has to be addressed by the minimization of the total waiting time of passengers. The focus in this contribution is, besides the minimization of travel cost, on the maximization of customer satisfaction by the minimization of the total waiting time of passengers.

4   The Proposed Simulation Model

In the following subsections, we will first describe the used simulation software. Then, we describe the developed PRT simulation model.

4.1   The Used Simulation Software

Different simulation software was evaluated in order to develop our multi agent simulation model for the PRT system. Among evaluated software we could note

Entreprise dynamics[4], Jadex[5], etc. Our decision was made in favor of the Any-logic software[6]. The Anylogic is a java based simulation software. It offers the advantages of combining three major simulation methodologies: Discrete event simulation; System Dynamic and Agent based simulation. The Anylogic offers modular and hierarchical modeling of complex models. The Anylogic provides also different tools such as diverse library which helps users to better build their models. This software offers also the possibility to work with action chart, state chart and a huge number of statistics tools. This makes possible for any developed simulation model to evaluate their output using the different built-in statistical tools.

4.2 Agent Based Simulation for Modeling Trips in PRT System

To have a specific simulation model that allows us to model all the designs of a single trips, we choose agent based modeling using the Anylogic simulation software. Intuitively, the PRT vehicles are the only agents that need to be rep-resented in our model. However, we used in our model two types of agents:

1. PRT vehicles are the agents representing the fleet of vehicles in the PRT system. The number of these agents is determined by the strategic decisions related to PRT system.
2. Passengers represent the specified users of the PRT system.

These different agents developed in this works are considered as the percep-tive entities having the ability to think, take decisions and react according to the current situation of the system. The PRT vehicles mainly achieves four main functions:

1. Passengers'transportation and Request satisfaction,
2. Charging operation,
3. Collecting travel statistics.

The passengers'agents mainly imitate the passengers'behavior. Each PRT vehi-cle day begins in the depot. The passengers'transportation demands will trigger a series of events and make the vehicle agents' properties and behaviors change. For a single trip, the PRT'passengers customer ask to be transported from their specific station to their destination station. A vehicle agent takes the request and handles it according to the principle of Close first. This means that the empty vehicle available in the station of the passengers will handle the transportation request. If there is more than one empty vehicle in the station of the transporta-tion request, the vehicle agent with the high level of energy in its battery will handle the transportation request. Otherwise, if there isn't any vehicle in the

[4] Source: http://www.incontrolsim.com/enterprise-dynamics/
enterprise-dynamics.html
[5] Source: http://www.activecomponents.org/bin/view/AC+Tool+Guide/
09+Simulation+Control
[6] Source: www.anylogic.com/

station of the transportation request, the closest empty vehicle to this location will be assigned to serve the specific trip. Details about PRT'vehicle behavior are shown in Algorithm 1. We should note also that if a vehicle agent finished serving a transportation request and there isn't any passengers waiting to be transported a principle of first come first serve is applied to serve transportation requests in others stations in the network.

Algorithm 1. Algorithm of a Agent Vehicle()

 1: **if** CurrentState=Waiting **then**
 2:     **for all** Waiting Passengers P_i in this.CurrentStation **do**
 3:         **if** $this.Batterylevel$ Allows the vehicle to serve P_i **then**
 4:             Assign P_i to Vehicle
 5:             Exit FOR
 6:         **end if**
 7:     **end for**
 8: **end if**
 9: **if** CurrentState=Waiting **then**
10:     MinDistance=$Big - M$.
11:     AffectedPassenger=$NULL$.
12:     **for all** Waiting Passengers P_i in the PRT network **do**
13:         **if** $this.Batterylevel$ Allows the vehicle to serve P_i and P_i isn't in the current station of the vehicle **then**
14:             MinDistance= Distance Between Current Station of Vehicle and the current station of P_i
15:             AffectedPassenger=P_i
16:         **end if**
17:     **end for**
18:     **if not** $(AffectedPassenger == NULL)$ **then**
19:         Assign P_i to Vehicle
20:     **end if**
21: **end if**

After the vehicle agent successfully deals with a transportation request, its level of energy in its battery is updated. The vehicle will begin to check its battery'energy level as soon as it successfully deals with an order. If it found that its level of energy is less or equal to the energy needed to returning to the depot in addition to a specific reserve value, the vehicle will then go back to its depot station to charge its battery. The passengers' agent mainly simulates the behavior of actual PRT users in stations. They also simulate the process of asking for a PRT'vehicle in order to study its behavior.

5 Computational Results

In this section, we report the computational results obtained for testing the multi agent simulation model for the PRT system. As for the network configuration,

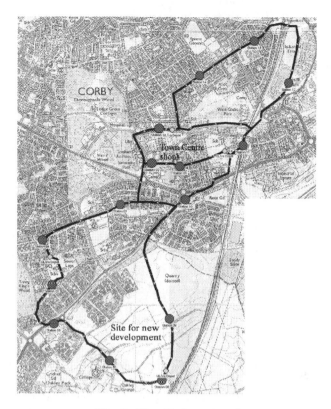

Fig. 1. The Corby network

we used the Corby use case which represents a real PRT network [2]
(see Figure 1). This configuration is based on a multiple depots shape. As we
supposed in our works to have a single depot network topology,**we generated
4 different networks while taken into consideration only one depot.**

As for PRT' transportation requests, we used carefully generated scenarios
based on the already developed PRT works [7] [6]. More specifically to obtain
the different scenarios, traveling requests from any station i to station j were
generated according to a Poisson process with rate $\lambda_{ij} \in [0.789, 17.902]$. These
rates are publicly available and are given the ATS/CityMobil software[7]. For each
tested network, **we used 5 different generated scenarios.** In our simulation
tests, **we supposed to have 200 as a PRT' fleet size.** The battery capacity
was taken as 40 minutes [10]. The reserve parameter(Algorithm 1) was supposed
to be equal to be the tenth of the total battery capacity of the PRT vehicles. The
results are shown in Table 1. The estimated wasted energy as well as effective
energy are reported in Table 1. We report also for each scenario the average
waiting time for passengers. Wasted energy denotes the energy used for the

[7] ATS/CityMobil   PRT   source: http://www.ultraprt.com/prt/implementation/
simulation/

Table 1. Computational Results of our Multi-agent Decentralized Strategy

Scenario	Network	Wasted Energy in %	Effective Energy in %	Average Waiting Time in Seconds
1	D1	20.434	79.566	937.078
2	D1	34.943	65.057	700.699
3	D1	34.855	65.145	755.855
4	D1	35.187	64.813	773.932
5	D1	31.645	68.355	578.453
6	D2	34.708	65.292	747.547
7	D2	38.511	61.489	683.355
8	D2	40.369	59.631	754.456
9	D2	39.016	60.984	859.082
10	D2	39.902	60.098	786.457
11	D3	40.438	59.562	280.051
12	D3	35.191	64.809	256.676
13	D3	35.874	64.126	297.712
14	D3	41.846	58.154	403.273
15	D3	36.660	63.340	262.621
16	D4	37.040	62.960	822.613
17	D4	40.949	59.051	780.078
18	D4	42.119	57.881	752.612
19	D4	35.836	64.164	797.523
20	D4	38.879	61.121	748.360
Average		36.720	63.280	648.922

empty movements of vehicles. Waiting Time of passengers denotes the difference in time between the rise of the demand and the fulfillment of this demand. To interpret this huge number of results, we conduct correlation analysis. We used the Multiple Pearson correlation tests to understand the effects of the design parameters in general. This latter includes the effects of network configuration, scenarios and their interactions. The effects of some of the studied parameters are intuitive and have already been reported in the literature.

In order to determine the design parameters that have the most significant effect on the wasted energy, multiple correlation Pearson tests was performed using GraphPad software[8]. Tables 2, 3 represent the resultant Pearson outcomes for the wasted energy and average waiting time. Values

Table 2. Results of the Correlation tests Related To The Scenario

Statistic	Scenario vs. Wasted Energy	Scenario vs. Average Waiting Time in Seconds
Pearson r		
r	0.5752	-0.2055
95% confidence interval	0.1778 to 0.8113	-0.5941 to 0.2608
R square	0.3308	0.04225
P value		
P-value (two-tailed)	0.008	0.3846
Significant? (alpha = 0.05)	Yes	No

---

[8] more details about GraphPad software could be found in http://www.graphpad.com/

Table 3. Results of the Correlation tests Related To The Network

Statistic	Network vs. Wasted Energy	Network vs. Average Waiting Time in Seconds
Pearson r		
r	0.5332	-0.1949
95% confidence interval	0.1186 to 0.7895	-0.5869 to 0.2711
R square	0.2843	0.03798
P value		
P-value (two-tailed)	0.0155	0.4103
Significant? (alpha = 0.05)	Yes	No

The multiple Pearson tests' results indicate that all main the two-way interactions are significant at a level of significance of 0.05 for the wasted energy. On the other hand, most of waiting time of passengers interactions are not significant. This significance of the two-way interactions for the wasted energy proves that the network topology and the scenario factors are interrelated. This proves the importance of the different strategic decisions on our PRT system. In the other hand, these factors have no real significant impact on the waiting time of passengers. Explaining the effects of the network topology on the wasted energy is simple and straightforward. An increase in the average distance between the depot and the different stations should be directly translated to an increase in the travel distance.

6 Conclusion and Future Research Directions

In this paper, we introduced a new Agent based simulation model for modeling PRT system. Based on agent method, this paper describes the PRT dispatching system simulation model using AnyLogic software. In this model the customers' demand can't be estimated ahead. That is why, it was important to consider specific rules for the different agent in order to reduce total traveled distance and waiting time of passengers. Simulation experiment verifies the exactness of this model and concludes that our simulation model by considering vehicles as autonomous agent is a powerful approach to model and optimize the PRT system. Extension to our work includes developing enhanced routing policies for the PRT system based on this model.

References

1. Anderson, J.E.: Some history of PRT simulation programs (2007)
2. Bly, P., Teychenne, P.: Three financial and socio-economic assessments of a personal rapid transit system. In: Proceedings of the Tenth International Conference on Automated People Movers, p. 39 (2005)
3. Daszczuk, W.B., Choromański, W., Mieścicki, J., Grabski, W.: Empty vehicles management as a method for reducing passenger waiting time in personal rapid transit networks. IET Intelligent Transport Systems (February 2014). http://digital-library.theiet.org/content/journals/10.1049/iet-its.2013.0084

 4. Gilbert, N.: Agent-based social simulation: dealing with complexity. The Complex Systems Network of Excellence **9**(25), 1–14 (2004)
 5. Kohn, A.: The ecall program: Overview and design considerations (2010)
 6. Lees-Miller, J.D.: Minimising average passenger waiting time in personal rapid transit systems. Annals of Operations Research 1–20 (2013)
 7. Lees-Miller, J.D., Wilson, R.E.: Sampling for personal rapid transit empty vehicle redistribution. Transportation Research Record: Journal of the Transportation Research Board **2216**, 174–181 (2011). http://dx.doi.org/10.3141/2216-19
 8. Li, J., Chen, Y.S., Li, H., Andreasson, I., van Zuylen, H.: Optimizing the fleet size of a personal rapid transit system: a case study in port of Rotterdam. In: International Conference on Intelligent Transportation, pp. 301–305 (2010)
 9. Mrad, M., Chebbi, O., Labidi, M., Louly, M.: Synchronous routing for personal rapid transit pods. J. Applied Mathematics **2014** (2014). http://dx.doi.org/10.1155/2014/623849
10. Mrad, M., Hidri, L.: Optimal consumed electric energy while sequencing vehicle trips in a personal rapid transit transportation system. Computers & Industrial Engineering **79**, 1–9 (2015). http://dx.doi.org/10.1016/j.cie.2014.09.002
11. Mueller, K., Sgouridis, S.P.: Simulation-based analysis of personal rapid transit systems: service and energy performance assessment of the masdar city PRT case. Journal of Advanced Transportation **45**(4), 252–270 (2011). http://dx.doi.org/10.1002/atr.158
12. Scharpf, F.W.: Games real actors play: Actor-centered institutionalism in policy research, vol. 1997. Westview Press, Boulder (1997)
13. Won, J.M., Lee, K.M., Lee, J.S., Karray, F.: Guideway network design of personal rapid transit system: a multiobjective genetic algorithm approach. In: 2006 IEEE Congress on Evolutionary Computation, vol. 1–6 (2006)
14. Won, J.M., Choe, H., Karray, F.: Optimal design of personal rapid transit. In: Intelligent Transportation Systems Conference, pp. 1489–1494, September 2006. http://dx.doi.org/10.1109/ITSC.2006.1707434

Optimal Fleet Sizing of Personal Rapid Transit System

Olfa Chebbi[1]([✉]) and Jouhaina Chaouachi[2]

[1] Institut Supérieur de Gestion de Tunis, Université de Tunis,
41, Rue de la Liberté - Bouchoucha, 2000 Bardo, Tunisie
[2] Institut des Hautes Etudes Commerciales de Carthage,
Université de Carthage, IHEC Carthage Présidence, 2016 Tunis, Tunisie
olfaa.chebbi@gmail.com

Abstract. In this paper, we address the problem of determining the optimal fleet size for Personal Rapid Transit system (PRT). In our problem, we consider electric battery and distance constraints which are found in real world application of the PRT system. To tackle this problem, we propose two valid mathematical formulations that are able to find optimal fleet size. Extensive computational experiments show that the edge based formulation performs impressively well, in terms of solution quality and computational time in comparison to the node based formulation.

Keywords: Personal Rapid Transit · Public transportation · Fleet-sizing · Vehicle routing problem

1 Introduction

1.1 Background

Private vehicles automobile are highly successful as a private transportation tool around the world. In fact, private vehicles provide their users with a nearly unlimited mobility option. Those who own and operate a vehicle could go almost anywhere. Private vehicles offer the advantage of offering an on-demand transportation service 24 hours a day between any origins and destinations in a pre-defined urban area. However, the increase in the use of private automobile has brought many environmental and social disadvantages. Among these, we could consider congestion, deaths and injuries, air pollution, increasing rate of carbon emissions and the continuing need for more roads, etc. Private vehicles are also responsible for a high percentage of the world's energy and oil usage. This results on a high pressure on the world petrol reserve and in an increase in the oil 'prices. We should note also that public transportation tools in cities such as buses and trains are losing ridership for many years. In fact, those public transportation tools offer a non-flexible transportation option where users need to adapt their transportation needs to a fixed non flexible schedule and routes. The latter results on small use' rate of public transportation tool. That is why

© IFIP International Federation for Information Processing 2015
K. Saeed and W. Homenda (Eds.): CISIM 2015, LNCS 9339, pp. 327–338, 2015.
DOI: 10.1007/978-3-319-24369-6_27

an increasing attention was focused on providing a viable public transportation system to urban areas that could replace private vehicles. Much attention in the United States and the European Union is being focused on the development of Personal Rapid Transit (PRT) systems. PRT is a class of automated fixed-guideway transit systems. Transportation service in PRT is provided by a set of small electric driverless vehicles (see Figure 1). PRT vehicles (also called pods) could take from one to six passengers. PRT' vehicles offers a set of auto-like characteristics (comfort, privacy, speed, etc). These features make PRT a viable alternative to the use of private automobile while being a public transportation system. PRT vehicles runs on a dedicated network of private guideways with stations positioned off the mainline. PRT' networks involves many guideways and closely spaced PRT' stations. This involves easy access of passengers to the PRT vehicles. Various descriptions and definitions of PRT are provided in the literature. Nowadays, there is general unanimity among PRT experts that there are five key characteristics that defines any PRT systems [1]:

1. On-demand, origin-to-destination service: transportation service in PRT is done on demand directly from an origin station to a destination station without any intermediate stops This is done through the specific topology of the PRT network that include offline stations which permit this feature.
2. Small, fully automated vehicles: PRT vehicles are driverless and small. As no driver is needed for a PRT system, a reduced operational cost in comparison with traditional transportation service is obtained.
3. Small, exclusive-use guideways: As the PRT vehicles are small, a use of small guideway is possible. This engenders a small construction costs for a PRT'network . Network of PRT is exclusive to the PRT pods. This helps to relieve congestion on the roads.
4. Off-line stations: This feature is one of the unique characteristics of PRT. In fact, stations are located on the sideline. It permits vehicles that don't need to stop at a specific station to by pass-it towards its destination. This results on a short transportation time.
5. A network of fully connected guideways: The network of PRT is fully connected. This feature allow any vehicles to go from any station to any another stations.

The PRT transportation mode has been first introduced in 1953. Nowadays there is different real implementation of PRT around the world. We could note the Heathrow Airport PRT, London UK, the Morgantown PRT , West Virginia, US or the Masdar City PRT, Abu Dhabi, UAE. Unfortunately, the transportation literature related to PRT is at early stages. Special focus was put on the feasibility of PRT system and only recently there were focus on strategic and operational issues related to PRT [2]; [3].

1.2 Objectives of The Paper

This paper focuses on a specific related problem to the strategic level of decisions. More specifically, we aim to treat the problem of fleet sizing of a PRT

Fig. 1. An Example of PRT Vehicle [1]

system under battery constraints. The fleet sizing is a really important problem for PRT. In fact, if the fleet size for PRT is large enough, small waiting time for passengers could be reached as passengers will always find empty vehicles available at stations. This engenders a high operational level for such an intelligent system. However, for real case and for rush hours, the fleet size of PRT is mainly subject to different constraints such as financial constraints which don't allow having a perfect zero waiting time for passengers. More specifically, in practice, for high peak demand, the fleet size is subject to financial constraints and will not be so large that all passengers can have zero waiting time. In fact, driverless PRT vehicles are expensive. The investment of purchasing PRT vehicles contributes mainly to the total investment of building PRT system. We could note for instance that purchasing' vehicles contributes on about 10% of the total investment of a PRT system [4].

That is why, optimizing of the fleet size of a PRT system is of a high importance for any PRT system. To the best of our knowledge, this problem was treated only by Li Jie [5]. However, their work doesn't consider battery constraints of PRT vehicles. Battery constraints involve that vehicles would be unavailable for serving passengers as they needs to periodically charge their battery. This could result on a pressure on the fleet of PRT vehicles in order to offers a high level of operational service.

To do so, we study in this paper a relative routing problem related to PRT in order to give decision related to the PRT' fleet size. We aim at our problem by minimizing the total number of used vehicles while respecting the battery capacity of the PRT vehicles.

To the best of our knowledge, there is no significant contribution in the literature to address the above PRT presented problem. In this paper to tackle the considered problem, we propose as a first step two valid mathematical formula-

---

[1] source: http://www.vincentabry.com/wp-content/uploads/2011/09/ Personal-Rapid-Transit.jpg

tions for solving our problem. Studying the performance of different valid mathematical formulations for our problem is of a high interest in order to perceive the general structure of the problem under study. The proposed formulations differs in term of defining the decisions variables. The proposed two valid mathematical formulations are numerically shown to be efficient to address small instances size for the treated problem.

1.3   Motivation of the Paper and Related Literature

Comparing valid mathematical formulations is of a high interest while studying new problems as the one treated in this paper. In fact as Demir and Isleyen state [6], *"although mathematical programming formulation is not efficient solution method due to the NP-hard structure of routing and combinatorial problems, it is considered as a first step prior to developing an effective heuristics and useful to understand the structure of the problem"* [6]. That is why scientists should be aware of the relative efficiency of routing models through studying the performance of valid mathematical formulations.

In the literature, several papers proposed to compare mathematical formulation for various problems. Kara [7] studied to compare two mathematical formulations for distance constrained vehicle routing problem (DCVRP). Fatnassi et al. [8] proposed to compare two valid mathematical formulations for the PRT case to minimize total traveled distance. Blazewichz et al. [9] proposed to study mathematical models for single-machine, parallel-machine and job shop scheduling problems. Focus on mathematical models for scheduling problems. Pan [10] proposed to compare mathematical formulations for both job-shop and flow-shop scheduling problems. Keha et al. [11] provided a comparison of various mixed integer linear programming (MILP) formulations for single machine scheduling problems. Other works on comparison between mathematical formulations for combinatorial problems include the works of Pan and Chen [12], Unlu and Mason [13], etc.

As presented above various survey papers have appeared on mathematical programming formulations for scheduling problems over the years. But in our search, only two papers focused on mathematical formulations for routing problems. The exceptions are the papers presented by Kara [7] and Fatnassi et al. [8]. They developed an integer linear programming model for DCVRP in order to minimize the total traveled distance.

In this paper, literatures related to routing problems are investigated in order to look for similarities between the proposed problem related to PRT and other works in the literature. By assuming the objective function is to reduce the fleet size of PRT vehicles, computational efficiency of the proposed two mathematical formulations models is compared and analyzed.

1.4   Contributions of The Paper

The contributions of this paper are several:

1. We propose a relative problem to the strategic level of decision for PRT system to reduce and minimize the use of PRT vehicles.
2. We propose two valid mathematical formulations to tackle our proposed problem.
3. We compare the efficiency of our two formulations in term of solution quality and computational effort through various analysis and statistical test.

1.5   Outline of The Paper

The remainder of this paper is organized as follows: in Section 2, problem definition of minimizing fleet size of PRT and notation of models are presented. In Section 3, a valid road based formulation is proposed. Sections 4 and 5 describe the two mathematical formulations for the proposed problem. In Section 6, computational results of models compared. Finally the conclusions of study are drawn in section 7.

2   Problem Definition

In this section, we present the problem definition as presented in [3],[14].

Let us consider a network of PRT N that contains

- a set of stations $S = \{s_1, s_2, ..., s_M\}$ of cardinality M.
- one depot D.
- We suppose also that the network N ensures connectivity constraints. This is possible by having enough guideways that make possible to reach any PRT station from any another one.
- We suppose also that a set of electric battery powered vehicles ensure the transportation service within the PRT network.
- Each vehicle have a limited electric battery capacity B.

In this paper, we treat the problem of fleet sizing in a static deterministic context. For that purpose, we suppose to have a deterministic list of trips (calendar or schedule) $T = \{1, 2, ..., n\}$ has to be performed. Each trip $i \in T$ is characterized by :

- Dt_i: the departure time of trip i.
- $Ds_i \in S$: the departure station of trip i.
- At_i : the arrival time of trip i.
- $As_i \in S$: the arrival station of trip i.

We suppose that the transportation service is done under the following assumptions:

- An unlimited number of PRT vehicles are available in the depot to guarantee all the trips. The exact number of vehicles needed will be the objective of our problem.
- The charging Operation of the batteries could be done only in the depot.

- The consumed energy for a vehicle from the depot visiting some stations in N and returning to the depot, must never exceed B
- We relax time needed to load and unload passengers at PRT stations.
- We suppose that the transportation move between any couple of stations is done following the shortest path. The cost of the shortest path between any pairs of stations is defined by the cost matric sp. The shortest paths between all stations could be determined by using the Floyd Warshall algorithm [15].

The objective of our problem is to assign the trips to vehicles in order to reduce the number of used PRT vehicles. For that purpose, three linear programming formulations are presented based on specific network representation.

Let $G = (V, E)$ be a graph, with V the set of nodes and E the set of the arcs. Each trip i is represented by a node, in addition of two dummy nodes s and t, thus $V = T \cup \{s, t\}$. $V^* = V \setminus \{s, t\}$. The set of the arcs E is defined as follows.

- If $i, j \in T$ such that $At_i + Sp_{(As_i, Ds_j)} \leq Dt_j$ then we add an arc (i, j) with cost c_{ij}, representing the required electric energy to move from arrival station As_i of trip i to depart station Ds_j of trip j in addition to the required electric energy to move from depart station Ds_j to the arrival station As_j of trip j.
- for each node i we add an arc (s, i) and the cost of this arc is c_{si}, representing the consumed electric energy to reach the arrival station As_i of trip i from the depot while passing through its departure station Ds_i .
- for each node i we add an arc (i, t) with cost c_{it} , representing the electric energy used to move from the arrival station As_i of trip i to the depot.

From this graph representation, we can see that our problem is similar to the asymmetric distance-constrained vehicle routing problem (ADCVRP). The distance-constrained vehicle routing problem is a variant of the vehicle routing problem (VRP) in which each route is assigned some maximum length or time constraint [16]. Here, this constraint is represented by the maximum distance that the battery capacity B allows each vehicle to run. The problem is asymmetric because the graph G is directed. In fact, the cost of arc (i, j) is generally different than that of arc (j, i). We can also note the low sparsity rate of the graph G, and this could be considered as the main difference between our PRT problem and the basic ADCVRP. In fact, for nodes $i, j \in V^*$, if the arc (i, j) exists, the opposite arc (j, i) does not exist. This problem is proven to be NP-hard [3]. As [17] state, the ADCVRP has not been studied as comprehensively as other versions of the VRP, such as the constrained VRP or the VRP with time windows. To the best of our knowledge, only two papers have studied to minimize the total distance traveled by vehicles for this problem [18],[17]. In this work, we present a novelty as we study to minimize the total number of used vehicles.

3   Road Based Formulation

In this section, we propose a road-based formulation to the PRT routing problem. The following indices variables and notations are introduced :

$$x_{ij} = \begin{cases} 1 \text{ if node } j \text{ is visited after node } i \\ 0 \text{ Otherwise} \end{cases}$$

- c_{ij} is the cost need to go from node i to node j.
- $\delta^+(i)$ is the set of edges that have i as a root.
- $\delta^-(i)$ is the set of edges that have i as a sink.
- $V^* = V \backslash \{s,t\}$.

For each $(l,k) \in E$ the following notations and definitions are given:

- $Road_{ab}$ represent a subsequence of connected edges in G starting from node a to reach node b. More specifically, $Road_{ab}$ is a sequence of selected edges from the graph G that connect the node a to node b.
- $InfR$ is the set of all infeasible Roads in G. $InfR$ represents all the roads in G where the total consumed energy exceed the battery capacity of PRT vehicles B.

The PRT model is written as follows:

$$\text{Minimize} \sum_{(s,i) \in E} x_{si} \tag{1}$$

$$\sum_{j \in \delta^+(i)} x_{ij} = 1 \qquad \forall i \in V^* \tag{2}$$

$$\sum_{j \in \delta^-(i)} x_{ji} = 1 \qquad \forall i \in V^* \tag{3}$$

$$\sum_{(i,j) \in Road_{ab}} x_{ij} \leq |Road_{ab}| - 1 \qquad \forall Road_{ab} \in InfR \tag{4}$$

$$x_{ij} \in \{0,1\} \qquad \forall (i,j) \in E \tag{5}$$

In this model, constraints (2),(3) are assignment constraints. They ensure that the degree of each node is equal to 1. Constraints (4) ensure that there exist no unfeasible roads in the final obtained solution. In fact, they eliminate any unfeasible roads by setting constraints on the cardinality of its related decisions variables. Unfortunately, there are an exponential number of constraints in (4) since the number of unfeasible roads is exponential. Therefore, we should employ reformulations and specific solution methods to be able to solve the problem in a reasonable time.

4 MTZ-Based Formulation

In this section a mixed integer programming formulation, which is based on the classical work of Miller, Tucker, and Zemlin (MTZ) (1960)[19] in the context of the *Asymmetric Traveling Salesman Problem* (ATSP), is presented. This is a valid mathematical formulation that was presented in [3],[14] for the case of energy minimization in the case of PRT. To that aim the following decision variables and notations are introduced.

- z_i is the consumed electric energy by the vehicle that reaches the depart station Ds_i of trip $i \in V^*$. This decision variable (z_i) is introduced to indicate the amount of the remaining electric energy for the vehicle arriving at Ds_i, in order to check the possibility of performing another trip before returning back to the depot.
- $a_i = c_{si}$ for $i \in V^*$.
- $b_i = B - c_{it}$ for $i \in V^*$.

Hence, the minimum electric energy assuring all the trips is the optimal value of the following programming model:

$$\text{Minimize} \sum_{(s,i) \in E} x_{si} \tag{6}$$

Equations 2,3.

$$z_i + c_{ij} \leq z_j + (b_i - a_j + c_{ij})(1 - x_{ij}) \quad \forall (i,j) \in E^* \tag{7}$$

$$a_i \leq z_i \leq b_i \quad \forall i \in V^* \tag{8}$$

$$x_{ij} \in \{0,1\} \forall \ (v_i, v_j) \in E^* \tag{9}$$

$$z_i \geq 0 \ \forall i \in V^* \tag{10}$$

The objective (6) is to minimize the number of used vehicles.

Constraints (7) are an MTZ constraints. They involve that the electric energy, for the vehicle visiting Ds_j immediately after As_i ($x_{ij} = 1$), satisfies $z_i + c_{ij} \leq z_j$ for $i, j \in T$. Clearly, for the other case $x_{ij} = 0$, the inequalities $z_i + c_{ij} \leq z_j + (b_i - a_j + c_{ij})$ holds since $z_i - b_i \leq 0 \leq z_j - a_j$ $(i, j \in T)$.

Constraints (8) present bounds on the electric energy needed to perform the trip i. They ensure that the electric energy consumed by the selected roads don't exceed the battery capacity. Finally, Constraints (9) indicates that x_{ij} are binaries variables and (10) z_i are real positive variables.

5   Flow-Based Formulation

In this section, we present a flow-based mathematical formulation (FB) for our problem. This formulation was presented in [7] for the Asymmetric Distance Constrained Vehicle Routing Problem (ADCVRP). We first introduce the following integer variable:

$z_{ij}=$ the electric energy used to travel from the depot to trip j as i is the predecessor of j.

$$\text{Minimize} \sum_{(s,i)\in E} x_{si} \tag{11}$$

Equations 2,3.

$$\sum_{(i,j)\in E'} z_{ij} - \sum_{(i,j)\in E'} z_{ji} - \sum_{j\in V^*} c_{ij}x_{ij} = 0 \quad \forall i \in T \tag{12}$$

$$z_{ij} \le (B - c_{jt})x_{ij} \quad \forall(i,j) \in E \tag{13}$$

$$z_{ij} \ge (c_{ij} + c_{si})x_{ij} \quad \forall i \ne \{s,t\}, \forall(i,j) \in E^* \tag{14}$$

$$z_{si} = c_{si}x_{si} \quad \forall i \in E^* \tag{15}$$

The objective (11) is to minimize the total number of used vehicles to cover all the trips.

Constraints (12) ensure that the energy consumed z_{ij} from any node i to any node j in a route is equal to the energy consumed between the depot to the node j in addition the electric energy consumed from node j to node i. Constraints (13) are battery constraints. In fact, they guarantee that the amount of electric energy a vehicle consumes to reach trip node j from the depot is less than its battery capacity minus the cost of returning to the depot.

In addition, according to constraints (14), the total electric energy consumed used to reach node j from the depot is greater than, or at least equal to, the direct link between the depot and node j. Finally, constraints (15) provide the initial values for z_{si}, which should be equal to the electric energy consumed while moving from the depot to trip node i.

6   Computational Results

We compared these two mathematical formulations in terms of GAP in %, CPU time and number of variables. For comparison, test problems' generator from the literature developed by Mrad and Hidri [3] and Mrad et al. [14] is used to generate 190 instances. The size of the problem instances varies from 10 to 100 in a multiple of 5. We generated randomly for each class'size 10 instances. The two models were coded in C++ and CPLEX 12.2. Test problems are run on PC with an Intel i3 CPU 2.53 GHz processor and 3 GB of RAM. **Cplex parameter were modified in such a way that the runs are terminated after 100 seconds.** This is made in order to test the efficiency of the two mathematical formulations.

We used two performance measures to assert the efficiency of our two tested mathematical formulations. These measures include:

Table 1. Results for the Flow-based formulation and the MTZ Formulation

Size	Number of variables	MTZ Formulation		Flow-based Formulation	
		GAP %	Time(sec)	GAP %	Time(sec)
10	41.80	0.00	0.32	0.00	0.24
15	80.40	10.85	0.39	10.85	0.23
20	131.20	11.59	2.33	11.59	0.84
25	197.80	11.21	30.45	11.21	1.36
30	271.00	14.85	82.99	8.32	24.04
35	356.50	19.46	103.76	14.21	44.88
40	455.80	19.41	109.47	11.69	49.06
45	556.20	22.14	105.94	12.44	84.35
50	684.00	23.98	104.31	12.51	86.55
55	812.70	25.76	105.25	13.56	90.29
60	976.80	28.50	105.48	12.38	93.87
65	1124.60	32.44	105.12	13.35	91.17
70	1290.70	35.92	103.13	11.43	92.88
75	1480.20	38.30	102.18	14.33	99.71
80	1656.30	38.25	101.33	11.03	86.04
85	1870.70	43.66	101.68	13.86	100.45
90	2116.40	43.45	101.45	12.98	93.12
95	2345.90	41.61	102.04	17.83	100.86
100	2546.80	41.75	101.50	18.26	100.64
Average	999.78	26.48	82.59	**12.20**	**65.29**

Table 2. Results of the comparison between the two formulations based on the Wilcoxon matched-pairs signed-rank statistical test

P value	< 0.0001
Significantly different? ($P < 0.05$)	Yes
One- or two-tailed P value?	Two-tailed
Sum of positive, negative ranks	0.0 , -8515
Sum of signed ranks (W)	-8515

– GAP $= (\frac{(SOL-LB)}{LB}) \times 100$, where LB is the maximum of the linear relaxation of the two mathematical formulations presented in this paper (MTZ and FB).
– CPU time is the time in seconds needed to find the obtained results.

Comparisons of these performance measurements are presented in Table 1.

In Table 1, for each instance size, the average value among the 10 instances is given in terms of gap and solution time. The last row of this table provides a global average assessment over all the instance sizes. Table 1 presents also information about the size of the generated graph expressed as the number of variables.

All the instances were not solved to optimality using the two mathematical formulations. **The MTZ formulation found the optimal solution 41 times**, and the **FB formulation found the optimal solution 80 times** out of 190 instances. We should note also that **mathematical formulations cannot obtain optimal solution as the size of the problem increase**. This latter proves that our problem is relatively hard to solve.

Statistical analysis using the Wilcoxon matched pairs signed rank test in term of solution quality is provided in Table 2. More details about this statistical test could be obtained from [20].

In terms of objective function, FB formulation is superior to the MTZ formulation. This was confirmed by statistical analysis provided in Table 2. Table 1 shows that for small size instances, the two formulations can find optimal solutions. Mathematical formulations cannot obtain optimum solution as the problems size increases in the limited time (100 seconds) due to the increasing number of variable. For the MTZ formulation, the use of decisions variables related to the nodes rather than the edges (as in the FB formulation) have contributed on the decrease number of constraints and the relatively bad quality solutions of this formulation in comparison to the FB. This is the reason of differences in the performance between the two formulations. We could note that the CPU time grows exponentially as the size of the problem increases. The second performance criterion is CPU times. As seen in the Table 1, Model FF is the best in terms of CPU time. In fact in term of CPU time, there occurs significant difference between the FB and the other MTZ models especially in medium-large sized problems due to the specific structure of the decisions variables related to the FB formulation. We should note that as we put a maximum limit of 100 seconds for both the mathematical formulations, the computing time seems rather constant between a problem size of 40 and 100. This is due to the fact that the mathematical formulation for instances great or equal to 40 trips don't find optimal solutions. In fact, the two mathematical formulations reach the maximum time limit of 100 seconds and exit with the best feasible solution. This confirms that our considered problem is hard to solve especially for medium and large size instance. Therefore, specific adapted heuristics could be developed to tackle large size instances of our problem.

A final conclusion obtained from our study and contrary to the case of minimization of total traveled distance for PRT [8], FB performs better than the MTZ formulation for the case of the minimization of the fleet size.

7   Conclusion

This paper proposes to study a related routing problem to optimize the fleet size for a PRT system. The proposed problem considers the battery constraints related to PRT which is a major operational issue for such a system. Two mathematical formulations are proposed to tackle this problem in order to provided valid fleet sizing for PRT system. Our formulations are applied on different sized test problems. For the proposed routing problem, good quality solutions are obtained. We remarked also that as the size of the problem increase the computation time increases exponentially. This work provides a good reference in order to analyze the cost-effectiveness of the PRT system. Our formulations also help us to determine an approximate fleet size of PRT system.

References

1. Carnegie, J.A., Hoffman, P.S.: Viability of personal rapid transit in New Jersey. Technical report (2007)

2. Lees-Miller, J.D.: Minimising average passenger waiting time in personal rapid transit systems. Annals of Operations Research 1–20 (2013)
3. Mrad, M., Hidri, L.: Optimal consumed electric energy while sequencing vehicle trips in a personal rapid transit transportation system. Computers & Industrial Engineering **79**, 1–9 (2015)
4. Rahimi-Vahed, A., Crainic, T.G., Gendreau, M., Rei, W.: Fleet-sizing for multi-depot and periodic vehicle routing problems using a modular heuristic algorithm. Computers & Operations Research **53**, 9–23 (2015)
5. Li, J., Chen, Y.S., Li, H., Andreasson, I., van Zuylen, H.: Optimizing the fleet size of a personal rapid transit system: a case study in port of rotterdam. In: 2010 13th International IEEE Conference on Intelligent Transportation Systems (ITSC), pp. 301–305. IEEE (2010)
6. Demir, Y., Kürşat İşleyen, S.: Evaluation of mathematical models for flexible job-shop scheduling problems. Applied Mathematical Modelling **37**(3), 977–988 (2013)
7. Kara, I.: Two indexed polonomyal size formulationsfor vehicle routing problems. Technical Report. BaskentUniversity, Ankara/Turkey (2008)
8. Fatnassi, E., Chebbi, O., Siala, J.C.: Comparison of two mathematical formulations for the offline routing of personal rapid transit system vehicles. In: The International Conference on Methods and Models in Automation and Robotics (2014)
9. Blazewicz, J., Dror, M., Weglarz, J.: Mathematical programming formulations for machine scheduling: a survey. European Journal of Operational Research **51**(3), 283–300 (1991)
10. Pan, C.H.: A study of integer programming formulations for scheduling problems. International Journal of Systems Science **28**(1), 33–41 (1997)
11. Keha, A.B., Khowala, K., Fowler, J.W.: Mixed integer programming formulations for single machine scheduling problems. Computers & Industrial Engineering **56**(1), 357–367 (2009)
12. Pan, J.C.H., Chen, J.S.: Mixed binary integer programming formulations for the reentrant job shop scheduling problem. Computers & Operations Research **32**(5), 1197–1212 (2005)
13. Unlu, Y., Mason, S.J.: Evaluation of mixed integer programming formulations for non-preemptive parallel machine scheduling problems. Computers & Industrial Engineering **58**(4), 785–800 (2010)
14. Mrad, M., Chebbi, O., Labidi, M., Louly, M.: Synchronous routing for personal rapid transit pods. J. Applied Mathematics **2014** (2014)
15. Floyd, R.W.: Algorithm 97: shortest path. Communications of the ACM **5**(6), 345 (1962)
16. Toth, P., Vigo, D.: The Vehicle Routing Problem. Monographs on Discrete Mathematics and Applications. Society for Industrial and Applied Mathematics (2002)
17. Almoustafa, S., Hanafi, S., Mladenovi, N.: New exact method for large asymmetric distance-constrained vehicle routing problem. European Journal of Operational Research (2012)
18. Laporte, G., Nobert, Y., Taillefer, S.: A branch-and-bound algorithm for the asymmetrical distance-constrained vehicle routing problem. Mathematical Modelling **9**(12), 857–868 (1987)
19. Miller, C.E., Tucker, A.W., Zemlin, R.A.: Integer programming formulation of traveling salesman problems. J. ACM **7**(4), 326–329 (1960)
20. Wilcoxon, F., Wilcox, R.A.: Some rapid approximate statistical procedures. Lederle Laboratories (1964)

Viability of Implementing Smart Mobility Tool in the Case of Tunis City

Ezzeddine Fatnassi[1], Olfa Chebbi[1(✉)], and Jouhaina Chaouachi[2]

[1] Institut Supérieur de Gestion de Tunis, Université de Tunis, 41, Rue de la Liberté, Bouchoucha, 2000 Bardo, Tunisia
olfaa.chebbi@gmail.com
[2] Institut des Hautes Etudes Commerciales de Carthage, Université de Carthage, IHEC Carthage Présidence, 2016 Tunis, Tunisia

Abstract. Nowadays, different changes from the economical, societal and environmental contexts are happen in cities. In fact, cities are generally the best place to endorse and enhance various experience in order to improve the quality of life of its citizens. In this context, the new vision of Smart Mobility fill into this context. The concept of Smart Mobility as a means to enhance the mobility experience of citizen has been gaining increasing importance in the agendas of cities stakeholder. It represents the best balance the economic, environmental and societal aspect of current transportation tools. The implementation of the smart mobility concept in the case of Tunis city is the subject matter of the paper. In fact, we focus on considering the Personal Rapid Transit system as an effective and efficient tool to bring smart mobility experience to Tunis city. This paper also presents and study the viability of implementing PRT in our specific context. An extensive simulation and economic feasibility study is conducted to validate our proposal. Computational results prove the different advantages of our proposal in the studied context.

Keywords: Smart city · Smart mobility · Personal rapid transit · Simulation

1 Introduction

It have been observed recently a tremendous increase of urbanization rate. In fact, more and more people tend to move to cities seeking for a better quality of life. The urban population is estimated to represent 53% of the whole world population. It is expected that 4.5 billion of peoples will be living in cities in 2025[1].

Many cities essentially in Asia and Latin America are expected to have more than 10 million inhabitants and 70% of the world population are expected to

---

[1] Source: UN World Urbanization Prospects, World Business Council for Sustainable Development.

© IFIP International Federation for Information Processing 2015
K. Saeed and W. Homenda (Eds.): CISIM 2015, LNCS 9339, pp. 339–350, 2015.
DOI: 10.1007/978-3-319-24369-6_28

be living in urban areas by 2050.Pressure generated by this high urbanization rate has a main impact on the mobility of peoples and goods in cities. As an example we could note that commuting delay is expected to double to over 100 hours per year per person in 2050. Consequently, it becomes necessary for cities stakeholders to organize and manage urban space and mobility tools to prevent all the negative impact of urbanization on cities.

Cities are generally considered as the right place to develop new initiatives and ideas. In fact, they can contribute to develop and build new innovative ecosystem which could develop new perspectives and opportunities. In this respect, the concept of smart city appears very promising. Smart city concept englobe mainly six different elements (see Figure 1). Among, these elements one could focus on smart mobility and smart environment concepts. These two essential elements of smart cities are closely related to urban mobility. They tends to promote the use of smart public transportation tools that have the least impact on environment.

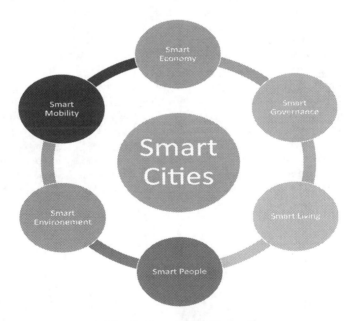

Fig. 1. Smart City Concepts

The recent experience related to smart mobility and smart environment concepts seem to shows that single and individual initiative of a single operating transportation mode to reduce energy consumption and CO2 emissions are note very effective approach is rather necessary to implement the concepts of smart mobility and smart environment. Generally, there is two ways to deal with urban sustainability issue: i) enhance the performance and quality of the already existent transportation tools. ii) Invest and build a completely new sophisticated smart transportation tool.

In our work, we focused on the second alternative. In fact, the paper is concerned by implementing the concept of smart mobility and smart environment in the case of Tunis city. We aim in our project to introduce a new intelligent transportation tool called Personal Rapid Transit (PRT) and Freight Rapid Transit in Tunis city. The different theoretical aspects related to PRT and FRT are subjects to a close identification in this paper.

The subject of this work is the feasibility of implementing PRT system in the specific context of Tunis city. For that purpose, we develop a new proposal for implementing PRT as an integrated part of a city. We also validate our proposal through simulation and economic feasibility.

In this work and based on the ideas of Smart city and mobility concepts, we propose a combined and integrated PRT/FRT system to be implemented and developed in the case of Tunis city. Next, a formalization of the treated problem is proposed. Then, we 'll focus on an strategic context of the PRT/FRT system to study the economic feasibility of our proposal through the tools of optimization and simulation. Finally, we conclude our paper with general conclusions and insights about our work and present our future research directions.

2 Smart City and Mobility Concepts

Smart city is concerned as a relatively new concepts. Smart city is also a highly context dependent. In the literature, there is no clear definition of what smart city is. In fact, in the literature the frontier between smart city concepts and other similar concepts such as intelligent city or creative city is not well defined. That is why many individuals claim that specific city is being smart without following specific directive and standards. However, one could consider that the smart city concept is the natural evolution of cities from a cities as a simple scientific center to a compact enhanced form in which cities use information and communication technologies to increase the efficiency of its different components such as infrastructure, mobility tools, etc [1].

Therefore, one could consider smart city as a conceptual urban development model which is mainly based on the human collective knowledge and technological advance in order to enhance the prosperity and the development of urban centers. That is why the concept of smart city should combine different elements such as the concept of knowledge based cities [2]. Literature about smart cities provides the six most common indicators of smart cities [3]:

- Smart economy: cities should offer a highly attractive economic environment. This should include highly innovative and productive climate as well as a flexible labor market.
- Smart people: Smart people are considered as the results of social and ethnic diversity, creativity, tolerance and so on [2]. To raise the global qualifications as well as a social capital cities could offers online courses or workshop [4].
- Smart governance: Specific city system management are required to reach development in this areas. Services such as e-government and social media

combined with a transparent decisions making process could lead to smart governance city.

- Smart living: This notion involves the improvement of the quality of live in term of service, environment and social infrastructure. Smart living includes also e-health, social services and specific developed public safety tools. This latter include specific emergency service and surveillance system network [5].
- Smart environment: an efficient smart city should optimize energy consumption as well as reduce the carbon emissions. This could be done through the use of renewable energy sources as well as the implementation of a specific resources management strategies based on sustainability principles.
- Smart mobility: Through specific planning practices, cities could effectively reach the objective of smart mobility. Urban planning strategies would necessarily imply to turn the focus from individuals to collective smart tool of transportation via the use of enhanced information shared and communication technologies.

Focusing on the latter principle, one could note that the idea of smart mobility is crucial for the development of smart cities. Development of smart mobility system means that a city is accessible for its different inhabitant through a safe, robust, eco-friendly and smart transportation tools. The emergence of smart mobility tool would necessarily imply to reach sustainable mobility.

Therefore, developing smart mobility concepts is necessary for any smart city. In the rest of this paper, we present the PRT as an enhanced sophisticated tool to reach the objective of smart mobility.

3   Personal and Freight Rapid Transit

The Personal Rapid Transit (PRT) provides a new and innovative system of transportation. PRT offers an ondemand direct transit from origin to destination stations. PRT is oriented to serve passengers in urban areas and is designed to work and act as any traditional taxi system. Therefore, the PRT is highly attractive for its users in comparison with traditional mass transit like bus or subway systems. The Personal Rapid Transit use small electric driverless vehicles (also called pod cars). PRT vehicles run on dedicated guide way in order to provide direct nonstop trips between origin and destination stations. This is made possible by the use of the offline station that is placed off the main line. This specific feature of PRT avoid for pod cars to stop at unnecessary stations. Guideways on such a system can be at grade, on tunnel or elevated and are segregated from other urban traffic and pedestrian. PRT systems contrary to other traditional tools run on a network of guideway rather than a group of simple lines. The network of guideway and the offline stations have the main advantage of being able to be integrated with existent building which reduce the visual intrusion and the time needed to get access to such a system. This is resulted from the small size of the infrastructure as the PRT system use small vehicles. Vehicles in PRT are made to take from 1 to 6 passengers. Therefore, the service quality of PRT is more similar to taxi rather than a bus.

Fig. 2. Example Of PRT[2]and FRT Vehicle[3]

On the other hand, Freight Rapid Transit is automated people movers that share the same infrastructure and characteristics of a PRT system. However, it is made and designed to transport goods and waste. FRT vehicles could handle up to 1500 Kg and could be adapted to handle different waste freight.

The combination of both PRT and FRT on the same network of guideways presents an interesting alternative for urban zone to mix the flow of passengers and goods on the same shared system. These two intelligent systems combined with all the new technologies that exist nowadays could represent a valid replacement for private vehicles and trucks. This is achieved mainly through different feature and specific characteristics of PRT and FRT:

- They both use electric energy which make them environmentally friendly and energy efficient.
- As the vehicles are driverless, it requires far less human power than other traditional mass transit system.
- As the transit operations are generally made on demand, PRT/FRT offer a better service quality than other transportation systems.
- PRT/FRT are faster than any other transit tools.

4   Formalization of the Treated Problem

Implementing PRT system in an urban context require to solve various problems and issue related to that specific urban context. However, these issues could be formalized into a PRT' guideway network design problem. Next, we present the formal problem definition of PRT' guideway network design problem[6].

Generally, a PRT/FRT system contains a guideways network (GN) and a set of PRT and FRT vehicles moving on the network. The GN could be modeled as a partition of a complete directed graph $G = S, \gamma$ where $S = 1, 2, ..., n$ represents the set of n stations and $\gamma = (i, j)|i, j \in S, i \neq j$ represents the set of $n(n-1)$ of possible directed links between each couple of stations in γ. The length of each possible link (i, j) is denoted by d_{ij}. The number of vehicles needed to travel from a location i to a location j is denoted by t_{ij}.

The input of the GN are the station locations, the set of d_{ij} and t_{ij} where i and $j \in S$ and $i \neq j$. For a GN, two main problems exists: the GN design and the

---

[3] source: http://www.ultraprt.net/multiVehicle.htm
[3] source: http://www.2getthere.eu/?pageid=912/

station design problems. The objective of the GN design is to find the least cost possible for building a PRT network while respecting connectivity constraints related to PRT. Connectivity constraints include the possibility for each vehicle to move from any station to any other station. On the other hand, the station design problem is to find the least cost option possible to design a PRT station subject to traffic constraint.

The formal GN design problem definition could be defined as follow:

- Given : G, S, γ, d_{ij} and t_{ij}.
- Minimize : $f_c(x)$, $f_t(x)$.
- Subject to connectivity constraints.

Where $f_c(x)$ represents the construction costs and $f_t(x)$ represents the traffic congestion over the PRT network.

We should note that $f_c(x)$ could be defined as follow :

$f_c(x) = \Sigma d_{ij} x_{ij}$, where x_{ij} is a binary variable equals to 1 if the link between i and j is selected in the final solution.

On the other hand, $f_t(x)$ is a function that aims to minimize the number of vehicles passing a point in the GN in a unit of time. This objective aims to ensure a fluid traffic in the GN.

To evaluate a designed GN, an empty vehicle problem (EVP) could be used. The EVP could be formulated as follow[7].

Given a PRT Network with (S) stations, one depot D and enough links to make possible the move between each couple of stations. This problem deals with empty vehicles movement over a designed GN in a static deterministic context. Therefore, we suppose to have a predefined list of trips (Θ) of size ν. Each trip i is defined by the following: i)Depart time Dt_i, ii) Depart station Ds_i, iii) Arrival time At_i, iv) Arrival Station As_i.

We suppose to have an unlimited number of vehicles initially located at the depot. Each vehicle have a Battery capacity B. The problem is defined on a Graph $\chi = V, E$ where V is the set of nodes and E the set of arcs.

The set V contains ν nodes that represent the ν trips plus two dummy nodes ς and τ that represent the depot. We define also $V^* = V/\{\varsigma, \tau\}$. The set of edges E defined on the following rules:

- for each node i, $j \in V^*$ with $j > i$ and , the arc (i, j) exists if $At_i + cost(As_i, Ds_j) <= Dt_j$ the cost of this arc will be the cost of moving from the arrival station of trip i to the arrival station of station j.
- for each node $i \in V^*$ the arc (ς, i) exists and have as a cost the energy used to go from the depot to the arrival of station of trip i.
- for each node $i \in V^*$ the arc (i, τ) exists and have as a cost the energy of moving from the arrival station of station i to the depot.

The objective of solving our problem is to evaluate a designed GN while treated a specific scenario determined by the list of trips Θ. Therefore, finding a set of least cost vehicles roads that satisfy the different trips in Θ could be used as a valid benchmark to evaluate a designed GN. Such a scenario could be obtained using historical data of traveling passengers in a predefined urban areas.

5 Proposal of Implementing PRT

This work aims to evaluate the feasibility of implementing PRT as a smart mobility tool in Tunis city. Tunis city is suffering like many a high urbanization rate phenomena with all its negative impact on people mobility. It is a strong intention from the city authorities to launch different measures that could relieve the already existent transportation tools. Thus making the urban center more attractive to visitors, tourists and residents.

5.1 Local Characterization

Tunis city is the capital of Tunisia located at the north east of the country. It presents a total area of 212,63 and it has a total population of 728, 453 which corresponds to a density of 3 426 $inhabitant/km^2$. The total Tunis metropolis area have a total number of 2 721 227 habitant. Considering only the areas regarded as the Tunis urban center (see Figure 3), it has been reported in [8] that it has a total of 10% of the whole population of the metropolitan area of Tunis with 30% of the total jobs [8]. It will remain for topographical reasons a center place of crossing for the main urban and goods flows within the metropolitan area. The main and only available public transportation tool to move in Tunis urban center is the light rail transit (LRT).

LRT (also called Metro Leger in French but it is more like a tramway than a metro) was first implemented in 1985 by operating the south line after it was decided in 1980. The implementation of the LRT network has suffered many uncertainties due to the various policies makers that disagreed its implementation. But finally, the whole project was implemented while constructing 6 different lines during the period 1988-2008. The LRT current network have a total length of 45 Km of double track, 6 lines, two main transfer stations (Barcelone and La République which are located at the urban center of Tunis). The total LRT ridership was around 35000 daily passengers[9]. The LRT in Tunis city suffers from many limits. Among them one could consider its limited capacity. The loading rate of the LRT cars is about 100% and for various lines, it excess 100% especially in the morning peak.

An estimation of the real modal share give the majority of the urban trips to private cars with 60%. This fact is suggested by the high ridership rate of 100% of the LRT line. This results of the difficulty for the private cars drivers to leave their cars for a public transportation tool.

Therefore, we could state that the context of Tunis urban center is characterized by a high use of private cars, a high rate of congestion with a limited option for implementing new mass transit solutions.

Following all these conditions, it becomes of a high interest to impose the quality and the capacity of public transportation tools in Tunis urban center. In the next, we propose an illustrative example and study into the urban center of Tunis with LRT to improve the quality of public transportation tools.

5.2   Integrated PRT Solution for the Urban Center of Tunis

After the different conclusion exposed in the last section, it appears necessarily to launch a new public transportation plan to overcome different issues. As underlined above, the systematic view of PRT is crucial for its integration in the current transportation practices. To append this systematic view on PRT, a mutualisation of the available resources (the LRT stations, available urban areas in the urban center, etc.) for a specific joint usage. It is also of a high interest to plan for a shared usage between PRT and LRT as it offers various options for city planner and managers. In fact, the opportunity to plan for a shared travels is among the recent trends in managing transportation systems.

We also foreseen a specific interest to design beforehand an integrated PRT network in order to allow persons to benefit from a highly sophisticated intelligent transportation tool fully connected to the LRT network. We should note also that the LRT network in the Tunis urban center is not dense and do not covers many essential commercial areas in the urban center and the last mile delivery has to be developed and implemented.

Therefore and to better explain our PRT implementation proposal, an example is depicted in Figure 3. In this illustration, we propose to implement a PRT network that follow the line of the LRT network. Our proposition aims to use elevated guideways in a specific way as shown in Figure 3. We also aim to use the already existent main station as intermodal facilities in order to allow users easily for LRT to PRT. Our option don't interfere with other urban projects as the areas that will be used for PRT is already in use by the LRT. Also, the small size of PRT guideways and station allows easy integration with its urban context. Our proposal encompass 8 stations and 4.5 km of one way guideways.

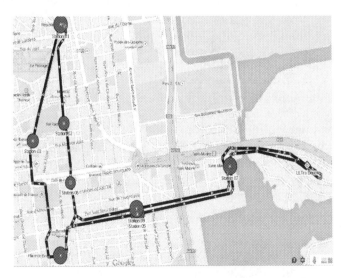

Fig. 3. Proposal Of Implementing PRT in Tunis City

This connected option between LRT and PRT in a high dense urban area is very beneficial for the users of LRT as they could easily be transferred from LRT vehicles to PRT vehicles in order to reach easily their destination.

This scheme is designed to solve the recurrent problem of congestion and capacity for LRT in urban center of Tunis. This option aims also to offer a smart mobility tool for the resident of Tunis and a new image for the city center which will be very beneficial as tourists could be attracted to the city center. It is clear from this proposal of an integrated LRT/PRT in the center of Tunis must go through three levels of decisions: It is clear that the implementation of an integrated PRT/FRT network, must go through a three levels decision-making process in order to determine:

- How to design the network and its transit capabilities (deployment, vehicles, stations).
- How to plan and schedule for the number of PRT/FRT and their capacities.
- How to optimize the travels in terms of energy use and transit time.

The rest of this paper will focus on the feasibility of such a proposal and its related economic benefits.

6   Simulation and Economic Feasibility

In order to test the feasibility of our proposal it was necessary to perform simulation study. In the literature, there are several simulation software for PRT. We used in this work, the ATS/mobile simulation software. In fact, this software enable its users to import specific maps and draw and test PRT feasibility. Demand scenarios was calibrated according to real condition on the LRT network. We run our simulation for 2 hours. We performed 10 different tests in order to eliminate any variability issues [4].

The simulation output shows that the PRT would offer an average waiting time of 19.354 seconds for its users(see Figure 4). The PRT in just 2 hours was able to perform and satisfy on average 1986.9 trips. This with a projection on a typical whole working day (7AM to 19 AM) makes the PRT able to satisfy up to 20,000 trips per day. This feature allows it to attract many users as it offers a really low waiting time.

6.1   Economic Feasibility

In this section, we present a preliminaries economic feasibility of implementing PRT in the PRT urban center. The overall proposed system costs are the sum of the annual capital costs, maintenance costs and day to day operations costs. In order to estimate the PRT fare which exceeds the total system costs, we performed a calculation based on the general costs and on the simulation results to estimate the operational costs.

---

[4] The experiments were performed on a computer with a 3.2 GHZ CPU and 8 GB of RAM.

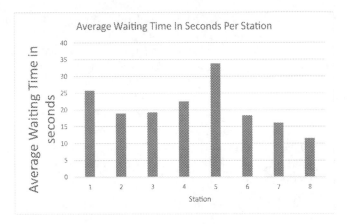

Fig. 4. Results of The Simulation

Computing system costs The system costs involves mainly all the different investments that need to be made in order to implement the proposed PRT system. The capital costs englobe the infrastructure costs (station, tracks, etc.), the cost for the different communication systems as well as the cost for the purchasing the PRT vehicles. The costs are then distributed over the period of time until that all the assets need replacement. Following this methodology allow us to obtain specific annual capital costs. We also supposed to use debt as a financing resources for the initial investment. Following these assumptions, interest rate should be considered.

Operating costs on the other hand are represented by the energy costs to run the PRT vehicles and the salaries for the workers on the PRT system. Finally, maintenance costs occurs for repairing, cleaning the vehicles and the different infrastructure. After obtaining all these values, the annual systems costs is computed as shown in table 1.

Computing the PRT fare After obtaining the costs for a PRT system, we need to estimate the PRT fare per Km which could cover the total system costs. For that purpose, we used the different simulation output in order to estimate the PRT fare which corresponds to the simulated PRT trips 'demand per day as well as the average trips length in Km.

From the obtained results, we should note that a minimum of 0.19$ per km is required to cover the total system costs. We should note that the system covers zones that are not mainly covered by other transportation tools except for LRT. We should note that buses and LRT in Tunis costs , LRT costs 0.16$ and taxi costs 0.59$ per km. Those transportation tools are less convenient than PRT. Hence, a fare between 0.2$ and 0.3$ per Km could be well acceptable by the population.

Table 1. PRT Cost

Interest rate	0.05					
Cost of	Number of items	Cost per Piece	Total Investment	Life expectancy	Annual Capital cost	Daily
Infrastructure		USD				
PRT Station	8	180000	1440000	20	75600	207.1232877
Hub Depot	1	250000	250000	20	13125	35.95890411
Track km	4.5	8000000	36000000	20	1890000	5178.082192
IT Systems						
Communications	1	500000	500000	7	26250	71.91780822
Navigation	1	300000	300000	7	15750	43.15068493
Control System	1	1200000	1200000	7	63000	172.6027397
Vehicles						
PRT vehicles	130	150000	19500000	7	1023750	2804.794521
Capital Costs			59190000			
Operation Costs						
Cost for	kwh/day	Cost USD/KWH	Operation Costs	Life expectancy	Annual Capital cost	Daily
Installing Solar Panel Energy Charging/Day Maintenance Costs		1577490.775		20	82818.26568	226.899358
Cost For	Number of items	Costs USD/item	Maintenance Costs			
Maintenance						
Vehicle Cleaning /days	130	2				260
Vehicles Repairs/Year	130	800	104000			284.9315068
Infrastructure/Year	10	5000	50000			136.9863014
System Costs					Cost in USD/day	9422.447303

7   Conclusions

During this study, it was possible to realize the importance of implementing smart mobility tool in dense urban area in a developing country. We presented PRT as a promising transportation tool to enhance the efficiency of the already existent transportation options. In that way, we proposed a specific PRT proposal which would integrate PRT to the urban context in Tunis city. We then performed a simulation and feasibility study in order to test the feasibility of our proposal. Our preliminaries results are very insightful on how our propositions could be improved. In our future work, the development of an enhanced simulation study could be done. Also, we would like to extend on managerial insight on how PRT could be successfully implemented and integrated with other transportation tools.

References

1. Dewalska–Opitek, A.: Smart city concept – the citizens' perspective. In: Mikulski, J. (ed.) TST 2014. CCIS, vol. 471, pp. 331–340. Springer, Heidelberg (2014)
2. Letaifa, S.B.: How to strategize smart cities: Revealing the smart model. Journal of Business Research (2015)
3. Allwinkle, S., Cruickshank, P.: Creating smart-er cities: An overview. Journal of Urban Technology **18**(2), 1–16 (2011)
4. Steinert, K., Marom, R., Richard, P., Veiga, G., Witters, L.: Making cities smart and sustainable. The Global Innovation Index 2011, p. 87 (2011)
5. Hielkema, H., Hongisto, P.: Developing the helsinki smart city: the role of competitions for open data applications. Journal of the Knowledge Economy **4**(2), 190–204 (2013)
6. Won, J.M., Lee, K.M., Lee, J.S., Karray, F.: Guideway network design of personal rapid transit system: a multiobjective genetic algorithm approach. In: 2006 IEEE Congress on Evolutionary Computation, vols. 1–6 (2006)
7. Mrad, M., Hidri, L.: Optimal consumed electric energy while sequencing vehicle trips in a personal rapid transit transportation system. Computers & Industrial Engineering **79**, 1–9 (2015)
8. Baltagi, A.: Projet d un reseau integre de transports collectifs dans la ville de tunis. In: CODATU XI: World Congress: Towards More Attractive Urban Transportation (2004)
9. Godard, X.: Some lessons from the lrt in tunis and the transferability of experience. Transportation Research Part A: Policy and Practice **41**(10), 891–898 (2007)

Optimal Input Signal Design
for a Second Order Dynamic System
Identification Subject to D-Efficiency Constraints

Wiktor Jakowluk[✉]

Faculty of Computer Science, Bialystok University of Technology,
Wiejska 45a, 15-351 Bialystok, Poland
w.jakowluk@pb.edu.pl
http://wi.pb.edu.pl/pracownicy/

Abstract. System identification, in practice, is carried out by perturbing processes or plants under operation. That is why in many industrial applications an
optimal input signal would be preferred for system identification. In this case,
the objective function was formulated through maximisation of the Fisher information matrix determinant (D-optimality) expressed in conventional Bolza
form. As setting such conditions of the identification experiment we can only
say about the D-suboptimality, we quantify the plant trajectories using the D-
efficiency measure. An additional constraint, imposed on D-efficiency of the
solution, should allow to attain the most adequate contents of information from
the plant which operating point is perturbed in the least invasive way. A simple
numerical example, which clearly demonstrates the idea presented in the paper,
is included and discussed.

Keywords: System identification · Optimal input signal · D-optimality ·
D-efficiency

1   Introduction

The choice of an input signal used for actuation of the system is critical in the task of
model building and parameter identification. System identification is the process of
constructing an accurate and reliable dynamic mathematical model of the system from
observed data and available knowledge. It is a common practice to perturb the system
of interest and use the resulting data to build the model [1, 2]. The accuracy of parameter estimates is increased by the use of optimal excitation signals [3].

The pertinence of a model is the critical factor for proper tuning of a controller,
usually performed as a model-based optimisation task. Inaccurate model can significantly influence the performance of the control loop, and finally deteriorate the quality of the plant product. The control performance assessment has a large impact on the
economic aspect of the production process. It was found that about 66% - 80% of the
advanced control systems are not able to achieve the desired performance [4].

The input design problem with respect to the intended model application, which is
often a control task, has received considerable attention in the last two decades [5, 6].

© IFIP International Federation for Information Processing 2015
K. Saeed and W. Homenda (Eds.): CISIM 2015, LNCS 9339, pp. 351–362, 2015.
DOI: 10.1007/978-3-319-24369-6_29

It was reported that model development absorbs about 75% of the costs associated with advanced control projects [7]. System identification, in practice, is carried out by perturbing processes or plants under operation. In many industrial applications a plant friendly input signal would be preferred for system identification. Plant friendly identification experiments are those that satisfy plant or operator constraints on experiment duration, input and output amplitudes or input rate [8, 9]. Techniques for synthesising multi-harmonic signals with low crest factors, which are attractive from a plant friendly perspective, have been reported in [2]. It was demonstrated that plant friendliness demands are often in conflict with requirements for accurate and reliable identification [10]. Hence, plant friendly input design is inherently multi-objective in nature. There have been some reports on multi-objective optimisation based methods, applied to identification and control [11, 12].

However, the papers mentioned above present the optimisation methods of designing the parametric signals which meet the assumed friendliness criteria. In the experiments described in this paper we present different approach – a design of an optimal input signal via the optimisation procedure with respect to the cost function D-efficiency constraint has been attempted. In some our previous works, in the design of optimal and plant friendly inputs for system identification the sensitivity of the state variable to the unknown parameter has been maximised. The results of optimal and plant friendly input signal design utilising Mayer's canonical formulation of the performance index for the simple first-order inertial system case study were presented in [13, 14]. In this study we present the formulation of the performance index for optimal dynamic system identification and assess the qualitative measure of accuracy of parameter estimation in the second-order torsional spring system case study. In order to design an optimal actuation signal for the one degree of freedom torsional spring system parameter estimation, it was necessary to scale the model of the system. One of the problems to be solved was to find the value of the scaling factor between the angular position and the angular velocity of the real plant.

2   The D-Efficiency Constraint Formulation

In the paper the design of optimal inputs for system identification with multiple unknown parameters is considered. In the design of optimal excitation signals for estimating more than one parameter, a suitable scalar function of the Fisher information matrix $\mathbf{M}$ must be selected as the performance criterion. The criterion, which is often used, is the trace of the matrix $\mathbf{M}$, wherein the sum of diagonal elements of the Fisher information matrix is maximised. Other measures of identification performance are as follows [15]:

- A-optimality: $tr(\mathbf{M}^{-1})$, minimises the average variance of the parameters,
- E-optimality: $\lambda_{max}(\mathbf{M}^{-1})$, minimises the maximum eigenvalue of $\mathbf{M}^{-1}$,
- D-optimality: minimises the volume of the ellipsoidal confidence region of parameter estimates.

However, the choice of the experiment criterion is important, as it is possible that inputs obtained based on some criteria may not be persistently perturbing [1].

The input signal employed in the identification experiment should simultaneously yield two results: the acceptable accuracy of the system parameter estimates and the system should be perturbed in the least invasive (the most friendly) way. Such a compromise can be reached applying an approach, which relies on the notion of the D-efficiency [15]. Any optimality criterion can be associated with the efficiency function, defined as a measure of the relative performance of any given experiment $\mathbf{e}$ compared to that of the optimal experiment $\mathbf{e}^*$. The D-efficiency, which may be considered as a measure of the D-suboptimality of given input trajectories, is specified by

$$E_D(\mathbf{e}) = \left\{ \frac{\det(\mathbf{M}(\mathbf{e}))}{\det(\mathbf{M}(\mathbf{e}^*))} \right\}^{1/k}, \qquad (1)$$

where k is the number of parameters to be identified, and $\mathbf{e}^*$ stands for the D-optimal trajectories which can be determined earlier. Following the reasoning and derivations presented in [16], we set a reasonable positive threshold $\eta < 1$ and impose the constraint on the D-efficiency value:

$$E_D(\mathbf{e}) \geq \eta. \qquad (2)$$

Such an approach will yield a D-suboptimal, yet reasonable solution. The inequality (2) is equivalent to the constraint:

$$\Psi[\mathbf{M}(\mathbf{e})] \leq D, \qquad (3)$$

where $\Psi[\mathbf{M}(\mathbf{e})] = \log(\det \mathbf{M}(\mathbf{e}))$ and $D = \Psi[\mathbf{M}(\mathbf{e}^*)] - k \log(\eta)$.

The objective of such an experiment is formulated through maximisation of the FIM determinant (D-optimality) with respect to D-efficiency inequality constraint (3).

The purpose of the current work is to formulate the optimisation problem for optimal input design with respect to the D-efficiency constraint. In that way (i.e. by setting such a constraint to control the level of the D-optimality loss) we can obtain the friendliest input signal, reducing the rapid changes of the mass or energy inflow to the system.

3   Optimal Input Design with Respect to the Cost Function D-Efficiency Constraints

To illustrate the properties of the above approach to parameter identification, using the optimal input signal and with respect to the assumed level of D-optimality, we have selected the second-order linear dynamic system. The mass-spring damper system represents many similar physical plants. Thus the plant model order may be as high as six with either four, two, or no zeros.

The dynamic model for the one degree of freedom (1 DOF) plant is shown in below figure.

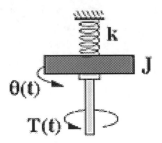

Fig. 1. The dynamic model for the one degree of freedom plant (free-clamped).

The equation of motion is as follows:

$$J_1\ddot{\theta} + c_1\dot{\theta}_1 + k_1\theta_1 = T(t), \tag{4}$$

where J_1, k_1, c_1, $T(t)$, θ_1 are, respectively: disk inertia, spring coefficient, damping ratio, force signal, position of the first disk of the plant. For notational convenience, let us introduce $x_1 = \theta_1$ and $x_2 = \dot{\theta}_1 = \dot{x}_1$. Then, the problem of synthesising an optimal input in the time domain for a torsional spring plant (1 DOF) can be described by the following single input, single output state space model:

$$\begin{aligned} \dot{x}_1 &= x_2; & x_1(0) &= x_{10}; \\ \dot{x}_2 &= ax_1 + bx_2 + cu; & x_2(0) &= 0; \\ y(t) &= x_1(t), & \end{aligned} \tag{5}$$

where $a = -k_1/J_1$, $b = -c_1/J_1$, $c = 1/J_1$. In order to design an optimal input signal, it was necessary to scale the model of the system as follows:

$$\begin{aligned} \xi_1 &= px_1 \rightarrow \dot{x}_1 = \frac{1}{p}\dot{\xi}_1; \\ \xi_2 &= gx_2 \rightarrow \dot{x}_2 = \frac{1}{g}\dot{\xi}_2. \end{aligned} \tag{6}$$

Utilising equation (6), the state space model (5) can be expressed as:

$$\begin{aligned} \dot{\xi}_1 &= \frac{p}{g}\xi_2; \\ \dot{\xi}_2 &= a\frac{g}{p}\xi_1 + b\xi_2 + cgu. \end{aligned} \tag{7}$$

Assuming that the parameter $p = 1$, from equation (6) we obtain $\xi_1 = x_1$. Then the above problem can be suitably modified by defining the state space model as:

$$\dot{x}_1 = \frac{1}{g}x_2;$$

$$\dot{x}_2 = agx_1 + bx_2 + cgu;$$ (8)

$$y(t) = x_1(t),$$

where $x_1 = x_1(t; a, b, c)$, $x_2 = x_2(t; a, b, c)$ and model parameters a, b, c are constant. The principle of the design of optimal input signals for system identification is to maximise the sensitivity of the state variable or the observation to the unknown parameter [3]. The justification for this approach is the Cramer-Rao lower bound, which provides a lower bound for the estimation error covariance. Providing this feature of the input, we obtain the parameter estimate or observation sensitivity which tends to be lowered for an optimal input

$$\mathrm{cov}([a, b, c]) \geq \mathbf{M}^{-1}.$$ (9)

The Fisher information matrix (FIM) for the torsional spring (1 DOF) model (8) can be expressed as:

$$\mathbf{M}(T) \cong \int_0^T \begin{bmatrix} x_{1a} \\ x_{1b} \\ x_{1c} \\ x_{2a} \\ x_{2b} \\ x_{2c} \end{bmatrix} [x_{1a} \quad x_{1b} \quad x_{1c} \quad x_{2a} \quad x_{2b} \quad x_{2c}] dt,$$ (10)

where: $x_{ia} = \partial x_i/\partial a$, $x_{ib} = \partial x_i/\partial b$, $x_{ic} = \partial x_i/\partial c$, $i = 1, 2$.

Then the problem can be suitably modified by defining the augmented state equations as [3]:

$$
\begin{array}{llll}
x_1 = x_1; & \dot{x}_1 = \dfrac{1}{g}x_2; & x_1(0) = x_{10}; & \\[2mm]
x_2 = x_2; & \dot{x}_2 = agx_1 + bx_2 + cgu; & x_2(0) = 0; & \\[2mm]
x_3 = x_{1a}; & \dot{x}_3 = \dfrac{1}{g}x_6; & x_3(0) = 0; & \\[2mm]
x_4 = x_{1b}; & \dot{x}_4 = \dfrac{1}{g}x_7; & x_4(0) = 0; & (11) \\[2mm]
x_5 = x_{1c}; & \dot{x}_5 = \dfrac{1}{g}x_8; & x_5(0) = 0; & \\[2mm]
x_6 = x_{2a}; & \dot{x}_6 = g(x_1 + ax_3) + bx_6; & x_6(0) = 0; & \\[2mm]
x_7 = x_{2b}; & \dot{x}_7 = g(ax_4) + x_2 + bx_7; & x_7(0) = 0; & \\[2mm]
x_8 = x_{2c}; & \dot{x}_8 = gax_5 + bx_8 + gu; & x_8(0) = 0. &
\end{array}
$$

An optimal input for exciting the torsional spring (1 DOF) system is formulated through maximisation of the Fisher information matrix determinant (D-optimality) in the form of a conventional integral-criterion optimal control problem. The problem of synthesising an optimal input signal for an inertial system, utilising Mayer's canonical formulation of the performance index, has been solved in literature [13, 14]

$$\mathbf{M}(t) = \int_0^t \begin{bmatrix} x_{1a} \\ x_{1b} \\ x_{1c} \\ x_{2a} \\ x_{2b} \\ x_{2c} \end{bmatrix} \begin{bmatrix} x_{1a} & x_{1b} & x_{1c} & x_{2a} & x_{2b} & x_{2c} \end{bmatrix} d\tau \ // \ \frac{d}{dt}, \qquad (12)$$

the FIM can be modified as follows:

$$\dot{\mathbf{M}}(t) = \begin{bmatrix} x_{1a} \\ x_{1b} \\ x_{1c} \\ x_{2a} \\ x_{2b} \\ x_{2c} \end{bmatrix} \begin{bmatrix} x_{1a} & x_{1b} & x_{1c} & x_{2a} & x_{2b} & x_{2c} \end{bmatrix}, \ \mathbf{M}(0) = 0, \qquad (13)$$

where

$$\mathbf{M}(t) = \begin{bmatrix} m_{11}(t) & \cdots & m_{16}(t) \\ \vdots & \ddots & \vdots \\ m_{61}(t) & \cdots & m_{66}(t) \end{bmatrix}, \qquad (14)$$

and $m_{ij} = m_{ji}$.

Then the equivalent optimal control problem utilising Mayer's canonical formulation, which maximises the performance index with respect to the D-efficiency equality constraint, is

$$J = \det[\mathbf{M}(T_f)], \qquad (15)$$

subject to:

$$\det[\mathbf{M}(T_f)] = D; \\ -5 \le u(t) \le 5, t \in [0, T], \qquad (16)$$

where D is D-efficiency constant.

4   Experimental Results for Torsional Spring Case Study

For numerical solution of the above optimal control problems one of existing packages for solving dynamic optimisation tasks, such as Riots_95, Dircol or Miser, can be employed. We were employing the Riots_95 package [17], which is implemented in Matlab, has efficient tools for solving the constrained problems of dynamic optimisation and can be easily merged with other Matlab facilities (e.g. simulation of models developed in Simulink environment, with graphical user interface). The Matlab toolbox Riots solves a very large class of finite-time optimal controls problems that includes: trajectory and end-point constraints, variable initial conditions, free final time tasks and problems with cost functions endpoint. System dynamics can be integrated with fixed step-size Runge-Kutta method, a discrete-time solver or a variable step-size method. The software automatically computes gradients for all functions with respect to the controls and any free initial conditions.

The main program in Riots is based on thick sequential quadratic programming (SQP). Hence, the program is not well-suited for high discretisation levels. One of the major limitations of Riots is that it is not well-appointed to deal with problems whose dynamics are unstable.

All computations were performed using low-cost PC (Atom, 1.66 GHz, 1 GB RAM) running Windows 7 and Matlab 7.12 (R2011a). Optimal and sub-optimal signals are computed for nominal values of parameters a = -88.95, b = -0.42, c = 52.02 assumed termination time T_f = 10 seconds and the scaling factor $g = 10^5$ utilising SQP algorithm. The system is assumed to be at an initial state $x_1(0)$ = 0.393, the initial value of the input signal is $u(0)$ = 1 and $-5 \leq u(t) \leq 5$. The system dynamics was integrated using the fixed step-size fourth-order Runge-Kutta method with grid intervals of 0.2 seconds. The D-optimal input signals obtained for different desired values of the D-efficiency constant D (according to (3)) are shown in below figures. As the minimisation algorithms implemented in RIOTS_95 guarantee convergence only to a local minimum, we made use of the typical way to reduce the risk of "trapping", i.e. repeating the computations several times, starting from different initial conditions from the range [-0.4, 0.4] around the 'nominal' initial state $x_1(0)$ = 0.393. The D-optimal excitation signal obtained when there was no constraint on the D-efficiency value (i.e. the coefficient η = 1 in the inequality (2)), is shown in black colour in Figure 1. It corresponds to the optimal experiment e^*, where the maximal possible value of the FIM determinant is obtained and in such a case the value D_{eff} = 100%·$D_{eff, opt}$. The control signals obtained for decreasing values of D-efficiency from the interval [70%, 100%] of its maximum value are shown in Figures 2-5. As we can see, when the desired value of D-optimality decreases, the shape of the optimal input signal substantially changes. While for the optimal experiment (in the sense of (2)) there are the abrupt changes of the input, the control signal obtained for $D_{eff} < 70\%·D_{eff, opt}$ is almost constant, so the FIM determinant component was dominated by D-efficiency constraint value of the maximised performance index.

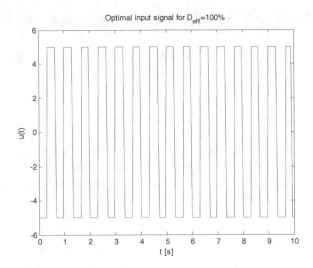

Fig. 2. Optimal input signal to the torsional spring system.

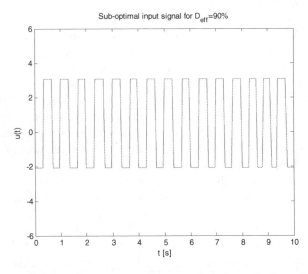

Fig. 3. Sub-optimal input signal to the torsional spring system for $D_{eff} = 90\% \cdot D_{eff. opt.}$

The optimal excitation signal obtained when there was no constraint on the D-efficiency component (i.e., for $D_{eff} = 100\%$ and $J = 4.14 \times 10^{32}$) is shown in Figure 2. The D-efficiency constraint value increased (Fig. 5) to obtain the critical value of the maximised performance index $J = 2.89 \times 10^{32}$ at the level of $D_{eff} = 70\%$. For comparison, Figure 3 shows the sub-optimal input signal, which corresponds to the objective function value $J = 3.72 \times 10^{32}$ at the level of $D_{eff} = 90\%$. Figure 4 contains the graphical display of the non-optimal signal obtained for $J = 3.10 \times 10^{32}$, where the FIM determinant component was maximised to the level of $D_{eff} = 80\%$.

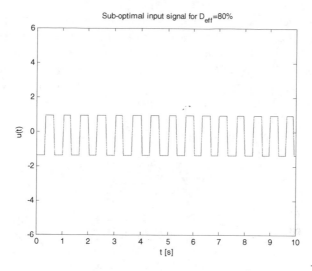

Fig. 4. Sub-optimal input signal to the torsional spring system for $D_{eff} = 80\% \cdot D_{eff, opt}$.

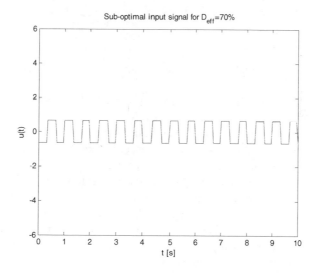

Fig. 5. Sub-optimal input signal to the torsional spring system for $D_{eff} = 70\% \cdot D_{eff, opt}$.

According to expectation, the constraint (16) was active in the optimal solution as shown in the above figures.

The signals $u(t)$ computed for different values of D-efficiency as solutions of the optimisation task (15) with the set of constraints (16), were then used as inputs in the parameter identification procedure. Figure 6 summarises the flow of information in the system identification process: we act on the physical system through the input $u(t)$ and collect information through the observations of its output $y(t)$. The presence of the white noise with different variance from the interval $0.0 \leq \sigma^2 \leq 0.7$ makes the observations random variables. The model corresponds to the theoretical representation of the system (8), which depends on a vector of unknown parameters $\boldsymbol{\theta} = [a, b, c]^\mathrm{T}$. The objective of the system identification task is to find the best values of model parameters $\boldsymbol{\theta}$ in terms of the performance criterion. The two hundred runs have been made for minimisation of the integral (within the time period from $t_0 = 0$ to the termination time $T_\mathrm{f} = 10$ sec) of the squared difference between the output of the system and the output of the model. The initial state of the torsional spring (1 DOF) model was chosen from the interval $-0.4 \leq x_1(0) \leq 0.4$ [rad] and angular velocity from the interval $0 \leq x_2(0) \leq 4$ [rad/s]. The optimisation was performed using the Nelder-Mead method.

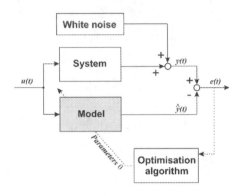

Fig. 6. Flow of information in the parameter identification system.

Figures 7(a)-7(d) show the result of the simulation experiments, i.e. the optimal values of parameters a and b computed as results of optimisation for each run, when the system starts from different initial state condition and the measurement noise influencing the system output has different variance. Figure 7(a) shows the results with the input signal obtained for the maximal value of FIM determinant (i.e. $D_\mathrm{eff} = 100\% \cdot D_\mathrm{eff,\ opt}$), the successive figures show the results (for the same combinations of initial states and noise variance) with the input signals were computed when a certain loss of D-optimality was assumed as ($D_\mathrm{eff} / D_\mathrm{eff,\ opt} = 90\%$, 80% and 70%, respectively). Analysis of the confidence regions of the torsional system parameter estimates confirms the following regularities. The optimal input signal, obtained for $D_\mathrm{eff} / D_\mathrm{eff,\ opt} = 100\%$, yields the minimal volume of the ellipsoidal confidence region of parameter estimates. When the desired ratio of $D_\mathrm{eff} / D_\mathrm{eff,\ opt}$ decreases (i.e. we accept bigger loss of D-optimality), the cluster occupied by the optimal values of identified model parameters increases its size – for the same initial conditions and noise characteristics as in the above experiment. Decreasing the desired ratio of $D_\mathrm{eff} / D_\mathrm{eff,\ opt}$ yields the input signal, which is more "friendly" for the plant, i.e. in that way we avoid abrupt changes of the control valve settings in the real-life identification experiments. The results of the simulation experiments for other combinations of the torsional system parameters a, b and c are very similar to those shown in Figure 7. The purpose of this case study was to show that the requirements of high friendliness of the input signal and the accuracy of parameter estimation are, in some sense, opposite.

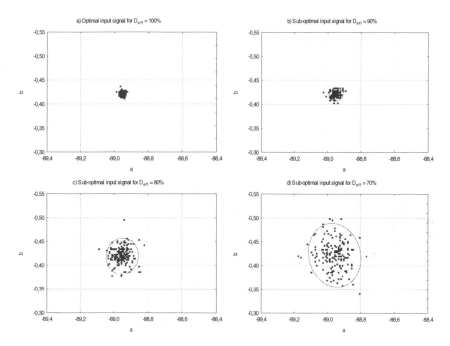

Fig. 7. Confidence regions of the torsional spring model parameter estimates; the model was excited utilising: (a) Optimal input signal $(D_{eff} = D_{eff, opt})$. (b) Sub-optimal input signal $(D_{eff} = 90\% \cdot D_{eff, opt})$. (c) Sub-optimal input signal $(D_{eff} = 80\% \cdot D_{eff, opt})$. (d) Sub-optimal input signal $(D_{eff} = 70\% \cdot D_{eff, opt})$.

5   Conclusions

An optimal input signal design problem for system identification was formulated in the paper and the method of the problem solution was outlined. In the presented approach the input signal is a solution of a dynamic optimisation problem, where the FIM determinant is maximised, at the same time providing a guaranteed level of D-efficiency. The second order dynamic system case study of optimal input signal design with guaranteed D-efficiency was presented in the paper. The experiments confirm that we can provide a compromise between the friendliness of the plant excitation in the identification process and the accuracy of estimates (observed as a reasonably small volume of the confidence ellipsoid) for a wide range of measurement noise at the system output. One of the most important steps in the approach presented in the paper was the transcription of the proposed problem formulation into an equivalent optimal control task expressed in the Lagrange form with the appropriate set of constraints. The optimal input trajectories were then computed using one of existing packages for solving dynamic optimisation problems. An optimal input signal design for solving free final time parameter estimation problem in the time domain will be presented.

Acknowledgement. The work was supported by the Dean's Project No. S/WI/1/13, Faculty of Computer Science, Department of Digital Media and Computer Graphics, Bialystok University of Technology.

References

1. Ljung, L.: System identification: Theory for the user. Prentice Hall, USA (1999)
2. Pintelon, R., Schoukens, J.: System identification: A frequency domain approach. John Wiley & Sons, USA (2001)
3. Kalaba, R., Spingarn, K.: Control, identification, and input optimization. Plenum Press, New York (1982)
4. Hugo, A.J.: Process controller performance monitoring and assessment. Control. Arts Inc. http://www.controlarts.com
5. Hildebrand, R., Gevers, M.: Identification for control: Optimal input design with respect to worst-case v-gap cost function. SIAM Journal on Control Optimization **41**, 1586–1608 (2003)
6. Pronzato, L.: Optimal experimental design and some related control problems. Automatica **44**, 303–325 (2008)
7. Hussain, M.: Review of the applications of neural networks in chemical process control-simulation and on-line implementation. Artificial Intelligence in Engineering **13**, 55–68 (1999)
8. Narasimhan, S., Rengaswamy, R.: Multi-objective input signal design for plant friendly identification of process systems. In: Proceeding of the American Control Conference 2006, Boston, Massachusetts, pp. 4891–4896 (2004)
9. Narasimhan, S., Rengaswamy, R.: Multi-objective optimal input design for plant friendly identification. In: Proceeding of the American Control Conference 2008, Seattle, Washington, pp. 1304–1309 (2008)
10. Rivera, D., Lee, H., Braun, M., Mittelmann, H.: Plant friendly system identification: a challenge for the process industries. In: SYSID 2003, Rotterdam, Netherlands (2003)
11. Steenis, R., Rivera, D.: Plant-Friendly Signal Generation for System Identification Using a Modified Simultaneous Perturbation Stochastic Approximation (SPSA) Methodology. IEEE Transactions on Control Systems Technology **19**, 1604–1612 (2011)
12. El-Kady, M., Salim, M., El-Sagheer, A.: Numerical treatment of multiobjective optimal control problems. Automatica **39**, 47–55 (2003)
13. Jakowluk, W.: Design of an optimal input signal for plant-friendly identification of inertial systems. Przegląd Elektrotechniczny **85**(6), 125–129 (2009)
14. Jakowluk, W.: Plant friendly input design for parameter estimation in an inertial system with respect to D-efficiency constraints. Entropy **16**(11), 5822–5837 (2014)
15. Atkinson, A., Donev, A., Tobias, R.: Optimum experimental design with SAS. Oxford University Press, Oxford (2007)
16. Uciński, D., Chen, Y.Q.: Sensor motion planning in distributed parameter systems using turing's measure of conditioning. In: Proceedings of the 45th IEEE Conference on Decision and Control 2006, San Diego, CA. WeB03.6, pp. 759–764. CD-ROM (2006)
17. Schwartz, A.. Polak, E., Chen, Y.: A Matlab toolbox for solving optimal control problems. Version 1.0 for Windows, May 1997. http://www.schwartz-home.com/~adam/RIOTS/

Modelling Human Cognitive Processes
Unipolar vs Bipolar Uncertainty

Agnieszka Jastrzebska[1]([⊠]), Wojciech Lesinski[2], and Mariusz Rybnik[2]

[1] Faculty of Mathematics and Information Science, Warsaw University
of Technology, ul. Koszykowa 75, 00-662 Warsaw, Poland
a.jastrzebska@mini.pw.edu.pl
[2] Faculty of Mathematics and Computer Science, University of Bialystok,
ul. Konstantego Ciolkowskiego 1M, 15-245 Bialystok, Poland

Abstract. The article presents an application of fuzzy sets with triangular norms and balanced fuzzy sets with balanced norms to decision making modelling. We elaborate on a vector-based method for decision problem representation, where each element of a vector corresponds to an argument analysed by a decision maker. Vectors gather information that influence given decision making task. Decision is an outcome of aggregation of information gathered in such vectors. We have capitalized on an inherent ability of balanced norms to aggregate positive and negative premises of different intensity. We have contrasted properties of a bipolar model with a unipolar model based on triangular norms and fuzzy sets. Secondly, we have proposed several aggregation schemes that illustrate different real-life decision making situations. We have shown suitability of the proposed model to represent complex and biased decision making cases.

Keywords: Decision making · Balanced fuzzy sets · Balanced norms ·
Fuzzy sets · Triangular norms

1 Introduction

Consumer decision making is an area extensively studied by specialists in various domains. In the pursuit of gaining the ability to model and predict human behavior neuroscientists unravel mysteries of human brain, social scientists study decisions in their social context, while economists relate decisions with money, markets and economies. The role of information science in research on decision making is critical, as it provides language for formal description and application of findings of the aforementioned domains. Information science faces a very challenging task, because quality of formal models could either hinder or enhance research in the other domains. Hence, it is of an utmost importance to work on frameworks for decision making modelling that are flexible and able to reflect real-world phenomena well.

It has been established that consumer decision making is a stimuli-driven process. Decision is an outcome of various influences recorded and evaluated

© IFIP International Federation for Information Processing 2015
K. Saeed and W. Homenda (Eds.): CISIM 2015, LNCS 9339, pp. 363–374, 2015.
DOI: 10.1007/978-3-319-24369-6_30

consciously or unconsciously. Stimuli driving our actions are often called needs, premises, factors, etc. We can generalize by saying that the decision making process is an outcome of information processing.

In this light, objective of the research underpinning this article is to elaborate on selected methods for describing and processing unipolar and bipolar information. We take under investigation fuzzy sets with triangular norms and balanced fuzzy sets with balanced norms. We apply a straightforward method for formal description of a decision problem, where forces influencing given decision are gathered in vectors. Secondly, we propose new information aggregation schemes for this model, which mimic consumer decision making processes.

The novelty aspect presented in this paper is the discussion on various information aggregation schemes for processing with balanced fuzzy sets and balanced norms. This analysis covers not only issues of information polarity, but also order of arguments' aggregation. Though the area of decision making itself is well-recognized, problems raised in this paper have not been analyzed in the context of consumer decision making.

The organization of this article is as follows. In Section 2 we introduce theoretical background of our decision making modelling framework. In particular, we elaborate on operators of interest. Section 3 presents application of standard and balanced norm to different decision making problems. A brief case study is provided to illustrate our approach. Section 4 concludes the paper and highlights future research directions.

2   Methodology

2.1   Brief Literature Review

Multiple criteria decision making is a thriving area of research with a wealth of contributions. Research relevant to the content of this study has been reported in [3], where a clear distinction between unipolar and bipolar information in a decision making problem has been addressed and elaborated on. A comprehensive perspective on fuzzy decision making could be found in [2], where the author summarizes key contemporary research streams of the domain. Interesting survey of multi-criteria decision-making can also be found in [6].

In a wealth of studies on multi-criteria decision making we can distinguish:

– unipolar,
– bipolar univariate,
– unipolar bivariate models.

Unipolar approach focuses on processing information of the same nature only, for example fuzzy sets, [13]. Bipolar univariate approaches, for example balanced fuzzy sets, [5], use single scale, typically divided by a neutral point to two zones to represent bipolar information. Unipolar bivariate models models, for example intuitionistic fuzzy sets, [1], use two separate scales, one for positive, second for negative information representation.

In this paper we look closely at the first two approaches. We are interested in modelling consumer decision cases, where attitudes could be expressed flexibly and intuitively. The unipolar bivariate models are a viable alternative to the bipolar models. Both share the ability to describe information of different nature (positive and negative). However, in our opinion, the bipolar univariate model is more straightforward. Its advantage is that information is always related to the same scale.

2.2   Decision Problem

Let us discuss certain decision problem. We have a decision maker, who is able to recognize all forces influencing give decision. Let us denote the number of such forces as n. Let us gather all these forces in an n-elements vector X:

$$X = [\, a_1, \, a_2, \, ..., \, a_n \,]$$

The decision maker is able to evaluate polarity and intensity with which each force influences given decision. In this paper we discuss fuzzy sets and balanced fuzzy sets. Hence, scale is either $[0, 1]$ in the first case or $[-1, 1]$ in the second.

Causality is captured by introducing consecutive input arguments vectors. Following schema is modelled: input arguments are evaluated twice. Initially, they are gathered and processed in premises vector. Secondly, in priorities vector.

Premises describe attitudes towards certain features or possibilities associated with an object of the decision. In terms of cognitive perspective on decision making, premises are motivational stimuli, which elicit, control, and sustain certain behaviours. They are general factors relevant to the current motivational state. Premises can be somehow called an initial or an *a priori* motivation.

Priorities is the second term we use. This term is applied in the context of a second set of beliefs (second set of motivational stimuli evaluations). Priorities concern qualitatively exactly the same arguments as premises, but they are evaluated later, in the context of a particular product. Priorities allow to take into account reassessed attitudes towards a particular choice. Priorities provide a perspective of how one particular choice satisfies stated conditions. In this context, they may be perceived as an *a posteriori* motivation, arising when the decision maker reasons about a particular item. Of course, a set of priorities evaluations might be drastically different than premises.

Priorities are moderating premises. We are able to capture causality, because the decision takes into account not only final attitudes towards one particular product (priorities), but also general attitudes (gathered in premises vector). On such input data processing with chosen aggregators is performed.

Proposed technique mimics real consumer decision making processes, as reported by psychologists, for example in [10], where a decision could be viewed as an outcome of prior beliefs (here represented with premises) and current stimuli encouraging or discouraging us (priorities). Roots of mathematical representation of a decision making processes with two or more vectors representing causality could be found in [8].

2.3 Fuzzy Connectives

Let us recall basic notions of fuzzy sets and generalization of fuzzy connectives min and max to triangular norms and conorms. We are expressing fuzzy sets in the form of membership functions. Namely, a fuzzy set A defined in the universe X is a mapping $\mu : X \to [0,1]$ or $\mu_{A,X} : X \to [0,1]$, if the names of the set and the universe should be explicitly stated. The Zadeh's model of fuzzy sets is clearly interpreted as $([0,1]^X, \max, \min, 1-)$, where $[0,1]^X$ states for mappings from the universe X into the unit interval $[0,1]$, i.e. $[0,1]^X$ is the space of membership functions, and max, min and $1-$ applied to membership functions implement qualitatively different operators on imprecise information.

Triangular Norms and Conorms. Triangular norms have been introduced in [9] and then studied in [7,11].

Triangular norms and conorms (t-norms and t-conorms in abbreviated form) are mappings $q : [0,1] \times [0,1] \to [0,1]$, where q stands for both t-norm t and t-conorm s, satisfying axioms of associativity, commutativity, monotonicity and boundary conditions. t-norms and t-conorms are dual operations in a sense that for any given t-norm t, we get the dual t-conorm s using the De Morgan's laws: $s(a,b) = 1 - t(1-a, 1-b)$ and $t(a,b) = 1 - s(1-a, 1-b)$

Let us focus on one well-known pair of dual t-norm and t-conorm: Lukasiewicz and bounded sum $(\max(0, x+y-1)/\min(x+y, 1))$ and on one pair of strict triangular norm and conorm generated by additive generators. We do not discuss decision making based on other standard triangular norms and conorms, because it is a topic thoroughly reported in the literature.

It is worth to recall that t-norms and t-conorms are bounded by min t-norm and max t-conorm, i.e. for any t-norm t, any t-conorm s and any $x, y \in [0,1]$ the following inequality holds:

$$t(x,y) \leq \min(x,y) \leq \max(x,y) \leq s(x,y) \tag{1}$$

Additive Generators. Triangular norms can be generated by additive or multiplicative generators, c.f. [7,11]. Let us focus on additive generators for defining triangular norms and conorms. Let $f : [0,1] \to [0,d]$ be a non-decreasing mapping with $[0,d]$ being closed subintervals of the extended real semiline $[0,+\infty]$. Then the formula $f^{-1} : [0,+\infty] \to [0,1]$ such that $f^{-1}(y) = \sup\{x \in [0,1] : f(x) < y\}$ defines the pseudo-inverse of the mapping f. Similarly, if the mapping f is non-increasing, then the pseudo-inverse is defined by the formula $f^{-1} : [0,+\infty] \to [0,1]$ such that $f^{-1}(y) = \sup\{x \in [0,1] : f(x) > y\}$. We restrict our discussion to strictly monotonic and continuous bijections with $f(0) = 0$ for increasing mapping and $f(1) = 0$ for decreasing mapping f. Therefore we get $(f^{-1})^{-1} = f$ in the interval $[0,1]$ and $f^{-1}(y) = 1$ for $y > d$ for increasing mapping f and $f^{-1}(y) = 0$ for $y > d$ for decreasing mapping f. A mapping $q : [0,1]^2 \to [0,1]$ such that $q(x,y) = f^{-1}(f(x) + f(y))$ is a t-norm for decreasing f and t-conorm for increasing f. Moreover, such norms are monotonic and continuous, hence they are called *strict* norms as they are assuming strict monotonicity. Detailed discussion on additive generators is in [7].

We apply following additive generator of t-conorm and its pseudo-inverse mapping:

- $f : [0, 1] \rightarrow [0, +\infty]$ and $f^{-1} : [0, +\infty] \rightarrow [0, 1]$ such that:
  - $f(x) = \arcsin(x)$ and $f^{-1}(x) = \sin(\min(x, \pi/2))$.

2.4 Balanced Connectives

Classical models of information processing were generalized by introducing new connectives defined on the unipolar unit interval and the unipolar unit square as well as the bipolar unit interval and the bipolar unit square. The former ones are uninorms and nullnorms with domain and codomain based on the unipolar unit interval, c.f. [7,12]. The latter ones are balanced norms and conorms (b-norms and b-conorms) with domain and codomain based on the bipolar unit interval. Initial considerations on bipolar connectives were published in [4] and then balanced norms and conorms were introduced in [5]. Uninorms/nullnorms are fuzzy sets connectives, while b-norms/b-conorms are balanced fuzzy sets connectives.

Balanced Fuzzy Sets. Fuzzy sets in represent both positive and negative information. Positive information is dispersed in the unit interval $(0, 1]$ while negative information is concentrated in the crisp point 0. The idea behind balanced fuzzy sets is to disperse negative information over the interval $[-1, 0]$. Such dispersion is analogical to the dispersion of positive information accumulated in the numeric value 1 into the (fuzzy) interval $[0, 1]$, c.f. [5].

Let us illustrate with a simple example what positive, negative and neutral information stands for. A customer needs to buy a car for transporting goods and for travelling with family. A lorry would provide superior cargo transportation (strong positive evaluation), but it would not be a good fit for travelling with the family (strong negative evaluation). In contrast, a notchback would be a good fit for travelling with the family (strong positive evaluation), but it would not be useful for goods transportation as its trunk space is not that impressive (strong negative evaluation). Finally, purchasing a minivan is a compromise as it meets moderately positive information in both aspects. On the other hand, a brand of the minivan may be unimportant, what would create a neutral information (neutral purchasing argument). Notice that strengths of arguments may differ and depend on circumstances, c.f. for instance [5].

Recalling basic notions, balanced fuzzy set is a system $\mathcal{F} = ([-1, 1]^X, \text{bmin},$ bmax, bneg, $I)$, where with X is a universe of discourse, bmin, bmax and bneg are balanced counterparts of min, max and $1-$ fuzzy connectives, c.f. Section 2.3:

- bmin equals min for positive arguments, equals max for negative arguments and vanishes for arguments of different signs,
- bmax equals to max for positive arguments, equals to min for negative arguments. bmax is in-between arguments of different signs and may be defined as equal to argument of greater absolute value. For arguments of opposite values it is undefined,
- bneg is the counterpart of $1-$ and may be defined as changing sign,

- I is a one place binverse operator. It does not have its fuzzy counterpart and may be defined as $I(a) = \text{sgn}(x) - x$ for $x \neq 0$ and undefined for $x = 0$.

In this paper connectives bmin and bmax are replaced with balanced norms and conorms, an inverse operator is not used.

Balanced Norms and Conorms. Notice, that until the standard system $\mathcal{F} = ([-1,1]^X, \text{bnorm}, \text{bconorm}, -)$ is considered, the concepts of balanced norms and conorms (b-norms and b-conorms for short) are isomorphic with uninorms and nullnorms. Roughly speaking, a binverse operator I distinguishes systems $([0,1]^X, \text{uninorm}, \text{nullnorm}, \text{negation})$ and $([-1,1]^X, \text{b-norm}, \text{b-conorm}, \text{b-negation}, \text{b-inverse})$ and in this way its implementation may distinguish between b-norms/b-conorms and uninorms/nullnorms, c.f. [5,12] for details. We use balanced norms and conorms rather than uninorms and nullnorms, because they model positive and negative information in a more intuitive way. Moreover, balanced norms and conorms represent positive and negative knowledge in a straightforward fashion, with the use of a single $[-1,1]$ scale, c.f. [4,5].

In this paper we employ operations corresponding to triangular norms and conorms, which are generated by additive generators. A balanced norm T and balanced conorm S are mappings $Q : [-1,1] \times [-1,1] \rightarrow [-1,1]$, which are associative, commutative, increasing, and satisfy boundary conditions, c.f. [5]. Note that Q stands for both balanced norm and conorm. Boundary condition of balanced conorms is: $S(0,a) = a$ for all $a \in [-1,1]$. Due to associativity problem, the values $S(-1,1)$ and $S(1,-1)$ are both defined either as -1, or as 1, or as undefined, for instance c.f. [7]. For balanced norm T we have $T(1,a) = a$ whenever $a \in [-1,0]$ and $T(-1,a) = a$ whenever $a \in [-1,0]$. It is worth to underscore, that balanced norms <u>must</u> vanish for arguments of different signs. This is a direct conclusion drawn from monotonicity and boundary conditions. Note, that balanced norms and conorms restricted to the unipolar square domain $[0,1]$ are t-norms and conorms, respectively. Alike, balanced norms and conorms restricted to the unipolar negative square domain $[-1,0]$, when linearly transformed to the unit interval $[0,1]$, are t-conorms and t-norms, respectively.

Additive Generators. Alike in the case of triangular conorms, we can construct balanced triangular conorms using additive generators. Roughly speaking, an odd function being an additive generator of a symmetric balanced conorm (i.e. $S(a,b) = -S(-a,-b)$) is obtained by reflection of an additive generator of a triangular conorm in the origin of coordinate system, c.f. [5]. Additive generators of non-symmetric balance conorms are composed of different generators for nonpositive and nonnegative arguments. Namely, a function $F : [-1,1] \rightarrow [-d,d][-\infty,+\infty]$, which is strictly increasing continuous mapping with $[-d,d]$ being closed subintervals of the extended real line $[-\infty,+\infty]$, $F(-1) = -d$, $F(1) = +d$ and $F(0) = 0$. The function $S : [-1,1] \times [-1,1] \rightarrow ([-1,1] - \{(-1,1),(1,-1)\}$, $S(a,b) = F^{-1}(F(a) + F(b))$, is a balanced conorm, where F^{-1} is the pseudo-inverse of F (defined by analogy to Section 2.3), i.e. the function defined as follows: $F^{-1}(y) = \sup\{x \in [0,1] : F(x) < y\}$ for $y \geq 0$ and $F^{-1}(y) = \inf\{x \in [-1,0] : F(x) > y\}$ for $x < 0$.

In this study authors consider balanced conorm and norm generated by tangent additive generator:

- $F : [-1, 1] \rightarrow [-\infty, +\infty]$ and $F^{-1} : [-\infty, +\infty] \rightarrow [-1, 1]$ such that:
  - $F(x) = \tan(\pi/2 * x)$ and $F^{-1}(x) = 2/\pi * \arctan(x)$,

Additive generators of balanced norms are defined analogously to additive generators of balanced conorms. Reflection of an additive generator of a triangular norm in the origin of the coordinates' system gives an additive generator of a balanced symmetric norm. Gluing two different generators gives a generator of a non-symmetric balanced norm. It is worth to notice, that additive generators of balanced norms are undefined for 0. Additive generators of balanced norms are not discussed here. For the study presented in this paper De Morgan laws are sufficient for switching from balanced conorms to balanced norms.

3   Comparative Overview of Modelling Capabilities of Selected Triangular and Balanced Norms and Conorms

The goal of this section is to illustrate how the discussed theoretical framework could be employed for decision making modelling. To achieve clarity of presentation the discussion is limited to simple examples: fixed number of premises and priorities (either 5 or 10), repeated values of premises/priorities, computationally simple norms/conorms and derived operators, etc.

Such examples could be easily extended by adding more arguments or by analyzing various operators. A real-world source of information needed to conduct such study could be, for example, a survey.

3.1   Modelling Decision Making with Triangular Norms

The decision is obtained with a 2-step procedure. First, we aggregate premises with priorities. Second, we compute the final decision. Selected pairs of dual t-norms/t-conorms are involved in the process. Considering vectors of premises $[p_1, \ldots, p_5]$ and priorities $[r_1, \ldots, r_5]$, we come to the decision support (decision in the form of a number from the $[0, 1]$ interval):

$$d = s\Big(t(p_1, r_1), t(p_2, r_2), t(p_3, r_3), t(p_4, r_4), t(p_5, r_5)\Big) \tag{2}$$

where d is a decision support, t is a t-norm and s is the dual t-conorm. Here, associativity of the t-conorm s is assumed, which guarantees validity of this notation. Otherwise, since s is a two place operator, this formula should be rewritten, for instance, in the form $s(t(p_1, r_1), s(t(p_2, r_2), s(t(p_3, r_3), s(t(p_4, r_4), t(p_5, r_5)))))$.

Assuming that all premises are set to the value b and that k priorities change in the unit interval $x \in (0, 1]$ and other are equal to b:

$$p_1 = p_2 = p_3 = p_4 = p_5 = b, \quad r_1 = \ldots = r_k = x, \quad r_{k+1} = \ldots = r_5 = b \tag{3}$$

and utilize the formula 2 we get:

$$d = s\Big(t(b, x), t(b, \cdot), t(b, \cdot), t(b, \cdot), t(b, b)\Big) \tag{4}$$

where $\cdot$ stands either for x, or for b, depending on the value k.

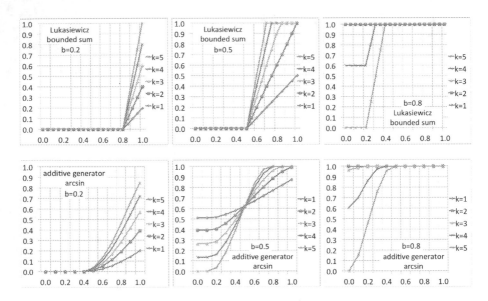

Fig. 1. Modelling decision making with Lukasiewicz/bounded sum (top row) and arcsine generated dual norms (bottom row). Decision is based on 5 pairs of premise/priority. All premises are equal b. Priorities are vectors with k arguments of strength x, remaining $5 - k$ elements are equal b.

Standard Triangular Norms. Let us start with presentation of decision making results with selected pair of dual t-norms/t-conorms: Lukasiewicz/ bounded sum. We consider vectors of premises and priorities and utilize the scheme for computing decision support as in Formulas 2 and 3.

Figure 1 demonstrates how a modification of arguments of one type influences the decision assuming other type arguments on a fixed level for a variety of operators. The following observations regarding plots in Figure 1 can be made: Lukasiewicz t-norm/bounded sum t-conorm are insensitive for values of arguments low (t-norms) or high (t-conorms) enough. These operators achieve lower/upper saturation state for values of arguments smaller/greater than some threshold. The impact of upper and lower thresholds is distinctly visible in differences between plots, where $b = 0.2$ and $b = 0.8$. The first one has all premises equal to 0.2. As a result, only for very strong priorities (greater than 0.8) we can get the decision greater than 0. In contrast, for strong arguments (like $b = 0.8$) the decision gets drawn to the upper threshold level and it is equal to 1, unless premises are combined with very small priorities. It happens only for $k = 5$ and $k = 4$, which are in this decision problem relatively big numbers of weak priorities. The middle plot (for $b = 0.5$) shows decisions for moderate arguments and transition between the extremes. In this case both lower and upper thresholds are clearly visible. Right plot concerns strong positive premises ($b = 0.8$). For such strong premises set the only case where the consumer is not able to make a positive decision is when all priorities are very small (for $k = 5$ and x in the range $[0, 0.2]$).

Second pair of operators of interest are arcsine generated dual norms, for which decision making results are in the second row of Figure 1. We see similarity between plots in the first and the second row. For both pairs of operators decisions vanish (are set to 0) for small input arguments and get saturated (to 1) for high arguments. In the case of Lukasiewicz t-norm and bounded sum the critical (threshold) point is sharp and easy to identify on the plot, while for arcsine generated dual norms the transition between 0 and 1 is smooth.

First column in Figure 1 shows that if positive premises influencing the decision are of weak intensity (first column, $b = 0.2$), then the consumer makes a positive decision only if all priorities are close to 1. This agrees with a common sense. We expect weak positive premises to vote over priorities. In contrast, if premises were higher at the beginning (middle and right plots, $b = 0.5$ and $b = 0.8$ respectively) it is easier to reach positive decision. Also in real life, we would expect that if our convictions about certain issue were high at start, we would have necessary motivational background to encourage certain decisions. In our model, priorities could be interpreted as the hot system described by W. Mischel in [10]. Evaluation of priorities under biased or emotional circumstances could lead to unexpected strong feelings towards certain products, for example chocolates. Though the rational cold system, here represented with premises, knows that in order to be healthy we should not be eating chocolate, strong positive stimuli of the hot system (priorities) could outvote it.

3.2   Discussion on Selected Balanced Norms

The application of balanced norms and conorms is an objective of this paper and it is an original input of the authors to the field of decision making based on both positive and negative forces. We use balanced norm and conorm associated with $\tan(\pi/2 \cdot)$ in the $[-1, 1]$ domain.

We consider vectors of premises $[p_1, \ldots, p_{10}]$ and priorities $[r_1, \ldots, r_{10}]$. The elements of both vectors are assumed to hold positive and negative values. It is assumed that the corresponding elements in vectors of premises and priorities are either both positive or both negative. Any case of different types of values (negative and positive) in corresponding elements is not considered.

Alike in Section 3.1, there are 5 pairs of positive premises/priorities. Positive values of premises are constant and equal b. k priorities change in the unit interval $x \in [0, 1]$ - the reference is on the OX axis. $5 - k$ positive values of priorities remain fixed at the same level as premises (b). There are j pairs of negative premises/priorities. Pairs of negative premises and priorities are set to the same negative constant value c, while the other $5 - j$ pairs of premises and priorities are not considered.

Unlike in Section 3.1, computing decision support may not be straightforward. Balanced norms obtained with generators such as arctangent hyperbolic and tangent are associative and commutative with the only exception for numeric values of different signs, c.f. Section 2.4. However, associativity and commutativity are not satisfied by norms generated, for instance, by arcsine. Therefore, computing with balanced norms following Formulas 2 and 3 is not valid. Instead we employ more complex assumptions.

Let us remind that at first corresponding premises and priorities are moderated with a balanced norm. Secondly, results of such balanced norm aggregation are aggregated with a balanced conorm. Let us introduce two different schemes of aggregation with a balanced conorm are applied: batch aggregation and one-by-one aggregation.

Batch Aggregation - positive and negative results moderated with a balanced norm are aggregated separately with a balanced conorm. Then, both results computed by the balanced conorm are aggregated with the same conorm:

$$S\Big(S\big(T(p_{i_1}, r_{i_1}), \ldots, T(p_{i_5}, r_{i_5})\big), S\big(T(p_{i_6}, r_{i_6}), \ldots, T(p_{i_{5+j}}, r_{i_{5+j}})\big)\Big) \qquad (5)$$

where:

- $p_{i_1}, r_{i_1}, \ldots, p_{i_5}, r_{i_5} \geqslant 0$ and $p_{i_6}, r_{i_6}, \ldots, p_{i_{5+j}}, r_{i_{5+j}} \leqslant 0$
- T is a balanced norm and S is a balanced conorm.

This formula is valid due to associativity of balanced triangular norms for non-negative arguments and for non-positive arguments as well as commutativity of balanced conorm for two arguments.

One-by-one Aggregation - consecutive results of a moderation with balanced norm are aggregated with a dual balanced conorm according to the following formula:

$$S\Big(S\big(\ldots\big(S\big(T(p_1, r_1), T(p_2, r_2)\big), T(p_3, r_3)\big), \ldots\big), T(p_{5+j}, r_{5+j})\Big) \qquad (6)$$

Following orderings of negative and positive values and corresponding vectors of premises and priorities are proposed:

1. 5 positive values first and then 5 negative ones:
   $p_1 = p_2 = p_3 = p_4 = p_5 = b$ and $p_6 = p_7 = p_8 = p_9 = p_{10} = c$
   $r_1 = r_2 = r_3 = r_4 = r_5 = x$ and $r_6 = r_7 = r_8 = r_9 =_{10} = c$
   $Prem = [b, b, b, b, b, c, c, c, c, c]$ and $Prior = [x, x, x, x, x, c, c, c, c, c]$

2. 5 negative values first and then 5 positive ones:
   $p_1 = p_2 = p_3 = p_4 = p_5 = c$ and $p_6 = p_7 = p_8 = p_9 = p_{10} = b$
   $r_1 = r_2 = r_3 = r_4 = r_5 = c$ and $r_6 = r_7 = r_8 = r_9 = r_{10} = x$
   $Prem = [c, c, c, c, c, b, b, b, b, b]$ and $Prior = [c, c, c, c, c, x, x, x, x, x]$

3. 5 positive values first and then j negative ones:
   $p_1 = \ldots = p_5 = b$ and $p_6 = \ldots = p_{5+j} = c$
   $r_1 = \ldots = r_k = x, \quad r_{k+1} = \ldots = r_5 = b$ and $r_6 = \ldots = r_{5+j} = c$
   $Prem = [b, b, b, b, b, c, c, \ldots]$ and $Prior = [x, \ldots, x, b, \ldots, b, c, c, \ldots]$

4. alternate positive/negative values beginning with a positive one:
   $p_1 = p_3 = p_5 = p_7 = p_9 = b$ and $p_2 = p_4 = p_6 = p_8 = p_{10} = c$
   $r_1 = r_3 = r_5 = r_7 = r_9 = x$ and $r_2 = r_4 = r_6 = r_8 = r_{10} = c$
   $Prem = [b, c, b, c, b, c, b, c, b, c]$ and $Prior = [x, c, x, c, x, c, x, c, x, c]$

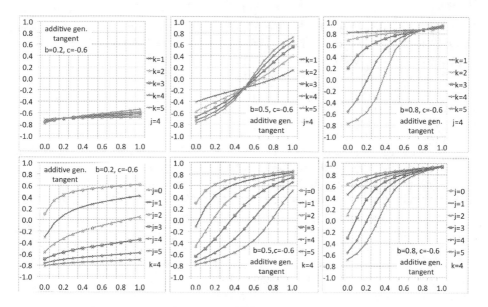

Fig. 2. Decision making modelling with dual balanced norms associated with tangent. Batch aggregation with scheme no. 3 is applied. Decision problems are based on 5 pairs of positive premises of strength b and priorities of strength x (on the OX axis) and j negative pairs of premise/priority both of strength c.

5. alternate positive/negative values beginning with a negative one:

$p_1 = p_3 = p_5 = p_7 = p_9 = c$ and $p_2 = p_4 = p_6 = p_8 = p_{10} = b$

$r_1 = r_3 = r_5 = r_7 = r_9 = c$ and $r_2 = r_4 = r_6 = r_8 = r_{10} = x$

$Prem = [c, b, c, b, c, b, c, b, c, b]$ and $Prior = [c, x, c, x, c, x, c, x, c, x]$

Various aggregation scenarios are constructed to represent different real-world decision making problems. We aimed at proposing processing schemes that would have the capacity to illustrate a wealth of real-life situations.

Figure 2 illustrates decision making results based on balanced norms associated with tangent additive generator. Tangent-based norms overestimate weak arguments. Emphasizing effect is clearly visible in two top lines (for zero or few negative input pairs: $j = 0$, $j = 1$ and $j = 2$) in the bottom row. Emphasizing effect causes also that in the top left plot (for $b = 0.2$ and $c = -0.6$) decisions computed with tangent are higher, than if we would have had applied arcsine or arctangent hyperbolic-based connectives. Tangent-based operators reflect well consumer behaviour. Overestimation of weak arguments is a behavioural bias of decision making - persistent deviation we observe. If we aggregate strong premises/priorities the strengthening effect is not present and results are in-between decisions computed with arcsine and arctangent hyperbolic norms.

With growth of the number of negative arguments decisions become weaker. Lines on the left plot in the bottom row of Figure 2 are placed one above another. For $j = 0$ lines are higher than for $j = 1$, $j = 2$, $j = 3$, $j = 4$ and $j = 5$ and so on. Decisions computed with tangent are relatively high, but with an upper boundary. Saturation effect is well-visible in right plots, which present decision cases with strong positive result. Similarly, we see a clear threshold for a negative decision in top left plot (for $j = 4$, $b = 0.2$ and $c = -0.6$).

Other norms are not considered here due to space constraints.

4   Conclusion

The article presents an approach to decision making modelling. The method is based on aggregation of premises influencing given decision. We emphasize the distinction between the two schemes: unipolar and bipolar. The unipolar approach, which could be represented with fuzzy sets and triangular norms, is able to process positive information only. The bipolar approach realized with balanced fuzzy sets and balanced norms overcomes this limitation and could be applied to represent positive and negative premises of different intensity. Building on the assumption that there is a relation between decision and an order, in which consumer acknowledges premises influencing this decision we have discussed various aggregation schemes that mimic different real-life decision making scenarios. Presented ideas have been illustrated with a brief case study, where we apply and compare different operators in several decision making problems. The study confirms advantageous modelling capability of the proposed methods. In future, we plan to continue the development of this framework. In particular, we plan to use it to describe basic behavioral biases in decision making.

References

1. Atanassov, K.T.: Intuitionistic fuzzy sets. Fuzzy Sets and Systems **20**, 87–96 (1986)
2. Dubois, D.: The role of fuzzy sets in decision sciences: Old techniques and new directions. Fuzzy Sets and Systems **184**, 3–28 (2011)
3. Grabisch, M., Greco, S., Pirlot, M.: Bipolar and bivariate models in multicriteria decision analysis: Descriptive and constructive approaches. International Journal of Intelligent Systems **23**(9), 930–969 (2008)
4. Homenda, W., Pedrycz, W.: Processing of uncertain information in linear space of fuzzy sets. Fuzzy Sets & Systems **44**, 187–198 (1991)
5. Homenda, W.: Balanced Fuzzy Sets. Information Sciences **176**, 2467–2506 (2006)
6. Ho, W., Xu, X., Dey, P.K.: Multi-criteria decision making approaches for supplier evaluation and selection: A literature review. European Journal of Operational Research **202**, 16–24 (2010)
7. Klement, E.P., Mesiar, R., Pap, E.: Triangular norms. Kluwer Academic Publishers, Dordrecht (2000)
8. Lewin, K.: Field theory in social science; selected theoretical papers. In: Cartwright, D. (ed.). Harper & Row, New York (1951)
9. Menger, K.: Statistical Metrics. Proceedings of the National Academy of Sciences, USA **28**, 535–537 (1942)
10. Mischel, W.: The Marshmallow Test: Mastering Self-Control. Little, Brown and Company (2014)
11. Schweizer, B., Sklar, A.: Probabilistic Metric Spaces. North Holland, New York (1983)
12. Yager, R.R., Rybalov, A.: Uninorm aggregation operators. Fuzzy Sets and Systems **80**, 111–120 (1996)
13. Zadeh, L.A.: Fuzzy sets. Information and Control. **8**(3), 338–353 (1965)

Experiments on Minimization Method of Incompletely Specified Finite State Machines for Low Power Design

Adam Klimowicz[(✉)] and Valery Solov'ev

Bialystok University of Technology, Bialystok, Poland
{a.klimowicz,v.salauyou}@pb.edu.pl

Abstract. This paper presents a heuristic method for minimization of incompletely specified finite state machine with unspecified values of output variables. The proposed method is based on two states merging. In this method, such optimization criteria as the power consumption and possibility of merging other states are taken into account already at the stage of minimizing internal states. In addition to reduction of the finite state machine (FSM) states, the method also allows reducing the number of FSM transitions and FSM input variables. Experimental results for various styles of state assignment are presented. The results show that this approach to minimization of FSM in most of cases is more effective than classical methods in respect of power consumption.

Keywords: Finite State Machine (FSM) · State minimization · Low power design

1 Introduction

A finite state machine (FSM) is a model used in the design of various computation structures like sequential circuits, digital control systems, microprocessor control circuits, digital communication systems, iterative networks, communication protocols, etc. For various reasons the transitions between the FSM states or the FSM outputs may be not completely specified. An incompletely specified finite state machine (ISFSM) is the one where either the next state or the output is not specified for at least one input vector. Minimization of ISFSMs is an important task in the optimal design of sequential circuits.

A general theory for incompletely specified machines was first developed in [1]. The standard approach to solution of the problem of ISFSM's state reduction is based on a generation of sets of compatible states (or compatibles) and finding of a minimal closed cover. The problem of minimization of ISFSMs is an NP-complete problem [2] and has been studied by a number of authors. In [3], a program called STAMINA that runs in exact and heuristic modes and uses explicit enumeration for the solution of state minimization problem is presented. In [4], an exact state minimization algorithm based on mapping of ISFSMs to FSMs tree is presented. In [5], a branch-and-bound search technique for the identification of sets of compatible states is described.

The conventional approach to the synthesis of FSMs includes the following stages, which are executed sequentially: minimization of the number of internal states, state

© IFIP International Federation for Information Processing 2015
K. Saeed and W. Homenda (Eds.): CISIM 2015, LNCS 9339, pp. 375–385, 2015.
DOI: 10.1007/978-3-319-24369-6_31

assignment and synthesis of the combinational part of the FSM. However, classical approach often contradicts the FSM optimization goal at the stage of logic synthesis because both the minimization of the number of internal states and their assignment completely ignore the features of the technological base and the requirements of logic synthesis. In [6-8], the implementation cost is minimized simultaneously with the minimization of the power consumption at the stage of state assignment. In the majority of these works, genetic algorithms are used. In [9], the minimization of power consumption and delay is considered for asynchronous FSMs. The concept of a low power semi-synchronous FSM operating on a high frequency is proposed that can be implemented and tested as an ordinary synchronous FSM. In [10], a two-level structural model is proposed to minimize the power consumption, area, and delay. The first level of this model consists of sequential units, while the second level consists of combinational units of limited size.

The analysis of available studies showed that there are no works in which the number of internal states and power consumption are simultaneously minimized. In this paper, we propose a heuristic method for minimization of incompletely specified FSMs with unspecified values of output variables. This method is based on an operation of two states merging. In this method, such optimization criteria as the power consumption and possibility of merging other states are taken into account already at the stage of minimizing internal states. In addition to reduction of internal states this method minimizes the number of FSM transitions and FSM input variables.

2   Preliminaries

An ISFSM can have incompletely specified outputs and incompletely specified transitions. Incompletely specified outputs take place when the value of the output variable does not influence on functioning of the controlled object, e.g. when a carry voltage is not applied to the controlled object. Incompletely specified transitions arise when some input vectors never appear on FSM inputs, e.g. the codes of hexadecimal figures A-F at work in a decimal notation.

In practice, designers usually redefine the unspecified transitions by transitions to the present state, or to the reset state, or to an additional state, where an error signal is generated. It makes it possible to increase the functional reliability of the digital systems. In the offered approach we define the unspecified values only of the output variables and do not change the unspecified transitions.

Let us denote by L the number of FSM input variables of a set $X = \{x_1,...,x_L\}$, by N the number of FSM output variables of a set $Y = \{y_1,...,y_N\}$, by M the number of FSM internal states of a set $A = \{a_1,...,a_M\}$, and by R the minimal number of bits required to encode internal states, where $R = \text{intlog}_2 M$.

A FSM behavior is described by the *transition list*. The transition list is a table with four columns: a_m, a_s, $X(a_m,a_s)$, and $Y(a_m,a_s)$. Each row of the transition list corresponds to one FSM transition. The column a_m contains the state where the transition begins (*a present state*), the column a_s contains the state where the transition ends (*a next state*), the column $X(a_m,a_s)$ contains the set of values of the input variables that initiates this transition (*a transition condition* or *an input vector*), and the column $Y(a_m, a_s)$ contains the set of values of the output variables that is generated by FSM at this transition (*an output vector*). An ISFSM output vector is represented by ternary vector. For example, $Y(a_m, a_s)$="01-0", where 0 denotes zero value, 1 denotes unity value, and dash ("-") denotes a don't care value of the corresponding output variable.

The transition condition may be described in the column $X(a_m, a_s)$ in the form of conjunction of FSM input variables. The transition condition can also be represented by a ternary vector. For example, $X(a_m, a_s)$ = "1-10-0" where unit (1) means that the corresponding input variable is included in conjunction in the direct form, zero (0) means that the corresponding input variable is included in conjunction in the inversed form, and dash ("-") means that the value of the input variable does not affect the FSM transition. Since the FSM behavior is deterministic, all the transition conditions from every FSM state should be mutually orthogonal. Two transition conditions are orthogonal if they have different significant values (0 or 1) at least in one position.

Two FSM states a_i and a_j can be merged, i.e. replaced by one state a_{i_j}, if they are equivalent. Equivalency of two FSM states means that FSM behavior does not change when these states are merged in one. FSM behavior does not change after states a_i and a_j merge, if the transition conditions from the states a_i and a_j that lead to different states are orthogonal. If there are transitions from states a_i and a_j that lead to the same unique state, then the transition conditions for such transitions should be equal. Moreover, the output vectors that are generated at these transitions should be not orthogonal. Note also that under two FSM states merging *wait states* can be formed.

Under FSM states merging the output vectors with unspecified values can be merged only if they are not orthogonal. Thus the significant values (0 or 1) remain without changes, and the unspecified values are replaced by the corresponding significant values. For example, let $Y(a_i, a_s)$ ="1-0-0" and $Y(a_j, a_s)$ ="-1010", and let the states a_i and a_j assume merging, then the output vector $Y(a_{i\_j}, a_s)$ ="11010" will be formed at the transition from the new state a_{i_j} to the state a_s.

The main strategy of the offered approach consists in finding the set D of all the pairs of FSM states satisfying the merging conditions. Then for each pair of states from D the trial merging is carried out. Finally a pair (a_i, a_j) for merging is selected in such a way that it leaves the maximal possibilities for other pairs of FSM states merging. The given process repeats as long as there exists a possibility for at least one pair of FSM states merging. The method was described more precisely in paper [11].

In distinction from [11], in the present paper we chose for merging at each step the pair (a_i, a_j) that best satisfies the optimization criteria in terms of power consumption, and leaves the maximum possibilities for merging other pairs in G. This procedure is repeated while at least one pair of states can be merged.

Let (a_s, a_t) be a pair of states in G, where P_{st} is the estimate of power consumption, and M_{st} is the estimate of the possibility to merge other states. Then, with regard to the above considerations, the FSM minimization algorithm can be described as follows.

Algorithm 1 (general algorithm for FSM minimization)

1. Using the method described in [11], form the set G of pairs of states that admit merging. If $G = \varnothing$ (no pairs can be merged), go to step 5
2. For each pair of states (a_s, a_t) in G, calculate the estimates P_{st}, and M_{st} of the optimization criteria.
3. According to the specified order of optimization criteria, choose a pair of states (a_i, a_j) for merging. Among all the pairs in G, choose a pair (a_i, a_j) for which $P_{ij} =$ min; if there are several such pairs, then choose among them the one for which M_{ij} = max.
4. Merge the pair of states (a_i, a_j). Store the results of minimization (transition list and corresponding P_{st} value). Go to step 1.
5. Among all saved results of minimization select one with minimal P_{st} value.
6. Minimize the number of transitions in the FSM.
7. Minimize the number of input variables in the FSM.
8. Stop.

Merging of the states a_i and a_j (step 4 of Algorithm 1), minimization of the number of transitions (step 6 of Algorithm 1) and minimization of the number of input variables (step 7 of Algorithm 1) are performed as described in [11].

Algorithms of minimization of the number of transition an input variables are based on some observations. Suppose, for instance, that one transition from a state a_1 under condition x_1 leads to a state a_2 and the second transition from a_1 under condition $\overline{x}_1$ leads to another state a_3 and on each of these transitions not orthogonal output vectors are formed ($\overline{x}_1$ is an inversed form of the variable x_1). Suppose that the states a_2 and a_3 can be merged. After merging a_2 and a_3, a new state a_{23} is formed. Now two transitions lead from a_1 to a_{2_3}, one under condition x_1 and the second under condition $\overline{x}_1$. The latter means that the transition from a_1 to a_{23} is unconditional and two transitions can be replaced by one unconditional transition. Notice that in general transition conditions from a state a_1 can be much more complicated.

At minimization of the number of FSM transitions one can arrive at a situation when certain input variables have no impact on the transition conditions. Suppose, for instance, that one transition from a state a_1 under condition x_1 leads to a state a_2 and another transition from a_1 under condition $\overline{x}_1$ leads to a state a_3 and the variable x_1 does not meet anywhere else in transition conditions of the FSM. Suppose that after the states a_2 and a_3 have been merged, the transition from the state a_1 to the state a_{23} becomes unconditional, i.e. it does not depend on values of input variables. The latter means that the variable x_1 has no impact on any FSM transition and therefore it is redundant.

3   Estimation of Optimization Criteria

To estimate the optimization criteria, all pairs of states in G are considered one after another. For each pair of states (a_s, a_t) in G, a trial merging is performed. For the resultant FSM, its internal states are encoded using one of the available methods that will later be used in the synthesis of the FSM, and the system of Boolean functions corresponding to the combinational part of the FSM is built. Next, for the pair (a_s, a_t), power consumption P_{st}, and the possibility of minimizing other states M_{st} are estimated. The optimization criteria for each pair of states (a_s, a_t) in G are estimated at step 2 of Algorithm 1 using the following algorithm.

Algorithm 2 (estimation of optimization criteria)

1. Sequentially consider the elements of the set G.
2. For each pair of states $(a_s, a_t) \in G$, make a trial merging.
3. Encode the internal states using one of the available methods.
4. Estimate the power consumption P_{st}.
5. Estimate the possibility of other states minimization M_{st}.
6. Return to the original FSM (before merging at step 2).
7. Execute steps 2-9 for all pairs of states in G.
8. Stop.

The estimate M_{st} is determined by the number of pairs of the FSM that can be merged after merging the pair (a_s, a_t). To provide the best possibilities for merging other states, M_{st} should be maximized. Using the method described in [11], the set G_{st} of pairs of states that can be merged upon merging the pair (a_s, a_t) must me find. After that, the parameter M_{st} can be calculated as the cardinality of the set G_{st} ($M_{st} = |G_{st}|$).

To estimate the power consumption of an FSM, we use the procedure proposed in [12] because it is the most universal and suitable for any hardware components. In addition, this procedure is adapted for the CMOS technology. The procedure described in [12] makes it possible to calculate the dynamic power consumption of an FSM based on the encoding of its internal states and the probability of occurrence of one (zero) at each input of the FSM. The power consumption depends on the encoding of internal states. For performing experiments the binary and one-hot encoding styles are used. In the one-hot encoding only one bit of the code has '1' value and all other bits have '0' value. In addition, the sequential encoding algorithm for low power design [13] is proposed to use.

According to [12], the power consumption of the FSM is determined by the rule:

$$P = \sum_{r=1}^{R} P_r = \frac{1}{2} V_{DD}^2 fC \sum_{r=1}^{R} N_r \tag{1}$$

where P_r is the power consumed by the flip-flop r, V_{DD} is the supply voltage, f is the frequency at which the FSM operates, C is the capacity of flip-flop output, and N_r is the activity of the flip-flop r.

Let k_i be a binary code of a state $a_i \in A$. Denote by k_r^i the value of the bit r in the code k_i of the state a_i. Then, the activity N_r of switching the memory flip-flop r of the FSM satisfies the equation

$$N_r = \sum_{m=1}^{M} \sum_{s=1}^{M} P(a_m \to a_s)(k_m^r \oplus k_s^r) \tag{2}$$

where $P(a_m \to a_s)$ is the probability of transiting from the state a_m to the state a_s (a_m, $a_s \in A$) and $\oplus$ is the XOR operation. The FSM must be encoded first to find the activity of each flip-flop.

The probability $P(a_m \to a_s)$ of transiting from the state a_m to the state a_s (a_m, $a_s \in A$) is given by the rule:

$$P(a_m \to a_s) = P(a_m) P(X(a_m, a_s)) \tag{3}$$

where $P(a_m)$ is the probability of the FSM to be in the state a_m and $P(X(a_m, a_s))$ is the probability of appearing the vector $X(a_m, a_s)$ initiating the transition from a_m to a_s at the input of the FSM.

The probability $P(X(a_m, a_s))$ of the vector $X(a_m, a_s)$ to appear at the input of the FSM is given by the rule:

$$P(X(a_m, a_s)) = \prod_{b=1}^{L} P(x_b = d) \tag{4}$$

where $d \in \{0, 1, \text{'-'}\}$ and $P(x_b = d)$ is the probability that the input variable x_b in the input vector $X(a_m, a_s)$ takes the value d. In this paper, we assume that 0 and 1 appear at each input of the FSM with the same probability; therefore, $P(x_b = 0) = P(x_b = 1) = 0.5$ and $P(x_b = \text{'-'}) = 1$ (the probability that 0 or 1 appear at each input of the FSM is equal one because symbol '-' means logic zero or logic one and any other values cannot appear at input). For a specific FSM, $P(x_b = 0)$ and $P(x_b = 1)$ may be different; however, it must hold that $P(x_b = 0) + P(x_b = 1) = 1$.

The probability $P(a_i)$ to find the FSM in each state a_i can be determined by solving the system of equations

$$P(a_i) = \sum_{m=1}^{M} P(a_m) P(X(a_m, a_i)), \ i \in [1, M] \tag{5}$$

If there are no transitions between the states a_m and a_i, then we set $P(X(a_m, a_i)) = 0$. If there are several transitions, then $P(X(a_m, a_i))$ is the sum of the probabilities of appearing each input vector initiating the transition from a_m to a_i.

System (5) is a system of M linear equations with M unknowns $P(a_1), \ldots, P(a_M)$, which can be solved by any available method, for example, by the Gauss method. Since the FSM is always in one of its internal states, it holds that

$$\sum_{m=1}^{M} P(a_m) = 1 \tag{6}$$

To simplify the solution of system (5), one equation in (5) can be replaced with (6).

4   Experimental Results

The method for minimization of incompletely specified finite state machines was implemented in a program called ZUBR. To estimate the efficiency of the offered method we used MCNC FSM benchmarks [14]. Each of tested FSM benchmarks was encoded using binary and one-hot encoding and sequential low power algorithm [13]. A power consumption estimation parameter was calculated using following values: output capacitance $C = 3pF$, frequency $f = 5MHz$, supply voltage $V_{CC} = 5V$, input probability $P(x_i = 1) = 0,5$. The power was calculated for the initial FSM, the FSM after minimization using method described in paper [11], the STAMINA program [3] and the method described in this paper.

The experimental results for binary encoding are presented in Table 1, where M_0 and P_0 are, respectively, the number of internal states and dissipated power (in mW) of the initial FSM; M_1 and P_1 are, respectively, the number of internal states and dissipated power (in mW) after minimization without taking in consideration power consumption (method described in [11]); M_2 and P_2 are, respectively, the number of internal states and dissipated power (in mW) after minimization using STAMINA and M_3, and P_3 are, respectively, the number of internal states and dissipated power (in mW) after minimization using proposed method (with taking in consideration power consumption). P_0/P_3, P_1/P_3, and P_2/P_3 are ratios of the corresponding parameters; and *Average* is the geometric mean value.

Table 1. The experimental results for binary encoding

Name	M_0	P_0	M_1	P_1	M_2	P_2	M_3	P_3	P_0/P_3	P_1/P_3	P_2/P_3
bbara	10	62.141	7	62.090	7	57.812	8	61.706	1.01	1.01	0.94
bbsse	16	226.014	13	226.014	13	232.976	13	226.014	1.00	1.00	1.03
beecount	7	113.275	5	91.889	4	75.116	5	91.889	1.23	1.00	0.82
lion9	14	192.569	4	93.750	4	109.375	4	84.375	2.28	1.11	1.30
s27	6	192.751	5	163.078	5	157.300	5	163.078	1.18	1.00	0.96
sse	16	226.014	13	226.014	13	232.976	13	226.014	1.00	1.00	1.03
tma	20	158.348	18	135.475	18	122.372	19	126.884	1.25	1.07	0.96
train11	12	101.902	4	78.125	4	93.750	6	68.452	1.49	1.14	1.37
Average									1.26	1.04	1.04

The analysis of Table 1 shows that application of the proposed method using binary encoding allows to reduce the number of internal states of the initial FSM. Similarly, the average reduction of the power consumption of the FSM makes 1.26 times, and on occasion (example *lion9*) 2.28 times. In comparison to method from [11] the number of states is higher in 3 cases, but the average reduction of the power consumption of the FSM makes 1.04 times, and on occasion (example *train11*) 1.14 times. In comparison to STAMINA the number of states is higher in 4 cases but the average reduction of the power consumption of the FSM makes 1.04 times, and on occasion (example *train11*) 1.37 times.

The experimental results for one-hot encoding are presented in Table 2, where all parameters have the same meaning as in Table 1.

Table 2. The experimental results for one-hot encoding

Name	M_0	P_0	M_1	P_1	M_2	P_2	M_3	P_3	P_0/P_3	P_1/P_3	P_2/P_3
bbara	10	83.476	7	82.325	7	82.236	7	82.325	1.01	1.00	1.00
bbsse	16	252.442	13	252.442	13	252.443	13	252.442	1.00	1.00	1.00
beecount	7	169.563	5	168.899	4	146.739	5	168.899	1.00	1.00	0.87
lion9	14	129.522	4	140.625	4	156.250	6	128.906	1.00	1.09	1.21
s27	6	255.251	5	226.102	5	226.103	5	226.102	1.13	1.00	1.00
sse	16	252.442	13	252.442	13	252.443	13	252.442	1.00	1.00	1.00
tma	20	130.134	18	140.384	18	99.033	19	119.320	1.09	1.18	0.83
train11	12	124.320	4	109.375	4	136.364	4	109.375	1.14	1.00	1.25
Average									1.05	1.03	1.01

The analysis of Table 2 shows that application of the proposed method using one-hot encoding allows to reduce the number of internal states of the initial FSM. Similarly, the average reduction of the power consumption of the FSM makes 1.05 times, and on occasion (example *train11*) 1.14 times. In comparison to method from [11] the number of states is higher in two cases, but the average reduction of the power consumption of the FSM makes 1.03 times, and on occasion (example *tma*) 1.18 times. In comparison to STAMINA the number of states is higher in 3 cases but the average reduction of the power consumption of the FSM makes 1.01 times, and on occasion (example *train11*) 1.25 times.

Table 3. The experimental results for encoding using the sequential algorithm

Name	M_0	P_0	M_1	P_1	M_2	P_2	M_3	P_3	P_0/P_3	P_1/P_3	P_2/P_3
bbara	10	52.389	7	52.664	7	52.664	8	52.171	1.00	1.01	1.01
bbsse	16	146.468	13	146.468	13	146.469	13	146.468	1.00	1.00	1.00
beecount	7	89.421	5	91.889	4	75.116	6	89.339	1.00	1.03	0.84
lion9	14	64.762	4	70.313	4	78.125	5	63.919	1.01	1.10	1.22
s27	6	168.330	5	148.634	5	148.634	5	148.634	1.13	1.00	1.00
sse	16	146.468	13	146.468	13	146.469	13	146.468	1.00	1.00	1.00
tma	20	65.250	18	71.117	18	53.106	19	63.970	1.02	1.11	0.83
train11	12	63.519	4	70.313	4	85.227	10	62.840	1.01	1.12	1.36
Average									1.02	1.04	1.02

The experimental results for encoding using the sequential low power algorithm [13] are presented in Table 3, where all parameters have the same meaning as in Table 1 and Table 2.

The analysis of Table 3 shows that application of the proposed method with low power encoding allows to reduce the number of internal states of the initial FSM on the average by 1.24 times, and on occasion (example *lion9*) by 1.75 times. Similarly, the average reduction of the power consumption of the FSM makes 1.02 times, and on occasion (example *s27*) 1.13 times. In comparison to method from [11] the number of states is 1.28 times higher, occasionally even 2.5 times higher (example *train11*). The average reduction of the power consumption of the FSM makes 1.04 times, and on occasion (example *train11*) 1.12 times. In comparison to STAMINA the number of states is higher, occasionally even 2.5 times higher (example *train11*). The average reduction of the power consumption of the FSM makes 1.02 times, and on occasion (example *train11*) 1.36 times.

It can be noticed that the greater reduction of states in most cases leads to increased power consumption of FSMs (in 62.5% of cases). Only for one example (*s27*) a FSM of lesser power consumption was obtained using the method from [11]. In contrast, using the method, taking into account the criterion of minimizing the power consumption, there are always obtained machines with less or the same power consumption as the initial machines. Additional minimization of the number of transitions in accordance with the method [11] does not cause further reduction in power consumption.

Table 4 presents the average power consumption for all three encoding styles. P_{AV0}, P_{AV1}, P_{AV2} and P_{AV3} parameters stand for the average power consumption of the initial FSM, the FSM after minimization using the method [11], the FSM after minimization using the STAMINA program and the method from this paper accordingly.

Table 4. Average power comparison for all tested encodings

Encoding	P_{AV0}	P_{AV1}	P_{AV2}	P_{AV3}
Binary	159126.75	134554.38	135209.63	131051.50
One-hot	174643.75	171574.25	168951.38	167476.38
Sequential	99575.88	99733.25	98226.25	96726.13

The analysis of the Table 4 shows that results obtained using presented approach are better than results obtained from the STAMINA and method from paper [11] in all styles of encoding used. Also, the one-hot encoding style was the most power consumable for all minimization algorithms used and sequential algorithm was the least power consumable method of encoding for all considered cases.

Table 5 presents ratios of power consumption for sequential encoding method in relation to binary encoding (P_{AVB}/P_{AVS}) and one-hot encoding (P_{AVO}/P_{AVS}) styles for all considered minimization methods, where parameters P_{AVB}, P_{AVO}, P_{AVS} are the average power consumption for binary encoding, one-hot encoding and sequential encoding, accordingly.

Table 5. Average power consumption ratios for all tested methods of minimization

Ratio	Initial FSM	Method [11]	STAMINA	This method
P_{AVB}/P_{AVS}	1.60	1.35	1.38	1.35
P_{AVO}/P_{AVS}	1.75	1.72	1.72	1.73

The analysis of the Table 5 shows that sequential algorithm for low power encoding is the most efficient in comparison to one-hot encoding (similar values for all minimization methods and not minimized FSMs). For binary encoding style, the power consumed by FSM is higher for the initial FSM than for FSMs after minimization.

5   Conclusion

Minimization of incompletely specified finite state machines is an important step in the FSM synthesis. In this paper we presented an efficient method for FSM minimization. In contrast to traditional approaches, the proposed method allows to minimize not only the number of FSM states and consumed power, but also the number of FSM transitions and input variables.

The main goal of this method is not to find the minimal number of states but the such representation of the FSM, which consumes minimal amount of power. Of course we obtain in most cases the worse results for state minimization in comparison to methods [11] and [3], but much better for power consumption. The most important conclusion from experiments is that the FSM with minimal number of states is not in most cases the best solution in respect of power consumption.

In the offered method of FSM minimization only two states merging is considered. The given algorithm can be modified so to merge a group of states containing more than two states. Besides, the further perfection of the presented algorithm can be implemented by consideration of incompletely specified values for the transition functions as additional conditions for merging possibility of FSM internal states.

Performed experiments are only the part of work on the complex minimization method [15], where not only power consumption, but also speed and area parameters are taken in consideration. In future, this method will serve to diminish power and cost and increase speed for FSM realization on programmable logic devices.

References

1. Paull, M., Unger, S.: Minimizing the number of states in incompletely specified state machines. IRE Trans. Electron. Comput. **EC-8**, 356–367 (1959)
2. Pfleeger, C.F.: State reduction in incompletely specified finite state machines. IEEE Trans. Comput. **C-22**, 1099–1102 (1973)
3. Rho, J.-K., Hachtel, G., Somenzi, F., Jacoby, R.: Exact and heuristic algorithms for the minimization of incompletely specified state machines. IEEE Trans. Computer-Aided Design **13**, 167–177 (1994)
4. Pena, J.M., Oliveira, A.L.: A new algorithm for exact reduction of incompletely specified finite state machines. IEEE Trans. Computer-Aided Design **18**, 1619–1632 (1999)
5. Gören, S., Ferguson, F.: On state reduction of incompletely specified finite state machines. Computers and Electrical Engineering **33**(1), 58–69 (2007)
6. Xia, Y., Almaini, A.E.A.: Genetic algorithm based state assignment for power and area optimization. IEE Proc. Comput. Digital Techn. **149**(4), 128–133 (2002)
7. Aiman, M., Sadiq, S.M., Nawaz, K.F.: Finite state machine state assignment for area and power minimization. In: Proc of the IEEE Int Symposium on Circuits and Systems (ISCAS), pp. 5303–5306. IEEE Computer Society (2006)
8. Chaudhury, S., Sistla, K.T., Chattopadhyay, S.: Genetic algorithm-based FSM synthesis with area-power trade-offs. Integration, VLSI J. **42**, 376–384 (2009)
9. Lindholm, C.: High frequency and low power semi-synchronous PFM state machine. In: Proc. of the IEEE Int. Symposium on Digital Object Identifier, pp. 1868–1871. IEEE Computer Society (2011)

10. Liu, Z., Arslan, T., Erdogan A.T.: An embedded low power reconfigurable fabric for finite state machine operations. In: Proc. of the Int. Symposium on Circuits and Systems (ISCAS), pp. 4374–4377. IEEE Computer Society (2006)
11. Klimowicz, A., Solov'ev, V.V.: Minimization of incompletely specified Mealy finite-state machines by merging two internal states. J. Comput. Syst. Sci. Int. **52**(3), 400–409 (2013)
12. Tsui, C.-Y., Monteiro, J., Devadas, S., Despain, A.M., Lin, B.: Power estimation methods for sequential logic circuits. IEEE Trans. VLSI Syst. **3**, 404–416 (1995)
13. Grzes, T.N., Solov'ev, V.V.: Sequential algorithm for low-power encoding internal states of finite state machines. J. Comput. Syst. Sci. Int **53**(1), 92–99 (2014)
14. Yang, S.: Logic synthesis and optimization benchmarks user guide. Version 3.0. Technical Report. North Carolina. Microelectronics Center of North Carolina (1991)
15. Solov'ev, V.V.: Complex minimization method for finite state machines implemented on programmable logic devices. J. Comput. Syst. Sci. Int. **53**(2), 186–194 (2014)

Designing of Hierarchical Structures
for Binary Comparators on FPGA/SoC

Valery Salauyou[✉] and Marek Gruszewski

Faculty of Computer Science, Bialystok University of Technology, Bialystok, Poland
{v.salauyou,m.gruszewski}@pb.edu.pl

Abstract. The article considers the general synthesis technique of hierarchical tree structures on FPGA/SoC for binary comparators. Designing of first level comparators is given. The best hierarchical comparator structure for the specific FPGA/SoC family is found empirically by experimental researches. The offered method allows reducing an area from 5.3% to 43.0%, and for high bitwidth comparators (with an input word length 1024) by 2.225 times. In the conclusion additional opportunities of the offered method are marked, and main directions of further researches are presented.

Keywords: Binary comparator · Synthesis · FPGA · SoC · Hierarchical tree structure · Verilog language

1   Introduction

At present, there is a constant tendency to increase the length of words in computer systems. The length of words increases rapidly in telecommunication systems and data transmission and processing devices. On the other hand, integrated circuits of a programmable logic such as Complex Programmable Logic Devices (CPLDs), Field Programmable Gate Arrays (FPGAs), and System on Chips (SoCs) are widely used in building digital systems [1]. Digital systems as a rule include different standard functional blocks one of which is the comparator of binary numbers [2]. The binary comparator is one of the fundamental components in digital systems with many applications such as the decoding of the microprocessor instruction sets, the renaming of the register files in a superscalar system, and the number magnitude comparison in an arithmetic logic unit.

When high bitwidth comparators are constructed, it is sufficient to implement only function G "greater-than" and function E "equal", because function L "less-than" can always be determined on the basis of two first functions: $L = \overline{G} \,\&\, \overline{E}$.

The design problem of binary comparators is examined in many articles. In [3], the comparator is offered to build like an adder by using of a generate function and a propagate function which can be realized by the Manchester carry chain.

In some designs, a pipeline processing of signals and a mechanism of power off are used to increase performance and reduction of energy consumption. In [4], the comparator using two-phase clocking dynamic CMOS logic with modified non-inverting all-

© IFIP International Federation for Information Processing 2015
K. Saeed and W. Homenda (Eds.): CISIM 2015, LNCS 9339, pp. 386–396, 2015.
DOI: 10.1007/978-3-319-24369-6_32

N-transistor block is presented. The compared output of two 64-bit binary numbers is performed in 3.5 clock cycles. In [5], the comparator is based on the priority-encoding (PE) algorithm. The circuit is realized with a latch-based two-stage pipelined structure. The comparator designed with the proposed techniques is 16% faster, 50% smaller, and 79% more power efficient as compared with the all-n-transistor comparator [4]. In [6], the prefix tree structure's area and power consumption can be improved by leveraging two-input multiplexers at each level and generate-propagate logic cells at the first level, which takes advantage of one's complement addition. In [7], a priority encoding (parallel-MSB-checking) algorithm along with a new priority encoder design and a MUX-based comparator structure is proposed; the method allows to increase performance by 22% in comparison with [5]. In [8], other architectures use a multiplexer-based structure to split a comparator into two comparator stages; the method allows to increase performance by 28% in comparison with [7]. In [9], to reduce the long delays suffered by bitwise ripple designs, an enhanced architecture incorporates an algorithm that uses no arithmetic operations. This scheme detects the larger operand by determining which operand possesses the leftmost 1 bit after pre-encoding, before supplying the operands to a bitwise competition logic (BCL) structure. The BCL structure partitions the operands into 8-b blocks and the result for each block is input into a multiplexer to determine the final comparison decision. In [10], the comparator project combines a tree structure with a two phase domino clocking structure for speed enhancement. In [11], binary comparator is based on a novel parallel-prefix algorithm. The proposed design shows an energy dissipation reduction of 23% and a speed improvement of 7%. In [12], the comparator exploits a novel scalable parallel prefix structure that leverages the comparison outcome of the most significant bit, proceeding bitwise toward the least significant bit only when the compared bits are equal. This method reduces dynamic power dissipation by eliminating unnecessary transitions in a parallel prefix structure.

All of the aforementioned works achieve high-performance operations using dynamic logic. While dynamic logic has demonstrated superior performance, as compared with static logic, it is not suitable for low-power operation. On the other hand, using of static logic allows reducing power consumption significantly. In [13], a new tree structure comparator with a pre-encoding scheme is proposed; one is particularly suitable for implementation on static logic to ensure low-power consumption. In [14], some modifications have been done in binary comparator [13] design to improve the speed of the circuit. In [15], a single-cycle tree-based binary comparator with constant-delay (CD) logic is presented. The proposed comparator with CD logic is 20% faster or 17% more energy-efficient compared to a comparator implemented with just the static logic.

In [16], the design of digital comparator with two different parallel architectures is proposed. These comparators are realized in Verilog and simulated with Xilinx ISE 8.2i platform. Simulation results show that the first proposed architecture has 23.769 % less combinational delay and the second proposed architecture has a combinational delay of 35.218 % less compared to the traditional design.

Reviewing of known methods of comparator designing showed that the majority of the methods (except for [16]) are intended to implement of the comparators on application specific integrated circuits (ASICs) and are not suitable for designing the comparators on the programmable logic.

This paper presents a universal method for designing of hierarchical tree structures of comparators on the programmable logic. Universality of the offered method is that the design of the comparator is described entirely in Verilog language; it is applicable to all classes of the programmable logic: CPLD, FPGS and SoC; it is also applicable to all CMOS process. The offered method allows changing the number of logical levels in a tree structure of the comparator in a broad range, as a result the user can select a trade-off of cost against performance. The comparator diagram is completely combinatorial circuit which does not contain clock signals therefore it does not require additional circuits for generating clock signals (unlike the considered known methods). Besides, in the offered approach there are no bitwise carries, and parallelism of the diagram provides high speed.

Section 2 executes the review of related researches. Section 3 describes the general synthesis technique the hierarchical structures for the binary comparators. Section 4 considers synthesis the comparators of the first level. Section 5 discusses experimental results. Conclusions presents additional opportunities of the offered method and also represent the main directions of further researches.

2   Related Research

This work is a continuation of researches to find the effective design methods for binary comparators based on a programmable logic [17,18,19,20]. In [17], the following methods of the comparator synthesis are considered: parallel, sequential, parallel-sequential, and with adder using. For each method two ways of implementation are offered: graphic and in the AHDL (Altera Hardware Description Language) language. The experimental researches are performed by the Altera MAX+PLUS II platform for 64-bit comparators and the results are compared to the Altera parametrized function lpm_compare.

In [18], the method of the comparator design in the form of a hierarchical structure is offered. The experimental researches are executed by Altera MAX+PLUS II platform. The offered method is compared to the sequential and parallel methods [17], and also to the Altera parametrized function lpm_compare, and to the method that implemented in the AHDL language compiler. At the first level of the hierarchical structure the 4-bit comparators are used. These comparators are built by four methods: the lpm_compare function, the AHDL language, and the parallel and sequential method [17].

In [19], the hierarchical structures of 64-bit comparators were researched by Quartus II 13.1 platform for Altera CPLDs and FPGAs. The 4-bit comparators formed a first level of the hierarchical structure. Two methods for building the first level comparators are used: Verilog language and pm_compare function. A connection of the comparators in the hierarchical structures for different configurations was executed by the graphics editor of Quartus II platform. By this method 15 hierarchical structures of the 64-bit comparator were constructed. The second group of the comparators is made by similar structures, but LCELL [21] buffers were set on outputs of the comparators of the first level. Such parameters as the implementation cost, the performance, and the power consumption were researched. Results were compared to the lpm_compare function. For CPLDs the offered method allows reducing the implementation cost by 32%, the delay by 44%, and the power consumption by 18%. For FPGAs the method allows reducing the implementation cost by 17% and the delay by 26%, thus power consumption does not change.

In [20], the combined technique was used for designing the 128-bit and 256-bit comparators. The 64-bit comparators made the first level. The 64-bit comparators were built by a parallel-sequential method [17] from sections on 2-, 4-, 8-, 16-, and 32-bit. The hierarchical structure of the 128-bit and 256-bit comparators was designed by the graphics editor of Quartus II platform. The offered method, in comparison with the lpm_compare function, allows reducing the implementation cost by 13% and the delay by 18% for 128-bit comparators, and for 256-bit comparators, respectively, by 19% and by 54%.

In [18,19,20], the methods of designing comparators generally on 64 bits were considered. In [18], for researches the outdated MAX+PLUS II platform and the AHDL language that supported only by Altera tools was used. In [18,19], the lpm_compare function and the AHDL language were used to implement comparators of the first level. Besides, the graphics editor of Quartus II platform was used to design hierarchical structures of comparators. The specified shortcomings do not allow the synthesis method [18,19,20] of the hierarchical comparator structures to be the universal method claiming for broad application.

This paper offers the synthesis method of the hierarchical structures of the high bitwidth comparators in Verilog language. This method has next distinctive features: all elements of hierarchical structure are described only in Verilog language, the graphics editor is not used, and the lpm_compare function is not used. Therefore the offered method is universal and can be used for the implementation of the binary comparators on any integrated circuits (CPLD, FPGA, SoC or ASIC) by design tools of any vendors. Single restriction is that these design tools must support the Verilog language.

3   A General Synthesis Technique of the Hierarchical Structures for Binary Comparators

The proposed hierarchical structure for binary comparators is shown in Fig. 1. It consists of modules of the first level comparators $CMP_1,...,CMP_N$ and the combinatorial circuit CL. Each comparator of the first level CMP_n represents the binary T-bit comparator which realizes two functions: the function "greater-than" g_n and the function "equal" e_n, where $n = \overline{1, N}$.

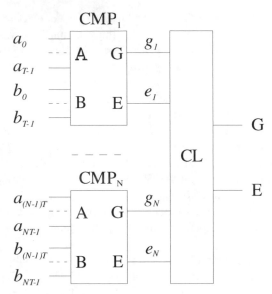

Fig. 1. The generalized hierarchical two-level structure of the comparator C_M_NxT

The combinatorial circuit CL calculates values of the output functions "greater-than" G and "equal" E for entire hierarchical structure. Inputs for the combinatorial circuit CL are values of output functions of first level comparators. For computing the values of the G and E functions the following equations are used:

$$G = g_N + e_N \& g_{N-1} + e_N \& e_{N-1} \& g_{N-2} + \ldots + e_N \& e_{N-1} \& \ldots \& e_2 \& g_1; \qquad (1)$$

and

$$E = e_1 \& e_2 \& \ldots \& e_N. \qquad (2)$$

The hierarchical structure in Fig. 1 is described by the formula:

$$C\_M\_NxT, \qquad (3)$$

where C is the abbreviation of the word "Comparator", M is the width (the number of bits) of input words of the comparator, N is the number of the first level comparators, and T is the width of input words of first level comparators. In the formula (3) the following condition must be executed: M = NT.

The hierarchical two-level structure in Fig. 1 can be used as comparators of the first level. By similar way the hierarchical structure for the comparator with the high value of the M can be constructed. The example of the multi-level hierarchical design for the comparator C_16_2x8_2x4_2x2 is shown in Fig. 2. Here the 2-bit comparators C_2 are located at the first level, and the combinatorial circuits CL make all subsequent comparator levels.

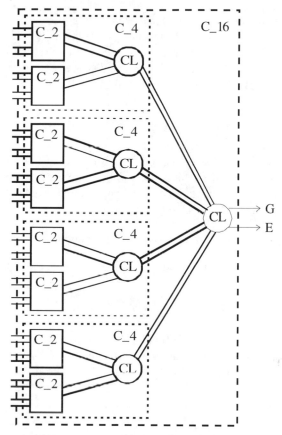

Fig. 2. Implementation a multi-level structure of the comparator *C_16_4x4_2x2*

The generalized hierarchical structure of the binary comparators is described by the formula:

$$C\_M\_N_Q x T_Q\_N_{Q-1} x T_{Q-1}\_ \ldots \_N_1 x T_1, \tag{4}$$

where Q is the number of levels in the comparator structure, N_q is the number of the comparator modules on the level q, and T_q is the bitwidth for comparators on the level q, $q = \overline{1, Q}$.

In a formula (4) the following conditions must always be satisfied:

$$M = N_Q T_Q;$$

$$T_q = N_{q-1} T_{q-1}, \forall\, q = \overline{1, Q}. \tag{5}$$

The number Q of the levels in the formula (4) determines a depth of the combinatorial circuit CL in Fig. 1. Taking into account the first level comparators, the total number of the logic levels in the hierarchical structure (4) is equaled of the Q + 1.

The synthesis method of the hierarchical structures of comparators is based on the formula (4) and the conditions (5). Note that several hierarchical structures can correspond to one comparator. These structures can have the different numbers of levels and vertices at each level. Besides, the hierarchical structures can have different comparators at the first level which are distinguished by the lengths of input words.

4   The Synthesis of the First Level Comparators

In the considered approach for all hierarchical structures of the comparators at the first level it is offered to use the 2-bit comparators. Let $A = (a_2, a_1)$ and $B = (b_2, b_1)$ be input words of the 2-bit comparator. The Boolean function "equal" for the 2-bit comparator is not minimized and it has the form:

$$E = \bar{a}_2 \& \bar{a}_1 \& \bar{b}_2 \& \bar{b}_1 + \bar{a}_2 \& a_1 \& \bar{b}_2 \& b_1 + a_2 \& a_1 \& b_2 \& b_1 + a_2 \& \bar{a}_1 \& b_2 \& \bar{b}_1. \tag{6}$$

The Boolean function "greater-than" for the 2-bit comparator after minimization has the following form:

$$G = a_2 \& \bar{b}_2 + a_1 \& \bar{b}_2 \& \bar{b}_1 + a_2 \& a_1 \& \bar{b}_1. \tag{7}$$

The logical equations (6) and (7) for the 2-bit comparators of the first level, the logical equations (1) and (2) for the combinatorial circuit CL in Fig. 1, and the formula (4) with constraints (5) are used to build the hierarchical tree structures of the comparators.

The hierarchical structure by the nature has the smallest time delay of the signal passing in comparison with the linear decomposition or the sequential implementation. Therefore it is possible to expect that hierarchical structures of the designed comparator will have low implementation cost and high performance.

It is an open question: what formula of the hierarchical comparator structure is the best at implementation for a particular comparator bitwidth on specific FPGA family. The response to this question is defined empirically by experimental researches.

5   Experimental Results

The following designs of hierarchical comparator structures were developed in Verilog language to check the efficiency of the offered method:

one structure of the 4-bit comparator

C_4_2x2;
two structures of the 8-bit comparators

C_8_2x4_2x2;
C_8_4x2;

four structures of the 16-bit comparators

C_16_2x8_2x4_2x2;
C_16_2x8_4x2;
C_16_4x4_2x2;
C_16_8x2;

eight structures of the 32-bit comparators

C_32_2x16_2x8_2x4_2x2;
C_32_2x16_2x8_4x2;
C_32_2x16_4x4_2x2;
C_32_2x16_8x2;
C_32_4x8_2x4_2x2;
C_32_4x8_4x2;
C_32_8x4_2x2;
C_32_16x2;

and similar 16 structures of the 64-bit comparators.

From the designed hierarchical comparator structures on 8-, 16-, 32-, and 64-bits the structures with the best results in implementation cost were selected. The following comparator structures were constructed from the selected comparator structures:

21 structures of the 128-bit comparators;
25 structures of the 256-bit comparators;
17 structures of the 512-bit comparators;
17 structures of the 1024-bit comparators.

For designing the hierarchical structures of comparators on 128 bits all the structures of comparators on 8, 16 and 32 bit, and the structure C_4_2x2 (in all 15 structures) were considered. From the structures of comparators on 64 bits the 6 structures, which are the best at an implementation cost at least for one family FPGA/SoC, were selected. Thus it was constructed 21 hierarchical structures of comparators on 128 bits. The hierarchical structures of comparators on 256-, 512-, and 1024 bits were similarly built.

All designed hierarchical comparator structures are described in Verilog and realized with Altera Quartus II 13.1 platform. The implementation cost was measured by the number of the functional generators LUT (Look-Up Table). The results received by the hierarchical comparator structures were compared to the standard (traditional) description of the comparator in Verilog language [22]. Note that the results obtained by the standard description exactly match the results received by the parametrized function lpm_compare.

Some families FPGA/SoC have the identical implementation cost for the offered hierarchical structures of comparators and for the standard description. Therefore all FPGA/SoC families can be divided into three groups:

group 1 – Arria II GX, Stratix III, and Stratix IV;

group 2 – MAX II, MAX V, Cyclone III, and Cyclone IV;
group 3 – Arria V GZ and Cyclone V.

The results of experimental researches are given in Table 1, where C_m is the comparator with a width of words on m bits, C_S is the implementation cost in case of standard approach, C_H is the smallest implementation cost received by using hierarchical structures, and C_S/C_H is a relation of the corresponding parameters.

Table 1. Research results of the hierarchical comparator structures for Altera FPGA/SoC

Comparator	Arria II GX Stratix III Stratix IV			MAX II MAX V Cyclone III Cyclone IV			Arria V GZ Cyclone V		
	C_S	C_H	C_S/C_H	C_S	C_H	C_S/C_H	C_S	C_H	C_S/C_H
C_2	2	2	1.000	2	2	1.000	2	2	1.000
C_4	4	4	1.000	6	6	1.000	3	3	1.000
C_8	8	9	0.889	13	11	1.182	6	6	1.000
C_16	20	19	1.053	27	24	1.125	12	12	1.000
C_32	41	37	1.108	53	48	1.104	28	23	1.217
C_64	82	74	1.108	107	96	1.115	59	46	1.283
C_128	141	149	0.946	213	194	1.098	119	96	1.240
C_256	254	302	0.841	427	392	1.089	236	165	1.430
C_512	521	587	0.888	853	794	1.074	(1)	(1)	-
C_1024	2645	1189	2.225	1707	1590	1.074	(1)	(1)	-

(1) – the compiler issues the message: not enough external outputs

The analysis of Table 1 shows that in all groups for comparators C_2 and C_4 the standard approach and the proposed hierarchical method show identical results. In group 1 the hierarchical method is better for comparators C_16, C_32 and C_64, and the implementation cost decreases from 5.3% to 10.8%. For the comparator C_1024 the hierarchical method exceeds the standard method by 2.225 times. In group 2 since the comparator C_8 and to the comparator C_1024 the hierarchical method is better than the standard method, and the implementation cost decreases from 7.4% to 18.2%.In group 3 the hierarchical method is better than the standard method for comparators from C_32 to C_256, and the implementation cost decreases from 21.7% to 43.0%.

In this work the efficiency of the considered synthesis method of the comparators was researched only concerning the implementation cost. Similar approach can be also used to minimize the delay or the power consumption.

6   Conclusions

In the provided approach 2-bit comparators were used at the first level of hierarchical structures. Comparators with different number of bits (e.g. 3, 4, 5) can also be used at the first level.

The offered synthesis method of hierarchical comparator structures can be also used to implement of comparators in other languages of hardware description, for example VHDL and SystemVerilog. The provided method can be used to find the best hierarchical comparator structure of a certain size for a specific FPGA or SoC family. The offered method can be enhanced by using of architectural features of the FPGA/SoC, for example fast carry chains, fast cascade chains, buffers LCELL.

Acknowledgements. This research was partially supported by Bialystok University of Technology, Poland, grant no. S/WI/1/2013.

References

1. Salauyou, V.V.: Designing of digital systems based on programmable logic integrated circuits. Hot line-Telecom, Moscow (2007) (Соловьев В.В. Проектирование цифровых систем на основе программируемых логических интегральных схем. - Москва: Горячая линия-Телеком, 2007. - 636 с. Второе издание.)
2. Salauyou, V.V.: Designing of functional blocks of digital systems on programmable logic devices. Bestprint, Minsk (1996) (Соловьев В.В. Проектирование функциональных узлов цифровых систем на программируемых логических устройствах. - Минск: Бестпринт, 1996. - 252 с.)
3. Guangjie, W., Shimin, S., Lijiu, J.: New efficient design of digital comparator. In: 2nd International Conference on ASIC, pp. 263–266. IEEE Press, Shanghai (1996)
4. Wang, C.C., Wu, C.F., Tsai, K.C.: 1 GHz 64-bit high-speed comparator using ANT dynamic logic with two-phase clocking. IEE Proceedings-Computers and Digital Techniques. IET **145**(6), 433–436 (1998)
5. Huang, C.H., Wang, J.S.: High-performance and power-efficient CMOS comparators. IEEE Journal of Solid-State Circuits **38**(2), 254–262 (2003)
6. Cheng, S.W.: A high-speed magnitude comparator with small transistor count. In: 10th IEEE International Conference on Electronics, Circuits and Systems, vol. 3, pp. 1168–1171. IEEE Press, Sharjah (2003)
7. Lam, H., Tsui, C.: High performance single clock cycle CMOS comparator. In: IEEE International Symposium on Circuits and Systems, pp.779–782. IEEE Press, Island of Kos (2006)
8. Lam, H.M., Tsui, C.Y.: A MUX-based high-performance single-cycle CMOS comparator. IEEE Transactions on Circuits and Systems II: Express Briefs **54**(7), 591–595 (2007)
9. Kim, J.Y., Yoo, H.J.: Bitwise competition logic for compact digital comparator. In: IEEE Asian Solid-State Circuits Conference, pp. 59–62. IEEE Press, Jeju (2007)
10. Perri, S., Corsonello, P.: Fast low-cost implementation of single-clock-cycle binary comparator. IEEE Transactions on Circuits and Systems II: Express Briefs **55**(12), 1239–1243 (2008)
11. Frustaci, F., Perri, S., Lanuzza, M., Corsonello, P.: A new low-power high-speed single-clock-cycle binary comparator. In: 2010 IEEE International Symposium on Circuits and Systems, pp. 317–320. IEEE Press, Paris (2010)
12. Abdel-Hafeez, S., Gordon-Ross, A., Parhami, B.: Scalable digital CMOS comparator using a parallel prefix tree. IEEE Transactions on Very Large Scale Integration (VLSI) Systems **21**(11), 1989–1998 (2013)

13. Chuang, P., Li, D., Sachdev, M.: A low-power high-performance single-cycle tree-based 64-bit binary comparator. IEEE Transactions on Circuits and Systems II: Express Briefs **59**(2), 108–112 (2012)
14. Hauser, A., Chichester, I.: High-Speed 64-Bit Binary Comparator using Two Stages. European Journal of Engineering and Innovation **11**(2), 29–38 (2013)
15. Chuang, P.I.J., Sachdev, M., Gaudet, V.C.: A 167-ps 2.34-mW Single-Cycle 64-Bit Binary Tree Comparator With Constant-Delay Logic in 65-nm CMOS. IEEE Transactions on Circuits and Systems I: Regular Papers **61**(1), 160–171 (2014)
16. Deb, S., Chaudhury, S.: High-speed comparator architectures for fast binary comparison. In: Third International Conference on Emerging Applications of Information Technology, pp. 454–457. IEEE Press, Kolkata (2012)
17. Salauyou, V.V., Posrednikova, A.A.: An implementation on programmable logic comparators with high bitwidth. Chip-News, Engineering microelectronics. 9, 20–25 (2005) (Соловьев В.В., Посредникова А.А. Реализация на ПЛИС компараторов большой размерности. – Chip-News, Инженерная микроэлектроника, 2005, №9, с.20-25.)
18. Solov'ev, V.V., Posrednikova, A.A.: The hierarchical method of synthesis of large-capacity comparators with the use of programmable logic integrated circuits. Journal of Communications Technology and Electronics. **54**(3), 338–346 (2009)
19. Salauyou, V., Gruszewski, M.: An implementation on CPLD/FPGA hierarchical comparators by parallel-sequential synthesis. Measurements, Automation, Control. **60**(7), 474–476 (2014). (Salauyou V., Gruszewski M. Implementacja w strukturach CPLD/FPGA komparatorów hierarchicznych z wykorzystaniem równoległo-szeregowej syntezy // Pomiary, Automatyka, Kontrola, V.60, nr 7, 2014, s. 474-476.)
20. Salauyou, V., Gruszewski, M.: Hierarchical comparators – describe styles, synthesis results. Measurements, Automation, Control **60**(7), 498–500 (2014). (Salauyou V., Gruszewski M. Komparatory hierarchiczne – metody opisu, wyniki syntezy // Pomiary, Automatyka, Kontrola, V.60, nr 7, 2014, s. 498-500.)
21. Designing with Low-Level Primitives: User Guide. Altera Corporation, San Jose (2007)
22. Salauyou, V.: Bases of the hardware description language Verilog. Hot line-Telecom, Moscow (2014) (Соловьев В.В. Основы языка проектирования цифровой аппаратуры Verilog. - Москва: Горячая линия-Телеком, 2014. - 208 с.)

Pattern Recognition and Image Processing

Registration and Sequencing of Vessels Section Images at Macroscopic Levels

Aneta Górniak and Ewa Skubalska-Rafajłowicz[(✉)]

Faculty of Electronics, Department of Computer Engineering,
Wrocław University of Technology, Wrocław, Poland
{aneta.gorniak,ewa.rafajlowicz}@pwr.edu.pl

Abstract. In this paper we present a new approach to registration and sequencing of microscope images obtained from serial sections of large blood vessels at macroscopic levels of magnification. It is assumed that subsequent section images may be located inadequately in the image series. Translations and rotations of the object of interest can occur. Some images can be also reflected vertically or horizontally. The proposed algorithm is based on the center of gravity estimation and the phase-only correlation (POC) and uses standard image normalization as a preprocessing procedure. The method is fully-automatic and robust to common image distortions. The quality of registration is measured by the mean value of the sum of absolute difference between images. This criterion can be used also for slide images sequencing, when the image acquisition is performed independently for each section. A set of experiments, carried out using sampled microscopic images of a vein section, proves experimentally the effectiveness of the proposed approach.

Keywords: Image processing · Microscopic image · Rigid image registration · Image normalization · Object matching · Phase-only correlation

1 Introduction

Medical images are widely used within healthcare for diagnosis, planning treatment, guiding treatment and monitoring disease progression. In many cases, multiple images are acquired from subjects at different times and with different imaging modalities. There is also a notion of comparing images obtained from patient cohorts in place of single subjects captured multiple times [6].

A medical image can refer to various types of images that possess very different underlying physical principles and very different applications. It covers images varying from microscopic images of histological sections to video images used for remote consultation. It becomes crucial to find ways of accurately aligning the information in the different images and providing tools for visualizing the combined images.

© IFIP International Federation for Information Processing 2015
K. Saeed and W. Homenda (Eds.): CISIM 2015, LNCS 9339, pp. 399–410, 2015.
DOI: 10.1007/978-3-319-24369-6_33

Image registration is a very important step in processing sequences of images [6], [11], [16]. A large number of algorithms have been developed to perform registration of medical and biological images. Image registration is the process of aligning multiple images representing the same scene that were captured at a different time, at or by a different set of modalities [6]. The process involves the transformation of the coordinate systems of the reference image and the input image into the joint coordinate system. It must ensure that the corresponding structures are precisely located at the same positions in the images to be matched [3]. One type of approach in image registration consists of estimating the geometric transformations of translation, rotation, scaling or perspective between the reference and input images, based on the pixel intensity. The process is iterative and aims to optimize the elected measure of similarity between the images. Other approaches may involve the identification of corresponding points or areas in the images [5], [11], [16].

The most common problems of medical image registration cover the varying deformations and distortions of the imagined tissues, the alignment of images with different dimensionality, the alignment of images from different subjects or the geometric distortion formed in the imaging process.

The other set of problems is finding the correct ways of assessing the registration accuracy. The required accuracy may vary between applications. The most promising approach in ensuring acceptable accuracy is visual assessment of the registered images before they are used [6], [9].

Image registration has application in many fields. It is used in remote sensing for multi-spectral classification, environment monitoring, change detection or weather forecasting. In medicine, it is used in signal fusion from multiple sources to acquire more accurate information about the patient, to monitor tumor growth or to compare patient data with anatomical atlases [6]. In [4], a method of MRI image registration with sub-pixel accuracy and its application in fMRI is presented. Other applications in biomedical image registration are presented in [2], [10].

In this paper we present a new approach to the registration and sequencing of microscope images [9], [13], [16] obtained from serial sections of large blood vessels at macroscopic levels of magnification. It is assumed that subsequent section images may be located inadequately in the image series. Furthermore, not only translations and rotations of the object of interest can occur. Some images can be also reflected vertically or horizontally. In general, the process of acquiring the data is imperfect and leads to geometric and pixel intensity-based distortions in the images. Due to the macroscopic levels of magnification (less than 100) we can restrict the rigid registration of images, since object deformation obtained during sectioning is here negligible. The small differences between geometry of the subsequent images should not be corrected, because these differences are caused by the natural morphological structure changes and their viability depends on section thickness. The proposed algorithm is based on the center of gravity estimation [1] and the phase-only correlation (POC) [3], [8], [15], [12] and it uses a standard image normalization as preprocessing procedure [7].

The method is fully-automatic and robust to common image distortions. The quality of registration is measured by the mean value of the sum of absolute difference between images (23). This criterion can be used also for slide image sequencing, when image acquisition is performed independently for each section.

In the next Section the problem of microscopic section images registration is formulated. Section 3 provides a concise description of specialized methods used in the proposed registration procedure. Section 4 presents the detailed registration procedure adapted to the blood vessel section images obtained at macroscopic levels of magnification. Section 5 describes a set of experiments for evaluating the performance of the proposed algorithm. The experimental data consists of two sets of microscopic images containing vein sections. Finally, in Section 6 some brief conclusions are presented.

2   Image Registration

An image is a two-dimensional sampled function $f(x, y)$ with a discrete set of coordinates $x = 1, ..., N_1$ and $y = 1, ..., N_2$, where N_1 and N_2 denote the width and the height of the image. Color intensity of the pixels in the image takes up values from the interval $[0, 1]$. Images are presented in greyscale.

Images f and g represent the same type of an object, captured with the same or different modalities. The acquisition can result in the appearance of differences between acquired objects. We may classify the differences into the following categories: naturally occurring differences, noise-induced differences, geometric distortions and intensity distortions.

The first type of differences stems from the two acquired objects being naturally different from each other. It translates into the lack of correspondence between the pixels of the two objects and the difference in intensity values of those pixels. The difference is described with the value $\beta(x, y)$

$$\beta(x, y) = | f(x, y) - g(x, y)|. \qquad (1)$$

If the objects in the images are non-identical, the sum of $\beta(x, y)$ values will be grater than zero. These differences should be retained, because they contain true information about subsequent changes of the morphological structure under consideration.

The other type of naturally occurring differences comes in the form of noise induced during the acquisition process. This type of difference is always present in the images.

The second group of differences, called distortions, corresponds to geometric displacement of the captured scene and disparity of intensity levels in the image.

The difference in intensity levels of the images results in the objects appearing in the images with varying intensity. Let us consider that each image's intensity changes can be described with parameters α and γ, which are called scaling factor and offset, respectively. The intensity transformation is denoted with $\mathcal{F}$ and describes the following dependency

$$\mathcal{F}\{f(x, y)\} = \alpha f(x, y) + \gamma. \qquad (2)$$

The result of the intensity transformation $\mathcal{F}$ of the image $f(x,y)$ is the image $\alpha f(x,y) + \gamma$. These image differences can be easily removed by the image normalization procedure [7].

The geometric distortion in the acquired objects requires the geometric transformation to map an object from one image to another, because the corresponding points in the images do not match the corresponding points on the objects in these images. The adequate geometric transformation is denoted with $\mathcal{T}$ and maps both position and the intensity at that position from one image to another. This dependency is given by

$$f(x,y) = \mathcal{T}\{g(x,y)\}. \tag{3}$$

We assume that the image $g(x,y)$ is a translated, rotated and possibly reflected (vertically or horizontally) replica of the image $f(x,y)$.

The difference between these two images can be described by an unknown displacement function $(d_1(x), d_2(y))$. So, we obtain

$$g(x,y) = f(x + d_1(x), y + d_2(y)) \tag{4}$$

or

$$f(x,y) = g(x - d_1(x), y - d_2(y)).$$

The objective of the image registration is to estimate the affine displacement function $(d_1(x), d_2(y))$. We assume that the displacement is a result (sum) of geometric transformations of translation, rotation and reflection in a prescribed order. We also assume that the values of the displacement $(d_1(x), d_2(y))$ can be obtained by estimating the parameters of the respective composite geometric transformations.

1. Rotation of the image by the angle θ around the point (x_0, y_0)

$$f(x,y) = g(x_\theta, y_\theta) \tag{5}$$

where x_θ and y_θ are given by

$$\begin{aligned} x_\theta &= (x - x_0) \cdot \cos\theta + (y - y_0) \cdot \sin\theta + x_0 \\ y_\theta &= -(x - x_0) \cdot \sin\theta + (y - y_0) \cdot \cos\theta + y_0. \end{aligned} \tag{6}$$

2. Translation of the image by the translation vector (τ_1, τ_2)

$$f(x,y) = g(x - \tau_1, y - \tau_2). \tag{7}$$

3. Reflection of the image. We consider two types of reflections: vertical and horizontal. Reflection about a vertical axis of abscissa x_0 is

$$f(x,y) = g(-x + 2x_0, y) \tag{8}$$

and the reflection about a horizontal axis of ordinate y_0 is

$$f(x,y) = g(x, -y + 2y_0). \tag{9}$$

The displacement $(d_1(x), d_2(y))$ is a sum of displacements generated by each of the transformations. The order by which the transformations are performed is significant and it may influence the accuracy of the results of displacement function estimation.

3   Used Methods

We have used normalization of the intensity levels in the image as a preprocessing step.

3.1   Normalization of the Intensity Levels in the Image

The purpose of the normalization of the intensity levels in the image is elimination of the intensity-based distortion so the images that differ only in intensity become identical [7]. Let f_1 and f_2 be two images which differ in the pixel intensity space (see (2)). For arbitrary values of α and γ, the following dependency holds

$$\mathcal{N}\{\alpha_1 f + \gamma_1\} = \mathcal{N}\{\alpha_2 f + \gamma_2\} \tag{10}$$

where α_1 and α_2 are the intensity levels of the images f_1 and f_2, and γ_1 and γ_2 are offsets of pixel intensities in both images, respectively. $\mathcal{N}$ denotes the normalization function of the intensity in the image.

To normalize the intensity level of the image, the influence of α and γ coefficients needs to be eliminated. The standard normalization function [7] is given by

$$\mathcal{N}\{f(x,y)\} = \frac{\alpha f(x,y) - \alpha\mu}{\alpha f_{max} - \alpha f_{min}} = \frac{\alpha(f(x,y) - \mu)}{\alpha(f_{max} - f_{min})} = \frac{f(x,y) - \mu}{f_{max} - f_{min}}, \tag{11}$$

where f_{max} is a maximum intensity value and f_{min} is a minimum intensity value in the image. The μ parameter is the mean value of intensity in the image

$$\mu = \frac{1}{N_1 N_2} \sum_{x,y} f(x,y) \tag{12}$$

where $\sum_{x,y}$ denotes $\sum_{x=1}^{N_1} \sum_{y=1}^{N_2}$.

3.2   The Center of Gravity of the Object in the Image

Calculating the position of the center of gravity in an image allows us for detection of the object and estimation of its position in the image. In practice it allows us to reduce the size of the processed image to the area where the object is localized.

We assume that a set of coordinates (x, y) in the image is the center of the object to be detected. A detection algorithm, defined with a probability-based function $c(x, y)$, which results in a local maximum of $c(x, y)$ around the center of each detected object [1].

For an object in a greyscale image the center of gravity is weighted and is defined as

$$(x_c, y_c) = \left(\frac{\sum_{x,y} x w(x,y)}{\sum_{x,y} w(x,y)}, \frac{\sum_{x,y} y w(x,y)}{\sum_{x,y} w(x,y)} \right) \tag{13}$$

where $\sum_{x,y}$ describes $\sum_{x=1}^{N_1}\sum_{y=1}^{N_2}$. The weight function $w(x,y)$ is defined as

$$w(x,y) = a(f(x,y) - m) \tag{14}$$

where $m < \min_{x,y}(f(x,y))$, when $a > 0$ and $m > \max_{x,y}(f(x,y))$, when $a < 0$. Parameter a decides if (x_c, y_c) drifts toward bright pixels $(a > 0)$ or dark pixels $(a < 0)$ in the image.

The results give a sub-pixel estimate of the central coordinates of an object. However, since we are not working with sub-pixel precision the results are rounded to pixels. Of course, sub-pixel accuracy can be used, when more subtle precision of image registration is necessary.

3.3 Rotation

We propose a simple, but relatively accurate, method of rotation estimation. The image under consideration is rotated around the center of gravity (x_c, y_c) for different θ values. New pixel values are calculated

$$\begin{aligned}
x_\theta &= (x - x_c) \cdot \cos\theta - (y - y_c) \cdot \sin\theta + x_c \\
y_\theta &= (x - x_c) \cdot \sin\theta + (y - y_c) \cdot \cos\theta + y_c
\end{aligned} \tag{15}$$

and used subsequently in the algorithm presented in detail in the next Section.

3.4 The Phase-Only Correlation (POC) Function

Correlation between phase-only versions of the two images to be aligned is used for image registration. This matching technique uses the phase component of two-dimensional discrete Fourier Transform (2D-DFT) of the two images [3], [8]. Furthermore, the POC method can be also-used for rotation estimation [12].

We assume that $f(x,y)$ is the reference image and $g(x,y)$ is the translated image of $f(x,y)$ by (τ_1, τ_2), both of the size $N_1 \times N_2$. For mathematical simplicity we assume that the index ranges are $x = -M_1 \cdots M_1$ $(M_1 > 0)$ and $y = -M_2 \cdots M_2$ $(M_2 > 0)$ with $N_1 = 2M_1 + 1$ and $N_2 = 2M_2 + 1$ [15].

The 2D Discrete Fourier Transforms (2D DFTs) of the images $f(x,y)$ and $g(x,y)$, denoted $F(k,l)$ and $G(k,l)$, are defined as follows

$$F(k,l) = \sum_{x,y} f(x,y) W_{N_1}^{kx} W_{N_2}^{ly}, \tag{16}$$

$$G(k,l) = \sum_{x,y} g(x,y) W_{N_1}^{kx} W_{N_2}^{ly}, \tag{17}$$

where $k = -M_1 \cdots M_1$, $l = -M_2 \cdots M_2$, $W_{N_1} = e^{-j\frac{2\pi}{N_1}}$, $W_{N_2} = e^{-j\frac{2\pi}{N_2}}$, and operator $\sum_{x,y}$ describes $\sum_{x=-M_1}^{M_1}\sum_{y=-M_2}^{M_2}$. For the 2D DFTs of the images, the cross-spectrum $R(k,l)$ is given by

$$R(k,l) = F(k,l)\overline{G(k,l)}, \tag{18}$$

where $\overline{G(k,l)}$ is the complex conjugate of $G(k,l)$. The cross-phase spectrum $\hat{R}(k,l)$ is a normalized cross spectrum $R(k,l)$ defined as

$$\hat{R}(k,l) = \frac{F(k,l)\overline{G(k,l)}}{\left|F(k,l)\overline{G(k,l)}\right|}. \tag{19}$$

The Phase-Only Correlation function $\hat{r}(x,y)$ is the 2D Inverse Discrete Fourier Transform (2D IDFT) of $\hat{R}(k,l)$ and is given by

$$\hat{r}(x,y) = \frac{1}{N_1 N_2} \sum_{k,l} \hat{R}(k,l) W_{N_1}^{-kx} W_{N_2}^{-ly}. \tag{20}$$

If the images $f(x,y)$ and $g(x,y)$ are the same, i.e., $f(x,y) = g(x,y)$, the POC function is defined as

$$\hat{r}(x,y) = \frac{1}{N_1 N_2} \sum_{k,l} W_{N_1}^{-kx} W_{N_2}^{-ly} = \delta(x,y) = \begin{cases} 1 & \text{for } x = y = 0 \\ 0 & \text{for others} \end{cases} \tag{21}$$

where $\delta(x,y)$ is the Kronecker's delta function. If the images are translated by some values (τ_1, τ_2) as in (7) then $\hat{r}(x,y)$ is a translated Kronecker's delta function [17] given by

$$\hat{r}(x,y) = \begin{cases} 1 \text{ for } (x,y) = (-\tau_1, -\tau_2) \\ 0 \text{ for others} \end{cases} \tag{22}$$

The position of the maximal value of POC function $\hat{r}(x,y)$ identifies the translation vector $(-\tau_1, -\tau_2)$. It has an opposite sign to (τ_1, τ_2). Of course, there are known many other methods of translation estimation (see for example [14] and references cited therein). We have used the POC method, since it is relatively robust to the images differences.

4   Algorithm Implementation

This section presents the proposed algorithm of object matching in the series of vessel section images with the use of the Phase-Only Correlation function, the center of gravity calibration and intensity levels correction. The algorithm matches the input image to the reference image by estimating the values of the parameters of the geometric transformations (5)-(9) forming the displacement between the images.

In the proposed algorithm we can list the following steps: estimation of the object position in the image, normalization of intensity in the image, rotation alignment, displacement alignment, reflection alignment and assessment of the match. The algorithm has a modular structure that allows for easy inclusion of new procedures or modification and removal of already applied procedures.

The main loop of the algorithm consists of the following steps:

1. Input the series of images
2. Normalize the images with the function (11).
3. **for each** pair of normalized images $f(x, y)$ and $g(x, y)$ in the series **do**:
   Calculate the new position of the image center (x_c, y_c) for $f(x, y)$ and $g(x, y)$ using the center of gravity function (13).
   Extract the $W_1 \times W_2$ window with the center at (x_c, y_c) from $f(x, y)$ and $g(x, y)$.
4. **loop for** θ on range $[-\theta_{max}, \theta_{max}]$ **do**: Rotate image $g^W(x, y)$ around its (x_c, y_c) coordinates by the angle θ. The rotated image is denoted $g_\theta^W(x, y)$.
5. **for** the non-reflected image $g^W(x, y)$ **do**: Estimate the displacement (τ_1, τ_2) with the POC function for the images $f^W(x, y)$ and $g_\theta^W(x, y)$.
   Translate image $g_\theta^W(x, y)$ by the displacement (τ_1, τ_2).
   Evaluate the match of $f^W(x, y)$ and $g_\theta^W(x - \tau_1, y - \tau_2)$ per criterion (23).
   Record the results.
6. **repeat for** the vertically and horizontally reflected image $g_\theta^W(x, y)$.
7. **repeat loop for** the next value of θ.
8. Return the best result.

Estimating the center of gravity of an image allows for the initial detection of the object in the image. The center of gravity (x_c, y_c) drifts toward the center of the object. The estimation allows us to reduce the size of the processing images $f(x, y)$ and $g(x, y)$ to the area around (x_c, y_c). The new set of images $f^W(x, y)$ and $g^W(x, y)$ of size $W_1 \times W_2$ (where $W_1 < N_1$ and $W_2 < N_2$) is focused on the mass of the object in the image and has most of the peripheral values removed, making it better suited for the POC function. For $f^W(x, y)$ and $g^W(x, y)$ further adjustments of the image center can be made.

Estimation of the center of gravity of the object in the image consists of the following steps:

1. Calculate the preliminary coordinates of the center of gravity points (x_c^f, y_c^f) and (x_c^g, y_c^g) of images $f(x, y)$ and $g(x, y)$.
2. Assign values to indexes x_W and y_W of window $W_1 \times W_2$ with the center at (x_c, y_c): $x_W = x_c - \frac{W_1}{2}, \dots, x_c + \frac{W_1}{2}$ and $y_W = y_c - \frac{W_2}{2}, \dots, y_c + \frac{W_2}{2}$
3. Extract the window area from images $f(x, y)$ and $g(x, y)$. The new set of images, named $f^W(x, y)$ and $g^W(x, y)$, is the size of $W_1 \times W_2$ with centers in (x_c^f, y_c^f) and (x_c^g, y_c^g) respectively; $x = x_W$ and $y = y_W$ for $f^W(x, y)$ and $g^W(x, y)$.

The rotation procedure is performed on $g^W(x, y)$. The new image is rotated by the angle θ around the center point of $g^W(x, y)$. For the rotated image $g_\theta^W(x, y)$ a new space of coordinates is assigned (see (5)). The new values are interpolated from $g(x, y)$ using a linear method. The angular range of θ is $-\theta_{max} \leq \theta \leq \theta_{max}$. In practical application, we used $\theta_{max} = 180°$ with $1°$ spacing.

Estimation of object translation with the POC function provides the translation vector (τ_1, τ_2) for the rotated by the angle θ image. This part consists of the following steps:

1. Calculate DFT for images $f^W(x,y)$ and $g_\theta^W(x,y)$. $F(k,l) = \text{DFT}[f^W(x,y)]$, $G(k,l) = \text{DFT}[g_\theta^W(x,y)]$.
2. Calculate $\hat{R}(k,l)$ for $F(k,l)$ and $G(k,l)$.
3. Calculate $\hat{r}(x,y)$ of $\hat{R}(k,l)$.
4. Find coordinates of maximum value of $\hat{r}(x,y)$. It will be the vector of translation (τ_1, τ_2).

The value of translation vector (τ_1, τ_2) is obtained from the POC function $\hat{r}(x,y)$ of $f^W(x,y)$ and $g_\theta^W(x,y)$. The image $g_\theta^W(x,y)$ is translated by $(-\tau_1, -\tau_2)$. The estimation with the POC function is repeated for the image $g_\theta^W(x,y)$ reflected horizontally and vertically.

The evaluation of the match is performed on the images $f^W(x,y)$ and $g_\theta^W(x-\tau_1, y-\tau_2)$. The criterion is the mean value of the sum of absolute difference between $f^W(x,y)$ and $g_\theta^W(x-\tau_1, y-\tau_2)$ given by

$$\frac{1}{W_1 W_2} \sum_{x,y} \left| f^W(x,y) - g^W(x-\tau_1, y-\tau_2) \right| \tag{23}$$

The smaller the value of (23), the better the match is.

The final result consists of the value (23) and the set of parameters describing the transformed image $g^W(x,y)$. These are the translation vector (τ_1, τ_2), the rotation angle θ, the center of gravity point (x_c, y_c) and the information on the type of reflection. The parameters allow for the geometric transformation of the image g into the image f by using the set of equations (5)-(9).

5   Experiments and Discussion

This section describes a set of experiments for evaluating the performance of the proposed algorithm. The experimental data consists of two sets of microscopic images containing vein sections. We can distinguish two types of shapes for these sections. The sets consist of six and five images of sizes 690×615 pixels and 746×1144 pixels respectively. The sample images of each set are shown in Fig. 1 and Fig. 2. The testing of the algorithm is performed on each image sequence. The acquired results consist of the estimated values of the parameters

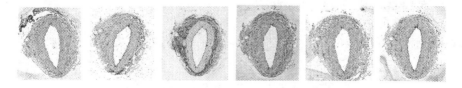

Fig. 1. The image set I consisting of 6 vein section images (I-1,I-2,I-3,I-4,I-5,I-6) of the size 690×615 pixels.

408   A. Górniak and E. Skubalska-Rafajłowicz

Fig. 2. The image set II (II-1,II-2,II-3,II-4,II-5) consisting of 5 vein section images of the size 746 × 1144 pixels.

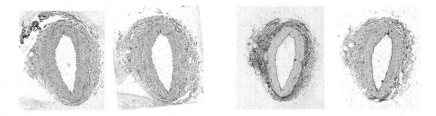

Fig. 3. The results of the section images registration using the proposed method. I-5 registered with respect to I-1 (on the left) and I-2 registered with respect to I-3 (on the right).

needed to match the input image to the reference image using the basic geometric transformations. The parameters include: the center of gravity point (x_c, y_c), the rotation angle θ, the translation vector (τ_1, τ_2) and the type of reflection applied.

The final results were chosen based on the value of the error criterion (23) used to measure the accuracy of the match for each pair of images in the sequence. The results are shown in Tables 1 and 2. A row in the table denotes the reference image and a column denotes the input image to be matched. From these tables, we can see that the error value varies depending on the reference image and the input image used. The cause of this disparity lies in the initial differences between the objects in the images. Therefore, assessing the value of the error criterion (23), we have to consider evaluating each result based on which pair of images it comes from. There is no constant threshold that applies to all results. The best considered course of action is to choose the best match at the cross-section of the analyzed image, i.e., the best result in both the row and the column containing the image. The most reliable assessment remains the visual confirmation of the acquired results.

Table 1. The value of criterion (23) for the best match of the pair of images in set I.

I-1	0.0708	0.0781	0.0716	0.0569	0.0611
0.0651	I-2	0.0633	0.0708	0.0528	0.0511
0.0825	0.0690	I-3	0.0853	0.0787	0.0706
0.0669	0.0720	0.0776	I-4	0.0688	0.0616
0.0594	0.0526	0.0714	0.0717	I-5	0.0546
0.0650	0.0459	0.0619	0.0665	0.0557	I-6

Table 2. The value of criterion (23) for the best match of the pair of images in set II.

II-1	0.1175	0.0895	0.0639	0.0676
0.1225	**II-2**	0.0979	0.1238	0.1265
0.0732	0.0953	**II-3**	0.0768	0.0733
0.0576	0.1062	0.0751	**II-4**	0.0627
0.0612	0.1248	0.0832	0.0605	**II-5**

The sample application of the acquired results to match the input image to reference image is presented in Fig. 3. The matched image was obtained by geometrically transforming the input image using the required parameters.

It should be noted that the method allows for the retrieval (building) of the match for a pair of images using the composition of geometric transformations from the corresponding pairs. Considering equation (4), it is also possible to acquire a reverse match by transforming the reference image to match the input image.

6   Conclusion

The paper presents a proposed algorithm of object matching for a series of images. The approach makes use of the distinctive features of the objects to estimate the match. The algorithm is shown to perform on the objects that are not identical, different on intensity level and geometrically transformed. It estimates the parameters of the geometric transformation differentiating the images without the influence of natural differences between the objects and the intensity of the images. It should be indicated, that the proposed approach is rather simple. It works in the image space domain and in the frequency domain consecutively, reducing distortion introduced by images displacements.

The method allows for further series analysis of the images. There is a possibility of applying the method to image scheduling and sequence construction.

References

1. van Assen, H.C., Egmont-Petersen, M., Reiber, J.H.C.: Accurate object localization in gray level images using the center of gravity measure; accuracy versus precision (2011)
2. Berberidis, K., Evangelidis, G.D., Karybali, I.G., Psarakis, E.Z.: An efficient spatial domain technique for subpixel image registration. Signal Processing: Image Communication **23**, 711–724 (2008)
3. Brunelli, R.: Template matching techniques in computer vision. Theory and practice. Wiley, Southern Gate, Chichester (2009)
4. DeLaPaz, R.L., Ma, Q.Y., Perera, G.M., Tang, H., Wu, E.X.: FFT-based Subpixel MRI Image Registration and Its Application in FMRI. Proc. Intl. Sot. Mag. Reson. Med. **8**, 1751 (2000)

5. Fitzpatrick, J.M., Sonka, M.: Handbook of Medical Imaging. Medical Image Processing and Analysis (SPIE Press Monograph, Vol. PM80/SC), vol. 2. SPIE Publications (2009)
6. Flusser, J., Zitova, B.: Image registration methods: a survey. Image and Vision Computing **21**, 977–1000 (2003)
7. Gonzalez, R.C., Woods, R.E.: Digital Image Processing. Prentice Hall (2007)
8. Hwang, J.J., Kim, D.N., Rao, K.R.: Fast Fourier Transform: Algorithms and Applications. Springer (2010)
9. Ourselin, S., Roche, A., Subsol, G., Pennec, X., Ayache, N.: Reconstructing a 3D structure from serial histological sections. Image and Vision Computing **19**(1), 25–31 (2001)
10. Lippolis, G., Edsjo, A., Helczynski, L., Bjartell, A., Overgaard, N.: Automatic registration of multi-modal microscopy images for integrative analysis of prostate tissue sections. MBC Cancer **13**, 408 (2013)
11. Modersitzki, J.: Numerical Methods for Image Registration (Numerical Mathematics and Scientific Computation). Oxford University Press, Oxford (2004)
12. Reddy, B., Chatterji, B.: An FFT-based technique for translation, rotation, and scale-invariant image registration. IEEE Transactions on Image Processing **5**, 1266–1271 (1996)
13. Schwier, M., Böhler, T., Hahn, H.K., Dahmen, U., Dirsch, O.: Registration of histological whole slide images guided by vessel structures. Journal of Pathology Informatics **4**(2 Suppl.), S10 (2013)
14. Skubalska-Rafajłowicz, E.: Estimation of horizontal and vertical translations of large images based on columns and rows mean energy matching. Multidimensional Systems and Signal Processing **25**(2), 273–294 (2014)
15. Takita, K., Aoki, T., Sasaki, Y., Higuchi, T., Kobayashi, K.: High-Accuracy Subpixel Image Registration Based on Phase-Only Correlation. IEICE Trans. Fundamentals of Electronics, Communication and Computer Sciences **E86–A**(8), 1925–1934 (2003)
16. Wang, C.W., Ka, S.M., Chen, A.: Robust image registration of biological microscopic images. Scientific Reports **4**, 6050 (2014)
17. Zhang, X., Abe, M., Kawamata, M.: An efficient subpixel image registration based on the phase-only correlations of image projections. In: The 2010 International Symposium on Communications and Information Technologies, pp. 997–1001 (2010)

Comprehensive Performance Evaluation of Various Feature Extraction Methods for OCR Purposes

Dawid Sas[1](✉) and Khalid Saeed[2]

[1] Faculty of Physics and Applied Computer Science,
University of Science and Technology, Krakow, Poland
dawsas@wp.pl
[2] Faculty of Computer Science, Bialystok University of Technology, Bialystok, Poland
k.saeed@pb.edu.pl

Abstract. Optical Character Recognition (OCR) is a very extensive branch of pattern recognition. The existence of super effective software designed for omnifont text recognition, capable of handling multiple languages, creates an impression that all problems in this field have already been solved. Indeed, focus of research in the OCR domain has constantly been shifting from offline, typewritten, Latin character recognition towards Asiatic alphabets, handwritten scripts and online process. Still, however, it is difficult to come across an elaboration which would not only cover the topic of numerous feature extraction methods for printed, Latin derived, isolated characters conceptually, but which would also attempt to implement, compare and optimize them in an experimental way. This paper aims at closing this gap by thoroughly examining the performance of several statistical methods with respect to their recognition rate and time efficiency.

Keywords: OCR · Feature extraction · Shape descriptors

1 Introduction

A simple taxonomy of OCR systems can be presented schematically as in Fig. 1. Online OCR concentrates on recognition of handwriting in real time. It employs digital devices like electronic pads and pens, which allow to acquire data and extract information not only from sheer shape, but also from dynamics of writing. The offline counterpart processes only static contents – the form of glyphs. It can be further divided based upon nature of text it operates on. Heavy variations of style and possible character overlapping account for the main problems related to handwritten OCR, especially while handling cursive scripts, like Arabic alphabet. OCR designed for machine text does not have to handle these issues as the characters are usually well separated and have uniform or at least highly predictable shape. Handwritten subsystems, both offline and online, are often referred to as Intelligent Character Recognition (ICR).

Offline OCR processing consists of the following stages. In the beginning, image is acquired by scanning or taking a photo of a document. Then it undergoes preprocessing. The term encompasses a set of techniques aiming to improve the quality of

© IFIP International Federation for Information Processing 2015
K. Saeed and W. Homenda (Eds.): CISIM 2015, LNCS 9339, pp. 411–422, 2015.
DOI: 10.1007/978-3-319-24369-6_34

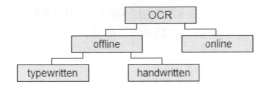

Fig. 1. Taxonomy of OCR systems

the scan. The next stage is binarization to convert the grayscale image to the form that features only two intensity levels. Binarization is followed by segmentation of lines, words and finally single glyphs or glyph fragments. As characters have been isolated, they are subject to feature extraction which means encoding a shape in a sort of numerical representation. Based upon the features, each glyph is subsequently classified, or labelled, as a member of one of predefined classes. At the final stage of OCR, the whole text is examined word by word against lexical and syntactical compliance with the given language rules.

1.1   Approaches to Feature Extraction

There are two main approaches to the feature extraction process: statistical and structural. Statistical methods transform a shape into a strictly ordered set of specified length, the so called *feature vector*, which represents a point in multidimensional *feature space*. They cannot work without a training set, serving as a database of mappings between cases and corresponding classes. Based upon the set, a decision is made into which class a new, hitherto unknown, case should be incorporated. On the other hand, structural approach is directed towards decomposing shapes into simpler pieces and establishing relationships between them. Detailed description of structural techniques can be found in [1].

1.2   Criteria of Statistical Coding Techniques

The attributes of a well-performing statistical feature extraction technique include capability of grouping all instances of the same class into tight clusters in feature space in order to aid classification. In [2] this is formulated as "*minimizing the within class pattern variability while enhancing the between class pattern variability*". Also, high robustness to noise and distortions as well as invariance to geometric transformations are demanded. The code format should be compact which means shape information to be carried by as few features as possible. Dimensionality reduction is essential as to guarantee that the computational expense of classification process does not exceed acceptable values. The same remark, regarding execution speed, applies as well to the extraction process algorithm.

1.3   Motivation

One of the most extensive surveys concerning statistical feature extraction methods for OCR purposes was covered in [3]. The authors put considerable efforts to set together multiple techniques, considering perspectives of their application to different forms of glyphs. They also discussed the aspects of feature invariance and reconstructability of the shape from a descriptor. The researchers, however, did not show any comparison of the described methods in an experimental way. The present paper is prepared with a view to complement the aforementioned survey with relevant tests. Numerous description techniques were also listed out by [4] (Arabic handwriting) and [5] (Devanagari script).

The paper is organized as follows. The review of shape description techniques is conducted within Section 2. Section 3 explains the scope of the research. Section 4 gives the results of the tests. Finally, the work is summarized in Section 5.

2   Feature Extraction Techniques

Within the family of statistical descriptors one can distinguish classes utilizing concepts like [6]:

- pixel distribution (i.e. zoning, crossings, projection methods),
- moment invariants (i.e. central moments, Hu moments),
- series expansion (i.e. Zernike moments),
- unitary transforms (i.e. Fourier transform, Hadamard transform, cosine transform),
- contour description (i.e. Freeman chaincodes, polyline approximation, elliptic Fourier descriptors).

There are other approaches to the concept of feature extraction techniques like the method based on Toeplitz matrix minimal eigenvalues for script feature extracting and description [7, 8] or soft computing approaches. In this paper, however, the authors have limited their research to the most relevant methods and algorithms.

2.1   Zoning

Glyph bounding box is divided into rectangular areas. A parameter is computed inside each rectangle and treated as a single feature (Fig. 2a). The authors of [9] partition an image of size 60×90 into 54 10×10 squares. Pixels along each of the 19 diagonals of a zone are summed up and the amounts are eventually averaged. Further, average values of the zones stacked horizontally and vertically contribute to extra 15 features. In this paper the image is zoned as suggested in [9] and pixel density in each region, row and column serves as a quantity.

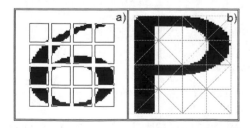

Fig. 2. a) Zonal division, b) Grid used in crossings technique

2.2   Crossings

A custom grid of lines is superimposed on the image and the spots where lines meet glyph pixels are used to form features. In the authors' implementation images are scaled to $(4n + 3) \times (4n + 3)$ squares $(n \in \mathbb{N})$ and quartered so that one-pixel-wide gap is left between the pieces. Four lines are stretched through each quarter: one horizontal, one vertical and two oblique, each going through the center. Additional four sections run from the middle of the image, orthogonally towards its edges (Fig. 2b). Along each line pixels are registered and their positions are averaged. The obtained pairs of numbers are dependant on each other and hence only one value is selected towards the feature vector. Thus, vector dimensionality is the same as the number of lines – 20. To prevent the algorithm from getting stuck due to undefined situations, several emergency scenarios must be taken into account.

2.3   Projection Histograms

Pixels are counted column-wise and row-wise, thus two histograms: H_x and H_y are created. Consider cumulative histograms V_x and V_y. Their kth bin expresses a total of first k bins of H_x and H_y, respectively [3]. By concatenating V_x and V_y, we get the feature vector, which is to some extent tolerant to shifting of glyph fragments.

2.4   Projection Axes

Image is fragmented into cells. Pixels present within each cell are cast orthogonally onto dedicated axes. In this approach features are identified with degrees of projection axes filling. The authors of [10] studied this technique coupled with Toeplitz model. Figure 3 depicts the cell system used by the authors.

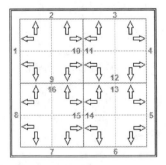

Fig. 3. A variant of projection axes technique

2.5   Central Moments

A moment is a scalar quantity that internally describes the shape of a function using powers of spatial variables. Potential application of moments in pattern recognition was first discovered by Hu and derives from the *uniqueness theorem* given in [11]. If we interpret an image as a pixel intensity function, then a set of moments becomes shape descriptor. Translational invariance can easily be obtained by introducing central moments, which for discrete 2D function $f(x, y)$ are expressed by (1):

$$\mu_{pq} = \sum_x \sum_y f(x, y)(x - \overline{x})^p (y - \overline{y})^q , \tag{1}$$

where $p + q$ is the order of the moment and $\{x, y\}$ is the centroid of the shape. Attention must be paid to the different orders of moment values magnitudes. This leads to unequal contribution from particular dimensions that hinders statistical classification. In order to compensate for this drawback, all components are multiplied by ten to the power of $m - (p + q)$, where m is the maximal order used (here: 5). The solution yields far better classification results than the logarithming and the normalization of features.

2.6   Hu Moments

From central moments Hu derived similitude invariants (2):

$$\eta_{pq} = \frac{\mu_{pq}}{\mu_{00}^\Gamma} , \tag{2}$$

where $\Gamma = (p + q + 2) / 2$ and $p + q > 1$. On the basis of η_{pq} Hu constructed seven expressions invariant under general linear transformations (translation, scale and rotation), the final one also being invariant under skew [11].

Unfortunately, seven-dimensional descriptor may fail when paired with a statistical classifier. This is due to the incommensurability between vector elements caused, similarly to what was pointed out in Section 2.5, by varying and hardly predictable orders of magnitude. As a remedy, the authors multiply each invariant by arbitrarily chosen factor 10^n, where $n = 0, 1, 1, 1, 2, 2, 3$, respectively.

2.7   Zernike Moments

The Zernike moment of order n and repetition m (A_{nm}) is given by the inner product of a function $f(x, y)$ and the Zernike polynomial $V_{nm}(x, y)$. For images the expression unfolds as in (3):

$$A_{nm} = \frac{n + 1}{\pi} \sum_x \sum_y f(x, y) V_{nm}^*(x, y) , \tag{3}$$

$$x^2 + y^2 = \rho^2 \leq 1 ,$$

with "*" to denote complex conjugate. For purposes of this definition, we assume that images are of unitary size. The confinement to the unit disk is a consequence of the definition of Zernike polynomials, which are a set of two-dimensional, orthogonal, complex functions. The properties and applications of Zernike moments were broadly investigated in [12].

Zernike moments owe their role in pattern recognition to two properties. First, their magnitudes are invariant to rotation. Second, the orthogonality of V_{nm} basis enables reconstruction of an image from a set of moments by summing up consecutive image contributions (eq. 14 in [12]).

2.8   Unitary Transforms

Unitary transforms are a class of linear transformations which are both orthogonal and invertible. One major example of a unitary transform is Discrete Fourier Transform (DFT), which is widely utilized in digital signal processing. Thanks to orthogonality, the signal can be represented as a finite series expansion without any information redundancy. Thus, one may extract desired frequencies whilst discarding the other. As the transform is invertible, one can subsequently return with the modified signal to the original domain by simple addition of terms. Main motivations to do so are signal filtering and data compression. Low-pass filtering is a method for eliminating the number of variables needed for successful description and identification. A procedure of shape coding requires transforming an $N \times N$ image into $N \times N$ frequency components and selecting only a limited number of transform coefficients from the low frequency part of spectrum to build the feature vector.

The other worth mentioning members of unitary transforms group are: Karhunen-Loève Transform (KLT), Discrete Cosine Transform (DCT) and Discrete Hadamard Transform (DHT). According to [13], KLT emerges as the ultimate in terms of compactness, but we are short of an efficient way to compute it. The authors of the comparison concluded that DCT most closely matches the performance of KLT and they also developed a fast DCT algorithm. The transform together with DFT and DHT are thus investigated in this work as a tool of shape description. Selected unitary transforms were previously considered in [14] as global features for recognition of online handwritten numerals and Tamil characters.

If we represent a finite, periodic set of N complex samples by $f(n)$, then, as a result of DFT, we obtain an equinumerous set of complex coefficients $F(k)$, given by (4):

$$F(k) = \sum_{n=0}^{N-1} f(n) e^{-i2\pi k \frac{n}{N}} . \tag{4}$$

Hadamard transform matrix of size $2N \times 2N$ ($\mathbf{H_{2N}}$) consists solely of positive and negative ones and is defined recursively by (5):

$$\mathbf{H_1} = [1] , \quad \mathbf{H_{2N}} = \frac{1}{\sqrt{2}} \begin{bmatrix} \mathbf{H_N} & \mathbf{H_N} \\ \mathbf{H_N} & -\mathbf{H_N} \end{bmatrix} . \tag{5}$$

Discrete Cosine Transform $G(k)$ of set $g(n)$ is given by (6):

$$G(0) = \frac{\sqrt{2}}{N} \sum_{n=0}^{N-1} g(n) ,$$

$$G(k) = \frac{2}{N} \sum_{n=0}^{N-1} g(n) \cos \left(\frac{(2n+1)k\pi}{2N} \right) , \quad k = 1, 2, ..., N - 1 . \tag{6}$$

2.9   Polyline Approximation

Freeman (1961) [15] proposed a method of encoding contours as a sequence of numbers, expressing relative segment positions. Pixels are labelled with digits 0-7, dependant on where the adjacent pixel is situated. Freeman chain codes effectively describe the shape of a curve with segments connected with each other at a multiple of $45°$ angle. The concept can be easily extended by dividing a contour into N fragments of equal length and connecting the division points with vectors v_l ($l = 1, ..., N$). If the curve cannot be divided without a remainder, it remains open. Each v_l phase φ_l contributes to the feature vector $V = [\varphi_1, \varphi_2, ..., \varphi_N]$, which represents the coarse shape of the outline. The angular distance d_ϕ serves for comparing two feature vectors U and V:

$$d_\phi(\vec{U}, \vec{V}) = \sum_{l=1}^{N} d_l(\vec{U}, \vec{V}) = \sum_{l=1}^{N} \left(1 - \left| \frac{|\Delta\phi_l| - \pi}{\pi} \right| \right), \tag{7}$$

where $\Delta\varphi_l$ denotes the phase difference between v_l and u_l in radians. It should be noted that the technique is appropriate for encoding single contours only, which proves inconvenient for representing glyphs that can occur with a diacritic.

2.10   Elliptic Fourier Descriptors

Description of closed contours via parametric equations was considered among others in [16]. As a result of expanding a parametric curve in Fourier series, one gets coefficients that strictly depend on size, orientation and selection of starting point on a curve [17]. The essence of the problem is to construct expressions relating the expansion terms which would be free of undesired information and thus could be considered as pure shape features.

Kuhl-Giardina elliptic descriptors [16] approximate a contour by superposition of harmonic phasors that encircle ellipses reflecting particular sine-cosine pairs of x and y projection expansions as in (8) and (9):

$$x(t) \approx \frac{a_0}{2} + \sum_{n=1}^{N} \left[a_n \cos \left(\frac{2\pi nt}{T} \right) + b_n \sin \left(\frac{2\pi nt}{T} \right) \right], \tag{8}$$

$$y(t) \approx \frac{c_0}{2} + \sum_{n=1}^{N} \left[c_n \cos \left(\frac{2\pi nt}{T} \right) + d_n \sin \left(\frac{2\pi nt}{T} \right) \right], \tag{9}$$

where N is the highest order and T is the total contour length. Expansion coefficients a_n, b_n, c_n, d_n have to be normalized with respect to three factors: phase shift θ, orientation ψ and the semi-major axis length E of the first harmonic ellipse. The final outcome is a set of invariant coefficients a_n**, b_n**, c_n**, d_n**, which can be expressed in matrix notation (10):

$$\begin{bmatrix} a_n^{**} & b_n^{**} \\ c_n^{**} & d_n^{**} \end{bmatrix} = \frac{1}{E} \begin{bmatrix} cos\psi & sin\psi \\ -sin\psi & cos\psi \end{bmatrix} \begin{bmatrix} a_n & b_n \\ c_n & d_n \end{bmatrix} \begin{bmatrix} cos(n\theta) & -sin(n\theta) \\ sin(n\theta) & cos(n\theta) \end{bmatrix} . \quad (10)$$

The authors of [18] applied Kuhl-Giardina Fourier descriptors in their system for identification of handwritten Arabic characters.

3   Matter of Study

The authors undertake implementation and testing of the methods presented in Section 2. The works were conducted using the Java programming language with the support of *Apache Commons Math* library (fast transform algorithms, Section 2.8) [19]. All issues were related to binary images – glyphs of triple form: solid, thinned and outlines. K3M algorithm was utilized for thinning [20]. The task was targeted at relative comparison of description techniques, highlighting their strengths and weaknesses and optimization of performance by adjustment of parameters.

The tests were carried out on own collection of 2460 typewritten glyphs including Latin letters and numerals. The dataset is divided into 33 font subsets. Ten of them comprise 52 Latin alphabets (both upper and lower case) and ten digits. The remaining 23 scripts contain additional 18 Polish-specific characters (Ą, Ć, Ę, Ł, Ń, Ó, Ś, Ź, Ż and ą, ć, ę, ł, ń, ó, ś, ź, ż). The selection of fonts provides broad diversity of styles which is responsible for high representativeness of test results. The following font styles are present: serif (e.g. *Times New Roman*), sans-serif (e.g. *Arial*), console (e.g. *Consolas*), decorative (e.g. *Comic Sans)* and exaggerated (e.g. *Elephant)*.

From the broad spectrum of classification algorithms, the authors decided to employ the simple k-nearest neighbor classifier with Manhattan metric and $k = 2$. The authors' implementation increases k each time there is a tie and repeats the procedure. The classifier is not designed to return "not recognized" response. $k = 2$ is also used together with angular metric (refer to Section 2.9).

$$x_i \rightarrow \frac{x_i - \mu}{\sigma} , \quad (11)$$

Feature vectors may be subject to standarization:

where μ denotes mean of components and σ is their standard deviation. The goal of this operation is elimination of significant differences between components, which can reach orders of magnitude, while keeping relations between them.

3.1   Recognition Rate

Main quality criterion of a feature extraction technique is the percentage of correct identification. The examination tool is leave-one-out cross-validation. The analysis of recognition rate based upon the whole collection of glyphs may be unreliable due to the problems emerging while trying to distinguish lower and upper case counterparts of letters: C, O, S, V, W, X, Z, Ć, Ó, Ś, Ź, Ż. Therefore, any attempts of doing so are discarded and the corresponding classes are merged into one class, i.e., c ≡ C, z ≡ Z, etc. Individual subcategories of the complete set are also examined: letters, lower case letters, upper case letters and digits. Polish-specific alphabets are excluded from tests of contour descriptors due to strong presence of diacritics.

3.2   Execution Speed

The efficiency of a method is measured by the average time it takes to extract feature set from a single character. The value does not encompass previous operations of thinning and size normalization. The additional information is mean classification time, correlated to the dimensionality of descriptor. Both quantities are given with a precision of 1 ms. Alternative indices are: the number of identifications per second and the time needed to process one A4 page with 30 lines of text, each containing 70 characters in average (2100 characters per page). The computations are carried out on processor *Intel Core 2 Duo T6600*, 2.2 GHz. Two factors which may negatively affect the speed are: object-oriented nature of the Java programming language and suboptimal quality of algorithms.

4   Experimental Results

In this section results of investigation categories described in Section 3 are given and discussed. Table 1 sets together the characteristics of particular descriptors. Image size, glyph form and the dimensionality of descriptors were adjusted with a view to achieving highest possible rates.

Table 1. Descriptor parameters. In column <Image form>: 'S' stands for 'solid', 'T' for 'thinned' and 'C' for 'contour'.

Technique	Descriptor constituents	No. of features	Image form	Image size	Vector standarized?
Zoning	pixel density in each zone, row and column	69	S	60×90	yes
Crossings	averaged coordinates of crossing points	20	S	63×63	yes
Projection Histograms	cumulative bin counts from both histograms	130	T	65×65	yes
Projection Axes	lengths of projections	16	S	64×64	yes
Central Moments	all central moments of orders 2-5	18	S	32×32	no
Hu Moments	seven Hu moment invariants	7	T	41×41	no
Zernike Moments	all Zernike moments of orders 2-8 and $m \geq 0$	23	T	48×48	no
Fourier Transform		224	S	32×32	yes
Hadamard Transform	a number of low-frequency samples	416	S	32×32	yes
Cosine Transform		320	S	32×32	yes
Polyline Approximation	polyline segment phases	12	C	any	no
Elliptic Descriptors	seven first invariant series coefficients	25	C	any	no

4.1   Results of Classification

Table 2 shows the percentages of correct classifications for each feature extraction method with regard to particular glyph class. The examination makes it obvious that pixel distribution methods have clear edge over other classes in terms of recognition rate of glyphs with known orientation. The crossings technique seems to be the method of choice. Cosine Transform and Zernike moments are not far behind despite the latter inability to correctly recognize pairs like 6 and 9. The rotation invariance is thus partially responsible for classification errors. Contour description methods are rather uncompetitive. Low rates can be explained by awkwardness of closed contour labelling algorithm, which is no silver bullet against many ambiguities and nontypical cases emerging while encoding chain of curve points. The least promising description technique is the one based on Hu moments, which suffers from low dimensionality.

Table 2. Classification results

Technique	All glyphs	Letters	Lower case letters	Upper case letters	Digits
Zoning	89.8%	91.9%	95.4%	93.3%	97.0%
Crossings	90.9%	93.5%	95.6%	95.5%	95.8%
Projection Histograms	90.9%	93.1%	94.3%	92.9%	93.6%
Projection Axes	89.7%	92.3%	94.6%	92.7%	96.7%
Central Moments	81.5%	84.5%	90.1%	85.3%	91.8%
Hu Moments	47.0%	n/a	n/a	n/a	n/a
Zernike Moments	86.5%	89.2%	89.0%	93.5%	92.4%
Fourier Transform	76.5%	79.5%	81.7%	84.1%	81.8%
Hadamard Transform	78.1%	79.7%	80.9%	80.5%	90.3%
Cosine Transform	87.2%	88.8%	91.4%	88.7%	95.8%
Polyline Approximation	78.5%	79.5%	82.6%	83.0%	89.4%
Elliptic Descriptors	75.7%	78.1%	80.5%	80.7%	78.2%

4.2   Time Efficiency

The superiority of zoning, crossings and histograms was reassured by average identification rates not exceeding 4 ms per glyph. Descriptors based on unitary transforms owe their agility to well-known fast processing algorithms. Regretfully, because of their high dimensionality, the techniques are slightly delayed by lengthy classification process. Previously asserted high accuracy of projection axes is severely hindered by relatively low time efficiency. As before, contour-based descriptors heavily suffer from drawbacks of chain encoding algorithm. Extreme complexity of Hu invariants is again reflected by unacceptable extraction rates. It cannot be negated that the benefits brought by geometric invariance may not compensate for the price one has to pay for them. Table 3 aggregates average identification rates of a single glyph together with the alternative quantities to better imagine the potential of particular techniques.

Table 3. Time efficiency rates

Technique	Extraction rate	Classification rate	No. of identifications per 1 sec	Time of one A4 page analysis
Zoning	1 ms	2 ms	333	6.3 s
Crossings	2 ms	2 ms	250	8.4 s
Projection Histograms	1 ms	3 ms	250	8.4 s
Projection Axes	12 ms	2 ms	71	29.6 s
Central Moments	14 ms	2 ms	62	33.6 s
Hu Moments	75 ms	n/a	13	157.5 s
Zernike Moments	17 ms	2 ms	52	39.9 s
Fourier Transform	< 1 ms	5 ms	200	10.5 s
Hadamard Transform	< 1 ms	7 ms	142	14.7 s
Cosine Transform	< 1 ms	5 ms	200	10.5 s
Polyline Approximation	31 ms	3 ms	29	71.4 s
Elliptic Descriptors	32 ms	1 ms	30	69.3 s

5   Conclusion

Tests conducted in the presented work identified contenders for the most useful feature extraction method for OCR purposes with application to machine-printed Latin text. Pixel distribution techniques boast the highest number of successful classifications and the time efficiency rates. Recognition rate peaks of 90% may not impress in absolute terms, nevertheless one should consider the number of glyph classes and the high diversity of font styles. The DCT descriptor emerged as a very close competitor, also thanks to the application of fast algorithm. Zernike moments also seem to be successful, albeit their rotational invariance may prove a curse. The computational expense of the technique is also not very appealing. The authors judge that contour description techniques should perform better in combination with real object outlines.

Acknowledgment. The research was supported by the Rector of Bialystok University of Technology in Bialystok, grant number S/WI/1/2013.

References

1. Sazaklis, G.N.: Geometric Methods for Optical Character Recognition. PhD dissertation. State University of New York at Stony Brook (1997)
2. Devijver, P.A., Kittler, J.: Pattern Recognition: a Statistical Approach, p. 12. Prentice-Hall, London (1982)
3. Trier, O.D., Jain, A.K., Taxt, T.: Feature Extraction Methods for Character Recognition – a Survey. Pattern Recognition **29**(4), 641–662 (1996)
4. Lorigo, L.M., Govindaraju, V.: Offline Arabic Handwriting Recognition: a Survey. IEEE Trans. on Pat. Anal. and Mach. Int. **28**(5), 712–724 (2006)

5. Jayadevan, R., Kolhe, S.R., Patil, P.M., Pal, U.: Offline Recognition of Devanagari Script: a Survey. IEEE Transactions on Systems, Man, and Cybernetics - Part C: Applications and Reviews **41**(6), 782–796 (2011)

6. Eikvil, L.: OCR – Optical Character Recognition. Norsk Regnesentral. Report No. 876 (1993)

7. Saeed, K., Tabedzki, M.: Cursive-character script recognition using toeplitz model and neural networks. In: Rutkowski, L., Siekmann, J.H., Tadeusiewicz, R., Zadeh, L.A. (eds.) ICAISC 2004. LNCS (LNAI), vol. 3070, pp. 658–663. Springer, Heidelberg (2004)

8. Saeed, K.: Carathéodory-Toeplitz based mathematical methods and their algorithmic applications in biometric image processing. Applied Numerical Mathematics **75**, 2–21 (2014). Elsevier

9. Pradeep, J., Srinivasan, E., Himavathi, S.: Diagonal Based Feature Extraction for Handwritten Alphabets Recognition System Using Neural Network. IJCSIT **3**(1), 27–38 (2011)

10. Saeed, K.: A projection approach for arabic handwritten characters recognition. In: Sincak, P., Vascak, J. (eds.) Quo Vadis Computational Intelligence? New Trends and Applications in Computer Intelligence, pp. 106–111. Physica-Verlag, Berlin - Kacprzyk J. (EiC) (2000)

11. Hu, M.K.: Visual Pattern Recognition by Moment Invariants. IRE Transactions on Information Theory **IT-8**, 179–187 (1962)

12. Khotanzad, A., Hong, Y.H.: Invariant Image Recognition by Zernike Moments. IEEE Trans. on Pat. Anal. and Mach. Int. **12**(5), 489–497 (1990)

13. Ahmed, N., Natarajan, T., Rao, K.R.: Discrete Cosine Transform. IEEE TC **C-23**(1), 90–93 (1974)

14. Ramakrishnan, A.G., Urala, K.B.: Global and local features for recognition of online handwritten numerals and tamil characters. In: MOCR 2013 Proceedings of the 4th International Workshop on Multilingual OCR (2013)

15. Freeman, H.: On the Encoding of Arbitrary Geometric Configurations. IRE Trans. Elec. Comp. **EC-10**, 260–268 (1961)

16. Kuhl, F.P., Giardina, C.R.: Elliptic Fourier Features of a Closed Contour. Computer Graphics and Image Processing **18**, 236–258 (1982)

17. Granlund, G.H.: Fourier Preprocessing for Hand Print Character Recognition. IEEE TC **C-21**(2), 195–201 (1972)

18. Maddouri, S.S., Amiri, H., Belaid, A., Choisy, Ch.: Combination of local and global vision modelling for arabic handwritten words recognition. In: Proceedings of the Eighth International Workshop on Frontiers in Handwriting Recognition, pp. 128–135 (2002)

19. Commons Math: The Apache Commons Mathematics Library, ver. 3.3, June 22, 2015. http://commons.apache.org/proper/commons-math/

20. Saeed, K., Tabedzki, M., Rybnik, M., Adamski, M.: K3M: A Universal Algorithm for Image Skeletonization and a Review of Thinning Techniques. AMCS **20**(2), 317–335 (2010)

Lagrange Piecewise-Quadratic Interpolation Based on Planar Unordered Reduced Data

Ryszard Kozera and Piotr Szmielew[✉]

Faculty of Applied Informatics and Mathematics, Warsaw University
of Life Sciences - SGGW, Nowoursynowska Str. 159, 02-776 Warsaw, Poland
{ryszard_kozera,piotr_szmielew}@sggw.pl

Abstract. This paper discusses the problem of fitting non-parametric unordered reduced data (i.e. a collection of interpolation points) with piecewise-quadratic interpolation to estimate an unknown curve γ in Euclidean space E^2. The term reduced data stands for the situation in which the corresponding interpolation knots are unavailable. The construction of ordering algorithm based on *e-graph of points* (i.e. a complete weighted graph using euclidean distances between points as respective weights) is introduced and tested here. The unordered set of input points is transformed into an ordered one upon using a minimal spanning tree (applicable for open curves). Once the order on points is imposed a piecewise-quadratic interpolation $\hat{\gamma}_2$ combined with the so-called *cumulative chords* is used to fit unordered reduced data. The entire scheme is tested initially on sparse data. The experiments carried out for dense set of interpolation points and designed to test the asymptotics in γ approximation by $\hat{\gamma}_2$ result in numerically computed cubic convergence order. The latter coincides with already established asymptotics derived for γ estimation via piecewise-quadratic interpolation based on ordered reduced data and cumulative chords.

1 Introduction

In a classical interpolation setting, a sampled ordered data points $Q_m = \{q_i\}_{i=0}^m$ with $\gamma(t_i) = q_i \in E^n$ define the so-called parametric data $(\{t_i\}_{i=0}^m, Q_m)$. Here we also assume to deal with a parametric curve $\gamma : [0, T] \to E^n$ with $t_0 = 0$ and $t_m = T < \infty$. Once the corresponding interpolation knots $\{t_i\}_{i=0}^m$ are missing the set Q_m represents the so-called non-parametric data (or reduced data). Under such circumstances the unknown knots $\{t_i\}_{i=0}^m$ must be first somehow estimated by properly guessed $\{\hat{t}_i\}_{i=0}^m \approx \{t_i\}_{i=0}^m$. The latter combined with Q_m permits to apply a given interpolation scheme $\hat{\gamma} : [0, \hat{T}] \to E^n$, with $\hat{t}_0 = 0$ and $\hat{t}_m = \hat{T}$. It is also required here that $t_i < t_{i+1}$ and $q_i \neq q_{i+1}$. In addition, the curve γ is assumed to be regular (i.e. $\gamma' \neq \mathbf{0}$) and of class C^3. From now on we consider and discuss the situation when $n = 2$, i.e. the case of interpolating planar curves.

We introduce now an interpolation scheme based on non-parametric unordered data $\bar{Q}_m = \{\bar{q}_i\}_{i=0}^m$ (with permuted points from Q_m) for which natural order of points in Q_m (dictated by the condition $q_i = \gamma(t_i)$) is somehow lost.

© IFIP International Federation for Information Processing 2015
K. Saeed and W. Homenda (Eds.): CISIM 2015, LNCS 9339, pp. 423–434, 2015.
DOI: 10.1007/978-3-319-24369-6_35

Clearly, in order to estimate the unknown curve γ with an arbitrary interpolant $\hat{\gamma} : [0, T] \rightarrow E^2$ based on $\bar{Q}_m$ it is necessary to propose a proper ordering of points in $\bar{Q}_m$ (accounting for the geometry of $\bar{Q}_m$) converting $\bar{Q}_m$ into an ordered set $\hat{Q}_m = \{\hat{q}_i\}_{i=0}^m$. This paper discusses a method designed to find such ordering for open curves serving subsequently as an input to piecewise-quadratic interpolation $\hat{\gamma} = \hat{\gamma}_2$ used with the guessed knots $\{\hat{t}_i\}_{i=0}^m$ according to the so-called cumulative chords [1]. Initially, we present the examples for different planar curves illustrating the proposed data fitting scheme implemented on sparse data $\bar{Q}_m$. Finally, we test numerically the convergence order α in approximating γ by $\hat{\gamma}_2$ based on dense $\bar{Q}_m$ converted into $\hat{Q}_m$ as prescribed in this paper. The conducted tests suggest cubic order of convergence.

Specific examples for interpolating real life ordered (or unordered) reduced data Q_m (or $\bar{Q}_m$) in *computer graphics* (light-source motion estimation or image rendering), *computer vision* (image segmentation or video compression), *geometry* (trajectory, curvature of area estimation) or in *engineering and physics* (fast particles' motion estimation) can be found among all in [1], [2] and [3].

2   Problem Formulation and Motivation

Frequently, once dealing with real life reduced data (i.e. the collection of multi-dimensional points) the exact ordering of the points (whatever they represent) remains unknown. Indeed, consider e.g. recognizing a shape in the picture as shown in Fig. 1. A desired output forms an image of a dog built from various curves (or lines). However, upon detecting data points $\bar{Q}_m$ it is almost impossible to be certain of the proper intrinsic ordering. Nevertheless, still the latter is a prerequisite to any interpolation scheme subsequently chosen to fit $\bar{Q}_m$. Thus a strong need for a scheme to fit such unordered data arises naturally here.

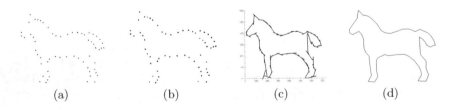

(a)   (b)   (c)   (d)

Fig. 1. a) Original image, b) points deducted from image using Mathematica tools, c) points connected using curves, d) points connected using lines.

The second example refers to a medical image processing application. Consider e.g. a problem of encircling a tumor in the USG image (a classical segmentation problem). A physician marks a border of a tumor and the system automatically passes an interpolating curve through it as seen in Fig. 2. This curve is meant to mimic the tumor boundary and serves as an automatic tumor segmentation tool. As it stands the data forms an ordered set Q_m provided the physician stores the order of the marked points. This may not be the case. Additionally, another specialist may add later a point (or points) in the middle (judged by him/her as vital for further medical examination). This would result in unordered points $\bar{Q}_m$ for which a need of imposing an appropriate ordering reappear again.

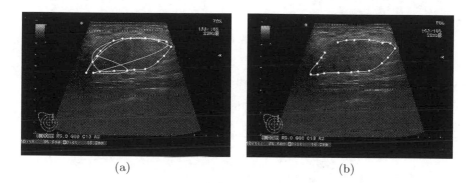

(a)   (b)

Fig. 2. *Hamartoma mammae* a) encircled without and b) with points ordering.

Before passing to the detailed description of the proposed algorithm designed to order an unordered set of points $\bar{Q}_m$ we recall a definition of the *e-graph of points* (see [4]) which in turn is used as an auxiliary tool in the subsequent interpolation scheme.

Definition 1. *We call an e-graph of points based on the set of planar points* $P = \{(x_1, y_1), (x_2, y_2), \ldots, (x_n, y_n)\}$ *as the graph* (V, E, f) *with* $V = \{1, 2, \ldots, n\}$, $E = V^2$, $f : \{1, \ldots, n\} \times \{1, \ldots, n\} \rightarrow \mathbb{R}$, *where* $f(i, j) = \sqrt{(x_i - x_j)^2 + (y_i - y_j)^2}$.

Obviously e-graph of points P has the corresponding adjacency matrix $A \in M_{n,n}(\mathbb{R})$, $A = [a_{i,j}]_{i,j=1}^n$, where $a_{i,j} = \sqrt{(x_i - x_j)^2 + (y_i - y_j)^2}$.

Lemma 1. *E-graph of points and the corresponding adjacency matrix can be easily constructed from each other.*

Proof. Step 1: Constructing adjacency matrix from given graph:
Let $(V, \overline{E, f})$ be e-graph of points, $n = \text{card}(V)$. Define $A \in M_{n,n}(\mathbb{R})$, $A = [a_{i,j}]$, where $a_{i,j} = f(i, j)$. A is a needed matrix.
Step 2: Constructing graph from given adjacency matrix
$\overline{\text{Let}}$ $A \in M_{n,n}(\mathbb{R})$, $A = [a_{i,j}]_{i,j=1}^n$. Define $f : \{1, \ldots, n\} \times \{1, \ldots, n\} \rightarrow \mathbb{R}$, $f(i, j) = a_{i,j}$. $(\{1, 2, \ldots, n\}, \{1, 2, \ldots, n\}^2, f)$ is a needed graph.

$\square$

Remark 1. Note that due to Lemma 1 an e-graph and adjacency matrix can be used interchangeably.

Once the order of interpolation points is fixed with $\hat{Q}_m = \{\hat{q}_i\}_{i=0}^m$ (appropriately permuted ordered points from $\bar{Q}_m$) the corresponding approximating knots $\{\hat{t}_i\}_{i=0}^m$ can be chosen in accordance with *cumulative chords* (see [5]), for $i = 1, 2, \ldots, m$:

$$\hat{t}_0 = 0, \qquad \hat{t}_i = \hat{t}_{i-1} + \|\hat{q}_i - \hat{q}_{i-1}\|. \tag{1}$$

Based on $(\{\hat{t}_i\}_{i=0}^m, \hat{Q}_m)$ an interpolation scheme $\hat{\gamma}$ (in this paper chosen as a piecewise-quadratic curve $\hat{\gamma}_2$) can be applied. A detailed description of piecewise-quadratic Lagrange interpolation can be found e.g. in [6] or [7].

3   Description of the Algorithm

3.1   Example of Curves and Samplings

We introduce now the curves and samplings used later for testing both on sparse and dense data $\bar{Q}_m$ (and thus on $\hat{Q}_m$). In particular the case when $m \to \infty$ is needed to perform numerical experiments to estimate the convergence order in γ approximation by $\hat{\gamma}_2$.

a) Curves

Example 1. (i) Define first a simple planar spiral γ_{sp} - see Fig. 3a:

$$\gamma_{sp}(t) = ((t + 0.2)\cos(\pi(1 - t)), (t + 0.2)\sin(\pi(1 - t))) \in E^2, \text{ for } t \in [0, 1], \tag{2}$$

and also another planar spiral γ_{spl} - see Fig. 3b:

$$\gamma_{spl}(t) = ((6\pi - t)\cos(t), (6\pi - t)\sin(t)) \in E^2, \text{ for } t \in [0, 5\pi].$$

As easily verifiable both γ_{sp} and γ_{spl} are regular curves, i.e. curves for which $\dot{\gamma} \neq \mathbf{0}$.   □

b) Samplings

Three types of testing samplings (other random samplings can be found in [5]) are considered in this paper. They are needed to simulate the points $q_i = \gamma(t_i)$ (here $\{Q_m\}_{i=0}^m$) on the trajectory of γ. Once the points are generated their implicit order marked by the ascending order of the interpolation knots $\{t_i\}_{i=0}^m$ is erased which renders the unordered set of reduced data $\bar{Q}_m$. This set in turn will be latter converted to the ordered set $\hat{Q}_m$.

The first selected sampling for our tests is a uniform sampling (for $0 \le i \le m$):

$$t_i = \frac{i}{m}. \tag{3}$$

The second sampling applied reads as:

$$t_i = \begin{cases} \frac{i}{m}, & \text{if } i \text{ is even,} \\ \frac{i}{m} + \frac{1}{2m} & \text{if } i = 4k + 1, \\ \frac{i}{m} - \frac{1}{2m} & \text{if } i = 4k + 3. \end{cases} \tag{4}$$

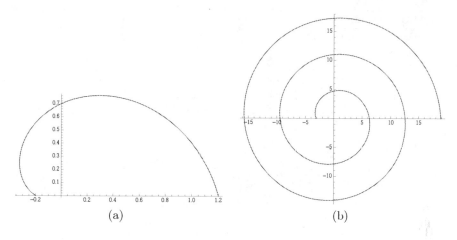

Fig. 3. The trajectories of the testing curves: a) γ_{sp}, b) γ_{spl}.

The last sampling considered here is defined as follows:

$$t_i = \frac{i}{m} + \frac{(-1)^{i+1}}{3m}. \tag{5}$$

Note that all samplings (3), (4) and (5) meet a requirement on general samplings permitting legal distribution of $\{t_i\}_{i=0}^m$. Namely, the following necessary *admissibility condition* must hold (if asymptotical analysis is to be later performed):

$$\lim_{m\to\infty} \delta_m = 0, \quad \text{where} \quad \delta_m = \max_{0\le i\le m-1}(t_{i+1} - t_i). \tag{6}$$

$\square$

3.2 Open Curves

In this subsection we assume to deal with the open curves. First let us define an open curve.

Definition 2. *The curve $\gamma : [a, b] \to \mathbb{E}^n$ is called* open *if $\gamma(a) \neq \gamma(b)$ (see [8]).*

If curve γ is closed (i.e. $\gamma(a) = \gamma(b)$), the experiments showed that our algorithm converting $\bar{Q}_m$ into $\hat{Q}_m$ does not perform so well and this remains an open problem.

The algorithm enforcing an order in a given set of points $\bar{Q}_m$ (rendering ordered set $\hat{Q}_m$) is formulated below. Subsequently this procedure is used later for interpolating $\hat{Q}_m$ (and thus also $\bar{Q}_m$).

In Algorithm 1, ε is to be chosen arbitrarily small (to prevent loops to appear).

One can easily see that Algorithm 1 is also well defined for an arbitrary Euclidean E^n space. However, the effectiveness in E^n spaces other than E^2 is not a subject of this paper.

Algorithm 1. Finding order of interpolation points for open curves

---
1: **function** FIND ORDERING OF POINTS(point_set : set of points)
2:      graphMatrix ← {}
3:      **for** i = 1; i ≤ Length(point_set); i++ **do**
4:          Append {} to end of graphMatrix
5:          **for** k = 1; i ≤ Length(point_set); k++ **do**
6:              e ← euclidean distance between i-th and k-th points in point_set
7:              **if** e < ε **then**
8:                  e ← ∞
9:              **if** i == k **then**
10:                  e ← ∞
11:              Append e to end of graphMatrix[i]
12:      g ← graph based on graphMatrix as its weighted adjacency matrix
13:      tree ← minimal spanning tree of graph g
14:      root ← first node of tree
15:      ordering ← order of vertices in g based on depth first scan using root as starting point
16: **return** point_set ordered by ordering

At this point we illustrate the execution of the above Algorithm 1. In doing so, consider γ_{sp} defined as in (2) to be sampled uniformly (3) with $m = 10$ (the number of interpolation points is 11). The interpolation knots $\{t_i\}_{i=0}^{10}$ are as follows:

$$A = \left(0, \frac{1}{10}, \frac{1}{5}, \frac{3}{10}, \frac{2}{5}, \frac{1}{2}, \frac{3}{5}, \frac{7}{10}, \frac{4}{5}, \frac{9}{10}, 1\right),$$

which ultimately yields the points $\{(t_i, \gamma_{sp}(t_i))\}_{i=0}^{10}$ positioned on the trajectory of the curve γ_{sp}:

$$
\begin{aligned}
Q_{10} = \gamma_{sp}(A) = \{ & (-0.2000, 0.0000), (-0.2853, 0.09271), (-0.3236, 0.2351), \\
& (-0.2939, 0.4045), (-0.1854, 0.5706), (0.0000, 0.7000), \\
& (0.2472, 0.7608), (0.5290, 0.7281), (0.8090, 0.5877) \\
& (1.0461, 0.3399), (1.2000, 0.0000)\} \subset \mathbb{E}^2.
\end{aligned}
$$

To simulate now the unordered set $\bar{Q}_{10}$ we apply an arbitrary permutation of the set of $\{0, 1, 2, \ldots, 10\}$:

$$P = \begin{pmatrix} 0 \; 1 \; 2 \; \; 3 \; \; 4 \; 5 \; 6 \; 7 \; 8 \; 9 \; 10 \\ 5 \; 6 \; 4 \; 10 \; 0 \; 3 \; 9 \; 2 \; 1 \; 8 \; \; 7 \end{pmatrix}.$$

This permutation results in the following random ordering of points:

$$
\begin{aligned}
\bar{Q}_{10} = \gamma_{sp}(A)^P = (& (0.0000, 0.7000), (0.2472, 0.7608), (-0.1854, 0.5706), \\
& (1.2000, 0.0000), (-0.2000, 0.0000), (-0.2939, 0.4045), \\
& (1.0462, 0.3399), (-0.3236, 0.2351), (-0.2853, 0.0927), \\
& (0.8090, 0.5877), (0.5290, 0.7281)).
\end{aligned}
$$

In the next step, based on $\bar{Q}_m$ (see also Definition 1), an e-graph $G_{\bar{Q}_m}$ from these points can be created with the corresponding adjacency matrix (see Remark 1):

$$
A_{\bar{Q}_m} =
\begin{pmatrix}
\infty & 0.255 & 0.226 & 1.39 & 0.728 & 0.417 & 1.11 & 0.566 & 0.671 & 0.817 & 0.53 \\
0.255 & \infty & 0.473 & 1.22 & 0.883 & 0.648 & 0.903 & 0.776 & 0.854 & 0.588 & 0.284 \\
0.226 & 0.473 & \infty & 1.5 & 0.571 & 0.198 & 1.25 & 0.363 & 0.488 & 0.995 & 0.732 \\
1.39 & 1.22 & 1.5 & \infty & 1.4 & 1.55 & 0.373 & 1.54 & 1.49 & 0.706 & 0.99 \\
0.728 & 0.883 & 0.571 & 1.4 & \infty & 0.415 & 1.29 & 0.266 & 0.126 & 1.17 & 1.03 \\
0.417 & 0.648 & 0.198 & 1.55 & 0.415 & \infty & 1.34 & 0.172 & 0.312 & 1.12 & 0.884 \\
1.11 & 0.903 & 1.25 & 0.373 & 1.29 & 1.34 & \infty & 1.37 & 1.35 & 0.343 & 0.647 \\
0.566 & 0.776 & 0.363 & 1.54 & 0.266 & 0.172 & 1.37 & \infty & 0.147 & 1.19 & 0.985 \\
0.671 & 0.854 & 0.488 & 1.49 & 0.126 & 0.312 & 1.35 & 0.147 & \infty & 1.2 & 1.03 \\
0.817 & 0.588 & 0.995 & 0.706 & 1.17 & 1.12 & 0.343 & 1.19 & 1.2 & \infty & 0.313 \\
0.53 & 0.284 & 0.732 & 0.99 & 1.03 & 0.884 & 0.647 & 0.985 & 1.03 & 0.313 & \infty
\end{pmatrix}.
$$

The respective e-graph $G_{\bar{Q}_m}$ together with the associated weights (taken accordingly from $A_{\bar{Q}_m}$) can be seen in Fig. 4.

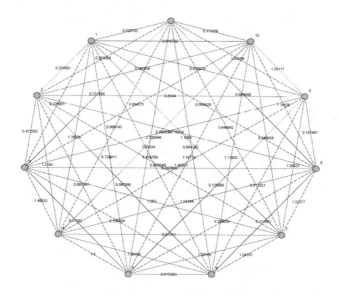

Fig. 4. E-graph created from points $\gamma_{sp}(A)^P$.

The minimal spanning tree (see [4]) generated from this graph can be seen on Fig. 5.

Fig. 5. Minimal spanning tree of e-graph created from points $\gamma_{sp}(A)^P$.

The minimal tree from Fig. 5 is highlighted on graph in Fig. 6.

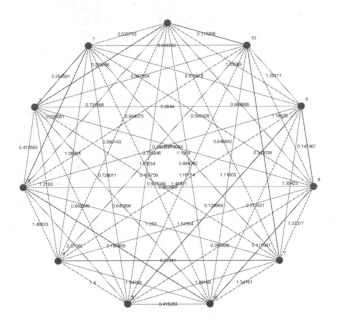

Fig. 6. E-graph created from points $\gamma_{sp}(A)^P$ with highlighted minimal spanning tree.

Having found the minimal tree, we can naturally enforce the ordering in $\bar{Q}_m$ since the depth first scan through graph yields the desired points in order (see [4]). Consequently our scheme results in the explicit ordering of the points (rendering therefore the set $\hat{Q}_m$):

$$((1.2000, 0.000), (1.0461, 0.3399), (0.8090, 0.5878),$$
$$(0.5290, 0.7281), (0.2472, 0.7608), (0.0000, 0.7000),$$
$$(-0.1854, 0.5706), (-0.2939, 0.4045), (-0.32360, 0.2351),$$
$$(-0.2853, 0.09271), (-0.2000, 0.0000)).$$

In the last step a piecewise-quadratic Lagrange interpolation $\hat{\gamma}_2$ is invoked (with $\{\hat{t}_i\}_{i=0}^m$ defined according to (1)) and based on either ordered or unordered set of reduced data i.e. either on $\hat{Q}_m$ or on $\bar{Q}_m$, respectively. The interpolating curves are presented in Fig. 7.

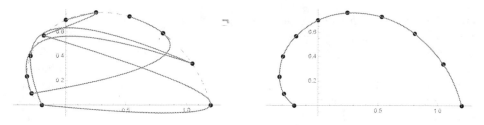

Fig. 7. a) Interpolation based on $\gamma_{sp}(A)^P$ without and b) with points ordering

One can easily see that ordering of points is the reverse original order. Which does not matter for the interpolation - trajectory is the same, however the curve $\hat{\gamma}_2$ passes in the opposite direction. Therefore the generated interpolant is optimal for these points, i.e. the same as generated from the points with original ordering.

□

We exploit here one particular phenomenon - when given points are forming open curve, it is safe to assume that minimal spanning tree of e-graph is actually a linear graph. Therefore from our observation and asymptotic testing, minimal spanning tree of e-graph generates an optimal ordering of points. This result combined with proven theorem from [7] lay foundations to the formulation of the following conjectured result (to hold asymptotically):

Theorem 1. *Let a regular $\gamma \in C^3$ be sampled according to the admissibility condition (6). Assume Algorithm 1 for unordered reduced data $\bar{Q}_m$ yields $\hat{Q}_m$ with ordering coinciding with the unknown interpolation knots $\{t_i\}_{i=0}^m$. Then a piecewise-quadratic interpolant $\hat{\gamma}_2 : [0, \hat{T}] \to E^2$ fitting $\hat{Q}_m$ with $\{\hat{t}_i\}_{i=0}^m$ (see (1) built on $\hat{Q}_m$) renders:*

$$\hat{\gamma}_2 \circ \psi = \gamma + O(\delta_m^3), \tag{7}$$

where $\psi : [0, T] \to [0, \hat{T}]$ is a piecewise-quadratic Lagrange interpolant defined as in [9].

It should be underlined here that ψ is not needed for the construction of the Algorithm 1 and the interpolant $\hat{\gamma}_2$ based on unordered data $\bar{Q}_m$. However, to test numerically (or for proving analytically Th. 1) it is necessary to introduce such reparameterization as both curves γ and $\hat{\gamma}_2$ need to be compared only over the same domain $[0, T]$. The interpolant in question $\hat{\gamma}_2$ is evidently defined over external domain $[0, \hat{T}]$, which generically does not coincide with the internal one i.e. with $[0, T]$. The function ψ is defined here a sum-track of the $\psi_i : [t_i, t_{i+2}] \to [\hat{t}_i, \hat{t}_{i+3}]$ (with $i = 2k$), where each ψ_i is a quadratic satisfying $\psi_i(t_{i+j}) = \hat{t}_{i+j}$, for $j = 0, 1, 2$. Note also that if the order of $\hat{Q}_m$ is the same as $\{t_i\}_{i=0}^m$ then ψ_i preserves the γ motion along t and (7) examines a real difference between the interpolant $\hat{\gamma}_2$ and the curve γ. Our conjecture is that for reasonable curves, admissible samplings $\{t_i\}_{i=0}^m$ and dense data $\bar{Q}_m$ the Algorithm 1 determines the set $\bar{Q}_m$ having the same order as original interpolation knots $\{t_i\}_{i=0}^m$ - this remains still an open problem to be resolved analytically. However, the numerical tests performed in the next section confirm the above fact, at least for all samplings and curves considered in this paper. Once the latter is achieved the asymptotics in (7) follows from [9]. Finally, note that ψ should be a re-parameterization, which also is proved not always to hold in [9]. A recent result [10] formulates sufficient conditions imposed on $\{t_i\}_{i=0}^m$ to guarantee that ψ is a genuine reparameterization. Note that the corresponding result established for ordered data points Q_m is also discussed in [7]. In the next section the numerical verification of Theorem 1 is experimentally accomplished.

4   Experiments

Our tests are performed in *Mathematica* 10.0.0 using Intel Core i7 3.5 GHz processor with 32 GiB of RAM.

We introduce now a formal definition of convergence orders.

Definition 3. *Consider the family* $F_{\delta_m} : [0, T] \to E^n$ *(in our case* $F_{\delta_m} = (\hat{\gamma} \circ \psi - \gamma)(t))$. *We say that* $F_{\delta_m} = O(\delta_m^\alpha)$ *if* $\|F_\alpha\| = O(\delta_m^\alpha)$ *(where* $\|\cdot\|$ *denotes the Euclidean norm). The latter can be reformulated to:* $\exists_{K>0} \exists_{\bar{\delta}} \|F_{\delta_m}\| \leq K\delta_m^\alpha$, *for all* $\delta_m \in (0, \bar{\delta})$ *and* $t \in [0, T]$.

Since $T = \Sigma_{i=1}^m (t_{i+1} - t_i) \leq m\delta_m$ the following holds $m^{-\alpha} = O(\delta_m^\alpha)$, for arbitrary $\alpha > 0$ mentioned in Definition 3 (see also [7]). Therefore, for the verification of any asymptotics expressed in terms of $O(\delta_m^\alpha)$ it is sufficient to examine the claims of Th. 1 in terms of $O(1/m^\alpha)$ asymptotics.

Recall that for a parametric smooth planar curve $\gamma : [0, T] \to E^2$ (with $[0, T]$ compact) and m varying between $m_{min} \leq m \leq m_{max}$ the i-th component of the error for γ estimation by $\hat{\gamma}^i$ is defined as follows:

$$E_m^i = \sup_{t \in [t_i, t_{i+2}]} \|(\hat{\gamma}^i \circ \psi_i)(t) - \gamma(t)\| = \max_{t \in [t_i, t_{i+2}]} \|(\hat{\gamma}^i \circ \psi_i)(t) - \gamma(t)\|. \qquad (8)$$

The maximal value E_m for each $m = 2k$ is found by using *Mathematica* numerical optimization function: *NMaximize* [11]. From the set of *absolute errors* $\{E_m\}_{m=m_{min}}^{m=m_{max}}$ the numerical estimate of α is calculated using a linear regression applied to the collection of points $(\log(m), -\log(E_m))$ (where $m_{min} \leq m \leq m_{max}$). The *Mathematica's* built-in function *LinearModelFit* renders the estimated coefficient α from the computed regression line $y(x) = \hat{\alpha}x + b$. The results estimating α from (7) are presented in Table 1 for three types of samplings: (3), (5), (4) and two testing curves γ_{sp} and γ_{spl} using $\varepsilon = 0.001$ introduced in Algorithm 1.

Tests (performed with $m \in \{151, \ldots, 181\}$) shown in Table 1 visibly confirm Theorem 1.

Table 1. Result of numerical experiments

Curve	Sampling	$\hat{\alpha} \approx \alpha$
γ_{sp}	(3)	3.017
γ_{sp}	(5)	3.021
γ_{sp}	(4)	3.015
γ_{spl}	(3)	3.015
γ_{spl}	(5)	3.017
γ_{spl}	(4)	3.02

5   Conclusion

In this paper we verify numerically the asymptotics (7) from Theorem 1. In doing so, first an Algorithm 1 for generating an interpolation scheme $\hat{\gamma}_2$ based on planar unordered reduced data set $\bar{Q}_m = \{\bar{q}_i\}_{i=0}^m$ is introduced. More specifically, Lagrange piecewise-quadratic interpolation $\hat{\gamma}_2$ combined with cumulative chords and a procedure of converting unordered reduced data $\bar{Q}_m$ into ordered reduced data $\hat{Q}_m$ are introduced. More specifically, Lagrange piecewise-quadratic interpolation $\hat{\gamma}_2$ combined with cumulative chords and a procedure of converting unordered reduced data $\bar{Q}_m$ into ordered reduced data $\hat{Q}_m$ are introduced and tested on both sparse and dense data. Additionally, our experiments confirm cubic order of convergence in trajectory approximation by the proposed data fitting scheme. This asymptotic results coincides with already proved one for the ordered data Q_m - see [9]. Naturally, the data fitting scheme in question is extendable to other interpolation schemes and to multidimensional unordered reduced data.

The open problems include interpolating the ordered reduced data positioned on the trajectory of closed curve γ. The theoretical proof of asymptotics observed and verified here forms another possible research task. This would immediately follow once we find sufficient conditions guaranteeing that asymptotically the ordering in $\hat{Q}_m$ coincides with the order of interpolation knots. This is our conjecture and it remains as another open problem. One can also analyze the asymptotics in approximating other geometrical features including length (see e.g. [12] or [13]) or curvature of γ. Finally, the next open problem may include testing effectiveness of our data fitting algorithm in E^3 (or in E^n).

More discussion on applications (including real data examples - see [2] or [14]) and theory of non-reduced data interpolation can be found in [3], [5], [15], [16], [17], [18], [19], [20] or [21]. In particular different parameterizations $\{\hat{t}\}_{i=0}^m$ of the unknown interpolation knots $\{t\}_{i=0}^m$ are discussed e.g. in [1], [22], [23] or [24].

References

1. Kvasov, B.I.: Methods of Shape-Preserving Spline Approximation. World Scientific Publishing Company, Singapore (2000)
2. Janik, M., Kozera, R., Kozioł, P.: Reduced data for curve modeling - applications in graphics, computer vision and physics. Advances in Science and Technology **7**(18), 28–35 (2013)
3. Piegl, L., Tiller, W.: The NURBS Book. Springer, Heidelberg (1997)
4. Ross, K.A., Wright, C.R.B.: Discrete Mathematics. Pearson (2002)

5. Kozera, R.: Curve modeling via interpolation based on multidimensional reduced data. Studia Informatica **25**(4B–61), 1–140 (2004)
6. De Boor, C.: A Practical Guide to Splines. Springer, Heidelberg (2001)
7. Kozera, R., Noakes, L., Szmielew, P.: Trajectory estimation for exponential parameterization and different samplings. In: Saeed, K., Chaki, R., Cortesi, A., Wierzchoń, S. (eds.) CISIM 2013. LNCS, vol. 8104, pp. 430–441. Springer, Heidelberg (2013)
8. Krantz, S.G.: Handbook of Complex Variables. Springer Science+Business Media, New York (1999)
9. Noakes, L., Kozera, R.: Cumulative chord piecewise quadratics and piecewise cubics. In: Klette, R., Kozera, R., Noakes, L., Weickert, J. (eds.) Geometric Properties for Incomplete Data Computational Imaging and Vision, vol. 31, pp. 59–76. Springer (2006)
10. Kozera, R., Noakes, L.: Piecewise-quadratics and reparameterizations for interpolating reduced data. In: Gerdt, V., Koepf, W., Seiler, W., Vorozhtsov, E. (eds.) CASC 2015. LNCS, vol. 9301, pp. 260–274. Springer Int. Pub. Switzerland (2015)
11. Wolfram Mathematica 9, Documentation Center. http://reference.wolfram.com/mathematica/guide/Mathematica.html
12. Kozera, R., Noakes, L., Klette, R.: External versus internal parameterizations for lengths of curves with nonuniform samplings. In: Asano, T., Klette, R., Ronse, C. (eds.) Geometry, Morphology, and Computational Imaging. LNCS, vol. 2616, pp. 403–418. Springer, Heidelberg (2003)
13. Noakes, L., Kozera, R.: More-or-less uniform sampling and lengths of curves. Quarterly of Applied Mathematics **61**(3), 475–484 (2003)
14. Bator, M., Chmielewski, L.: Finding regions of interest for cancerous masses enhanced by elimination of linear structures and considerations on detection correctness measures in mammography. Pattern Analysis and Applications **12**(4), 377–390 (2009)
15. Kozera, R., Noakes, L.: Piecewise-quadratics and exponential parameterization for reduced data. Applied Mathematics and Computation **221**, 620–638 (2013)
16. Kozera, R., Noakes, L., Szmielew, P.: Length estimation for exponential parameterization and ϵ-uniform samplings. In: Huang, F., Sugimoto, A. (eds.) PSIVT 2013. LNCS, vol. 8334, pp. 33–46. Springer, Heidelberg (2014)
17. Farin, G.: Curves and Surfaces for Computer Aided Geometric Design, 3rd edn. Academic Press, San Diego (1993)
18. Epstein, M.P.: On the influence of parameterization in parametric interpolation. SIAM Journal of Numerical Analysis. **13**, 261–268 (1976)
19. Kozera, R., Noakes, L.: C^1 interpolation with cumulative chord cubics. Fundamenta Informaticae **61**(3–4), 285–301 (2004)
20. Homenda, W., Pedrycz, W.: Processing uncertain information in the linear space of fuzzy sets. Fuzzy Sets and Systems **44**(2), 187–198 (1991)
21. Budzko, D.A., Prokopenya, A.N.: Symbolic numerical methods for searching equilibrium states in a restricted four-body problem. Programming and Computer Software **39**(2), 74–80 (2013)
22. Mørken, K., Scherer, K.: A general framework for high-accuracy parametric interpolation. Mathematics of Computation **66**(217), 237–260 (1997)
23. Kocić, L.M., Simoncelli, A.C., Della Vecchia, B.: Blending parameterization of polynomial and spline interpolants, Facta Universitatis (NIŠ). Series Mathematics and Informatics **5**, 95–107 (1990)
24. Lee, E.T.Y.: Choosing nodes in parametric curve interpolation. Computer-Aided Design **21**(6), 363–370 (1987)

A Novel Phase-Based Approach to Tear Film Surface Quality Assessment Using Lateral Shearing Interferometry

Piotr Szyperski$^{(\boxtimes)}$ and D. Robert Iskander

Department of Computer Engineering, Wrocław University of Technology,
Wybrzeże Wyspiańskiego 27, 50-370 Wrocław, Poland
{piotr.szyperski,robert.iskander}@pwr.edu.pl
http://www.tearfilm.pwr.wroc.pl/index.php/en/research
http://dri.pwr.edu.pl/research/

Abstract. Lateral shearing interferometry (LSI) can be used for assessing the properties of tear film. In particular, it has the capability of acquiring dynamic variations in tear film surface quality (TFSQ) during an interblink interval in an *in"-vivo* fashion. The purpose of this study was to assess the suitability of LSI based two"-dimensional (2"=D) phase estimation procedures in the analysis of tear film dynamics. The paper discusses the main difficulty in 2"=D phase estimation "+ the problem of phase unwrapping, proposes a modification of one of the popular phase unwrapping algorithms, and suggests a set of phase parameters that could be exploited as LSI"-based TFSQ descriptors.

Keywords: *in-vivo* interferometry · Takeda's algorithm · two-dimensional phase unwrapping · Goldstein's algorithm

1 Introduction

Background. Lateral shearing interferometry (LSI) is one of the most sensitive methods for measuring tear film surface quality (TFSQ) *in"-vivo* in human eyes [1]. Current analysis of LSI"-based interferograms essentially includes parameters derived based on the analysis of the first harmonic of the amplitude Fourier spectrum [2]. It was of interest to ascertain whether the phase contained in the spectrum can be used to extract additional information from the interferogram that can be further utilized for the assessment of TFSQ. A classical method for phase estimation in interferometry and profilometry is based on the Takeda approach [3]. The main problem in LSI is that the spatial phase requires two-dimensional (2"=D) unwrapping, for which the algorithms are not trivial [4] and computationally very intensive. Furthermore, the results of 2"=D phase unwrapping are highly dependent on the particular algorithm used. The aim of this work was to assess the applicability of 2"=D phase estimation for LSI and design a set of phase parameters for the characterization of the dynamics in TFSQ analysis both on the eye's cornea and contact lens surface.

© IFIP International Federation for Information Processing 2015
K. Saeed and W. Homenda (Eds.): CISIM 2015, LNCS 9339, pp. 435–447, 2015.
DOI: 10.1007/978-3-319-24369-6_36

1.1 Hardware Setup of Experiments

The LSI hardware setup under consideration comprises single set optical wedge with predetermined shear angle. Conversely, Twyman"+Green utilizes the reference mirror that allows measuring wavefront deformations in a direct manner [5–7]. The drawback of this setup reducing its applicability in TFSQ assessment is the fact that it is more sensitive to even slight vibrations of the test surface (e. g. saccadic movements of the eye). These are inevitable during *in"-vivo* experiments whereas LSI experimental setup is capable of mitigating their impact on the interference pattern [2].

Figure 1 depicts a typical LSI configuration employed for corneal and contact lens tear film surface topography data acquisition while Sec. 1.1 shows few examples of output interferograms.

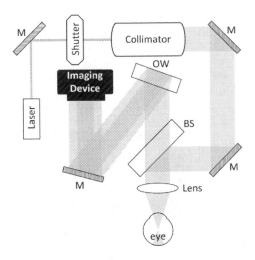

Fig. 1. LSI scheme: M "+ mirrors, BS "+ beam splitter, OW "+ optical wedge

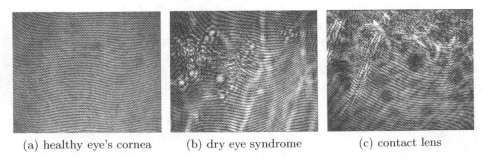

(a) healthy eye's cornea   (b) dry eye syndrome   (c) contact lens

Fig. 2. Typical cases of tear film interferograms showing pre-corneal tear film in good condition 2a, slightly deteriorated 2b and pre"-lens tear film 2c

Until now the analysis of the LSI images concerned only the amplitude information and little attention was paid to the phase [8]. The purpose of this work was to examine the applicability of phase"-based methods in the analysis of tear film.

2   Methods

The true wavefront phase cannot be estimated directly from LSI images [9], although some methods of evaluating an unknown wavefronts have been developed, e. g. Saunders method or Rimmer"+Wyant method with Okuda improvements. The main limitation of these methods is that the wavefront evaluation is confined only to points separated by a distance of S that is the lateral shear in the sagittal ($0x$) direction [7, Sec. 1.5.2, 1.5.3].

2.1   Indirect Retrieval of Phase Information

There is some visual similarity between interferometric images in the single direction LSI and those of *profilometry*. Hence, it was of interest to ascertain whether methods developed for phase estimation in profilometry would be applicable also to LSI. The basic principle of phase estimation in profilometry has been outlined by Takeda [3,10] in which both 1"=D and 2"=D phase estimation algorithms were considered. In profilometry, such algorithms are usually followed by a phase unwrapping procedure which reveals the true surface of the wavefront exhibiting the shape of the scanned object. In case of 3"=D objects, an algorithm for 2"=D phase unwrapping has been proposed by Goldstein's et al. [11] for application in satellite radar interferometry to measure ground surface deformation or terrain elevation. Goldstein's algorithm is considered as a good trade"-off between trivial direct phase unwrapping methods and more sophisticated but also computationally very expensive procedures [4,12]. Furthermore, for which there are few ready implementation routines.

The Takeda's Phase Reconstruction Algorithm. This method was proposed by M. Takeda *et al.* in 1981 to enable automatic discrimination between elevation and depression of the object or wavefront form [3]. The chain of the operations constituting the routine is depicted by Sec. 2.1 and discussed below in greater detail.

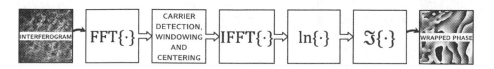

Fig. 3. Image processing chain in Takeda's algorithm

Assumptions on fringe pattern periodicity and phase disruptions. When a periodic fringe pattern is considered, it can be represented in the form of:

$$g(x, y) = a(x, y) + b(x, y) \cos[2\pi f_0 x + \phi(x, y)], \tag{1}$$

where $\phi(x, y)$ contains the desired phase information and $a(x, y)$ and $b(x, y)$ are unwanted irradiance variations that, together with $\phi(x, y)$, in most cases present much slower spatial frequency than the variation introduced by f_0. Equation (1) can be rewritten equivalently as:

$$g(x, y) = a(x, y) + c(x, y) \exp(2\pi i f_0 x) + c^*(x, y) \exp(-2\pi i f_0 x), \tag{2}$$

where

$$c(x, y) = \tfrac{1}{2} b(x, y) \exp[i\phi(x, y)], \tag{3}$$

with $\cdot^*$ denoting a complex conjugate.

Carrier sideband detection and extraction in spectral domain. During the analysis of 2"=D interferogram, the following procedure can be performed in either of the two dimensions as well as in both. Since the operation in 2"=D do not differ significantly from 1"=D case, the latter is described to maintain simplicity of the notation. The Fast Fourier Transformation (FFT) algorithm can be applied to the fringe pattern along the axis of abscissæ. The result of transforming Eq. (2) into spatial frequency domain is:

$$G(f, y) = A(f, y) + C(f - f_0, y) + C^*(f + f_0, y), \tag{4}$$

with capital letters denoting the Fourier spectra (and C used for the carrier side bands) and f being the spatial frequency in $0x$ direction.

In a typical case of an interferogram with low distortion grade, the sidebands Fourier spectra from Eq. (4) would be well"-separated from the carrier frequency f_0. This is ensured as long as the variations of $a(x, y)$, $b(x, y)$ and $\phi(x, y)$ are sufficiently slower than the spatial frequency f_0. Either of the two sidebands spectra on the carrier can be used for phase information retrieval, and the commonly used is $C(f - f_0, y)$.

A few simple operations are applied on the periodogram to mask and extract the carrier sideband spectrum. Then it is translated by $-f_0$ on the frequency axis toward its origin to obtain $C(f, y)$. Note that the unwanted background variation $a(x, y)$ representing has been filtered out in this stage. As $A(f, y)$ represents the value of the 0th order harmonic component in Fourier spectrum, this reduction can be further improved by shifting the interferogram brightness values during the preprocessing to reduce its mean to have zero value.

Fringe phase reconstruction. The Inverse FFT (IFFT) algorithm is used to compute $c(x, y)$, the inverse Fourier transform of $C(f, y)$ with respect to f. It is defined by Eq. (3) and a complex natural logarithm of it can be computed:

$$\ln[c(x, y)] = \ln[\tfrac{1}{2} b(x, y)] + i\phi(x, y). \tag{5}$$

The phase $\phi(x,y)$ constitutes the imaginary part of the result, as Eq. (5) shows. Furthermore, it is completely separated from the real part that comprises the unwanted amplitude variation $b(x,y)$. The phase obtained in this manner is in fact the angular coordinate of $C(f,y)$ represented in polar form. Thus, it is indeterminate to a factor of 2π, which is often referred to as *wrapped phase*. In most cases, a computer"-generated function subroutine gives a principal value ranging from $-\pi$ to π. This can lead to presence of discontinuities in reconstructed phase that sometimes need to be eliminated to allow further analysis of the absolute phase value in a process commonly referred to as *phase unwrapping* that is described further.

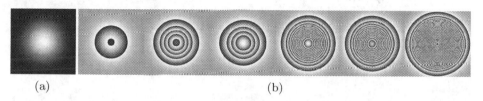

(a)   (b)

Fig. 4. Gaussian phase disruption to be reconstructed by Takeda's algorithm: 4a unwrapped, used for phase modulation of fringes, and 4b wrapped mod 2π for mimicking the error"-less output (disruption scale increases from left to right)

Advantages and Limitations of Takeda's Algorithm. The method described above is more accurate and sensitive than e. g. moiré topography or conventional fringe-contour interferometry and does not require any moving components in experimental setup nor involve interpolation of the data in the regions between contour fringes [3,10]. Nevertheless, under specific circumstances, its results can be inaccurate. This was investigated on synthetic data involving Gaussian phase disruptions of maximum intensities of $\phi_{max}(x,y)$ varying from low to high as well as low, intermediate and high fringe frequencies f_0.

The phase disruption surface used for investigation of Takeda's algorithm implementation has maximum value in the center and zeros in the corners, q. v. Sec. 2.1. The wrapped phase surfaces in Fig. 4b were generated for comparison with actual results. Sections 2.1 to 2.1 show (clockwise): Takeda's algorithm inputs, intermediate results and reconstructed wrapped phase surfaces. In, e. g. Figs. 5a and 5b there is the synthetically generated interferometric input image and its wrapped phase calculated directly from the disruption, in Figs. 5c and 5d "+ periodograms of interferogram and extracted carrier sideband, in Fig. 5e "+ the algorithm output: retrieved information about phase (in this case properly reconstructed) and in Fig. 5e "+ fringe pattern generated on the basis of the reconstructed wrapped phase surface.

In a typical case, low and intermediate (relatively to f_0) phase disruptions were reconstructed properly irrespective of fringe frequency (q. v. Sec. 2.1). For odd fringes count, there was a phase shift of $-\pi$, but further analysis showed that

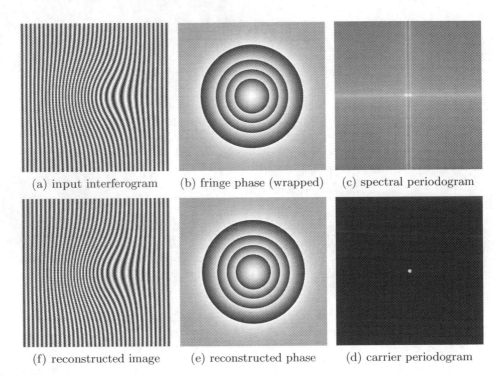

(a) input interferogram   (b) fringe phase (wrapped)   (c) spectral periodogram

(f) reconstructed image   (e) reconstructed phase   (d) carrier periodogram

Fig. 5. Takeda's algorithm with medium fringe frequency and moderate phase disruption

it was caused by the specificity of the fringe generator that was fixed to have zero phase and the local maximum of the cosine fringe function (i.e., $x = 0$) in the image center. In the leftmost pixel, there was a half"-period of the cosine function and the local minimum of the fringe value. When the FFT is evaluated, this local minimum is equivalent to $\pm\pi$ phase offset in the leftmost pixel associated with spatial point having $x = 0$ coordinate.

Furthermore, for non-integer fringes count, there are some errors in the unwrapped phase that tend to accumulate near the border of the image, at the side from which the carrier side band was extracted (q.v. Sec. 2.1). The influence of above mentioned reconstruction faults is significant for small fringe frequencies and becomes almost negligible in the intermediate or higher bands. The significance of inter-pixel location of the true 1st order spectral peak is the most important cause of this effect, and the relative inaccuracy of peak localization, which in this case had 1 px precision, is inversely proportional to the value of f_0. Some overcomes have been proposed to mitigate this undesired property, i.a. by determining Fourier peaks at sub"-pixel level [13] (one attempt may be to infer about the peak exact location by utilizing the information of side band contour map). The applicability of these attempts is usually strongly restricted to interferograms with sufficiently low phase noise level and therefore the problem remains unsolved

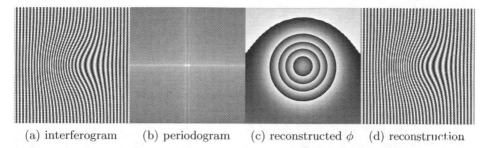

(a) interferogram   (b) periodogram   (c) reconstructed ϕ (d) reconstruction

Fig. 6. Takeda's algorithm: non"-integer fringe frequency, moderate phase disruption

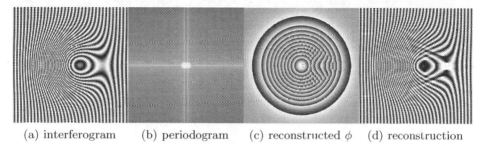

(a) interferogram   (b) periodogram   (c) reconstructed ϕ (d) reconstruction

Fig. 7. Takeda's algorithm: medium fringe frequency, intense phase disruption

when the interferogram periodicity is strongly deteriorated (e. g. for tear film evaporating from contact lens surface).

Sections 2.1 and 2.1 depicts the conditions, in which proper phase reconstruction was impossible and the result was distorted by the excessive level of phase disruption. When there are closed loops in the interference pattern, it means that there is a region where decrease of instantaneous phase introduced by the disruption is too fast and cannot be compensated by the increase from constant frequency f_0 component. An area of local phase descent in one direction exhibits negative instantaneous frequency in that direction, as $f_x(x,y) = \frac{\partial \phi(x,y)}{\partial x}$. Negative frequency components from the $C(f - f_0, y)$ carrier side band superimposes on the conjugate symmetric $C^*(f + f_0, y)$ side band negative frequency component and vice versa for positive frequencies. This introduces ambiguity in at least part of the area between two 1st order Fourier peaks. Thus, the side bands become partially indistinguishable and in general case it is impossible to eliminate the overlapping components from the chosen band. When the band is extracted using circular mask, a part of it still maintains information about its conjugate counterpart. IFFT of spectrum extracted in such manner amplifies or weakens some frequency components when compared to the unobtainable pure single band transformation. This eventually leads to asymmetry and some artefacts occurring in the reconstructed wrapped phase and also distorts the reconstructed fringe pattern. Although the visual disturbance is not necessarily of a substantial extent, in many cases it breaks some of the phase discontinuity loops

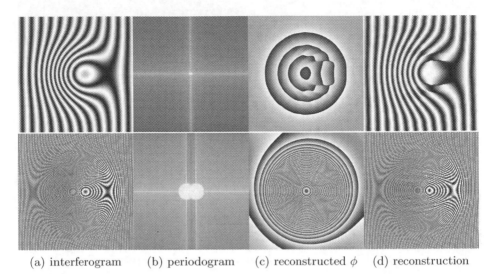

(a) interferogram   (b) periodogram   (c) reconstructed ϕ (d) reconstruction

Fig. 8. Takeda's algorithm: low (top row) and high (bottom row) fringe frequencies, intense phase disruption

or introduces open areas of such discontinuity. Such structures are associated with phase residues and the presence of such residues is a sign of improper phase surface reconstruction. What is more, it is impossible to remove phase discontinuities by unwrapping the phase along any close loop encompassing a single residue. This makes the phase unwrapping task non"-trivial for residue"-afflicted surfaces and its result will always be imperfect. Various phase unwrapping algorithms, however, can diminish residues influence to a different degree. Nonetheless, as a rule of thumb one can state that the more effective in accomplishing this task a method is, the more complicated its implementation would be and its computational complexity may be also disproportionately higher than the achieved improvement [4, 12].

In preceding examples involving synthetic fringe pattern, windowing was not applied, both in the spatial division (before FFT) and in the frequency division (before carrier side band masking) due to its negligible role as the perfect fringes periodicity and lack of spectral background noise were guaranteed.

The Goldstein's Phase Unwrapping Algorithm. Whereas phase unwrapping is trivial in 1"-D problems, this is not true for higher dimensionality. In an ideal situation of perfectly reconstructed wrapped phase this would still be a relatively simple task. However, it is not the case applicable to most *in vivo* measurements. The phase in a complex images is subject to many factors that can disrupt its values. The influence of these phenomena reduces the useful signal detectability. Procedures have been developed that try to achieve a trade off between solution accuracy under these adverse conditions and computational requirements. No *standard procedure* to solve the phase unwrapping problem has been established, thus a large variety of algorithms are in use. Given the failure of a straightforward integration when applied to noisy data, other methods utilizing residue detection and branch cuts, quality maps or error minimization are commonly used. They can be divided into two main types [14]: *a*) path"-following methods and *b*) minimum"-norm methods. They differ in efficacy and computational complexity. Detailed explanation of their quality, robustness and execution time is presented in [4].

Goldstein's method (sometimes referred to as *Goldstein"=Zebken"=Werner algorithm*) has a fairly complex procedure structure [15]. Firstly, the polarity is computed for the phase residues. This involves phase gradient calculation, residues detection and residue charge determination (± 1). Subsequently, the branch areas to cut are located, along which a phase integration path may not intersect. These are, i. a. lines linking residues of opposite polarity and, in some implementations, isolated residues located near image borders together with their connections. Typical LSI contact lens image produces a numerous amount of branch cuts as compared to the corneal interferograms, what indicates much higher level of image disruption caused by the drying of the tear film. Finally, the instantaneous phase surface is reconstructed during flood fill procedure that prevents every integration path from crossing the branch cuts.

Advantages and Limitations of Goldstein's Algorithm. Goldstein's algorithm takes a relatively short time to execute that makes one of the fastest phase unwrapping procedures. It also tries to reduce defects significance relative to a trivial phase unwrapping approach as depicted by Sec. 2.1 that shows failures during the unwrapping of imperfectly reconstructed phase. It takes measures to minimize the number of discontinuities and optimizes branch cuts location to locally minimize their length (q. v. Fig. 9b). Nonetheless, branch cuts placement can isolate segments of the image and thereby prevent them from being unwrapped. This occurs especially in datasets containing many residues. Figure 9b also reveals that the algorithm is subject to numerical pitfalls. In the utilized implementation, residues placed close to image borders are connected with them by two branch cuts directed at the angle of 45 instead of one at 90 . Thus a separated triangular areas are formed where no information about unwrapped phase was retrieved.

There are some more efficient alternatives, but they are also of much higher computational complexity [4,16]. Much better (i. e. the most discontinuity"-free) solution is produced by, e. g. the minimum $\ell^{p"}$=norm algorithm. Average background noise is also minimized in comparison to other algorithms. However, this is the second slowest algorithm after the mask cut approach with execution time usually longer than Goldstein in about one to two orders of magnitude (actual value vary greatly, as it depends on the convergence speed [4]).

Some additional steps can be performed to locally improve the quality of this method results. The modification of the Goldstein's algorithm described below allows complete reduction of significant branch cuts at the expense of losing phase information in some image parts outside its central area.

(a) a trivial approach without branch cuts (b) Goldstein's algorithm with branch cuts

Fig. 9. examples of phase unwrapping results (without phase residues masking). Discontinuities of the surface are present where the algorithms were unable to unwrap phase due to residue-induced ambiguities

Algorithm Modification. After determining the residue polarities, the image is preliminary masked to achieve a region, where the mask contains only regions with no residues. Also accepted are the areas with pairs opposite charge residues separated by a short distance. All subsequent actions may be performed only within the masked region. This condition ensures lack of any significant discontinuities in unwrapped phase. The mask is calculated as a circle expanding (by default from the image center) as long as it fulfils the above conditions. Then, four more circles are created on its border and expanded. This subroutine is performed in a recursive manner and thus the modification is called a *recursive bubble* approach.

2.2   Phase Parameters as TFSQ Descriptors

Three phase components were derived from the phase coordinates (two spatial and one intensity component). The variance of all of them was significantly different than the variance of the phase itself. However, after applying the linear detrending of the unwrapped phase, the variance of phase was much smaller than of spatial components. Thus, PCA combined and transformed the coordinates into first two principal components, whilst the intensity of the phase map was assigned virtually intact to last component. Therefore phase and 3rd component variations were the same. This indicates that PCA procedure is redundant and phase variance is equally adequate TFSQ descriptor.

3   Results

There was an application developed that underwent tests on a set of static and dynamic data. The initial input data set consisted of 19 static PNG images and 13 AVI video sequences. Results for the synthetic undistorted images were consistent with theoretically predicted results. The output for *in vivo* LSI (q. v. Sec. 3) has shown that the algorithm is capable of reconstructing phase for slightly distorted images, but gives ambiguous output in case of strongly deteriorated film. Processing of a single movie in MATLAB environment lasted between 30 min and 16 h depending on disorder level.

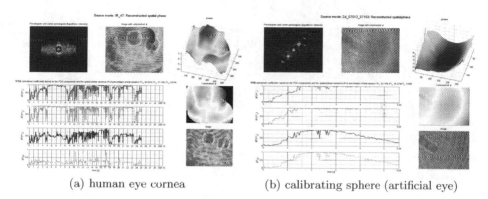

        (a) human eye cornea   (b) calibrating sphere (artificial eye)

Fig. 10. Exemplary outputs of the tear film surface quality assessing system

4   Discussion and Conclusions

Spectral representation of LSI images provide mostly information of sub"-global character related to the frequency of fringes. On the other hand, the phase extracted from those images carries information of local character. The unwrapped phase has no simple physical interpretation. Although it is not directly related to the wavefront, it is causally associated with it. However, there are similarities between the two considered representations. In case of deteriorating quality of tear film covering the eye cornea, the spectral representation of LSI images becomes less regular and the phase representation starts to loose its continuity.

Conclusions. Analysis of the measurements and theoretical background suggests that the method joining Takeda's and Goldstein's algorithms with phase variability analysis as tear film surface quality descriptor is capable of supplying useful information. Still, along with the increase of the phase noise occurring when tear film dries up, the efficacy of this solution decreases significantly.

Tests on LSI images, frequently exhibited saddle"-shaped formation in phase surface and chessboard-like structures in the phase maps. They were consistent with the visible input phase variations. Their occurrence might arise due to optical aberrations of objective lens and the natural corneal asphericity. Thus the method has a potential for serving in other closely"-related applications, like testing and calibration of medical diagnostic equipment.

Future Recommendations. As a way of overcoming issues encountered, a enhanced or new method of interferogram analysis may be adapted. In particular an extended set of both wrapped and unwrapped phase parameters might be considered, e. g.: *a*) excess kurtosis; *b*) texture statistics derived from gray"-level co"-occurrence matrix (GLCM): homogeneity, energy/uniformity, correlation and contrast; *c*) Rényi entropy and *d*) Kass"-Witkin coherence [17]. Thereafter a modification of hardware in experimental setup can be taken into account to improve the input data quality.

Acknowledgments. The authors would like to express their gratitude to **Prof. Ewa Skubalska"-Rafajlowicz** and **Dr. Dorota Szczesna-Iskander** for extensive and fruitful cooperation and for their encouragement, advice and support.

Supported by the European Regional Development Fund within Innovative Economy Operational Program co-financed by the Foundation for Polish Science (POMOST/2012-5/8/0072).

References

1. Szczęsna, D.H., Alonso-Caneiro, D., Iskander, D.R., Read, S.A., Collins, M.J.: Lateral shearing interferometry, dynamic wavefront sensing and high-speed video-keratoscopy for noninvasive assessment of tear film surface characteristics: A comparative study. J. Biomed. Opt. **15**(3:037005), 1–9 (2010)
2. Szczęsna, D.H., Iskander, D.R.: Robust estimation of tear film surface quality in lateral shearing interferometry. J. Biomed. Opt. **14**(6), 064039-1–064039-4 (2009)
3. Takeda, M., Ina, H., Kobayashi, S.: Fourier-transform method of fringe-pattern analysis for computer-based topography and interferometry. J. Opt. Soc. Am. **72**(1), 156–160 (1982)
4. Braganza, S.: Analysis of phase-unwrap quality of OQM images, May 2006. http://www.coe.neu.edu/Research/rcl/projects/phaseunwrap/Analysisofphase-ver2.html
5. Rottenkolber, M., Podbielska, H.: High precision Twyman-Green interferometer for the measurement of ophthalmic surfaces. Acta Ophthalmol. Scand. **74**(4), 348–353 (1996)
6. Licznerski, T.J., Kasprzak, H.T., Kowalik, W.: Application of Twyman-Green interferometer for evaluation of in vivo breakup characteristic of the human tear film. J. Biomed. Opt. **4**(1), 176–182 (1999)
7. Malacara, D., Servín, M., Malacara, Z.: Interferogram analysis for optical testing, 2nd ed., vol. 84. Taylor & Francis Group, Ed., ser. Optical engineering (Marcel Dekker, Inc.), CRC press, Boca Raton, FL (2005)
8. Szczęsna, D.H., Jaroński, J., Kasprzak, H.T., Stenevi, U.: Interferometric measurements of dynamic changes of tear film. J. Biomed. Opt. **11**(3), 034028-1–034028-8 (2006)
9. Licznerski, T.J.: Interferencyjne i modelowe badanie filmu łzowego oka ludzkiego. Polish, Ph.D. thesis, Politechnika Wrocławska, Wrocław (1998)
10. Takeda, M., Muto, K.: Fourier transform profilometry for the automatic measurement of 3-D object shapes. Appl. Opt. **22**(24), 3977–3982 (1983)
11. Goldstein, R.M., Zebker, H.A., Werner, C.L.: Satellite radar interferometry: Two-dimensional phase unwrapping. Radio Sci. **23**(4), 713–720 (1988)

12. Ghiglia, D.C., Pritt, M.D.: Two-dimensional phase unwrapping: Theory, algorithms, and software, ser. Wiley–Interscience. Wiley (1998)
13. Mainsah, E., Greenwood, J.A., Chetwynd, D.G.: Metrology and properties of engineering surfaces. In: Mainsah, E., Greenwood, J.A., Chetwynd, D.G. (eds.) ser. Optoelectronics, Imaging and Sensing. Springer (2001)
14. Gens, R.: Phase unwrapping. http://www.asf.alaska.edu/~rgens/teaching/geos639/phase_unwrapping.pdf (2006)
15. Goldstein, R.M., Werner, C.L.: Radar ice motion interferometry. In: Proceedings of 3rd European Remote Sensing Symposium Space at the Service of our Environment, vol. 2, pp. 969–972, Florence, Italy (1997)
16. Gens, R.: Two-dimensional phase unwrapping for radar interferometry, Developments and new challenges. International Journal of Remote Sensing **24**(4), 703–710 (2003)
17. Kass, M., Witkin, A.: Analyzing oriented patterns. Computer vision, graphics, and image processing **37**(3), 362–385 (1987)

Various Aspects of Computer Security

The Impact of the TPM Weights Distribution on Network Synchronization Time

Michał Dolecki[1($\boxtimes$)] and Ryszard Kozera[1,2]

[1] The John Paul II Catholic University of Lublin, ul. Konstantynów 1H 20-708, Lublin, Poland
michal.dolecki@kul.pl
[2] Warsaw University of Life Sciences – SGGW,
ul. Nowoursynowska 159 02-776, Warsaw, Poland
ryszard.kozera@gmail.com, ryszard_kozera@sggw.pl

Abstract. Two neural networks with randomly chosen initial weights may achieve the same weight vectors in the process of their mutual learning. This phenomenon is called a network synchronization, and can be used in cryptography to establish the keys for further communication. The time required to achieve consistent weights of networks depends on the initial similarity and on the size of the network. In the previous work related to this topic the weights in TPM networks are randomly chosen and no detailed research on used distribution is performed. This paper compares the synchronization time obtained for the network weights randomly chosen from either the uniform distribution or from the Gaussian distribution with different values of standard deviation. The synchronization time of the network is examined here as a function of different numbers of inputs and of various weights belonging to the intervals with varying sizes. The standard deviation of Gaussian distribution is selected depending on this interval size in order to compare networks with different weights intervals, which also constitutes a new approach for selecting the distribution's parameters. The results of all analyzed networks are shown as a percentage of the synchronization time of a network with weights drawn from uniform distribution. The weights drawn from the Gaussian distribution with decreasing standard deviation have shorter synchronization time especially for a relatively small network.

Keywords: Neural networks · Tree Parity Machine · Key exchange protocol

1 Introduction

Cryptographic algorithms permit the data encryption and decryption with the use of the cryptographic keys [1]. These cryptographic keys are special data forming additional input to the encryption and decryption functions. Depending on the keys applied, the cryptography can be divided into symmetric or asymmetric one [2, 3]. In the first approach, the sender and receiver use the same secret key to encrypt and decrypt data. In the asymmetric cryptography the pair of keys is used, where one of them is kept secret whereas the other is available publicly. In order to use a secret key, a

© IFIP International Federation for Information Processing 2015
K. Saeed and W. Homenda (Eds.): CISIM 2015, LNCS 9339, pp. 451–460, 2015.
DOI: 10.1007/978-3-319-24369-6_37

secure communication channel is needed facilitating a possible transfer of the secure key to the both communicating partners. Consequently, this leads to the well-known paradox which in essence amounts to the necessity of creating a secure communication channel based on the assumption of the existence of secure channel. Such difficulty is solved by the Diffie – Hellman [2, 4], where a key exchange algorithm in an open communication channel is proposed. Alternatively, another recently investigated interesting approach is to generate a relatively secure [5, 6] cryptographic key exchange protocol, which is based on special artificial neural network tool [7-11].

Artificial intelligence methods are used in cryptography in various ways. For example genetic algorithms can be used in crypto-analysis or in protocol design [12]. Similarly to the artificial neural networks constituting an important element of artificial intelligence, the neuro-cryptography forms an interesting subfield of the cryptography. The term itself was first time used by Dourlens [13] in 1995. The neural networks are exploited to the realization of the cryptographic operations such as the S-BOX operation [14]. In addition they can be used in cryptographic context as a supporting tool e.g. in cryptographic keys exchange procedure [7-9]. The key exchange protocol over an open communication channel using artificial networks is particularly interesting as it is based on a new phenomenon of the so-called TPM network synchronization. Two special artificial neural networks during the mutual learning are able to establish consistent values of weights, which can in turn be used as cryptographic keys [15].

The key exchange protocol resorts to the Tree Parity Machine (TPM) network [7, 8, 16]. TPM is a specific artificial multilayer, feed-forward neural network. Its input topology is characterized by disjointed inputs. In conventional neural networks, each input reaches each neuron of the first hidden network's layer [17-19]. In this case, each neuron has its own impulses received from the fixed collection of input neurons. Values of all the first layer neurons inputs can be seen together as the one input vector for the entire network. This modification is introduced due to the cryptographic usage of the TPM network. If every impulse had an impact on the result of each hidden layer neuron, there would be a potential danger of reasoning about the results of the inner layer based on input pulses. Such separation gives the network distinctive tree-like look. Figure 1 shows the topological structure of the typical TPM network. Each input $x_{ij} \in \{-1, 1\}$ and weight is an integer number $w_{ij} = -L, -L + 1, \dots, 0, \dots, L - 1, L$.

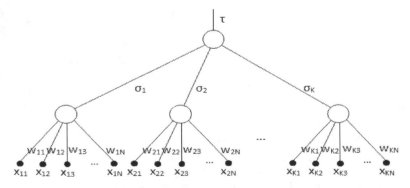

Fig. 1. Structure of Tree Parity Machine network.

The first layer networks are typical neurons which input pulses are multiplied by the corresponding weights and determine the value of its activation function [20], according to the following formula:

$$\sigma_i = f\left(\sum_{j=1}^{N} x_{ij} w_{ij}\right),$$

where $1 \leq i \leq K$. Activation function f is taken as a signum function given by the formula:

$$f(x) = \begin{cases} -1, for\ x \leq 0 \\ 1, for\ x > 0 \end{cases}.$$

Next, the results of the neurons of the first hidden layer are passed as inputs to the last layer neuron, which calculates the product of all incoming impulses:

$$\tau = \prod_{i=1}^{K} \sigma_i,$$

since $\sigma_i \in \{-1, 1\}$, a result of the network $\tau \in \{-1, 1\}$.

TPM networks are trained according to one of three methods: Anti-Hebbian, Hebbian or Random Walk rule [5, 7, 8, 11]. The synchronization process of the TPM network with discrete weights involves $(2L + 1) \times (2L + 1)$ parameters, which variations in turn forms the Markov chain. The pertinent theoretical analysis can be found in [9].

In key exchange protocol TPM networks undergo a process of mutual learning, in which both play simultaneously the role of a teacher and of a student. This learning process decomposes into the following consecutive steps:

1. Trusted parties A and B shall determine e.g. through an open channel, the parameters K, N and L describing the TPM topology and interval which contains a network weight. Both parties establish also a common method for TPM learning.
2. Each party creates its own TPM network (according to the previously agreed topology) with randomly chosen initial weights w^A and w^B, kept in secret.
3. Both A and B obtain the same, publicly known input vector $x \in X^{KN}$ and compute TPM's results τ^A and τ^B, respectively.
4. Next two involved parties exchange their networks results.
5. A treats received value τ^B as an expected result for its TPM and analogously B uses τ^A as an expected result for its own network.
6. Two parties modify their TPM's weights according to chosen learning method.
7. Both parties compare the results of both networks τ^A and τ^B to determine the number of consecutively occurring consistent results. If this value is greater than the pre-determined threshold, the algorithm ends and the network are considered as synchronized, otherwise it is necessary to continue such learning/teaching process and return to step 3.

The synchronization status achieved by both networks is a state, in which they have compatible weight vectors (which may change on each iteration but remain equal in a given pair). Such networks remain synchronized regardless of the time of their further learning. Their weight's values can be used directly as cryptographic keys or as a starting point for pseudo-random number generator that will be used as the keys.

In the first case, the generated key is a sequence of $K \cdot N$ weights within the range of -L to L, which involves $K \cdot N \cdot \log_2(2L + 2)$ bits. For example, synchronization of the networks of 3 neurons with 100 entrances to each of them and weights ranging from -15 to 15 (represented by 5 bits) enables to generate 1500 bit key. Similarly, in general the keys with the required length can be achieved by modifying the networks' parameters. It is important to note that once the networks are synchronized they change their weights (equal in each pair) at each subsequent learning step. Consequently, the latter immediately permits to generate next keys with a priori specified length.

The main problem for the potential attacker is the lack of knowledge of the inner layer's outputs so that he/she has no idea how to modify the weights of the attacking TPM. During the learning process, the respective weights are changed only when the networks produce either the same results (Hebbian and Random Walk Rule) or the opposite results (Anti-Hebbian). In addition, only neurons that have the same result as the entire network modify their weights. For each output of the network (-1 or 1) it is possible to have $2^{(K-1)}$ variants of its inner layer, which attacker should consider in each learning step when weights are modified.

At the beginning of the synchronization procedure both TPM networks have randomly chosen weights. The authors of this key exchange protocol have identified various types of learning steps for each pair of the corresponding neurons in both networks. More specifically, three steps are distinguished: an attracting, a repulsive and quiet steps. The respective names of each step emphasize its impact on the weights of both networks. In an attractive step both TPMs have the same output and the weights of both neurons move along the same direction. If one would exceed the limit value -L or L, it stays on the border, and the other moves to this value decreasing distance. In a repulsive step the weight of one network is not changed whereas the other can increase the distance between both weights. There are also cases in which weight reduce distance in repulsive step [21]. The last category is a silent step, when neurons results are different from the results for the entire network so the weight of neurons does not change. The synchronization time is dependent on the frequency of occurrence of the attractive and repulsive steps. Usually, at the beginning of synchronization process, when both weights are drawn and their compliance is low, more frequently the repulsive steps appear. In contrast at the end of synchronization they occur sporadically. Therefore, the closer to each other the weight vectors are, the more frequently synchronization step occurs permitting both weights getting closer.

2   Results

In this paper the relationship between the random distribution from which the initial weights are drawn and the network synchronization time is analyzed. Short time synchronizations are more secure and occur more often than long ones [22-24]. The research performed here is focused on two commonly used distributions: namely the uniform one and the Gaussian distribution. Due to the symmetry of the weight's interval [-L, L], the Gaussian distribution is taken with the mean zero, whereas different values of standard deviation are tested instead. Since the simulations in questions are conducted on networks with different sizes (i.e. different topologies dependent on parameter N and weights interval size determined by the parameter L) a standard deviation depends here on the maximum/minimum weight values of TPM examined. This in turn as indicated above is determined by the parameter L. Here various distributions with selected standard deviation $s \in \left\{L, \frac{L}{2}, \frac{L}{5}\right\}$ are admitted and tested. The latter enables to compare different networks of various sizes. The networks tested here use different topologies parameterized here by $K = 3$ and $N \in \{11, 50, 100\}$. As outlined above, the parameter L is related to a standard deviation s taken for the Gaussian distribution as $s = L$. The value of L is assumed to belong to the following set $L \in \{2, 3, 4, \ldots, 10\}$. In addition, for the normal distribution with $s = \frac{L}{2}$ only even values of L are tested and for a standard deviation $s = \frac{L}{5}$ only values for L which are divisible by 5 are considered i.e. $L \in \{5, 10\}$. This gives 75 possible variants of parameters of the examined networks. Each network is tested with random initial weights draw and synchronization 5000 times. The latter renders a total number of 375 000 investigated cases. The results presented below are obtained upon using own simulation program, which enables to draw the initial weights for the TPM network and its synchronization.

The distribution, from which the initial weight values of both learned TPMs are drawn affects their weights compatibility [25]. In addition, the compliance at the beginning of synchronization impacts on the duration of the learning process. An increase of the number of each first layer neuron's input pulses determined by the parameter N together with widening the interval [-L,....,L] containing the respective weights, extends the average synchronization time in accordance with the exponential growth. The analyzed time is expressed in the number of the networks' learning cycles as described above in seven step procedure. This relationship is evident for all analyzed distributions of initial weights. Table 1 presents detailed results for the uniform distribution for TPMs with different values of parameter N and L. The graphs enclosed in the figure 2 represent the results for the uniform distribution and Gaussian distribution with standard deviation set to either s = 0 and s = L / 2.

Table 1. An average synchronization time in learning cycles for uniform distribution.

L	UNIFORM		
	N=11	**N=50**	**N=100**
2	106,11	143,50	154,10
3	235,95	320,48	345,52
4	421,31	585,87	629,55
5	668,64	946,04	1013,96
6	972,76	1393,71	1512,05
7	1342,04	1926,97	2100,38
8	1775,86	2611,55	2839,96
9	2296,15	3354,97	3654,78
10	2858,83	4251,63	4608,29

Noticeably, small differences in the obtained results visibly follow for different distributions. However, for all analyzed cases, a characteristic exponential growth in time required for reaching a full synchronization of the networks is conspicuously transparent.

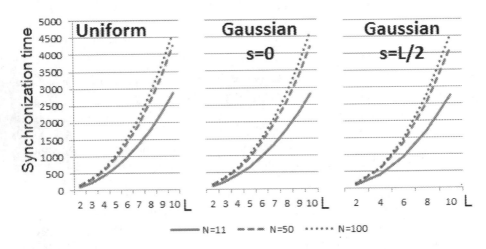

Fig. 2. Synchronization time in learning cycles for different distributions and TPM parameters.

For the clarity of the results of detailed synchronization time, the presented values are expressed in percentage, where the time obtained for uniform distribution as a reference point with 100% is considered.

Our analysis shows that the closer the initial weights are, the shorter synchronization time is. Table 2 enlists detailed results of the corresponding average synchronization time for each network obtained upon 5 000 simulations. In particular, these outcomes emphasize the impact of the selected initial weights distributions on the length of networks learning. Visibly, given a fixed distribution, if the initial weights values are drawn closer to the distribution mean, then the networks synchronize faster.

The results obtained for a fixed distribution in percentage are similar despite the change of parameter L. Note that the synchronization time significantly increases (see Table 1), but presenting the normal distribution with various standard deviations in relation to the synchronization time for uniform distribution permits to show the nature of the variability of synchronization time. This allows to average the results obtained for networks with different parameter L. Significant impact of this parameter's value on the distribution of the TPM synchronization time is studied in [21, 23]. Moreover, the analysis of the geometry of the distribution's histograms forms a further research topic, which is to be conducted in the context of numerical methods [26, 27]. Table 3 shows an average synchronization time for each analyzed distribution and weights interval which is determined by the parameter L.

Table 2. Synchronization time details in percentage.

L	UNIFORM	GAUSS 0	GAUSS 2
	N=11		
2	100%	100%	94%
4	100%	99%	95%
6	100%	99%	96%
8	100%	99%	96%
10	100%	98%	96%
	N=50		
2	100%	99%	95%
4	100%	99%	97%
6	100%	100%	97%
8	100%	99%	97%
10	100%	99%	97%
	N=100		
2	100%	99%	95%
4	100%	99%	97%
6	100%	100%	96%
8	100%	99%	97%
10	100%	100%	98%

Table 3. An average synchronization time for different distribution and number of inputs.

N	UNIFORM	GAUSSIAN s=0	GAUSSIAN s=L/2	GAUSSIAN s=L/5
11	2858,83	2814,28	2745,47	2422,38
50	4251,63	4219,30	4131,35	3714,64
100	4608,29	4594,18	4500,68	4133,94

Table 4. An average synchronization time percetage.

N	UNIFORM	GAUSSIAN s=0	GAUSSIAN s=L/2	GAUSSIAN s=L/5
11	100%	98%	96%	85%
50	100%	99%	97%	87%
100	100%	100%	98%	90%

Table 4 shows how the synchronization time decreases in comparison with the uniform distribution after 5000 simulations performed. The latter is conducted for the networks with three first layers and for the number of input signals given by parameter N.

The average synchronization time expressed in percentages takes the time obtained for the uniform distribution as 100%.

The drawing of the initial weights from the Gaussian distribution enables to reduce the respective network synchronization time. Upon comparing the results for a network of fixed parameter L, it can be seen that for the same range of weights the resulting weights' reduction is similar. In addition, having reduced the standard deviation for fixed number of TPM inputs the synchronization time can be even further reduced by 15% for the relatively small networks.

3   Conclusions

Neural cryptography like the other new methods such as quantum cryptography [28, 29] is an interesting alternative to the currently used algorithms [2]. The TPM network' synchronization time is the most important issue built in neural cryptography. In this paper a new topic is analyzed, namely the impact on synchronization time of the distribution, from which initial network's weights are drawn. We analyzed here the uniform and the Gaussian distributions with a standard deviation depending on the parameters of the synchronized TPM network. Clearly random drawing of the initial weights based on different distributions impacts on their compliance level. By setting uniform distribution as a reference point, it can be observed that the choice of the Gaussian distribution results in diminishing the networks' synchronization time. Additionally, the smaller standard deviation is, the shorter synchronization time follows. Generally, the greater synchronized network is, the whole process takes longer. Particularly noteworthy is the fact that the results are similar for networks of various sizes. The use of standard deviation dependent on the networks parameter enables to compare results obtained for TPMs with different sizes. Upon analyzing the results of a percentage of the synchronization time of network with the initial weights drawn from the uniform distribution it can be seen that similar decreases of synchronization time for networks with different numbers of inputs occurs. The presentation of the results percentage-like and the dependence of the standard deviation on the network parameters permits to compare the results for networks with various sizes. In this paper we demonstrated that the choice of initial weights distribution, according to which they are   drawn, has an impact on the synchronization time. Its reduction in turn may well facilitate the practical use of the TPM network synchronization to determine the encryption keys. These keys can be used in various sensitive data encryption including image [30, 31] or sound encryption [32].

References

1. Barker, E., Barker, W., Burr, W., Polk, W., Smid, M.: Recommendation for key management – part 1: general (revision 3), National Institute of Standards and Technology Special Publication 800-57 (2012)
2. Menezes, A., Vanstone, S., Van Oorschot, P.: Handbook of Applied Cryptography. CRC Press (1996)

3. Stinson, D.R.: Cryptography, Theory and Practice. CRC Press (1995)
4. Stokłosa, J., Bilski, T., Pankowski, T.: Data Security in Informatical Systems (in Polish). PWN (2001)
5. Klimov, A.B., Mityagin, A., Shamir, A.: Analysis of neural cryptography. In: Zheng, Y. (ed.) ASIACRYPT 2002. LNCS, vol. 2501, pp. 288–298. Springer, Heidelberg (2002)
6. Ruttor, A., Kinzel, W., Naeh, R., Kanter, I.: Genetic Attack on Neural Cryptography. Physical-Review E **73**(3), 036121–036129 (2006)
7. Kanter, I., Kinzel, W., Kanter, E.: Secure Exchange of Information by Synchronization of Neural Networks. Europhysics Letters **57**, 141–147 (2002)
8. Kanter, I., Kinzel, W.: The Theory of Neural Networks and Cryptography. In: Proceeding of the XXII Solvay Conference on Physics, The Physics of Communication, pp. 631–644 (2003)
9. Rosen-Zvi, M., Klein, E., Kanter, I., Kinzel, W.: Mutual Learning in a Tree Parity Machine and its Application to Cryptography. Physical Review E **66**, 066135 (2002)
10. Klein, E., Mislovaty, R., Kanter, I., Ruttor, A., Kinzel, W.: Synchronization of Neural Networks by Mutual Learning and its Application to Cryptography. Advances in Neural Information Processing Systems **17**, 689–696 (2005). MIT Press Cambridge
11. Ruttor, A.: Neural Synchronization and Cryptography, Ph.D. thesis, Wurzburg (2006)
12. Ibrachim, S., Maarof, M.: A review on biological inspired computation in cryptology. Jurnal Teknologi Maklumat **17**, 90–98 (2005)
13. Dourlens, S.: Neuro-Cryptography. MSc Thesis, Dept. of Microcomputers and Microelectronics, University of Paris, France (1995)
14. Kotlarz, P., Kotulski, Z.: On application of neural networks for s-boxes design. In: Szczepaniak, P.S., Kacprzyk, J., Niewiadomski, A. (eds.) AWIC 2005. LNCS (LNAI), vol. 3528, pp. 243–248. Springer, Heidelberg (2005)
15. Bisalapur, S.: Design of an efficient neural key distribution center. International Journal of Artificial Intelligence & Applications **2**, 60–69 (2011)
16. Volkmer, M., Wallner, S.: Tree Parity Machine re-keying architectures. IEEE Transactions on Computers **54**, 421–427 (2005)
17. Hassoun, M.: Fundamentals of Artificial Neural Networks. MIT Press (1995)
18. Osowski, S.: Neural Networks in Algorithmic Approach (in Polish). WNT (1996)
19. Rutkowski, L.: Methods and Technics of Artificial Intelligence (in Polish). PWN, Warsaw (2006)
20. McCulloch, W.: A logical calculus of the ideas immanent in nervous activity. Bulletin of Mathematical Biophysics **5**, 115–133 (1943)
21. Dolecki, M.: Klasyfikacja czasu synchronizacji sieci Tree Parity Machine używanych do uzgadniania kluczy kryptograficznych (in Polish), Ph.D. thesis, Gliwice (2014)
22. Dolecki, M., Kozera, R.: Threshold method of detecting long-time TPM synchronization. In: Saeed, K., Chaki, R., Cortesi, A., Wierzhoń, S. (eds.) CISIM 2013. LNCS, vol. 8104, pp. 241–252. Springer, Heidelberg (2013)
23. Dolecki, M., Kozera, R.: Distribution of the Tree Parity Machine synchronization time. Advances in Science and Technology Research Journal **18**, 20–27 (2013)
24. Dolecki, M., Kozera, R., Lenik, K.: The evaluation of the TPM synchronization on the basis of their outputs. Journal of Achievements in Materials and Manufacturing Engineering **57**, 91–98 (2013)
25. Dolecki, M., Kozera, R.: Distance of Tree Parity Machine initial weights drawn from different distributions. Advances in Science and Technology Research Journal **26**, 137–142 (2015)

26. Kozera, R., Noakes, L.: More-or-less-uniform sampling and lengths of curves. Quarterly of Applied Mathematics **61**, 475–484 (2003)
27. Kozera, R., Noakes, L.: C^1 interpolation with cumulative chord cubics. Fundamenta Informaticae **61**, 285–301 (2004)
28. Gerdt, V.P., Prokopenya, A.N.: Some algorithms for calculating unitary matrices for quantum circuits. Programming and Computer Software **36**, 111–116 (2010)
29. Gerdt, V.P., Prokopenya, A.N.: Simulation of quantum error correction by means of QuantumCircuit package. Programming and Computer Software **39**, 143–149 (2013)
30. Brooks, M.J., Chojnacki, W., Kozera, R.: Shading without shape. Quarterly of Applied Mathematics **50**, 27–38 (1992)
31. Kozera, R.: Uniqueness in shape from shading revisited. Journal of Mathematical Imaging And Vision **7**, 123–138 (1997)
32. Homenda, W.: Optical music recognition: the case study of pattern recognition. In: Kurzynski, M., Puchala, E., Wozniak, M., et al. (eds.) Computer Recognition Systems. Advances in Soft Computing, pp. 835–842 (2005)

Verification of Mutual Authentication Protocol for MobInfoSec System

Olga Siedlecka-Lamch[3], Imed El Fray[1], Mirosław Kurkowski[2],
and Jerzy Pejaś[1]([✉])

[1] Faculty of Computer Science and Information Technology,
West Pomeranian University of Technology, Szczecin, Poland
{ielfray,jpejas}@zut.edu.pl
[2] Institute of Computer Sciences, Cardinal Stefan Wyszynski University in Warsaw,
Warsaw, Poland
mkurkowski@uksw.edu.pl
[3] Institute of Computer and Information Sciences,
Częstochowa University of Technology, Częstochowa, Poland
olga.siedlecka@icis.pcz.pl

Abstract. This paper presents a detailed analysis of the mutual authentication protocol developed especially for the system MobInfoSec - for a mobile device to share and protect classified information. MobInfoSec uses fine-grained access rules described by general access structures. In this paper we describe the architecture and functioning of the system, and the requirements imposed on cryptographic authentication protocols, resulting from both: standards, the collection of good practices, as well as directly from the vision of the system. The article contains a description of the protocol's parts and formal analysis of its security.

Keywords: Authentication protocols · One-to-many protocol · Mobile device · Sensitive information · Secure communication channel

1 Introduction

The modern people process tens of gigabytes of information a day, most of which is transferred electronically, by mobile devices. Phones and tablets have become personal, handheld offices by which users download and often send sensitive content: emails, business and banking transactions, etc. Each participant of that mobile/distributed system wants one - security of transmitted and stored data. Security has many aspects: information is only accessible to the defined destination (it should not be stolen or intercepted), the encrypted information can not be lost or deciphered by inappropriate entity (see [7–9]).

Cryptographic protocols provide security relevant to the needs of information systems. This security concerns, inter alia: authentication of entities, session key agreement between the parties, provides confidentiality, integrity, anonymity and non-repudiation. Participants of cryptographic protocol exchange

© IFIP International Federation for Information Processing 2015
K. Saeed and W. Homenda (Eds.): CISIM 2015, LNCS 9339, pp. 461–474, 2015.
DOI: 10.1007/978-3-319-24369-6_38

messages through a specific communication channel. Communication channels can be divided into three types: channel point-to-point (or one-to-one) connecting the two participants, broadcast channels (one to many) connecting the sender and multiple recipients and conference channels (many to many) connecting all participants in the protocol and allow for exchange of messages between all participants.

Cryptographic protocols are subject of rigorous analysis, as they represent a critical component of any secure distributed computer system. They are easy to write, but on the basis of the code its very difficult to estimate their security level. Their simple structure is often confusing and leads to false conclusions in their security evaluation. Therefore, an important element in the selection and design of cryptographic protocol is to verify its correctness.

The article shows a mutual authentication protocol designed for system MobInfSec, which enables cryptographic protection of sensitive information in accordance with Originator Controlled access control rules [6,14]. The ORCON rules release a user from the obligation to monitor any information (especially against unauthorized copying). The information is removed when a user is no longer allowed to access it.

A description of the assumptions, architecture, and the rules of functioning of the system MobInfoSec are included in the next chapter. A further section describes the objectives and requirements for the proposed protocol. The next chapter describes its functioning and at the end the verification of its correctness. The whole is closed by summary, containing further directions of research.

2   Objective

The paper gives mutual authentication protocol under the name of SP2SP_Mutual_Auth (Secret Protection module of user A to Secret Protection module of user B mutual authentication) designed for MobInfSec system that allows protection of cryptographic confidential information in accordance with the ORCON rules.

This protocol is initialized by an entity A (called the chairman). The chairman executes (sequentially or simultaneously) n times the one-to-one protocol with every other member $B_1, B_2, ..., B_n$ from the group B. Successful completion of each instance of SP2SP_Mutual_Auth protocol enables to authenticate every pair of users (A, B_i), $i = 1, \ldots, n$, and to establish n independent secure communication channels between them with different key material used by each pair of participants.

The security analysis of SP2SP_Mutual_Auth protocol is based on its specification written in HLPSL and ProToc languages and next used in well-known tools of automatic protocol verification like AVISPA, VerICS and PathFinder (see [1,10,13]. We assume that the adversaries inside our system have many capabilities of the standard Dolev-Yao intruder, namely, they are able, within their bounded storage capacity, to compose, decompose, overhear, and intercept messages as well as update values with fresh ones. Hence, it is commonly believed that Dolev-Yao intruder is the most powerful attacker because following the seminal work of Dolev and Yao [4], the communication media are assumed to be under absolute control of the intruder. This intruder can in particular destroy all transmitted messages.

The results of our security analysis have showed the correctness of the proposed protocol for the different states of $SP.B_i$ and $SP.A_i$ tokens when performing cryptographic operations and during authentication.

3   Architecture of MobInfoSec System

MobInfoSec system can be seen as a set of cooperating applications, including trusted parts, that are distributed in different locations and communicate with each other. More detailed assumptions, the architecture and functioning of the system MobInfoSec are described in [5]. At this point, we focus only on a description of those elements that have an impact on SP2SP_Mutual_Auth protocol and its security analysis.

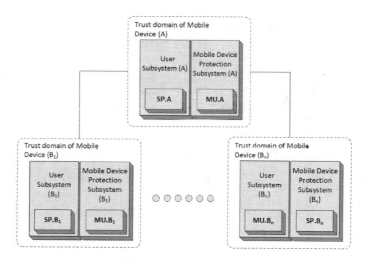

Fig. 1. Trust domains concept for different mobile devices

Applications can be closed in the domain of trust. A single domain is created around a trusted application or a group of trusted applications. We assume that communication between applications within the same trust domain is secure, could be caused by placing them in one location or the use of ready-made security technologies (eg. SSL).

Communication between domains therefore remains an open problem, namely: communication between components located in different domains, which will require the compilation of trusted paths and channels. Paths/channels created by the use of strong cryptography, allows applications from different domains to trust each other and accept their decisions. The main task is to define domains of trust and determine trusted paths and channels [5,7].

4   Basic Authentication Protocols

The aim of the cryptographic authentication protocol is to identify a particular or all of the participants of communication. Typically, the additional effect of the protocol is the key - established between the participants of the protocol, which will be used to build a trusted channel or a trusted path.

Another goal is to provide for messages exchanged during protocol execution the following (all or some) security features: confidentiality, authentication, integrity or non-repudiation. As mentioned earlier authentication protocols can be divided into unilateral, mutual and multilateral protocols of authentication of entities.

In the case of MobInfoSec system the secure communications between multiple entities is required. The main point is to ensure the proper authentication between the SP components which are located in different trust domains. One of the domains (a chairman) is the initiator of communication and should be mutually authenticate with each of the other domains of trust and establish a secure communication channel.

There are few potentially useful protocols (Table 1) that can be considered in MobInfoSec ([11, 15, 16]). All of them guarantee mutual authentication, key integrity, key authentication, key control or confirmation, but only the first has a formal security proof. None of them provides a common communication channel or the secret handling. No matching of existing solutions to the system assumptions forced to design a new mutual authentication protocol.

5   Mutual Authentication Protocol

Cryptographic protocol design must be preceded by a clear definintion of project objectives and a determination of the impact of violations of these assumptions on achieving planned objectives of security. Examination of protocol defects that were not included in the assumptions (e.g. due to the lack of knowledge related to a given defect) motivates and allows to understand the various design features of the protocol, and the knowledge of successful (and known) attacks helps designers to avoid standard attacks.

Principles of engineering design of cryptographic protocols are associated with the three phases [3]:

- analysis of the protocol requirements phase,
- detailed protocol design phase,
- proving protocol security phase.

Below, we present SP2SP_Mutual_Auth one-to-many group mutual authentication protocol. In this protocol the group members are authenticated by the chairman "one-by-one". That is, n authentication messages are required to authenticate n group members. Then, these members share individual keys for the communication with the group chairman.

Table 1. Authentication protocols comparison

No.	Property	Transport RSA (EN 14890) [15]	Key transport ISO/IEC 11770-3 Mechanism 5 [16]	Lim-Lee key agreement protocol 5 [11]
1.	Mutual authentication	+	+	+
2.	Multi-party authentication (one to many and many to one)	-	-	-
3.	Key integrity	+	+	+
4.	Key authentication	+	+	+
5.	Personal (independent) communication channels	$+^{1)}$	$+^{1)}$	$+^{1)}$
6.	Common communication channel	-	-	-
7.	Forward secrecy	-	-	-
8.	Backward secrecy	N/A $^{2)}$	N/A	N/A
9.	Liveness	$+$ $^{3)}$	$+^{3)}$	+
10.	Key control	+	$+^{4)}$	+
11.	Key freshness	$+^{3)}$	$+^{3)}$	$+^{3)}$
12.	Key confirmation	+	+	+
13.	Formal security proof	+	$+^{6)}$	+

Legend

+ Means that the protocol has indicated property, perhaps after meeting additional requirements presented in footnote
1) It applies also to the case when the protocol is used to authenticate the initiator of the protocol with other members of the participants group
2) N/A - not applicable
3) Applies to all participants of the protocol
4) Applies only to the initiator of the protocol
5) If session key is used by all members of the group
6) Lack of information about the existence of a formal security proof

5.1 Assumptions and Notations

For the proposed protocols the following assumptions have been made:

- types of connection and transmission medium (LAN, WLAN, WWAN, ...) used by the parties involved in the protocol are not significant,
- the term 'address' of the device means: complete and current information that helps to communicate with the device through the selected communication medium; method of processing and distribution of this information is beyond the scope of this paper,
- All parties involved in the described authentication protocol are equipped with SP, under their exclusive control,
- SP provides an interface compatible with the PKCS#11.

The protocol specification uses the following symbols and markings:

AUT	authentication
C	Certificate (X509 format or CVC card format)
CS	Signing certificate that contains the public part of the key used to submit and verify the signature
CS_AUT	Signing certificate used to authenticate other certificates; the private, key complementary to the public key contained in CS_AUT, may be used to sign other certificates
C.CAX.CS_AUT	A certificate issued by the main office RCA to intermediate CA certification authority used by this office to authenticate the public key of X
C.X.AUT	The certificate containing the public key of the entity X used in the authentication procedure
D[key](msg)	Decrypt a message <msg> with the key <key>
DS[key](msg)	Digital signature of messages <msg> with the key <key>
E[key](msg)	Encrypt a message <msg> with the key <key>
h(msg)	The message digest calculated for message <msg> using a hash function h
ID	id
MU.A	User Subsystem Authentication Module installed in the mobile device under the control of the user A
MDC.A	Protected Data Magazine of User A
MK.A	Keys Magazine of User A
PrK	The private key
PRND	Complementary random number
PuK	Public key
PuK.CAX.CS_AUT	The public key contained in the certificate C.MAX.CS_AUT used for authentication of public keys
Q||Z	Concatenation information of Q and Z
SK	Secret key (symmetric)
RCA	Root CA.
SP.A	Secret Protection Module installed in the mobile device user A
SP.SU	Secret Protection Module installed on the Authentication Server
SU	The authentication server (one of the functions of a Trusted Third Party Distribution and Authentication Users and Devices Server)
UM.A	Mobile device under the control of user A
X	Protocol participant
XC	Mutual certificate

We assume that for a given set of entities $P = A, B_1, ..., B_n$, where $n \geq 1$, the entity A is the preferred entity responsible for initiating the protocol. The aim of the protocol is the mutual authentication with each entity B_i, $i = 1, \ldots, n$, and generation of a key material necessary to ensure the confidentiality and authenticity of information exchanged between the parties. Additionaly we assume that:

- SP tokens have the same root CA certificate; the case of several certificates is not included in the protocol; however, if we assume that the two root CAs have issued cross certificates to each other, the protocol - after the introduction of minor modifications - will also work correctly;
- token SP.X of the entity X stores in its memory: the root CA's certificate C.RCA.AUT, the intermediate CA's certificate C.CASP.X.CS_AUT CA issued by root CA, and certificate C.SP.X.AUT of the token SP.X.

5.2 Protocol description

The SP2SP_Mutual_Auth$(A, B_1, ..., B_n)$ protocol provides authentication of each pair of entities (A, B_i), $i = 1, ..., n$ and consists of the following states:

State 0: SP.B_i and SP.A tokens do not possess the public keys of the opposite side.

1. Authentication MU.A module initiates the protocol, establishes a connection to authentication module MU.B_i of mobile device B_i and and carries protocol in the initial state.

2. If token SP.B_i do not have public key PuK.CASP.A.CS_AUT, then:

    2.1 MU.A requests through MU.B_i selection and verification of key PuK.RCA.AUT by SP.B_i:

     MU.A -> MU.B_i -> SP.B_i: select and verify(PuK.RCA.AUT)

    2.2 SP.B_i chooses and verifies PuK.RCA.AUT key, and then returns the confirmation:

     SP.B_i -> MU.B_i -> MU.A: conf.OK

    2.3 MU.A ask SP.A to read certificate C.CASP.A.CS_AUT:

     MU.A -> SP.A: get certificate (C.CASP.A.CS_AUT)

    2.4 SP.A gets certificate C.CASP.A.CS_AUT and returnt it to the MU.A:

     SP.A -> MU.A: C.CASP.A.CS_AUT

    2.5 MU.A requests through MU.B_i that SP.B_i verified certicate C.CASP.A.CS_AUT:

     MU.A -> MU.B_i -> SP.B_i: verify certificate (C.CASP.A.CS_AUT)

    2.6 SP.B_i verifies certificate C.CASP.A.CS_AUT, saves the public key PuK.CASP.A.CS_AUT and sends confirmation to the MU.A:

     SP.B_i -> MU.B_i -> MU.A: conf.OK

3. MU.A through MU.B_i requests SP.B_i to choose and verify the key PuK.CASP.A.CS_AUT:

    MU.A -> MU.B_i -> SP.B_i: select and verify(PuK.CASP.A.CS_AUT)

4. SP.B_i chooses and verifies PuK.CASP.A.CS_AUT key, and then returns the confirmation:

    SP.B_i -> MU.B_i -> MU.A: conf.OK

5. MU.A asks SP.A to read its authentication certificate C.SP.A.AUT:

    MU.A -> SP.A: get certificate (C.SP.A.AUT)

6. SP.A gets C.SP.A.AUT certificate and returns it to the MU.A:
   SP.A -> MU.A: C.SP.A.AUT

7. MU.A through MU.B_i requests SP.B_i to verify the certificate C.SP.A.AUT of token SP.A:
   MU.A -> MU.B_i -> SP.B_i: verify certificate (C.SP.A.AUT)

8. SP.B_i verifies the C.SP.A.AUT certificate, stores the public key PuK.SP.A.AUT and sends a confirmation to MU.A:
   SP.B_i -> MU.B_i -> MU.A: conf.OK

   State 1: Token SP.B_i has the public key C.SP.A.AUT of token SP.A

9. If SP.A does not have PuK.CASP.B_i.CS_AUT public key, then:
   9.1 MU.A requests the SP.A to select and verify key PuK.RCA.AUT:
       MU.A -> SP.A: select and verify(PuK.RCA.AUT)
   9.2 SP.A chooses and verifies PuK.RCA.AUT key, and then returns the confirmation:
       SP.A -> MU.A: conf.OK
   9.3 MU.A through MU.B_i requests SP.B_i to read C.CASP.B_i.CS_AUT certificate:
       MU.A -> MU.B_i -> SP.B_i: get certificate (C.CASP.B_i.CS_AUT)
   9.4 SP.B_i gets C.CASP.B_i.CS_AUT certificate and returns it to the MU.A:
       SP.B_i -> MU.B_i -> MU.A: C.CASP.B_i.CS_AUT
   9.5 MU.A requests to SP.A verified C.CASP.B_i.CS_AUT certificate:
       MU.A -> SP.A: verify certificate (C.CASP.B_i.CS_AUT)
   9.6 SP.A verifies the certificate C.CASP.B_i.CS_AUT, stores the public key PuK.CASP.B_i.CS_AUT and sends a confirmation to MU.A:
       SP.A -> MU.A: conf.OK

10. MU.A requests the SP.A to select and verify key PuK.CASP.B_i.CS_AUT:
    MU.A -> SP.A: select and verify(PuK.CASP.Bi.CS_AUT)

11. SP.A chooses and verifies PuK.CASP.B_i.CS_AUT key, and then returns the confirmation:
    SP.A -> MU.A: conf.OK

12. MU.A through MU.B_i requests SP.B_i to read authentication certificate C.SP.B_i.AUT:
    MU.A -> MU.B_i -> SP.B_i: get certificate (C.SP.B_i.AUT)

13. SP.B_i gets C.SP.B_i.AUT certificate and returns it to the MU.A:
    SP.B_i -> MU.B_i -> MU.A: C.SP.Bi.AUT

14. MU.A requests to SP.A verified the certificate C.SP.B_i.AUT of token SP.B_i:
    MU.A -> SP.A: verify certificate (C.SP.B_i.AUT)

15. SP.A verifies the certificate C.SP.B_i.AUT , stores the public key PuK.SP.B_i.AUT and sends a confirmation to MU.A:
    SP.A -> MU.A: conf.OK

    State 2: Token SP.A has the public key C.SP.B_i.AUT of token SP.B_i

16. `MU.A` through `MU.B_i` requests `SP.B_i` to activate (select) `PuK.SP.A.AUT` and `PrK.SP.B_i.AUT` keys:
    ```
    MU.A -> MU.B_i -> SP.B_i:
    acivate security key (PuK.SP.A.AUT, PrK.SP.B_i.AUT)
    ```

17. `SP.B_i` activates `PrK.SP.B_i.AUT` and `PuK.SP.A.AUT` keys and sends confirmation to the `MU.A`:
    ```
    SP.B_i -> MU.B_i -> MU.A: conf.OK
    ```

18. `MU.A` requests that `SP.A` activated (selected) `PuK.SP.B_i.AUT` and `PrK.SP.A.AUT` keys:
    ```
    MU.A -> SP.A: acivate security key (PuK.SP.B_i.AUT, PrK.SP.A.AUT
    ```

19. `SP.A` activates `PrK.SP.A.AUT` and `PuK.SP.B_i.AUT` keys and sends confirmation to the `MU.A`: `SP.A ->  MU.A: conf.OK`

    State 3: `SP.A` and `SP.B_i` tokens activated their keys, which are necessary during performing cryptographic operations; moreover, the public key of the `SP.A` is now known by the `SP.B_i` and *vice versa*, and can be trusted by both sides.

20. `MU.A` requests the `SP.A` to generate a random number and return it together with its ID:
    ```
    MU.A -> SP.A: get challenge
    ```

21. `SP.A` generates `RND.SP.A` and, together with its identifier `SN.SP.A` sends all to `MU.A`:
    ```
    SP.A -> MU.A: RND.SP.A||SN.SP.A
    ```

22. `MU.A` through `MU.B_i` requests to authenticate `SP.B_i`:
    ```
    MU.A -> MU.B_i -> SP.B_i: authenticate(RND.SP.A || SN.SP.A)
    ```

23. `SP.B_i` generates a random key `K.SP.B_i`, random padding `PRND.SP.B_i`, prepares `preToken.SP.B_i`, signs the concatenated data using its private key, encrypts it and then through `MU.B_i` return it to `MU.A`:
    ```
    SP.B_i -> MU.B_i -> MU.A:
    E[PuK.SP.A.AUT](DS[PrK.SP.B_i.AUT](preToken.SP.B_i))
    ```
    where:
    ```
    preToken.SP.B_i = textA.SP.B_i || PRND.SP.B_i || K.SP.B_i
    || h(PRND.SP.B_i || K.SP.B_i || RND.SP.A ||  SN.SP.A) || textB.SP.B_i
    ```

24. `MU.A` sends to `SP.A` the request for verification of authentication token:
    ```
    MU.A -> SP.A:
    verify(E[PuK.SP.A.AUT](DS[PrK.SP.B_i.AUT](preToken.SP.B_i)))
    ```

25. `SP.A` decrypts `E[PuK.SP.A.AUT](DS [PrK.SP.B_i.AUT](preToken.SP.B_i))` and after the verification by `SP.A` the signature of `SP.B_i` (after confirmation of compliance with the previously sent random challenge `RND.SP.A`) sends confirmation to the `MU.A`: `SP.A -> MU.A: conf.OK`

    State 4: `SP.B_i` token has been authenticated to the `SP.A`.

26. `MU.A` requests through `MU.B_i` that `SP.B_i` generated a random number and send it together with its ID:
    `MU.A -> MU.B_i -> SP.B_i: get challenge`

27. `SP.B_i` generates `RND.SP.B_i` challenge and, together with its identifier `SN.SP.B_i` sends all to `MU.A`:
    `SP.B_i -> MU.B_i -> MU.A: RND.SP.B_i || SN.SP.B_i`

28. `MU.A` requests authentication by `SP.A`:
    `MU.A -> SP.A: authenticate(RND.SP.B_i || SN.SP.B_i)`

29. `SP.A` generates a random key `K.SP.A`, random padding `PRND.SP.A`, prepares `preToken.SP.A`, signs the concatenated data using its private key, encrypts it and then sends to `MU.A`:
    `SP.A -> MU.A: E[PuK.SP.B_i.AUT](DS[PrK.SP.A.AUT](preToken.SP.A))`
    where:
    `preToken.SP.A = textA.SP.A || PRND.SP.A || K.SP.A`
    `|| h(PRND.SP.A || K.SP.A || RND.SP.B_i ||  SN.SP.Bi) || textB.SP.A`

30. `MU.A` sends via `MU.B_i` request to `SP.B_i` for verification of authentication token:
    `MU.A -> MU.B_i ->`
    `  verify(SP.Bi: E[PuK.SP.B_i.AUT](DS[PrK.SP.A.AUT](preToken.SP.A)))`

31. `SP.B_i` decrypts `E[PuK.SP.B_i.AUT](DS[PrK.SP.A.AUT](preToken.SP.A))` and after the verification by `SP.B_i` the signature of `SP.A` (after confirmation of compliance with the previously sent random challenge `RND.SP.B_i`), token `SP.B_i` sends confirmation to `MU.A`:
    `SP.B_i -> MU.B_i -> MU.A: conf.OK`

State 5: `SP.A` token has been authenticated now to the opposite party, i.e. to `SP.B_i`.

32. After performing of the protocol `SP.B_i` and `SP.A` have a confidential key material `K.SP.A` and `K.SP.B_i`. On this basis both parties calculate the symmetric difference:
    `  K.SP.A/SP.B_i = K.SP.A ⊕ K.SP.A`
    and then create session keys to ensure confidentiality and authentication of the message. It being understood that:
    `K.SP.A/SP.B_i = Ka(ENC) || Kb (ENC) || Ka (MAC) || Kb (MAC)`
    Other more general methods for generating keys to ensure the confidentiality and authentication can be found in [15] (see chap. 8.10).

State 6: `SP.B_i` and `SP.A` tokens are able to set the trusted channel.

5.3   Protocol's verification

Protocol analysis was performed using known automatic verification tools: Avispa [1], VerICS [10] and PathFinder [12,13]. In the case of communication over an insecure channel, in an open way, without any encryption, and in which the goal for subprotocol is not to maintain the confidentiality of the new data (keys, nonces) or user authentication, then automatic verification tools could not be used.

The need to introduce this type of communication results from the fact that the parties haven't established yet a secure communication channel. In these cases, the intruder can perform only flooding-type attack or disrupt communications. They are, however, risks faced by all communication systems. Justification of subprotocols' correctness, in such cases, is based on the analysis of the correctness of data transfer scheme, in order to achieve the objectives and the assumption of a trusted repository and duly signed certificates.

Fig. 2. Simplified diagram of subprotocol: State 3

Accordingly, only two parts of the protocol (subprotocols of states 3 and 4) are designed to maintain the confidentiality of the new data (keys, nonces), and providing authentication of users. These two subprotocols provides mutual entity authentication. Because the messages sent are independent of each other, it is important to note that the subprotocol of state 4 is unambiguously symmetrical (similar) to the subprotocol of state 3. Therefore, in the description of these subprotocols we will focus only on the subprotocol of state 3. It is easy to observe that in other subprotocols there is no possibility of possessing by Intruder important data, so correctness of the whole protocol from security and authentication point of view is assured. The analysis of the correctness and the security of subprotocol of state 3 is made on the basis of the data transmission diagram (Fig. 2) and the experimental results obtained by using formal methods and aforementioned automatic tools.

In conducted studies the Dolev-Yao Intruder model was used, which is widely considered in the literature. According to this model the Intruder has full access to the network and transmitted data, he can decompose and compose transmitted data according to held by him cryptographic keys. The only assumption that limits privileges of the Intruder is the perfect cryptography assumption - the

472 O. Siedlecka-Lamch et al.

inability to decode the corresponding ciphertext without knowing the encryption key.

Specifications were made according to the syntax of HLPSL and ProToc languages and the data transmission of tested subprotocol. Users participating in the protocol and security goals guaranteed by this protocol were also modeled. Specifications in HLPSL is extensive, and does not introduce no additional information in relation to the specifications in ProToc, which is demonstrated below (see Listing 1).

From the viewpoint of the tested security properties, all modules of AVISPA tool reported the SP2SP_Mutual_Auth protocol correctness for a limited number of sessions, and one of AVISPA module reported also the correctness to an unlimited number of sessions.

VerICS tool generated 18 hypothetical runs, and for each of them built an automata model, which was then encoded into the Boolean formula. The formula was verified by the SAT solver MiniSAT. The result showed that in the surveyed space and with the adopted assumptions, protocol is correct and no errors were found in its structure.

For generated runs the PathFinder tool created chains of states. An attempt to construct a tree of runs containing a path of attack failed. This proves the correctness of subprotocol.

Listing 1. Authentication protocol specification in ProToc language

```
BEGIN
    Users (2)
    Players (3)
    Steps (2)
    Intruder (DY)

    Protocol:
        A; N_A, i(A); N_A; N_A|i(A); B;
        B; +K_A, -K_B, K_AB, N_A, i(A); K_AB;
        <<K_AB, h(K_AB,i(A))>_-K_B>_+K_A;
    Session
        (A,B,I)
    Goals
        Authentication (B,A)
        Secrecy (K_AB)
End
```

Verification for selected parts of the protocol for all assumed parameters, fared well - the protocol is correct and secure.

All results and times are listed in the table 2.

Table 2. Summary of the results

Subprotocol	AVISPA				VerICS	PathFinder
	OFMC	CL-AtSe	SATMC	TA4SP		
State 3	SAFE	SAFE	SAFE	SAFE	SAFE	SAFE
	70 ms.	<10 ms.	30 ms.	661 ms.	15 ms.	<10 ms.
State 4	SAFE	SAFE	SAFE	SAFE	SAFE	SAFE
	70 ms.	<10 ms.	30 ms.	661 ms.	15 ms.	<10 ms.

6   Summary

In the paper a mutual authentication protocol was presented, it was designed specifically for MobInfoSEc system, to guarantee secure communication for mobile devices. The protocol provides mutual authentication between each pair of participants of communication, establishing a common key material, and thus setting up a secure communication channel.

The most important security properties of the described protocol were tested using three different automatic verification tools. During the verification perfect cryptography and the Dolev-Yao intruder model were assumed. The SP2SP_Mutual_Auth$(A, B_1, ..., B_n)$ protocol has passed verification and achieved its objectives.

Acknowledgments. This scientific research work is supported by NCBiR of Poland (grant No PBS1/B3/11/2012) in 2012-2015.

References

1. Armando, A., et al.: The AVISPA tool for the automated validation of internet security protocols and applications. In: Etessami, K., Rajamani, S.K. (eds.) CAV 2005. LNCS, vol. 3576, pp. 281–285. Springer, Heidelberg (2005)
2. Boyd, C., Mathuria, A.: Protocols for Authentication and Key Establishment. Springer-Verlag, Heidelberg (2003)
3. Dong, L., Chen, K.: Cryptographic Protocol Security Analysis Based on Trusted Freshness. Springer-Verlag, Heidelberg (2012)
4. Dolev, D., Yao, A.: On the security of public key protocols. IEEE Transactions on Information Theory **29**(2), 198–207 (1983)
5. El Fray, I., Hyla, T., Kurkowski, M., Maćków, W., Pejaś, J.: Practical authentication protocols for protecting and sharing sensitive information on mobile devices. In: Kotulski, Z., Księżopolski, B., Mazur, K. (eds.) CSS 2014. CCIS, vol. 448, pp. 153–165. Springer, Heidelberg (2014)
6. Hyla, T., Pejaś, J.: Certificate-based encryption scheme with general access structure. In: Cortesi, A., Chaki, N., Saeed, K., Wierzchoń, S. (eds.) CISIM 2012. LNCS, vol. 7564, pp. 41–55. Springer, Heidelberg (2012)
7. Hyla, T., Pejaś, J., El Fray, I., Maćków, W., Chocianowicz, W., Szulga, M.: Sensitive information protection on mobile devices using general access structures. In: ICONS 2014, The Ninth International Conference on Systems, pp. 192–196. IARIA (2014)

8. Hyla, T., Pejaś, J.: A practical certificate and identity based encryption scheme and related security architecture. In: Saeed, K., Chaki, R., Cortesi, A., Wierzchoń, S. (eds.) CISIM 2013. LNCS, vol. 8104, pp. 190–205. Springer, Heidelberg (2013)
9. Hyla, T., Maćków, W., Pejaś, J.: Implicit and explicit certificates-based encryption scheme. In: Saeed, K., Snášel, V. (eds.) CISIM 2014. LNCS, vol. 8838, pp. 651–666. Springer, Heidelberg (2014)
10. Kurkowski, M., Penczek, W.: Verifying Security Protocols Modeled by Networks of Automata. Fund. Inform. **79**(3–4), 453–471 (2007)
11. Lim, C.H., Lee, P.J.: Several practical protocols for authentication and key exchange. Information Processing Letters **53**, 91–96 (1995)
12. Kurkowski, M., Siedlecka-Lamch, O., Szymoniak, S., Piech, H.: Parallel bounded model checking of security protocols. In: Wyrzykowski, R., Dongarra, J., Karczewski, K., Waśniewski, J. (eds.) PPAM 2013, Part I. LNCS, vol. 8384, pp. 224–234. Springer, Heidelberg (2014)
13. Siedlecka-Lamch, O., Kurkowski, M., Piech, H.: A new effective approach for modeling and verification of security protocols. In: Proceedings of 21th international Workshop on Concurrency. Specification and Programming (CS&P 2012), pp. 191–202. Humboldt University Press, Berlin (2012)
14. Chen, Y.-Y., Lee, R.B.: Hardware-assisted application-level access control. In: Samarati, P., Yung, M., Martinelli, F., Ardagna, C.A. (eds.) ISC 2009. LNCS, vol. 5735, pp. 363–378. Springer, Heidelberg (2009)
15. prEN 14890–1 Application Interface for smart cards used as Secure Signature Creation Devices - Part 1: Basic services (2012)
16. ISO/IEC 11770–3:2008 Information technology - Security techniques - Key management - Part 3: Mechanisms using asymmetric techniques (2008)

AQoPA: Automated Quality of Protection Analysis Framework for Complex Systems

Damian Rusinek[1], Bogdan Ksiezopolski[1,2]([✉]), and Adam Wierzbicki[2]

[1] Institute of Computer Science, Maria Curie-Sklodowska University, Lublin, Poland
bogdan.ksiezopolski@acm.org
[2] Polish-Japanese Academy of Information Technology, Warsaw, Poland

Abstract. Analysis of security economics for the IT systems is one of the important issues to be solved. The quality of protection (QoP) of IT System can be achieved on different levels. One can choose factors which have a different impact on the overall system security. Traditionally, security engineers configure IT systems with the strongest possible security mechanisms. Unfortunately, the strongest protection (especially in low resource devices) can lead to unreasoned increase of the system load and finally influence system availability. In such a situation the quality of protection models which scales the protection level depending on the specific requirements can be used. One of the most challenging issues for quality of protection models is performing quality of protection evaluation for complex and distributed systems. The manual analysis of such systems is almost impossible to perform. In the article, we proposed the Automated Quality of Protection Analysis framework (AQoPA). The AQoPA performs the automatic evaluation of complex system models which are created in the Quality of Protection Modelling Language (QoP-ML). In the article the case study of complex wireless sensor network analysis is presented. The network is deployed on a roller-coaster.

Keywords: Modelling and protocol design · Security protocol analysis · Quality of protection · Applied cryptography

1   Introduction

The security analysis of the IT systems and simultaneously that of its influence on the system performance is one of the most important topics to be solved. On one hand, the traditional approach assumes that implementation of the strongest security mechanisms makes the system as secure as possible. Unfortunately, on the other hand, such reasoning can lead to the overestimation of security measures which causes an unreasonable increase in the system load [1–4]. The system performance is especially important in the systems with limited resources such as the wireless system networks or the mobile devices. Another example where such analysis should be performed is cloud architecture. The latest research indicates three main barriers for using cloud computing which are security, performance and availability [5]. Unfortunately, when the strongest security mechanisms are

© IFIP International Federation for Information Processing 2015
K. Saeed and W. Homenda (Eds.): CISIM 2015, LNCS 9339, pp. 475–486, 2015.
DOI: 10.1007/978-3-319-24369-6_39

used, then it will decrease system performance and further influence system availability. This tendency is particularly noticeable in complex and distributed systems. The latest results show [6,7] that in many cases the better way is to determine the required level of protection and adjust security measures to these security requirements [8]. Such approach is achieved by means of the Quality of Protection models where the security measures are evaluated according to their influence on the system security.

One of the most challenging issues for the QoP models is performing quality of protection evaluation for complex and distributed systems [12]. The manual analysis of such systems is almost impossible to perform. The analysis of any type of the security protocol is difficult when the experts do not use automated tools. In literature, we can indicate programs which helped the experts analyse the protocols. We can indicate the AVISPA tool [13,14] or ProVerif [15] application, which verifies security properties for cryptographic protocols. From the Quality of Protection analysis point of view, AVISPA and ProVerif have two limitations. The first one refers to the types of the function which can be modelled. One can model only cryptographic primitives and cryptographic algorithms. The full QoP analysis must refer to all security factors which affect the overall system security. The second limitation is that these languages do not provide the structure for evaluation of the security factors performance. In the literature one can indicate the tool for QoP analysis which are modelled in the UMLsec [16]. This tool can be used for automated analysis of simple models but when we would like to analyse the scenarios when thousands of hosts take part in the protocol, then the analysis is too complex and cannot be done properly. The UMLsec is used for model-driven security as the part of model-driven development.

The major contribution of this study is introduction of Automated Quality of Protection Analysis framework which performs the automatic evaluation of QoP-ML models created in the Quality of Protection Modelling Language [9,10]. It allows to analyse complex systems which may consist of thousands of hosts representing a wide area network which are actors in the cryptographic protocol or a complex IT system. One can balance security against performance. The full description of the AQoPA will be presented in the next sections. The AQoPA framework can be downloaded from the web page of the Quality of Protection Modelling Language Project [11].

2   Automated Quality of Protection Analysis Framework (AQoPA)

In this section we present the architecture of AQoPA and data flow of model during the analysis process. The architecture of AQoPA is presented in Fig. 1. The figure presents four successive stages: stage 1 - model creation, stage 2 - security metrics definition, stage 3 - scenarios definition and stage 4 - simulation. These stages refer to the methodology of creating QoP-ML models defined in the article [9] where the details about syntax and semantics can be found.

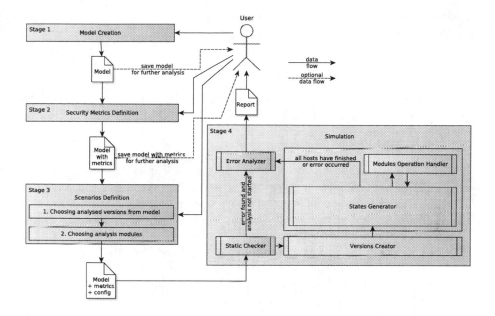

Fig. 1. AQoPA architecture and data flow

2.1   Stage 1 - Model Creation

Model creation stage is the first stage which must be performed in the AQoPA
framework. The goal of this stage is to create the QoP-ML model that will be
evaluated in the analysis process. The stage is divided into 4 phases. Initially
the designer has to define functions (phase 1), functions equations (phase 2) and
channels (phase 3). Later he can use them to create protocol flow (phase 4).

Protocol flow is defined for hosts as they are the highest level elements of the
analysis. Hosts contain processes and processes can contain subprocesses. Each
process and subprocess contain instructions list.

2.2   Stage 2 - Security Metrics Definition

The second stage is the security metrics definition stage which is divided into 4
phases, too. In the first phase the designer has to gather metrics and configurations of analysed devices (servers, sensors, etc.). In the second phase the designer
has to select subset of metrics for the functions that are used in the protocol
flow created in the first stage.

The aim of last two phases is to group selected metrics in sets and assign them
to hosts. The designer can model different devices therefore the metrics for the
same functions may have different values. For example, the encryption operations
are many times faster on high-performance servers than on the wireless sensors

nodes. The designer has to group metrics into sets representing one device and assign these sets to hosts created in the first stage.

2.3   Stage 3 - Scenarios Definition

The aim of the third stage is to define the scenarios of the analysis process. The protocol flow is already created and the designer has to define versions that he would like to evaluate.

Versions Selection. Versions represent different variants of the evaluated protocol. Versions include a list of executed hosts, their processes and subprocesses that will be included in independent evaluations. The designer does not have to choose all processes from the host, but any subset that will create the target protocol flow. The differences in versions may come from using different devices or security mechanisms resulting in different metrics or from different protocol flows (i.e.. including additional processes or subprocesses in the version that implement additional security mechanism). Versions allow to evaluate complex models with a large number of hosts using repetition. The designer can repeat hosts and processes. At the end of the analysis, the designer obtains results for all evaluations and can compare them.

Modules Selection. Besides versions, the designer must select modules that he would like to use in the analysis process. The AQoPA is module based what means that the designer can easily add modules to the analysis process. The core of AQoPA is responsible for generating next states according to the protocol flow. The additional operations that bring results of analysis are executed in modules.

2.4   Stage 4 - Simulation

Simulation stage is the core stage of AQoPA architecture. The analysis process is realized by this stage and proceeds automatically without the user's interaction.

Static Checker. Firstly, the provided model is passed to Static Checker which is responsible for syntax validation of the model. Any syntax error is passed to the Error Analyzer.

Versions Creator. When the model is validated by Static Checker, it is passed to the Versions creator. The task of this component is to create independent analysis process for each version selected in the Scenarios Definition stage. Creating versions involves the modification of protocol flow according to the list of executed hosts, processes and subprocesses in a particular version. As a result, AQoPA obtains as many protocol flows as many versions were selected. Each modified protocol flow is passed to the States Generator component and is analysed independently.

States Generator. In the States Generator component AQoPA generates successive states of evaluated hosts executing their instructions. This process is repeated until all hosts are finished or an error occurs. Each process of next state generation includes execution of the instruction that was modelled in the QoP-ML.

This component is also responsible for detection of QoP-ML model errors. These errors may result from the designer's mistake during modelling the system (or protocol) or from the limitations due to the metrics (i.e.. using sensors - devices with limited resources). These errors may lead to the situation when a variable is used before assignment, to deadlock in communication or to ambiguity of equations. This component detects these kinds of problems and passes them to Error Analyzer which outputs the information to the user.

QoP-ML introduces equations that are used to reduce complex function calls (nested function calls in parameters). Syntax validation checks all equations according to the syntax rules, finds and reports contradictory equations and checks if one equation contains the other one. The States Generator component finds ambiguity during the reduction process. All above situations pass an error to Error Analyzer.

Modules Operation Handler. Modules selected in the Scenarios Definition stage take part in the process of generating the next state of protocol. Execution of all instructions is passed to the modules so that they can retrieve information about the current state and prepare the results. Additionally, modules can change default instructions flow.

Error Analyzer. Error Analyzer is the last component of simulation stage. It outputs the information about the error received from Static Checker or States Generator. When the analysis finishes successfully, Error Analyzer creates a result report.

3   Case Study

In this section we present the analysis of complex system performed by means of the AQoPA framework. This case study presents the features of AQoPA as the tool used to analyse the wireless sensor networks in terms of security and efficiency.

We analyse the wireless sensor network used for structural health monitoring deployed on roller-coaster. Its main aim is to collect acoustic emission data during the ride which is transmitted to the gateway and analysed for cracks. This method has been studied in [18] and is still widely used as inspection method [19]. Using wireless sensor network gives a possibility to react to detected failures in real time.

In the case study we have used the Rougarou roller-coaster from Cedar Point theme park [17]. It is interesting example because the roller-coaster was opened in 1996 and named Mantis while now it is being rebuilt to be a floor-less coaster. Therefore the main structure remains and is going to be operated by new coaster.

The Rougarou is about 1200 meters length, 44 meters high and the speed goes up to 97 kmph. In Fig. 1ffig:rollercoaster we present an example of sensor placement on 270 degrees turn. Sensing nodes are placed every 3 meters on the track while the sink is mounted to the car and collects data from sensors during ride. During the analysis we would like to evaluate how the quality of protection of exchanging data influence the system efficiency and finally the lifetime of system.

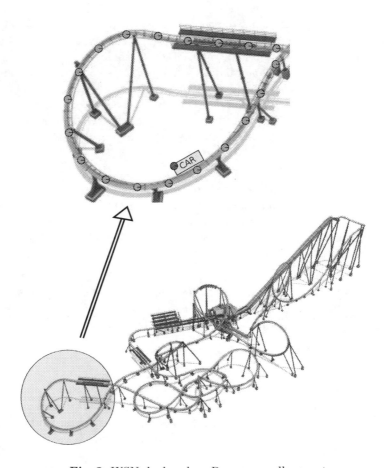

Fig. 2. WSN deployed on Rougarou roller-coaster.

3.1   Protocols

We propose three protocols to collect acoustic emission data presented in Fig. 3, 4 and 5. When data is collected the algorithms for fatigue cracks detection are used and report any suspicious results in real time. Protocols present communication between sink, which collects data, and sensor, which senses data. The wireless sensor network consist of many sensors mounted on the track and one sink mounted to the car. The technique of sink mobility is used to collect data from sensors [20].

The first protocol is the simple one where no security is guaranteed. The second and the third protocols are modified version of protocol presented in verified in [23] which is used to authenticate new nodes in a sensor network.

In the description of protocols we use the following notation:

S - Sensor,

$Sink$ - Sink,

R - empty request for SHM data,

D - acoustic emission data
          sampled by sensors,

n_I - nonce generated by I,

$sk(I)$ - private key of I,

$pk(I)$ - public key of I,

$\{M\}_K$ - encryption of M with
          symmetric or asymmetric key K.

Protocol 1

In the first protocol we analyse the network without security mechanisms. The protocol is presented in Fig. 3.

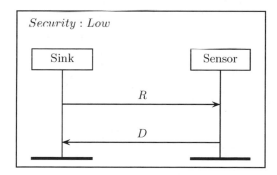

Fig. 3. Protocol 1: No security.

The sink node sends empty request for acoustic emission data to sensor when the car is near its place of mounting. In response the sensor collects acoustic emission data and returns it back unencrypted.

Protocol 2

The second protocol includes security mechanisms which provide confidentiality and authentication of sink and sensors. The communication is encrypted with pre-deployed, symmetric key NK. The presented is shown in Fig. 4.

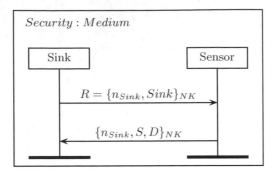

Fig. 4. Protocol 2: Symmetric cryptography

Protocol 3

The difference between second and third protocol is that the third one uses asymmetric cryptography to ensure security. We assume that the pairs of keys were pre-deployed and sink knows public keys of all sensors while sensors know the public key of sink. The protocol is presented in Fig. 5. The difference between

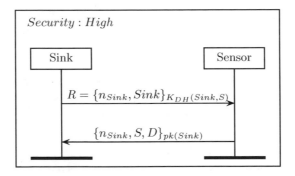

Fig. 5. Protocol 3: Asymmetric cryptography

original version from [23] and the third protocol is returned data. In the original version, the session key is returned while in the proposed protocol it is acoustic emission data. Additionally, in the second protocol data is encrypted with network key which has two advantages: encryption takes less time and protocol does not require asymmetric keys management. However, using network key gives possibility of reading and modifying packets to all nodes in network. Therefore, the assumption of all trusted nodes is required.

3.2   AQoPA Evaluation

As the result of the case study we want to estimate the lifetime of wireless sensor network deployed on the roller-coaster depending on the protocol and type of sensor node. Firstly, we have to define the assumptions about the monitoring system.

Assumptions:
- **Number of measurements.** We assume that there are 100 rides with measurement each day.
- **Number of sensors.** We assume that the network consists of one sink mounted to the car and 400 sensors mounted to the track at equal intervals.
- **Battery.** We assume that nodes are equipped with standard AA battery with 1200 mAh capacity.

After this, we defined two type of factors which influence the lifetime of the wireless sensor network monitoring system.

Factors:
1. **Protocol.** We want to check the lifetime depending on the type of protocol selected from three previously described.
2. **Hardware.** We estimate the lifetime for two types of nodes: MicaZ with 8MHz ATmega128L CPU and Imote2 with 104MHZ PXA271 XScale CPU.

In case of page limit we do not present the QoP-ML model of the roller-coaster but the QoP-ML model of the case study can be found on the QoP-ML Project web page [11] and in the AQoPA framework.

Presented model consists of hundreds of sensors and the analysis of such complex network is impossible to be performed manually. Using AQoPA the network can be analysed automatically in short time. The lifetimes of nodes (in days) estimated with AQoPA are presented in Table 1.

Table 1. Lifetime (in days) of nodes in SHM network.

	Lifetime (in days)			
	MicaZ		Imote2	
	Sink	Sensor	Sink	Sensor
Protocol 1 - NO security	87378	5378	86677	653
Protocol 2 - MEDIUM security	38	3974	61	636
Protocol 3 - HIGH security	5	1089	27	597

One can see that lifetime of sink node for protocol 1 (*NO security*) is very long. When we compare it with other protocols one can notice significant influence of security operations on lifetime of the network. When the security mechanisms are introduced (protocol 2 and 3) the sink becomes the bottle neck of the network. One can see that in case of MicaZ and *HIGH* security protocol the lifetime of network decreases to 5 days while for Imote2 it becomes 27 days.

One of the important factor which is worth for estimating is the wireless sensor network lifetime. We define the network lifetime as the minimum of nodes' lifetimes because we assume that each node must be operative in order to keep network working correctly. In case of *HIGH* security protocol using MicaZ sensors, lifetime of network could be extended five times only if the sink was replaced with Imote2 sensor (both nodes have the same radio chip CC2420).

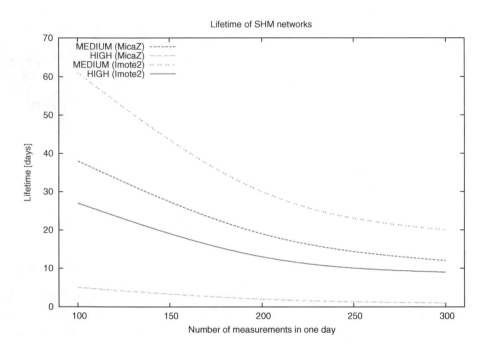

Fig. 6. The lifetime of networks depending on the number of daily measurements.

Another element which can be analysis by means of AQoPA framework is the influence of measurements granularity to the network lifetime. The lifetime results in Tables 1 were estimated with assumption that there are 100 rides with measurements during one day. Figure 6 presents the decrease of lifetime depending on daily number of measurements for the protocols which guarantees the security on *MEDIUM* and *HIGH* security level. The protocol 1 (*NO security*) has not been included on Fig. 6 because in this protocol the performance is obviously much more effective than other protocols.

4   Conclusions

In the article we proposed the Automatic Quality of Protection Analysis framework. One of the main contributions of AQoPA is quality of protection and efficiency analysis of complex systems which are modelled in QoP-ML (Quality of Protection Modelling Language). The complexity of models may result by e.g. a large number of hosts (actors) in the protocol flow which can be executed simultaneously or by a specifically defined order. For illustrating the capabilities of AQoPA we present an example of SHM wireless sensor network deployed on roller-coaster in order to find cracks in the track. The AQoPA has been used to estimate the lifetime of such network under different conditions depending on the level of security and hardware. The AQoPA can verify whether a proposed network which uses given protocol can be operative for questioned length of time under given, environmental circumstances. The presented in the article analysis of the wireless sensor network deployed on roller-coaster show that one can gather the results which can help designers for making the best decision about complex system parameters.

Modelling tools used for computer security applications may however be found to prospective co-existence and cooperation with modelling tools used in computational neuroscience [21,22]. We have undertaken some steps in order to merge security aspects of computer systems with hypothesised existence of brain activity fingerprint characteristic for particular users. These research will be continue as the future work. That kind of analysis of complex system cannot be prepared manually.

Acknowledgments. This work is supported by Polish National Science Centre grant 2012/05/B/ST6/03364.

References

1. Stubblefield, A., Rubin, A.D., Wallach, D.S.: Managing the Performance Impact of Web Security. Electronic Commerce Research **5**, 99–116 (2005)
2. Sklavos, N., Kitsos, P., Papadopoulos, K., Koufopavlou, O.: Design, Architecture and Performance Evaluation of the Wireless Transport Layer Security. The Journal of Supercomputing **36**(1), 33–50 (2006)
3. Ksiezopolski, B., Kotulski, Z., Szalachowski, P.: Adaptive approach to network security. Communications in Computer and Information Science **158**, 233–241 (2009)
4. Ksiezopolski B., Kotulski Z., Szalachowski P.: On QoP method for ensuring availability of the goal of cryptographic protocols in the real-time systems. In: European Teletraffic Seminar, pp. 195–202 (2011)
5. Jürjens J.: Security and Compliance in clouds. In: 4th Pan-European Conference on IT-Compliance 2011, Berlin (2011)
6. Ksiezopolski, B., Rusinek, D., Wierzbicki, A.: On the modelling of Kerberos protocol in the Quality of Protection Modelling Language (QoP-ML). Annales UMCS Informatica AI XII **4**, 69–81 (2012)
7. Ksiezopolski, B., Rusinek, D., Wierzbicki, A.: On the efficiency modelling of cryptographic protocols by means of the quality of protection modelling language (QoP-ML). In: Mustofa, K., Neuhold, E.J., Tjoa, A.M., Weippl, E., You, I. (eds.) ICT-EurAsia 2013. LNCS, vol. 7804, pp. 261–270. Springer, Heidelberg (2013)

8. Lambrinoudakis, C., Gritzalis, S., Dridi, F., Pernul, G.: Security requirements for e-government services: a methodological approach for developing a common PKI-based security policy. Computers & Security **26**, 1873–1883 (2003)
9. Ksiezopolski, B.: QoP-ML: Quality of Protection modelling language for cryptographic protocols. Computers & Security **31**(4), 569–596 (2012)
10. Ksiezopolski B.: Multilevel Modeling of Secure Systems in QoP-ML, pp. 1–256. CRC Press (2015)
11. The official web page of the QoP-ML project. http://www.qopml.org
12. Ksiezopolski, B., Zurek, T., Mokkas, M.: Quality of Protection Evaluation of Security Mechanisms. The Scientific World Journal **2014**, 18 (2014)
13. Blanco, V., Gonzalez, P., Cabaleiro, J.C., Heras, D.B., Pena, T.F., Pombo, J.J., Rivera, F.F.: AVISPA: visualizing the performance prediction of parallel iterative solvers. Future Generation Computer Systems **19**, 721–733 (2003)
14. Vigano, L.: Automated Security Protocol Analysis With the AVISPA Tool. Electronic Notes in Theoretical Computer Science **115**, 61–86 (2006)
15. Blanchet, B., Chaudhuri, A.: Automated formal analysis of a protocol for secure file sharing on untrusted storage. In: Proceedings of the 29th IEEE Symposium on Security and Privacy, pp. 417–431 (2008)
16. Jürjens, J.: Tools for Secure Systems Development with UML. International Journal on Software Tools for Technology Transfer **9**, 527–544 (2007)
17. Cedar Point web page. https://www.cedarpoint.com/
18. Yuyama, S.: Fundamental Aspects of Acoustic Emission Applications to the Problems Caused by Corrosion. Corrosion Monitoring in Industrial Plants Using Nondestructive Testing and Electrochemical Methods, American Society for Testing and Materials, 43–74 (1986)
19. ElBatanouny, M., Mangual, J., Ziehl, P., Matta, F.: Early Corrosion Detection in Prestressed Concrete Girders Using Acoustic Emission. J. Mater. Civ. Eng. **26**(3), 504–511 (2014)
20. Rault, T., Bouabdallah, A., Challal, Y.: Energy efficiency in wireless sensor networks: A top-down survey. Computer Networks **67**, 104–122 (2014)
21. Wojcik, G.M.: Electrical parameters influence on the dynamics of the hodgkin-huxley liquid state machine. Neurocomputing **79**, 68–78 (2012)
22. Wojcik, G.M., Garcia-Lazaro, J.A.: Analysis of the neural hypercolumnin parallel pcsim simulations. Procedia Computer Science **1**(1), 845–854 (2010)
23. Mansour, I., Rusinek, D., Chalhoub, G., Lafourcade, P., Ksiezopolski, B.: Multihop node authentication mechanisms for wireless sensor networks. In: Guo, S., Lloret, J., Manzoni, P., Ruehrup, S. (eds.) ADHOC-NOW 2014. LNCS, vol. 8487, pp. 402–418. Springer, Heidelberg (2014)

ICBAKE 2015 Workshop

Text Data Mining of English Interviews

Hiromi Ban[1(✉)], Haruhiko Kimura[2], Takashi Oyabu[3], and Jun Minagawa[4]

[1] Graduate School of Nagaoka University of Technology, Nagaoka, Niigata, Japan
je9xvp@yahoo.co.jp
[2] Graduate School of Kanazawa University, Kanazawa, Ishikawa, Japan
kimura@blitz.ec.t.kanazawa-u.ac.jp
[3] Kokusai Business Gakuin College, Kanazawa, Ishikawa, Japan
oyabu24@gmail.com
[4] Sanyo Gakuen College, Okayama, Japan
mendelmondel@gmail.com

Abstract. An "interview" is the technique to gain the particular data effectively which the interviewers want to know through the conversation. In this paper, we metrically analyzed some English interviews: *Larry King Live* on CNN, and compared these with English news (*CNN Live Today*) and the inaugural addresses of the three U.S. Presidents. In short, frequency characteristics of character- and word-appearance were investigated using a program written in C++. These characteristics were approximated by an exponential function. Furthermore, we calculated the percentage of American basic vocabulary to obtain the difficulty-level as well as the K-characteristic of each material.

Keywords: Analysis of English literary style · Interview · Metrical linguistics · Statistical analysis · Text data mining

1   Introduction

Human beings are always talking with other people. We are getting information from others as an everyday experience, using many effective arts in order to obtain a cooperative response. An "interview" is more specific way of talking, and it is the technique to gain the particular data effectively which the interviewers want to know through the conversation [1].

In this paper, we metrically analyzed some English interviews: *Larry King Live* on CNN, and compared these with English news (*CNN Live Today*) and the inaugural addresses of the three U.S. Presidents. In short, frequency characteristics of character- and word-appearance were investigated using a program written in C++. These characteristics were approximated by an exponential function: $[y = c * \exp(-bx)]$.

As a result, it was clearly shown that the interviews have the same tendency as English journalism in character-appearance. Moreover, we could show quantitatively that the interviews are a little easier to listen than CNN news.

K. Saeed and W. Homenda (Eds.): CISIM 2015, LNCS 9339, pp. 489–499, 2015.
DOI: 10.1007/978-3-319-24369-6_40

2   Method of Analysis and Materials

The materials analyzed here are as follows:

Larry King Live (Jan. 21, 2004-July 13, 2004; 20 materials in total)

Larry King Live is one of the CNN's highest-rated shows and Mr. King is regarded as the first American talk show host to have a worldwide audience.   He was born at Brooklyn in New York on November 19 in 1933, and educated at the Lafayette High School[2].   We selected 20 interviews, and analyzed interviewer's English, that is, the utterances of Mr. King.   For reference, the interviewees' data are shown in Table 1.

Table 1. Data of the Interviewees in *Larry King Live*.

No.	Interviewee's name	Status	Aired date	Gender
1	Bill Clinton	frm. President	June 24, 2004	m
2	Dan Rather	CBS news anchor	June 18, 2004	m
3	Macaulay Culkin	actor	May 27, 2004	m
4	Colin Powell	Secretary of State	May 4, 2004	m
5	Don Rickles	comedian	May 2, 2004	m
6	Dick Clark	TV personality	Apr. 16, 2004	m
7	Peter Jennings	broadcast journalist	Apr. 1, 2004	m
8	Donald Rumsfeld	Defense Secretary	Mar. 19, 2004	m
9	Ben Affleck	actor	Mar. 16, 2004	m
10	Toby Keith	country singer	Jan. 21, 2004	m
11	Theresa Saldana	actress	July 13, 2004	f
12	Ann Richards	frm. Texas Governor	May 20, 2004	f
13	Hillary Rodham Clinton	Senator	Apr. 20, 2004	f
14	Karen Hughes	one of Bush's closest advisers	Apr. 6, 2004	f
15	Tanya Tucker	country singer	Mar. 23, 2004	f
16	Tammy Faye Messner	TV personality	Mar. 18, 2004	f
17	Linda Evans	actress	Mar. 15, 2004	f
18	Katie Couric	TV news personality	Mar. 4, 2004	f
19	Veronica Atkins	widow of Dr. Robert Atkins	Feb. 16, 2004	f
20	Sharon Osbourne	rock star	Feb. 12, 2004	f

Thus, while the interviewees are male in Materials 1 to 10, they are female in Materials 11 to 20.

For comparison, we analyzed 20 English news materials from *CNN Live Today* aired on January 2-31 in 2003, as well as the inaugural addresses of the three U.S. Presidents: George Bush (Jan. 20, 1989), William J. Clinton (Jan. 21, 1993), and George W. Bush (Jan. 20, 2001).

The computer program for this analysis is composed of C++.   Besides the characteristics of character- and word-appearance for each piece of material, various information such as the "number of sentences," the "number of paragraphs," the "mean word length," the "number of words per sentence," etc. can be extracted by this program [3].

3   Results

3.1   Characteristics of Character-Appearance

First, the most frequently used characters in each material and their frequency were derived.   Then, the frequencies of the 50 most frequently used characters including capitals, small letters, and punctuations were plotted on a descending scale.

The vertical shaft shows the degree of the frequency and the horizontal shaft shows the order of character-appearance. The vertical shaft is scaled with a logarithm. As an example, the result of Material 1 is shown in Fig. 1.

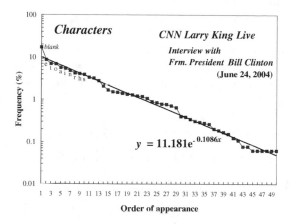

Fig. 1. Frequency characteristics of character-appearance in *Larry King Live*.

There is an inflection point caused by the difference of the degree of decrease between the 13th and the 14th ranked characters, and the degree of decrease gets a little higher after the 26th character.

This characteristic curve was approximated by the following exponential function:

$$y = c * \exp(-bx) \tag{1}$$

From this function, we are able to derive coefficients c and b[4]. In the case of Material 1, c is 11.181 and b is 0.1086. The distribution of coefficients c and b extracted from each material is shown in Fig. 2.

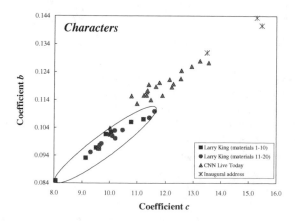

Fig. 2. Dispersions of coefficients c and b for character-appearance.

There is a linear relationship between c and b for all of the 43 materials. Previously, we analyzed various English writings and reported that there is a positive correlation between the coefficients c and b, and that the more journalistic the material is, the lower the values of c and b are, and the more literary, the higher the values of c and b[5]. The values of coefficients c and b for interviews are low: the value of c ranges from 8.0567 (Material 5) to 11.605 (Material 11), and that of b is 0.0848 to 0.1099, compared to the case of the CNN news (c is 10.009 to 13.548, b is 0.1039 to 0.1279) and inaugural addresses (c is 13.484 to 15.461, b is 0.1309 to 0.1434). Thus, while the interviews have a similar tendency to journalism, the inaugural addresses are similar to literary writings.

3.2   Characteristics of Character-Appearance

Next, the 20 most frequently used words in some of the materials are shown in Table 2.

Table 2. High-frequency words for each material.

	Larry King (Bill Clinton)	Larry King (Colin Powell)	Larry King (Theresa Saldana)	Larry King (Hillary Clinton)	CNN Live Today (Jan. 2, 2003)	Inaugural address (G.W. Bush)
1	the	the	you	you	that	and
2	you	you	the	the	to	of
3	to	that	to	to	the	the
4	of	in	a	of	this	our
5	and	to	and	and	at	a
6	a	a	did	do	police	we
7	that	of	he	in	in	to
8	do	and	was	with	of	in
9	it	it	what	is	he	is
10	I	have	do	a	they	not
11	in	is	that	what	and	will
12	is	he	were	think	are	are
13	president	I	in	be	a	that
14	was	with	with	it	here	it
15	on	do	who	on	on	this
16	back	be	have	back	case	but
17	be	at	I	that	point	for
18	Clinton	don't	Jeff	he	able	by
19	did	state	of	I	as	I
20	have	this	right	this	been	us

The definite article *THE*, the personal pronouns *YOU* and *I*, and auxiliary *DO* (*DID*) are often used in interviews. In addition, interrogatives such as *WHAT* and *WHO* are also used frequently in Materials 11 and 13. As for personal pronoun *YOU*, it ranks as the most frequently used word in the 8 interviews in which the interviewee was female, except for Materials 14 and 19, in which *YOU* ranks the 2nd. Thus, personal pronoun *YOU* tends to be more often used, when the interviewee is female. For interviews and CNN news, some content words such as *PRESIDENT* and *POLICE* are ranked high, because the number of words for each material is not so many.

Just as in the case of characters, the frequencies of the 50 most frequently used words in each material were plotted. Each characteristic curve was approximated by the same exponential function: [$y = c*\exp(-bx)$]. The distribution of c and b is shown in Fig. 3.

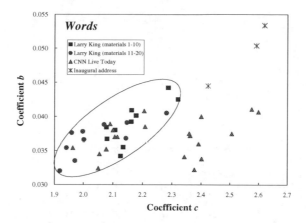

Fig. 3. Dispersions of coefficients c and b for word-appearance.

In this case, we can see a positive correlation between coefficients c and b for the interviews and inaugural addresses. The values of coefficients for the interviews are low, compared with the inaugural addresses. Especially, in the case of the interviewee was female, the value of c ranges from 1.9188 (Material 14) to 2.2815 (Material 11), and that of b is 0.0320 to 0.0405, which a little lower than the case of the males: the value of c ranges from 2.0772 (Material 8) to 2.3210 (Material 3), and that of b is 0.0342 (Material 2) to 0.0442 (Material 4). While the values of c for the CNN news have a wide range as much as from 1.9635 to 2.5988, the values of b for them are 0.0322 to 0.0411, which are very similar to the interviews in which interviewees were female.

As a method of featuring words used in writing, a statistician named Udny Yule suggested an index called the "K-characteristic" in 1944[6]. This can express the richness of vocabulary in writings by measuring the probability of any randomly selected pair of words being identical. He tried to identify the author of *The Imitation of Christ* using this index. This K-characteristic is defined as follows:

$$K = 10^4 \left(S_2 / S_1^2 - 1 / S_1 \right) \tag{2}$$

where if there are f_i words used x_i times in a writing, $S_1 = \Sigma x_i f_i$, $S_2 = \Sigma x_i^2 f_i$.

We examined the K-characteristic of each material. The results are shown in Fig. 4. According to the figure, the values for the interviews in which the interviewee was female are comparatively low except for one material (Material 11); they are 71.876 to 93.178. The highest values for interviews are almost equal to the values for the three inaugural addresses (106.230 to 113.541). On the other hand, the values for CNN news have a wide range from 69.875 to 136.149. Thus, the K-characteristic expresses a similar tendency to coefficient c for word-appearance in terms of the order and the interval of values. We would like to investigate the relationship between K-characteristic and the coefficients for word-appearance in the future.

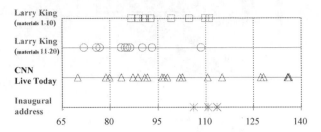

Fig. 4. K-characteristic for each material.

3.3   Degree of Difficulty

In order to show how difficult the materials for listeners are, we derived the degree of difficulty for each material through the variety of words and their frequency[7]. That is, we came up with two parameters to measure difficulty; one is for word-type or word-sort (D_{ws}), and the other is for the frequency or the number of words (D_{wn}). The equation for each parameter is as follows:

$$D_{ws} = (1 - n_{rs} / n_s)$$ (3)

$$D_{wn} = \{ 1 - (1 / n_t * \Sigma n(i)) \}$$ (4)

where n_t means the total number of words, n_s means the total number of word-sort, n_{rs} means the American basic vocabulary by *The American Heritage Picture Dictionary* (American Heritage Dictionary, Houghton Mifflin, 2003), and $n(i)$ means the respective number of each basic word.   Thus, we can calculate how many basic words are not contained in each piece of material in terms of word-sort and frequency.   The values educed are shown in Fig. 5.

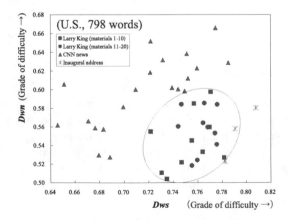

Fig. 5. Two types of difficulty using basic English vocabulary in the U.S.

The closer the value is to 1, the more difficult the material. As for the degree of word-sort (D_{ws}), when we analyzed the English textbooks in Japanese junior and senior high schools, the difficulty increases as the grades go up. Thus, the validity of using the variety of words and their frequency of the American basic vocabulary as the parameters to extract the difficulty was accepted[7]. According to Fig. 5, the difficulty of interviews ranges from 0.722 (Material 2) to 0.782 (Material 6), which is almost identical with the half of the news materials. The difficulties of the three inaugural addresses are high: 0.782 to 0.808. The most difficult interview (Material 6) is almost equal to the easiest of the inaugural address.

As for D_{wn}, because the most frequently used words in each material, that is, *THE, OF, TO, AND, IN, A*, etc., are common in every material, and the characteristics of word-appearance are also similar among them, the range of values for D_{wn} is assumed to be tight.

Thus, we calculated the values of both D_{ws} and D_{wn} to show how difficult the materials are for listeners, and to show which level of English the materials are compared with others. In order to make the judgments of difficulty easier for the general public, we derived one difficulty parameter from D_{ws} and D_{wn} using the following principal component analysis:

$$z = a_1 * D_{ws} + a_2 * D_{wn} \tag{5}$$

where a_1 and a_2 are the weights used to combine D_{ws} and D_{wn}. Using the variance-covariance matrix, the 1st principal component z was extracted: $z = 0.349 * D_{ws} + 0.9374 * D_{wn}$, from which we calculated the principal component scores. The results are shown in Fig. 6.

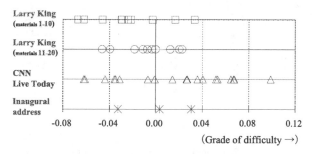

Fig. 6. Principal component scores for difficulty shown in one-dimension.

According to Fig. 6, we can judge that the eight news materials are more difficult than all of the interviews and inaugural addresses, using our way of measuring difficulty. The difficulties of the interviews in which the interviewee was female are from -0.0464 (Material 20) to 0.0226 (Material 19), which are similar to the inaugural addresses: -0.0325 to 0.0304. The easiest of all the materials is one of the interviews in which the interviewee's gender is the same as the interviewer's, Material 9; its principal component score is -0.0669.

3.4   Other Characteristics

Other metrical characteristics of each material were compared. The results of the "mean word length," the "number of words per sentence," etc. are shown together in Table 3.

Table 3. Metrical data for each material.

	Larry King (materials 1-10) (avg. of 10 materials)	Larry King (materials 11-20) (avg. of 10 materials)	CNN Live Today (avg. of 20 materials)	Inaugural address (avg. of 3 materials)
Total num. of characters	7,574	8,141	3,600	10,046
Total num. of character-type	63	64	56	57
Total num. of words	1,423	1,506	640	1,830
Total num. of word-type	496	516	273	646
Total num. of sentences	119	113	34	110
Mean word length	5.342	5.413	5.651	5.516
Words/sentence	13.248	13.505	19.660	16.629
Repetition of a word	2.850	2.896	2.287	2.810
Commas/sentence	0.770	0.778	1.428	1.181
Freq. of prepositions (%)	12.209	11.912	15.045	14.075
Freq. of relatives (%)	4.125	3.968	3.973	2.844
Freq. of auxiliaries (%)	0.922	0.915	1.142	2.261
Freq. of personal pronouns (%)	13.395	14.045	6.721	10.479

Although we counted the "frequency of relatives," the "frequency of modal auxiliaries," etc., some of the words counted might be used as other parts of speech because we didn't check the meaning of each word. Additionally, the results of the "mean word length" and the "number of words per sentence" for each material are shown in Fig. 7 and Fig. 8 respectively.

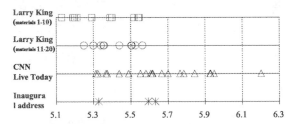

Fig. 7. Mean word length for each material.

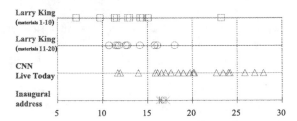

Fig. 8. Number of words per sentence for each material.

Mean Word Length. As for the "mean word length," it is 5.129 (Material 5) to 5.546 letters (Material 8) for Materials 1 to 10, and 5.249 (Material 20) to 5.562 letters (Material 13) for Materials 11 to 20, which are low, compared with the CNN news and inaugural addresses. As much as 13 materials of the 20 CNN news materials are longer than interviews. Moreover, 4 interviews in which the interviewee was male are shorter than the interviews in which the interviewee was female. Thus, we can see that when the interviewee is male, the male interviewer tends to use short-length words.

Number of Words per Sentence. The "number of words per sentence" for the interviews in which the interviewee was male is 7.092 (Material 5) to 15.054 words (Material 7), and it is exceptionally high: as much as 23.250 words for Material 8. When the interviewee was female, it is 10.718 (Material 14) to18.046 words (Material 20). In this case, as much as 12 materials of the 20 CNN news materials are longer than Material 20. Also from this point of view, the interview materials seem to be easier to listen than the CNN news and inaugural addresses.

Frequency of Auxiliaries. We also examined the "frequency of auxiliaries." There are two kinds of auxiliaries in a broad sense. One expresses the tense and voice, such as *BE* which makes up the progressive form and the passive form, the perfect tense *HAVE*, and *DO* in interrogative sentences or negative sentences. The other is a modal auxiliary, such as *WILL* or *CAN* which expresses the mood or attitude of the speaker[8]. In this study, we targeted only modal auxiliaries. As for the result, the "frequency of auxiliaries" is highest in the inaugural address, the average of the 3 materials is 2.261%, and lowest in interviews, the average of Materials 11 to 20 is 0.915%. As for Materials 1 to 10, it is 0.922%. Therefore, it might be said that while the President tends to communicate his subtle thoughts and feelings with auxiliary verbs, the style of Larry King's talking can be called more assertive.

Frequency of Personal Pronouns. As for the "frequency of personal pronouns," it is as high as 13.395% and 14.045% for Materials 1 to 10 and Materials 11 to 20 respectively. This is because the frequencies of *YOU* and *I* are rather high in the interviews, as was mentioned before.

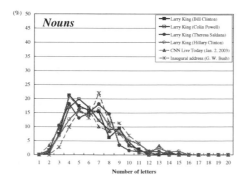

Fig. 9. Word-length distribution of nouns.

Word-length Distribution of Nouns, Verbs, Adjectives, and Adverbs. We also examined word-length distribution of "nouns," "verbs," "adjectives," and "adverbs." As examples, the results of Nouns and Adverbs are shown in Fig. 9 and Fig. 10 respectively. Judging from Fig. 9, we can see a tendency that in the case of Nouns, shorter words are used in the interviews, compared with the inaugural address. On the other hand, as for the case of Adverbs, the frequency of 4-letter words is rather high in the interview materials. It is as much as 48.837% in Material 1.

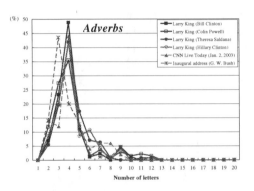

Fig. 10. Word-length distribution of adverbs.

3.5   Positioning of Each Material

We tried to make positioning all of the 43 materials, doing a principal component analysis of the educed data by the correlation procession. The results are shown in Fig. 11.

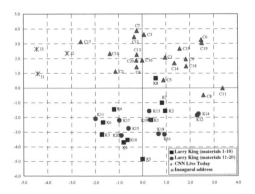

Fig. 11. Positioning of each material.

We could assume that while the first principal component expresses whether an utterance was turned to the public or to an individual, the second principal component defines whether an utterance is broadcast English or speech style English.

4   Conclusions

We investigated some characteristics of character- and word-appearance of interviews: *Larry King Live* on CNN, comparing these with English news and the inaugural addresses of the U.S. Presidents.   In this analysis, we used an approximate equation of an exponential function to educe the characteristics of each material using coefficients c and b of the equation.   Moreover, we calculated the percentage of American basic vocabulary to obtain the difficulty-level as well as the K-characteristic.   As a result, it was clearly shown that the interviews have the same tendency as English journalism in character-appearance.   Moreover, we could show quantitatively that the interviews are a little easier to listen than the CNN news.

In the future, we plan to apply these results to education.   For example, we would like to measure the effectiveness of teaching some characteristics of English materials before listening or reading them.

References

1. Ban, H., Dederick, T., Nambo, H., Oyabu, T.: Stylistic characteristics of English news. In: Proceedings of the 5th Japan-Korea Joint Symposium on Emotion and Sensibility, Korea, p. 4, June 4–5, 2004
2. The Museum of Broadcast Communications. http://www.museum.tv/archives/etv/K/htmlK/kinglarry/kinglarry.htm
3. Ban, H., Dederick, T., Oyabu, T.: Linguistical Characteristics of Eliyahu M. Goldratt's The Goal. In: Proceedings of the Fourth Asia-Pacific Conference on Industrial Engineering and Management Systems, Taiwan, pp. 1221–1225, December 18–20, 2002
4. Ban, H., Dederick, T., Oyabu, T.: Metrical analysis of english materials for business management. In: Proceedings of the 33rd International Conference on Computers and Industrial Engineering, CIE450, Korea, p. 6, March 25–27, 2004
5. Ban, H., Dederick, T., Nambo, H., Oyabu, T.: Relative Difficulty of Various English Writings by Fuzzy Inference and Its Application to Selecting Teaching Materials. An International Journal of Industrial Engineering & Management Systems 3(1), 85–91 (2004)
6. Yule, G.U.: The Statistical Study of Literary Vocabulary. Cambridge University Press (1944)
7. Ban, H., Dederick, T., Oyabu, T.: Metrical comparison of english textbooks in east asian countries, the U.S.A. and U.K. In: Proceedings of the 4th International Symposium on Advanced Intelligent Systems, Korea, pp. 508–512, September 25–28, 2003
8. Ban, H., Dederick, T., Nambo, H., Oyabu, T.: Metrical comparison of English materials for business management and information technology. In: Proceedings of the Fifth Asia-Pacific Industrial Engineering and Management Systems Conference 2004, Australia, pp. 33.4.1-33.4.10, December 12–15, 2004

Relationship of Terror Feelings and Physiological Response During Watching Horror Movie

Makoto Fukumoto[(✉)] and Yuuki Tsukino

Fukuoka Institute of Technology, 3-30-1 Wajirohigashi, Higashi-Ku, Fukuoka, Japan
fukumoto@fit.ac.jp

Abstract. Movie is one of the most popular media types. Horror movie is a kind of attractive movie contents which part of people want to watch very much. Although the users feel terror of the contents, the users want to watch the horror movies to have extraordinary feelings such as excitements. Therefore, terror feelings of the horror movies are considered as an important factor to establish more attractive movie contents, and the effect of horror movie is highly believed. However, few previous studies have investigated a relationship of horror movie and its terror feelings. This study aims to investigate psycho-physiological effects of horror movies on the user for clarifying the relationship. In the experiment, physiological data (electrocardiogram and respiration, and skin conductance) of ten male subjects were measured. Additionally, after watching movie contents, the experimenter asked the subjects points in movie affecting terror feelings on the subjects and how the subjects felt in these points. The experimental results shows that change in intensity and cycle of respiration: in the point affecting terror feelings on the subject, the intensity of respiration was augmented and the cycle of respiration was shortened.

Keywords: Horror movie · Terror feeling · Respiration · Skin conductance

1   Introduction

Movie is one of important media type which is very popular and has strong effects on people. Some movies makes people very exciting, on the other hand, some other movies makes people very sad. This must be come from effective combination of stimuli related to sight and hearing of the movies.

It is interesting that many people loves horror movie although they do not like to be in horror situation in their real life: of course, they can enjoy horror movies because of its hypothetic horror. From same point of view, positive effects of horror game were argued and applied on various situations [1].

Various previous studies have investigated the relationships of physiological change and subjective feelings including Kansei. As a representative of the studies, Picard et al. have investigated the relationships by employing multiple physiological indices [2]. It is very important to reveal the relationship for presuming the user's state without subjective evaluation for various objectives.

© IFIP International Federation for Information Processing 2015
K. Saeed and W. Homenda (Eds.): CISIM 2015, LNCS 9339, pp. 500–507, 2015.
DOI: 10.1007/978-3-319-24369-6_41

However, the relationship in horror movie was investigated by few previous studies. As one of the related studies, Nagano et al. have investigated the effects of Japanese horror game [3]. In a mean of investigating the physiological changes during the user feeling terror, this previous study and the present study have same objectives. However, during playing game, user's operation must be cause of physiological noise. To observe and investigate the relationship, it is better to affect the subject by only terror feeling without other tasks.

This study aims to investigate the relationship of terror feeling and physiological indices. An experiment is conducted to investigated the relationship, and a Japanese horror movie is selected as a stimulus that affecting the subjects terror. Respiration, electrocardiogram, and skin conductance were measured as the physiological indices. With a questionnaire, subjective terror feelings of the subjects during the stimulus were investigated.

2   Experimental Method

2.1   Subjects and Stimulus

The time length of physiological measurement was forty minutes. Beforehand of the measurement, the experimenter described the all of procedures of the experiment to the subject. The experiment was composed of three steps as shown in Fig. 1; prior rest period (5 min), movie period (32 min), and post rest period (3 min). During these three periods, the experimental room was kept quietly and dark. Immediately after these three periods, as questionnaire period, the experimenter asked the subject his terror feelings of the movie stimulus by replaying each of scenes of the stimulus considered as affecting terror feeling as described in the next subsection 2.2.

During the 40 min measurement, as physiological indices, respiration, Garvanic Skin Response (GSR), and electrocardiogram were measured. In the measurement, a device of physiological measurement and software (MT-BA-BM2 and Real-Time EFRP II, Melon Technos) and physiological amplifiers (RSP100C and GSR100C, BIOPAC Systems) were used. Prior to the experiment, these devices were attached on the subject by the experimenter. Band of RSP100C was attached on the subjects' chest, and electrodes of GSR100C were attached on index and middle fingers of left hand.

2.2   Experimental Procedure

Ten male students participated in the experiment as subjects. They participated in the experiment individually. As a movie stimulus, one of Japanese famous horror movies, "Juon 2" [4] was employed. In detail, time length of the movie was about 90 min and was composed of several related parts. Two successive parts of the movie was selected as the stimulus: these parts were merged into one stimulus. Time length of these parts was totally 32 min. All of the subjects had no experience of watching this movie.

The experimenter investigated contents of the stimulus and picked up eight scenes where the subjects seemed to feel terror (Fig. 2). Prior four of them were considered as scenes that affect the subjects sudden terror. On the other hand, latter four of them were considered as scenes make the subjects shiver. In other words, the scene makes the subjects shiver is also considered as scenes where the subjects can predict something will happen. These scenes were selected by the experimenters, and reasons of selection were sudden loud sounds, sudden scream, and sudden happenings after silent and/or dark scenes.

Fig. 1. Procedure of the experiment.

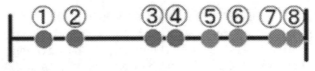

    Scene considered as affecting the subjects sudden terror

    Scene considered as making the subjects shiver

Fig. 2. Location of eight scenes affecting the subjects terror feeling in movie stimulus and type of these scenes.

3   Experimental Results

This section mainly shows results of change in respiration and show an example of GSR: analysis of electrocardiogram is not finished.

3.1   Result of Change in Respiration

Fig. 3 shows an example of respiration of subject who felt terror feelings around scenes 7 and 8. Upper figure shows intensity of respiration, and lower figure shows cycle of respiration. The intensity of respiration was measured by change in thoracic cavity, and it means deepness of respiration. The cycle of respiration means was obtained by analyzing intensity of respiration: band pass filter was applied on data of the intensity.

Around the scene 7, the intensity respiration began to increase by comparing to prior to the scene 7. The increase continues to the end of the scene 8, and sometimes the rapid changes of the intensity were observed. In accordance with the change in the intensity of respiration, the cycle of respiration began to accelerate around the scene 7 from 4 s to 3 s, and shortened cycle was kept till the end of the scene 8.

To compare the respiration between subjects who felt terror and who did not felt terror, Fig. 4 shows another example of subject who did not felt any terror around scenes 7 and 8. In this subject, the intensity of respiration did not change in the scene 7, the intensity decreased around the scene 8. The cycle of respiration did not change around the scenes 7 and 8. Note that the intensity of respiration is an index which cannot be compared between subjects, because the value of the intensity is defined by tightening of the band of GSR100C.

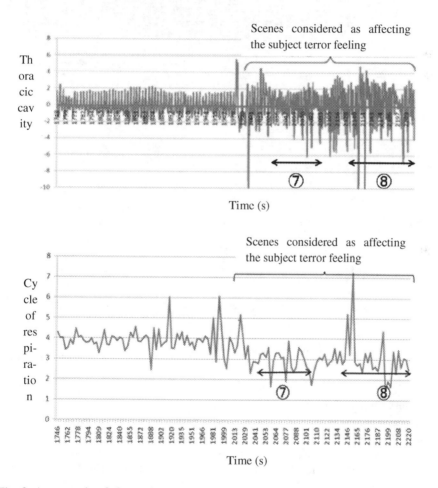

Fig. 3. An example of change in respiration of one subject who felt terror feeling around the scenes 7 and 8.

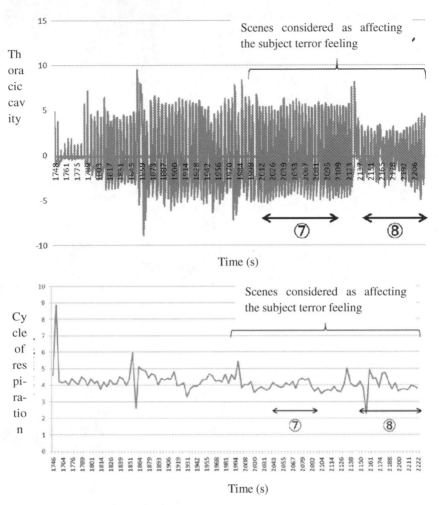

Fig. 4. An example of change in respiration of one subject who did not feel any terror around scenes 7 and 8.

To observe trend of the change in the cycle of respiration with covering all of the subjects, mean cycles of respiration prior to and during the horror scenes 7 and 8 were obtained by summarizing subjects who did not feel terror, subjects who felt terror, and all subjects, respectively (Table 1). The horror scene here means around scenes 7 and 8, and prior to horror scenes means general scene without horror just after changed from a certain scene. In all of the subjects, cycle of respiration was shortened in the horror scenes although in a case the subjects subjectively responded as they did not feel terror at all.

To investigate the change in the cycle of respiration, statistical analysis is applied to the data of all of the subjects in Table 1. In detail, Sign Test was employed. The difference in cycles of respiration was significantly different between prior to and during the horror scenes ($P<0.01$).

Table 1. Mean cycle of respiration (s) between subjects during prior to and during the horror scenes 7 and 8.

	Prior to Horror Scenes (4:07)	During Horror Scenes (3:45)
6 subjects who did not feel terror	4.68	4.11
4 subjects who felt terror	4.15	3.47
All of 10 subjects	4.47	3.85

3.2   Result of Change in Galvanic Skin Response

As result of change in GSR, only two examples of change in GSR are suggested, because analysis of GSR is not finished. Fig. 5 shows an example of change in GSR of one subject who felt terror. This example shows the change in GSR during all of the experiment (40 min) including prior and post rests, and time periods of the eight scenes considered as affecting terror are also described in the figures.

Conductance of GSR was low level in the prior rest, and increased from just after beginning the movie stimulus. In almost all of the scenes considered as affecting terror feeling to the subject, the conductance increased. This subject subjectively explained that he did not felt terror in scenes 3, 5, 6, and 7. In most of these scenes, relatively low reactions in the conductance were observed, especially in the scene 5. Moreover, in some periods like around 1100 s that is not related to the scenes, the conductance raised

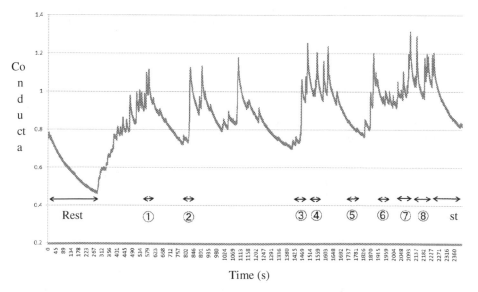

Fig. 5. An example of change in Galvanic Skin Response in one subject.

4   Discussion

During the scenes considered as affecting the subjects terror feeling, the intensity of respiration was increased in some samples of the subjects. Furthermore, the cycle of respiration was accelerated, and the cycle was statistically increased by comparing with prior to the scenes. The change in the cycle of respiration is considered as a result of change in autonomic nervous activity. We have to investigate the change in autonomic nervous activity by combining the analysis of GSR and heartbeat (which were not finished).

The cycle of respiration was accelerated in both of the subjects who felt terror and did not feel terror. If the subjects responded as felt no terror, the movie stimulus may affect to the subject. Moreover, there is a possibility that the subjects told a lie that they did not feel any terror although they felt terror. In such the case, pride of the subject must be a reason of the lie: feeling terror might be a shame feeling. This is a severe problem that makes difficult connecting the terror feeling and physiological information. Presuming the terror feeling via physiological information is possible to apply to user's terror in some simulations of safety system [5]. By improving the experimental procedure, we have to connect them.

5   Conclusion

In this study, we focused on the psycho-physiological effects of horror movie and investigated the relationship of terror feeling and physiological change. Intensity and cycle of respiration was mainly analyzed, and the intensity was augmented during the scenes considered as affecting the subjects terror feeling. The cycle was accelerated in accordance with the augmentation of the intensity. The change in the cycle was significant in all of the subjects although subjects subjectively explained that they did not feel any terror.

As next steps, we have to investigate the relationship after analyzing GSR and electrocardiogram. Combining various physiological data will dedicate to precise presuming subjects' psychological state as the previous study did [2]. In the use of GSR as skin conductance index, a recent study suggested that asymmetry of activity between right and left hands [6], therefore, the asymmetry should be considered and be utilized for further investigations.

Acknowledgment. This work was supported in part by Grant from Computer Science Laboratory, Fukuoka Institute of Technology.

References

1. Perron, B.: Coming to Play at Frightening Yourself: Welcome to the World of Horror Video Games. Aesthetics of Play (2005). http://www.aestheticsofplay.org/perron.php
2. Picard, R.W., Vyzas, E., Healey, J.: Toward Machine Emotional Intelligence: Analysis of Affective Physiological State. IEEE Transactions Pattern Analysis and Machine Intelligence **23**(10), 1175–1191 (2001)

3. Nagano, Y., Nakao, A., Kobayashi, H., Funaki, S., Sato, H., Takeuchi, T.: Investigation of effects of horror game on skin conductance, heart rate, and skin blood flow. In: Proc. Conf, of Japanese Society of Physiological Psychology and Psychophysiology, p. 132 (2010) (in Japanese)
4. Juon Official Site. http://www.juon-movie.jp/ (in Japanese)
5. Saito, Y., Suzuki, K., Nakano, Y., Nishioka, D., Takahashi, T., Murayama, Y.: A Study on a System for Generating a Near Miss Map utilizing Emotion Sharing. JSPS IOT 27(11), 1–6 (2014)
6. Picard, R.W., Fedor, S., Ayzenberg, Y.: Multiple Arousal Theory and Daily-Life Electro-dermal Activity Asymmetry. Emotion Review 1–14 (2015)

Estimation of User's Attention and Awareness in Occlusion-Rich Environments Using RGB-D Cameras

Jun-ichi Imai$^{(\boxtimes)}$ and Masanori Nemoto

Chiba Institute of Technology, 2–17–1 Tsudanuma,
Narashino-shi, Chiba 275–0016, Japan
imai@cs.it-chiba.ac.jp
http://www.imai.cs.it-chiba.ac.jp/

Abstract. Objective recognition by systems often does not agree with subjective recognition by users. Therefore, it is an important to estimate users' subjective states appropriately. Especially, in occlusion-rich environments, information on what a user can/cannot see, what he/she pays attention to, and what he/she is aware of or not in the environments is one of important clues to estimate his/her subjective states and predict next actions. In this paper, we propose a system for estimating maps of a user's attention and awareness in such environments based on the view estimation system using RGB-D cameras. The proposed system can estimate what the user sees, what he/she pays attention to, and what he/she is aware of in environments in pixels of captured images. Experimental results in a real environments show effectiveness of the proposed system. Furthermore, we discuss an extension of the proposed system to estimation for multiple users.

Keywords: Attention · Awareness · Occlusion-rich environment · RGB-D Camera · View estimation

1 Introduction

Human-symbiotic systems, which share humans' living spaces and assist with their activities by various means, have been increasingly studied in recent years (e.g. [1]). In order to realize such systems, a lot of techniques for recognizing states of users and their circumstances have been proposed. However, such *objective* recognition by the systems often does not agree with *subjective* recognition by users. Such a perception gap will cause disagreement between assistance provided by the systems and one which users really need. Therefore, it is an important problem to estimate users' subjective states appropriately.

Generally, in our living spaces, there are a lot of objects which can cause visual occlusion. Since a system and a user will observe the environment from different positions, it often occurs that one cannot see an object by occlusion while the other can. This is a typical example of the perception gap between

© IFIP International Federation for Information Processing 2015
K. Saeed and W. Homenda (Eds.): CISIM 2015, LNCS 9339, pp. 508–518, 2015.
DOI: 10.1007/978-3-319-24369-6_42

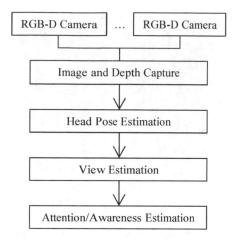

Fig. 1. Processing Flow of Proposed System

the systems and users [2]. In such environments, information on what a user can/cannot see, what he/she pays attention to, and what he/she is aware of in the environments will be one of important clues to estimate his/her subjective states and predict the next action.

In this paper, based on the view estimation using multiple RGB-D cameras [3], we propose a system for estimating maps of a user's attention and awareness in occlusion-rich environments. We simply define a user's *attention* as watching something continuously during a short period, and *awareness* as having seen something before and knowing that it is there. The proposed system can estimate what the user sees, what he/she pays attention to, and what he/she is aware of in environments in pixels of captured images. The system can estimate them without his/her wearing cameras or other equipments. This point is the advantage of our proposed method.

Fig. 1 shows the processing flow of the proposed system.

The flow can be divided into four parts; the image and depth capture module, the head pose estimation module, the view estimation module, and the attention/awareness estimation module. After capturing images and depth information from the cameras, the system estimates the user's head pose horizontally and vertically. Then, the user's field of view is estimated using the specified head pose. And finally, based on the specified field of view, maps of the user's attention and awareness in environments are estimated.

2   System Architecture

2.1   Hardware

The proposed system consists of multiple RGB-D cameras put in the environment and a PC. As RGB-D cameras, we adopt *Kinects*, manufactured by

Fig. 2. Examples of Head Pose Estimation

Microsoft Corporation. We assume that the system knows the number of cameras N, their positions and poses described in the world coordinate system. The cameras are put so that their optical axes will be parallel to the x-z plane.

2.2   Image and Depth Capture

In the first module, color images and corresponding depth information are captured from synchronized multiple RGB-D cameras. After the capture, three-dimensional Cartesian camera coordinates, which origin is placed in the position of the corresponding camera, are calculated for each pixel in each captured image using the measured depth z.

2.3   Head Pose Estimation

In the second module, the user's head pose is estimated from a set of images and depth information captured in the first module.

First, the position of the user's head is detected. We adopt the particle filter [4] for tracking the user's head. Then, based on the specified head position, the user's head pose $(\theta_{\text{pitch}}, \theta_{\text{yaw}})$ is estimated. In this paper, we assume that the roll angle $\theta_{\text{roll}} = 0$. They are estimated by using vertical integral projections v_x and v_y of horizontal edge components in the extracted head image are calculated as follows [5]:

$$v_x(x) = \sum_y |e_h(x,y)|, \quad v_y(y) = \sum_x |e_h(x,y)|, \tag{1}$$

where $e_h(x, y)$ denotes the horizontal edge component at the pixel (x, y). Then, histograms of v_x and v_y are smoothed ten times to extract rough features of the face. The positions of the maximum values of v_x, v_y are calculated as

$$x_{\text{max}} = \arg\max_x v_x(x), \quad y_{\text{max}} = \arg\max_y v_y(y). \tag{2}$$

Fig. 2 shows examples of the histograms of v_x and v_y. Blue lines denote the center of the head image and red lines denote positions of x_{max} and y_{max}. We can see from these examples that the point $(x_{\text{max}}, y_{\text{max}})$ corresponds to the center of the user's face.

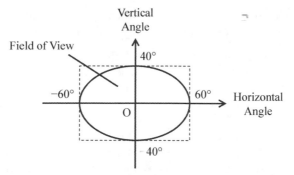

(a) Horizontal and Vertical Angles of View

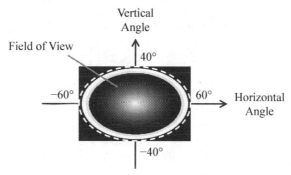

(b) Distribution of Relative Acuity of Visual Perception

Fig. 3. Model of Field of View

Although a lot of methods have been proposed for the head pose estimation [6], we give priority to achievement of estimation at high frame rate because this advantage enables the system to recognize even the user's glancing. Therefore, we adopt a simple method for the head pose estimation.

2.4   View Estimation

Next, based on the specified head pose, the user's field of view in pixels from three-dimensional point cloud data [3].

In this paper, we simply assume that the horizontal and vertical angles of view of human's eye are 120° and 80° respectively, as shown in Fig. 3 (a). The origin of the coordinates in Fig. 3 (a) denotes the user's head orientation.

Humans can see objects clearly near the center of view, but blurredly near the border. So we also assume that relative acuity of visual perception in the field of view is approximated as shown in Fig. 3 (b). The brighter color in Fig. 3 (b) denotes the higher relative acuity and the origin of the coordinates has the highest acuity 1.

The user's field of view in an environment is estimated according to the following procedure. This procedure is performed for each captured image.

1. The camera coordinate system which origin is placed in the position of the camera is transformed into the viewing coordinate system such that its origin is placed in the center of gravity of the user's head and its z-axis corresponds to the user's head orientation, using the specified head pose parameters θ_{pitch} and θ_{yaw}.

2. The Cartesian coordinate system (x, y, z) is transformed into the polar coordinate system (ρ, θ, ϕ). In this coordinate system, the field of view shown in Fig. 3 corresponds to $0° \leq \theta \leq T_\theta(\phi)$ and $0° \leq \phi \leq 360°$, where

$$T_\theta(\phi) = (2 + |\cos \phi|) \times 20°. \tag{3}$$

Furthermore, the relative acuity a shown in Fig. 3 (b) is formulated as

$$a(\theta, \phi) = \left(\frac{\theta - T_\theta(\phi)}{T_\theta(\phi)} \right)^2. \tag{4}$$

3. The θ-ϕ plane $(0° \leq \theta \leq T_\theta(\phi), 0° \leq \phi \leq 360°)$ is divided into bins at $0.5°$ intervals. For each bin, the nearest pixel to the user's eye, which has the smallest value of ρ, is decided. The set of these nearest pixels is defined as the user's *field of view*, that is, the regions that the user can observe from his/her position. Conversely, pixels out of the field of view are defined as the user's *blind regions*.

Pixels in the field of view are classified into the following three categories according to the positional relationship between the user's line of sight and the environment [3].

(A) Pixels that the corresponding camera and the user observe the same side.
(B) Pixels that the corresponding camera and the user observe the opposite side to each other.
(C) Pixels that the corresponding camera and the user *will* observe the same side, but it is also possible that the user cannot observe it by occlusion due to an obstacle in the camera's blind region.

2.5   Attention/Awareness Estimation

Finally, based on the estimated field of view, the maps of the user's attention and awareness in the environment on the captured images are estimated as follows:

1. The visual acuity map M_{acuity} at time step t is defined as

$$M_{\text{acuity}}(i, j, t) = a(\theta(i, j), \phi(i, j), t), \tag{5}$$

where (i, j) denotes a pixel in the map, $\theta(i, j)$ and $\phi(i, j)$ denote the parameters in the polar coordinate system for the point which corresponds to (i, j). M_{acuity} denotes a distribution of the user's visual acuity among his/her field of view. That is, it represents how well the user sees each pixel at the moment.

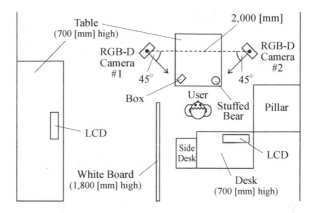

Fig. 4. Experimental Environment

2. The user's attention map M_{att} at time step t is defined as

$$M_{att}(i,j,t) = \beta \cdot M_{acuity}(i,j,t) + (1 - \beta) \cdot M_{att}(i,j,t-1), \quad (6)$$

where β denotes a mixture rate. In this paper, we set $\beta = 0.1$. M_{att} is a temporal accumulation of M_{acuity}, and it represents how well and how continuously the user sees each pixel for a period. So we define this map as the user's *attention*.

3. The user's awareness map M_{awr} at time step t is defined as

$$M_{awr}(i,j,t) = \max \{M_{acuity}(i,j,t), M_{awr}(i,j,t-1)\} \quad (7)$$

If depth z for the pixel (i,j) makes some change (we set a threshold at 50 [mm] in this paper) from the previous time step, then $M_{awr}(i,j,t)$ is reset at 0. M_{awr} denotes a map of maximum values of visual acuity until then. It represents pixels which has been included in the user's view. Therefore, it is probable that the user is aware of the objects and information corresponding to those pixels. So we define this map as the user's *awareness*.

3   Experiment

We carry out an experiment to confirm effectiveness of the proposed system.

3.1   Experimental Settings

Fig. 4 shows the experimental environment. The two RGB-D cameras are set in front of a user, who sits on a swivel chair, at interval of 2,000 [mm]. These cameras are set at a height of 1,050 [mm]. There are a white board and a pillar on the left and right side of the user respectively. There are also a box and a

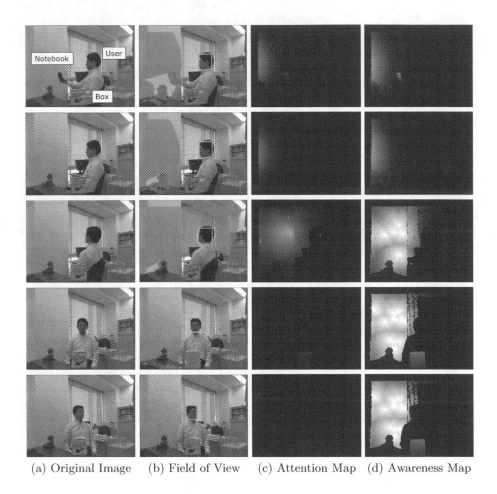

(a) Original Image   (b) Field of View   (c) Attention Map   (d) Awareness Map

Fig. 5. Experimental Results (Camera #1)

stuffed bear on the table in front of the user, an LCD on the desk behind him, and another LCD on the left table.

The size of both of image and depth information captured from the RGB-D camera is 640×480 pixels. The estimation of the maps of attention and awareness is performed to the resized image of 320 × 240 pixels to reduce computational time. The frame rate of the system is about 5–7 [fps] without any special optimization on a normal notebook PC (Intel Core i7, 2.60 [GHz]). The latency time from data capture to output of the estimated field of view is about 200 [msec].

3.2   Results

Fig. 5 and 6 show examples of the experimental results.

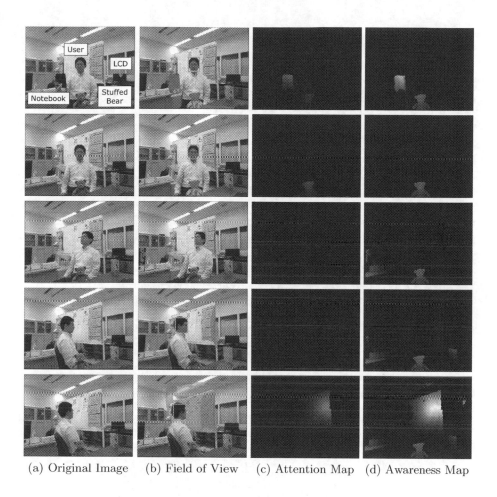

(a) Original Image   (b) Field of View   (c) Attention Map   (d) Awareness Map

Fig. 6. Experimental Results (Camera #2)

Fig. 5 (a) and 6 (a) show the original images of the same scene captured from the camera #1 and #2 respectively. These figures are arranged in time order. In the top figures, the user held his notebook and looked to it. Then he lowered the notebook and looked down to the stuffed bear (in the second rows). Next, in the third rows, he turned to his right and saw the pillar. Then he turned to his left and looks to the box (in the fourth rows). And finally, he further turned to his left and looked to the right side of the white board (in the bottom).

Fig. 5 (b) and 6 (b) show the estimated fields of view in the images captured from the camera #1 and #2 respectively. Red, blue and green regions in these figures correspond to Category (A), (B) and (C) respectively. Fig. 5 (c) and 6 (c) show the estimated attention maps, 5 (d) and 6 (d) show the estimated awareness maps on the images captured from the camera #1 and #2 respectively. (In Fig. 5 and 6, the field of view and the maps of attention and awareness are not estimated in the upper and left regions because the RGB-D cameras cannot capture the corresponding depth data.)

We can see from Fig. 5 and 6 that the proposed system could estimate the maps of the user's attention and awareness well. For example, in the top figures in Fig. 6 (c) and (d), the pixels which corresponds to the notebook and the stuffed bear near it are colored brighter gray because they must be seen clearly by the user. In the second rows, the notebook are removed from both maps because it moved and went out of his view. Furthermore, in the fourth and bottom figures, the LCD put on the table is not colored even if the user tuned to his left because it was occluded by the white board and out of his view. Therefore, the system could recognize that the user was not aware of the LCD. We can see from the attention maps (Fig. 5 (c) and 6 (c)) that the system can recognize the regions to where the user looks, that is, pays attention at the moment well. We can also see from the awareness maps (Fig. 5 (d) and 6 (d)) that the system can store pixels which the user has seen in the environment well. These stored pixels are expected to correspond to the objects of which the user will be aware.

These experimental results agree well with the user's subjective evaluation.

4   Extension to Estimation for Multiple Users

The proposed method can be extended to the estimation of joint attention among multiple users. Fig. 7 shows the extended processing flow. The processes of the head pose estimation and the view/attention/awareness estimation are

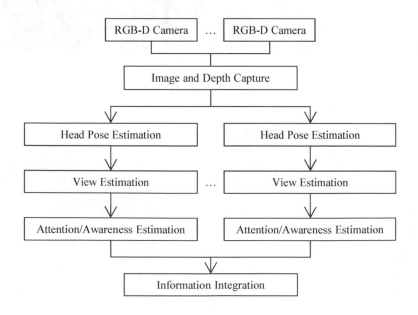

Fig. 7. Flow of Estimation for Multiple Users

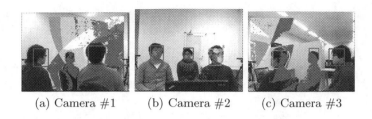

(a) Camera #1   (b) Camera #2   (c) Camera #3

Fig. 8. Example of View Estimation for Multiple Users

parallelized into threads for multiple users. The results of estimation are finally integrated.

Fig. 8 shows an example of the view estimation for multiple users. In this example, the system has three cameras and estimate three users' field of view simultaneously. In Fig. 8, the colors of red, green and blue are assigned to fields of view for each user. Furthermore, the overlapped regions in their view are painted the mixed color of their assigned colors. The system can obtain the regions where all users can see (i.e. their *joint attention*), ones where the only one user can see while the others cannot, and so on.

5   Conclusions

In this paper, we propose a system for estimating maps of a user's attention and awareness in occlusion-rich environments based on the view estimation system using multiple RGB-D cameras. The proposed system can estimate what the user sees, what he/she pays attention to, and what he/she is aware of in environments in pixels of captured images. Experimental results in a real environments show effectiveness of the proposed system. Furthermore, we discuss an extension of the proposed system to estimation for multiple users.

The maps of attention and awareness estimated by the proposed system are still only rough estimation. As a future task, we plan to investigate the accuracy of the proposed system through the subjective evaluation. It is expected that we can obtain the user's attention and awareness by subjective questionnaire. Furthermore, we also plan to introduce the saliency map to the system in order to estimate more detailed information on users' attention and awareness in environments.

References

1. Maeda, Y., Katagami, D., eds.: Special Issue on Human Symbiotic System. Journal of Advanced Computational Intelligence and Intelligent Informatics **14**(7) (2010)
2. Imai, J., Kaneko, M.: Human Interactions with a Robot that Recognizes Differences between Fields of View. Kansei Engineering International Journal **10**(1), 59–68 (2010)

3. Imai, J., Tamegai, M.: Three-dimensional estimation of user's field of view using multiple RGB-D cameras. In: Proc. SICE Annual Conference 2013, pp. 2347–2352 (2013)
4. Doucet, A., de Freitas, N., Gordon, N. (eds.): Sequential Monte Carlo Methods in Practice. Springer, New York (2001)
5. Brunelli, R., Poggio, T.: Face recognition: Features versus templates. IEEE Trans. Pattern Anal. Mach. Intell. **15**(10), 1042–1052 (1993)
6. Murphy-Chutorian, E., Trivedi, M.M.: Robust Head Pose Estimation in Computer Vision: A Survey. IEEE Trans. Pattern Anal. Mach. Intell. **31**(4), 607–626 (2009)

Factors to Affect Descriptions on Intra-Concept Relation in Introductory Concept Mapping

Jun Minagawa[1] and Hiromi Ban[2(✉)]

[1] Sanyo Gakuen College, Okayama, Japan
mendelmondel@gmail.com
[2] Nagaoka University of Technology, Nagaoka, Niigata, Japan
je9xvp@yahoo.co.jp

Abstract. Introductory Concept mapping is a method that property of association task is introduced to Concept Mapping. With a certain extent of freedom permitted to experiment participants for association, the method is advantageous in that motivation of participants to construct maps is enhanced higher than Concept Mapping. Experiment participants are supposed to write down concepts which are associated from the concept of developmental psychology around the word, "developmental psychology", written on a white paper. In an examination of correlation coefficient based on this method using score of intra-concept relation explanation as a dependent variable and previous (existing) knowledge score, number of mean expressed concepts, number of bifurcated concepts, number of cross-links, and number of forward reactions as independent variables, significant positive correlation was observed with all independent variables except for the number of cross-links. In addition, only number of bifurcated concepts and previous knowledge score remained as reasonable independent variable by a multi-regression analysis performed based on stepwise way.

Keywords: Concept map · Association task · Introductory concept map · Relation of concepts

1 Introduction

Concept Mapping is an externalizing strategy for a cognitive structure de-veloped by Novak & Gowin (1984) based on a learning theory of Ausubel (1968) as well as a learning strategy for forming more reasonable cognitive structure. With a focus put on a strict systematicity between concepts, in particular, hierarchical systematicity reaching from subordinate to superordinate concept among others, Novak et al. included links between concepts as well as explanation (linking label) described on the links as elements of concept map using a material of science education. Concepts to be written, way of linking, and linking label is strictly determined in the corresponding unit.

However, it was revealed in the subsequent development that non-hierarchical map could exist, and Novak himself proposed to perform association task in the course of introduction of concept map to learning. Further subsequently, even such opinion has also appeared in Japan that association task itself should be taken as a concept map resulting in diffusing the very meaning of the concept itself in a form of concept map.

© IFIP International Federation for Information Processing 2015
K. Saeed and W. Homenda (Eds.): CISIM 2015, LNCS 9339, pp. 519–526, 2015.
DOI: 10.1007/978-3-319-24369-6_43

There have been pros and cons regarding association task. For example, Cachapuz & Maskill (1987) performed association task in order to examine intra-concept relation held by subjects. As the result, it has been proved that there is a large difference between experts and beginners using a diagram with less cognitive load and an easily viewable method. At the same time, Cachapuz et al. have criticized such strategy that describes intra-concept relation in detail is a very time-consuming method. On the other hand, Stewart (1979, 1980) and Shinkai (1981) have criticized regarding association task that how subjects thought to link between concepts is unclear.

In the author's series of experiments, showing association task graphically really has an advantage to keep cognitive load lower and it is possible to assume how subjects though to link between concepts as long as they are able to endure strict experiment, but it has been proved that such strategy as to memorize the whole things of typical maps is used by subjects who have in-adequate previous knowledge or who are judged to lack of learning motivation required for understanding intra-concept relation. Therefore, it is desired to describe link-labels in detain from a perspective of learning support which is the true purpose of Concept Mapping. However, it has been revealed that when making subjects with less knowledge describe link-labels on the map during the experiment they get confused by the time consumed to think how to describe them resulting in great decrease in number of concepts to be de-scribed.

Amid such trend, Minagawa (2009) figured out a way to positively utilize association task by revising it. With appearance of various factors observed in association task similarly to a case of concept map, such as hierarchical property, concept bifurcation phenomenon (a few subordinate concepts to be bifurcated from specific concept and described), and cross-linking (a new relationship between subordinate concepts to be recognized after completing hierarchical upper and lower structures), it has been proved to be possible to obtain clues for recognizing cognitive structure of learners by rather considering these observation results and association task as such meaning has be-come to be called as "Introductory Concept Mapping."

Practically in this method, learners are handed over with a sheet of white paper and asked to write original concept for association on the center of it and additionally write down concepts associated from the original one in order. This method has characteristics such as

① to describe related concepts consecutively without caring for hierarchical intra-concept relation,

② to note re-called order by numbers,

③ to continuously describe concepts group in a direction free from the original concept for association at the center, and

④ to describe link-labels too similarly to a case of Concept Mapping, and it also demands efforts to find out cross links asking to describe link-labels too in principle in such a case. However, as it often becomes to be extremely complicated, such link-label and numbers to indicate order are often omitted. In this study, Minagawa has demonstrated in a multi-regression analysis using a test score of the corresponding field as the dependent variable that numbers of concept bifurcation and cross-linking are useful as independent variables. Fig. 1 and Fig. 2 below are examples of ordinary concept map and introductory concept map, respectively.

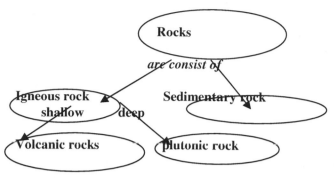

Fig. 1. An example of the Concept Map, "Rock"

The second rebellious age
The second of adolescence

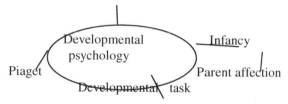

Fig. 2. An example of the Introductory Concept Map, "Developmental Psychology"

Then, why hierarchical property was not necessarily demanded between associated words groups in the Introductory Concept Mapping is based on a fact that recalled order of concept groups in association is random to some extent. That is, for example, in a concept of Ausubel's meaningful learning, subordinate concepts are believed to consist of systematization with several concepts and refining for which meaningfulness, understanding with profound contents and correlation are considered.

What is important is that association is not necessarily developed from superordinate concepts in association task even if subjects systematized them by Concept Mapping. For example, first response word for stimulus word, meaningful learning, may be "meaningfulness." Further, it may be often developed in order from correlation, refining to understanding with profound con-tents. Since these examples are often observed in association, any association should be determined to be correct as long as it is within the same super-ordinate concept.

Then, there is a problem of link-label. Link label should be described in de-tail as much as possible from a perspective of learning support, but it is inappropriate at early stage of unit learning due to tight time constraint. Therefore, adopting intra-concept relation (including a link-label to directly and indirectly link between concepts) as dependent variables in the present study, independent variable and dependent variables were considered from among various possible variables using examples from Minagawa (2009, 2015).

Variables ever considered in the previous studies include posttest score, number of correct associations, number of erroneous associations, total number of associations, number of cross-links, number of bifurcated concepts, related previous knowledge score, score of intra-concept relation explanation, and mean number of expressed concepts per series (total number of associated concepts/number of direct connection)

Of those items, number of erroneous associations and total number of associations were excluded from the study because the former had less importance for interpreting the corresponding experiment and the latter was difficult to be interpreted due to the concurrently included correct and erroneous associations.

As the result, previous knowledge score, score of intra-concept relation explanation, mean number of expressed concepts, number of bifurcated concepts, number of cross-links, and number of correct responses were adopted as variables, among which score of intra-concept relation explanation was used as a dependent variable because it corresponded to a link-label in a broad sense.

Our research hypotheses are as follows:

1. Subjects of the present study may be difficult to function as an independent variable because neither were they able to find out even a few cross-links nor were they instructed how to find out them in a concept mapping practice of previous lectures.

2. Mean number of expressed concepts per series may be difficult to function as an effective independent variable because number of concept maps is originally determined by the types of subordinate concepts.

3. Previous knowledge may work as an effective independent variable this time too because it was able to effectively function every time up to now.

4. Numbers of correct responses and bifurcated concepts may function as effective independent variables because they are indexes whether the whole concept groups is well understood or not.

Experiments are performed and the results are considered in order to verify these hypotheses.

2   Methods

1. Experiment participants: Totally 26 sophomores including 2 men and 24 women of B department in a private A university in Okayama prefecture
2. Date of experiment: December in 2014]
3. Venue of experiment: Class room within A university
4. Procedures: We performed a previous knowledge survey (scale of one to ten) a week before the experiment and a relation explanation test (scale of one to ten) a week after them without preliminary notice for both of them. The experiment was performed in a lecture of "Developmental psychology" as a part of class. First, students were handed with a sheet of A4 size white paper and instructed as follows: "We perform an association experiment now. Fill in your affiliation, student ID number and name at the top of the form. As a word "Developmental psychology" is written at the center, write down words associated from the word in order you associated in a

manner to connect them. In order to make the order of associated words clear, draw lines from the origin word for association to those associated. Also note numbers to indicate the order of association. You don't need to write link-label. You are allowed to use 30 minutes for writing. Then, let's get started!" Then, instructing, "Stop!" after 30 minutes elapsed, the forms were collected.

3   Results

A multi-regression analysis was performed based on stepwise way using relation explanation score as a dependent variable and number of bifurcated concepts/number of direct connections, number of correct responses, number of cross-links, and previous knowledge survey score as independent variables. Mean value and standard deviation of each variable is shown in Table 1. Correlation coefficients between each variable are shown in Table 2. In addition, Table 3 shows bifurcation number, standard partial regression coefficient β of previous knowledge, as well as significance probability p of t and VIF.

Table 1. Mean and standard deviation of each variable.

	M	S
related explanation score (max. =10)	3.4	2.6
remembrance concepts/ connection	3.1	1.3
number of positive reactions	35.6	11.3
number of branches	3.9	3.9
cross-links	0.5	1.2
prior knowledge score(max=10)	5.6	1.9

$*p{<}.05, **p{<}.01$

Table 2. Standard regression coefficient β of the number of branch and the preceding knowledge, score

	β	t	p	VIF
number of branches	.44	2.69	.013	1.571
prior knowledge	.43	2.63	.015	1.571

4   Discussion

Positive reaction counts refer to the appropriate number of vocabulary associated with conceptional relationship. It is a high number in considering the limited time of 30 minutes which indicates that students are keeping the memory of the study contents for a long time. On the other hand, Table 1 indicates that students do not have a deep understanding of intentional and extensional concepts as well as conceptional relationship despite of their low relative explanation score. In comparison with a concept divergent and a regular concept mapping, the introductory concept mapping (ICM) enables us to theoretically draw unlimited lines that are connected directly to the initial stimulus thereby it is reasonable to say why the number of lines become large. (See Fig. 3 and Fig. 4).

Fig. 3. Student A's Concept Map, "apparent movement" in Japanese

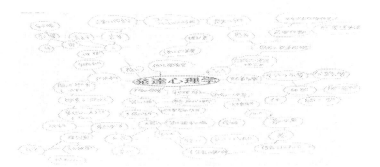

Fig. 4. Student B's   Introductory Concept Map, "Developmental Psycholpogy" in Japanese

Prior knowledge score is consisted of basic knowledge questions and it doesn't provide a high performance. On the other hand, Table 2 shows a significantly high relative explanation score for the prior knowledge, the positive reaction counts as well as the concept divergent just like the previous studies while its correlation for cross-link is low. It is assumed that cross-link was not sufficiently generated as they didn't have enough study contents and time for the course unit in order to discover a new relevance in conceptional relationships. This is why the cross-link was not extracted as a valid variable by multiple regression analysis as shown in Table 3.

Table 2 shows a significantly high relative explanation score for the prior knowledge and the concept divergent just like the previous studies. Because a number of memory concepts divided by a number indicates a high correlation for cross-link, it is assumed that correlation was enhanced due to the high average concepts associated with direct reaction words towards stimulus words. In Minagawa(2009, 2015), cross-link was largely found among students with high academic achievement which is believed due to the correlation of their high academic ability and creativity. However, it is hard to say cross-link happens naturally but requires for a professor to provide sufficient advice or training to students. It is also preferable to have a high motivation for study.

According to Novak et al., cross-link is believed to be an expression of extremely highly abstract thought. Therefore, it can be judged that participants in the present experiment were a bit lack of that aspect, but it may be true in any way that cross-link is the most difficult one to be created.

Among variables for which higher correlation between intra-concept relation is expected, number of bifurcated concepts and previous knowledge remained after a multi-regression analysis for the results of the experiment this time. Quantity and quality of previous knowledge is quite important for connecting intra-concept relation directly. In addition, as it is required for concept bifurcation a good deal of knowledge on what kinds of meanings the given concept can have, this result is believed to be rational.

As it is believed to lead to content understanding support by taking a strategy to instruct about cross-link and the like in advance in addition to recruiting more motivating experiment participants, we intend to study focusing on such aspect in the future. In this study, sophomore in nursing department were targeted, however, we have done similar experiments with college students in early childhood education department as well. Both majors are directly related to the practice, however, it is believed that proper study for developmental psychology and its theories are required.

References

1. Ausubel, D.P.: Educational Psychology : A Cognitive view. Holt, Rinehart & Winston, New York (1968)
2. Cachapuz, A.F.C., Maskill, R.: Detecting changes with learning in the organization of Knowledge: Using association tests to follow the learning of collision theory. International Journal of Science Educa-tion 9, 491–504 (1987)
3. Minagawa, J.: The Relation between Elements of Introductory Concept Map and the Score of Multiple-Choice Test. Tokyo Future University Bulletin. 2, 33–39 (2009). (in Japanese)
4. Minagawa, J.: The effect of the introductory concept map creation in short-time. In: The 1st International Symposium on Affective Science and Engineering (ISASE 2015) C1_3,Z000060 (2015)

5. Shinkai, K.: Of a cognitive construct check by a related description way during a concept-about junior high school creature teaching materials. University of Tsukuba pedagogy system collection of essays **5**, 145–157 (1981). (in Japanese)
6. Stewart, J.: Content and Cognitive Structure: Critique of Assessment and Representation Techniques Used by Science Education Re-searchers. Science Education **64**, 223–235 (1979)
7. Stewart, J.: Techniques for Assessing and Representing Information in Cognitive Structure. Science Education **64**, 223–235 (1980)

Investigation of Comfort of Uniform Shirt Made of Cellulose Considering Environmental Load

Hideaki Mizuhashi[1], Masayoshi Kamijo[1(✉)], Hiroaki Yoshida[1], and Harumi Tamaki[2]

[1] Faculty of Textile and Science Technology,
Shinshu University, 3-15-1 Tokida, Ueda, Nagano, Japan
kamijo@shinshu-u.ac.jp
[2] Tamaki Co., Ltd., 37-3 Honmokumakado, Naka-Ku, Kanagawa, Japan
harumi@tamac.co.jp

Abstract. The purpose of this study is to evaluate the wearing comfort of uniform-shirts and to investigate the suitable value for the preset temperature of air conditioners thorough measuring material properties and psychophysiological responses. The uniform shirt was made of cellulose materials such as rayon and tencel for wearing in hot conditions like summers in Japan. Material properties measurement were made according to Kawabata Evaluation System (KES), Japan Industrial Standards (JIS) and Moisture Management Tester (MMT). Physiological response measurements were electrocardiogram (ECG), respiration, skin temperature and the humidity inside the clothes. Psychological response measurements were by semantic differential method and ranking method. We concluded that the uniform shirts made of rayon are comfortable even in hot conditions like summer in Japan. 29°C as the temperature setting of air conditioners is too hot for people. Respiration seems to be an important factor for evaluation of wearing comfort.

1 Introduction

In Japan, the summer is a hot season with high humidity. For Japanese workers, thermal stress is a great annoyance in the summer. A uniform shirt is something that workers must wear. So the thermal stress of uniform shirts should be minimized. Cellulose materials such as tencel and rayon have characteristics such as high thermal conductivity and hydrophilicity suitable for reducing thermal stress. Cellulose also has low environmental impact since it can be turned back into soil. The purpose of this study is to develop comfortable uniform shirts made of cellulose. We used rayon and tencel as the cellulose materials. In terms of environment loading, tencel is lower than rayon because the waste fluid can be recycled as a soap. We manufactured trial uniform shirts and evaluated the wearing comfort by psychophysiological measurements and material properties evaluation.

The Japanese government recommends setting the air conditioner to 28°C in the summer. If the temperature setting of the air conditioner is increased by 1°C, power consumption will be reduced by 13%[1]. So we examined the temperature setting of air conditioners by comparing 28°C and 29°C from the viewpoint of wearing comfort.

© IFIP International Federation for Information Processing 2015
K. Saeed and W. Homenda (Eds.): CISIM 2015, LNCS 9339, pp. 527–538, 2015.
DOI: 10.1007/978-3-319-24369-6_44

2   Experiment

2.1   Samples

Table 1 shows the information of 3 types of samples with flat woven structure. Tencel, rayon, cotton and polyester were used to create the samples. R100 was composed of 100% rayon. The materials of R/T were rayon and tencel. The warp of R/T was 100% rayon. The weft of R/T was 100% tencel. P/C was composed of blended yarn made of 65% polyester and 35% cotton. P/C was the conventional product and R100 and R/T were the improved products.

Table 1. Samples

Symbol		R100	R/T	P/C
Material	Warp	Ray-on100%(Filamen	Ray-on100%(Filame	Polyes-ter65%/Cotton35%
	Weft	Ray-on100%(Filamen	Tencel100% (Spun)	Polyes-ter65%/Cotton35%
Yarn count	Warp	120 d ($\fallingdotseq$44.291S)	120 d ($\fallingdotseq$44.291 S)	45S
	Weft	120 d ($\fallingdotseq$44.291S)	40S	45S
Density	Warp	105 thread/inch	106 thread/inch	136 thread/inch
	Weft	77 thread/inch	85 thread/inch	72 thread/inch
Structure		Flat Woven Structure		

2.2   Material Properties Evaluation

This experiment was for evaluation of the heat and moisture transport properties of the 3 fabrics shown in Table 2. All items were measured 5 times. The mean value of those measurements was used as the representative value.

2.2.1   Japan Industrial Standards

For moisture transfer properties, moisture permeability and moisture content were measured. Moisture permeability was measured using the water method defined in JIS L 1099 A-2. A moisture-permeable cup is filled to 10mm of the upper rim of the cup with water at 40°C. The fabric is attached to the top of the cup so that the back side faces the water surface. Then, the cut surfaces of the test piece are covered with vinyl tape so that water vapors cannot escape. The cup prepared in this way is placed in a constant-temperature, constant-humidity environment at 40°C and 50%RH for 1 hour. Then the initial weight of the cup (a_1) is measured. Next, the weight of the cup after one hour has elapsed (a_2) is measured. The moisture permeability (MP) is then derived from the following equation. In this equation, S is the water-vapor-permeating surface area of the test piece.

$$MP = \frac{10 \times (a_1 - a_2)}{S} [g / m^2 \cdot h]$$

The moisture absorbency of textile products is determined according to the moisture ratio which is the percentage of atmospheric moisture that is absorbed. Dry-state textiles placed in the atmosphere absorb water vapors in the air to reach equilibrium. The moisture content (MC) defined in JIS L 1096 is expressed using Wd and Ww according to the following equation.

$$MC = \frac{Ww - Wd}{Wd} \times 100[\%]$$

In this equation, Wd is the weight of the textile in its absolute dry state, and Ww is the weight of the textile after being left in a constant-temperature, constant-humidity environment for more than 24 hours. In this research, the moisture content was measured at 28°C and 65% RH.

2.2.2 Kawabata Evaluation System

The air permeability property R was measured using KES-F8. R is the air flow resistance. The thermal properties q-max, K' and Qd were measured using KES-F7. q-max is the initial maximum heat flux when the copper plate heated to 30°C was put on the fabric. K' is the steady state thermal conductivity when a heat source at 30°C is placed on the fabric on top of a cool box at 20°C. Qd is the thermal insulation rate when air is blown on at an air flow of 0.3m/s. Measurement conditions were 20°C and 65% RH.

Table 2. Measurement items

Block property	Symbol	Property	Unit	Reference	Condition
Moisture transport	MC	Moisture content	%	JIS L 1096	28°C65%RH
	MP	Moisture permeability	g / m² · h	JIS L 1099 A-2	40°C50%RH
Thermal	q-max	Initial maximum heat flux	W/cm²		
	Qd	Thermal insulation rate (Dry method)	%	KES-F7	20°C65%RH
	K'	Steady state thermal conductivity	W		
Ventilation	R	Airflow resistance	KPa · s/m	KES-FB8	20°C65%RH
Water transport	Wt	Wetting time	s		
	Ar	Absorption rate	%		
	Mwr	Maximum wetted radius	mm	MMT	20°C65%RH
	Ss	Spreading speed	mm/s		
	$OWTC$	One way transport capacity	–		
	$OMMC$	Overall moisture management capacity	–		

2.2.3 Moisture Management Tester

The Moisture Management Tester (MMT) is the device for analyzing 3 dimensional water transport properties. Measurement items were *wetting time, water absorption rate, maximum wetted radius, spreading speed, one way transport capacity (OWTC)* and *overall moisture management capacity* (*OMMC*). Data were measured on both sides except for *OWTC* and *OMMC*. *OWTC* is the difference of the integral value of the time series data of moisture content calculated by subtracting the value of the bottom side from the value of the top side. *OMMC* is the calculated from the *absorption rate* of the top side, *spreading speed* of the bottom side and *OWTC*. As each value becomes greater, *OWTC* become greater. The measurement values were classified by software. Water injection time was 20 seconds. Observation time was 100 seconds. Water content of fabric at the end of the experiment could be confirmed by the images. Measurement conditions were 20°C and 65% RH.

2.3   Wearing Experiment

To evaluate the wearing comfort of the uniform shirts, psychological responses and physiological responses of subjects were measured while wearing the shirt. The items measured for the physiological responses were electrocardiograms (ECG), respiration, skin temperature and humidity inside the clothes. For the psychological response, impression data on the feelings of warmth and comfort were obtained by the SD method and ranking method.

This experiment aimed to observe the body temperature increase after moving from a room at 25°C and 50% RH to the room with hot condition. Experimental conditions were 28°C and 65% RH or 29°C and 65% RH.

Fig. 1 shows the protocol of the experiment. Each subjects participated for 2 days at the pace of 1 condition per day. 3 samples were evaluated for each condition. At first, subjects were in a room at 25°C and 50% RH for 13minutes wearing T-shirts, shorts, underwear and socks. In the next 2 minutes, subjects moved from 25°C and 50% RH to the hot conditions and then took off the T-shirts and put on the uniform shirts. After that, evaluation of the sample was carried out for 22 minutes. The subjects remained seated and relaxed in a chair except for 2 minutes of moving. Skin temperature and humidity inside the cloth were measured every minute from the beginning of the experiment. The temperature and humidity sensor was the Hygrochron from KN Laboratories. Skin temperature was measured by Ramanathan 4-points method. Humidity was measured at 4 points: On the chest, the abdomen, the upper part of the back and the lower part of the back. Measurement periods of ECG and respiration were 2 minutes. ECG and respiration measurements were taken twice, once at 5 minutes after the start of the experiment and again at the end of experiment. ECG was measured by the bipolar chest lead method. Respiration was measured by a thermistor (BIOPAC TDS202A) attached below the nose of subjects. Data of ECG and respiration were input to a BIOPAC MP100, and were recorded on the computer at a sampling frequency of 2000Hz. Table 3 shows the terms used for the SD method. The terms were selected to cover all feelings about wearing comfort. The evaluation scale was a seven-step scale (Word on left end of scale: Extremely ~ Very ~ Slightly ~ Neither ~ Slightly ~ Very ~ Extremely: Word on right end of scale). After examination, a score of -3 to +3 was given to quantify evaluation. The SD method was conducted 2 times: once immediately after putting on the sample shirt, and then again 15 minutes after putting on the sample shirt. Ranking was performed after the third sample had been evaluated. After all of the experiments had finished, subjects asked "Which was the day corresponding to 28°C or 29°C?" and "Please tell me the standards for comfort evaluation of the uniform shirts". The presentation order of samples and conditions were random. The subjects were 5 healthy male college students in their 20's. All samples were conditioned in an artificial weather room at the same conditions as the experiment for more than 24 hours before evaluation. The experiment time was unified for each subject taking into consideration their circadian rhythms. The experiment was conducted after 2 hours had elapsed since eating. The sample shape was a short-sleeved shirt with buttons in front. The size of each sample was essentially the same size as each subject normally wore.

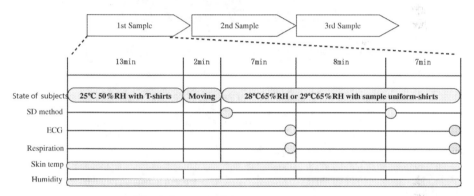

Fig. 1. Protocol of the wearing experiment

Table 3. Terms used in the SD method

Comfortable feeling overall	Comfortable⇔Uncomfortable
Thermal & moisture transport	Cool⇔Warm Refreshing⇔Hot Dry⇔Damp Well-ventilated⇔Poorly-ventilated
Mechanical properties	Good texture⇔Poor texture Rough ⇔Smooth Soft⇔Hard Restrictive⇔Not restrictive Thin⇔Thick

3   Result and Discussion

3.1   Material Properties Evaluation

Fig. 2 shows the results of evaluation by JIS and KES. R100 had high moisture content, high moisture permeability, high q-max, high K', low Qd and low R. R100 seemed to transfer heat and moisture easily to outside the garment. Fig. 3 shows the results by MMT. R100 and R/T ware easy to wet, and P/C was difficult to wet. The size of the variation was in the following order: R100 < R/T < P/C.

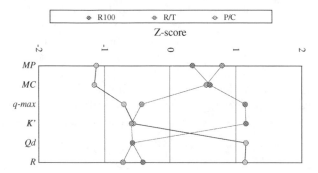

Fig. 2. Result of Japan Industrial Standards and Kawabata Evaluation System

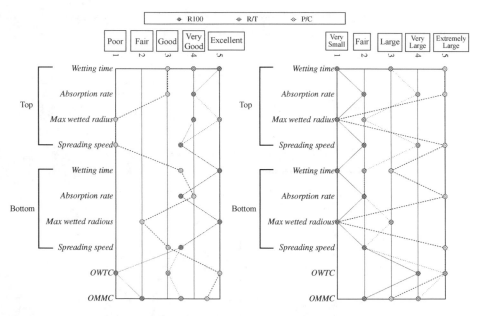

Fig. 3. Grade results by MMT: Left graph shows measured value and right graph shows variance

Fig. 4 shows a picture of the wetting by MMT[2]. R100 was the easiest to wet and had high diffusivity. The higher the variation of sample measurement values, the more difficult it was to wet the sample. R100 seems to be the most comfortable sample from the point of heat- and moisture-transfer properties.

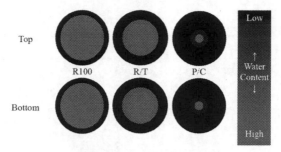

Fig. 4. Picture of fabric wetting

3.2   Wearing Experiment

Fig. 5 shows the mean values for subjects of the measurement results for temperature and humidity inside the shirts. Humidity data of one subject was expected because of noise. The mean skin temperature was low when R100 and R/T were worn. The humidity of P/C was higher than others in 29°C. The reason is considered to be it's low diffusion properties and starting temperature of sweating. Sweating of human begin when temperature become 29°C[3]. Skin temperature and humidity were both higher in the 29°C environment than in the 28°C one.

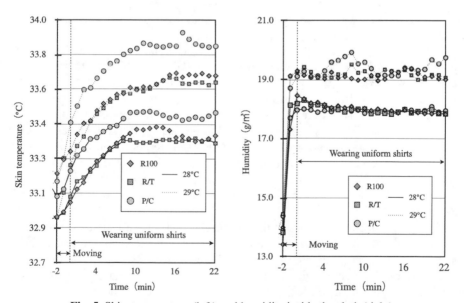

Fig. 5. Skim temperature (left) and humidity inside the cloth (right)

Table 4 shows the results of ranking of comfort criteria by introspection investigation. All subjects felt comfort with cool or chilly sensation except Subject 5. *W's* coefficient of concordance[4] matched significantly excluding Subject 5. The criteria of Subject 5 seem to be different from other subjects. The most comfortable sample was R100 because of its cool feeling and good texture.

Table 4. Results of ranking

Subject	Condition	R100	P/C	R/T	Comfort Criteria
Subject 1	28℃	2	1	3	When it's hot, cool is better.
	29℃	1	2	3	If it's thin, it becomes uncomfortable.
Subject 2	28℃	1	3	2	It's comfortable if it's well-ventilated,soft and not restrictive. Good texture against skin is
	29℃	1	3	2	also important.
Subject 3	28℃	1	3	2	It's comfortable if it feels a little chilly.
	29℃	2	1	3	
Subject 4	28℃	1	3	2	Comfort when feel soft,good texture & cool.
	29℃	1	3	2	
Subject 5	28℃	3	1	2	It's uncomfortable if it's cool.
	29℃	2	1	3	
Average except Subject 5		1	2	3	*W's* coefficient of concordance S=80>72 p<0.01

Fig. 6 shows the mean values of the scores for all subjects by SD method. Statistically significant differences were examined by ANOVA. 15 minutes after putting on samples, the effect of conditions were statistically significant for "Poorly-ventilated↔Well-ventilated". Stuffiness was felt more strongly at 29°C than at 28°C. R100 had the characteristics of being refreshing, cool, dry, well-ventilated, good texture, soft and thin. R/T was similar to R100 but the heat- and moisture-transfer characteristics were inferior compared to R100. One of the reason is considered to be it's low diffusion properties. Even though there were no difference of humidity inside the cloth between R100 and R/T, water diffusion property seem to effect human sensation from the result of MMT. P/C had characteristics which were the opposite of those of the others.

Fig. 7 shows the mean values of the respiration cycles for all subjects. Long respiration cycles reflect relaxation [5]. R100 is considered more comfortable than the others because the respiration cycles for R100 were marginally significant longer than for the others. Fig. 8 shows the mean values of the expiratory phase times for all subjects. The tendencies of the expiratory phase times were similar to the respiration cycles. They were significantly longer for R100 than for others. Respiration could be considered useful for evaluation of wearing comfort.

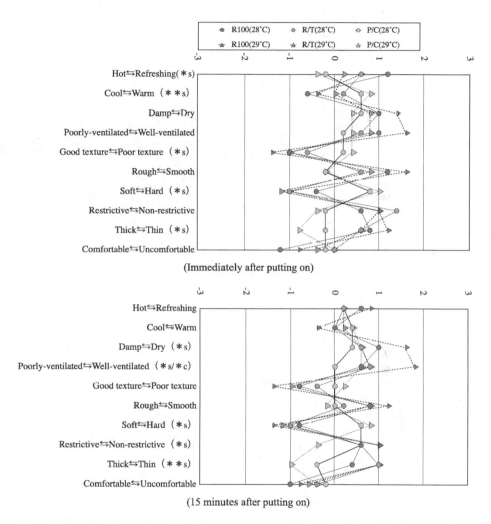

Fig. 6. Results of SD method: ** p<0.01 ANOVA, * p<0.05 ANOVA, s = Significant difference of sample, c = Significant difference of condition

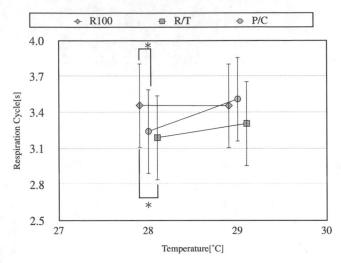

Fig. 7. Respiration cycles: * p<0.01 ANOVA and p<0.05 Tukey's test

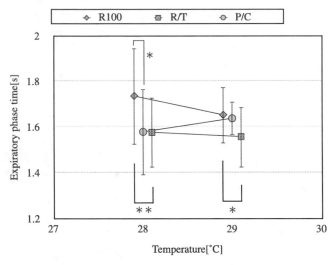

Fig. 8. Expiration phase times: * p<0.01 ANOVA and Tukey's test, * p<0.05 ANOVA and Tukey's test

Fig. 9 shows the results for skin temperature 13 minutes after the beginning of the experiments standardized by subtracting the first data. Skin temperature in the 29°C environment increased more than in the 28°C environment. Fig. 10 shows the results for heart rate by ECG. Marginally significant differences exist between 28°C and 29°C for each samples. Heart rate increased in the hotter conditions. Circulation could be considered to be increasingly active for heat dissipation. 4 subjects could distinguish between the 28°C and 29°C environments by introspection investigation. The temperature setting of 29°C seems too hot for people.

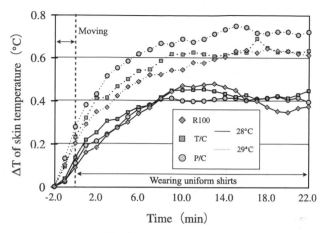

Fig. 9. Skin temperature

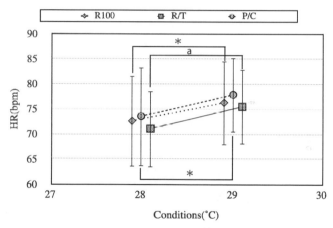

Fig. 10. Heart rate: * p<0.01 ANOVA and p<0.05 Tukey's test

4   Conclusion

R100 is the most comfortable uniform shirts because of its heat- and moisture-transfer properties. If R/T had been easier to wet, the result of evaluation would be more comfortable. The psychophysiological responses were different between the 28°C and 29°C environments. The temperature setting should be 28°C because 29°C was too hot for people. Wearing comfort could be evaluated by respiration.

Acknowledgments. This work was supported by Grant-in-Aid for Scientific Research (B) (No. 25280099) of the Ministry of Education, Culture, Sports, Science, and Technology of Japan.

References

1. Ministry of the Environment of Japan : Power-saving actions that can taken in the office. https://funtoshare.env.go.jp/setsuden/office/saving01.html
2. Junyan, H., Li, Y., Yeung, K.-W.: Anthony S. W. Wong, Weilin Xu : Moisture Management Tester : A Method to Characterize Fabric Liquid Moisture Management Properties. Textile Research Journal **75**(1), 57–62 (2005)
3. Yamaguchi, S.: Sensory Evaluation Handbook, pp. 301–304. Juse Press Ltd. (1973)
4. Ashoff, J.: Warmenhaushalt. In: Landois, L., Rosemann, R. (ed.) Lehrbunch der Physiologie des Menschen, Munchen, Berlin, pp. 331–369 (1960)
5. Umezawa, A., Terai, K.: Paradigm of relaxation evaluation : Respiration and relaxation. Japan Journal of Physiological Psychology and Psychophysiology **19**(2), 69–74 (2001)

Usability Evaluation for Continuous Error of Fingerprint Identification

Nobuyuki Nishiuchi[✉] and Yuki Buniu

Graduate School of System Design, Tokyo Metropolitan University, 6-6 Asahigaoka,
Hino, Tokyo 191-0065, Japan
nnishiuc@sd.tmu.ac.jp, buniu-yuki@ed.tmu.ac.jp

Abstract. It is generally quite difficult to apply the current usability evaluation methods to the interface for the biometric identification, because the operation time of the biometric identification is too short to analyze. In the current study, we conducted the interview research on the biometrics. From the results of the interview research, it was clarified that 71% users have an experience of continuous error while in use of the biometric identification. So, we conducted the evaluation experiments for continuous error of the fingerprint identification. In the experiment, the unsatisfaction which is one of the usability is evaluated from the aspect of the mental stress during the continuous error of fingerprint identification. Based on the results of the evaluation experiment, we can show a guideline that when the continuous error occurs X times, the fingerprint identification system should be changed to another identification method to avoid an increase in the user's unsatisfaction.

Keywords: Biometrics · Usability · Fingerprint identification · Continuous error

1 Introduction

In the current progress of the information society, the technologies which can identify a user specifically and real-time have been attracted. The biometric identification has been considered as one of the most powerful technologies. In the biometric identification, fingerprint, vein and iris are used as the physical characteristics. On other hand, signature, gait and voice are used as the behavioral characteristics. However, the physical characteristics, especially the fingerprint, is mostly used for the identification and the behavioral characteristics are not commonly used. Being one of reasons of this situation, it is considered that the usability of biometrics has not been sufficiently discussed.

On the other hand, it is quite difficult to apply the current objective methods to evaluate the usability of the interface [1]-[6] for the biometric identification, since the biometric identification step is having too short time to analyze. So, it is needed to innovate another approach to evaluate the interface of biometrics.

In the current study, the interview research on the usage of biometrics was conducted. Based on the results of the interview research, we conducted the evaluation experiments for continuous error of the fingerprint identification. The general

© IFIP International Federation for Information Processing 2015
K. Saeed and W. Homenda (Eds.): CISIM 2015, LNCS 9339, pp. 539–546, 2015.
DOI: 10.1007/978-3-319-24369-6_45

usability is evaluated from the three view points; effectiveness, efficiency, and satisfaction. In this study, we supposed that the efficiency is related with the continuous error, the unsatisfaction is evaluated from the aspect of the mental stress during the fingerprint identification. And, as for comparison, the unsatisfaction is evaluated during the continuous error of the password identification. Moreover, as a context of use which is mentioned in ISO 9241-11 [7], the time pressure was added as a condition of the evaluation experiment.

Based on the results of the evaluation experiment, we can show a guideline that when the continuous error occurs X times, the fingerprint identification system should be changed to another identification method before the user's unsatisfaction is increased.

The present study is organized as follows: in Section 2, a literature review is summarized; in Section 3, the interview research on biometrics is described in detail; in Section 4, the results of our evaluation experiment of continuous error are discussed; and in Section 5, our conclusions are noted.

2   Literature Review

Usability is defined by ISO9241-11 [7] as "The extent to which a product can be used by specified users to achieve specified goals with effectiveness, efficiency, and satisfaction in a specified context of use". Under this definition, there are three critical terms of usability: effectiveness, efficiency and satisfaction. In applying these terms to biometric identification, the effectiveness is about whether the identification is successful or not. The efficiency is for the number of trial and operation time to successful identification and the satisfaction is a kind of emotion arising from the usage of biometric identification.

The accuracy of the most biometric systems is still not high enough. For example, the fingerprint identification can be problematic if the user's finger is in different condition from the enrollment; such as wetness, dryness, or oiliness, moved during the reading of the fingerprint, or just a part of the fingerprint is presented. Boutella [8] reported that fingerprint image quality is of great importance for the fingerprint identification, and affects its performance. So, the continuous error is currently unavoidable. When the continuous error is considered from the viewpoint of the usability, the efficiency is mightily related with the continuous error.

Some studies on the usability of biometrics have been conducted. Theofanos [9] validated the elements of usability of biometrics; such as the method for feedback, the physical issues (angle and height of the devices for identification), and presence or absence of the usage experience on biometric identification. Matsumoto [10] discussed the balance between the security and usability. El-Abed [11] evaluated the biometric identification system from the viewpoint of users' acceptance and satisfaction. Though these studies were focused on the usability of biometrics, it was not evaluated with experimental approach or the continuous error was not concerned.

3   Interview Research on Biometrics

3.1   Method of the Interview Research

The interview research on the biometrics was conducted to 21 university students who were regularly using the biometric identification system. Following items were the interview questions;

(Q1) What type of biometrics have you used?
(Q2) Have you ever experienced an error of biometric identification?
(Q3) Have you ever experienced continuous error of biometric identification?
(Q4) If you have experienced continuous error, how did you respond to it?

3.2   Results of the Interview Research

The results of the interview research on the experience in using biometrics were shown in Table 1 and on the experience of error of biometrics identification in Table 2. 90% users have experienced an error of biometric identification while 71% users have experienced the continuous error. Most of the users who have experienced the continuous error feels unsatisfied about the accuracy of the biometrics.

Table 1. Experience in using biometrics

Biometric modality	Fingerprint	Face	Vein
Number of subjects	15	3	3

(The number of interviewees: 21)

Table 2. Experience of error of biometric identification

Experience of error	Single error	Continuous error
Number of subjects	19	15

(The number of interviewees: 21)

Similar research was conducted by Sasaki [12]. In his research, he mentioned that some students using the vein identification as the attendance management system have experienced the continuous error, and felt strong unsatiscfaction to the accuracy of identification system.

The summary of the responses regarding the continuous error in the fingerprint identification are noted below;

* Wipe finger, or heat it up by breathing on it.
* Ask someone who registers the system to login and then use the system.
* Give up the fingerprint identification and use another identification method (for example, password).

From these results, the problems of biometrics usage caused by the continuous error must not be ignored. It is necessary to evaluate the usability of biometrics from the aspect of the continuous error.

4   Evaluation Experiment of Continuous Error

4.1   Method of the Evaluation Experiment

In this experiment, users' mental stress was evaluated when the continuous error had occurred in the identification with fingerprint and password. The time pressure was also added as a condition of the evaluation experiment. The fingerprint reader of the swipe type (SREX-FSU2, RATOC Systems Inc., Japan) was used in the experiment. The experimental view is shown in Figure 1. On the interface for the identification was made by us (Figure 2).

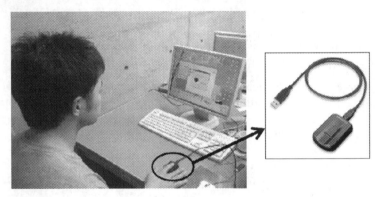

Fig. 1. Experimental View

In the identification system, there was no identification performed during that period. As the fingerprint reader is triggered by swiping the finger, the interface shows results randomly whether it's successful or not after one second. If the identification fails, the user clicks the retry button and tries it again, if the identification succeeds, a web browser pops up, and a task is finished. The password identification also has the same flow. Each subject used six characters to set the password.

The subjects of the experiment were 20 university students. The experimental task was conducted under four conditions below.

(C1) Fingerprint identification with time pressure
(C2) Fingerprint identification without time pressure
(C3) Password identification with time pressure
(C4) Password identification without time pressure

In each 4 conditions, 5 tasks (the successful identification is at the nth [n=1-5]) were conducted randomly. In the condition "with time pressure", the tense situation was assumed by the subjects in the task. The subjects were given 30 seconds to log in using the fingerprint identification while those who were using the password identification had 40 seconds. Both number of seconds were set to be able to login even if there were continuous error.

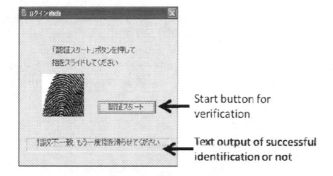

(a) Interface for fingerprint identification

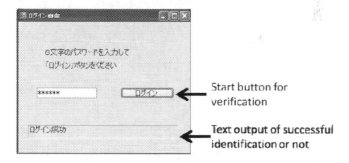

(b) Interface for password identification

Fig. 2. Interface for each identification for the evaluation experiment

After every task, user's mental stress about the 3 items was evaluated on 5-grade evaluation based on the evaluation method of Tamaki [13].

(E1) How much mental stress did you feel on the number of times of identification?
(E2) How much mental stress did you feel on the action of identification?
(E3) How much mental stress did you feel on the time of identification?

4.2   Results of Experiment and Consideration

The user's mental stress on the number of times of identification is shown in Figure 3, on the action of identification is shown in Figure 4 and on the time of identification is shown in Figure 5. In all graphs, the vertical axis shows the average score of the mental stress, and the horizontal axis shows that the successful identification is at the nth. Four lined graphs show the each conditions from C1 to C4.

In Figure 3, 4 and 5, it was shown that the users felt stronger mental stress from the password identification than the fingerprint identification. Especially on the mental stress on the action of identification in Figure 4, the difference of the mental stress between the fingerprint and password identification was clearly large. There was a statistically-significant difference ($p<0.01$) for the mental stress between the fingerprint identification and the password identification at each successful identification. These results were supported by the users' comments after the experiment that the fingerprint identification was easy to use and the password identification was bothering to type the password. Therefore, it is clarified that the usability regarding the satisfaction of the fingerprint identification is better than the password identification.

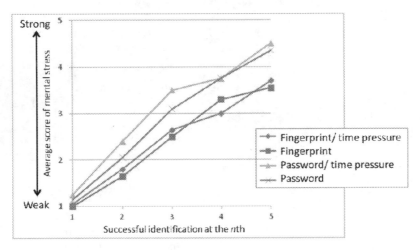

Fig. 3. Average score of mental stress on the number of times of identification

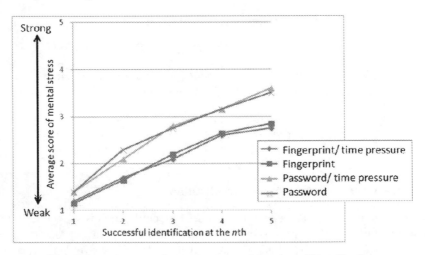

Fig. 4. Average score of mental stress on the action of identification

The analysis of variance and multiple comparison (Holm's method) were performed to the mental stress on the number of times of identification and the time of identification. In the result, in spite of the presence or absence of the time pressure, a statistically-significant difference ($p<0.05$) for the mental stress was shown in between the second and the third successful identification. Moreover, a statistically-significant difference was not shown in between neighboring conditions over the third successful identification. So, it was shown that the mental stress over the third successful identification is obviously lager than the second one. From these results, if a continuous error occurs twice, the fingerprint identification system should be changed to another identification method before the user's unsatisfaction is significantly increased.

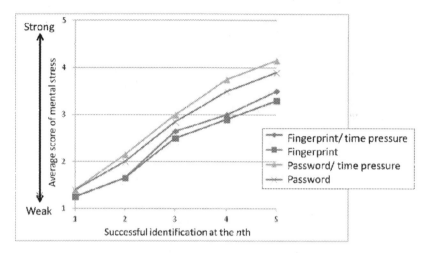

Fig. 5. Average score of mental stress on the time of identification

Finally, in Figure 3, 4 and 5, from the results of the analysis of variance, it was shown that the presence or absence of the time pressure didn't influence to the mental stress. There was no statistically-significant difference between the presence and absence of the time pressure. Though the tense situation was assumed with time pressure, it was consider that the users didn't feel the pressure, because the penalty against the failure of the task wasn't set in the experiment. This term will be discussed continuously as a future issue.

5   Conclusions

In this study, we conducted the evaluation experiments for continuous error of the fingerprint identification. By the advance interview research on the usage of biometrics, it was clarified that the problems of biometrics usage caused by the continuous error must not be ignored. From the results of the evaluation experiment for continuous error, three conclusions were obtained;

1) The usability regarding the satisfaction of the fingerprint identification is better than the password identification.

2) When the continuous error occurs twice, the fingerprint identification system should be changed to another identification method to avoid an increase in the user's unsatisfaction.

3) The presence or absence of the time pressure does not notably influence to the mental stress of the continuous error of fingerprint and password identification.

For future experiment, the change of pressure during the fingerprint identification should be measured and the relationship between the data gathered and the subjective assessment should be validated. The data of the changes in pressure will then be considered and be used for the improvement of the usability of biometrics. On the other hand, other physical or behavioral characteristics will be applied to the current proposed method.

Acknowledgement. This work was supported by JSPS KAKENHI Grant Number 25240017.

References

1. Nielsen, J.: Usability Engineering. Academic Press (1993)
2. Faulkner, X.: Usability Engineering. Palgrave (2000)
3. Barnum, C.M.: Usability Testing Essentials. Morgan Kaufmann (2011)
4. Urokohara, H., Furuta, K., Tanaka, K., Kurosu, M.: A usability evaluation method that compares task performance between expert and novice. In: Proceedings of Human Interface Symposium, pp.537–542 (1999)
5. MacDorman, K.F., Whalen, T.J., Ho, C., Patel, H.: An Improved Usability Measure Based on Novice and Expert Performance. International Journal of Human- Computer Interaction **27**(3), 280–302 (2011)
6. Nishiuchi, N., Takahashi, Y., Hashizume, A.: Development of a usability evaluation method based on finger movement. In: Stephanidis, C. (ed.) HCII 2013, Part I. CCIS, vol. 373, pp. 144–148. Springer, Heidelberg (2013)
7. ISO 9241-11:1998 Ergonomic Requirements for Office Work with Visual Display Terminals (VDTs) - Part 11: Guidance on usability
8. Boutella, L., Serir, A.: Fingerprint quality assessment based on wave atoms transform. Int. J. of Biometrics **6**(2), 143–165 (2014)
9. Theofanos, M.F., Stanton, B.: Usability of Biometrics Systems, Usability in Government Systems, pp.231–244 (2012)
10. Matsumoto, T.: Security and Usability in Biometric Authentication. Journal of Human Interface So-ciety **9**(1), 11–18 (2007)
11. El-Abed, M., Giot, R., Hemery, B., Rosenberger, C.: Evaluation of biometric systems: a study of users' acceptance and satisfaction. Int. J. of Biometrics **4**(3), 265–290 (2012)
12. Sasaki, T.: Some Problems of User Acceptability of Biometrics. Biomedical Fuzzy Systems Association **12**(1), 79–86 (2010)
13. Tamaki, H., Higashino, S., Kobayashi, M., Ihara M.: The Influence Exerted by Delay on Speech Contention and Psycho-logical Stress in Distributed Conferences, The Transactions of the Institute of Electronics, Information and Communica-tion Engineers D, pp.35–45 (2013)

Study of Cancelable Biometrics in Security Improvement of Biometric Authentication System

Sanggyu Shin[(⊠)] and Yoichi Seto

Advanced Institute of Industrial Technology, 1-10-40, Higashiooi,
Shinagawa-ku, Tokyo 140-0011, Japan
{shin,seto.yoichi}@aiit.ac.jp

Abstract. Recently, there is a widespread use of biometric authentication systems. This is because biometric systems have become open and large scale and enrolment and authentication systems are separate. Many methods have been proposed for cancelable biometrics technology in biometric systems. However, the security criterion in such is indefinite in cancelable biometrics technology. Moreover, there is still no work on the systematic study of the safety of biometric authentication systems. In this paper, we consider the cancelable biometric techniques from the perspective of the safety of the system. In addition, we also verify the effect on the security precaution of the liveness detection techniques using Fault Tree Analysis, a risk evaluation method about data protection and spoofing prevention techniques.

Keywords: Cancelable biometrics · Biometric · Authentication system

1 Introduction

In biometric authentication systems, the biometric data that becomes the reference for comparison is called template data. A template is biometric information that is used at authentication. The need for template sharing has been recognized because using the same template between applications makes inheriting trust among organizations (e.g., passports and back cards) possible. Furthermore, it enhances stability and reduces cost of system development and operation. Template protection technologies aim at preventing the prediction of raw biometrics data from templates and at preventing leaked templates from being reused by unauthorized users (cancelling leaked templates and reissuing new valid templates).

When the template data leaks, problems such as the spoofing of other users and leakage of private data occur. These problems are usually addressed by the cryptography technology and the system technology of tamper-proof devices such as smart cards.

Various methods have been published for security techniques now known as cancelable biometrics [1]-[7]. However, there has been no systematic study on the criteria for security in biometric authentication systems.

© IFIP International Federation for Information Processing 2015
K. Saeed and W. Homenda (Eds.): CISIM 2015, LNCS 9339, pp. 547–558, 2015.
DOI: 10.1007/978-3-319-24369-6_46

Paul proposed to tackle the problem and present a novel solution for cancelable biometrics in multimodal system. They developed a new cancelable biometric template generation algorithm using random projection and transformation-based feature extraction and selection. The performance of their proposed algorithm was validated on multi-modal face and ear database [11]. They also present a novel architecture for template generation in the context of situation awareness system in real and virtual applications [12]. In addition, Rathgeb presented comprehensive survey of biometric cryptosystems and cancelable biometrics [13].

The purpose of this paper is to discuss and evaluate the cancelable biometrics techniques from the viewpoint of ensuring safety of the systems.

First, the location and the type where the threat is generated on the biometric authentication systems model are explored, and the meaning of cancelable biometrics as the countermeasure technology to those threats is described.

Next, we propose a scheme for evaluating the effectiveness of cancelable biometrics. After that, the effectiveness of the security precaution with the liveness detection techniques is verified by using FTA (Fault Tree Analysis), which is a quantitative risk analysis and is the evaluation approach about the data protection and the proofing prevention technology then the superiority of the liveness detection technique is presented.

Finally, to know the open problems with the current template protection technologies, we summarize our evaluation result, especially from technical and security points of view.

2   Threat Medel for a Biometric Authentication System

Many biometric data is inherently exposed (e.g., faces and fingerprints). It has little value without linking information to person and it is a countermeasure preventing a leak. Liveness detection should be done at sensors and since it has no alternative technologies to it.

Fig. 1 shows the processing diagram of a biometric authentication system. At first, raw biometric data of an individual is captured from the user. For every input, biometric data changes due to the body and sensor device condition in the environment.

In the enrollment process, the correction processing is included in the feature extraction from raw biometric data of an individual, and the extracted characteristics of individual is stored in the database as template data.

In the authentication process, the identification data that specifies the user is inputted from a sensor device and the corresponding template data is selected from the database. Two sets of features are matched, then the degree of similarity is obtained by a matching process. It is assumed that the authentication succeeds if the degree of similarity exceeds a threshold. As a result, the user can access the application.

The number in Fig. 1 shows the location under the threats of attack in a biometric authentication system. The threats at each location are explained as follows.

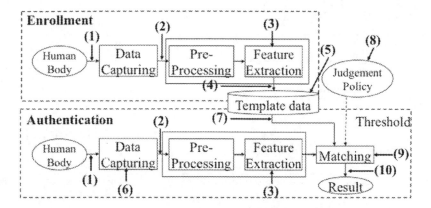

Fig. 1. Possible attack points in a biometric authentication system.

(**1**) Attack on sensor input of fake biometrics: The photograph of face, counterfeit fingerprint or signature are put on the sensor.

(**2**) Attack on the transfer data from sensor to feature extraction processing: Biometric data captured from the sensor is replaced with information attacking the network or the bus.

(**3**) Making replacement of extracted feature data: The feature extraction processing is attacked with the Trojan horse etc., and an arbitrary feature is set instead of an actual feature.

(**4**) Illegal conversion of body data: Body data is replaced with counterfeit data. It is very difficult to execute this attack because the feature extraction processing and the matching processing are often done in the same system. However, when an extracted feature data is transmitted to the matching processing by the Internet, this attack becomes possible by substituting the packet data.

(**5**) Tampering with stored template data: An illegal user makes the falsification of a template data stored in the database, such that an unfair user obtains an illegal attestation and gains access or a fair user obtains an illegal attestation and is denied access.

(**6**) Re-input of stored biometric data: Biometrics that remains on the sensor devices is automatically inputted again without user input.

(**7**) Attack on the transfer from template data storage to matching processing: When the template stored in the database is transferred to the matching processing through the communication channel, the template data is illegally changed.

(**8**) Replacement of threshold value: The threshold value is set to the given value by rewriting the judgment policy in order to get the intended result.

(**9**) Attack on matching process: The matching process is attacked, and the matching result is replaced with an arbitrary score.

(**10**) Substituting of final decision data: The judgment result of the authentication is substituted.

Table 1. Threats and countermeasures.

No	Threats	Countermeasures
(1)	Attack on sensor input of fake biometrics	Liveness detection
(2)	Attack to transfer data from sensor to feature extraction processing	Encryption
(3)	Making replacement of extracted feature data	Digital signature
(4)	Illegal conversion of body data	Encryption Cancelable biometrics
(5)	Tamper with stored template data	Physical security Cancelable biometrics
(6)	Re-input of stored biometric information	Liveness detection Challenge & Response
(7)	Attack to transfer from template data storage to matching processing	Encryption Cancelable biometrics
(8)	Tampering authentication parameters	
(9)	Replacement of threshold	Digital signature
(10)	Data	

The countermeasures shown in Table 1 are effective ways to prevent the above-mentioned attacks. The threats in categories (4), (5) and (7) relate to the theft of template data and those in categories (1) and (6) relate to counterfeit use (spoofing) when biometric data is captured and attested.

For example, the development of countermeasure techniques for the following attacks will become important in the future.

- Study of fabricating a counterfeit fingerprint with cheap material such as the gelatin, which can be made for a short time.
- A method of the transformation of biometric data of protection and each application of biometric data by the encryption for the template protection and storing.
- A peculiar attack that counters dictionary attack to the biometric authentication.

Another problem includes the copying process when the data used for the biometric authentication loses reliability.

When reliability is lost, the authentic method such as using the key, the token, and the password, etc. can nullify these attestation devices as many times as you want. But, there is a limit in the number of times of nullification for biometrics.

In the security requirement for a biometric authentication system, the cancelable biometric techniques are not exclusive but are one of the measures technologies.

The problem of the template data leakage is divided into the problem of spoofing due to reuse and privacy concerns. Biometrics was originally exposed, and at 1:1 matching, the individual can be specified if there is a link to other information. Therefore, there is an opinion that biometrics is not privacy.

As for the problem of reuse, the measures technique when reusing such as the liveness detection technique is more effective than the encryption of data and nullification of data if biometrics can specify the individual by the link information.

It is necessary to examine effectiveness compared with the competing measures techniques, for instance, cryptography. T he analysis of the effectiveness of the measures technique is described in Chapter 4.

3 Systematization of the Cancelable Biometrics Technique

3.1 Cancelable Biometrics Techniques

Cancelable biometrics is a collective term of template protection techniques that nullifies it when an original biometric data is made invisible from the template not to be restorable in the biometric authentication systems.

There are two kinds templates. One is for image (signal) data input from the sensor and the other is for the feature data that used for processing. There are two kinds of nullification methods: based on encryption techniques and on image processing.

Encryption-based approach stores encrypted templates and decrypts templates at authentication time. Image processing-based approach matches encrypted templates without decrypting the data and provides the abilities of invisibility of original biometric data and canceling lost templates. It is also a mixed technology of biometrics and encryption as various mechanisms are used to implement these functionalities. Generally, security strength is unclear.

Fig. 2 shows typical processing flow of the cancelable biometrics.

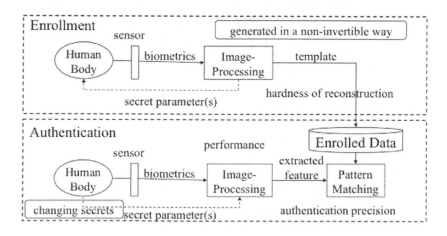

Fig. 2. The processing flow of cancelable biometrics.

The biometric data is distorted by the conversion processing using a one way transformation function in an enrollment or an authentication processing.

The template generated by a nonreciprocal method is stored in the smart card and the database.

The biometric data causes a different swerve at each registration. Therefore, when the reliability of biometric information is lost, the misinterpretation method used at that time is changed. Furthermore, it only has to register again based on a new conversion coefficient.

The technical details of a cancelable biometrics based on image processing is discussed thoroughly in [9].

The groupings by PET (Privacy Enhancing Technologies) [8]-[10] are classified techniques of privacy protection that can be applied to the systematization of cancelable biometrics. Techniques of cancelable biometrics and the dynamic key generation algorithm developed now can be classified into four categories (A to D) in reference to the classified techniques of PET, as shown in Table 2.

Table 2. Grouping by PET of template protection techniques.

Principle	Methods	Ref.
One-way function	A1. Non-reversible transformation of images	[6]
	A2. Non-reversible transformation of templates	
	B. Image morphing	
Common key cryptography	NA	
Public key cryptography	D1.	[5] [7]
Secret sharing function	NA	
Blind signature	NA	
Zero knowledge protocol	D2	[4]
Proxy network	NA	
Fake information	C1. Fuzzy vault	[1] [3]
	C2. Convolution random pattern	[2]
Privacy language	NA	

Category A is a method by noninvertible conversion. Conversion can be applied to both image (signal) and feature region. An example of conversion in the image area includes morphing and the block substitution. For example, the block structure is allocated in the block substitution according to a feature point in former image area, it arranges at every the block, and the scramble is done. However, not noninvertible conversion in this case but former image can often be computed reversibly.

Therefore, security strength is low, and the conversion in the image space is classified into category B.

Category C is the method to use information on fake data such as Fuzzy Vault.

Category D is the method of the data protection using the public key cryptography and zero knowledge proof technology. Furthermore, category D also proposes data protection techniques that use a general cryptographic protocol in ISO TC68 that is the technical committee intended for financial services.

Currently, data protection technologies in biometric data are perceived to be immature. Therefore, the empty column in Table 2 represents template protection technologies that could be proposed in the future.

3.2 Evaluation of Validity of the Cancelable Biometrics

There are two technologies for the protection of template data: image processing based methods and cryptographic based methods.

Cryptographic template protection technology is open to the public, which allows evaluation of security strength by third parties. For example, FIPS140-2 is maintained as a safety standard at the implementation level.

Application Existence of an application where image processing-based template protection methods have the precedence over cryptographic-based.

On the other hand, from a technical point of view, image processing-based template protection methods have the following problems..

- Proper evaluation of the template protection technique is insufficient.
- The third party evaluation cannot be done because the algorithm and the interface are unpublished.
- The security strength evaluation scheme is not established, and an objective evaluation concerning a one way transformation, accuracy preservation and the processing performance is not done (Refer to Table 3).
- There is a possibility that it is technically immature as described in paragraph 3.1, and a more effective method will be developed in the future.
- There is no appropriately applied actual case.
- The individual data not in the database but in the smart card model is general from a viewpoint of a restriction of law and safety.

Table 3. Evaluation axis of the cancelable biometrics.

Items	Description
Hardness of reconstructing original data	Proof of being essentially unable to reconstruct original biometric data from converted data by a one-way function etc.
Preservation of authentication precision	Proof that authentication precision over converted data is no lower than that over pre-converted (original) data
Performance	Demonstration of the performance of a conversion algorithm for practical use
Application	Existence of an application where image processing-based template protection methods have the precedence over cryptographic-based.

- Cancelable biometrics is a technology that assumes storage in a database, and a powerful application that can demonstrate superiority over template protection technology of cryptography based methods is not known.
- The priority is low in the viewpoint of the security risk. Details are presented in Chapter Chapter 4. Therefore, it is enough not to ensure that the template data is kept secret and discuss the safety of the system.

As a solution to these problems, security evaluation techniques will be established and an appropriate application will be developed.

4   Evaluation of Countermeasure Techniques for Securing the System

Two points should be considered: technical validity and standardization. If biometrics have been exposed. the possibility that it is acquired by a malicious person without the consent of the user is high. Therefore, for the safety of a biometric authentication system, measures against reuse are more important than those against theft.

In reusing the template data, there are two kinds of abuse such as the capturing of the biometrics of the counterfeit and spoofing due to hacking to the system. The liveness detection function is necessary for the former and it is necessary for data transfer to be secure for the latter.

Applying the standardized cryptography technology for the data protection in the channel is an advantage in terms of cost and safety. Moreover, liveness detection measures that should be carried out when body information is acquired from the sensor, and image processing techniques become indispensable, as no alternative technology exists.

Therefore, from a practical viewpoint, it is thought that the development of liveness detection technology is a higher priority than the data protection technique of the image processing based cancelable biometrics.

In this chapter, the liveness detection technique is discussed as a spoofing prevention in the sensor aiming to prove the above-mentioned hypothesis quantitatively. Then, encryption and cancelable biometrics are taken up as data protection techniques in the channel and the database. The effectiveness of each technique is evaluated with respect to safety.

In this study, FTA (Fault Tree Analysis) is adopted as a quantitative risk evaluation method. FTA is a technique for making a logic diagram with a tree structure known as the Fault Tree that shows the causal relation of the generation process of the threat, the calculation of the probability of occurrence of the threat based on this logic diagram, and evaluation of the risk.

Applied to the security measures in the information system, FT is composed of making the threat a root[8], and uniting events derived according to the causal relation hierarchically by using the logic gate of the logical add and the logical product. The probability of occurrence of the root threat can be obtained by giving the probability of occurrence for each lower event after the FT is made.

Fig. 3 shows FT made for the spoofing attack. The probability of occurrence of a basic event of the liveness detection, the encryption, and the cancelable biometrics was given to FT under assumption that each technology was applied, and the probability of occurrence of the threat was calculated.

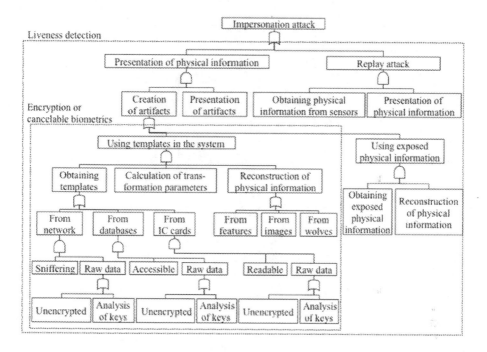

Fig. 3. Fault tree for an impersonation attack.

Table 4 shows the probability of occurrence of the basic event used by this analysis. It was roughly distinguished that the probability of occurrence obtained an actual figure in three stages because it was difficult. The living body detection technology was assumed to be the one that it was possible to detect it surely when body information not to be alive was presented.

Table 5 shows the numerical results. The risk type is usually defined by the product of the probability of occurrence and the size of the loss. Here it was assumed that the loss that occurred as a result of the spoofing was the same for each threat, and so the risk is evaluated only by the probability of occurrence.

It is understood to have lowered the liveness detection in addition while the cryptography and the cancelable biometrics lower the probability of occurrence (0.15 and 0.13, respectively) under the situation in which measures are not done compared with the probability 0.33 that the threat is generated from the results in Table 5. The following conclusions can be derived from above.

Table 4. Occurrence probabilities of basic events.

Events	Event probability (When a measure is applied)			
	Nothing	Cryptography	Cancelable biometrics	Liveness detection
Obtaining physical information from sensors	0.1	0.1	0.1	0.1
Obtaining exposed physical information outside the system	0.3	0.3	0.3	0.3
Reconstruction of physical information from exposed biological information	0.3	0.3	0.3	0.3
Derivation of transformation parameters of cancelable biometrics	-	-	0.1	-
Reconstruction of physical information from features	0.1	0.1	0.1	0.1
Reconstruction of physical information from images	0.3	0.3	0.3	0.3
Analysis of encryption keys	-	0.01	-	-
Data Encryption	1.0	0	1.0	1.0
Interception of communication	0.1	0.1	0.1	0.1
Database Access	0.2	0.2	0.2	0.2
Unauthorized reading of IC card	0.1	0.1	0.1	0.1
Presentation of not physical information that is not live	1.0	1.0	1.0	1.0

Table 5. Probability of occurrence of threats.

Applied technology	Probability of occurrence of threats	Range of Reduction Probability
Nothing	0.33	-
Cryptography	0.18	0.15
Cancelable biometrics	0.20	0.13
Liveness detection	0	0.33

- In these technologies, the liveness detection is the most effective.
- From viewpoint of prevention of reuse to effectiveness of this level cryptography and cancelable biometrics that is data protection technology.
- The cryptography technology is standardized, and it is an advantage if an objective evaluation approach for safety has been established.

The template protection technology currently proposed is still immature but it is possible that it would evolve sufficiently in the future. Technical merits and demerits can't be judged objectively because the precision and the security strengths aren't estimated enough.

5   Conclusions

Living body measure is most effective in these technologies. However, encryption technology is standardized and there is a merit by which objective evaluation technique is established about safety.

The viewpoint of an effective methodology that secured the safety of biometric authentication systems was considered. The cancelable biometrics technique was systematized based on Privacy Enhancing Technology, and the possibility that a new technology will be developed in the future was shown in Chapter 4.

It proposed the evaluation items such as one way transformation, accuracy preservation and processing performance that clarified the effectiveness of the cancelable biometrics. The effectiveness of the technologies were quantitatively compared by using FTA method for the reuse problem in a biometric authentication system, when biometrics data had been leaked and exposed. According to the FTA analysis, when compared the cryptography and liveness detection, the effect of cancelable biometrics on the safety of biometric authentication systems was small.

References

1. Clancy, T., Kiyavash, N., Lin, D.: Secure smartcard based fingerprint authentication. In: WBMA 2003 Proceedings of the 2003 ACM SIGMM workshop on Biometrics methods and applications, pp. 45–52 (2003)
2. Hirata, S., Takahashi, K., Mimura, M.: Vulnerability analysis and improvement of cancelable biometrics for image matching. In: The 2007 Symposium on Cryptography and Information Security, 3C1-2, Japan (2007)
3. Juels, A., Sudan, M.: A fuzzy vault scheme. In: Proc. IEEE Int. Symp. Inf. Theory, pp. 408–413 (2002)
4. Kikuchi, H.: On security of asymmetric biometrics authentication. In: The 2006 Symposium on Cryptography and Information Security, 2D3-2, Japan (2006)
5. Kwon, T., Lee, J.: Practical digital signature generation using biometrics. In: Laganá, A., Gavrilova, M.L., Kumar, V., Mun, Y., Tan, C.J.K., Gervasi, O. (eds.) ICCSA 2004. LNCS, vol. 3043, pp. 728–737. Springer, Heidelberg (2004)
6. Ratha, N., Connell, J., Bolle, R.: Enhancing security and privacy in biometrics-based authentication systems. IBM Systems J. 40(3), 614–634 (2001)

7. Soutar, C., Roberg, D., Stoianov, A., Gilroy, R., Kumar, V.: Biometric encryption. http://www.bioscrypt.com/assets/Biometric_Encryption.pdf
8. Shimizu, S., Seto, Y.: A study on the effectiveness of cancelable biometric technology in biometric authentication systems. In: The 2008 Symposium on Cryptography and Information Security, 2B3-2, Japan (2008)
9. Shimizu, S., Seto, Y.: An evaluation of biometric template protection methods. In: The Asian Biometrics Consortium Conference and Exhibition 2007 (ABC2007), Invited talk, Singapore (2007)
10. Seto, Y.: Proposal to develop and operate for useful biometric application systems. The Journal of the Institute of Electronics, Information and Communication Engineers **90**(12), 1025–1030 (2007)
11. Paul, P.P.: Multimodal cancelable biometrics. In: Cognitive Informatics and Cognitive Computing (ICCI*CC), Kyoto, pp. 43–49 (2012)
12. Paul, P.P., Gavrilova, M., Klimenko, S.: Situation awareness of cancelable biometric system. The Visual Computer **30**(9), 1059–1067 (2014)
13. Rathgeb, C., Uhl, A.: A survey on biometric cryptosystems and cancelable biometrics. EURASIP Journal on Information Security (2011)

Estimating a Shooting Angle in Ear Recognition

Daishi Watabe[⊠], Takanari Minamidani, Hideyasu Sai,
Taiyo Maeda, Takaharu Yamazaki, and Jianting Cao

Saitama Institute of Technology, 1690 Fusaiji, Fukaya, Saitama 369-0293, Japan
dw@sit.ac.jp

Abstract. To improve on our earlier work on single-view-based ear biometrics, an estimation method is presented for the shooting angle of an ear image based on the summation of similarity scores over a threshold within a database of known shooting angles. Experimental results indicate that the estimation method can improve the robustness of ear recognition in varied poses.

Keywords: Ear recognition · Normalizing shooting angle · Gabor feature

1 Introduction

1.1 Background

Ear shape is unique to every individual and has been used in forensic science over the past 40 years [1]. In particular, ear prints left on walls have been used in identification of criminals, most notably in the Netherlands [2]. A detailed survey on using ear shapes for forensic purposes is available in [2], where historical studies and present issues are detailed. Furthermore, detailed surveys of automatic ear recognition systems are available in [3][4][5], where databases, algorithms, experimental conditions, and accuracies are presented. Whereas masks and sunglasses often purposely obscure facial features, ear shapes can be all that is required to identify subjects. However, the shooting angle of an ear from a surveillance camera is usually not the same as that for a facial image. Hence, accounting for such differences is necessary [6][7].

1.2 Related Studies

Moriyoshi [6][7] thoroughly investigated the effect of differences in the shooting angle in the context of forensic science. As far as image processing and computer vision are concerned, a few studies have variations in the angle of the shot [8][9]. However, these studies were limited to in-plane rotations. In single-view-based ear recognition studies, the authors improved the robustness of the method for off-angle rotation [10][11], in which feature vectors of various poses are estimated from a single-view image and recognition processes are performed without using prior knowledge of shooting angles of the input images. This is done by taking a correlation against the averaged estimated feature vectors over various poses. Although this averaging process may contaminate final accuracy, we did not use information on the

© IFIP International Federation for Information Processing 2015
K. Saeed and W. Homenda (Eds.): CISIM 2015, LNCS 9339, pp. 559–568, 2015.
DOI: 10.1007/978-3-319-24369-6_47

shooting angle of input ear images because the estimation method of the shooting angle of an ear image is not established. One may point out the usability of the shooting angle of face images, for which various estimation methods are well-established. However, because individual variations in the ear overhang angle are considerable, the use of the estimated face angles as an ear angle is not feasible. We do not know, however, how promising it is to pursue the direction of seeking a method of estimating the shooting angle of an ear. If such an estimation method is established, it will be possible to improve the accuracy of the single-view-based ear recognition system, by taking the correlation against estimated feature vectors of a specified angle, but not against contaminated averaged feature vectors of unspecified shooting angles.

1.3   Aim of this Study

An initial attempt to estimate the shooting angle of an ear image is presented. Using these estimated shooting angles, a few estimation methods for the feature vector of other shooting angles are compared experimentally. We examine the possibility of improving the robustness of ear recognition by estimating the shooting angle of an ear image.

2   Proposed Method

2.1   Outline

In Subsections 2.2 and 2.3, our method for estimating the shooting angle of an input image is explained. For completeness, the method we used for ear recognition is summarized briefly in Subsections 2.4, 2.5, and 2.6.

2.2   Gabor Features of Ear Minutiae

To fix a baseline, we used the Gabor features for the various methods described below: Let $\mathbf{x} = (x, y)$ be a point in a plane. A 2D plane wave defined by wave vector $\mathbf{k} = (k_x, k_y)$ and modified by a Gaussian function is called a Gabor function (Eq. (1)):

$$\psi(\mathbf{x}) = \frac{|\mathbf{k}|^2}{\sigma^2} \exp\left(-\frac{|\mathbf{k}|^2 |\mathbf{x}|^2}{2\sigma^2}\right) \left[\exp(i\mathbf{k} \cdot \mathbf{x}) - \exp\left(-\frac{\sigma^2}{2}\right)\right]. \tag{1}$$

Here σ denotes the width of this function determined by the Gaussian function. The factor $\exp(-\sigma^2/2)$ is a compensation term that eliminates averages. This condition is required from wavelet theory, but if σ is large enough, the factor can be ignored. Gabor functions are characterized as localized wavy shapes in various directions determined by plane waves. Gabor filters, i.e., convolutions with these Gabor functions, extract the direction and wavelength of these localized wavy shapes of an image near the point under consideration. Wavy shapes in various directions also characterize the outer ear. Thus, endpoints, junctions, and protuberances of the ridges of the outer ear are selected as feature points. Wavy shapes near these feature points are measured and coded using Gabor filters.

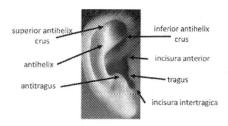

superior antihelix crus

inferior antihelix crus

antihelix

incisura anterior

antitragus

tragus

incisura intertragica

Fig. 1. Feature points of an ear.

2.3   Gabor Configurations

Five wavelengths, $4, 4\sqrt{2}, 8, 8\sqrt{2}, 16$, were adopted as Gabor filters to cover the various widths of ridges along the ear that appear in the experimental data. Furthermore, to cover all directions evenly, eight directions corresponding to $\pi/8$ rotations are employed. To realize these settings, we set $\sigma = 2\pi$ and

$$\mathbf{k} = \left(k_x, k_y\right) = \frac{2\pi}{\lambda}\left(\cos\frac{\pi}{8}\mu \, , \sin\frac{\pi}{8}\mu\right), \tag{2}$$

for $\lambda = 4, 4\sqrt{2}, 8, 8\sqrt{2}, 16$ and $\mu = 0, \dots, 7$ in Eq. (1).

We implemented these Gabor filters using a mask of 101×101 pixels for the convolution window, and this convolution was performed using the fast Fourier transform. Using this bank of Gabor filters, Gabor feature vectors were sampled at the feature points as indicated in Fig. 1 and then stacked into one vector with maximum dimensions of 560 (=80×7). Furthermore, when phases were ignored, that is only taking absolute values, these vectors became 280 (=40×7) dimensional.

2.4   Estimating Shooting Angles of an Input Image

Given an input ear image of unknown shooting angle, we can compute the similarity scores between this input ear image and the ear images of a known shooting angle from a database. Where this angle is close to the unknown shooting angle of an input ear image, it is anticipated that the number of ear images with higher scores for their similarities may be large. Based on this concept, we examined the following algorithm:

1. First, similarity scores between an input ear image and images of known shooting angles in a database are computed.
2. The summation scores for these similarity scores above a given threshold within a shooting angle are obtained. If there is no sample with a similarity score higher than the threshold, this algorithm returns a failure for the shooting angle estimation.
3. The above process 1-2 is repeated through various shooting angles in the database.
4. Finally, the shooting angle with the maximum summation is returned as an estimated shooting angle of an input image.

Similarity scores are given by normalized-cross-correlations to the phase-ignored Gabor feature vectors. A threshold is employed in order not to contaminate the estimation accuracy of shooting angle through using the lower scores of the similarities of non-similar ears. This threshold is obtained by maximizing the estimation accuracies of shooting angles through a survey of threshold-values using leave-one-out cross validation strategy.

2.5 Estimation of Gabor Features After Off-Angle Rotation for a Single Registration Image Using a Linear Jet Transformation

For completeness, the method used in [11] is outlined. Locally, near the feature points, the subject is approximated by a tangent plane. The tangent plane does not have depth. Hence, the image of this plane rotated in depth can be estimated. This estimated image reflects local features under pose variations near the feature points. Similar to the tangent plane, Gabor jets only represent local features. Motivated by this, we explore the benefits of Gabor jets for subjects rotated in depth. The following outlines the reproduction method using Gabor jet estimates of subjects with different poses [11][10]. Let the x-y coordinates be set on the camera plane and the z-axis set perpendicular to this plane. Suppose that a subject plane, initially placed parallel to the camera plane, is rotated by ϕ around its x-axis and then θ around its y-axis. By observing the transformations of unit vectors, a point on the subject plane initially at $\mathbf{u}=(x,y)$ is transformed to $\mathbf{x}$ given by:

$$\mathbf{x}=\mathbf{Au}, \qquad \mathbf{A}=\begin{pmatrix} \cos\phi & \sin\theta\sin\phi \\ 0 & \cos\theta \end{pmatrix}. \tag{3}$$

If this plane is initially placed at (ϕ_1,θ_1) and not parallel to the camera plane, the above transformation is:

$$\mathbf{x}=\mathbf{A}(\phi_2,\theta_2)\mathbf{A}(\phi_1,\theta_1)^{-1}\mathbf{u}. \tag{4}$$

Under this transformation, the transformation of the Gabor jets corresponding to the pose change can then be estimated. In what follows, $\mathbf{A}(\phi_2,\theta_2)\mathbf{A}(\phi_1,\theta_1)^{-1}$ is denoted as $\mathbf{A}$ for simplicity. Components of the transformed Gabor jets are obtained by convoluting the Gabor function with the transformed image $I(\mathbf{A}^{-1}\mathbf{x})$. Using $\mathbf{x}=\mathbf{Au}$, $\mathbf{x}'=\mathbf{Au}'$, this is

$$j'_k(\mathbf{x})=\int I(\mathbf{A}^{-1}\mathbf{x}')\Psi_k(\mathbf{x}-\mathbf{x}')d\mathbf{x}'$$
$$=\int I(\mathbf{u}-\mathbf{u}')\Psi_k(\mathbf{Au}')|\mathbf{A}|d\mathbf{u}. \tag{5}$$

Assuming the following approximation:

$$\Psi_k(\mathbf{Au}')|\mathbf{A}|\approx\sum_{k'}c_{kk'}(\mathbf{A})\Psi_{k'}(\mathbf{u}'), \tag{6}$$

the Gabor jet transformation is simply written as:

$$j'_k(\mathbf{x}) \approx \sum_{k'} c_{kk'}(\mathbf{A}) j_k(\mathbf{u}) \cdot \tag{7}$$

Once $\mathbf{C}^{(A)} = (c_{kk'}(\mathbf{A}))$ is obtained, the transformation of the Gabor jets can be estimated using:

$$\mathbf{j}'(\mathbf{x}) \approx \mathbf{C}^{(A)} \mathbf{j}(\mathbf{u}) \cdot \tag{8}$$

Matrix $\mathbf{C}$ is obtained by multiplying both sides of Eq. (6) by $\overline{\Psi_{k''}}(\mathbf{u}')$ and integrating both sides. Two of the variables are difficult to determine. One is (ϕ_2, θ_2), which depends on the poses of input images. This is an unknown in real scenarios. In [11], we solved this issue by producing the Gabor feature of many other poses in advance. The other unknown variable is (ϕ_1, θ_1), which represents the normal vector of the tangent plane at each feature point. Because this variable is difficult to determine from a single-view-image, some type of statistical modeling is necessary. In [11], this model was produced using an exhaustive search of smaller equal error rates in the variable ϕ and θ using a five-fold cross validation strategy.

2.6   Estimation of Gabor Features After Off-Angle Rotation for a Single Registration Image Using Principal Component Analysis (PCA)

To estimate the Gabor feature vectors for other poses, the feature vectors taken at the registration and input angles are stacked into one feature vector for the same person in a training set. Because phases are ignored and absolute values taken, a 560 (=40×7×2) dimensional vector is obtained. Such stacked feature vectors are created for all training datasets and subjected to PCA. For testing the sample, the Gabor feature vector at the registration angle and the null data are stacked into one vector. Using the principal component subspace, the Gabor feature vector at the input angles are estimated as a sub-vector of the back-projected stacked feature vector. Similar to Subsection 2.5, a five-fold cross validation is used to create training and test sets. The principal component subspaces serves 3D statistical modeling for estimating feature vectors of other poses.

2.7   Estimation of Gabor Features After Off-Angle Rotation for a Single Registration Image Using Multiple Regression Analysis (MRA)

To estimate the Gabor feature vectors taken from different shooting angles, the normal equation is solved to obtain the regression coefficients that describe each component of the Gabor feature as a linear combination of the components of Gabor features of the registration angle. With phases ignored, a set of 280(=40×7) normal equations is solved for training sets and used to estimate the Gabor features of the input angles for test sets. Similar to Subsection 2.5, a five-fold cross validation is used to create training and test sets. The regression coefficients obtained serve 3D statistical modeling that can be used to estimate feature vectors for other poses.

2.8   Creating the Linear Discriminant Analysis Matrix Using the Estimated Features for Input Images with Unknown Poses

To fix a baseline for comparison, similar to the method described in [12], all the estimated feature vectors, as illustrated in Subsections 2.5, 2.6 and 2.7, are subject to multiple linear discriminant analysis (LDA), thereby creating the LDA matrix of discriminant vectors. After applying this LDA matrix to both the input and registration feature vectors, a normalized correlation is computed to obtain the similarity between the input and registration feature vectors taken from different shooting angles.

3   Experiment

3.1   Database of Feature Vectors for the Experiment

Experiments were performed using the database of Gabor feature vectors at ear feature points of images from the human and object interaction processing (HOIP) database [12] obtained in our previous studies [11]. The HOIP database consisted of facial images of 300 subjects photographed from 504 (72 yaw angles every 5° and 7 roll angles every 15°) directions, where the size of the ear fitted approximately within a 70×90 pixel window. By mirror reflecting images, left profile images of 600 people were subjected to Gabor feature computations. Thus a database of Gabor feature vectors for 600 people was obtained.

3.2   Shooting Angles and Number of Visible Feature Points in the Experiments

To examine robustness against yaw-angle pose variations, verification experiments were performed using an ear image of the true left profile of a registration image taken from 85°. Input data were taken from yaw angles varying from 40° to 80°, every 10°.

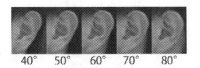

40°   50°   60°   70°   80°

Fig. 2. Example of input images.

(Yaw angles 0°, 90°, and 180° corresponding to frontal face, true left profile, and back)

One hundred and sixty-two subjects corresponding to images with seven visible feature points at all angles were selected for input, registration, and training data. In these datasets, there was a single biometric sample for each identity in each angle.

3.3   Experiment for Estimating the Shooting Angle

For the algorithm presented in Subsection 2.4, a threshold was determined by maximizing the estimation accuracy of the shooting angle using a leave-one-out cross validation strategy as follows:

1. First, the set of images at a 40° angle were selected as input images. An image from this image set was selected and treated as an input image of an unknown shooting angle. All other images with the same identity as this input image were removed from the image sets of yaw angles varying from 40° to 80°, every 10°.
2. Second, the shooting angle for this input image was estimated using the algorithm presented in Section 2.4.
3. Repeating this process over all the images in the image sets at 40° angles provided an estimation accuracy at a 40° angle.
4. Performing the above steps 1-3 similarly on sets of images at 50° to 80° angles provided estimation accuracies for each angle. The accuracies from 40° to 80° angles were averaged.
5. A survey search of threshold-values that maximized the averaged accuracy was performed based on the coarse-to-fine approach.

3.4 Experiment for Examining Robustness

The effect of our proposed method using the estimated shooting angle, robustness was examined as follows:

1. From the feature vectors of registration data taken from 85°, feature vectors for the yaw angles 40°, 50°, 60°, 70° and 80° were estimated using algorithms LJT, PCA and MRA as demonstrated in 2.5-2.7.
2. As in Subsection 2.8, the LDA matrix was created using these estimated and registration datasets. Using this matrix, the registration, input and estimated datasets were all transformed into a coordinated dataset where discrimination was easier.
3. Similarity scores were obtained using normalized cross correlations taken against the 85° angle registration feature vector, and the estimated feature vector of the estimated shooting angle. Equal error rates were obtained from ROC using the algorithm in Section 3.5.

In summary, the following six cases were compared;

- LJT, 85° angle registration of the feature vector
- LJT, estimated feature vector of the estimated shooting angle.
- PCA, 85° angle registration of the feature vector
- PCA, estimated feature vector of the estimated shooting angle
- MRA, 85° angle registration of the feature vector
- MRA, estimated feature vector of the estimated shooting angle

Similarity scores obtained using the 85° registration feature vector corresponded to our previous method in [11]. Where the shooting angle estimation failed, the registration angle for 85° was used instead for correlation computation. A small number of such cases depended on the shooting angle (~2%).

3.5 The Validity Metrics for the Experiments

As validity metrics for the verification experiments, the ROC, and the equal error rate EER are commonly used (10.6.3 of [13]). For computing these metrics, we used the algorithm recommended in Annex. F.1–2 of [13].

3.6 Results of the Experiment for Estimating Shooting Angle

The accuracy at each threshold is demonstrated in Fig. 3. When the threshold value is 0.88, the maximum averaged accuracy is 46.6%. This is a somewhat encouraging result as an initial attempt, because this accuracy far exceeds that of a random answer (20%) to the question of five selective answers (40°, 50°, 60°, 70°, 80°). However, there seems to be considerable room to improve the estimation accuracy of the shooting angle.

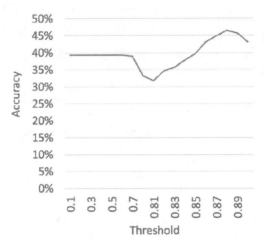

Fig. 3. Accuracy at various thresholds.

3.7 Result of the Experiment to Examine Robustness

Using the estimated shooting angle as determined in Subsection 3.6, equal error rates at various input yaw angles were obtained, as in Fig. 4.

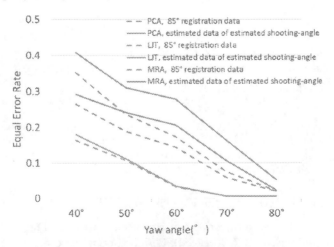

Fig. 4. Equal error rate at various yaw angles.

The results using PCA and MRA were not particularly good. Equal error rates for the estimated data of the estimated shooting angles were worse than the equal error rates using registration data without shooting angle normalization. Similar to our previous report [14], the number of subjects may not be sufficient for accurately determining the principal component subspace and regression matrix. However, using LJT, the estimated data for the estimated shooting angle perform as accurately as our previous method using averaged estimated feature vectors of various poses.

4   Discussion and Conclusions

An initial attempt to estimate the shooting angle of an ear image is presented. Although the estimation accuracy was 46.6% and far exceeds the accuracy of a random answer (20%) to a question of five selective answers, there seems to be considerable room to improve it because the presented estimation algorithm for the shooting angle is not sophisticated. Using this estimated shooting angle, the estimation method of feature vector of other poses—PCA MRA and LJT—are examined. Although none perform beyond the accuracy of our previous method using averaged estimated feature vectors of various poses, LJT performs as accurately as our previous result. Hence, using LJT and refining the accuracy of the estimated shooting angle by improving the algorithm, there may be a chance to improve the robustness of single-view-based ear recognition.

Acknowledgments. The facial database was used with the permission of Softopia Japan Foundation. This work was supported by KAKENHI 22700219, 24500260 and 15K00191.

References

1. Iannarelli, A.V.: Iannarelli system of ear identification. Foundation Press, Brooklyn (1989)
2. Meijerman, L., Thean, A., Maat, G.: Earprints in forensic investigations. Forensic Sci. Med. Pathol. **1**, 247–256 (2005)
3. Abaza, A., Ross, A., Hebert, C., Harrison, M.A.F., Nixon, M.: A Survey on Ear Biometrics. ACM Trans. Embed. Comput. Syst. **9**, 39:1–39:31 (2010)
4. Pflug, A., Busch, C.: Ear biometrics: a survey of detection, feature extraction and recognition methods. IET Biometrics. **1**, 114 (2012)
5. Yuan, L., Mu, Z.-C., Yang, F.: A review of recent advances in ear recognition. In: Sun, Z., Lai, J., Chen, X., Tan, T. (eds.) CCBR 2011. LNCS, vol. 7098, pp. 252–259. Springer, Heidelberg (2011)
6. Moriyoshi, H., Miyoshi, M., Hino, D., Nakayama, H., Morikawa, T., Nakaki, S., Itohara, K.: Morphological Classification of the Ear Components and the Correlation between Morphological Characteristics in Each Component. Japanese J. Forensic Sci. Technol. **14**, 61–70 (2009)
7. Moriyoshi, H., Miyoshi, M., Hino, D., Nakayama, H., Morikawa, T., Nakaki, S., Itohara, K.: Personal Identification from Ear Images in the Different Orientations. Japanese J. Forensic Sci. Technol. **12**, 27–34 (2007)

8. Watabe, D., Sai, H., Ueda, T., Sakai, K., Nakamura, O.: ICA, LDA, and Gabor Jets for Robust Ear Recognition, and Jet Space Similarity for Ear Detection. Int. J. Intell. Comput. Med. Sci. Image Process. **3**, 9–29 (2009)
9. Watabe, D., Sai, H., Sakai, K., Nakamura, O.: Ear biometrics using jet space similarity. In: Proc. of the IEEE Canadian Conference on Electrical and Computer Engineering. CCECE 2008, pp. 1259–1264. Niagara Falls, Canada (2008)
10. Watabe, D., Wang, Y., Minamidani, T., Sai, H., Sakai, K., Nakamura, O.: Empirical Evaluations of a Single-view-based Ear Recognition when Rotated in Depth. Kansei Eng. Int. J. **11**, 247–257 (2012)
11. Watabe, D., Minamidani, T., Sai, H., Sakai, K., Nakamura, O.: Improving the robustness of single-view-based ear recognition when rotated in depth. In: Huang, T., Zeng, Z., Li, C., Leung, C.S. (eds.) ICONIP 2012, Part V. LNCS, vol. 7667, pp. 177–187. Springer, Heidelberg (2012)
12. Yamamoto, K., Niwa, Y.: Human and Object Interaction Processing (HOIP) project. In: Joho Shori Gakkai Shinpojiumu Ronbunshu (in Japanese), pp. 379–384 (2002)
13. ISO/IEC: Information technology — Biometric performance testing and reporting — Part 1: Principles and framework. In: ISO/IEC 19795-1 (2006)
14. Watabe, D., Minamidani, T., Sai, H., Cao, J.: Comparison of ear recognition robustness of single-view-based images rotated in depth. In: 2014 Fifth International Conference on Emerging Security Technologies (EST), pp. 19–23. IEEE, Alcala de Henares (2014)

Music Information Processing Workshop

Mobile System for Optical Music Recognition and Music Sound Generation

Julia Adamska, Mateusz Piecuch, Mateusz Podgórski,
Piotr Walkiewicz, and Ewa Lukasik[✉]

Institute of Computing Science, Poznan University of Technology, Poznań, Poland
Piotr.Walkiewicz@yahoo.com, Ewa.Lukasik@cs.put.poznan.pl

Abstract. The paper presents a mobile system for generating a melody based on a photo of a musical score. The client-server architecture was applied. The client role is designated to a mobile application responsible for taking a photo of a score, sending it to the server for further processing and playing mp3 file received from the server. The server role is to recognize notes from the image, generate mp3 file and send it to the client application. The key element of the system is the program realizing the algorithm of notes recognition. It is based on the decision trees and characteristics of the individual symbols extracted from the image. The system is implemented in the Windows Phone 8 framework and uses a cloud operating system Microsoft Azure. It enables easy archivization of photos, recognized notes in the Music XML format and generated mp3 files. An easy transition to other mobile operating systems is possible as well as processing multiple music collections scans.

Keywords: Optical Music Recognition · OMR · Mobile applications · Windows Phone

1 Introduction

Optical Music Recognition (OMR) is an automatic recognition and classification of symbolic music notation. It is usually performed on scanned musical sheets and uses specialized methods of image processing and classification. The research in the domain of OMR has a long history that began in sixties of last century [21,22], was popularized by Bainbridge [4,5,6] and Fujinaga [8,9] and continued through the years [10, 11] up to nowadays [12,19,23] leaving still open issues for further research. The advanced algorithms are used not only for printed scores, but also for handwritten music notation [1,17,18,23]. Various methods of musical symbols recognition have been applied, e.g. statistical classification methods using support vector machines (SVMs), neural networks (NN), k-nearest neighbours (kNN) and hidden Markov models (HMM) compared by Rebelo [30]. Decision trees have been used by Baumann [29] and for mobile technology by Keon-Hee Park et al [31], unfortunately the paper is available only in Korean. It is difficult to compare results of OMR, as a ground truth database does not exist. The mobile part of the system performance

© IFIP International Federation for Information Processing 2015
K. Saeed and W. Homenda (Eds.): CISIM 2015, LNCS 9339, pp. 571–582, 2015.
DOI: 10.1007/978-3-319-24369-6_48

evaluation has been proposed by Szwoch [27], who introduced a method for comparing and evaluating results of recognition systems stored in MusicXML format [15].

MusicXML is a digital sheet music interchange and distribution open format invented by M. Good at 2000 and since then developed collaboratively by a community of musicians and software developers [15]. It has already been used by numerous sites offering sheet music in this format, or formats that may be easily converted to it.

Despite the fact that many research problems have not been fully solved yet, as e.g. recognition of hand written scores, there exist computer applications that perform this task for users. Well known are e.g. commercial programs, like SmartScore [26], PhotoScore Ultimate [20], SharpEye [25] and open source –Audiveris [3]. Each of them processes an image of a music sheet and transcribes it to MusicXML format. However, as it might be deduced from various internet forums, users are hardly satisfied with existing systems and this should push researchers to pursue towards finding some other reliable solutions in this domain.

Wider popularization of OMR systems may be expected from mobile technology. Smartphones, with their ability to take pictures, are replacing personal scanners. The rise of cloud computing enhances possibilities of storing and sharing digital sheet of music. First mobile OMR applications are already on the market. The most popular is iSeeNotes [13] available for Android and iOS, NoteReader [14] - available for iOS and PhotoScore Ultimate that has its version for Android and iOS. As the best of authors' knowledge in the moment of writing this paper none of mobile OMR applications are available for Windows Phone. The presented solution tries to fill this gap.

The paper presents a mobile system for generating a melody from a photo of a musical score. The system has an educational purpose and is addressed to a large group of people that cannot read music notation. The presented solution is complete, i.e. applies all stages of musical symbols recognition using the original method based on decision trees, applies MusicXML format for storing the semantic information and enables playing the recognized melody with a timbre of various popular musical instruments. An easy archivization of photos, and MusicXML documents is also possible. Thanks to its client-server architecture the proposed solution enables its easy transition to other mobile operating systems and to process multiple scans of music collection. While being complete, the system still enables introducing the improvements to the algorithm of musical symbols recognition.

The paper is structured as follows. Section two describes the OMR and music sound generating system architecture. Section three is devoted to the presentation of music notation recognition algorithm. Section four presents the experiments results and Section five concludes the paper.

2   Mobile OMR and Sound Generating System Architecture

The discussion of problems presented in the Introduction shows, that many issues of OMR is not solved yet and the proposed solutions have their limitations. The goal posed by the authors of this paper was to built a mobile OMR application employing up-to-date elements of software technology able to serve users with no musical background to give them possibility to listen to the music encoded in musical notation.

The client-server architecture presented in Figure 1. has been employed. The image processing is at the server side giving the possibility to modify musical notes recognition procedure without any interventions on the mobile client side.

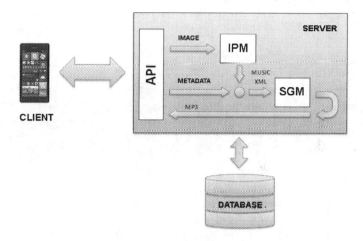

Fig. 1. Architecture of the OMR and sound generation system

The Client. The client role is designated to a mobile application (built on Windows Phone 8 platform) responsible for taking a photo of a score, sending it to the server for further processing and playing mp3 file received from the server. Figure 2 presents the screenshot of a score before and after starting the playback. The note being played is highlighted on the photo of the score by a round marker (Figure 2b). The pictures of the scores may be stored in the database on the server, the same procedure of playing music on the client side is possible for items from the repository.

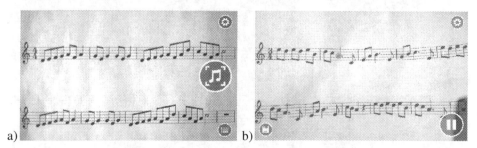

Fig. 2. The photo of a score a) before and b) at the time of playing sound (the note being played is highlighted)

The Server. The server communicates with the client through the API created in the REST architectural style (Representational State Transfer) [24]. First an image is sent to the Image Processing Module (IPM) that recognizes musical symbols and outputs them in MusicXML format. Combined with the additional metadata obtained from the client concerning e.g. tempo and musical instrument they are further processed by the Sound Generation Module,SGM (see Section 3). The resulting mp3 file is sent back to the client and the information about the file is stored in the database. A relational database – an SQL Server – stores users' login information and all other resources including analyzed musical pieces in Music XML format accessible through the website.

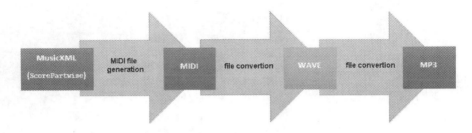

Fig. 3. Generating an .mp3 music file from MusicXML notation.

Sound Generation Module. In the time of building the application, MIDI APIs for Windows Phone 8.1 were still in preview and there was a chance that they might have changed when the final version was released. Therefore it was decided to apply a safer and stable solution in the Sound Generation Module (SGM) – to convert MIDI file to .mp3 format. First a MIDI file is created from MusicXML notation. Then it is converted to .wav format, compressed and sent as mp3 file. Since MIDI is an intermediate stage of sound generation, it is possible to change its several attributes, like playing instrument or tempo in bpm (beats per minute). The flowchart of the sound generation procedure is presented in Figure 3.

Fig. 4. Elements of user interface: a) file description, b) processing history review, c) settings (the prototype application has been prepared in Polish)

User Interface. A user can navigate between several views and has access to previously opened pages. At the start of the application the user or registers to the system, or logs in, or, if she is already logged in, may start scanning the score (2a). If the user receives the phone call while using the application, it gets into the *dormant* state and may be accessed again later. The generated melody may be played, paused, restarted and stopped (Figure 2b). User may also store the processed musical piece together with textual descriptions (Figure 4a), access history of the processed files (Figure 4b) and navigate to the settings of the system (Figure 4c).

3   Algorithm for Optical Music Recognition

The key element of the system is the program realizing the algorithm of musical symbols recognition. It is based on the rules based decision trees. The procedure follows the typical OMR scenario consisting of the following steps:

- image preprocessing,
- staff lines detection and removal,
- merging broken elements,
- recognition of musical notation elements,
- semantic reconstruction.

In the subsequent subsections each of the above steps will be described from the applied algorithm perspective.

3.1   Image Preprocessing

Since the system is devoted to recognize the photographic images, their quality may substantially differ, e.g. the luminance may be too low, or staves may be skewed or rotated. Therefore the preprocessing of the image is, like in many other image processing applications, indispensable. The operations chain is following:

- conversion of the image to the grayscale,
- filtering for sharpening the lines of staff,
- noise reduction using median filter,
- elimination of skewness and rotation of an image based on Hough transform,
- image binarization using adaptive filtering.

All those steps are performed using the elements of the AForge.Net [2] software library with or default, or experimentally adjusted parameters. The conversion of the color image to the grayscale is performed with the values: R - 0,2125, G - 0,7154 and B - 0,0721. Filtering for sharpening the lines of staff is performed by convolving the image with a 3x3 points kernel: {-2,-1,0}, {-1,1,1}, {0,1,2}

For noise reduction a median filter with the same size 3x3 pixels window is used. Image binarization is made using adaptive filtering. We quote after [2]:" The brief idea of the algorithm is that every image's pixel is set to black if its brightness is t percent lower than the average brightness of surrounding pixels in the window of the specified size". The default values are t = 0.15 and window size – 41 pixels.

Hough Transform determines the angle of the document by detecting the most distinct straight lines, in this case – staff lines. It uses polar coordinate system to represent lines: distance of its closest point from the origin and an angle. With the angle detected, the whole image may be rotated to get horizontal lines (Figure 5).

Fig. 5. Example of staves rotation based on straight lines detection using Hough Transform

3.2   Staff Lines Detection and Removal

Staff lines, fundamental elements of western musical notation, enabling symbolic notation of musical pitch, distort the shape of musical symbols and in most OMR systems are objects to be removed [7]. On the other hand staff line thickness and staff space height are reference values to find out the size of other music symbols. Therefore the detection of staves and their thorough analysis is the crucial part of the algorithm.

The most common algorithm is based on the horizontal projections [8]. A binary image is horizontally mapped into a histogram by accumulating the number of black pixels in each row. To indicate the line, a local maximum is searched. Since lines mostly are not entirely straight, are undulated, may be broken and have some other distortions, they are analyzed in segments and then a procedure ensuring continuity of line segments is applied. Such approach was proposed i.a. by Szwoch [28].

3.3   Merging Broken Elements

The operations performed during the preprocessing step, as well as the staff lines removal cause the continuity of musical symbols shapes to be distorted or broken (Figure 6). In order to make the algorithm recognize them, the broken parts have to be connected again. This task is difficult, as there are symbols that are very close one to another and should not be connected. Finding a rule that is not computationally demanding and able to distinguish a broken element from small parts inherent to musical notation is difficult.

Typical points at which continuity is interrupted are upper and lower parts of the whole notes, half notes head, stems, flags or beams. Thus those primitive symbols are first extracted. The principle is simple: a set of connected black pixels is treated as one coherent object. The rules for merging objects are following:

- a rectangle boxes bounding objects are close enough each other (at a distance of three times the thickness of the line).
- the height of the bounding box after the merge of several elements does not exceed the height of the staff or exceeds it, but one of the components shape suits linked notes, and the size of the second one is the same as a single note (this rule concerns a group of eighths/sixteenths that have to form a single object).
- none of the rectangles bounding connected objects is equal in shape to the rectangle bounding a box.

All fragments are sorted according to their distance. For a given fragment a match is sought in the order of this list. If any of them match up, then the two are combined and next match is sought for, without returning to fragments previously browsed. In practice this limitation does not influence correctness of the merge and covers most cases while speeding up processing time.

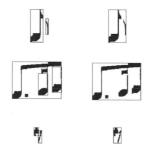

Fig. 6. Merging broken elements of music symbols after staff lines removal and filtering

3.4   Recognition of Music Notation Elements

The recognition of musical notation elements is performed using a decision tree based on rules related to musical symbols construction. Each musical object may be described by a set of characteristic features. For example, the whole notes may be described by the height of its bounding box that is approximately equal to the distance between the staff lines, the center of gravity located near the center of the bounding box and a relatively small number of black pixels in comparison with the white pixels in that box.

Descriptive Features. After analyzing the entire set of musical symbols that were to be recognized according to the system requirements the following set of features was distinguished:

1. *object bounding box height (or width) in relation to a staff line space* - allows for an initial segregation of objects;
2. *center of gravity* of an object - allows to specify whether the notes are directed upwards or downwards.
3. *black-to-white pixels number ratio* – e.g. this ratio for whole note- and half note-pauses or dots are above 70%;

4. *object bounding box aspect ratio;*
5. *number of intersections of vertical or horizontal lines with black elements of the objects;* this parameter is useful for distinguishing between eighth and sixteenth notes at their flags.

The number of features may be increased in the future.

Decision Tree Construction. The root of the tree performs the operation according to the feature 1. - *object bounding box height (or width) in relation to the staff line space.* Exemplary fragment of the decision tree from which the decision rules may be acquired is presented in Figure 7. A branch on the left provides to the recognition of the dot symbol. The algorithm in its current form recognizes: bar lines, whole notes, half notes, quarter notes, eighths, sixteenths single or linked, corresponding pauses and a dot. The tree may be further expanded in along with new characteristic features for new music symbols.

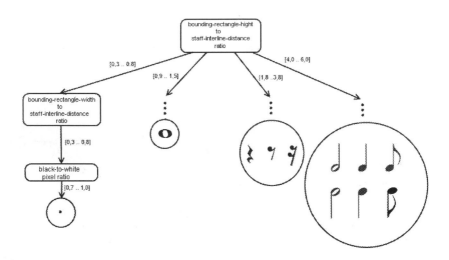

Fig. 7. Fragment of rule based decision tree recognizing musical objects

Recognition of Linked Notes. Linked notes are recognized outside a decision tree. The features taken into account are the size of a bounding box and a number of stems. First the stems are removed to separate the notes heads in linked notes. Then using the set of vertical lines for each head and counting the number of intersections with beams their number may be found: one for eighths and two for sixteenths (Figure 8).

By marking the lines as follows (from left to right): LL1, LL2, LL3, LC1, LC2, LC3, LR1, LR2, LR3, the number of intersections of line Lij with black pixels as b(Lij), the number of intersections with beams α is calculated as follows: α=max{min[b(LL1),b(LL2), b(LL3)], min[b(LC1), b(LC2), b(LC3)]-1, min[b(LR1), b(LR2,b(LR3)]} One is subtracted from a minimum of central lines intersections number to eliminate the intersection with the note head.

Fig. 8. Linked notes without stems and sets of lines to recognize eighths and sixteenths

3.5   Semantic Reconstruction and Generation of Output Data

Another set of heuristic rules is used to perform the semantic reconstruction of musical information and to code it to MusicXML format. First all elements other than
musical symbols have to be removed (text, some notes etc.). Then the musical object
position relating to a staff is calculated. A so called characteristic point of the element
is calculated. For notes it is the center point of a note head and for the pause it is the
center of its bounding box. Musical object maximum distance from the staff is also
defined. For a pause – only the duration time is calculated. Additionally the coordinates of the notes have to be found in order to highlight them when playing the melody received from the server.

4   Experimental Results

A test data set was collected comprising images presenting musical notation of varying difficulty. Images were taken from both music textbooks and specially prepared
sheet music using MuseScore [16] program. Six musical pieces were tested: three
prepared in the MuseScore and three taken from music manual. Processed examples
had a variety of notes. Three photos were taken for each musical piece, containing
two, three and four staves in a horizontal position. They were taken in daylight, during a dark whether, using a Nokia Lumia 730 Phone. This camera is equipped with a
6.7 megapixel sensor and Carl Zeiss optics. The pictures were taken at a resolution of
316 dpi. The size of photo files in JPEG format was about 1.3 MB.

The quality of music recognition depends on the symbols to be recognized, number
of linked notes and on the number of staves in the image. The average recognition
rate for all test examples was 78,85%. The errors concerned both: musical symbols
and their pitch. It is worth noting, that the error rate for misclassified symbols is only
5,29%, i.e. the symbols are well defined by the rules.

Figure 9 a) presents a musical score of Fryderyk Chopin piece, that was the most
difficult example to recognize. This is a photo of a book page – the staff lines are
rounded, the background is not homogeneous – with the shadow of a photographer.
Also the set of notes to be recognized is demanding: there are many linked eighths
and sixteenths, notes with dots is a challenge. The intermediate steps of musical symbols recognition are presented in Figure 9b) and 9c).

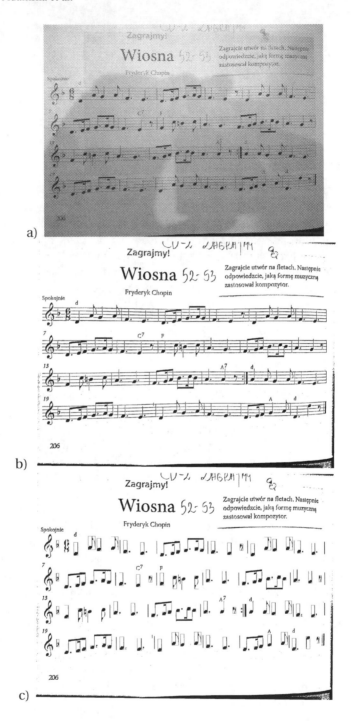

Fig. 9. The stages of the procedure of optical music recognition using smartphone illustrating a) the original photo, b) after preprocessing, c) at the stage of musical objects recognition.

However the overall recognition rate was quite high: 86,11% for two staves, 88,46% for three staves and 85,21% for four staves.

Basically, the more detailed testing has not been performed, as the proposed application is rather a proof of concept to be further developed in many aspects – first of all within the Image Processing Module, where the algorithms will be significantly changing. Also steps towards reducing processing time will be undertaken. Now the average data transfer time (from the device to the server and back) is approximaely 10 seconds, whereas the approximate processing time on the server (image and music) is 5 seconds. This is acceptable by users.

5   Conclusions

The goal of the project presented in this paper was twofold. First – to built a reliable multi-user mobile system to perform Optical Music Recognition and playing the recognized melody on the smartphone with any, chosen by the user, tempo and with a sound of a favorite musical instrument. The second goal was to test the new algorithm of the optical music recognition based on a decision tree and heuristically created rules describing symbols' shapes - no learning algorithms were needed to recognize musical symbols.

The proposed system with a modular architecture based on the client-server paradigm proved to be a correct solution. The implementation of the server performed in line with modern technologies providing its services via REST API ensures transparent communication with the mobile application. Server running on Microsoft Azure provides high degree of scalability. The Sound Generation Module is designed to support files MusicXML compatible, therefore data, from which it can generate sound, is not limited only to that from the system. It may process multiple music tracks and allows selection of musical instrument to be played and serve to other purposes, like e.g. style recognition.

The system is still being developed. The main directions are: enlarging the set of musical symbols that can be recognized, providing music documents e.g. in pdf format from recognized musical symbols, creating a music database in MusicXML format and adaptation to handwriting. The system architecture enables also rather easy implementation in other operational systems (Android and iOS).

Acknowledgements. Authors thank the reviewers for their insightful comments.

References

1. Alirezazadeh, F., Ahmadzadeh, M.R.: Effective staff line detection, restoration and removal approach for different quality of scanned handwritten music sheets. JACST **3**(2) (2014)
2. AForge.NET. http://www.aforgenet.com
3. Audiveris. https://audiveris.kenai.com
4. Bainbridge, D.: Extensible Optical Music Recognition. Ph.D. thesis. Department of Computer Science, University of Canterbury, Christchurch (1997)

5. Bainbridge D.: An extensible optical music recognition system. In: Proceedings of the Nineteenth Australasian Computer Science Conference, pp. 308–317 (1997)
6. Bainbridge D, Bell T.: The challenge of optical music recognition. Comp.H. **35**(2) (2001)
7. Dalitz, C., Droettboom, M., Pranzas, B., Fujinaga, I.: A comparative study of staff removal algorithms. IEEE Trans. PAMI **30**(5), 753–766 (2008)
8. Fujinaga, I.: Optical Music Recognition Using Projections. M.Sc. thesis, McGill University, Montreal (1988)
9. Fujinaga, I.: Adaptive Optical Music Recognition. Ph.D. thesis, Department of Theory, Faculty of Music, McGill University, Montreal (1997)
10. Homenda, W.: Optical music recognition: the case study of pattern recognition. In: Kurzynski M., et al. (eds.) Computer Recognition Systems. Advances in Soft Computing, vol. 30, pp. 835–842. Springer, Heidelberg (2005)
11. Homenda, W., Lesinski, W.: Optical music recognition: case of pattern recognition with undesirable and garbage symbols. In: Choras, et al. (eds.) Image Processing and Communications Challenges, pp. 120–127. Exit.Warsaw (2009)
12. Lesinski, W., Jastrzebska, A.: Optical music recognition as the case of imbalanced pattern recognition: a study of single classifiers. In: Skulimowski, A.M.J. (ed.) Proc. of KICSS 2013, pp. 267–278. Progress & Business Publishers, Kraków (2013)
13. iSeeNotes. http://www.iseenotes.com/
14. NoteReader. http://www.musitek.com/mobile/
15. MusicXML. http://www.musicxml.com/
16. MuseScore. https://musescore.org/pl
17. Ng, K.C., Cooper, D., Stefani, E., Boyle, R.D., Bailey, N.: Embracing the composer: optical recognition of handwritten manuscripts. In: Proc. of the ICMC, pp. 500–503 (1999)
18. Ng, K.: Optical music analysis for printed music score and handwritten music manuscript. In: George, S.E. (ed.) Visual Perception of Music Notation: On-Line and Off Line Recognition, pp. 108–127. IGI Global (2004)
19. Novotny, J., Pokorny, J.: Introduction to optical music recognition: overview and practical challenges. In: Necasky, M., et al. (eds.) Datseo 2015, pp. 121–130 (2015)
20. PhotoScore. http://www.neuratron.com/
21. Prerau, D.S.: Computer Pattern Recognition of Standard Engraved Music Notation. Ph.D. thesis, Massachusetts Institute of Technology, Cambridge (1970)
22. Pruslin, D.: Automatic Recognition of Sheet Music. Sc.D. dissertation, Massachusetts Institute of Technology, Cambridge (1966)
23. Rebelo, A., Fujinaga, I., et al.: Optical music recognition: state-of-the-art and open issues. Int. J. Multimed. Info. Retrieval. **1**(3), 173–190 (2012)
24. RESTful Tutorial. http://www.restapitutorial.com/
25. Sharp Eye. http://www.visiv.co.uk/
26. SmartScore. http://www.musitek.com/
27. Szwoch, M.: Guido: A Musical Score Recognition System, Document Analysis and Recognition. In: ICDAR 2007, vol. 2, pp. 809–813 (2007)
28. Szwoch, M.: A robust detector for distorted music staves. In: Gagalowicz, A., Philips, W. (eds.) CAIP 2005. LNCS, vol. 3691, pp. 701–708. Springer, Heidelberg (2005)
29. Baumann, S., Dengel A.: Transforming Printed Piano Music into MIDI, ASSPR World Scientific (1992)
30. Rebelo, A., Capela, G., Cardoso, J.S.: Optical recognition of music symbols. A comparative study. IJDAR **13**(1), 19–31 (2010)
31. Park, K.-H., et al.: Decision-Tree Algorithm for Recognition of Music Score Images Obtained by Mobile Phone Camera. The J. of the Korea Contents Ass. **8**(6), 16–25 (2008)

Audio Features Dedicated to the Detection of Four Basic Emotions

Jacek Grekow[✉]

Faculty of Computer Science, Bialystok University of Technology,
Wiejska 45A, 15-351 Bialystok, Poland
j.grekow@pb.edu.pl

Abstract. In this paper, we decided to study the effect of extracted audio features, using the analysis tool Essentia, on the quality of constructed music emotion detection classifiers. The research process included constructing training data, feature extraction, feature selection, and building classifiers. We selected features and found sets of features that were the most useful for detecting individual emotions. We examined the effect of low-level, rhythm and tonal features on the accuracy of the constructed classifiers. We built classifiers for different combinations of feature sets, which enabled distinguishing the most useful feature sets for individual emotions.

Keywords: Music emotion recognition · Audio feature extraction · Music information retrieval

1 Introduction

One of the most important elements when listening to music is the expressed emotions. The emotions contained in music can alter or deepen the emotional state of the listener. For example, the Funeral March listened to during a funeral deepens the emotional state of the departed's loved ones; while light and relaxing music listened to at home after a hard day's work can restore the listener's good mood. The elements of music that affect the emotions are timbre, dynamics, rhythm, and harmony. Changes in the types of instruments used, the dynamics, rhythm, and harmony change the emotions found in the music.

In the era of the Internet, searching music databases for emotions has become increasingly important. Automatic emotion detection enables indexing files in terms of emotions [1]. Automatic emotion detection also enables creating visual emotion maps of musical compositions [2].

In this paper, we decided to study the effect of extracted audio features, using the analysis tool Essentia [3], on the quality of constructed music emotion detection classifiers. We selected features and found sets of features that were the most useful for detecting individual emotions. We examined the effect of low-level, rhythm and tonal features on the accuracy of the constructed classifiers.

Studies on emotion detection in music are mainly based on two popular approaches: categorical or dimensional. The categorical approach [4][5][6][7]

© IFIP International Federation for Information Processing 2015
K. Saeed and W. Homenda (Eds.): CISIM 2015, LNCS 9339, pp. 583–591, 2015.
DOI: 10.1007/978-3-319-24369-6_49

describes emotions with a discrete number of classes - affective adjectives. In the dimensional approach [8][9][10], emotions are described as numerical values of valence and arousal. In this way, the emotion of a song is represented as a point on an emotion space. In this work, we used the categorical approach.

An important phase in emotion detection is feature extraction. There are several other studies on the issue of emotion detection using different audio tools for musical feature extraction. Studies [6][11][12] used a collection of tools that use the Matlab environment called MIR toolbox [13]. Feature extraction library jAudio [14] was used in studies [7][9]. Feature sets extracted from PsySound [15] were used in paper [12], while studies [8][16] used the Marsyas framework [17]. The Essentia [3] library for audio analysis was used in studies [18][19].

There are also papers devoted to the evaluation of audio features for emotion detection within one program. Song et al. [6] explored the relationship between musical features extracted by MIR toolbox and emotions. They compared the emotion prediction results for four sets of features: dynamic, rhythm, harmony, and spectral features.

An important paper in the area of music emotion recognition was written by Yang et al. [20], who did a comprehensive review of the methods that have been proposed for music emotion recognition. Kim et al. [21] presented another paper surveying the state of the art in automatic emotion recognition.

2   Music Data

In this research, we use four emotion classes: energetic-positive, energetic-negative, calm-negative, calm-positive. They are presented with their abbreviations in Table 1 and cover the four quadrants of the two-dimensional Thayer model of emotion [22]. They correspond to four basic emotion classes: happy, angry, sad, and relaxed.

Table 1. Description of mood labels

Abbreviation	Description
e1	energetic-positive
e2	energetic-negative
e3	calm-negative
e4	calm-positive

To conduct the study of emotion detection, we prepared two sets of data. One set was used for building one common classifier for detecting the four emotions, and the other data set for building four binary classifiers of emotion in music. Both data sets consisted of six-second fragments of different genres of music: classical, jazz, blues, country, disco, hip-hop, metal, pop, reggae, and rock. The tracks were all 22050Hz Mono 16-bit audio files in .wav format.

The author of this paper, a music expert with a university musical education, labeled the music samples. The music expert listened to six-second music samples and then labeled them with one of the emotions (e1, e2, e3, e4). In the case when the music expert was not certain which emotion to assign, such a sample was rejected. In this way, each file was associated with only one emotion/label.

The first training data set for emotion detection consisted of 324 files, 81 files labeled as e1, 81 files labeled as e2, 81 files labeled as e3, and 81 files labeled as e4.

We obtained the second training data from the first set. It consisted of four sets of binary data. For example, data set for binary classifier e1 consisted of 81 files labeled e1 and 81 files labeled not e1 (27 files each from e2, e3, e4). In this way, we obtained four binary data sets (consisting of examples of "e" and "not e") for four binary classifiers e1, e2, e3, e4.

3   Feature Extraction

For feature extraction, we used Essentia [3], a tool for audio analysis and audio-based music information retrieval. Essentia is an open-source C++ library, which was created at Music Technology Group, Universitat Pompeu Fabra, Barcelona.

We used Essentia version 2.0.1 (published in 02/2014), which contains a number of executable extractors computing music descriptors for an audio track: spectral, time-domain, rhythmic, tonal descriptors, and returning the results in YAML and JSON data formats.

The use of Essentia software entailed getting through installation procedures and the documentation. Launching the program required compiling the source code (C ++) and installing additional libraries.

Extracted features by Essentia are divided into three groups: low-level, rhythm and tonal features (Table 2).

Essentia also calculates many statistic features: the mean, geometric mean, power mean, median of an array, and all its moments up to the 5th-order, its energy, and the root mean square (RMS). To characterize the spectrum, flatness, crest and decrease of an array are calculated. Variance, skewness, kurtosis of probability distribution, and a single Gaussian estimate were calculated for the given list of arrays.

The previously prepared, labeled by emotion, music data sets served as input data for the Essentia tool used for feature extraction. For each 6-second file from the music data set, we obtained a representative single feature vector. The obtained lengths of feature vectors had 471 features.

4   Results

4.1   The Construction of One Classifier Recognizing Four Emotions

We built classifiers for emotion detection using the WEKA package [23]. During the construction of the classifier, we tested the following algorithms: J48, RandomForest, BayesNet, IBk (K-nn), SMO (SVM). The classification results were calculated using a cross validation evaluation CV-10.

Table 2. The feature set obtained from Essentia

Group	Group Abbreviation	Features
Low-level features	L	Average Loudness
		Energy of the Barkbands
		Energy of the Erbbands
		Energy of the Melbands
		Dissonance
		Dynamic Complexity
		HFC (High Frequency Content)
		Pitch Salience
		Silence Rate
		Spectral Centroid
		Spectral Complexity
		Spectral Energy
		Spectral Energy Band High
		Spectral Energy Band Low
		Spectral Energy Band Middle High
		Spectral Energy Band Middle Low
		Zero Crossing Rate
		GFCC (Gammatone Feature Cepstral Coefficients)
		MFCC (Mel-Frequency Cepstral Coefficients)
Rhythm features	R	Beats Loudness
		Beats Loudness Band Ratio
		BPM (The mean of the most salient tempo)
		BPM Histogram
		Danceability
		Onset Rate
Tonal features	T	Chords Changes Rate
		Chords Number Rate
		Chords Strength
		Key Strength
		Chords Histogram
		HPCP (Harmonic Pitch Class Profile)

Table 3. Accuracy obtained for SMO algorithm

	Accuracy
Before attribute selection	59.26%
After attribute selection	**64.50%**

The first important result was that during the construction of the classifier we obtained the highest accuracy among all tested algorithms for SMO algorithm. SMO was trained using polynominal kernel.

The results obtained for SMO algorithm are presented in Table 3. The result (classifier accuracy) improved to **64.50%** after applying attribute selection (attribute evaluator: WrapperSubsetEval [24], search method BestFirst).

The confusion matrix (Table 4), obtained during classifier evaluation, shows that the most recognized emotion was e2 (F-measure 0.727), and the next emotions were e1 and e3 (F-measure 0.653 and 0.65). The hardest emotion to recognize was e4 (F-measure 0.544).

From the confusion matrix, we can conclude that usually fewer mistakes are made between the top (e1, e2) and bottom (e3, e4) quadrants of the Thayer model. At the same time, recognition of emotions on the valence axis (positive-negative) is more difficult.

Table 4. Confusion matrix for the best result

classified as –	a	b	c	d
a = e1	**62**	9	4	6
b = e2	19	**56**	3	3
c = e3	9	4	**51**	17
d = e4	19	4	18	**40**

The most important features (with group abbreviation) after applying attribute selection were:

- Energy of the Erbbands (L),
- MFCC (L),
- Onset Rate (R),
- Beats Loudness Band Ratio (R),
- Key Strength (T),
- Chords Histogram (T).

In the selected features, we have a representative of low-level (L), rhythm (R) and tonal (T) features. This means that features of each of the three groups are important/useful during emotion detection.

The results were not satisfactory; classifier accuracy was too low (**64.50%**). It is difficult to build a good classifier that differentiates four emotions equally well. Some emotions have better recognition (e2) and others worse (e1, e3, e4), which lowers total classifier accuracy.

4.2   The Construction of Binary Classifiers

To improve emotion detection accuracy, we decided to build specialized binary classifiers for each emotion. A binary classifier algorithm can better analyze data sets for the presence of a given emotion.

During the construction of the binary classifiers, we tested the following algorithms: J48, RandomForest, BayesNet, IBk (K-nn), and SMO (SVM) on the prepared binary data. We calculated the classification results using a cross validation evaluation CV-10.

Table 5. Classifier accuracy for emotions e1, e2, e3, and e4 obtained for SMO

	Classifiers for e1	Classifiers for e2	Classifiers for e3	Classifiers for e4
Before attribute selection	66.05%	87.04%	77.16%	65.43%
After attribute selection	80.86%	**90.74%**	87.03%	77.16%

Once again, we obtained the best results for SMO algorithm. The results are presented in Table 5. Accuracy improved (3-14 percentage points) for all four classifiers after applying attribute selection (attribute evaluator: WrapperSubsetEval, search method BestFirst).

The best results were obtained for emotion e2 (90.74%) and the worst results for emotion e4 (77.16%). We can conclude that in our case, emotions with a negative valence (e2, e3) are recognized better by approx. 10 percentage points than emotions with a positive valence (e1, e4). The obtained binary classifier accuracy results were higher (12-26 percentage points) than the accuracy of one classifier recognizing four emotions.

Table 6 presents the most important features obtained after feature selection (attribute evaluator: WrapperSubsetEval, search method BestFirst) for each emotion. In each feature set, we had a representative of low-level, rhythm features, even though we had different sets for each emotion. Only in the case of classifier e4, tonal features were not used. The energy of the bands was important for e1, e2, and e4 classifiers, but they differed as to which bands they pertain: e1 - Barkbands, e2 - Erbbands, and Melbands, e4 - Barkbands and Erbbands. High Frequency Content, which is characterized by the amount of high-frequency content in the signal is important for e3 and e4 classifiers. Beats Loudness Band Ratio (the beat's energy ratio on each band) was very important for emotion detection because it was used in all sets. Another important feature was the tonal feature: Chords Histogram, which was used by e2 and e3 classifiers.

Feature sets seem to logically describe the nature of each emotion. More energetic emotions are described by features pertaining to energy and rhythm, and more calm emotions by parameters such as rhythm and the amount of high frequency.

4.3   Evaluation of Different Combinations of Feature Sets

During this experiment, we evaluated the effect of various combinations of feature sets - low-level (L), rhythm (R), tonal (T) - on classifier accuracy obtained for SMO algorithm. We calculated the classification results using a cross validation evaluation CV-10. To improve the classification results, we used attribute

Table 6. Selected features used for building binary classifiers

Classifier	Selected features
e1	Energy of the Barkbands (L)
	Onset Rate (R)
	Beats Loudness Band Ratio (R)
	Key Strength (T)
e2	Average Loudness (L)
	Dissonance (L)
	Energy of the Erbbands (L)
	Energy of the Melbands (L)
	MFCC (L)
	Beats Loudness Band Ratio (R)
	Chords Changes Rate (T)
	Chords Histogram (T)
e3	High Frequency Content (L)
	Silence Rate (L)
	Spectral Energy Band Middle Low (L)
	Beats Loudness Band Ratio (R)
	Key Strength (T)
	Chords Histogram (T)
e4	Energy of the Barkbands (L)
	Energy of the Erbbands (L)
	High Frequency Content (L)
	Pitch Salience (L)
	Beats Loudness Band Ratio (R)

selection (attribute evaluator: WrapperSubsetEval, search method BestFirst). The obtained results are presented in Table 7.

The obtained results indicate that the use of all groups (low-level, rhythm, tonal) of features resulted in the best accuracy in most cases (e1, e2, e3). The only exception was classifier e4, where using the set L+T (low-level, tonal) had better results (80.24%) than using all features - accuracy 77.16%.

The use of individual feature sets L, R or T did not have better results than their combinations. Combining feature sets R+T (rhythm and tonal features)

Table 7. Classifier accuracy for emotions e1, e2, e3, and e4 obtained for combinations of feature sets

Features set	Classifiers for e1	Classifiers for e2	Classifiers for e3	Classifiers for e4
L	72.22%	88.27%	79.62%	77.77%
R	73.45%	82.09%	81.48%	72.83%
T	72.22%	81.48%	76.54%	69.75%
L+R	77.16%	88.88%	77.77%	77.16%
L+T	79.01%	**90.74%**	**86.41%**	**80.24%**
R+T	**80.86%**	90.12%	79.01%	73.45%
All (L+R+T)	**80.86%**	90.12%	87.03%	77.16%

improved classifier results in the case of classifiers e1 and e2. Combining feature sets L+T (low-level and tonal features) improved classifier results in the case of classifiers e2, e3 and e4.

5   Conclusions

In this paper, we studied the effect of extracted audio features, using the analysis tool Essentia, on the quality of constructed music emotion detection classifiers. The research process included constructing training data, feature extraction, feature selection, and building classifiers.

We built a classifier recognizing four basic emotions, but its accuracy was not satisfactory (64.50%). We then built binary classifiers dedicated to each emotion with accuracy from 77% to 90%. We obtained information on which features are useful in the detection of particular emotions.

We examined the effect of low-level, rhythm and tonal feature sets on the accuracy of the constructed binary classifiers. We built classifiers for different combinations of feature sets, which enabled distinguishing the most useful feature sets for individual emotions. The obtained results present a new and interesting view of the usefulness of different feature sets for emotion detection.

Classifier accuracy could be better. The process of searching for and assessing new features describing audio files continues.

Acknowledgments. This paper is supported by the S/WI/3/2013.

References

1. Grekow, J., Raś, Z.W.: Emotion based MIDI files retrieval system. In: Raś, Z.W., Wieczorkowska, A.A. (eds.) Advances in Music Information Retrieval. SCI, vol. 274, pp. 261–284. Springer, Heidelberg (2010)
2. Grekow, J.: Mood tracking of musical compositions. In: Chen, L., Felfernig, A., Liu, J., Raś, Z.W. (eds.) ISMIS 2012. LNCS, vol. 7661, pp. 228–233. Springer, Heidelberg (2012)
3. Bogdanov, D., Wack, N., Gomez, E., Gulati, S., Herrera, P., Mayor, O., Roma, G., Salamon, J., Zapata, J., Serra, X.: ESSENTIA: an audio analysis library for music information retrieval. In: Proceedings of the 14th International Conference on Music Information Retrieval, pp. 493–498 (2013)
4. Lu, L., Liu, D., Zhang, H.J.: Automatic mood detection and tracking of music audio signals. IEEE Transactions on Audio, Speech and Language Processing 14(1), 5–18 (2006)
5. Grekow, J., Raś, Z.W.: Detecting emotions in classical music from MIDI files. In: Rauch, J., Raś, Z.W., Berka, P., Elomaa, T. (eds.) ISMIS 2009. LNCS, vol. 5722, pp. 261–270. Springer, Heidelberg (2009)
6. Song, Y., Dixon, S., Pearce, M.: Evaluation of musical features for emotion classification. In: Proceedings of the 13th International Society for Music Information Retrieval Conference (2012)
7. Xu, J., Li, X., Hao, Y., Yang, G.: Source separation improves music emotion recognition. In: ACM International Conference on Multimedia Retrieval (2014)

8. Yang, Y.-H., Lin, Y.-C., Su, Y.-F., Chen, H.H.: A regression approach to music emotion recognition. IEEE Transactions on Audio, Speech, and Language Processing **16**(2), 448–457 (2008)

9. Lin, Y., Chen, X., Yang, D.: Exploration of music emotion recognition based on MIDI. In: Proceedings of the 14th International Society for Music Information Retrieval Conference (2013)

10. Schmidt, E.M., Turnbull, D., Kim, Y.E.: Feature selection for content-based, time-varying musical emotion regression. In: Proc. ACM SIGMM International Conference on Multimedia Information Retrieval, Philadelphia, PA (2010)

11. Saari, P., Eerola, T., Fazekas, G., Barthet, M., Lartillot, O., Sandler, M.: The role of audio and tags in music mood prediction: a study using semantic layer projection. In: Proceedings of the 14th International Society for Music Information Retrieval Conference (2013)

12. Aljanaki, A., Wiering, F., Veltkamp, R.C.: Computational modeling of induced emotion using GEMS. In: Proceedings of the 15th International Society for Music Information Retrieval Conference (ISMIR), pp. 373 378 (2014)

13. Lartillot, O., Toiviainen, P.: MIR in Matlab (II): a toolbox for musical feature extraction from audio. In: International Conference on Music Information Retrieval, pp. 237–244 (2007)

14. McKay, C., Fujinaga, I., Depalle, P.: jAudio: a feature extraction library. In: Proceedings of the 6th International Conference on Music Information Retrieval (ISMIR05), pp. 600–603 (2005)

15. Cabrera, D.: PSYSOUND: a computer program for psychoacoustical analysis. In: Proceedings of the Australian Acoustical Society Conference, pp. 47–54 (1999)

16. Grekow, J.: Mood tracking of radio station broadcasts. In: Andreasen, T., Christiansen, H., Cubero, J.-C., Raś, Z.W. (eds.) ISMIS 2014. LNCS, vol. 8502, pp. 184–193. Springer, Heidelberg (2014)

17. Tzanetakis, G., Cook, P.: Marsyas: A framework for audio analysis. Organized Sound **10**, 293–302 (2000)

18. Laurier, C.: Automatic Classification of Musical Mood by Content-Based Analysis. Ph.D. thesis, UPF, Barcelona, Spain (2011)

19. Sarasua, A., Laurier, C., Herrera, P.: Support vector machine active learning for music mood tagging. In: 9th International Symposium on Computer Music Modeling and Retrieval (CMMR), London (2012)

20. Yang, Y.-H., Chen, H.H.: Machine Recognition of Music Emotion: A Review. ACM Transactions on Intelligent Systems and Technology **3**(3), Article No. 40 (2012)

21. Kim, Y., Schmidt, E., Migneco, R., Morton, B., Richardson, P., Scott, J., Speck, J., Turnbull, D.: State of the art report: music emotion recognition: a state of the art review. In: Proceedings of the 11th International Society for Music Information Retrieval Conference, pp. 255–266 (2010)

22. Thayer, R.E.: The Biopsychology of Mood and Arousal. Oxford University Press (1989)

23. Witten, I.H., Frank, E.: Data Mining: Practical machine learning tools and techniques. Morgan Kaufmann, San Francisco (2005)

24. Kohavi, R., John, G.H.: Wrappers for feature subset selection. Artificial Intelligence **97**(1–2), 273–324 (1997)

AutoPRK - Automatic Drum Player

Filip Biedrzycki, Jakub Knast, Mariusz Nowak, and Jakub Paszkowski[✉]

Institute of Computing Science, Poznan University of Technology, Poznań, Poland
Mariusz.Nowak@put.poznan.pl,
Jakub.Paszkowski@student.put.poznan.pl

Abstract. The paper presents the new solution of the robot playing percussion. There are two ideas of such robots: imitating a human body and realizing its function in an artificial way - without imitating a human. The presented solution belongs to the second group. It consists of 8 arms and two peripherials for control two pedals. Authors developed of entire construction of the robot and they write the software in Java for control the device.The sticks and pedals are excited with electromagnets controlled by the microcontroller ATmega328 on an Arduino board which interprete MIDI files. Authors declare full success of the project.

Keywords: Musical robotics · Drum · Percussion · MIDI · Solenoid

1   Introduction

Robotic drummers are devices which can play the percussion using specially designed peripherals moving with the usage of electromagnets or pneumatics. There were many projects that tried to achieve that phenomenon. For instance, people used simple controlled microprocessor percussion sticks installed on drums or complicated humanoid robots. The problem is complicated, because percussions often have many elements such as central bass drum, snare, tom-toms, big floor tom, hi-hat and cymbals [1].

The main challenge of this project was to create a robotic drummer which playing skills would be equivalent to human ones, or even better. The quality has to be good enough to let other instruments accompany (e. g. a guitar) like it was a real musician. The machine has to be customizable to be useful– it should match any percussion without any interference in the structure of the instrument and it must handle any possible element of the instrument. Hence, changing location of the drums only to set this up is unacceptable. The robot was designed in such a way that its shape can be altered to be fitted to the instrument. Everything ought to be easy to use for any person, and the configuration has to be as quick as possible - the whole process has to take less than an hour. It means that installing and setting percussion sticks needs to be fairly easy and operating the software and loading songs has to be quick and intuitive.

A lot of robotic drummers are not one-part machines. There are many separated sticks connected to elements setting them in motion. However, each of them has to be installed on their drums so there is a need for interference in the structure of the percussion. A good example can be "Thelxiapeia" created by N.A. Baginsky.

K. Saeed and W. Homenda (Eds.): CISIM 2015, LNCS 9339, pp. 592–600, 2015.
DOI: 10.1007/978-3-319-24369-6_50

More ambitious constructions try to replicate human by moving human-shaped arms with elbows and hands ended with sticks. The robot created by MIT Researchers (named "Cog") has even got a head on its torso. There are robots controlled by MIDI files too, like "TibetBot" designed by Eric Singer and LEMUR. All these solutions are described by Ajay Kapur in [2].

AutoPRK name is a shortened form of phrase automatic percussion (pol. automatyczna PeRKusja). AutoPRK, the robotic drummer has eight stable arms connected to one central stem with specially designed and created ponds that allow to set each of them up and block them when the setting is complete. The only moving element is the percussion stick on the end of every arm. Moreover, there are two peripherals for controlling pedals of the percussion - hi-hat and central bass drum. Everything moves with the usage of electromagnets connected to the microcontroller using relays. A specially created application allows to load MIDI file tracks.

The paper is structured as follows. In the second Section an overview of various robotic drummer constructions is given. Next Section introduces the autoPRK Automatic Drum Player - details of its construction, electronics and software are presented. Fourth section is dedicated to the tests and experiments that were carried out throughout the whole process of autoPRK construction and their results. Fifth Section concludes the paper.

2   Related Work

There are few ways of generating movement for robotic drummers. J. Long et al. shows the most commonly used solutions in [3]. One of these groups contains solenoid-based mechanism (rotary or linear). Durability of the parts, low latency and cost make them good choice for parts to apply - opposed to RC Servos. The only disadvantage is that they cannot play as loud as it is needed (Servos are better here). Pneumatic mechanisms are often used in robotics too- they represent the highest capabilities of loudness, but are more expensive than solenoids. According to this research, 50W linear solenoids were used in autoPRK.

Ajay Kapur from University of Victoria presents materials related to some projects about this topic in [2]. Definitely, the most advanced of them is the robot called "Cog" - a humanoid moved thanks to the hydraulics, and it can play the percussion like a real man, using only two arms. The team of Mitsuo Kawato (the creator of Cog) found an interesting solution to constructing hands imitating human ones. A drum stick is installed only by a pivot at quarter of its length and can freely move while playing. The movement of the stick is produced in the whole arm - not at its end, in a hand. Chico MacMurtie in [2] suggests different solutions to drum stick moving problems. The robot he created has got no sticks, but silicon hands, which are used to hit the membrane.

A different approach to the problem, presented by Baginsky in [2], assumes building a robot without any construction imitating a human body. The construction is rather simple. A percussion stick is installed on the drum and there is an element making it move.

Some of the robots can play more than one instrument. Good example of this is "Shimon" which can be set up to play drums or marimba. This is only one example. Marcelo Cicconet et al. presents more in [4].

Topic of robotic instruments is very wide. Some examples are presented by Kishan Kumar et al. who show   a robotic Pan Flute in [5] and Wonse Jo et al. who propose a Violin Playing Robot in [6].

3   Detailed Solutions in autoPRK

3.1   Construction

Structurally the robot consists of a high (approx. 160cm) pipe and eight independent, fully-configurable arms attached to special connectors (Fig. 1). This means that if needed, there is possibility to put two arms on one connector or remove the ones that are not used while playing a given song. Furthermore, for each of them the length of the arm can be set, as well as the individual angle at which it will be tilted to the drum kits. All eight arms of autoPRK are constructed identically. Each arm can be positioned over various percussion elements, such as a drum or a plate. A single stick hits the drum element after receiving a signal from the Arduino.

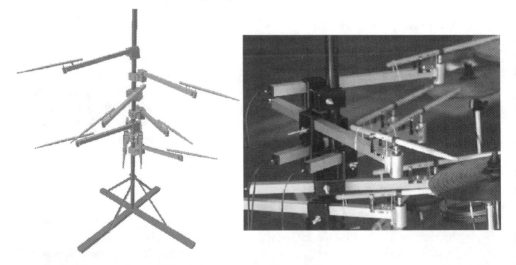

Fig. 1. Construction of the autoPRK robot

In addition, the composition of the robot consists of two elements simulating the drummer's feet (Fig. 2). After proper configuration and placement on the floor, they can handle the bass drum and a hi-hat foot.

Every end effector is moved by the same electromagnet so each of them has the same strength of hitting. The difference between the parts for drums and parts for percussion feet is in the way the electromagnets are located. In arms, there are pulling solenoids installed below the sticks, which are activated to make a hit. On the other hand, to play on bass drum or hi-hat, pushing solenoids are used. The percussion pedal is pressed directly by them, to make a sound.

Fig. 2. Feet of the autoPRK robot

3.2   Electronics

Electronics contains two different circuits. First of them - controlling circuit which is operating on 5V is powered by USB port. It consists of a microcontroller ATmega328 on an Arduino Uno Compatible board and is connected to ten relays. The second circuit, controlled by relays, uses 12V current generated by three PC supplies. Each relay is connected directly with one of ten 50W electromagnets located at the end of every arm or on foot. All the elements of electronics are located on a transparent board, which is presented in figure 3.

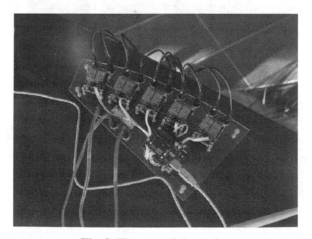

Fig. 3. Elements of electronics

3.3   Software

Software is divided into two different parts, one is Java application KuKuFi, that provides user interface, process data, and send them via USB port to the second part which is microcontroller Arduino. Task of the Arduino is to control relays using the obtained from KuKuFi data. Figure 4 shows data flow diagram.

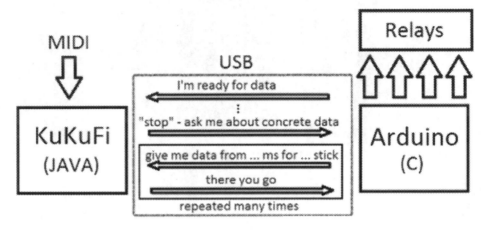

Fig. 4. Data flow diagram

KuKufi Overview

KuKuFi is a program written by the authors of autoPRK for the purpose of an easy control and KuKuFi name comes from the first letters of the names of the creators (Kuba, Kuba, Filip). The task of the program is to display and manage a graphic user interface and communicate via USB serial port with a microcontroller Arduino. KuKuFi works in such a way that the user will control autoPRK in an uncomplicated way.

KuKuFi is written in Java. It uses several free libraries, for example Swing, to build the GUI, RXTXcomm to communicate via the USB port, GSON to manage files in JSON format and a very important package - javax.sound.midi - to decode MIDI files.

Fig. 5. Selecting the MIDI file

When the program is activated, a form with separate fragments illustrating the four steps that one should take to start autoPRK is presented to the user.

The first step (Fig. 5) contains a selection of MIDI files that the program has to play - clicking on the button "Open" displays a file selection dialog from a hard drive.

After selecting a file, the program searches all stored MIDI tracks in the file.

The second step (Fig. 6), which the user must take, is selecting from a dropdown list the drum kit track. The program suggests the correct option. After confirming the selection, it starts to operate a specially designed algorithm. It is the task of selecting all elements that are in the track of the drum kit. Then the program selects from the track the moments in which drums are playing. These moments are read as the MIDI ticks and they are not clear moments of time. To convert them to a unit of milliseconds, respectively algorithm multiplies them by BPM (Beats Per Minute) and PPQ (Pulse Per Quarter note) [7].

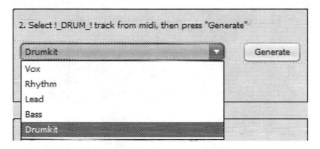

Fig. 6. Selecting the drum kit track

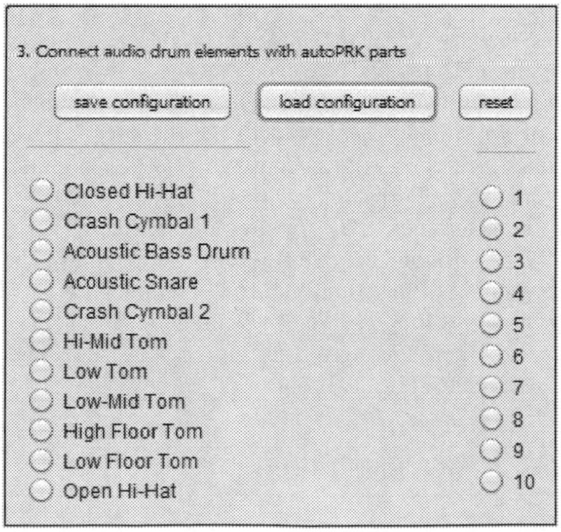

Fig. 7. Pairing drum kit elements with autoPRK's arms

Obtained in this way time stamps are stored sequentially in arrays - but each percussion element has its own array. Now, the moments when the stick will hit are stored in tables and they can be later sent to Arduino.

In the third step (Fig. 7), the user must pair the drum kit elements selected from the MIDI file with the numbers of autoPRK's arms. From the user's perspective, this process takes the longest period of time, so in order to improve it, there is a possibility of saving the prepared configuration and load it later.

When all percussion tracks are connected with numbers, the user must press the stop button (Fig. 8). Then signal is sent to the Arduino to ask about the data. Arduino will begin recording in the memory first moments of drum beats. When the data is received, the user goes to the final fourth step and can press the "play" button to start autoPRK.

Fig. 8. Buttons for controlling the robot

There is also the "pause" button to stop autoPRK in the middle of the song.

Arduino Overview
Microcontroller Arduino is used in order to control relays. Due to the limited working memory to 2kB microcontroller ATmega328, only 400 next hits can be stored (40 per track) in 10 cyclic buffers (one for each track). This is only enough for a few seconds of the song. It begins working after receiving a stop signal. In the beginning, the first moments of drum beats are stored in the memory. Then Arduino waits for "start" signal and after receiving it, microcontroller starts to operate relays checking if the time to the next hit on each track elapsed. If it did, it gives logical HIGH signal to the corresponding track number relay for 40 milliseconds. This interval of time is long enough to make percussion stick hit powerfully enough to produce a loud sound. Because only the beginning of the song is stored in the memory, Arduino must collect data while playing the song. It is resolved by sending small packets of data (64kB) in real time. In each packet there are eight consecutive beats sent. The size of the packet is caused by small size of the serial port buffer.

4   Experiments and Their Results

The tests were carried while building the robot. The decision how to install the parts was based on earlier trials. A good example of it was searching for a place to place the pivot for drum sticks – about ten different places were tried before making the final decision.

To confirm if all applied solutions are correct and if the robot is able to play the drums in a way allowing other instruments to accompany, there was a presentation of its capabilities after finishing the construction. Primarily, there was a need to analyse durability of used relays, because they had caused problems in the past.

The presentation was very successful - autoPRK was playing for about 30 minutes without a break, including dynamic and requiring tracks, and all the elements worked correctly, without any faults. The strength of hitting drums was balanced, the speed of playing – appropriate, and the construction - stable.

Based on the number of visitors participating in the presentation it can be said that the show was a success. It means that the listening experience was on high level and listening to the robot playing was as pleasurable as listening to a human musician.

The project and the presentation is attractive for the potential recipients not only as a novelty, but can be seen as a product that can be used in life due to the way it is made – good-looking, easy to use, with almost unlimited capabilities of music to play. All those factors make this robot practical and possible to exploit in a large-scale music making projects.

5   Conclusions

The final construction meets all the assumptions. AutoPRK plays as well as a human - in some cases results are even better. It can easily play sixteenth note of 180bpm song using only one bass malleus or snare tremolo on one drum stick. All the elements work correctly, and in effect the sounds of drums are clear, loud and the pace is regular all the time. The tests show that the robot can be customised to every percussion, without changing locations of the drums, and setting everything up takes about 40 minutes. All the arms can be flexibly changed and each of them can handle every percussion element. Easy application allows the user to load the MIDI file and stream data to the robot to start playing.

AutoPRK project connects popular solutions for percussion playing robots, such as assigning each stick to only one drum, using linear solenoids to move them with practical, aesthetic construction. What is more, the cost of building the robot is relatively low. This can provide wide capabilities of songs to play on every percussion and a user-friendly service. There were no constructions similar to this.

Future plans connected with this project involve rebuilding it into a different machine, with two moving arms, for playing drums, legs for the percussion pedals and a head for making construction more humanlike. It will be equipped with a camera or other kind of sensors and appropriate algorithms allowing the robot to customize itself to the percussion without any help of the user. What is more, the robot will be connected to a microphone in order to listen to other instruments and - when it is asked - improvise playing with them in the same pace, metre and fixed style.

References

1. http://perkusja.rockmetal.art.pl/800/co_to/co_to_jest.html
2. Kapur, A.: A History of Robotic Musical Instruments. ICMC (2005)
3. Long, J., Murphy, J.W., Kapur, A., Carnegie, D.A.: A comparative evaluation of percussion mechanisms for musical robotics applications. In: Proceedings of the 6th International Conference on Automation, Robotics and Applications, pp. 173–178 (2015)
4. Cicconet, M., Bretan, M., Weinberg, G.: Human-Robot Percussion Ensemble. IEEE Robotics & Automation Magazine 105–110 (2013)
5. Kumar, K., Chand, P., Carnegie, D.A.: Pan piper 1.0 an overview of a robotic pan flute for Pacific music. In: IEEE Asia-Pacific World Congress on Computer Science and Engineering (2014)
6. Wonse, J., Hyeonjun, P., Bumjoo, L., Donghan, K.: A study on improving sound quality of violin playing robot. In: Proceedings of the 6th International Conference on Automation, Robotics and Applications, pp. 185–191 (2015)
7. http://www.midi.org/techspecs/

Optical Music Recognition: Standard and Cost-Sensitive Learning with Imbalanced Data

Wojciech Lesinski[1]([✉]) and Agnieszka Jastrzebska[2]

[1] Faculty of Mathematics and Computer Science,
University of Bialystok, ul. Konstantego Ciolkowskiego 1M, 15-245 Bialystok, Poland
wlesinski@ii.uwb.edu.pl
[2] Faculty of Mathematics and Information Science, Warsaw University of
Technology, ul. Koszykowa 75, 00-662 Warsaw, Poland

Abstract. The article is focused on a particular aspect of classification, namely the issue of class imbalance. Imbalanced data adversely affects the recognition ability and requires proper classifier's construction. In this work we present a case of music notation as an example of imbalanced data. Three classification algorithms - random forest, standard SVM and cost-sensitive SVM are described and tested. Feature selection based on random forest feature importance was used. Also, feature dimension reduction using PCA was studied.

Keywords: Cost-sensitive learning · SVM · Random forest · Feature selection · Optical music recognition · Imbalanced data

1 Introduction

The problem of pattern recognition is an important area of data mining, which has been studied and developed for many years now. In a number of its applications, satisfying results have already been achieved. However, in many fields it is still possible to obtain better results. Among many other important issues of this domain, studies on class imbalance have gained popularity.

Recently, the class imbalance problem has been recognized as a crucial obstacle in machine learning and data mining. It occurs when the training data is not evenly distributed among classes. Class imbalance is also especially critical in many real applications, such as credit card fraud detection when fraudulent cases are rare or medical diagnoses where normal cases are the majority. In these cases, standard classifiers generally perform poorly. Classifiers usually tend to be biased towards the majority class and ignore the minority class samples. Most classifiers assume an even distribution of examples among classes and an equal misclassification cost. Moreover, classifiers are typically designed to maximize accuracy, which is not a good metric to evaluate effectiveness in the case of imbalanced training data. Therefore, we need to improve traditional algorithms so as to handle imbalanced data and choose other metrics to measure performance instead of accuracy.

© IFIP International Federation for Information Processing 2015
K. Saeed and W. Homenda (Eds.): CISIM 2015, LNCS 9339, pp. 601–612, 2015.
DOI: 10.1007/978-3-319-24369-6_51

Most of the publications concerning imbalanced data focus on binary classification problems, for example [4], [5]. Far less articles (inter alia [1], [15]) address multiclass problems.

Automatic recognition and classification of music notation is a case of optical character recognition. It may have many applications. First and foremost, digital versions of musical scores popularise and simplify access to art. Availability of digital music notation and dedicated processing tools widens possibilities not only, but also for learning and appreciation of music. It also contributes to limitation of barriers for those, who experience difficulties in accessing standard, printed music notation, for example those, who are visually impaired. With electronic record of music notation we can make an attempt to computerize musical synthesis, we can also, by using the voice synthesizer, read music scores. Electronic music notation could also be used to verify the performance correctness of the musical composition, and to detect potential plagiarism. These applications lead to the conclusion that the optical recognition of music notation is an interesting and worthy research topic. General methodology of optical music recognition has been already researched and described in [6] and [13]. We would like to highlight that studied problem of imbalance of classes is an original contribution of this paper to the field of music symbol classification. In particular, application of cost-sensitive learning is a new element, not yet present in the literature devoted to optical music recognition.

The paper is organized as follows. Section 2 lists basic information about applied classification technique. Section 3 describes our data set, feature vector and empirical tests. Section 4 concludes the paper and indicates future research directions.

2   Preliminaries

2.1   Support Vector Machine

Support Vector Machine [14] (SVM) is a statistical classification method that forms a separation hyperplane with maximized margin between classes. The optimal margin is necessary to support generalization ability. Because some classification problems are too complicated to be solved by a linear separation, kernel functions are used to transform data set into a new one where such separation is possible. Classification decision is given by the function:

$$f(X) = \sum_{i=1}^{M} \alpha_i y_i K(X_i, X) + b \tag{1}$$

where M is the number of learning samples, y_i is the class label assigned to features vector X_i. Parameters α_i and b are calculated in learning process. Coefficients α_i are calculated as the solution of QP problem limited by the hypercube $[0, C]^{dimension}$. C is the capacity constant that controls error. The larger the C, the more the error is penalized. Function K is a kernel function.

In our work we use cost-sensitive SVM. The main approach to cost-sensitive learning is rescaling. Rescaling [3], is a general approach that can be used to make cost-blind learning algorithms cost-sensitive. The principle is to enable influences of the higher - cost classes to be larger than that of the lower - cost classes. The rescaling approach can be realized in many ways, for example by assigning to training elements of different classes different weights, sampling the classes according to their costs or moving the decision threshold.

2.2 Feature Selection Using Random Forest

In machine learning feature selection, also known as variable selection, attribute selection or variable subset selection, is a process of selecting a subset of relevant features for use in model construction. The central assumption when using any feature selection technique is that the data contains redundant or irrelevant features. Redundant features are those, which provide no more information than the currently selected feature set, and irrelevant features provide no useful information in any context.

In the case of feature selection a criterion function J(.) is optimized:

$$\begin{bmatrix} x_1 \\ \vdots \\ \vdots \\ x_d \end{bmatrix} \rightarrow \begin{bmatrix} x_{i_1} \\ \vdots \\ x_{i_d} \end{bmatrix} = argmax[J(\{x_i | i = 1, \ldots, D\})] \qquad (2)$$

Where D is the dimension of the whole feature set and d is the dimension of given feature subset. Unfortunately, comprehensive search of all possible subsets of D is usually impossible due to computational complexity of such endavour. Therefore, algorithms that approximate function J(.) are applied. We can distinguish two groups of such algorithms: filter and wrapper methods.

Wrapper methods use a predictive model to score feature subsets. Each new subset is used to train a model, which is tested on a hold-out set. Counting the number of mistakes made on that hold-out set (the error rate of the model) gives the score for that subset. As wrapper methods train a new model for each subset, they are very computationally intensive, but usually provide the best performing feature set for that particular type of model. An example of wrapper methods is random forest feature selection.

Filter methods use a proxy measure instead of an error rate to score a feature subset. This measure is chosen to be fast to compute, whilst still capturing the usefulness of the feature set. Common measures include the Mutual Information, Pearson product-moment correlation coefficient, and the inter/intra class distance. Filters are usually less computationally intensive than wrappers, but they produce a feature set which is not tuned to a specific type of predictive model. Many filters provide a feature ranking rather than an explicit best feature subset selection, and the cut off point in the ranking is chosen via cross-validation.

The Random Forest [2] method uses a collection of decision tree classifiers, where each tree in the forest has been trained using a bootstrap sample of individuals from the data, and each split attribute in the tree is chosen from among a random subset of attributes. Classification of individuals is based upon aggregate voting over all trees in the forest. Each tree in the random forest is built as follow:

- Let the number of training objects be N, and the number of features in features vector be M.
- Training set for each tree is built by choosing N times with replacement from all N available training objects.
- Number $m \ll M$ is an amount of features on which to base the decision at that node. This features are randomly chosen for each node.
- Each tree is built to the largest extent possible. There is no pruning.

Repetition of this algorithm yields a forest of trees, which all have been trained on bootstrap samples from training set. Thus, for a given tree, certain elements of training set will have been left out during training.

Prediction error and attribute importance is estimated from these "out-of-bag" elements. This part of training set is used to estimate the importance of particular attributes according to the following logic: if randomly permuting values of a particular attribute does not affect the predictive ability of trees on out-of-bag samples, that attribute is assigned a low importance score. If, however, randomly permuting values of a particular attribute drastically impairs the ability of trees to correctly predict the class of out-of-bag samples, then the importance score of that attribute will be high. By running out-of-bag samples down entire trees during the permutation procedure, attribute interactions are taken into account when calculating importance scores, since class is assigned in the context of other attribute nodes in the tree.

2.3   Reduction of Problem Dimensionality - Principal Component Analysis

One of dimension reduction algorithms is called Principal Component Analysis (PCA). PCA is a statistical procedure that uses orthogonal transformation to convert a set of observations of possibly correlated variables into a set of values of linearly uncorrelated variables called principal components. The number of principal components is less than or in the worst-case-scenario equal to the number of original variables. This transformation is defined in such a way that the first principal component has the largest possible variance (that is, accounts for as much of the variability in the data as possible), and each succeeding component in turn has the highest variance possible under the constraint that it be orthogonal to (i.e., uncorrelated with) the preceding components. Principal components are guaranteed to be independent if the data set is jointly normally distributed. PCA is sensitive to the relative scaling of original variables.

2.4   Evaluation of Solution

Evaluation of classification methods applied to imbalanced pattern recognition problem is the principal goal of this research. First of all, classification quality from a perspective of single classes is considered. We adopt parameters of binary classification evaluation and parameters and quality measures used in signal detection theory. Since these parameters are widely utilized, we do not refer to original sources, but of course we do not claim to be their authors. In this point we recall employment of these factors in an imbalanced two-class problem, c.f. [4].

Two-Class Problem. We share an opinion that evaluation of just a single factor cannot truly express classification quality. This is valid in general, as well as in the two-class problem. For instance, it is not only important to account the proportion of the number of correctly recognized symbols of a class to the number of all symbols of this class. Let us point out that, for example, the number of symbols falsely accounted to this class affects intuitive meaning of quality. Especially, when we consider a class of small number of elements, falsely classified symbols significantly decrease intuitive evaluation of quality. Therefore, we should look for formal evaluations compatible with intuition. Let us recall that in the case of imbalanced two-class problem, the minority class is often called positive one while majority class - negative one.

Such intuitive measures, as indicated above, provide a simple way of describing classifier's performance on a given data set. However, they can be deceiving in certain situations and are highly sensitive to changes in data. For example, consider a problem where only 1% of the instances are positive. In such situation, a simple strategy of labelling all new objects as members of other classes would give a predictive accuracy of 99%, but failing on all positive cases. In [4] the following confusion matrix was used in evaluating classification quality of a two-class problem, c.f. Table 1. Parameters presented in this table were then used to define several factors, which outline classification quality.

Table 1. Confusion matrix for *two-class* problem

	Positive prediction	Negative prediction
Positive class	True Positives (TP)	False Negatives (FN)
Negative class	False Positives (FP)	True Negatives (TN)

Multiclass Problem. For a better classification quality measuring, let us first consider the following parameters of a *multiclass problem*. The parameters given in Table 2 are numbers of elements of a testing set, which have the following meaning:

- TP - the number of elements of the considered class correctly classified to the considered class,
- FN - the number of elements of the considered class incorrectly classified to other classes,
- FP - the number of elements of other classes incorrectly classified to the considered class,
- TN - the number of elements of other classes correctly classified to other classes (no matter, if correctly, or not).

Table 2. Confusion matrix for a *multiclass* problem

	Classification to the considered class	Classification to other classes
The class	True Positives (TP)	False Negatives (FN)
Other classes	False Positives (FP)	True Negatives (TN)

Using parameters showed in Table 1 and Table 2 we can calculate some measures valid to evaluate performance even when we deal with imbalanced data:

$$Sensitivity = \frac{TP}{TP + FN} \tag{3}$$

$$Miss\ Rate = \frac{FN}{TP + FN} = 1 - Sensitivity$$

$$Accuracy = \frac{TP + TN}{TP + FN + FP + TN} \tag{4}$$

$$Error = \frac{FP + FN}{TP + FN + FP + TN} = 1 - Accuracy$$

$$Precision = \frac{TP}{TP + FP} \tag{5}$$

$$False\ Discovery\ Rate = \frac{FP}{TP + FP} = 1 - Precision$$

3 Experiment and Results

3.1 The Data Set

The recognized set of music notation symbols had about 27.000 objects in 20 classes. There were 12 classes defined as numerous and each of them had about 2.000 representatives. Cardinality of the other eight classes was much lower and various in each of them. Part of the examined symbols was cut out from chosen Fryderyk Chopin's compositions. Other part of the symbols' library comes from our team former research projects [6]. The following elements form regular classes: flat, sharp, natural, G clef, F clef, forte, piano, mezzo forte, quarter rest, eight rest, sixteenth rest, and flagged stem. The set of irregular classes includes breve note, accent, crescendo, diminuendo, tie, fermata, C clef and thirty-second rest were included. Each regular class in training sets consisted of 400 elements. Cardinality of irregular classes is shown in Table 3. Recognized symbols arc illustrated in Figure 1.

3.2 Feature Vector

Performance of every classifier is conditioncd by an appropriate description of objects used for its training. In the case of image classification feature vectors

Table 3. Cardinality of learning and testing sets for irregular classes

class	learning set	testing set
accent	30	65
breve	1	2
crescendo	55	100
diminuendo	51	97
fermata	35	46
clef C	100	178
tie	100	155
thirty-second rest	20	35

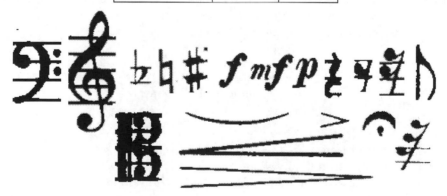

Fig. 1. Symbols being recognized: 1) numerous classes in the upper row, left to right: clefs (F and G), chromatic symbols (flats, naturals and sharps), dynamic markings (forte, mezzo forte and piano), rests (quarter, eight, sixteenth), flagged stem, 2) rare symbols in the bottom row, left to right, top to down: clef C, tie (arc), crescendo, diminuendo, accent fermata, 32nd rest.

describe objects subjected to recognition. Many publications on pattern recognition propose to use different features extracted from an image. Those are: histograms, transitions, margins, moments, directions and many more. It may seem that creating a vector of all known features would be the best solution. Unfortunately such vector could cause a huge load of computation and in turn, it might result in an unacceptable consumption of resources. On the other hand, often adding more features does not increase classifier efficiency.

In this study we used a group of known features often used in optical character recognition. These were: projections, transitions, margins, directions, regular moments, central moments, Zernike moments, field and perimeter of symbol, Euler's vector and other. For accurate description of those features please see [9].

We have experimented with different approaches to feature vector construction. In the first step possibly biggest vector, which included all features, was created. It had 300 components. Next, we employed random forest to evaluate importance of features. Feature vectors comprising of most important features were constructed. We studied feature sets of the following cardinalities: 200, 150, 100, 75, 50, 40, 30, 25, 20, and 15. Lastly, PCA was studied. We used it with 99%, 95% and 90% transferred variance.

3.3   Results

Three different classifiers were used to perform prediction. These were: random forest, SVM and cost-sensitive SVM (with weights). To evaluate the classifiers three measures were calculated: sensitivity, accuracy and precision. For these calculations our multi class problem was turned to m two-class problems (*one class contra all others*). All measures were calculated for each class. Average measure was determined in the end. Also, standard error and accuracy (Formulas 6 and 7) were calculated. In our previous works we have elaborated on application of decision tree, kNN, bagging, and other methods. One may consult [8], [12] and [10] to compare different techniques.

$$accuracy = \frac{\text{number of all correctly classified}}{\text{number of all elements}} \qquad (6)$$

$$error = 1 - accuracy \qquad (7)$$

Standard Measures. The best prediction rate was achieved, when we employed feature selection procedures. Optimal number of characteristics were 50 and 40. For these vectors random forest and SVM obtained 98%. These two classifiers had similar efficiency. Slightly worse results were achieved by SVM with weights. Feature vectors obtained using PCA gave worse results. All results are gathered in Table 4.

Accuracy. Accuracy informs about the influence of given class on the whole testing set. The best accuracy was in minority classes. Accuracy of classifiers

Table 4. The influence of different feature vectors on recognition accuracy (in percent).

feature vector	random forest	SVM	cost-sensitive SVM
whole set	96	96	95
best 200	96	96	95
best 150	97	96	95
best 100	97	97	95
best 75	98	97	96
best 50	98	98	97
best 40	98	98	97
best 30	97	98	96
best 25	96	96	95
best 20	95	95	93
best 15	93	92	90
PCA 99%	94	93	91
PCA 95%	94	95	91
PCA 90%	93	93	91

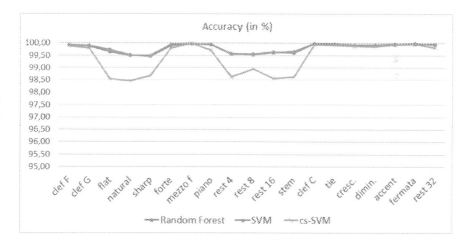

Fig. 2. Accuracy (in percent) for all classes

without weights in the case of the breve note was 99.99%. In the case of SVM with weights it was a little worse. In contrast, sensitivity in this class was 0%! Other rare classes were also recognized with good accuracy. It varied between 99.89% and 99.99%. The worst accuracy was in natural and sharp classes. These classes had relatively poor sensitivity and had many elements in testing set. Similar results were noted in the rest group (quarter, eighth , sixteenth, thirty-second rest). Rests belonging to regular classes were classified with better accuracy, but worse than rare ones. Accuracy of cost-sensitive SVM was a little worse, especially in rare classes. Figure 2 summarizes the results for all classes.

Sensitivity. Sensitivity shows the recognition effectiveness in the given class. The highest value of this factor, 100%, was obtained in forte, mezzo-forte and piano classes. Random forest and SVM reached high values of this factor for all regular classes. Among the rare classes the best sensitivity was achieved in the C clef class. The worst sensitivity (0%) was in breve note class. This symbol was not recognized by any classifier. Cost-sensitive SVM reached better sensitivity for rare classes. Results for all classes and all classifiers are illustrated on Figure 3.

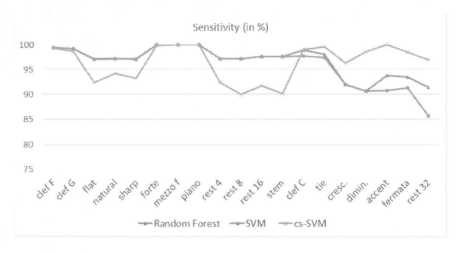

Fig. 3. Sensitivity (in percent) for all classes

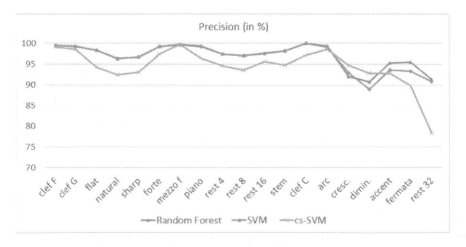

Fig. 4. Precision (in percent) for all classes

Precision. Precision shows the influence of other classes on a given class. The highest values of this measure were in classes with dynamics symbols and clefs' classes. When we applied random forest and SVM we achieved better precision for regular classes than for rare ones. The worst precision were in crescendo, diminuendo and thirty-second rest classes. This measure was significantly worse for cost-sensitive SVM for rare classes. Figure 4 shows precision for all classes.

4 Conclusion

The problem of pattern recognition for imbalanced data was tackled in this paper on an example of music notation symbols. Authors presented results of classification experiments performed with standard and cost-sensitive classifiers on a dataset consisting of 27.000 elements of 20 classes. 12 of them have been considered as regular classes, the other 8 as irregular classes.

The recognition effectiveness of regular classes was very satisfying. Results obtained by random forest and SVM were similar. Cost-sensitive SVM achieved better sensitivity for rare classes, but all in all they were worse than other factors. We may conclude this study by saying that better recognition of rare classes causes worse recognition of regular classes.

In addition, different versions of feature selection procedures were tested. In particular, for this study feature selection based on random forest feature importance and PCA were used. Best results were achieved by random forest feature selection. Vector with 50 most important features, selected from 300 features, gave the best recognition accuracy performance.

Despite the fact of high efficiency of the proposed techniques, we believe that better results can be achieved. In the next step of our research we will take a closer look at other cost-sensitive classifiers. Also another sets of algorithms for feature selection will be tested. Conducted studies indicate that a vital issue for pattern recognition tasks are "garbage" elements. Existence of garbage elements is often due to errors that occur at the point of image segmentation. There is an urgent need for methods that deal with rejection of such garbage. This issue is not easy though, as garbage elements are not know at the point of classifier construction. We come towards conclusion that involvement of imprecise knowledge representation schemes, for example balanced fuzzy sets, [7] or fuzzy sets [11] in classification might help us to deal with this problem.

References

1. Abe, N., Zadrozny, B., Langford, J.: An iterative method for multi-class cost-sensitive learning. In: Proc. ACM SIGKDD Int. Conf. Knowledge Discovery and Data Mining, pp. 3–11 (2004)
2. Breiman, L.: Random Forests. Machine Learning **45**, 5–32 (2001)
3. Elkan, C.: The foundations of cost-sensitive learning. In: Proc. of the 17th International Joint Conference on Artificial Intelligence, Seattle, pp. 973–978 (2001)

4. Garcia, V., Sanchez, J.S., Mollineda, R.A., Alejo, R., Sotoca, J.M.: The class imbalance problem in pattern recognition and learning. In: II Congreso Espanol de Informatica, pp. 283–291 (2007)
5. He, H., Garcia, E.A.: Learning from imbalanced data. IEEE Transactions on Knowledge and Data Engineering **21**(9), 1263–1284 (2009)
6. Homenda, W.: Optical music recognition: the case study of pattern recognition. In: Computer Recognition Systems, pp. 835–842. Springer Verlag (2005)
7. Homenda, W.: Balanced Fuzzy Sets. Information Sciences **176**, 2467–2506 (2006)
8. Homenda, W., Lesinski, W.: Optical music recognition: case of pattern recognition with undesirable and garbage symbols. In: Choras, R., et al. (eds.) Image Processing and Communications Challenges, pp. 120–127. Exit, Warsaw (2009)
9. Homenda, W., Lesinski, W.: Features selection in character recognition with random forest classifier. In: Jędrzejowicz, P., Nguyen, N.T., Hoang, K. (eds.) ICCCI 2011, Part I. LNCS, vol. 6922, pp. 93–102. Springer, Heidelberg (2011)
10. Homenda, W., Lesinski, W.: Decision trees and their families in imbalanced pattern recognition: recognition with and without rejection. In: Saeed, K., Snášel, V. (eds.) CISIM 2014. LNCS, vol. 8838, pp. 219–230. Springer, Heidelberg (2014)
11. Homenda, W., Pedrycz, W.: Processing of uncertain information in linear space of fuzzy sets. Fuzzy Sets & Systems **44**, 187–198 (1991)
12. Lesinski, W., Jastrzebska, A.: Optical music recognition as the case of imbalanced pattern recognition: a study of single classifiers. In: Skulimowski, A.M.J. (ed.) Proceedings of KICSS 2013, pp. 267–278. Progress & Business Publishers, Krakow (2013)
13. Rebelo, A., Fujinaga, I., Paszkiewicz, F., Marcal, A.R.S., Guedes, C., Cardoso, J.S.: Optical music recognition: state-of-the-art and open issues. International Journal of Multimedia Information Retrieval **1**, 173–190 (2012)
14. Vapnik, V.: The nature of statistical learning theory. Springer-Verlag (1995)
15. Zhou, Z.H., Liu, X.Y.: On Multi-Class Cost-Sensitive Learning. Computational Intelligence **26**, 232–257 (2010)

Emotion-Based Music Information Retrieval Using Lyrics

Akihiro Ogino[✉] and Yuko Yamashita

Kyoto Sangyo University, Motoyama, Kamigamo, Kita-ku, Kyoto-City 603-8555, Japan
ogino@cse.kyoto su.ac.jp

Abstract. In this paper, we present a study on emotion-based music information retrieval using lyrics information. Listeners want to search the lyrics of music suitable for his/her emotion (impression of music), by using an information system from music libraries. As a solution of listeners' needs, we have designed a system that retrieve the lyrics of music based on the emotion (or the impression) suitable for a listener's feelings that the listener has selected, from 9 emotions and 9 impressions. We select the words, i.e. verb and adjective, from the bridge part of the lyrics of music that express emotion in lyrics by using natural language processing. We summarize the words into the representative words by using a dictionary of synonyms. We make a model that estimates a listener's 9 emotion/impression of the representative words by using a machine learning method. And listeners want to understand why the recommended music by a system is suitable for his/her emotion/impression. Therefore, we select the representative words most related to a listener's emotion/impression and we use the selected words as the explanation of reason to a listener. We have made each model of emotion and impression for 9 subjects and have evaluated the accuracy of the model. We also have investigated the selected representative words related to emotion/impression.

Keywords: Affective computing · Music information retrieval · Text mining

1 Introduction

In order to retrieve the music suitable for listener's emotion/impression from the digital music libraries that store tremendous music, we propose a method of emotion/impression-based music retrieval using lyrics for Japanese music.

As listeners' behaviors for searching music, Lee [1] shows that listeners search the music by the bibliographic information of music, such as singer, title and genre. The query by bibliographic information is useful in when he/she has the accurate information of the targeted music. However, when he/she searches new music, it is difficult to find the music that he/she wants to listen because he/she does not have the information of music. As listeners' important factor for choosing music, the survey also shows that he/she pays attention to the contents of music, such as the lyrics of music and the relationship with emotional state of them, when he/she searches music. A listener understands the meaning of the lyrics of music and selects the music suitable for his/her current feelings or moods.

© IFIP International Federation for Information Processing 2015
K. Saeed and W. Homenda (Eds.): CISIM 2015, LNCS 9339, pp. 613–622, 2015.
DOI: 10.1007/978-3-319-24369-6_52

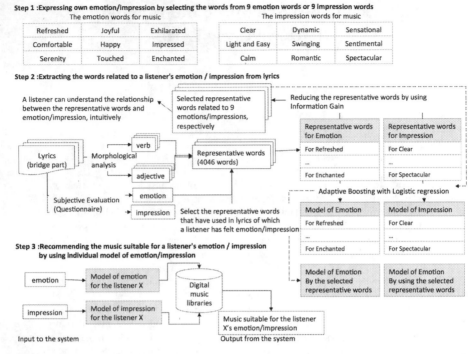

Fig. 1. The framework of our approach for recommending the music suitable for a listener's emotion/impression

Therefore, detecting the listener's emotion/impression of music through analyzing lyrics is useful for a listener to search music that touches his/her minds. There are a number of researches on music retrieval based on emotion/impression by using lyrics [2, 3, 4, 5, 6, 7, 8].

On the other hand, a listener checks the news, reviews and etc. in Internet as a reference because they want to get reasons to select the music. Therefore, for a listener, we think that a music information retrieval system has to have a mechanism that shows the candidate music with the reason.

We propose an approach that estimates a listener's emotion/impression of the music by analyzing the relationship between the lyrics of it and the listener's emotion/impression. We offer the music suitable for his/her emotion/impression with the selection reasons, which are the words of the lyrics more related to emotion/impression, of the music. The framework of our approach is shown Figure 1. It consists of three sections. The first section is the definition of the emotional words that show a listener's emotion/impression. We have selected 9 words for expressing emotion and 9 words for expressing impression in order to support queries by emotion/impression that he/she feels from music. The second section is to extract the words of lyrics related to a listener's emotion/impression.

Table 1. Words for expressing emotion and impression of lyrics of music

Emotion words for music		
Refreshed	Joyful	Exhilarated
Comfortable	Happy	Impressed
Serenity	Touched	Enchanted

Impression words for music		
Clear	Dynamic	Sensational
Light and Easy	Swinging	Sentimental
Calm	Romantic	Spectacular

In order to estimate a listener's emotion of lyrics, we have used the lyrics of the bridge part of music because the bridge has a high likelihood that a listener feels emotion/impression from lyrics in Japanese pop songs. We have inquired a listener's emotion/impression of the lyrics in the bridge part through subjective evaluation test. We have made a model of the relation between the listener's emotion/impression words and the lyrics using a machine learning method.

The third section is to retrieve the music suitable for a listener's emotion/impression from the digital music libraries by using the model automatically. Our system searches the music suitable for the listener's emotion/impression and offers the music to a listener with the words related to the listener's emotion/impression.

The rest of this paper is organized as follows. Section 2 describes a method of emotion-based music retrieval using lyrics. Section 3 presents the evaluation of the proposed method. Section 4 is conclusion of our work.

2   Estimating Listener's Emotion/Impression of Lyrics

2.1   Definition of Emotional Words

We assume that there are the needs of two types in emotional music search: one is a search by emotion and another is a search by impression. For example, one case is that a listener wants to search the music that changes his/her emotion to "Happy", directly. In this case, a listener has clearly the needs, such as "I want to change my sad emotion to happy". Another case is that a listener wants to search the music that offers "Uplifting impression" to his/her mind and to change his/her mind to positive. In this case, a listener's needs are ambiguous and his/her emotion may change to happy or exhilarated. Therefor, we have selected 9 words for expressing emotion and 9 words for expressing impression in order to support queries by emotion/impression that he/she feels from music as shown Table 1.

We select the emotion words from positive words of Russell's model and add words for expressing music, such as "Impressed". We select the impression words that are likely to cause emotion of the emotion words by authors.

2.2   Detecting the Words Related to Emotion/Impression from Lyrics

We pay attention to adjective and intransitive verb to extract a listener's emotion/impression of lyrics. For example, a human laughs when he/she feels happy. The "laugh" which is intransitive verb expresses happy feelings. We use an adjective word, such as cheerful, when we want to express a happy feeling in the writing. The word of "cheerful" which is adjective expresses happy feelings of a human in the writing. We do not use noun because noun is used to express the surroundings where we are, such as summer, park and sea.

The detecting of the words related to a listener's emotion/impression is composed of four steps:

1. Extracting adjective and intransitive verb from lyrics;
2. Summarizing the extracted words to the representative word based on synonym dictionary of Japanese.
3. Vectorizing of an appearance of representative words.
4. Selecting the representative words related to emotion / impression by using the criteria of information gain

First, we carry out word segmentation of lyrics with the help of natural language processing (NLP) tool for Japanese, i.e. Mecab[11]. We select the adjective and the intransitive verb from the segmented words. Second, we summarize the extracted words to the representative word based on the synonym dictionary. The representative words are 4626 words that are composed by noun, adjective and verb. For example, a representative word includes 67 words. Third, we vectorize the representative words based on an appearance of the word. We set a true flag when a representative word includes an adjective and intransitive verb. We also set a false flag when a representative word does not include an adjective and intransitive verb. Four, we select the representative words, which are more related to emotion/impression than other words, by using the criteria of information gain. We have selected the representative words of which the information gain is over zero.

2.3   Making a Model for Estimating Emotion/Impression

We make a model that estimates a listener's emotion/impression of lyrics of music by using a machine learning method. As a machine learning method, we have selected the adaptive boosting with the decision stump as weak classifier. We make one model for one emotion / impression and we make 18 models (9 models of emotion and 9 models of impression) for a listener. For example, when a listener wants to listen to the music of lyrics that affords happy feelings to the listener, we select the model of "happy" from 18 models and retrieve the music of the lyrics from a music library by using the model of "happy".

Table 2. The accuracy rates of models and the number of which subjects have felt emotions, as for Refreshed, Exhilarated and Comfortable (All sample music are 79).

Subjects	Refreshed		Exhilarated		Comfortable	
	Number	Accuracy Rate	Number	Accuracy Rate	Number	Accuracy Rate
A	1	98.7	4	86.1	3	92.4
B	5	84.8	2	97.5	2	94.9
C	12	74.7	16	55.7	18	62.0
D	11	75.9	3	92.4	9	86.1
E	9	78.5	0	---	6	83.5
F	9	83.5	8	78.5	14	70.9
G	13	77.2	14	65.8	11	67.1
H	5	83.5	1	98.7	2	89.9
I	0	---	3	94.9	7	73.4
Baseline	16	48.1	11	86.1	17	58.2

Table 3. The accuracy rates of models and the number of which subjects have felt emotions, as for Joyful, Impressed, Touched and Enchanted (All sample music are 79).

Subjects	Joyful		Impressed		Touched		Enchanted	
	Number	Accuracy Rate	Number	Accuracy Rate	Number	Accuracy Rate	Number	Accuracy Rate
A	6	82.3	35	51.9	14	55.7	14	60.8
B	28	50.6	29	58.2	5	87.3	7	79.7
C	18	62.0	32	46.8	28	63.3	28	43.0
D	11	84.8	37	45.6	16	65.8	15	55.7
E	20	50.6	31	50.6	17	64.6	26	54.4
F	19	58.2	9	83.5	15	77.2	30	57.0
G	17	68.4	16	68.4	14	65.8	5	68.4
H	12	81.0	18	55.7	14	70.9	23	65.8
I	15	68.4	30	59.5	13	73.4	14	77.2
Baseline	36	48.1	52	43.0	32	58.2	49	50.6

3   Evaluation

In order to simulate listener's emotion/impression of lyrics of music on a system, we have made 18 (9 emotion and 9 impression) models for 9 individual subjects. We have asked 9 individual subjects about the emotion/impression of 79 sample lyrics of music through a web questionnaire system. We used 79 Japanese pop songs in the RWC music library [9] as sample lyrics. The subjects do not listen to the music and only read the lyrics of music on the web page and answer emotion/impression of the lyrics. We have made a individual model from the individual's questionnaire data and the representative words of individual by using Adaptive Boosting with Logistic regression model on the Weka [10].

Table 4. The accuracy rates of models and the number of which subjects have felt impressions, as for Clear, Light and easy, Sensational and Calm (All sample music are 79).

Subjects	Clear		Light and easy		Sensational		Calm	
	Number	Accuracy Rate	Number	Accuracy Rate	Number	Accuracy Rate	Number	Accuracy Rate
A	1	98.7	4	89.9	9	81.0	7	91.1
B	1	98.7	1	98.7	9	78.5	1	96.2
C	10	83.5	14	72.2	20	58.2	12	72.2
D	12	75.9	6	86.1	12	69.6	22	65.8
E	14	68.4	3	96.2	21	50.6	7	87.3
F	3	93.7	1	88.6	1	91.1	36	48.1
G	9	77.2	5	78.5	18	65.8	16	67.1
H	3	86.1	2	89.9	5	88.6	6	74.7
I	0	---	4	83.5	4	94.9	3	78.5
Baseline	13	67.1	9	79.8	20	58.2	29	50.6

Table 5. The accuracy rates of models and the number of which subjects have felt emotions, as for Joyful, Impressed, Touched and Enchanted (All sample music are 79).

Subjects	Dynamic		Swinging		Sentimental		Romantic	
	Number	Accuracy Rate	Number	Accuracy Rate	Number	Accuracy Rate	Number	Accuracy Rate
A	5	92.4	20	64.6	33	44.3	13	55.7
B	15	60.8	16	65.8	33	40.5	8	79.7
C	21	49.4	24	58.2	25	58.2	35	49.4
D	22	59.5	11	78.5	45	60.8	31	55.7
E	12	68.4	11	78.5	37	41.7	31	46.8
F	24	55.7	21	55.7	8	83.5	15	67.1
G	22	63.3	19	70.9	18	55.7	17	57.0
H	11	81.0	4	94.9	38	54.4	16	77.2
I	14	73.4	25	50.6	45	63.3	12	64.6
Baseline	34	48.1	39	59.5	61	65.8	42	58.2

In order to evaluate individual model, we have made a baseline model by using the data that two subjects out of all subjects feel emotion/impression of lyrics. We have evaluated the estimate accuracy of individual model based on the 10-hold cross-validation.

3.1   Result and Consideration Concerning Emotion Model

Following tables show the number of which each subject has experienced emotions, and the rate of correctly classified data of the individual model.

Table 2 is the result concerning "Refreshed", "Exhilarated", and "Comfortable". The result shows that the accuracy rate of them is over 70%. Individual models are more effective than the base model. The accuracy rates of individual models are better than the base model. However, many subjects do not feel these emotions from sample lyrics. Therefore, we think that the individual models only estimate their emotion concerning the limited representative words.

Table 3 is the result concerning "Joyful", "Impressed", "Touched" and "Enchanted". All subjects have experienced these emotions from sample lyrics and have felt same emotion from same lyrics. However, the accuracy rate of individual model is over 60% and is not good. We could pick up a number of representative words that are related to these emotions. For example, as for the representative words related to "Joyful", we have picked up the words that show human action (e.g. "run" and "sing") and the words positive impression (e.g. "laugh" and "beautiful"). However, we also have picked up the words that afford negative impression to us (e.g. "afraid" and "wondering"). One reason of which we have picked up the word not related to the emotion is that there are many kinds of the representative word related to a word.

For example, there are words (e.g. "outstandingly", "sweet voice" and "splendor") as representative words of "beautiful" in a synonym dictionary. Therefore, we estimate the context of lyrics and have to select the representative word suitable for the word.

3.2   Result and Consideration Concerning Impression Model

Table 4 is the result concerning "Clear" and "Light and easy". The result shows that almost same tendency of table 1. The accuracy rate of them is over 70% but many subjects do not feel these impressions from sample lyrics. As for "Clear", we have picked up the representative words from a number of lyrics (e.g. "search", "look at" and "believe"). As for "Light and easy", we could not detect the good representative words. We think that one of reasons is that subjects have paid attention to except for verb and adjective. Table 4 also shows the result concerning "Sensational" and "Calm". The number of which each subject experienced impression is different but we have detected a number of common representative words in subjects. We think that some subjects have same criteria about these impressions and feel same impressions from the lyrics.

Table 5 is the result concerning "Dynamic", "Swinging", "Sentimental" and "Romantic". Subjects have felt these impressions from many sample lyrics. The representative words related to "Dynamic" are "move", "dance", "take a step" and "run". The representative words related to "Swinging" are "laugh", "shine" and "believe"

4   Selecting the Representative Words More Related to Emotion/Impression

Our aim is to recommend the lyrics with the representative words as the reason of recommendation. In order that a user evaluates the candidate lyrics through the representative words, our system has to reduce the representative words to the number at which they can take a glance.

Table 6. The comparison of the accuracy rate between the normal baseline model and the reduction baseline model

	Emotion / Impression	Normal baseline model (Using all representative words)	Reduction baseline model (Using the selected representative words)
Emotion	Joyful	48.1	65.8
	Comfortable	58.2	86.1
	Happy	62.0	83.5
	Impressed	43.0	79.7
	Serenity	44.3	72.2
	Touched	48.2	72.2
	Enchanted	50.6	79.7
Impression	Dynamic	48.1	70.9
	Sensational	58.2	78.5
	Swinging	59.5	74.7
	Sentimental	65.8	84.8
	Clam	50.6	72.2
	Romantic	58.2	54.4
	Spectacular	51.9	74.7

In order to reduce representative words with maintaining explanation ability, we have selected the representative words more related to emotion/impression of which the value of information gain is over 0.0, from all 4626 representative words. We have evaluated efficiency of selection of representative words by comparing the accuracy rate of the normal model and the reduction model. In this experiment, we evaluate only the baseline model of each emotion/impression and we do not evaluate the each subject's model. We also do not evaluate the baseline models based on data of which two subjects out of all subjects do not have experienced emotion/impression in over 20% of all sample lyrics. Therefore, we have evaluated the baseline models of seven emotions and the seven impressions, as shown in table 6.

As for emotion, for example, the selected representative words of "serenity" are "keep" and "think" and this model recommends the lyrics that included these words as serenity. The selected representative words of "touched" are "reach", "feel" and "gaze". We think that a user can be satisfied with the recommend reason concerning above representative words.

As for "Joyful", the authors think that "run", "laugh" and "sing" are relevant to joyful, but these words have not been chosen as the selected representative words by information gain.

As for impression, the accuracy rates of the six reduction models except for "romantic" are good than normal model. For example, the selected representative words of "dynamic" are "dance" and "encounter". The selected representative words of "calm" are "feel" and "keep". On the other hand, the accuracy rate of the reduction model of "romantic" is down than normal model. The selected representative words of "romantic" are "sweet", "reach" and "beautiful". The one of reasons is that we cannot have deleted the useless words (e.g. "go out" and "can do").

5   Conclusion

We have introduced the model of emotion/impression based on analyzing lyrics of music in order to recommend the music suitable for a user's emotion/impression. Our method explains the recommendation reason of music to a user through showing the words related to the emotion/ impression of the lyrics. We have selected the verb and adjective of lyrics in order to analyze the relationship between user's emotion/impression of lyrics. We have summarized the verb and adjective to the representative words. We have used the 4626 representative words of lyrics that are related to emotion/impression to make the models of 9 emotions and 9 impressions by using Adaptive boosting with logistic regression. We have gotten 9 subjects of 9 emotions and 9 impressions concerning 79 sample lyrics through a subjective evaluation experiment. We have made the models for 9 subjects and the baseline model and evaluate the models through 10-hold cross-validation.

The evaluations of the models have shown that the almost personalized models are better than the baseline model. The result shows that each subject has the personal relationship between his/her emotion/impression and the representative words in lyrics. We also have detected the representative words more related to emotion/impression by using information gain. We can use the representative words to explain the reason to a user.

In future works, we will try to improve the method of the summarizing of words in lyrics to the representative words by estimating the context of lyrics. We also will try to detect the representative words related to individual emotion / impression.

Acknowledgement. This work was supported by JSPS KAKENHI Grant Number 25330331.

References

1. Lee, J.H., Downie, J.S.: Survey of music information needs, uses, and seeking behaviours: preliminary findings. In: 5th International Conference on Music Information Retrieval, pp. 441–446 (2004)
2. Yang, D., Lee, W.: Music emotion identification from lyrics. In: 11th IEEE International Symposium on Multimedia, pp. 624–629 (2009)
3. Guo, Z., Wang, Q., Liu, G., Guo, J., Lu, Y.: A music retrieval system using melody and lyric. In: 2012 IEEE International Conference on Multimedia and Expo Workshops, pp. 343–348 (2012)
4. Hu, Y., Chen, X., Yang, D.: Lyric-based song emotion detection with affective lexicon and fuzzy clustering method. In: Proceedings of the 10th International Society for Music Information Retrieval Conference, pp. 123–128 (2009)
5. Laurier, C., Crivolla, J., Herrera, P.: Multimodal music mood classification using audio and lyrics. In: Proceedings of ICMLA 2008, pp. 688–693 (2008)
6. Wang, T., Kim, D., Hong, K., Youn, J.: Music information retrieval system using lyrics and melody information. In: 2009 Asia-Pacific Conference on Information Processing, pp. 601–604 (2009)

7. Seungwon, O., Minsoo, H., Jinsul, K.: Music mood classification using intro and refrain parts of lyrics. In: 2013 International Conference on Information Science and Applications, pp. 1–3 (2013)
8. Chung-Yi, C., Ying-Shian, W., Wei-rong, C., Wu, D.C., Hsu, J.Y.-j., Tsai, R.T.-H.: The power of words: enhancing music mood estimation with textual input of lyrics. In: 3rd International Conference on Affective Computing and Intelligent Interaction (ACII 2009), pp. 1–6 (2009)
9. Goto, M., Hashiguchi, H., Nishimura, T., Oka, R.: RWC music database: popular, classical, and jazz music databases. In: Proceedings of the 3rd International Conference on Music Information Retrieval (ISMIR 2002), pp. 287–288 (2002)
10. Weka. http://www.cs.waikato.ac.nz/ml/weka/
11. MeCab. http://taku910.github.io/mecab/

Author Index

Printed in the United States
By Bookmasters